KNIVES
2013

EDITED BY
Joe Kertzman

Published by

Krause Publications, a division of F+W Media, Inc.
700 East State Street • Iola, WI 54990-0001
715-445-2214 • 888-457-2873
www.krausebooks.com

To order books or other products call toll-free 1-800-258-0929
or visit us online at www.shopblade.com

Cover photography by Kris Kandler

ISSN: 0277-0725

ISBN-13: 978-1-4402-3060-8
ISBN-10: 1-4402-3060-9

Designed by Sharon Bartsch
Edited by Corrina Peterson

Printed in the United States of America

Dedication and Acknowledgments

Looking at the knives in this book, collectors and enthusiasts everywhere are reminded of something that they and hunters, outdoorsmen and outdoorswomen, sportsmen and sportswomen, farmers, linesmen, utility workers, ranchers, cabinet makers, construction workers and millions of other people have pondered for centuries. How could anyone, no matter their political slant, motivation or agenda, want to outlaw knives of any kind, shape or form? Thumbing through the pages of *Knives 2013*, it seems absurd to even consider banning such handcrafted works of art. It's implausible that a single piece be considered a dangerous weapon in the hands of anyone but the most deranged of human beings.

Yet, there are people, as witnessed for decades, who want to make it illegal to own and carry anything from daggers to switchblades, from swords to one-hand-opening spring-assisted flipper folders. In the name of concerned citizenry and self-righteous politicians, they lobby to outlaw edged tools, to permanently ink their demise through laws, on dockets and by manipulation of the court system. There are those who want to forever ban knives from public ownership and carry.

It is for these reasons and more that I not only acknowledge Knife Rights and the American Knife & Tool Institute (AKTI), but also dedicate this book to these two organizations that actively protect the rights of knife-carrying citizens in this country and across the globe. The American Knife & Tool Institute (www.akti.org) is a nonprofit association that has been a voice of advocacy for the entire knife community since 1998, ensuring that Americans will always be able to make, buy, sell, own, carry and use knives and edged tools. The AKTI is recognized worldwide and respected as a credible, accurate source of knife legislation information, legislative input and industry information. The organization has a successful, proven record of accomplishments in making effective changes to restrictive knife laws and promoting reasonable and responsible laws and enforcement.

Knife Rights (www.kniferights.org) provides knife and edged-tool owners an effective voice to influence public policy and to oppose efforts to restrict the right to own, use and carry knives and edged tools. It encourages safe, responsible and lawful use of knives through education and outreach, enhancing positive perceptions of knives and edged tools and their owners and users. It encourages the marketing of knives in a responsible manner conducive to the organization's goals, and it cooperates with advocacy organizations that have complementary interests and goals.

It is with pleasure that I recognize the work of Doug Ritter of Knife Rights and Jan Billeb of the American Knife & Tool Institute, as well as all their members, board members, presidents, vice-presidents, contributors and supporters.

Additionally, I'd of course be remiss if I didn't dedicate this book to the F&W Media staff that helps make the *Knives* annual a reality each year—Jim Schlender, Corrina Peterson, Steve Shackleford, Sharon Bartsch, Lori Hallman and Bruce Wolberg. And finally to my wife, Tricia, our kids, Danny and Cora, and my parents Jack and Cathy, all of whom have helped shape me into the editor and man that I am today. Thank you to each and every one of you.

Joe Kertzman

Contents

On The Cover

There's something for everyone to like on the front cover of *Knives 2013*, starting with a Nathan Carothers fully integral dagger (far left) machined from a single piece of CPM-154 steel, heat treated by Paul Bos, then given four handle scales of resin-impregnated maple burl made by "Simply Nicholas." The pins are hidden, the steel hand finished with stones before polishing, and the maple burl a dark green. Standing to its right is "Seeing Scarlet," a Ron Appleton creation including a 440C blade with spherical contours, a red-anodized 6061-T6-aluminum handle and a titanium InfiLock™ mechanism with "soft close modification" in a fashion only Appleton could

accomplish. Looming large to its right is an impressive Steven Rapp knife, his interpretation of a circa-1800-1850 Sheffield Wostenholm IXL piece—a bowie, but Rapp's is a dagger—shown at the Crystal Palace Exhibition, which eventually became the World's Fair. Rapp's version includes a 13.5-inch, double-ground 440C blade, a cast guard and pommel by Mark DeGraffenried, and an ancient-ivory handle. So engraved and gorgeous we had to look at it lying down (the knife, not us) is an Emmanuel Esposito "Rhino" tab-lock folder showcasing Brian Hochstrat's incredible Italian bulino-style engraving and gold-appliqué depicting scenes from Homer's poems the *Iliad* (one side

of the handle) and the *Odyssey*. It also sports an RWL-34 blade and 416 stainless steel frame. If that doesn't satisfy the knife lover in you, nothing will.

Introduction

Honestly, knifemakers are helping to revive the U.S. economy. It's a theory I've heard and read about, one that's been bandied around lately in newspapers, on television news and within online forums and articles. Knifemakers are not specifically mentioned or pinpointed, but they might as well be. The thought process goes like this: after the bank bailouts, housing collapse and stock market crash (or at the least the "great recession"), the unemployment rate skyrocketed and people found themselves out of work, forced from their homes, in debt, bankrupt or suffering extreme poverty. Large corporations like General Motors, Lehman Brothers and Delta Airlines were also bankrupt, and no one was hiring. There wasn't a quick fix for reviving the economy, and the only thing, theorized some, that would at least help jump-start a recovery would be innovation, self starters—entrepreneurs opening their own small businesses.

Enter the innovative knifemaker.

Starting a business is never easy, but the American spirit is not about taking the easy way out, and knifemakers have been going it alone for as long as hammers have been hitting anvils. Few of those hammerheads strike gold, but there is pride in workmanship, in being a craftsman. The quality of workmanship that modern custom knifemakers exhibit is unsurpassed, and the innovation in custom knives has never been more widespread. People unfamiliar with the state of custom knifemaking find themselves flabbergasted by the knives made today, blown away by the quality, craftsmanship and artistry. Those who are familiar still find themselves in awe at the beauty of the knives and ability of the knifemakers.

To say that knifemakers have a hand in reviving the U.S. economy is not such a stretch after all, and to go further and say they're working on the world economy is not so farfetched. Knifemakers listed in the "Custom Knifemaker Directory" of Knives 2013 represent 30 countries around the world. Innovations in knives often coincide with those in the steel industry. Yet there's more to a knife than a blade, and thus advancements in materials, mechanisms and patterns further propel custom knives into the technology sector here and abroad.

In the "Trends" section of Knives 2013 are "21st-Century Fold-Downs"—folders that incorporate meteorite or Stellite™ handles, bolsters and blades; titanium frames; "lightning strike" carbon fiber grips;

Ikoma Korth bearing systems; and more locks than a bike rack at the Tour de France. Speaking of American innovation, check out the "American Stickers" entry in "Trends" for a look at custom knives fashioned by makers living in each of the 50 states.

"Dress Folders" and "High-Art Handle Work" get play in the "State Of The Art" section of the book, as do "Mecca-Worthy Mosaics," "Double-Take Damascus," "Stone-Cold Steel Austenites" and "Cast Guards and Pommels." That doesn't include features on engraving, sheath making, scrimshaw, wire inlay and carving. Other trends involve knife designs from the Far East; "Bowie Birthrights" and "Blow-The-Door-Hinges-Off Bowies;" camp knives; horsemen's, falconer's and huntsmen's swords; "Easy-Handlin' Hunters" and "Fiery Fighters."

How else can knifemakers lend a hand in the economic recovery? How about writing their own feature articles about knives? Knifemaker and director of the Knifemakers' Guild, Kevin Hoffman pens a feature on the Guild as a strong alliance of independent artists. Knifemaker Michael Burch tells us why the "Latest Friction Folders Are Freaky Good," and knife collector Don Guild gets into the act with "Art Knive$ A$ Inve$tment$." Fellow collector Roger Pinnock gives "Tips for Knifemakers" from his own unique perspective.

Other makers leave the writing to the world's best knife wordsmiths, with such including Pat Covert who explains why these are "Fat Times for Slip-Joint Followers;" Dexter Ewing, who covers "Formidable Tactical Folders;" Attorney At Law Evan F. Nappen who describes a "Miracle in New Hampshire;" Mike Haskew and his "The Knife Aquatic" feature on models with pearl, shell, coral and even fossil-walrus-ivory handles; James Morgan Ayres, giving us a history lesson on the "Arms of Malta;" and Richard D. White who reminds us that the "Large Folding Hunters" of yesteryear literally "Swallowed the Hand."

Who needs bank bailouts and government subsidizing? Why depend on Wall Street executives to make wise and sound investments? We'll just make the best knives in the world, market and sell them, and display the edged wonders right here, within the color, glossy pages of Knives 2013.

Joe Kertzman

2013 WOODEN SWORD AWARD

Experienced knife collectors and general enthusiasts have likely seen small knives that slide into the pommels or butt ends of swords, bowies or large daggers, similar to how tweezers and toothpicks slide into milled-out compartments in the red handles of Swiss Army Knives. Some knife companies also offer two knives that fit into one sheath, or a piggyback knife that rides in the handle, on the spine or in the bolster area of another, maybe a hunter and skinner, or a hunter and caper combo. Then there are scissors that come apart to create two separate knives. The innovation is endless.

A "first ever" for this *Knives 2013* editor, though, is a double-action automatic folder that snaps—in the open position, mind you—into the handle and full-tang area of a large Persian fixed blade. We're talking about a perfect pocket not only pierced through the handle scales, but the full tang of the large knife, a total package that is held to tight tolerances, and exhibits fine fit and gorgeous finish.

The guilty and dynamic knifemaking duo is Shaun and Sharla Hansen, who, together, fashioned the 21-inch Persian art knife to incorporate a Turkish-damascus blade, gilded white mother-of-pearl handle, a sculpted guard, and engraved and gold-inlaid ferrule and pommel. It comes with a stainless steel sheath with pierced and carved stainless caps wrapped over each end, 24k-gold inlay and Victorian-style engraving. Mechanical latches hold the small double-action automatic snuggly in place.

The auto folder is 3.75 inches open and sports a 1095-and-203E-damascus blade, a 416 stainless steel frame, carved guard, mother-of-pearl handle scales, and engraved and gold-inlaid bolsters.

In addition to fashioning fine knives, Shaun and Sharla are teammates when it comes to work, play and family. They love the outdoors, ride horses on pack trips, hunt and fish, and fly aircraft they, of course, build themselves. Some of the awards they've won include "Best Of Show" and "Best Art Knife" at the 2010 BLADE Show, the Jim Schmidt Award at the East Coast Custom Knife Show, and now the 2013 Wooden Sword Award. Congratulations to a great knifemaking team, and keep the momentum going!

Joe Kertzman

Eric Eggly, PointSeven Studios photo

Tips for Knifemakers–
A Collector's Perspective

How does a maker promote his knives in what has become a crowded and competitive market?

By Roger Pinnock

Having been a collector and custom knife enthusiast for over 25 years, I have had the opportunity to observe that, while the fundamentals of the industry have remained the same—quality construction and innovative design—much else has changed, and quite dramatically so.

The information superhighway is not only open, but also expanding at a near exponential rate with increasing traffic moving at ever-higher velocity. The sheer number of custom makers, and good makers at that, vastly exceeds that which could have been reasonably forecast a quarter-century ago. So how does a maker manage to stand out and connect with potential buyers in what has become a crowded and competitive market? What follows will hopefully provide some insight, from a collector's perspective, on that very question.

Where Do You Find Collectors?

The first step is to make it as easy as possible for them to find you. To that end, a well produced website has become an increasingly key component in a successful marketing and promotion strategy. It will only become more so going forward. The days of stuffing an envelope with $3 and mailing it in for a maker's brochure are well and truly over. For the newer knife collectors of today who were born into the computer age, if you're not on the Net, you simply don't exist.

Even for those who, like me, actually walked this earth in the days between the discovery of fire and the creation of the World Wide Web, the first step in following up on a tip about a terrific new knifemaker is to check online for his website. If there isn't one, the inquiry just might come to an early end.

The site itself should be simple, clear and easy to navigate. It should introduce you to potential customers and, more importantly, introduce them to your work. There should be a gallery of quality photographs of your work, and I fully endorse the phrase coined by professional photographer Jim Cooper: quality photographs don't cost, they pay.

If only a maker and buyer see the latest and best knife creation, the marketing potential of that piece has been utterly squandered. And if your Web gallery contains poorly lit, blurry images of your knife resting on the bathroom floor mat, you are definitely not putting your best foot forward, even if you do manage to keep them (your feet) out of the frame. Keep your

Dan Farr's combat knife in a black-powder-coated Cru Forge V blade features a contoured, stippled walnut handle laminated with carbon fiber for additional strength. *(SharpByCoop. com photo)*

With no alignment pin, yet of takedown construction, the guard and spacer alignment of David Wesner's camp knife is accomplished using a precision boss/pocket system. It sports a 1084-and-15N20-damascus blade, a Turkish-twist-pattern damascus guard, and a stabilized-koa-wood handle. Recently, on www.bladeforums.com, Wesner presented a detailed work-in-progress (WIP) thread detailing the many steps taken in creating the damascus camp knife, from the forging of the steel itself to the final polishing of the handle and all stages in between. *(SharpByCoop.com photo)*

site updated and give viewers a reason to come back, such as occasionally making a knife available for sale exclusively through the site.

Also, use your site to build client lists by inviting subscriptions to future updates. Remember, it's not "spam" if subscribers voluntarily sign up and can easily opt out. There are many good examples of quality sites out there, including those of Burt Foster (www.burtfoster.com), Don Hanson III (www.sunfishforge.com) and Kyle Royer (http://kyleroyerknives.com).

Engage Potential Buyers

Web forums provide a tremendous low-cost (or no-cost) opportunity to engage with potential buyers and make them aware of your work. While there are potential pitfalls, the marketing upside is far too great to ignore. Recently, on www.bladeforums.com, Michigan bladesmith David Wesner presented a detailed work-in-progress (WIP) thread detailing the many steps taken in creating a damascus camp knife, from the forging of the steel itself to the final polishing of the handle and all stages in between.

That thread generated well over 13,000 discreet views, and according to the maker, generated orders for similar knives as well. His primary investment was time, and it paid off admirably. Other forms of social media, such as Facebook and Twitter, are increasingly being employed by makers as a virtual means of keeping in contact with existing customers, and more significantly, introducing their work to potential new customers.

While the Internet has had an impact on knife shows from the standpoint of competing purchase opportunities, it can never and will never replace the experience of seeing and handling the work of a variety of makers all at one place and time, or the camaraderie of a shared experience with people who love knives just as much as you do. And this should amount to a statement of the obvious, though experience suggests otherwise—try to actually have knives available for sale on your table.

If you are in the fortunate position of having your knives be in such demand that you regularly sell out at each show, don't pre-sell everything the night before in your hotel room. Keep at least a few pieces available for those lined up at the show opening, and consider asking some early buyers to let you continue to display sold pieces.

Don't treat your prices as a highly classified secret—the price should be legibly displayed near the knife itself. I know some makers are of the view that hiding the price forces the potential buyer to ask, hence granting the maker the opportunity to engage in salesmanship. This, in my view, alienates more potential buyers than it attracts.

While you will obviously want to bring examples of your work that you feel will be the most saleable, also consider displaying at least one piece that represents your best work—your personal state-of-the-art piece de resistance that shows buyers what you can accomplish.

One of the successful show strategies of Rochester, N.Y., maker Dan Farr is to always strive to have something new to show potential buyers visiting his table. At successive shows he has introduced engraving as an upgrade embellishment on some pieces, carbon fiber on handles, laminated wood handles for increased strength and a unique aesthetic touch, and external "strong shoulders" for added strength on hidden-tang, fixed-blade pieces. A maker who demonstrates continued drive to improve his craft invariably creates a positive resonance with collectors.

Pricing is an area that has long presented significant challenges to makers, but in today's highly competitive market, getting the price right has never been more important. And the key to setting prices that are not only sustainable, but provide a foundation upon which to build, rests on understanding your market position. Simply looking at a comparable piece from another maker and concluding that your knife should command the same price is not a workable pricing strategy. You need to have an understanding of a broad cross-section of work in your particular genre, the range of prices commanded by various makers, and some understanding of what factors contribute to price variations within a given segment.

Pricing Is Crucial

The information superhighway is your friend here, because much data can be gained from dealer sites, maker sites and forum sales, as well as the more traditional venues such as knife shows. Understanding the importance of the secondary market is key as well. How do your knives perform compared with those of your competitors? This is a subject that could form the basis of an entire article unto itself, but if one message can be communicated, it should be this: Pricing is a crucially important factor in a saturated market.

The following isn't meant to suggest a predominantly negative perception of makers and their work.

Burt Foster presents a wide cross-section of his work to browsers of his website, including many of his signature stainless-over-carbon steel laminated blades.

Indeed, my experiences over the years have been overwhelmingly positive. But when collectors get together and chat at the bar after the show closes or online anytime, there are some consistent themes that emerge as to why a particular piece, or the work of a particular maker, had been passed over. I've selected just five of the more common examples.

1. Handle materials—get the good stuff. Too often a superb blade is painstakingly created, and then finished with some block of lifeless mystery wood that happened to be lying in a dusty corner of the shop. Whatever material you choose, make it the best quality you can get and a premium example of its kind.

2. Sharp matters. Embellishments are great on the right piece, but no matter how fancy you make the knife, make certain it leaves your shop with a keen edge. The buyer should be able to stake his life on that edge from the moment he opens the box.

3. Pass on the snake oil. While it's more than okay to engage in the romanticism that attaches itself to custom knives, understand that today's buyer is far more informed (all those WIP [Work In Progress] threads on knife forums are most educational) and thus not likely to believe that your secret quench in virgin goat's blood by the light of a full moon will impart magical properties to your blade.

4. Never speak ill of another maker's work. This doesn't happen often, but results in a lingering turn-off when it does. By all means promote what's good about your knives, but do not point out what you feel is bad about the work of others. In fact, makers who take the opportunity to both praise and recommend the work of others tend to gain credibility.

5. Price. As discussed above, the most beautifully crafted knives will not maintain saleability in the primary and secondary markets if the pricing is out of line.

From a collector's perspective, we are quite arguably living in the golden age of custom knifemaking. Never before have we been so spoiled for choice of quality handmade knives available through multiple venues. That this creates a corresponding challenge for newer and established makers alike is obvious. It's harder for the new guy to make his voice heard and all too easy for the old hand to get lost in the crowd. But the challenge can be met.

As ever, understanding the goal and having a plan to accomplish it are key prerequisites. While I don't envy makers the task, I have no doubt that today as in days past talent combined with a drive to succeed will ultimately bear fruit.

Latest Friction Folders Are Freaky Good!

Long before pockets were invented, early man put a rivet between a blade and a handle, and a friction folder was born ... just not for pants carry yet

By Michael Burch

One of the many great things about the knifemaking industry is that it is always looking for ways to re-invent itself and keep its customers coming back for more. Old designs are raised from the depths to be modernized and that is part of what makes custom knives so fascinating. Trends come and go, and right now one of the oldest and simplest folding knife designs is making a comeback—

the friction folder—but you won't recognize it in its new form. This isn't the primitive-styled friction folder with a metal collar around the front of an antler-tip handle you might remember from yesteryear.

"Friction folder" is a fairly loose term for such a knife. Throughout history it has had many

Deryk Munroe's "Revenant N Model" comes in a variety of colors, shapes and blade finishes, and features a deep-pocket carry clip, among other amenities.

names, a "peasant's knife," "penny knife" or "tobacco knife," just to name a few. It is basically any folding knife that employs a tight pivot to regulate the ease of opening and closing the blade. The knife style is certainly the earliest folder known to man. With the advent of the Iron Age, the simplest folders were invented—a rivet (pivot) through the blade and handle, and "voila," early man had his first pocket-knife, and long before pockets were invented!

The knives were simple utilitarian pieces put to work cutting up food, gardening and accomplishing related chores. The Romans also utilized a simple folder for eating on the go, as explorers and travelers carried such portable knives during excursions. The folding knife was still relatively rare until around the 1700s when cutlery was produced at a slightly quicker pace. Those blades evolved into the peasant's knife and penny knife (called such because of the cost).

The mechanics of the modern friction folder include an extension off the tang of the blade that presses against a stop pin or back bar in the open position, and is used to open the folder from the closed position. Older pieces incorporated a metal collar around the front of the handle that would act as the blade stop in the open position.

In the world of knifemakers trying to outdo each other with the latest, greatest locking mechanisms for folding knives, the friction folder is like a breath of fresh air with a beautiful aura that lies in its simplicity. Years ago blacksmiths who forged steel blades and those who made neo-primitive pieces were the only ones fashioning friction folders. They infused antler tines with forged blades (beautiful pieces in their own right), but now you can find a wide variety of makers putting together their version of the ancient folder using some of the latest and greatest materials.

Brian Fellhoelter

A machinist by trade, Brian Fellhoelter utilized his skills to start creating folders in 2006 because he wanted to make a knife for his own pocket, but folks took notice, and orders rolled in. And though relatively new to knifemaking, he has already stacked up several awards, including the "Best Tactical Folder" Award at the 2011 BLADE Show. He now has one year under his belt as a full-time knifemaker.

Fellhoelter approached friction folders from a unique direction. He wanted to use the stop bar as a bottle opener, and to make a folder small enough to fit in a coin pocket, and thus the "Frikky" was

born. When asked why he thought customers were drawn to friction folders, Fellhoelter replied, "The usefulness, and novelty of the package, and the price. How many other quality, handmade folding knives can you find at this price?" He went on to say, "Also, they're legal, fit right in, and aren't intimidating in places like much of Western Europe where locking knives are banned."

Utilizing synthetic materials such as carbon fiber and G-10 for the handle scales, and CPM-154 for the blade, the "Frikky" is a fresh look at the old style. The knife features a 1.8-inch blade and comes in at 4.125 inches overall. To help keep cost down, Fellhoelter makes the "Frikky" in batches.

Deryk Munroe (Munroe Knives)

Based out of Montana and an avid outdoors-man, Deryk Munroe has made a variety of styles of knives, including forged pieces and fixed blades, but he's probably best known by current collectors for his stylistic folders that feature layers of high-tech materials.

This year, Munroe debuted the "Revenant N Model" folder that features a 2.9-inch CPM-154 blade in a variety of finishes, and an overall length of 6.75 inches. The standard folder sports an anodized-titanium frame with contoured and milled G-10 handle slabs. It also comes with a deep-pocket carry clip, for which Munroe folders have become known. When asked why he decided on this pattern, Munroe offered, "I wanted to make a folder that was simple, lightweight and legal to carry almost anywhere." When deciding on a friction folder, his criteria included "high-tech materials with good ergonomics." He definitely met and exceeded his customer's wants and needs, as collectors snatch up every piece as soon as it's posted for sale. Munroe is currently not taking orders, but makes the knives in batches to sell. His list price for the base Revenant N Model: $325.

Mike Snody

The "Money Friction Folders" by Mike Snody are the epitome of "old meets new," with the "new" being the best materials available to knifemakers. A choice of blade materials includes Chad Nichols stainless damascus or knifemaker's-grade titanium infused with a special Black Diamond carbide edge. Snody employs 6AL4V titanium for some of the frames and handle scales, and usually anodizes them and brings them up to a high polish. He took the friction folder design a step further by adding an extra hole

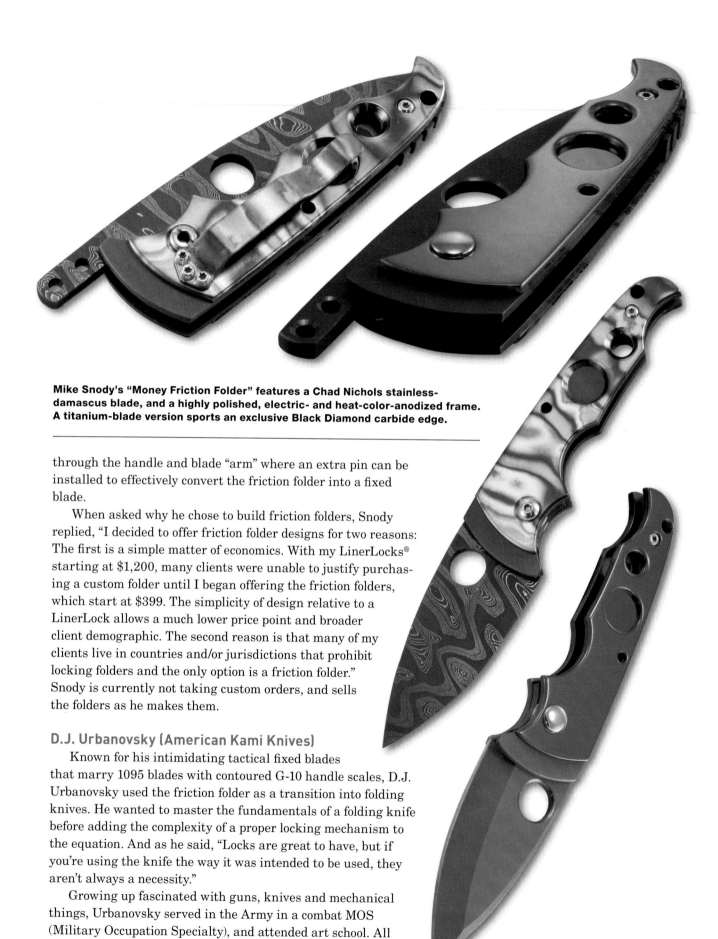

Mike Snody's "Money Friction Folder" features a Chad Nichols stainless-damascus blade, and a highly polished, electric- and heat-color-anodized frame. A titanium-blade version sports an exclusive Black Diamond carbide edge.

through the handle and blade "arm" where an extra pin can be installed to effectively convert the friction folder into a fixed blade.

When asked why he chose to build friction folders, Snody replied, "I decided to offer friction folder designs for two reasons: The first is a simple matter of economics. With my LinerLocks® starting at $1,200, many clients were unable to justify purchasing a custom folder until I began offering the friction folders, which start at $399. The simplicity of design relative to a LinerLock allows a much lower price point and broader client demographic. The second reason is that many of my clients live in countries and/or jurisdictions that prohibit locking folders and the only option is a friction folder." Snody is currently not taking custom orders, and sells the folders as he makes them.

D.J. Urbanovsky (American Kami Knives)

Known for his intimidating tactical fixed blades that marry 1095 blades with contoured G-10 handle scales, D.J. Urbanovsky used the friction folder as a transition into folding knives. He wanted to master the fundamentals of a folding knife before adding the complexity of a proper locking mechanism to the equation. And as he said, "Locks are great to have, but if you're using the knife the way it was intended to be used, they aren't always a necessity."

Growing up fascinated with guns, knives and mechanical things, Urbanovsky served in the Army in a combat MOS (Military Occupation Specialty), and attended art school. All

The "SHFF" (Space Hornet Friction Folder) from D.J. Urbanovksy gets its name because it "looks like it came from outer space." The SHFF parades a chisel-ground 1095 blade, a hefty G-10 handle and a back spacer with a "skull-crusher" pommel.

Brian Fellhoelter wanted to use the stop bar of a friction folder as a bottle opener, and to make a folding knife small enough to fit into a coin pocket, and thus the "Frikky" was born.

this led him to launch the American Kami custom knife company with 70 bucks in his pocket, a drill press and a Dremel tool. He has since become a full-time maker for the past six-plus years.

The "SHFF" (Space Hornet Friction Folder) gets its name because it "looks like it came from outer space," he says. "If aliens visited Grandpa on the farm back in the '40s, and they made a knife together, this is what it would look like." When building the folder, Urbanovsky wanted the blade to be as "bombproof" as possible, so he utilized a steel back spacer with an integral open/closed blade stop and an exposed "skull-crusher" pommel. The 3.5-inch 1095 blade is chisel-ground. To further the modern look, Urbanovsky offers a choice of G-10 or carbon fiber handle scales. His base price for the piece: $400.

Urbanovsky continues to accept orders and has a waiting time of 12-18 months. He also has an "Available" page on his website.

Not only has the friction folder evolved into a new form, but it has also taken a whole new material makeup, look, feel and direction. Only a handful of knifemakers are showcased herein, but there are plenty more out there putting modern spins on ancient-era knives. Whether using your "high-speed" friction folder to open up boxes, or slice up an afternoon snack, you'll find a modern friction folder to be a welcome addition to any knife collection, and much easier on the wallet, too.

Contact:

Brian Fellhoelter
760-223-2503
Brian@knifewerks.com
www.knifewerks.com

Deryk Munroe
P.O. Box 11698
Bozeman, MT 59719
www.munroeknives.com
info@munroeknives.com

Mike Snody
361-443-0161
Snodyknives@yahoo.com
www.snodyworld.com

D.J. Urbanovsky
402-813-0508
info@americankami.com
www.americankami.com

Arms of Malta ...
Sally Forth Into Pitched Battle

Tools and weapons teach their own lessons during a day spent at Malta's Palace Armory

A magnificent display in The Palace Armoury showcases a collection of armor worn by the Knights of Malta in the 16th century.

By James Morgan Ayres

Steel remembers. I'm holding the grip of a 500-year-old rapier in my right hand. The Milanese steel blade lies across my left palm, and with that, visions flash before me—the heat and crush of battle, the Ottoman Turkish warrior slashes at my belly and misses as I draw back, then thrust the rapier's point into his throat. Quickly I withdraw my blade and beat another Ottoman's scimitar out of line, and as he comes through the breach in our wall, I slash his sword arm. The knight beside me, my comrade in arms, strikes him down with a blow of his mace. Yet more of the Turks pour through our breach, behind them an army of thousands press forward, and we drive them from the breach and sally forth into pitched battle.

Although my imagination traveled to the chaos

The impressive close-up reveals a Maltese cross embossed on a 14th-century rapier.

of the Siege of Malta in 1565, a key battle in the defense of Europe, my physical being is in the curator's workroom of the Palace Armory in Valetta, Malta. The rapier in my hand once belonged to a knight of the Sovereign Order of Saint John, also known as the Knights of Malta, and is marked with their symbol: the Maltese Cross. These knights, along with auxiliaries and Spanish reinforcements defeated the army of Suleiman the Magnificent when they attacked Malta.

This victory was a turning point in the centuries-long wars between East and West. Malta repelled the Turkish assault, thereby preventing Suleiman's armies from capturing a strategic location from which to launch an invasion of Europe. Across Europe people celebrated their deliverance. Although it was not known then, this would be the last epic battle involving crusader knights.

The curator of the Palace Armory, Robert Cassar, and curator emeritus Michael Stroud generously allowed me to handle one of the many rapiers in their care. The 500-year-old weapon balanced perfectly as I moved to en garde*, then to other fencing positions: tierce, quarte, seconde, prime, and then brought my point back in line. I moved slowly out of respect for the antique sword, the close confines of the museum

workroom and the sensibilities of my hosts. But the 48-inch, double-edged blade has a life of its own. It incites, and I have to hold myself back from a sharp balestra and a full power lunge.

The memory in the steel guides me. My movements bear only slight resemblance to modern sport fencing with its rules and protocols. The rapier's grip is smooth and oval shaped, and it fits my hand comfortably, the blade only slightly pitted. The fine-grained steel blade retains a deadly cutting edge and point, and is to a modern sport fencing foil as a Colt .45 automatic is to a water pistol.

The rapier I handled was a work a day weapon, not a fine court sword that never saw battle, and is but one of dozens of rapiers in the museum, along with pole arms, scimitars, sabers, cutlasses, daggers, muskets, cannons, full suits of amour, everything but gunpowder needed to repel a medieval invasion.

Cassar and Stroud were generous with their time and knowledge, spending the better part of a day with my wife and me, and allowing us unlimited photographic access to the treasures in their charge. They were also heroically patient with my many, many questions.

The Palace Armory is unique in that while it's a museum today, it is the actual building where many

Grand Master Martino Garzes, Knight of Malta, wore the full suit of armor between 1595 and 1601. The Milanese-made armor, shown from the knees up, is circa 1590.

of these arms have been stored for centuries, the armory where the knights and other soldiers went to arm themselves for war. The two wings of the building contain an extraordinary collection of arms and armor—all manner of edged weapons, full plate and partial armor, crossbows, pole arms, firearms including handguns and muskets, and enormous canons weighing tons.

Decisive Siege of Malta

Sworn and consecrated knights came to Malta, a critical strategic point from all of Europe, to defend against the Ottoman Turks and Barbary Pirates. It was a long-running series of battles, skirmishes and wars that lasted for centuries and culminated in the decisive Siege of Malta. Most of the swords and other edged weapons came from the famed workshops in Milan, the most prominent weapons fabrication city in its day. Others were made in Solingen, Toledo and lesser-known centers.

Firearms were in common use in the 16th century, but were single-shot weapons and had not entirely replaced steel

A collection of pole-arms includes halberds, lances, short poles and stabbing spears.

crossbows and edged weapons. Pole arms, with strong but flexible ash wood shafts, were a primary weapon of war. Swords of various kinds were the premier personal weapon, decisive in many battles and countless hand-to-hand combats.

In addition to an extensive collection of European arms, the Palace Armory also displays a large collection of Turkish weapons, many of them captured in battle. Prominent is the signature weapon of the East, the scimitar. There are dozens on display, some with ivory handles, and others of ebony and various hardwoods.

Many of the blades appear to have been folded in their forging, some are engraved. The sword and the scimitar symbolize the cultural and religious differences between Christians and Muslims that led to centuries of warfare. These two weapons are also emblematic of differences in tactics.

The sword as typified by the rapier went through centuries of evolution. The rapier was slimmed down from the broadsword for speed. The guard evolved from a simple cross guard through various forms and into the later bell-shaped guard that provided full hand protection. Often described

as a thrusting weapon, the rapier also had sharp double edges and was used as a cut-and-thrust weapon against unarmored or lightly armored opponents. When faced with an armored opponent, a swordsman used the rapier to thrust into joints and weak spots in the armor.

The scimitar, a Turkish sword, was primary a slashing weapon, although it did have an effective point. Turks and others from the East preferred the slash, or cut, for certain tactical reasons, including the perception that the slash was superior in a melee. The eastern methods of fighting were different from western fencing, and included a good deal of circular movement in which the slash was paramount. In addition, eastern amour, if any, was chain or leather and often a scimitar could cut through such light amour.

The tribes and nations of the East, similar to those of the West, fought each other as often as against the Christian knights. Only knights could afford full armor, and they were few in

Robert Cassar, curator of The Palace Armoury, holds a 14th-century rapier.

*Fencing Terms:

Balestra: a forward hop or jump, typically followed by an attack such as a lunge or fleche.

Beat: an attempt to knock the opponent's blade aside or out of line by using one's foible or middle against the opponent's foible.

Cut: an attack made with a chopping motion of the blade, landing with the edge or point.

En Garde, also on guard: the fencing position; the stance that fencers assume when preparing to fence.

Lunge: an attack made by extending the rear leg and landing on the bent front leg.

Prime: parry #1; blade down and to the inside, wrist pronated.

Quarte: parry #4; blade up and to the inside, wrist supinated.

Quinte: parry #5; blade up and to the inside, wrist pronated. In sabre, the blade is held above the head to protect from head cuts.

Rapier: a long, double-edged thrusting sword popular in the 16th and 17th centuries.

Seconde: parry #2; blade down and to the outside, wrist pronated

Thrust: an attack made by moving the sword parallel to its length and landing with the point.

Tierce: parry #3; blade up and to the outside, wrist pronated.

Scimitar: a backsword or sabre with a curved blade, originating in Southwest Asia (Middle East)

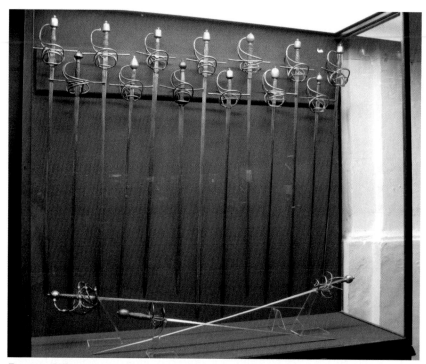

Famous Milanese swordsmith Antonio Piccinino, 1509-1589, reportedly made the rapiers.

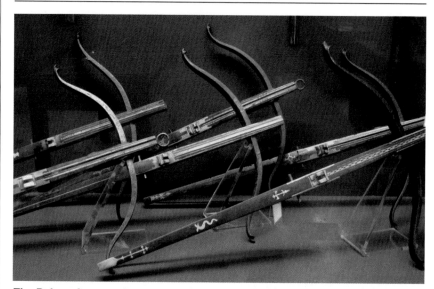

The Palace Armoury has amassed a nice collection of steel crossbows.

number. Most western soldiers were unarmored or lightly armored with a *cuirass* (chest amour) and helmet, which left them vulnerable to a slash that could and at times did literally "disarm."

The full plate amour worn by the knights was virtually impervious to the slashing scimitar. Some of the armor and helmets in the Palace Armory bear dents from powerful slashes or musket balls in battle, and simple testing by the maker. One suit of armor I examined had eight dents from musket balls in the chest; only one would have been from testing. Obviously such protection provided an advantage, but not always a decisive one.

No Light Knights

Fully armored knights were well protected in stationary combat, such as when they stood to defend a breach in the walls. But the weight of the

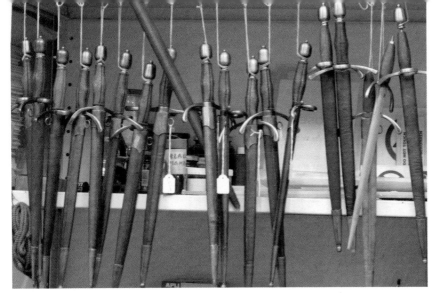

Michael Stroud, curator emeritus of The Palace Armoury, fashioned the replicas of period daggers used in movies.

plate armor hampered agility and led to fatigue even in the well-conditioned knights who had trained since childhood. Siege amour, used primarily in stationary defense, ran to 90 pounds. A full suit of battle armor, which was worn in changes and melees, weighed about 60 pounds and would wear down even a strong, well-conditioned knight in a short period of time. As firearms became more effective and more common, armor lost its utility. The Siege of Malta was one of the last major battles in which armor played an important tactical role.

Many varieties of swords are on display here, but they all have certain things in common: they are light, quick in the hand, and the blades smooth and free of saw teeth or anything that would hang up clothing, armor or flesh. Ignore the ivory grips, the engraving, decorative touches, differences in design, and even the fine-grained, polished and lustrous steel. To the trained and discerning eye, their purpose is clear—these are weapons.

What about knives? This is, after all, the *Knives* annual book. Amidst all the war weaponry and daggers by the dozen, I spotted

a simple knife with a single, dropped edge and a 14-inch blade accompanied by a leather sheath. To most it would appear to be an oversized chef's knife. While there were dozens of rapiers, scimitars, sabers, yatagans, daggers and cutlasses, there was only one lonely knife in the entire museum. Why, I wondered? Were they uncommon, rare even? Robert and Michael explained that, to the contrary, knives like this were the most common edged implements in daily use during the 16th century and for centuries before and after because this was an all-purpose design.

Knives like this were used in the hunt, not only to dress game, but also to dispatch it, and for everything from woodwork to food preparation. It was also an everyman's self-defense weapon. Swords were often restricted to the nobility and soldiers, and in any case were expensive single-purpose items. There are not many examples of these knives today simply because they were used so much in daily life—used, sharpened and used up.

Little has changed in terms of the utility of the big knife, even in today's world. As I wrote in the

book I authored for F&W Media, *The Tactical Knife*, "In every climatic zone on our planet where people live close to the earth, they use big knives as their daily tool: machete, bolo or parang in the tropics, the Leku or Sammi in the arctic. The big knife is also the preferred field blade at SERE (Survival, Escape, Resistance & Evasion) schools."

I was unable to determine the exact composition of the various steels used in the swords, but clearly none of them were made of any kind of modern stainless steel. They are all high-carbon forged blades, and they are still in good condition, functional after centuries. Today highly educated curators and scientists care for these blades and use sophisticated preservation methods, including specially formulated varnishes. But these weapons did not have that level of care over the centuries. They were cleaned after use and simply wiped down with oil, usually olive oil.

Yet here they are, tangible artifacts from centuries past.

Much can be learned by spending a day in the Palace Armory and by carefully observing the blades on display, by considering the implications of design and use, by meditating on what our world would be like today if Malta had fallen and Europe had been conquered by the East. Tools and weapons teach their own lessons. For any aficionado of the blade, or anyone interested in how our world came to be what it is today, a trip to Malta will be well rewarded. The entire island is soaked in history. You may not experience an imaginary journey to the 16th century, but you will be entertained and enlightened by visiting this historical monument.

Fat Times for Slip-Joint Followers

Just as people display antiques to create a warm mood in the home, a slip joint draws on that same appreciation of our past

By Pat Covert

The lure of the slip-joint folder is one of the strongest forces in the knife industry. Slip joints, or pocketknives as they're commonly known, remain a popular part of the knife arena despite the overwhelming amount of press paid to modern tactical folders. They have one of the strongest collector bases in all the land, a fervent group that includes buyers of new and antique models.

A trek to the annual BLADE Show in Atlanta reveals hungry knife enthusiasts packing the aisles and perusing cases of slip joints—with no blade locks, spring-assisted openers or auto mechanisms—of every description. The slip joint is over 175 years old, and the number of manufacturers who have come, gone and stayed is well into the hundreds, giving enthusiasts endless possibilities in collecting brands, patterns, handle materials and blade styles.

In addition to collectors, there is a strong customer base of folks who just like the advantages of carrying and using a slip-joint folder. One of the most obvious reasons is blade selection. Modern folders almost universally feature single blades, which limits their versatility. The user of a multi-blade pocketknife can chose from two or more blades, and several more in the case of the Swiss Army

The classic Folding Hunter, one of the largest of the slip joints, is a viable workhorse for field chores, as well as a highly valued pattern. Shown here is Boker's version, done up nicely in stag handle slabs.

This pair of Great Eastern Cutlery slip-joint folders, sporting burnt-stag handles, shows the versatility of the cigar-knife-design platform. At top is a harness jack, and at bottom a two-blade jack.

Hot, hot, hot! The latest collaboration between Tony Bose and W.R. Case & Sons, dubbed the "Back Pocket Knife," features a trapper-inspired design.

Knife, to best suit the chore at hand. Often there is a large blade for beefy chores and smaller blades that specialize in peeling, carving, slicing and dicing with more efficiency than a single-blade style can offer.

Folding knives were manufactured to an extremely high standard by the beginning of the 20th century when factories geared their slip-joint folders to a variety of professions. Electricians, doctors, cowboys, trappers and others benefited from blade styles and options tailored to their work.

Some continue to carry a traditional slip joint because it is easily concealed in the pocket, and a pocketknife does not have the perceived intimidation factor of modern tactical folders. Virtually all slip-joint enthusiasts are bound by one key factor—tradition. Most of us had a pocketknife passed down to us from our fathers or grandfathers, and the thought of that first knife brings back fond memories. Just as people collect and display antiques to create a warm mood in the home, a slip joint draws on that same appreciation of our past.

For sheer selection, no other type of knife offers the wide range of patterns and styles as the slip joint. A plethora of manufacturers such as W.R. Case & Sons, Queen Cutlery, Schatt & Morgan, Buck Knives and Boker of Germany have been manufacturing slip joints for many decades. More recently,

companies like A.G. Russell Knives, Canal Street Cutlery, Great Eastern Cutlery and Columbia River Knife & Tool have joined the revival, while storied names such as Ka-Bar (and the original Union Cutlery label), Remington, Winchester and Utica Cutlery (Kutmaster) are revitalized.

In addition, legendary brands that went under in recent years, including Kissing Crane, Schrade, Robert Klaas and Camillus, have had their trademarks picked up by other companies and rejuvenated.

Adding excitement to the mix is a cornucopia of patterns available to the slip-joint lover.

A Salacious Selection

The most common traditional styles like the trapper, Arkansas toothpick, stockman and whittler have

There will always be a demand for upscale handle materials. Shown here is a slick Queen Cutlery Wharncliffe Half Whittler in beautiful, iridescent abalone scales.

Ka-Bar's recently resurrected Union Cutlery label includes this handsome pair. Shown at top is a Swing Guard in burnt-licorice "roofline" jigged bone, at bottom a Sunfish in brown "worm-grooved" bone.

always been in abundance, followed by less-common but popular ones like the peanut, Barlow, folding hunter and Scout. These are joined by a host of more obscure patterns, such as the sleeve-board, gunstock, sowbelly, sunfish, cotton sampler, and harness jackknife, a good sign that users and collectors are growing and broadening their bases.

For some, the manufacturer is not as important as the quality and materials. One group of collectors prefers natural handle materials like bone and stag. On the other hand, slip-joint users may opt for something more affordable or durable, like Delrin®, and any number of woods such as cocobolo or rosewood. There will always be a market for upscale mother-of-pearl, black-lip-pearl and abalone handle scales.

Another factor that can weigh in a buyer's decision is whether to go with high-carbon or stainless steel blades. Some prefer the old-fashioned carbon variety for its ease of sharpening, while others forego the extra trouble for the corrosion resistance of stainless steel. Fortunately there are plenty of slip joints on the market to allow customers choices.

Slip joints do not follow trends like modern incarnations of tactical folders and chef's knives. While these seem to be centered on the hottest designs and newest steels, slip-joint users and collectors tend to view other factors such versatility and rarity in making their purchases.

The overall hottest-selling slip joint is the trap-

per, hands down. Not only is this true among production folders, but also in custom knives, which should not come as a surprise. Getting its name from the old fur trapping industry, the trapper has a rich tradition as a versatile knife around the farm or ranch, and its sleek lines make it one of the most attractive patterns.

A recent visit to a Website that specializes in Case knives revealed 150 iterations of the standard 4 1/8" trapper, many of them special editions, and that doesn't count popular offshoots such as the mini, tiny and slim-line trapper. The trapper has been morphed into other siblings, as well, including the jumbo trapper and "Mountain Man." Tony Bose's newest addition to the Case line, the "Back Pocket Knife," takes its design cues from the trapper. At last check on eBay, there were over 4,800 listings for trappers, with the closest contender being the stockman at slightly over 3,000 posts.

In the *2012 BLADE®'s Complete Knife Guide*, industry experts were consulted as to trends they saw in slip-joint sales. One of those was Kenny Wilson, owner of Sooner State Knives, an Internet dealer that sells a truckload of slip-joint folders annually. Upon going back to Kenny for a little more insight, he said, "As far as trends, it seems that any new pattern is immediately popular because a collector can now get one of each new handle color or variation as they are produced. Case seems to be the leader in introducing new patterns."

The utilitarian stockman will always be a big seller because it is a pattern often associated with traditional pocketknives. It typically sports three blades, making it a favorite among those who need a versatile utilitarian carry knife. Right up there with the stockman is the cigar pattern, a ubiquitous equal-end wonder that has spawned more offspring than a rabbit ranch.

Most people associate the Scout knife with the cigar pattern, and that's certainly the best way to describe it, but there are so many variations of the knife that a collector could never accumulate them all. Jack, pen, cattle (in three- and four-blade versions), harness jack, and even trapper and muskrat styles have all spun off from the cigar platform, and every traditional slip-joint maker worth their salt has paid homage to the pattern in some form or fashion.

The Corpulent Sunfish

Just because a pattern moves, however, doesn't mean it brings the highest dollar. Obscure patterns—ones a user or collector may never have a second opportunity to purchase again—bring high prices. A case in point is the corpulent sunfish, or "elephant toenail," as it is sometimes called. Buyers fall all over themselves bidding for these on Internet auctions, and you don't see a lot of them hanging around the sellers' tables at shows.

Other large slip joints such as the folding hunter and Coke Bottle command high prices, as well, due to the fact that, like the sunfish, they are produced in much smaller quantities and less frequently than their common brethren.

Limited editions and special issues continue to heat up the slip-joint market. Few companies do this as well as Great Eastern Cutlery, which manufactures limited editions of 50-100, and sometimes even less, of a pattern in a specific handle material. Given that manufacturers typically ramp up for sales of a SKU in multiples of thousands, knowing that you can own one of only 50 knives is enough to make any collector salivate.

Case has been extremely successful selling its Tony Bose premium editions, not to mention the regular production models sporting Tony's name, and these bring top dollar anywhere you can find them. Not surprisingly, Case remains the hottest-selling brand for current and vintage models.

The manufacturer's dating system, which began

Remington offers several old reproductions of its early, officially licensed Boy Scout knives. This one is based on the original RS3333 Cigar pattern created in 1923.

with its use of dots to identify the year of manufacture in 1970, has been a boon for the company and collectors alike. While other manufacturers have tried to spark interest in their knives by following suit, nobody does it like Case. Remington comes in a close second regarding historic interest. Old Remingtons, including the much sought-after Bullet series, command top dollar among collectors.

As mentioned, new steels have not been a major factor that drives the slip-joint market, but that could be changing. According to Wilson, "Any of the stainless steels are popular with collectors because they are easy to care for. Many older 'using' customers still prefer carbon steel because of the misconception that a blade that doesn't rust will not hold an edge. As the tactical knifemakers introduce new blade steels, they seem to eventually trickle down to slip-joint folders. As an example, Case employs 154CM for its high-end Tony Bose knives. It will be interesting to see when or if CPM S30V is used. Canal Street Cutlery and Queen both incorporate quite a lot of D2 tool steel."

Kenny also gives his take on what's hot in handle materials: "The most popular handle materials are stag, jigged bone, wood and mother-of-pearl, with jigged bone being hottest, probably because of the variety and the lower cost [as compared to stag or mother-of-pearl.]"

It would be remiss not to mention modernly styled slip joints. Spyderco rules the roost in producing high-tech slip-joint folders for enthusiasts who reside in certain foreign countries, such as England, and in some parts of the U.S. (New York State), where oppressive knife laws prohibit the sale and carry of

Spyderco leads the pack when it comes to modern slip joints. This is the company's popular Bob Terzuola model in a carbon fiber handle and premium CPM S30V blade steel.

A.G. Russell Knives labels this its Sowbelly Trapper. At 4 1/4" closed, it's a handful of a slip joint, nicely outfitted in a brown cocobolo handle.

folding knives with locks or spring-assisted openers. Other manufacturers are following suit, offering modern slip joints as an alternative to their locking fare. It will be interesting to see if this becomes a full-blown trend!

No matter your budget, chances are there's a slip joint that will satisfy your needs. Affordable slip joints produced offshore can be obtained in the $20 range, and for an extra $10

a stag-handle beauty awaits. High-quality knives produced stateside can be had in the $50-$100 range. Limited and special editions are available for as little as $100, but can escalate to four times that amount in some cases, such as the Case Tony Bose models. Regardless, whether you need a good using knife or strive to collect only the finest, these are fat times for slip joint followers!

Obscure patterns like this Schatt & Morgan Cotton Sampler have become increasingly popular in recent years. This knife sports "mountain moss green" worm-groove handle scales and upscale ATS-34 stainless steel.

The Knifemakers' Guild–
A Strong Alliance of Independent Artists

As the oldest organization in the United States dedicated to handmade knives, the Guild deserves some recognition

By Kevin Hoffman, Director, the Knifemakers' Guild

The Knifemakers' Guild is the oldest organization in the United States dedicated to promoting and preserving the art of the handcrafted knife. It and the American Bladesmith Society are the two largest organizations for knifemakers in this country, and likely worldwide. At 43 years old, the Guild has members all over the states and in several foreign countries, and has matured into a strong alliance of independent artists with a unified goal.

Our mission is to raise the awareness of our work, to support and challenge each other in the quest for excellence in craftsmanship, to foster responsible professional business practices and to sponsor the annual Knifemakers' Guild Show. The

KMG Show is a premier all-custom knife show that's open to the public and held in conjunction with the Guild's business meeting each September.

How did this all come to pass? Well, back in the late 1960's, independent knifemakers were few and far between, and largely isolated from one another. At that time A.G. Russell was in the business of selling Arkansas sharpening stones. In the course of his travels, he had met a number of knifemakers who plied their trade around the country. Having gotten to know them and admiring their work, it occurred to him that they could benefit from getting to know each other. So in February 1970, A.G. bought a block of tables at the Sahara Gun Show in Las Vegas, and invited them to come to the show and display their knives.

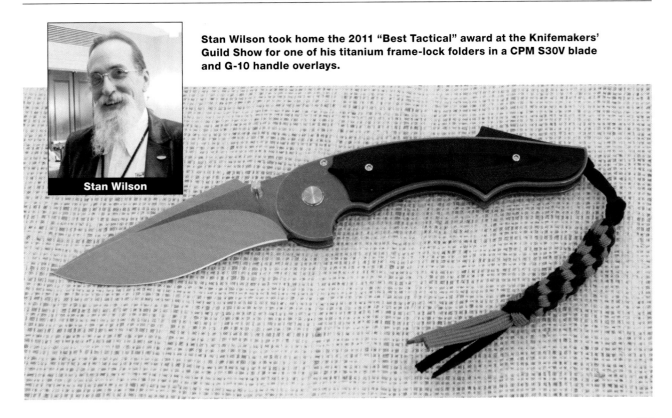

Stan Wilson took home the 2011 "Best Tactical" award at the Knifemakers' Guild Show for one of his titanium frame-lock folders in a CPM S30V blade and G-10 handle overlays.

Stan Wilson

Wesley Hibben

Winner of the 2011 Guild Show "Best Art" knife was Wesley Hibben for an Alabama Damascus sword with a 26-inch blade, a carved damascus guard with Mike Sakmar mokumé overlay, an amber handle and damascus pommel. Check out that snakeskin-inlaid sheath!

This provided them with the opportunity to share ideas and techniques, as well as start new friendships. By the end of the show they agreed that they wanted to get together again. Later that same year another meeting was arranged, and 11 knifemakers met at a show in Tulsa, Okla., to form the Knifemakers' Guild. The founding members were John Applebaugh, Walter "Blackie" Collins, John Nelson Cooper, Dan Dennehy, T.M. Dowell, Chubby Hueske, Jon Kirk, R.W. Loveless, John Owens, Jim Pugh and G.W. Stone. Loveless was elected secretary for a year, and Russell was made honorary president.

The fact that the founders chose to use the word "guild" as opposed to "association" or "organization" speaks to the kinship they felt with generations of master craftsmen over the ages, and the values they wanted to promote. The purpose of the Knifemakers' Guild is to promote the creation and use of handcrafted, custom-made knives as superior tools and valuable collectibles, and assist knifemakers in the development of their skills through the sharing of information about techniques, tools and materials. The KMG strives to provide access and education to the public about issues of craftsmanship, what constitutes quality, and what things to look for when buying fine cutlery. It is an effort to enforce ethical and professional business conduct, and if need be, help mediate in the event of a conflict. Last but not least the KMG provides an atmosphere of camaraderie.

Over the years the Guild Show has called many

cities home—Kansas City, Dallas, Orlando, Las Vegas, New Orleans and back to Orlando. Moving the show around the country was done as a way of broadening our exposure. In 2009 we moved it to the Seelbach Hilton Hotel in Louisville, Ky., to take advantage of the city's centralized location, putting us within a one day's drive to about two thirds of the country's major population centers. It's been a great move to a gracious city and a fabulous venue to call home each September.

Guests of the Gala

On Thursday night before the start of the show, the Guild hosts the complimentary President's Gala for honorary members, knifemakers and their spouses who feast on fine food, desserts and drinks. Live music by a string quartet and door prizes make for great conversation. Honorary members who attend the gala also get the opportunity to see and purchase some of the show's best knives at the special pre-show. Some of the other benefits of honorary membership are free early admission to the show each day, the quarterly newsletter and a free chance to win one of four knives fashioned by knifemakers and used in all of the advertising for the show.

There are five categories of membership in the Knifemakers' Guild:

1. Voting Members - for knifemakers who have completed the probationary membership requirements.

2. Probationary Members - They must be engaged in the making of bench-made knives for sale to the

Libor Tobolak

The blade of Libor Tobolak's knife, which took home the "Judges Choice" award at the 2011 Knifemakers' Guild Show, is fashioned from Egyptian jade using modern techniques.

Gil Hibben (left), President of the Knifemakers' Guild, presents the "Best Display" award to Paul Lansingh for assembling a collection of knives made by the Guild's leadership over the years.

public, including the grinding and/or forging of their own knives. Before attaining probationary status, they have filed an application signed by four voting members, have submitted promotional material representing his or her handmade knives, and have displayed their knives at the annual show where their work has been inspected by a technical committee. Probationary period is two years, at which time their knives must be displayed and inspected at the annual show before voting status can be granted.

3. Youth Members - Young people over the age of nine, who make knives under the supervision of a parent or mentor, may be admitted as probationary members under this classification.

4. Associate Members - This category of membership is reserved for those who are not knifemakers, but rather are engaged in a knife-related trade. Examples are, but not limited to, suppliers, photographers, publishers, purveyors, engravers and scrimshanders. Associate members do not have voting privileges and are not required to display at the annual show.

5. Honorary Members - These are the individuals, mainly collectors and a number of writers, who support the Knifemakers' Guild, promote custom knives and knifemakers, and advance the purposes of the Guild. Honorary members must be sponsored by a voting or probationary member. Knifemakers are not eligible for honorary membership.

When I joined in the early 80's, the sponsoring makers reviewed my work at the time they signed my application. Then when a new probationary member attended their first Guild Show, one or two

of the Board members would stop by his or her table, welcome him or her and do a quick check of their knives. Knives didn't undergo any further inspection unless there was some type of problem. One of the major problems facing the fast-growing custom knife business at the time was knifemakers who were taking orders and deposits, but not delivering on their promises. As a result, the KMG was highly vigilant to make sure that its members were adhering to ethical business practices, both during the probationary period and after earning voting status. This became an important thing for the collectors—the knowledge that the KMG would police its members and mediate any potential disputes.

Because of the confidence these policies gave collectors, membership in the KMG became important to a knifemaker's business prospects. When collec-

Rob Hudson was all smiles after winning the "Best Hunter" award (three years running!) for a clip-point fixed blade in an ancient-ivory grip.

Rob Hudson

tors attended other shows they would ask makers they didn't know if they were a member of the KMG, and if they were not, they were often asked "Why not?"

The Guild is made up of independent, strong-willed, unbelievably talented artists, yet when I asked them to give me some of their reasons for being KMG members they spoke with a surprisingly singular voice, echoing the same basic themes. They spoke of the friendships that they've made, the business contacts, and their pride in earning membership into an organization that stresses such high standards for quality, craftsmanship and ethical practices.

One thing that came up unanimously was the gratefulness to have access to the breadth and depth of so many tremendously generous and fantastically talented knifemakers who are willing to help each other improve. This open mentorship is remarkable. If you ask a fellow member about something, they'll not only explain how to do it, but they'll (more times than not) invite you to their shop to show you how. Try that with Ford or Chevy.

Stiff Competition

One of the highlights of the show each year is the judging of the awards competitions. This is an opportunity for the makers to compare their work to that of fellow makers, and win or lose it's a revelation. It's also a tremendous opportunity to pick the brains of the winners. The competition is judged by two fellow knifemakers for quality, technical innovation, design and artistic merit. The competition is stiff and getting tougher each year. The makers also have the opportunity to talk with the judges if they want to find out what, if any, deficiencies may have

kept them out of the winner's circle.

Wolfgang Loerchner joined the Guild in 1984 and has been making knives for 30 years. Winner of the 2011 "Best Folder" award, he said, "Joining the Guild and being accepted by the membership felt like joining a new family. The encouragement I received from other members was greatly responsible for getting my knifemaking career started. I feel that the Guild stands for and promotes the very best of our craft."

Winner of the 2011 "Best Fighter" award, Steven R. Johnson joined the Guild in 1971, worked with Loveless and has been making knives for 45 years. "The Guild, in many ways, started it all," he said, "at least as far as the organized custom knifemakers go. Early on, the feeling was that the Guild was a brotherhood where one could feel welcome and supported by the members. It's 2011, and watching the show, the leaders and the members, I get that same feeling. I don't see self promotion, I see efforts to, as the original purposes outlined: encourage ethical practices, help each other, promote knives and knifemaking, and hold an annual show and business meeting.

"The leadership is promoting the Guild and its members, not themselves as they fulfill their duties," Johnson added. "I think the new members still feel welcome and supported, and that they can walk into a room of 100 competitors and leave that weekend with a lot of new friends and mentors. That old feeling is still here!"

Rob Hudson, who has won the "Best Hunter" award at the show three years running, joined the Guild in 2004 and has been making knives since 2001. The truth is that his knives have the most flawless finish and just feel so darned good in your hand.

"Only at the custom level can you find the true artistry, imagination and design you have in today's cutlery world," Hudson remarked. "I feel that being a member of the KMG helps set a standard for a handmade knife and assures a purchaser that he or she is getting a quality knife. I believe this integrity sets a goal for a new maker and helps form a direction for his artistry."

Calvin Robinson, who has only been making knives for six years, joined the Guild in 2009 and landed the 2011 "Best Multi-Blade Folder." He had only this to say, "I joined the Guild in order to be associated with and to learn from the best knifemakers in the world!"

Libor Tobolak has been making knives for 30 years, but just joined the Guild in 2011, and won the "Judges Choice" award his first time entering. His knives are a unique combination of ancient and new. The blade of his winning entry was fashioned from Egyptian jade using modern techniques to shape the oldest of man's blade materials. A recent immigrant to the United States, he said, "I joined the KMG because it was my lifelong dream."

Jerry Johnson won the 2011 "Frazier Museum's Choice" award, which is judged and chosen by Owsley Brown Frazier, founder of the Frazier International History Museum in Louisville. Johnson, who has been making knives for 20 years, joined the Guild in 2009 and became a voting member in 2011. He remarked, "This is where world-class makers congregate. The organization stands for excellence, it has standards both ethical and technical for entry. It's about friendship, sharing and inspiration."

The "Best Display" award went to collector Paul Lansingh, who has been a long-time supporter of the Guild as an honorary member. He has put together a beautiful collection that chronicles the history of the Guild by assembling a display of knives made by the Guild's leadership over the years.

The formation of the Knifemakers' Guild was the spark plug that really ignited the modern custom knife movement. Later, Bill Moran, a KMG member and former Guild President, founded the American Bladesmith Society to champion the interest in the forged blade. Today, KMG members are active in state and local knife clubs and organizations all across the country that are helping to increase public interest in handcrafted knives.

Steven R. Johnson

"Best Fighter" went to Steven R. Johnson at the 2011 Knifemakers' Guild Show for his sub-hilt bowie/fighter with a full, tapered tang.

Wolfgang Loerchner

Upon winning the 2011 Knifemakers' Guild Show award for "Best Folder," Wolfgang Loerchner said, "I feel that the Guild stands for and promotes the very best of our craft."

THE KNIFEMAKERS' GUILD **31**

Art Knive$ A$ Inve$tment$

The author finds the price behavior of art knives a fascinating and challenging mystery, and attempts to address it

By Don Guild

Only 10 o'clock in the morning and this place is jammed! International buyers and onlookers focus their attention on the 100-plus art knives sitting on aligned white-linen-covered tables. How serious can adults get about a few pocketknives and a couple of kitchen knives? Very! The room buzzes with the buyers' prospects of fulfilling one of the two goals: 1. Buy a knife to keep in a collection; 2. Buy a knife to sell for a profit.

The scene is tense because the buyers fall into two competing groups, each motivated to win over the other. The first group, made up of genuinely seasoned collectors from all over the world, hopes to own a peerless art knife for its beauty and rarity. The second group, a crowd that means business, wants to buy a one-of-a-kind art knife in order to flip it on the spot to one of the ogling collectors and make a tidy profit, often doubling an investment of $12,000 to more than $20,000. Quite a motivation!

At this 2011 Art Knife Invitational (AKI), held every other year in San Diego, I'm talking about the most rare art knives in the world, not tactical fixed blades and folders, not hunting knives, not prune pickers, nor antique knives, but the finest of the finery. No underwhelming knives here. At this Mt. Everest of art knife shows, innovations and record prices are seen first. It's where 25 of the most skillful knifemakers on the planet are invited to converge at the end of October and present their wares.

Today 170 buyers vie for a little over 100 of these knives. Sure, anyone can place an order with one of the knife artisans at any time, but to wait five to 10 years for delivery puts a bit of a restraint on instant gratification. This show makes instant gratification possible for the select fortunate few whose names are drawn or whose bidding prices are not topped. Virtually every knife in the room is sold in a couple of hours, with prices that span from $1,800 to over $50,000.

As a collector who's bought and sold well over a thousand knives of virtue (as well as scads with diminished virtue), I seem to have rather strong opinions, yet I've had experience making mistakes in this art knife arena, since I collect and trade knives for my love of the art, not necessarily for a profit. But as my wife says, "It's better that you trade knives

This is it—the Jack Levin "Scroll" knife that, in 2005, sold for $5,700, yet brought $18,000 five years later! *(Dr. David Darom photo)*

rather than wives." I find the price behavior of art knives a fascinating and challenging mystery. I'll attempt to address it. Out of the thousands of knifemakers in the U.S., only a few climb to the top. Let's find out why.

I sought objectivity and a true consensus for this article on art knife prices, so I asked some of the most accomplished knife purveyors and collectors to pick their top six makers of art knives, and they came up with a list of dependable makers whose edged artworks show consistent price increases year after year, and who have consistent batting averages.

Therefore, based on the experience of the most knowledgeable specialists in the art knife world, who daily put their money where their mouths are, they collectively named these 19 makers:

- Nine votes each for Wolfgang Loerchner and Jim Schmidt
- Eight votes each for Juergen Steinau and Michael Walker
- Seven votes for Emmanuel Esposito
- Three votes each for Tony Bose, Ron Lake and Buster Warenski
- One to two votes each, in alphabetical order, for Ray Appleton, Thad Buchanan, Antonio Fogarizzu, Tore Fogarizzu, Elizabeth Loerchner, Bob Loveless, Bill Moran, Salvatore Puddu, Scott Sawby, Ken Steigerwalt and Owen Wood

Exception for Every Rule

But why do some knives constantly go up in price year after year, while others stay flat or decrease in value? Opinion varies considerably on this subject, and for every rule mentioned there's an exception. No single attribute is responsible for consistent value increases, but rather mélange of constituents work synergistically to create a champion.

Two important qualifiers combine to elevate an art knife to the top: 1. Aesthetically pleasing art and 2. Precise mechanics. When the two elements integrate in a manner that produces originality and excitement, the collector and the knife establish an emotional bond during the first few microseconds of the encounter, as in, "It speaks to me. What a fabulous knife!"

The cognitive part comes later. Most art knives of virtue exhibit easily discernible eye appeal along with smooth operation. For a top knife, two essentials validate the old adage, "Form follows Function," requiring an artistic blend of form and function to be a winner.

Once superior form and function are confirmed, several other factors come into play to influence the price of a knife. The secondary market is of utmost importance. A maker will be left behind, even if his work is superior, if he's unaware of how his knives' prices are trending. Having studied the art knife market for years, another constant has occurred to me. It's absolutely essential that, in order for his wares to consistently increase in price year after year, the maker's initial selling price must be below the secondary market price. Violate this rule and buyers drop like flies.

Take for example the knifemaking and marketing genius, Bob Loveless, who told me he carefully watched the way J.W. Denton, the world's largest purveyor of Loveless knives, priced knives. Loveless applied this as a conscious strategy, selling his wares at least

The sculpted and flowing Wolfgang Loerchner "Wing" sold in 2004 for $3,400, and again in 2011 for $20,000. *(David Darom image)*

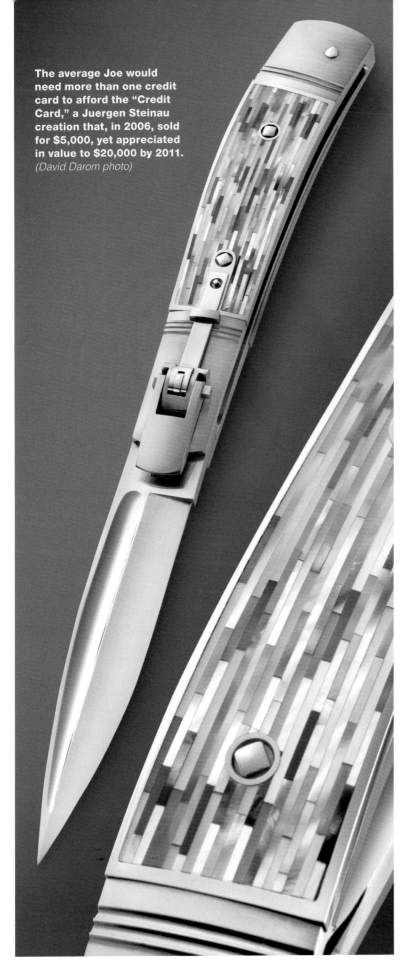

The average Joe would need more than one credit card to afford the "Credit Card," a Juergen Steinau creation that, in 2006, sold for $5,000, yet appreciated in value to $20,000 by 2011. *(David Darom photo)*

15 percent below the secondary market. In contrast, but with an identical result, Wolfgang Loerchner does something similar; he simply sells his knives at a fair but low price. Thusly, the market drives his prices up every year. A powerful four-word truism works here: "Performance rewarded is repeated."

In contrast to price-it-below-secondary-market logic, a phenomenon has happened to a few talented makers. Based on the fact they were backordered for a year or two, they priced their knives at the top of what the market would bear, but after a while purveyors and collectors backed off. Even the wealthiest collectors don't want to take a bath if they decide to sell on the secondary market. Little did these talented makers realize they were shooting themselves in the foot by bumping their prices too soon and too high.

I've seen several knives of these makers on the Web that can be purchased for half of what they sold for originally. It's a real purse string puller. And there are makers who erroneously price their knives "based on time and material." However the smart ones watch the secondary market and use that measure to set their initial selling price. The secondary market mandates a harsh but honest appraisal of true worth.

What are the characteristics of the six to 10 makers whose secondary market has consistently gone up most? What principles keep these makers in front of collectors to make them drool? Once a maker is in demand, well priced and backordered, smart makers don't just give in to the squeaky-wheeled collector who takes a knife home and stuffs it in a safe. That knife won't see daylight for five to 10 years. Out of sight means out of mind.

Exposure is key to staying on top. Therefore by having a strategy of selling some knives to selected purveyors, a maker leaves a little on the table and gets invaluable exposure on a hot purveyor's Website. Publicity is a powerhouse for establishing a maker's image and desirability. Ways of accomplishing this are well known, such as pictures in *BLADE® Magazine* and the *Knives* annual book, having a Website, personally appearing at quality knife shows and on knife forums, having knives in auctions, and being showcased in David Darom's art knife collector books.

Victors Top All Comers

Although auctions set market prices in the stratospheric world of fine art, this vehicle seldom exists in our relatively young world of art knives. Yet at art knife shows, one can find fully visible bid-up sheets, where buyers continue to bump each preceding offer until the final victors top all comers. Or secret bids can be placed in boxes for the highest bidders to be determined later. The use of bid-up sheets and secret-bid boxes at knife shows has established new highs for makers, and they are the closest things to an auction for setting market prices.

Another recent trend in setting art knife prices is growth in the overseas markets. Some of today's hottest collectors live in Russia, Taiwan, China, Europe and Indonesia. For example, a knife of Jack Levin that sold for $5,700 four or five years ago brought $18,000 on the current Russian art knife market.

The fact that the top five or 10 art knife makers have plied their craft for 20 or more years provides another component of price appreciation. Consistency, when all other factors are present, evidently predicates an increase in desirability and therefore increased dollar value. Yet once a top maker's backorder time becomes several years, the only

Not only did Michael Walker's "Zipper" sell at the 2011 Art Knife Invitational for $80,000, but also there were three offers pending for it later in the fall of the year. *(Francesco Pachi photo)*

way to acquire one of his knives quickly is to buy it on the secondary market. Supply and demand drive up the price.

Is crafting knives at least 20 years or more an earmark of a top maker? Not so! As with most things there are exceptions. Take the 29-year-old Emmanuel Esposito, who smashes this precept. How can his art be deemed by experts to be up there with Jurgen Steinau and Michael Walker so soon? Magnified by his 15 years of machining experience, this svelte Italian creative artist not only puts in 80-hour weeks, but he possesses the eye of a Leonardo da Vinci. He constantly conjures up exciting new designs, and with the use of fine watchmaking machinery, his knives feature exacting inlays and velvet

mechanics. A true virtuoso!

Do all top knifemakers turn out only four to 15 knives a year? Again not so! "Bob Loveless produced over 10,000 knives during his career," Denton told me. This contrasts with Jim Schmidt, who is said to have made up to 300 knives in his lifetime.

Nevertheless virtually every top maker is limited as to how many knives he can fashion. Walker, a full-time knifemaker, said when I interviewed him that some years he has made only three knives. As one of the top five or so knifemakers in the world, the price for Walker's knives reaches new heights year after year. By the time the final bell had rung at the 2011 AKI, the wining bid on Walker's 8-inch "Zipper" had ascended to $80,000,

driven by the 30 or so collectors bidding in mortal combat for the fair damsel. That's $10,000 per inch! Could an exceptional art knife be a better place than Wall Street in which to invest one's money?

Although intangibles seem difficult to define, how much influence do they have on prices? Many collectors (especially the newer ones) watch to see what longtime, sage collectors buy, and then follow their example. So the charade goes like this: "If the big guys want them, so do I, because the big guys don't make mistakes." Yet sometimes even a collector will buy a big name simply to impress his peers. A saying often heard is, "Buy the maker not the knife, if you want to make money." It probably works okay if you have no passion for the art and it's only the bucks you're chasing. Are you a flipper or a lover?

And then there are the tire kickers at leading knife shows, dropping their names in the lottery box for a particular knife, hoping to flip a winning knife for a profit. At the 2009 AKI, I stood next to collector Walter Hoffman and purveyor Dan Favano of IQ Knives at Steinau's table. Just after the drawing for Steinau's dagger, at the fixed price of $10,000, along came the fellow whose name was drawn. Favano offered him $16,000, and the guy made a quick $6,000 profit with no investment. This happens over and over at better shows. Today, retail for that dagger is $20,000, weird but true!

Confused yet? Sure, we all are. If you seek appreciation, look for a knife with intrinsic qualities from a dependable maker, whose knives show a consistent price rise. The acid test lies in the secondary market. But don't stay past midnight if you're in it for a profit. Follow the legendary Wall Streeter Bernard Baruch who said, "I made my money by selling too soon."

Large Folding Hunters Swallow the Hand

Substantial pocketknives excelled at skinning deer, cutting saplings and building shelter

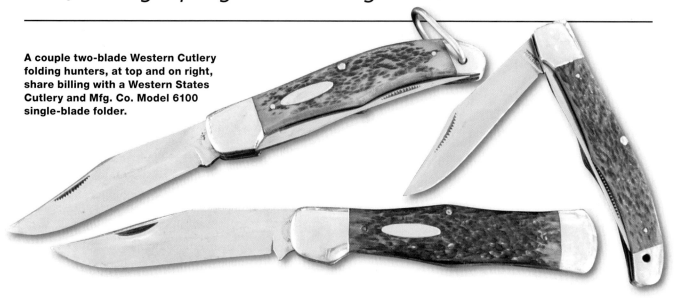

A couple two-blade Western Cutlery folding hunters, at top and on right, share billing with a Western States Cutlery and Mfg. Co. Model 6100 single-blade folder.

By Richard D. White

These knives are the "monsters of the midway," the "stop and take notice" knives that attract a small crowd when displayed. The largest of early folding hunters swallow up the hands of those who pick them up. Enthusiasts who dare open the blades are advised to keep a firm grasp on the knives themselves. The larger of early folding hunters frequently measure over 5 inches long when closed, and are an impressive 9 inches long opened.

Significantly larger than trappers or big jack-knives, folding hunters, "Coke Bottle folding hunters," or "American clasp knives," as they are known, hold a place of honor in American cutlery history. The mammoth folding knives were the standard for most outdoorsmen in the early 20th century, and remained popular until fixed-blade hunters gradually replaced them in the early 1940's.

Most were used to skin and dress out wild game, and were generally single blades with exceptionally strong back springs. The stiff springs resulted in a resounding "snap" or "click" as blades closed. The blades were usually much wider than those of other production knives, and often featured a clip point with a "match striker" nail pull.

The pointed clip blades were described in one brochure as "the perfect shape for sticking game." For the hunter, they became the perfect companion—heavy enough for belt carry, and with blades thick enough to not only skin deer, but cut saplings and stakes to make temporary shelters or stretch fur hides. The size allowed users to get firm grips on the knives when game was freshly slaughtered or the weather turned to sleet and rain.

Generally curvaceous, knives fit the hands like gloves, allowing a secure grip without danger of them dropping into flowing streams or thick underbrush. Enthusiasts often referred to them as "clasp knives" for how they were clasped in the hand.

W. R. Case & Sons Cutlery pioneered the style as early as the 1920's with the Model 62100 two-blade folder. Case has continued to produce a similar example through the decades, known to enthusiasts

Circa-1930's Colonial Cutlery single-blade folding hunters showcase colorful interlace-geometric-pattern celluloid handles. The blade spines of the top and bottom pieces are designed for scaling fish. Despite being 75 years old, the threesome is considered to be in mint condition.

as the popular Model #6265 Folding Hunter. The knife, like many clasp-type folding hunters, has an enlarged or swelled bolster on the top end. This exaggerated bolster gives significant strength to the blade end of the hunter.

Mellowed Yellow

Genuine stag was the preferred handle material, which tended to mellow into an almost transparent yellow surface with deep, dark grooves after being exposed to the moisture and lanolin present in the human palm. The knives can be found with other handle materials, most often ebony, rosewood or jigged bone. Some of the Coke Bottles were produced with celluloid handles, the most desirable being "cracked ice celluloid."

Most featured leather belt pouches, but others had holes through the bottom bolsters for leather lanyards that helped in removing them from their leather

sheaths. Indicative of their widespread outdoor use, some were advertised as: "Frontier Knife," "Western Favorite," "The Forest Ranger," "Yukon" and "Campers Knife." An example from a Maher and Grosh Catalog was touted as being "General Custer's Favorite Hunting Knife." One of the best known, made by Cattaraugus Cutlery Co., was called the "King of the Woods." That trademark just about sums it up.

Whatever name given to the folding hunters or clasp-style folders, the number of major knife companies that produced them is indicative of their popularity. Such would include Ulster Knife Co.; W. R. Case & Sons; New York Knife Co.; Napanoch; Miller Brothers; Challenge Cutlery Co.; Western States Cutlery and Mfg. Co.; Union Cutlery Co.; Utica Cutlery; Winchester; Cattaraugus Cutlery Co.; Maher and Grosh; Ulster Knife Co.; and probably a few others. Of those, perhaps the most collectible is the Winchester Model 1920, a 5 ¼" swell-center folding hunter with stag handle slabs. Current prices range from $1,200-1,500 apiece.

The New York Knife Co., known for many years as the maker of the "finest knives in America," went one better by adding a lock to the blade of its large folding hunter. The center locking mechanism

Among many other models, KA-BAR Cutlery manufactured the "Grizzly" (top) and a standard folding hunter in stag handle slabs.

ensured that the blade would not fold onto the user's fingers while in use. Unfortunately, New York Knife Co. went out of business during The Great Depression in 1931, meaning that anyone owning a knife stamped with the name or logo—a clenched arm and fist—owns a knife made during the 1920's, making it at least 82 years old.

In addition to its locking mechanism, the bottom bolster of the Coke Bottle folding hunter is exceptionally thick and engraved with "NYK" for "New York Knife." The shield on the jigged bone handle is similarly large and quite ornate, with the jigging pattern itself distinctive and immediately identifiable to collectors.

Another New York Knife folding hunter is stamped "Chipaway Cutlery Company," with initials "CCC" engraved on the bottom bolster. The stamp was used on knives sold by the famous E.C. Simmons Hardware Co. located in St. Louis. E.C. Simmons is known best for the "Keen Kutter" trademark, and merging with Winchester in the early 1920's.

Cattaraugus Cutlery Co. fashioned the "King of the Woods" pattern in six variations, all folding hunters etched with the blade logo "King of the Woods." While massive in size, the knives differed in specific features. One had a swing guard that opened simultaneously with the blade. Another showcased a massive swell-end bolster and a lanyard hole. The Model 12919 sported an unusually small bottom bolster, and distinctive curve to the knife itself. The Cattaraugus Cutlery catalog refers to it as a "Yukon" model, a reference to its possible use in Alaska. Each had a distinctive "worm groove" bone handle with deep grooves running along the scales and doubling as traction.

Coke-Bottle Shape

As their name implies Coke Bottle swell-centered folding hunters are shaped like Coca-Cola bottles. Offered by Colonial, Paris Bead,

Cattaraugus manufactured six "King of the Woods" folding hunters in "worm groove" jigged-bone handles. This model has a small bottom bolster and a swelled-center shape that allows for a firm grip.

Golden Rule Cutlery, Valley Forge, Western Cutlery (West Cut), Imperial and KA-BAR Cutlery Co., Coke Bottles paraded a range of celluloid handles, from "cracked ice" to colored swirls, plain yellows and reds, checkerboards, and stripes of all sorts. The plain yellow and lighter celluloid handles were ideal for corporate advertising and logos, with engraved knives gifted to the best customers or suppliers. Imagine the look on a customer's face as they were handed such an extra-large, impressive pocketknife.

Western Cutlery, once located in Boulder, Colo., produced quite a few models with various advertisements engraved on celluloid handle scales. The rather lucrative practice of manufacturing large numbers of identical knives with identical advertising became more appealing during the darker times of The Great Depression.

In terms of collectability, they follow the rule "larger is better." Although some marvel at the intricacies of smaller knives with multiple blades, most collectors are drawn to the massive size of knives measuring over 5 inches. Large size means longer and wider blades, and thicker and stronger backsprings, not to mention the sizeable slabs of stag or jigged bone needed to handle the monsters.

Maybe it's the call of the American frontier and what it represents that draws enthusiasts to folding hunters. Together with trappers and muskrats, they represent the most highly sought-after pocketknife patterns in the country, particularly in Texas and the southern states.

Overall condition is a major factor in determining value. As they saw heavy use, repeated sharpening,

A KA-BAR stag-handle folding hunter features a "match striker" nail pull and would have been the constant companion of any hunter or trapper.

and all kinds of weather conditions, folding hunters are often found in terrible condition. Opened and closed frequently, and not oiled regularly, many suffer from worn backsprings and blade pivots, making the distinctive blade snap almost non-existent. Misused more than other knife patterns, many show significant pitting. Inherent in the very design of such highly collectible pieces is that they handled the biggest chores and most strenuous tasks.

Stag-handle examples, as the antler has mellowed sweetly over time, have undoubtedly become the most desirable, with such pieces commanding the highest prices, followed closely by jigged-bone folding hunters. Ebony- or other wood-handle versions have found their way into admirable collections, and celluloid models are not far behind.

The patterns with locking blades feature a split backspring that was somewhat more difficult and costly to manufacture, limiting supply. A folding swing guard is a rare feature, initially or primarily offered by Cattaraugus, and can command higher prices. Folding hunters with original blade etchings are often considered to be in mint or near-mint condition, and remain at the top of collectors' "want lists." Used daily, few etched knives still exist, and quickly become the centerpieces of collections.

Although the era of the folding hunters has long passed, examples of the impressive knives remain to be found. Substantial collections are passed down from generation to generation, many of whom have little-to-no interest in the knives. Without knowing the history behind them or anything about the companies that produced them, newcomers relegate the folders to sales in a variety of places. Being in the right place at the right time can often result in a collection that would be the envy of any knife enthusiast.

The Knife Aquatic

The ocean offers a rich variety of natural handle materials that are vibrant, durable and beautiful

By Mike Haskew

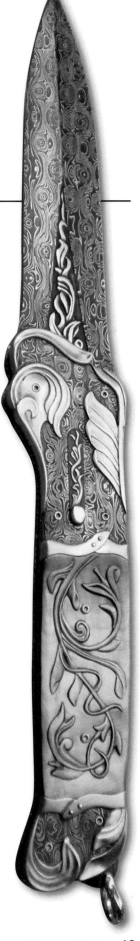

The handle of Donald Vogt's folder is carved black-lip pearl book-ended by carved Rob Thomas damascus bolsters, blade and spine, with emeralds in gold settings along the spine, carved 14k-gold accents and a gold lanyard ring.

A translucent rainbow of color, a contrast from light to dark, and a luster like no other have drawn artists and collectors to mother-of-pearl and her oceanic offspring for centuries. Capturing the allure of the sea and the conceptual interpretation of the knifemaker, handle materials from the world's oceans combine the best of Mother Nature's creative hand and the finest in custom knife artistry.

Mother-of-pearl, gold-lip pearl, black-lip and brown-lip pearl, black Pen shell, pink pearl, abalone, coral and even fossil-walrus ivory are among those handle materials that elevate a knife's stature from conventional to extraordinary. The wonder of natural beauty and the romance of the sea are reflected in a timeless fashion.

"After hundreds of years of cutlery, there are few mainstays," asserts Karen Culpepper of Culpepper & Co., a knife materials supplier based in North Carolina. "Stag and bone are two of these, but mother-of-pearl and shell have been used as long or probably longer than the other materials. Mother-of-pearl and shells are more versatile in their use and lend more value to the pieces they appear on. Pearl is prized for its historical significance, association with treasures of the sea, cost to obtain, rarity, unlimited uses and pure beauty."

Such versatility transcends the knife industry alone. Pearl and shell accents are found in furniture, musical instruments, jewelry and artwork.

"Natural materials are wonderful to look at, comfortable to hold, and every piece is absolutely unique," remarks Matt Conable of William Henry Studio. "The ocean happens to offer a rich variety of natural materials that are durable and beautiful, a rare and necessary combo when it comes to knife design and production. When you can find a material that is tough, beautiful and has a romantic story behind it, you have a winner."

Two of William Henry's most dazzling knives are the Caledonia, featuring stunning abalone handle inlays, and the Key Largo, showcasing a grip of 100,000-year-old fossil brain coral. Among the company's more specialized pieces is the golf divot tool, also sporting a fossil-brain-coral inlay.

"Ocean materials have been in the mix for as long as people have been putting handles on edged tools," Conable asserts, "and they are still in the mix today, and will be 500 years from now. Ocean-based materials are fundamental to the art of knifemaking. We are always working with these materials in combination with others like mosaic damascus, engraved stainless steel and inlaid gold.

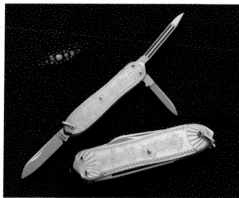

Gray C. Taylor's "Candle End Lobsters," one in carved and checkered black-lip pearl, the other in carved and scalloped gold-lip pearl, each feature 14k-gold bolsters, milled liners, and a spear-point blade, pin blade and manicure blade of CPM-154. *(PointSeven photos)*

William Henry Knives offers the Caledonia gent's folder with stunning abalone handle inlays.

"Our collection is based on short-run limited editions, so people will see new offerings with ocean-based materials almost every month from William Henry," he promises. "Recently, we won the 2011 *BLADE Magazine* Investor/Collector Knife of the Year® Award with our B12 Rising Sun that features gold maki-e [Japanese lacquer sprinkled with gold or silver powder] applied over black-lip pearl in breathtaking results!"

For many custom knifemakers, pearl, coral and abalone are standard handle options for customers. Under his Sunfish Forge trademark, Don Hanson III has worked with a variety of pearly offerings.

Pearl Says Upscale

"It really is just beautiful," he reasons, "and it fits with the types of knives I make, such as damascus folders, gent's folders and even larger models. These are all upscale, and mother-of-pearl or black-lip pearl seems to say that to people. Among the guys who buy from me, they are largely asking for black-lip pearl right now.

"Mother-of-pearl, or white pearl, is not as popular as it was 10 years ago," Hanson informs. "I have also used pink pearl and brown lip that has a lot of fiery color in it. Walrus has really good colors like blues, black and reddish brown, and one way to describe the good stuff is 'calico cat' with marble colors running through it."

Donald Vogt began making knives in 1996, and a couple years later he used gold-lip pearl on the handle of a small folder. Then, he was hooked. He appreciates not only the color, but also its stability, which is more reliable than a number of other natural materials.

"My favorite handle material today is black-lip pearl," says Vogt. "It looks great with any steel and comes in many shades, from almost black to an array of colors. A select piece of black lip can make a knife colorful, and the darkness of it goes equally well with dark steel, such as damascus, or a light stainless steel. The material doesn't warp or shrink over time and doesn't degrade."

While the aesthetic rewards of pearl-handled

knives are well known, the material does present challenges, both in and out of the shop. Decades of harvesting have rendered large pearl and abalone shell suitable for a workable pair of handle scales scarce. Many knifemakers have resorted to using the material only on small knives or as inlay options.

Also scarce are fossil walrus ivory and oosic (fossil walrus penile bone), and thus, they are more expensive than readily available handle materials. A high quality set of black-lip-pearl handle scales, even for a small pen knife, can run as high as $200.

"It is tough to get pearl these days because the larger shells have been used up," says Hanson. "You can obtain some small scales, but it is especially hard to get the black lip. You need it one inch wide by three inches long for a good set of knife scales. Walrus is still available, but it is difficult to get nice colors."

Vogt acknowledges that sea-borne handle materials can be pricey. "The cost of a knife," he notes, "is determined by the amount of time spent making it, and the cost of the materials. Handle materials from the sea are expensive, especially when looking for the best quality pieces. The best grades of pearl have no fractures. Some fractures are immediately visible, while others are hard to see."

Depending on the rarity of the material the ocean has to offer, and the time involved in making a particular knife, prices can jump 20 percent or more. Beauty and affordability are in the eye of the beholder, and years from today such an enhancement might net financial rewards many times over. Other such knives remain in families and become priceless heirlooms.

Rare Has Its Price

"All things rare and beautiful have their price," comments Culpepper. "Mother-of-pearl, coral, or even whale bone are no exception to this rule. Black-lip pearl is the most expensive per square inch. The shells are limited to the region of the South Pacific, limited in availability, hard to obtain, expensive to transport to the U.S., and many are not suitable for handle purposes.

"Black lip is the most expensive of the pearls. Gold lip, black Pen, brown lip, pink pearl and other inlay materials are the least expensive, but they are also limited in size and availability," Culpepper reminds. "White mother-of-pearl is on the lower end of the price spectrum.

"Abalone is above average in price," she adds. "With new diving restrictions on the shells, many professional shell divers do not even bother with this industry, and hobbyists cannot gather enough to ensure yield. Abalone shells need to weigh from 1.5-to-2 pounds each in order to yield enough for knife handles. Although we have a large stock of abalone shells at this time, we restrict it to special orders and trade shows for the larger material, meaning pieces that are 3 inches-by-1 inch-by-1/8-inch."

A 35-year knifemaking veteran, C. Gray Taylor advises that working with natural oceanic materials is a painstaking process. "You can easily chip a piece of

Though not exactly borne from the sea, but rather from a creature who lives in the sea, a good example of fossil walrus ivory is the handle of Don Hanson III's "Wicked" clip-point bowie with an 11-inch 1086 blade and wavy temper line.
(SharpByCoop.com photo)

William Henry Knives uses fossil brain coral for everything from its Key Largo folder to high-end pens and golfer's divot tools.

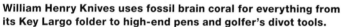

pearl, and then it is gone. You need to learn how to peen pins into a pearl handle and should get it worked down and finished before you put the pins in," he suggests. "This is difficult to do, and I use a microscope. If I plan to carve pearl, as was done on some of the old Sheffield knives, I use three or four little hand gravers, and that takes quite a bit of time."

Taylor has enjoyed using pearl and abalone on dirks and bowie knives, and considers his tour de force to be a dagger with 240 pieces of pearl inlaid in a spiral pattern around the handle. It reinforces his assertion that a considerable investment of time is required to become a master of pearl.

While Don Lozier likes working with pearl, he has

ventured into apple and tiger coral, non-fossilized materials that work similar to wood with the added dimension of porosity that the maker must seal.

"You have to finish out a coral handle on a polishing belt, but don't take it to the buffing wheel with polishing compound on it," he advises. "If you do, polishing compound can get into the pores, and you will never get it out. You need to totally saturate it with thin Super Glue and let it dry on its own, then take medium viscosity Super Glue and cover it with that."

When it comes to working with mother-of-pearl, abalone and others of the ocean's offerings, some additional precautions must be taken. Culpepper warns that drill bits should be new or as sharp as possible, and that the surface of the bit and the material should be kept cool to avoid overheating and a telltale burn mark. Holes should be drilled slightly larger than the pins themselves, and sanding must be done with caution. The beautiful surface of some shells is literally "skin deep," and overzealous sanding can race through the lustrous material.

Conjecture related to the hazards of sanding or grinding shells, particularly abalone and pearl, persists. Culpepper states emphatically that mother-of-pearl is not hazardous. Nevertheless, a good vacuum system and working with hands and shell under water to reduce the amount of airborne dust that can be inhaled just make good sense. Further, a fan set up near the grinding area could help ensure that fewer dust particles are produced.

"There are some things to consider when working with pearl," warns Vogt, "and this holds true for walrus, as well. You should always use sharp or new tools. When you drill into it, use a new bit. If you carve it, make sure your chisels are sharp. Dull tools can cause the pearl to chip. Also, when grinding pearl, too coarse a grit will cause chipping, or one that is too fine will cause the pearl to overheat. Using a buffer on oosic will fill the material with buffing compound that you won't be able to remove.

"I am not sure how dangerous working with pearl or abalone is," he concludes. "I have heard from knifemakers that it is danger-ous to breathe the dust, and have read an article that it is not dangerous. So, to be on the safe side, I wear a respirator when grinding pearl or carving it. I feel it is better to be safe than sorry."

Although working with pearl, coral, fossil ivory or abalone may present challenges and require some additional preparation, those who have become familiar with the process readily agree that the dividend is worth the investment. Their treasures of timeless beauty from the sea remain highly coveted from generation to generation.

White mother-of-pearl contrasts beautifully with the damascus, gold and sapphires of Donald Vogt's Floral Art Dagger. *(Rudolph Lopez photo)*

Formidable Tactical Folders

These rogue warriors have become the test subjects for advanced blade steels, mechanisms and materials

By Dexter Ewing

Tactical folders have made up a hot segment of the knife industry for close to 20 years, and there is no denying the progressive designs and usefulness of such knives. Tactical folders are the testing grounds for the latest and greatest in blade and handle materials in the knife industry. Big-name companies pull out their freshest models, earning public accolades at events like the S.H.O.T. Show and BLADE Show. What makes these knives such a hot commodity today? It's the use of cutting-edge materials with new lock mechanisms, coupled with custom collaborations between the hottest tactical knifemakers and production knife companies to bring forth mass-produced versions of the makers' best-selling pieces.

There are many big names in the tactical folder genre, and no one as well known and synonymous with tactical folders as Ernest Emerson. A custom knifemaker turned CEO of Emerson Knives, Inc. he sits at the helm of one of the most progressive tactical folder companies. Since its humble beginnings in 1997, Emerson Knives has steadily grown over the years in tactical knife models and sales.

For 2011, Emerson and crew unleashed two folders at opposite ends of the spectrum in terms of appearance and design philosophy. The Roadhouse showcases an aggressive, low-slung blade of which, Emerson says, the inspiration came from an equally aggressive fixed-blade tactical fighter he made some years ago. It was "based on a warrior design for a rogue warrior," he stated. Emerson explained that he has always been enamored with Japanese swords, and thus they served as inspiration for the pattern. The Roadhouse's tanto blade, like Japanese swords,

A Shane Sibert design, the Benchmade Adamas features a D2 blade, tan G-10 handle scales, and an Axis Lock. *(Benchmade photo)*

is a shape known for its piercing abilities. "It has the same gentle curve on the cutting edge that a Samurai katana has," he noted.

The blade edge of the Roadhouse dips below the bottom of the handle. "This protects the hand and knuckles," Emerson began. "With the 'dropped-blade' design, the edge always arrives first no matter how you present your hand. Combined with the integral guard, it feels so good in the hand and the knife looks like it wants to jump forward."

The blade, less than 4 inches in length, is ground from 1/8-inch-thick 154CM stainless steel, and an ergonomic G-10 handle and metal liners provide the backbone. Emerson's patented "Wave" feature facilitates rapid blade deployment as the knife is withdrawn from the pocket. The Roadhouse is an aggressive, don't-mess-with-me design that is all Emerson.

Emerson Knives also debuted the Journeyman in 2011. "The Journeyman is more of a straight-ahead, utility-class folding knife that does not scream 'aggression,'" Emerson surmised. It is a design that

▶ The Kershaw Knockout has a sub-frame lock embedded into the G-10 handle that provides the strength and lockup of a frame lock, while retaining the slimness and light weight of a standard LinerLock® folder. A deep-carry pocket clip is standard equipment.

◀ Designed as a workingman's folder, the Emerson Knives Journeyman also excels at tactical applications for law enforcement and military.

features nice, clean lines and a good and secure feel to the handle. Emerson also noted that it makes a perfect knife for law enforcement, military and those employed in the trades. "We have shipped large numbers to the SEALs," he noted. "There are many of them floating around Afghanistan right now."

The Journeyman sports a 3.5-inch 154CM drop-point blade, the Wave opener, a large index-finger groove, and a down-turned handle butt for secure hand purchase. Handle scales are G-10 with metal liners. Emerson builds high-quality, U.S.-made knives, and the Roadhouse and Journeyman are prime examples.

Benchmade also engineers quality U.S.-built tactical folders, and in early 2012 launched the Shane Sibert-designed model 275 Adamas, as well as the first automatic opener under the Harley-Davidson banner—the 13800 Nonconformist. "Style and functionality are key elements in the Harley-Davidson brand," said Alicia Hunt, Benchmade's public relations coordinator. "The aggressive handle design of the Nonconformist is stylish, yet practical."

The Nonconformist does its nonconforming in a 3.5-inch, drop-point 154CM stainless steel blade that is coated black for non-reflective and corrosion-resistant properties. The ergonomic, machined 6061-T6-aluminum handle curves in all the right places and lies sweetly in the user's grasp. It is also available in an optional tanto blade. Hunt said, "The blade variants are functional for any preference. It is a great push-button automatic knife for the Harley-Davidson enthusiast who appreciates style, quality and functionality."

An Imposing Figure

The 275 Sibert Adamas strikes an imposing figure with its forward-raked handle. "With a name derived from the Greek word for 'invincible' or 'unconquerable,' the Adamas is a heavy-duty tool for tactical situations," Hunt informed.

It features a 4-inch, drop-point blade of D2 tool steel, well known for its ability to hold an edge yet remain easy to sharpen. Benchmade's Axis Lock secures the blade in the open position with rock-solid precision each and every time, and self-adjusts to compensate for any wear that occurs over time. Desert-tan G-10 handle scales are textured for a sure grip, and the tan handle married with the black blade is not only a nice-looking combination, but also a great alternative to the all-black look that is so prevalent in tactical folders.

Those familiar with Sibert's custom work know that he likes to incorporate a fuller, or blood groove, in his blades, and the 275 Adamas is no exception. "Designed to honor the courage and commitment exhibited by our fighting heroes, Benchmade is proud to donate a portion of the proceeds from the sale of these knives to the Ranger Assistance Foundation," Hunt concluded.

Columbia River Knife & Tool (CRKT) recently unleashed two of its most-exciting folders in company history. Take for example the Sampa, designed by Brazilian knifemaker Flavio Ikoma. It follows CRKT's Onion Eros and Onion Ripple into the "gentleman's tacticals" category, particularly considering its slender size and comfortable pocket carry,

► Low slung and delightfully aggressive in appearance, the Roadhouse is a typical Emerson Knives design that showcases the engineering prowess of the man at the company helm.

▲ The Columbia River Knife & Tool NIRK Tighe features a pierced or skeletonized blade and handle, as well as a flipper mechanism that provides fast one-hand blade deployment.

▲ The Columbia River Knife & Tool Sampa, fashioned by Brazilian knifemaker Flavio Ikoma, is slender in nature and useful by design.

yet retaining all the features that make tactical folders popular.

With a 3 1/8-inch AUS-8 blade, the Sampa is a great size for daily carry. "We took Flavio Ikoma's custom knife and replicated it almost to a 'T,'" said Doug Flagg, CRKT's vice president of sales and marketing. "We were even able to do the two-tone finish that Flavio did on the custom version by bead blasting the handles and then machining the flat spots of the handle so the shiny aluminum would show. The handle is cold-forged aluminum, making it lightweight yet durable, and features a variety of texturing to aid in hand purchase."

For quick blade deployment, the Sampa is de-signed with an IKBS (Ikoma Korth Bearing System) pivot. By firmly pressing the flipper mechanism, the blade opens smoothly.

CRKT's NIRK Tighe incorporates Glenn Klecker's NIRK folder design that Canadian custom knifemaker Brian Tighe transformed into a one-hand-opening, lock-back folder with a flipper. The knife showcases an array of weight-reducing, aesthetically pleasing holes in the blade and handle. "When Brian Tighe showed us his custom knife we were speechless!" Flagg said. "The knife is large, but the slim design makes it incredibly easy to carry."

With an AUS-8 blade close to 4 inches in length, the NIRK Tighe is up to any task, while the pierced-

The first automatic in the company's Harley-Davidson line, the Benchmade Nonconformist is stylish and unique. *(Benchmade photo)*

steel handle, integral hand guard and pronounced finger recesses allow for maneuverability and hand indexing. The blue-anodized cutouts contrast nicely with the satin-finished flats of the frame. One of the neat things about the NIRK Tighe is that the lock-back mechanism and spring are integral to the handle, not merely add-on components. The open-channel construction of the lock bar permits the use of a flipper, one of the few production lock-back flippers.

"Seeing the custom and wanting to manufacture it is one thing. Actually making it is another," Flagg stressed. "We broke at least three sets of stamping dies trying to match Brian's intricate design. However with time and patience we were able to manufacture the knife so it is nearly identical to his custom knife in appearance."

Kershaw and Zero Tolerance (ZT) Knives are two high-quality tactical folder lines that fall under the parent company umbrella of Kai USA. Two fresh tactical models include the Kershaw 1870 Knockout and ZT Rick Hinderer-designed 0560/0561. The 1870 Knockout is an in-house design featuring progressive styling, a highly useful blade shape, and a nice overall size and feel. The frame-lock folder parades a 3.25-inch, modified-drop-point Sandvik 14C28N stainless steel blade and a G-10 handle.

What a Knockout!

"The Knockout actually gets its name from the fact that we 'knocked out' a piece of the textured G-10 handle and inset a stainless-steel plate to create a sturdy frame lock," noted Chris Brooks, advertising and marketing manager for KAI USA. "The handle is contoured slightly to fit the arc of the palm, and has an additional index finger contour for a secure grip."

Built into the handle, a lock-bar limiter prevents the locking mechanism from being pushed over too far when disengaging the blade. Still another issue addressed with the Knockout, according to Brooks, is the deep-carry pocket clip. "Our new deep-carry clip is seated as far down the handle as possible, and is shaped so that the knife is nearly invisible when it's in the pocket. Plus, the handle is drilled for tip-up, tip-down, left- or right-handed carry," he explained.

While the Knockout is slim and stylish, the ZT 0560 and 0561 models are big and brawny. A renowned tactical folder maker, Hinderer loosely based the design—only bigger—on his popular XM-18 folder. The nearly 4-inch blade is ground from ELMAX powdered steel, an alloy high in chromium, vanadium and molybdenum content.

"ELMAX is easily hardened and offers extreme edge retention, high strength, toughness, and wear and corrosion resistance. Knowing this would be a hard-use knife, we chose steel that would stand up to such use," Brooks stated.

The lock side of the handle is titanium, and the non-lock side G-10, each 3-D machined for enhanced appearance and grip. "Both the titanium back handle and frame lock have machined weight-relief pockets, and the liner on the G-10 side is skeletonized to ensure the big knife carries at a comfortable weight," Brooks interjected.

A flipper mechanism and the company's KVT pivot bearing system make blade deployment smooth and effortless, and as quick as using a Kershaw Speed Safe assisted opener. "The bearings are seated in a durable collar that fits around the pivot," Brooks pointed out.

Otherwise, the 0560/0561 is standard Hinderer fare, embodying the maker's attention to detail and handle ergonomics, and including his Lock Bar Stabilizer, a small disc that prevents the frame-lock bar from overriding the blade tang. A deep-carry clip keeps the knife snug in the pocket, and can be mounted in one of four positions.

Tactical folders are refined in every sense of the word, entailing more sophisticated designs, advanced materials and attention to detail. It seems that manufacturers offer up tactical folders only after intently listening to their customers about what works, what doesn't, and what knife designs and makers are most popular.

"Big" is in the Blood of the Claymore User

Two-hand swords are cutting and slashing weapons, with velocity and power expressed toward the ends of the blades

Carried on the shoulder, the claymore is in a near-ready position for combat.

By Greg Bean

"What do you do with that thing?" That's a question that every knife collector will hear at some time, and it's usually a fair question even if the collector comes to dread it. If you collect knives, there's always a practical use. You can skin a deer, clean fish, cut string, open packages, strip insulation, repair furniture and carve meat, even if you'd never do such a thing with your handmade, folded-steel, fixed-blade hunter with a gold-inlaid narwhal-tusk grip that's displayed in an ebony and rosewood case, signed by the knifemaker, and placed prominently on your fireplace mantle. If worse comes to worst and your boss's wife is looking over your shoulder in horror, you can say it's a letter opener.

Sword collectors have a more difficult time finding an answer that makes sense to the non-believer. In general there isn't much you can do with a sword, except own it and talk about it, which is enough for the true believers.

I've found my own solution, which is to hear a different question. I don't answer, "What do you do with that thing?" because the answer is almost nothing. I answer the questions: "What did the warriors and soldiers do with that thing? What country is it from and when was it used? What was their culture like, and what affect did it

have on history? Has it influenced anything about the way we live today?" Those are the questions I answer, and on a good day I can make a case for having a sword collection that's as reasonable as having a shelf of history books or a subscription to *National Geographic*.

Most swords look generic to the general public, without suggesting a time, place or culture. The Scottish two-handed claymore isn't one of those generic "others." It has a look that is all its own, because of both its size and its geometry.

The down slope of the guard is the giveaway. The angled guard pieces, called quillons, give a sleek look to the weapon that you don't expect from a sword of its size. If there were such a thing as aerodynamics for sword designs, this sword would have come from a wind tunnel. The four-leaf clovers at the end of the quillons are distinctive and not found on any other sword in the world. The shape is called a quatrefoil and while common in medieval design, it proclaims a Scottish origin when found on a sword.

The quillons serve several purposes; they protect

Two-handed swords were a specialty item wielded by high-status elite warriors. Combining form and function, the guards gave the sword makers a chance to show off their skill at the forge.

Two hands spread apart on the grip shows how to leverage the weapon for maximum effect.

If you have to carry a slaughter sword, or any sword that's taller than you are, the back scabbard is essential. Notice the quatrefoil in the side rings and the acorns at the ends of the blade catchers.

the fighter's hand from their opponent's blades as the first priority. They also keep the fighter's hands from sliding onto his own blade if the weapon meets any resistance. The angled quillons could be used to catch the opponent's blade so it could be manipulated out of the way. These are defensive considerations, but you can't hold a shield while using one of these things so the sword has to be your defense as well.

The two-handed Scottish claymore is a cumbersome piece to explain historically and tactically, because there isn't a lot of documentation on how it was used compared to other pieces of military hardware. Its period of use was between 1400 and 1700 A.D., roughly the medieval period with some hangover into more modern times. This corresponds with the development of artillery from catapults to muskets, although there's less written about the claymore than either catapults or muskets.

Deploying the Troops

The type of troops used during this period and how they were deployed has been recorded from all of the major battles. The standard troops of the time were the light and heavy cavalry, light and heavy infantry, archers and pikemen. The pikes were between 10 and 15 feet long and used defensively more often than offensively. The claymore-armed soldiers have not been well documented so there is more conjecture than concrete about what they did. It's likely they were used similarly to how the two-handed swordsmen of the continental armies were used, which was as shock troops breaking through the opposing lines of pikemen to allow the cavalry and infantry past the enemy defenses. At some point the battle would degenerate into the chaos of a general melee but the victor was often the one with the momentum, so an aggressive front line was an advantage, and these specialists were often mercenaries.

The Scots produced their own mercenary exports, the Gallowglass, who favored the two-hand swords. Elite troops of Norse and Gaelic background, the Gallowglass came from the Scottish highlands and the Scottish western islands called the Hebrides.

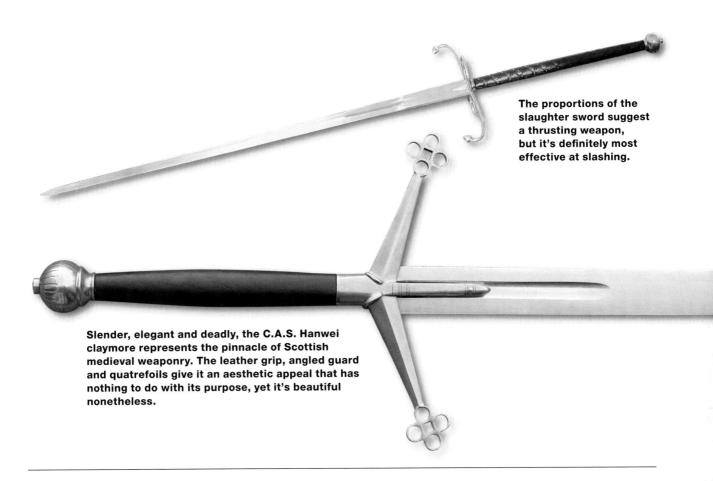

The proportions of the slaughter sword suggest a thrusting weapon, but it's definitely most effective at slashing.

Slender, elegant and deadly, the C.A.S. Hanwei claymore represents the pinnacle of Scottish medieval weaponry. The leather grip, angled guard and quatrefoils give it an aesthetic appeal that has nothing to do with its purpose, yet it's beautiful nonetheless.

From the 13th to the 16th century they were favored troops in Ireland in the perpetual warfare between the Irish and the English. Since mercenaries usually went to the highest bidder, the English occasionally employed the Gallowglass, who could be found in the armies of a few of the mainland countries. The Gallowglass did use the claymore and a two-handed axe so outsized ambitions must have been in the blood.

A second sword with a Scottish element forged into its guard was a fairly typical mercenary's weapon that you would find on the continent. Along with the outsized guard, the grip had two side rings that added to the protection for the hands. One example has the quatrefoil forged into the side rings, identifying it as Scottish.

The German's called these swords zweihanders, meaning two-hand [swords], and the soldiers of fortune who used them qualified for double pay in the German mercenary forces called the Landsknecht. The Swiss, Spanish and Italians all had their own take on the great swords and how to use them, and there was an intense rivalry, which isn't surprising since the stakes were life and death. The English had their own term when the swords were applied to English troops, calling them slaughter swords.

One of the great moments of owning a two-handed sword comes when someone picks one up and spits out his or her first thoughts. If they pick it up with one hand and try a few fencing moves while quoting lines from the *Princess Bride*, they end up in shock, rubbing their wrists and complaining about how heavy it is. If they pick it up with both hands and hold it like an ax or baseball bat, they comment on how light it is. Both comments are valid. I haven't seen anyone try a golf swing with it; that probably wouldn't go down so well.

The claymore shown in this article is 55 inches long and weighs close to 5 lbs. The blade length is 51 inches, and the handle about 14 inches. While it dwarfs the usual broadsword or rapier, it is dwarfed by the slaughter sword at 69 inches and almost 7 pounds.

Hands Spread, Arms Extended

Two-handed swords are meant for both hands, spreading them as far apart as the grip allows. There's a lot of leverage that comes with the correct grip. They are essentially cutting weapons, with an impressive level of velocity and power expressed towards the end of the blade.

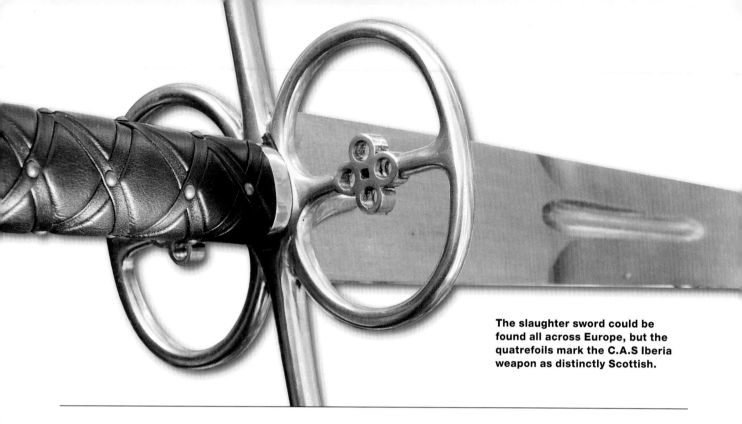

The slaughter sword could be found all across Europe, but the quatrefoils mark the C.A.S Iberia weapon as distinctly Scottish.

When held properly and used at the distance they were intended for, they aren't awkward or heavy. Five or six pounds—less than a gallon of milk—feels well balanced and natural when hefted between two hands, and the basic moves flow readily.

The two-handed swords were definitely not optimal weapons for close combat, but in-your-face encounters were certain to happen, and there was a plan for that too. One of the soldier's hands could be placed part way up the blade, called half-swording, shortening its reach and creating a thrusting weapon. A substantial glove or gauntlet was essential, if you expected to use this technique more than once, although some blades weren't sharpened close to the grip—a part of the blade called the ricasso. On the other end of the weapon, the pommel is substantial and has probably served up a few blunt traumas in hand-to-hand fighting.

The swords were too long to go into scabbards that were suspended around the waist. It would take arms the length of an NBA player to draw one, and maybe not even then. The swords were not worn as a constant sidearm, as they were too heavy and cumbersome, so a side scabbard wasn't needed anyway. The higher-status soldiers would have one or two men or boys to assist them and at least a couple of horses. If swords were carried they were slung over the back or carried on the shoulder.

Surviving scabbards from 500-600 years ago are rare. They were made of leather, cloth and wood, and rotted long before finding their way to a museum. Quite a number of modern manufacturers have contributed their own versions of how to carry the weapons. For the illustrations for this article, a back scabbard from C.A.S. Hanwei has been used for both types of swords, showing how they could have been carried.

If given half a chance, I will tell an eager listener that the Scottish mercenaries would till and seed their fields at home, then sail to their overseas employers to fight for the war season, and subsequently return for harvest. The last recorded battle in which the claymore was used was the Battle of Killiecrankie in 1699. I'll talk about my ancestor Gillies MacBean holding a breach in a wall against the British in the Battle of Culloden and killing 14 British soldiers until being shot, run-through and horse stomped, earning a place in the history books.

I'll explain that German mercenaries were fashion leaders during their era with colorful flamboyant clothing, and that the Swiss mercenaries are still employed by the Vatican. And that the development of firearms took the edge off of edged weapons and bayonets, and muskets replaced pikes and bowmen. On a good day, my audience will ask questions that keep me talking and reaching for my history books and *National Geographic* magazines. On a bad day their eyes glaze over and they change the subject. Then I tell them the swords are letter openers.

TRENDS

Trends may come and go but it would be dangerous to disregard them as inconsequential. On the contrary. Each knife trend identified in the *Knives* annual books, from the inception of the series in 1981, was a stepping stone in the advancement of knives to the next level. Trends in knives are styles, patterns, materials, steels, mechanisms or technological advancements that more than a few knifemakers adopt within the same few years, and that they feel are useful and important enough to incorporate the features into their knives.

These are not knives that are stamped out by the hundreds or thousands, but pieces that a single maker has designed, cut out, patterned, held, forged, ground, beveled, painstakingly deburred, polished and put his or her tang stamp or mark on. A craftsman does not go through that trouble for something believed to be here today, gone tomorrow and considered irrelevant.

So what's happening in 2013? How about folders so hi-tech they could only be made in the 21st century? Flip to page 76 and enjoy a knife from each of the 50 states in the "American Stickers" section, or peruse the "Automatics for the People" on page 89. Don't miss the "Horseman's, Falconer's & Huntsmen's Swords," the "Amber Waves of Stag," "Fiery Fighters," "Runaway Grains," or "Finger Nick'n Good Knives." Find out who is "Channeling Loveless" or building "Blow-the-Door-Hinges-Off Bowies." Trendy? Sure, and how nice it is to be up on everything happening in today's modern knife arena.

Foray Into the Far East

The Far East is the epitome of exoticism to Americans, and even to Europeans, Africans, Italians, Australians, Scandinavians, Indians, Russians and Spaniards. The food, architecture, clothing, music, traditions, religions and hierarchy of the people of the Far East compose a fascinating cultural study, one that triggers the imagination and piques curiosity.

In the United States, kids are known to try to "dig to China," rationalizing that since the two lands are on opposite ends of the earth, one should be able to dig a hole straight through the planet to the other side. It's not the digging that brings out the inner child, but rather the lure of a faraway place so unlike his or her own, one that is mysterious and exotic. The history of the United States is like that of a newborn or infant compared to most places in the Far East, and that is hard to grasp for those of the New World unless they experience the Southeast Asian land, people and culture themselves.

Perhaps that all explains the fascination with the weaponry of the Far East, and the desire to replicate that which predates a good number of other knife and sword styles. Maybe it's the exotic style that accounts for the allure, but logic says it goes beyond that. True weapons masters were born and raised in China, Cambodia, Japan, Malaysia, Nepal, Indonesia, Hong Kong, Thailand, Singapore, Taiwan, Korea and the Philippines.

They passed their bladesmithing, swordsmithing, blacksmithing, forging, grinding, fitting and finishing techniques down to apprentices, from generation to generation, over thousands of years. The styles are unique in the world, and the secrets of steel revealed only in the finished blades. A foray into the Far East is the trip of a lifetime, one we should all take with the open mind and natural curiosity of a child.

◄ **DAVID GOLDBERG:** Amenities include a carved and pierced tsuba (guard), wispy hamon (temper line), leather-wrapped, maroon ray-skin hilt, and silver menuki (handle charm). *(PointSeven Studios photo)*

▲ **DAN KEFFELER:** With CPM-3V blade steel reigning supreme, the maker toiled in titanium and "Timascus" for the fuchi (ornamental hilt ring), kashira (pommel cap), tsuba (guard) and menuki (handle charm). *(Eric Eggly, PointSeven Studios photo)*

▶ **PAUL JARVIS:** Textured nickel and bronze accent an upswept 1095-and-nickel-damascus blade, while a mammoth-ivory grip completes the Far Eastern ensemble. *(Eric Eggly, PointSeven Studios photo)*

▶ **PEKKA TUOMINEN:** The art version of a traditional Shanghai fighting knife sports an "explosion"-pattern damascus blade, a mosaic-damascus guard and pommel, and an ebony handle. *(Yrjo Korhonen photo)*

▲ **DAVID BRODZIAK:** The Australian knifemaker tackled a damascus tanto with an ebony, sandalwood and weeping myall (wood native to Australia) hilt and scabbard. Carol Ann O'Connor painted the cherry blossoms.

▲ **RICHARD VAN DIJK:** The Wing Chung swords, or Chinese martial arts butterfly swords, grace us with 400-layer damascus blades, ebony handles, brass fittings, iron guards and a side-by-side ebony scabbard.

▶ **ZACK JONAS:** The 1095 tanto may have its roots in Japan, but the rosewood hilt is all Bolivia. *(SharpByCoop.com photo)*

▶ **MICHAEL BELL:** The forge-welded and folded cable steel blade is orchestrated via the osaraku-zukuri style, complemented by a copper habaki (blade collar), silk-wrapped hilt, dragon menuki (handle charm) and purple-lacquered saya (sheath).

Bowie Birthrights

▲ TOSHIAKI MICHINAKA: The exhibition bowie knife regales its audience with an ATS-34 blade, nickel-silver furniture and a stag handle.

◄ STEVE CULVER: The Searles/Fowler reproduction includes a checkered-blackwood handle with 24k-gold pins, nickel-silver fittings and a 1095 blade. *(Ward photo)*

▲ FOREST "BUTCH" SHEELY: The rosewood coffin-style handle in a nickel-silver wrap is a classic design, accompanied by an 8.5-inch 5160 blade. *(Eric Eggly, PointSeven Studios photo)*

STEVEN RAPP and ALEX DANIELS: Two makers' interpretations of a Michael Price dress bowie differ only slightly, each in ivory handles and nickel silver fittings, with Rapp's version (left) sporting a CPM-154 blade, and Daniels' in 440C stainless steel. Julie Warenski-Erickson engraved the sheath for Rapp, while Daniels employed the engraving services of Billy Bates. *(Hoffman photos)*

▲ **LARRY FUEGEN:** With carved-walrus-ivory handle and engraved gold band, the Sheffield Bowie is the belle of the ball. *(Francesco Pachi photo)*

◀ **ALAN TIENSVOLD:** Not only is it a replica of a Henry Shivley bowie, but the 5160 blade is treated with an aged patina, and the checkered elephant ivory grip could have come straight out of the 19th century.

▼ **RICK "BEAR BONE" SMITH:** A classic I*XL Wostenholm Bowie is brought to life in a file-worked and mirror-polished O1 tool steel blade, a nickel silver guard and escutcheon plate, and sambar-stag handle scales.

◀ **MICHAEL VAGNINO:** If the walrus ivory handle of the California bowie isn't worthy enough for a loving squeeze, the engraved pins and silver edge wrap should work their magic. *(Mitch Lum photo)*

▶ **BRIAN THIE:** The Daniel Searles bowie in ivory, nickel silver and 5160 is as sweet as its 1800's ancestors. *(Ward photo)*

◀ **J.R. COOK:** Born a Carrigan Bowie, the damascus piece is strikingly handsome in a coffin-style blackwood handle and fine silver fittings. *(Ward photo)*

TRENDS **61**

21st-Century Fold-Downs

► RON APPLETON: The ATS-34 "Legacy" folding push dagger integrates a "Multalock" mechanism and a mirror-polished, tastefully grooved, hardened and tempered blade and frame.

▲ TODD REXFORD: Blue "Mokuti" handle rods rise above the titanium frame of the "Injection" tactical folder that also features a Chad Nichols "fade"-pattern stainless-damascus blade, and a Mokuti pivot insert, thumb studs and pocket clip. *(SharpByCoop.com photo)*

▲ THOMAS HASLINGER: The "Campo Del Cielo" (From the Sky) folder emits mammoth ivory hues, and those of meteorite, ammonite, ruby and gold. The meteorite blade dons an O1-tool-steel edge. To the moon!

▼ SCOT MATSUOKA: All the edges are rounded off—with the exception of the leaf-shaped CPM-154 blade—including those on the gorgeous wood grip, and titanium frame and bolsters of the flipper folder. *(SharpByCoop.com photo)*

► GUS CECCHINI: They are not cracks—the aesthetically 21st-century lines are supposed to run the length of the titanium frames on a couple dress tactical folders, one in damascus. *(SharpByCoop.com photo)*

▶ **JOHN W. SMITH:** Let 10 inches of CPM-S35V and carbon fiber take over for a while. *(Eric Eggly, PointSeven Studios photo)*

◀ **MIKKEL WILLUMSEN:** The "Blondie" flipper folder sports a sand-color and brown G-10 handle, and a rock-tumble-finished, multi-ground, hog-nose CPM-154 blade.

▶ **JOHN BARTLOW:** A desert-Micarta®-handle folding version of a "Green River Skinner," it includes an ATS-34 blade, jeweled, file-worked and anodized-titanium liners, and heat-blued screws and pivot. *(Eric Eggly, PointSeven Studios photo)*

◀ **PETER CAREY:** I'll flip ya for the dress tactical flipper folder, this one in Stellite 6K™, titanium and mammoth ivory. *(SharpByCoop.com photo)*

▲ **MICHAEL WALKER:** The inventor of the LinerLock®, Walker has been building them a long time, but his newest renditions—this one in damascus, carbon fiber and titanium—are all 21st century. *(Eric Eggly, PointSeven Studios photo)*

◀ **CALVIN ROBINSON:** And would you like black or brown paper Micarta® with that D2 folder? *(Ward photo)*

◀ **ALLEN ELISHEWITZ:** "Bumblebee" carbon fiber is sticky sweet on the double-ground, two-tone-finished XHP tactical stinger with curved titanium bolsters.

▶ **EMMANUEL ESPOSITO:** The maker gave the knife what he calls a "watch finish," and the intricacies of a patent-pending "C-Lock" system are like those of fine Swiss watches. Carbon fiber and RWL-34 blade steel coalesce comfortably. *(Francesco Pachi photo)*

◀ **ERIC OCHS:** A large custom mosaic pin, milled traction grooves on the maroon linen-Micarta® handle scales, and a wide, multi-ground CPM-S30V blade characterize the locking-liner folder. *(Jamie Piekkola photo)*

▶ **LAURENT DOUSSOT:** The texturing of the titanium handle is golden, the Devin Thomas herringbone damascus orchestrated perfectly, and the pen-style pocket clip perfect. *(SharpByCoop.com photo)*

◀ **SHANE SIBERT:** The "Pocket Rocket" will put the blue in your jeans with its hued and grooved G-10 handle, not to mention the bulging CPM-S30V blade. *(SharpByCoop.com photo)*

▲ **BILL KELLER:** Blued bolsters were called in to break up the etched Chris Marks "lizard-skin"-damascus blade and Llannoite handle, one more alive than the next. *(Johnny Stout photo)*

▶ **BRIAN TIGHE:** The technologically advanced "Tighe Rod" flipper folder exhibits a grooved Damasteel blade, a Klecker lock (Glenn Klecker), a CNC-machined, pierced titanium handle and a needle thrust bearing system. *(Eric Eggly, PointSeven Studios photo)*

▲ **SEAN O'HARE:** Like a fine suit, the locking-liner folder wears the silver twill G-10 well, accessorizing with black G10 and gray CPM-154.

▼ **BRUCE BUMP:** Pre-ban elephant ivory and hand-forged damascus play significant roles on the "Port Royal" .36-caliber black-powder muzzleloader/folding knife. *(BladeGallery.com photo)*

▶ **GRANT and GAVIN HAWK:** When the flipper of the "Beetle" folder is pressed, a silicone rubber bungee moves the lower part of the frame back and forth. The unusual material combination includes "lightning strike" carbon fiber, anodized titanium and Devin Thomas "bubble wrap" damascus. *(BladeGallery.com photo)*

▼ **KEITH OUYE:** "Crazy lace" damascus by Mike Norris is given a nice double grind, while Superconductor bolsters lend color, and "lightning strike" carbon fiber handle scales anchor the flipper folder. *(SharpByCoop.com photo)*

▶ **PETER CAREY:** So, how 21st century is a flipper folder in a Superconductor bolster and pocket clip, bronze-anodized liners, "lightning strike" carbon fiber handle and CPM-S3VN blade?

▲ **DARREL RALPH:** A 3D-carved and anodized titanium frame is butted up against a bowie-style Chad Nichols stainless-damascus blade that works off an assisted opener.

▶ **JIM and JOYCE MINNICK:** The all-gray tactical is sleek, sharp, swedged and edged. *(Eric Eggly, PointSeven Studios photo)*

▼ **MICHAEL VAGNINO:** An engraved bronze bolster in a dragonhead motif is one highlight, along with "lightning strike" carbon fiber, but what is unseen is a new slip-joint split-spring feature in which, unlike traditional pocketknives, the spacer does not rise above the handle spine when opening and closing the blade. *(Hiro Soga photo)*

▲ **JEFF HALL:** A pair of frame locks in carbon fiber, titanium and steel blur the lines between black and gray, opened by discs and pocketed via clips. *(Eric Eggly, PointSeven Studios photo)*

▲ **RICHARD S. WRIGHT:** The double-edge, modified-tanto CPM-154 flipper folder with textured-titanium frame, ball-bearing pivot and four-position pocket clip stands on its own.

Finger Nick'n Good

Only a knifemaker, enthusiast or collector would understand the "finger nick'n good" pun. So it's a good thing the *Knives 2013* book is largely absorbed by knifemakers, collectors and enthusiasts. But just in case, a finger nick, or nail nick, is a fingernail-shaped recessed notch on the top face of a pocketknife blade used to open the blade. On older knives it takes a good tug or pull, one strong enough to break fragile nails, to override the spring holding the stubborn blade closed. A fancy multi-blade folder might have several nail nicks, one for each blade, and the fun begins.

There's an expression, this one not a pun, that says "everything old is new again." Knifemakers like that expression, and in fact are rather obsessive about it. Just when knife technology advances into spring-assisted folders with thumb studs, high-tech locks, thrust-bearing washers, hardened pivots, half-stops, safeties and flipper mechanisms, custom knifemakers revert back to building old-fashioned pocketknives, albeit of modern materials and makeup.

The driving force is craftsmanship. Some things are just built better the old way. Think automobiles, John Deere tractors, refrigerators, furniture and houses, to name a few. Other things were just more fun to operate in the old days. Just as every young adult under the age of 30 was putting all their music on iPods, a fresh batch of high school and college students were overturning antique stores looking for turntables and .33 records. And unless you're enjoying this text on a digital book reader, you have a paper book in your hands, imagine that! The knives the craftsmen fashion, the ones with folding blades, stiff springs, tight tolerances and tighter liners, are of the finger nick'n good variety, and oh so fun to play with and enjoy.

▼ **RICHARD ROGERS:** If a five-blade sowbelly is on your wish list, look no further than this ATS-34 beauty in a checkered mother-of-pearl grip. *(SharpByCoop.com photo)*

▲ **TOM PLOPPERT:** The hollow-ground CPM-154 blades are as modern as the knife pattern is old, and the stag handle slabs and acorn shield just feel right. *(SharpByCoop.com photo)*

▲ **JEFF CLAIBORNE:** An "elephant toenail" model is forged from 52100 steel and includes half-stops, long pulls, swedge grinds and stainless steel bolsters and liners, not to mention mammoth-ivory handle scales. *(Hoffman photo)*

▶ **DON HANSON III:** The dress slip-joint folder features a hand-rubbed blade, polished bolsters and a stag handle. *(SharpByCoop.com photo)*

▲ **JERRY HALFRICH:** The maker's take on a Case bulldog pattern is done up in CPM-154 blade steel, 416 stainless steel bolsters and liners, and stag handle slabs. *(SharpByCoop.com photo)*

▶ **T.R. OVEREYNDER:** The maker updates the traditional sowbelly pattern with Carpenter CST-XHP steel, and then plants an 18k-rose-gold acorn shield in the middle of the jigged bone grip. *(SharpByCoop.com photo)*

▲**YOSHIO SAKAUCHI:** You can poke, prod, pick, saw, cut, tweeze, notch and open a wine bottle with the multi-implement ATS-34 pocketknife in a stag grip. *(Eric Eggly, PointSeven Studios photo)*

▲ **MIKE ZSCHERNY:** The dog points as well as the ATS-34 blade. *(SharpByCoop.com photo)*

Finger Nick'n Good

▼ **RYUICHI KAWAMURA:** The highly fit and finished two-blade ATS-34 lock-back folder comes in old jigged bone. *(Eric Eggly, PointSeven Studios photo)*

▲ **CALVIN ROBINSON:** Two nail-nick locking-liner folders come together in 2 5/8-inch 13C26 stainless steel blades, mammoth-ivory-core handle slabs and carbon-fiber and bronze bolsters. *(Eric Eggly, PointSeven Studios photo)*

▼ **EUGENE SHADLEY:** A lock-back swing-guard folder parades stag and stainless steel.

▼ **BRET DOWELL:** If you're going to break a nail, it might as well be on a two-blade ATS-34 folder with smooth ivory grips and clean stainless steel fittings. *(Ward photo)*

▲ **RICKY MENEFEE:** What a pair these two make—a dogleg (top) and Wichita trapper with plenty of nail pulls and "pop." *(Eric Eggly, PointSeven Studios photo)*

▲ J.R. PRESTON: The stag-handle folder showcases fancy file work, amber-stag handle scales and an oval name shield. *(Ward photo)*

▲ CRAIG BREWER: The two-blade sowbelly gets the hand-rubbed CPM-154 treatment, jigged bone handle scales and 416 stainless steel bolsters. *(Johnny Stout photo)*

▼ RON NEWTON: Roll out the pearl-handle eight-blade barrel knife. *(Ward photo)*

▶ DURVYN HOWARD: Satiny smooth steel and gold-lip pearl pretty up the girls. *(Eric Eggly, PointSeven Studios photo)*

Finger Nick'n Good

▶ **CHICCI K. YONEYAMA:** The mother-of-pearl is bookended by M3 bolsters and complemented by file work and ATS-34 steel. *(SharpByCoop.com photo)*

▲ **STANLEY BUZEK:** One pull is all it takes to extract the 3.25-inch CPM-154 blade from the mill-relieved 416 stainless steel liners of the Amboyna-burl handle. *(Kayla Minchew photo)*

▲ **BILL RUPLE:** A stag handle, CPM-154 blades and stainless steel bolsters round up the cattleman offerings. *(Ward photo)*

▲ **GUY STAINTHORP:** The pinch-joint folder in Damasteel is all modern and good, and includes the obligatory nail nick and finger notch to make it even nicer.

▶ **JERALD NICKELS:** Some floral engraving by Mike Tarango accents the stainless steel handle frame of a one-blade pocketknife in CPM-154 steel and mammoth-ivory handle slabs. *(Kayla Minchew photo)*

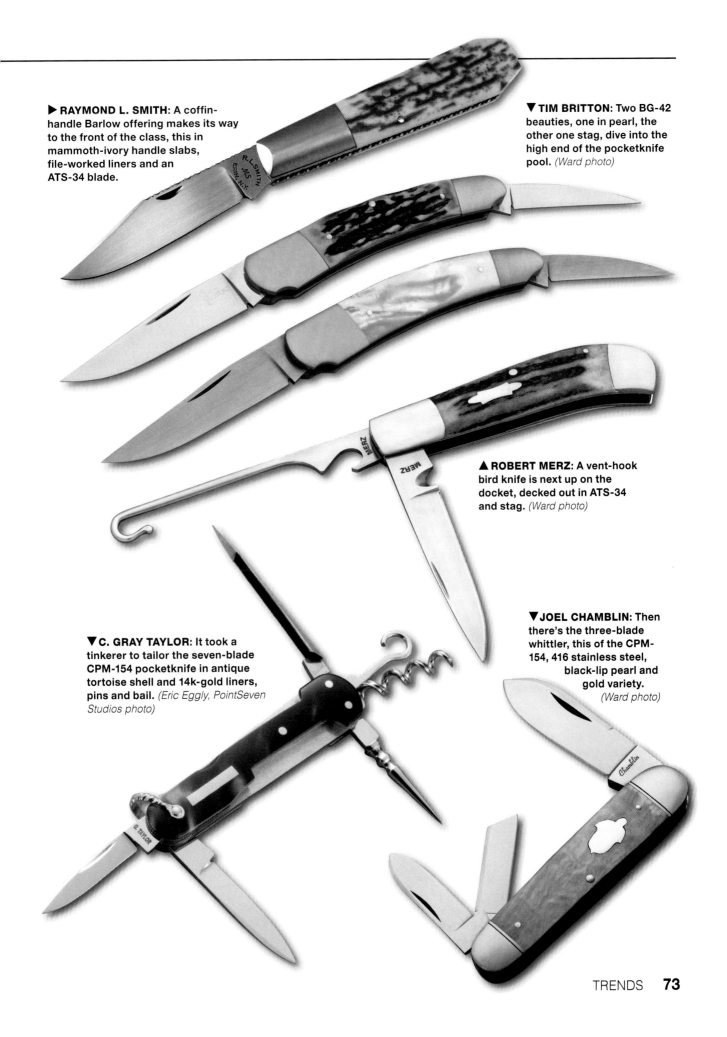

► RAYMOND L. SMITH: A coffin-handle Barlow offering makes its way to the front of the class, this in mammoth-ivory handle slabs, file-worked liners and an ATS-34 blade.

▼ TIM BRITTON: Two BG-42 beauties, one in pearl, the other one stag, dive into the high end of the pocketknife pool. *(Ward photo)*

▲ ROBERT MERZ: A vent-hook bird knife is next up on the docket, decked out in ATS-34 and stag. *(Ward photo)*

▼ C. GRAY TAYLOR: It took a tinkerer to tailor the seven-blade CPM-154 pocketknife in antique tortoise shell and 14k-gold liners, pins and bail. *(Eric Eggly, PointSeven Studios photo)*

▼ JOEL CHAMBLIN: Then there's the three-blade whittler, this of the CPM-154, 416 stainless steel, black-lip pearl and gold variety. *(Ward photo)*

Edged Combatants

As many art knives as there are in the world, and as many beautiful interpretations of hunting knives, swords, daggers and all blades in between, one tends to forget that there's still knife work to be done, or working knives to make so that they can perform the work. In other words, we still need knives that cut, slice, chop, poke and even prod. Try not to pry or you'll end up with a chisel-like tool with no tip. Some say that early tanto designs came from broken sword blades.

Combat knives could be the most important of the knife bunch. Lives really do depend on them. In an effort to avoid the broken-sword-tip-turned-tanto dilemma, knifemakers become metallurgists and aspire for unbreakable steel blades, a target that is elusive to say the least. Synthetic handle material is most often chosen over aesthetic natural offerings, while gemstones and precious metals tend to be saved for the collector's showcase. Pearl, mammoth ivory and tortoise shell are seldom seen in the war zone.

And just as real heroes rarely appear on the silver screen, in television commercials, on basketball courts or on football fields, rarely do the knives of soldiers make it into coffee-table books … until now. It's time they got their day in the sun, and this is just the sunny source to let them shine.

So take off your hats, tuck in your shirts and stand while *Knives 2013* allows the makers of these edge combatants to sing their national anthems and wave their flags. It's the least we can do for those who serve their country and fight for freedom.

▲ **LARRY LUNN:** The Scottish dirk is a presentation piece fit for an officer and showcasing a carved ebony handle, silver dollar pommel, engraved guard and a foot-long damascus blade. *(Eric Eggly, PointSeven Studios photo)*

▶ **LAWRENCE LITTLE:** A brass knuckle bowie boasts an 8-inch 1080 blade, a brass D-guard and pommel, and red fiber spacers.

▶ **LEE OATES:** Called a "Sand Snake" by soldiers in Iraq referring to the textured pattern of the Teflon™-coated 5160 spring-steel blade, it is a fitting description for the double-edged knuckle knife with a rag Micarta® grip.

▶ **DOC WACHOLZ:** A differentially heat-treated 52100 blade takes care of the business end, while a nickel-silver guard and black-linen-Micarta® handle anchor the piece. *(Eric Eggly, PointSeven Studios photo)*

◀ **DANIEL WINKLER:** Measuring 9.75 inches overall, the edged combatants feature extended "striker pommels," camouflage finishes, and cord-wrapped and otherwise synthetic handles. *(Eric Eggly, PointSeven Studios photo)*

▼ **JERRY HOSSOM:** A black-and-green linen-Micarta® grip leverages the hollow-ground CPM-3V fixed-blade. *(SharpByCoop.com photo)*

▶ **JAY FISHER:** A tactical, combat and survival knife all wrapped into one, the "Imamu" includes a bead-blasted, ATS-34 blade with saw-tooth serrations, a stainless steel guard and pommel, and a fiberglass-reinforced G-10 composite handle. The knife locks into a black Kydex® sheath, and comes with a fire starter, sharpening pad and MagLite™.

▲ **MACE VITALE:** Integral 1084 and 1095 fighters adopt Paracord-wrapped handles and edgy attitudes. *(SharpByCoop.com photo)*

American Stickers...
One Knife from Each of the 50 States

▶ **BILL LANCE, Alaska:** Expect nothing less from the Land Of The Midnight Sun than an Alaskan ulu in Devin Thomas damascus and a mammoth-ivory handle scrimshawed by John Fish in a polar bear motif. *(Ward photo)*

▶ **BRIAN FELLHOELTER, Arizona:** Grooves in the "lightning-strike" carbon fiber handle and CPM-S35VN blade add depth to a smooth frame-lock folder. *(Eric Eggly, PointSeven Studios photo)*

◀ **TOM UPTON, Arkansas:** Grab hold of a 9-inch utility fixed blade in stag and D2 blade steel. *(Ward photo)*

▲ **JONATHAN MCNEES, Alabama:** The differentially heat-treated blade of the MCK1 Utility piece showcases a hamon (temper line) that dances with the dimples of a G-10 handle. *(SharpByCoop.com photo)*

▶ **IRA E. DIXON JR., California:** Harkening back to the Gold Rush days, the clean bowie boasts a burly handle, file-worked spacers and a sweet demeanor.

◀ **JERRY HOSSOM, Georgia:** You would have the most handsome fillet knife on the Chattahoochee with this CPM-3V and ivory-Micarta® trophy. *(SharpByCoop.com photo)*

▶ **MIKE ZIMA, Colorado:** Bolsters engraved by Russ Zima and India stag dress up a mirror-polished and file-worked ATS-34 lock-back folder.

◀ **TERRY LEE RENNER, Florida:** What's the most unusual aspect, the Doug Ponzio "feather"-damascus blade pattern, the mammoth-tooth handle scales, the multi-plane-ground blade, Joel Davis damascus bolsters, folding skull-point latch, or the fact that the butterfly knife incorporates all these features? *(SharpByCoop.com photo)*

◀ **GERALD WILLEY, Delaware:** A drop-point hunter features a 4.5-inch 154CM blade, a nickel-silver guard, laminated-wood handle, and black and white Micarta® spacers. Gerald keeps busy sharpening over 500 knives every week at his Delaware retail store, Willey Knives, and rarely has time for his true love of knifemaking.

▲ **DAVID LOUKIDES, Connecticut:** The 5160 bowie with smooth and curvaceous desert-ironwood grip will have you singing Yankee Doodle in no time. *(SharpByCoop.com photo)*

▶ **JEFF CLAIBORNE, Indiana:** A maker from the Hoosier State builds a two-blade 52100 congress in nickel-silver bolsters and liners, and abalone handle scales. *(Hoffman photo)*

◀ **KEITH OUYE, Hawaii:** Like a humpback whale off the coast of Waipahu, the CPM-S30V blade dives sharply at the nose, allowing its embellished body to speak for itself. Bruce Shaw is credited for the engraving on the titanium handle frame. *(SharpByCoop.com photo)*

▲ **DWIGHT TOWELL, Idaho:** The "Hitt Mountain Hunter" incorporates a 3-inch, hand-rubbed blade, a sheep-horn handle, and engraved and gold-inlaid bolsters in a ram's-head motif. *Esto perpetua* (May it endure forever).

▲ **MIKE ZSCHERNY, Iowa:** A two-blade offering from the Hawkeye State is fashioned in stainless steel and ivory. *(SharpByCoop. com photo)*

▲ **RON ROSENBAUGH, Illinois:** A flinted finger-choil pack knife in CPM-S35VN stainless steel, a Dall-sheep-horn handle and mosaic pins will get you a long way in the Land Of Lincoln.

▶ **GENE BASKETT, Kentucky:** The damascus locking-liner folder showcases ivory handle scales, gold screws and blue-anodized-titanium bolsters engraved by Paul Markous. The liners are also anodized cobalt blue and gold. *(Hoffman photo)*

◀ **SCOTT GOSSMAN, Maryland:** A "Big Boar Tusker" involves a 10-inch blade and brown-Micarta® handle.

▲ **LAMONT COOMBS, Maine:** Mammoth tooth leaves its mark on the "Persian Immortal" fighter, designed by Paul Rohaly of Rohaly Cutlery, that also features a sculpted 416 stainless steel guard and 7.5-inch re-curved ATS-34 blade. *(SharpByCoop.com photo)*

▲ **DAVE DARPINIAN, Kansas:** Brass, forged and heat-colored 9150 steel and ironwood lend hot hues to a Persian fixed blade. *(Ward photo)*

▲ **REGGIE BARKER, Louisiana:** Damascus rises and falls along the edge of a stag-handle fighter. *(Ward photo)*

▶ **JERRY VAN EIZENGA, Michigan:** Whitetail crown antler and an arrowhead shield define the friction folder in O1 blade steel. *(Ward photo)*

▶ **JOHN COHEA, Mississippi:** The unusual and beautiful wharncliffe hunter dons random-pattern damascus, mammoth ivory, copper and rawhide. *(Ward photo)*

▲ **PAUL COOPER, Massachusetts:** The words *Manus haec inimica tyrannis ense petit placidam*, etched on the blade of the stag-handle bowie, are Latin for "This hand, an enemy to tyrants, seeks with the sword calm peace in freedom." In another adopted form, *Ense petit placidam sub libertate quietem*—"It seeks by the sword a calm peace in freedom"—it is part of the official motto of the U.S. Commonwealth of Massachusetts. *(Eric Eggly, PointSeven Studios photo)*

▶ **EUGENE SHADLEY, Minnesota:** Why wouldn't the Land of 10,000 Lakes produce a 10-blade sportsman in ATS-34 steel and sambar-stag handle scales? *(Eric Eggly, PointSeven Studios photo)*

◀ **RUSS ANDREWS II, Missouri:** Let the Show Me State show off a random-pattern-damascus bowie handled in black walnut. *(SharpByCoop.com photo)*

▼JOHN DOYLE, Montana: The "Stormy Night Bowie," in a 10-inch 1084 blade with cloud-like temper line and a carbon-fiber and silver-twill handle, will take what Mother Nature dishes out in Big Sky Country. *(BladeGallery.com photo)*

▶BRUCE BINGENHEIMER, Nevada: The clean sambar-stag-handle bowie boasts a 5160 blade and nickel-silver hardware. *(BladeGallery.com photo)*

▶ALAN TIENSVOLD, Nebraska: A Barns & Huber bowie knife reproduction is treated to a 5160 high-carbon-steel blade, brass fittings and a dark walnut handle that reflects a bygone era.

▶LANCE FISHER, New Jersey: Fresh from the Garden State is a 13C26 integral bird-and-trout knife with pinned paper-Micarta® handle slabs and a handy finger-hole pommel.

▲HOWARD HITCHMOUGH, New Hampshire: A fine folder features 24k-gold twisted wire over a black-lip-pearl grip, a Damasteel blade and 18k-gold fittings and screws. *(Eric Eggly, PointSeven Studios photo)*

▶ **JAY FISHER, New Mexico:** The Land Of Enchantment produces a knifemaker who fashions a "Manaya Sculpture" including a hand-engraved ATS-34 hatchet with a polished nephrite jade handle.

▼ **MIKE CRADDOCK, North Carolina:** The laminated blade (top) is a combination of 416 stainless steel and 1095, while the W2 bladed beauty sports a raised clip and smoky temper line. *(SharpByCoop.com photo)*

▲ **JOEL WORLEY, Ohio:** The raindrop-pattern damascus blade includes an integral choil, vine file work and a full, tapered tang sandwiched by sheep-horn handle scales. *(Eric Eggly, PointSeven Studios photo)*

▼ **RAYMOND L. SMITH, New York:** Carrying on the American theme is a one-blade ATS-34 barlow with a Stanhope lens near the butt of the desert ironwood handle. Look inside to see the American flag and read the Pledge of Allegiance.

▼ **RUSS KOMMER, North Dakota:** A handmade drop-point hunter that Russ built for Browning, it features a hollow-ground ATS-34 blade, dovetailed 416 stainless steel bolsters and desert-ironwood handle scales.

▲ **C.R. MILES JR., South Carolina:** From the Palmetto State comes a Native American-style skinner in a blade ground out from a farrier's rasp, a curly maple handle, and brass screws and thong-hole liner.

▲ **BEN MIDGLEY JR., Oklahoma:** The Sooner State offers up an English-scroll-engraved 154-CM lock-back folder. *(Ward photo)*

◄ **RICHARD S. WRIGHT, Rhode Island:** An ambidextrous bolster-release auto, this one has a CPM-154 blade in a modified tanto point, a textured G-10 handle, and titanium bolsters, liners, back bar, kick spring and pocket clip.

▼ **ROBERT L. APPLEBY JR., Pennsylvania:** Clip-point and spear-point 440C bowies boast cast-white-bronze guards and pommels framing stag handle slabs and nickel escutcheon plates. *(Ward photo)*

▲ **ALAN WARREN, Oregon:** It's 7 inches of orange, black and a humped back. *(BladeGallery.com photo)*

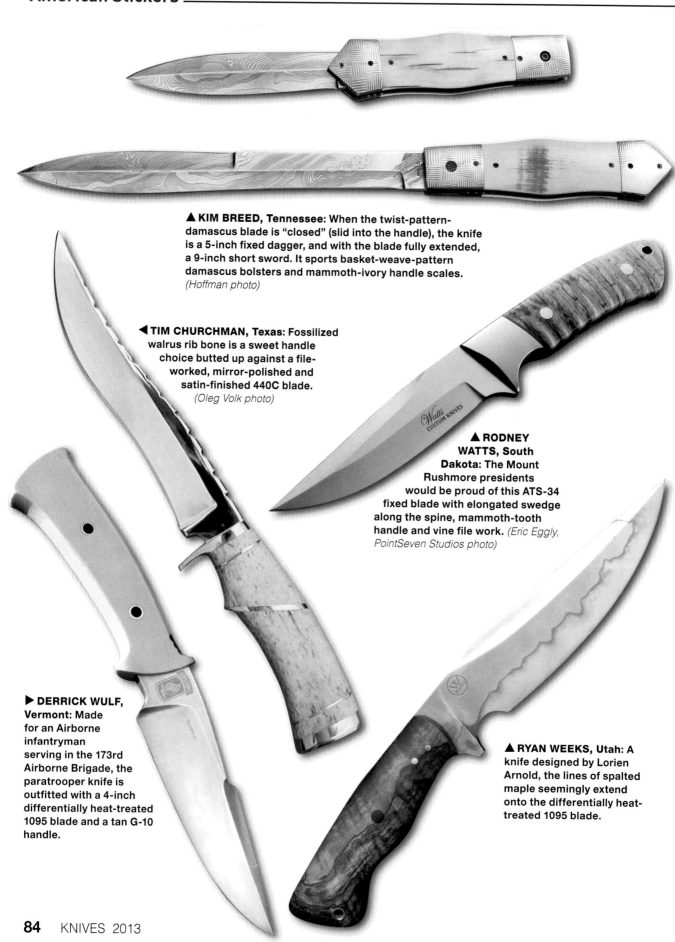

▲ **KIM BREED, Tennessee:** When the twist-pattern-damascus blade is "closed" (slid into the handle), the knife is a 5-inch fixed dagger, and with the blade fully extended, a 9-inch short sword. It sports basket-weave-pattern damascus bolsters and mammoth-ivory handle scales. *(Hoffman photo)*

◀ **TIM CHURCHMAN, Texas:** Fossilized walrus rib bone is a sweet handle choice butted up against a file-worked, mirror-polished and satin-finished 440C blade. *(Oleg Volk photo)*

▲ **RODNEY WATTS, South Dakota:** The Mount Rushmore presidents would be proud of this ATS-34 fixed blade with elongated swedge along the spine, mammoth-tooth handle and vine file work. *(Eric Eggly, PointSeven Studios photo)*

▶ **DERRICK WULF, Vermont:** Made for an Airborne infantryman serving in the 173rd Airborne Brigade, the paratrooper knife is outfitted with a 4-inch differentially heat-treated 1095 blade and a tan G-10 handle.

▲ **RYAN WEEKS, Utah:** A knife designed by Lorien Arnold, the lines of spalted maple seemingly extend onto the differentially heat-treated 1095 blade.

► **T.K. STEINGASS, West Virginia:** Take the CPM-S30V drop-point hunter in stabilized spalted maple along the Appalachian Ridge, and you'll never be without the daily staples. *(SharpByCoop.com photo)*

► **PETER MARTIN, Wisconsin:** Roll out the barrel knife, this one in damascus, titanium, nickel silver and an ancient kauri wood handle. *(Cory Martin Imaging)*

▲ **JOHN BARTLOW, Wyoming:** The ATS-34 hunter in bark-elephant ivory traveled from Wyoming to Colorado to win the Judge's Choice Award for a Hunting/ Utility Knife at the 2011 Denver PKA Show. *(Eric Eggly, PointSeven Studios photo)*

◄ **CHARLES VESTAL, Virginia:** The stag and CPM-154 steel fighter will carry you back to old Virginia. *(SharpByCoop.com photo)*

► **MATTHEW CALDWELL, Washington:** Chopping Walla Walla sweet onions would be no sweat using the stonewash-finished 5-inch 154CM blade while holding the 3D-textured, black and orange, paper-Micarta® handle. *(BladeGallery. com photo)*

Ride Into the Dagger Zone

JOHN H. DAVIS: The rounded and sculpted ebony handle, and nickel silver guard and pommel, transition into a straight, narrow and sharp 8-inch twist-damascus dagger blade. (*Hoffman photo*)

◄ BILLY MACE IMEL: Only mother-of-pearl interrupts the shapely, integral, blackened O1-tool-steel dagger. (*SharpByCoop.com photo*)

◄ ANDERS HOGSTROM: The maker has become adept at combining bronze, black ebony and clay-tempered steel in a most appealing manner. (*SharpByCoop.com photo*)

► MIKE QUESENBERRY: The coffin-style ebony handle hints at what happens when the 11-inch damascus blade gets busy. (*SharpByCoop. com photo*)

► ADAM DESROSIERS: While damascus makes up the bulk of the dagger, even it can't totally distract from the fluted African blackwood handle with twisted silver wire overlay. (*SharpByCoop. com photo*)

▶ **GEORGE GARNER:** The pommel points one direction, the twist-pattern-damascus blade another, and leather and desert ironwood are stacked in the middle. *(Hoffman photo)*

▶ **JERRY VAN EIZENGA:** Ebony spirals, steel straightens and nickel silver rounds it all off. *(Ward photo)*

▶ **J.R. COOK:** Someone quench it—that dagger blade's on fire. Check out the carved overlay of the stylish sheath. *(Ward photo)*

▶ **JOE ZEMITIS:** The exotics include a nickel-damascus blade, Tasmanian-burl handle, cast pewter fittings, nickel silver and buffalo horn.

▲ **GAWIE HERBST:** Bronze fittings bring out the color of the bird's-eye-maple handle, leaving the K110 blade to speak for itself. And it does.

▶ **BILL HERNDON:** Fellow knifemaker Herman Schneider is given credit for the design, but Herndon slimmed it down a bit, gave it a black-oxide-treated 5160 steel blade, and added some pearl and gold inlay. He says it's the prettiest knife he's ever made, and who could argue?

◀ **SCOTT ROUSH:** The "Manzanita Dagger" is done up in manzanita wood, a copper habaki (blade collar), and a blade of 304 stainless steel, nickel and W2.

▶ **MIKE WILLIAMS:** "La Petite Mort" is a deadly little bugger in damascus and ivory. *(Ward photo)*

▲ **OWEN WOOD:** The damascus blade, guard and pommel are equally thorny. *(Eric Eggly, PointSeven Studios photo)*

▲ **CHARLES VESTAL:** Bark mammoth ivory makes its presence known on a CPM-154 Bob Loveless-style dagger. *(SharpByCoop.com photo)*

Automatics for the People

▶ **PETER MARTIN:** Of the large Italian auto stiletto variety, it stretches 17 inches overall and includes a ladder-pattern-damascus blade, blued-steel bolsters, titanium liners, an elephant-ivory handle, and an 18k-gold and pearl button. *(Cory Martin Imaging)*

◀ **LARRY NEWTON:** The tiger-coral handle of the "toothpick auto" is a perfect bedfellow for the gold-inlaid Larry Donnelly damascus bolsters and Rob Thomas raindrop-damascus blade. *(PointSeven Studios photo)*

▶ **RALPH TURNBULL:** A 13C27 automatic folder enlists Alabama damascus bolsters, a tiger-eye-inlaid button, grooved blackwood handle and gold-plated screws.

▼ **LARRY HOSTETLER:** The first two bolster-release autos the maker has attempted are orchestrated in mother-of-pearl handles, Damasteel blades, file-worked spines and lock bars, and 24k-gold screws. Sheila Hostetler engraved the bolsters. *(Hoffman photo)*

▲ **CALVIN ROBINSON:** Orange G-10 sweetens a Sandvik 14C28N drop-point auto folder with a stainless steel frame. *(Hoffman photo)*

Runaway Grains

Did you ever hear the expression, "He wouldn't know a good thing if it hit him over the head?" I often wonder if people recognize the miracles that happen every day, or take time to appreciate the picturesque landscape that surrounds them. Do they see the goodness in other people, or recognize the tragedies of life, the ironies, or beauty of even the saddest things, with puzzlement, wonderment and awe?

Knifemakers have a way of pulling beauty to the surface, whether by hand rubbing and satin finishing blade steel, anodizing titanium, or sanding, oiling, stabilizing and finishing wood. The artist in them brings out the grains, and wants others to see the rings, the inner sanctum of sultry swirls, the colors, contrasts and character.

Just like pearl, mammoth ivory, mastodon tooth, elephant ivory, abalone, stag, stone, and even Micarta®, carbon fiber and celluloid, wood is its own entity. Highly figured wood is nature's own way of painting a picture and growing a masterpiece. For millennia artists have attempted to capture nature on canvas, and even the masters bow graciously before the original, Mother Nature, nurturer of all living things.

So when building edged tools or weapons, knifemakers mimic and harvest their surroundings, the shapes, flowing lines, colors, elements and natural bounty. They channel forces beyond their realm, bringing forth and offering nacreous pearl, fossilized ivory, faceted stone, dyed stag and the runaway grains of highly figured flora.

▶ **ROB HUDSON:** Buffalo horn frames the maple-burl handle, allowing the well-shaped CPM-154 blade to speak for itself. Harry Limings Jr. lent his hand at engraving and 24k-gold inlay.

▲ **BILL AMOUREUX:** So after the box elder burl was stabilized, the only logical thing to do was engrave flowers on the finger guard of the D2 drop-point hunter. (BladeGallery.com photo)

▲ **SAMUEL LURQUIN and LIN RHEA:** Here we have one bowie knife, a heat-treated and hand-finished W2 blade, a drop-dead-gorgeous desert ironwood handle, and two proud knifemakers. (SharpByCoop.com photo)

► **MICKEY YURCO:** The full-tang 440C fixed blades are outfitted in winsome wooden .45 ACP Colt pistol grips. *(Hoffman photo)*

▲ **LEE OATES:** The drop-point hunter includes a 5-inch "topographic"-damascus blade, a water-buffalo-horn guard, and a to-die-for dyed-maple and stag handle.

► **TED OTT:** California buckeye burl makes for the palpable pulp of a flat-ground CPM-D2 drop-point hunter with a nickel guard. *(Frank Brabec photo)*

► **THOMAS HASLINGER:** Hold on tight, the stabilized maple burl will make you lose all control.

► **HENRY TORRES:** The character of the stabilized maple burl shouldn't be so surprising considering how many years it took the tree to grow. The kitchen/utility knife also sports a 52100 blade and mosaic pins. *(BladeGallery.com photo)*

▲ **MARK NEVLING:** Tiger-skin-like stabilized and spalted maple is g-r-r-r-r-e-a-a-a-t! And so is the chainsaw-chain blade and nickel silver guard.

◄ **DAN RAFN:** This serpentine little number sports a Sleipner steel blade and a snakewood grip. *(Jette Schulz photo)*

◄ **MIKE MOONEY:** The redwood burl handle of the "Coho" model fillet knife is more blue than red after dying, stabilizing and butting up against a CPM-S30V blade and 416 stainless steel guard. *(Thomason photo)*

▶ **HARVEY KING:** You could just as easily poke your eye out with California buckeye burl handle as with the D2 blade. *(Thomason photo)*

▶ **ALBERT TRUJILLO:** The ATS-34 blade steel is cryogenically treated, and the amboyna and dyed box elder burl stabilized for a handsome pair of hunters. *(PointSeven Studios photo)*

▲ **DAN FARR:** Goncalo alves, also known as zebrawood or tigerwood, is given a carved and textured treatment, helping enliven a Cru-Forge V fixed blade. *(SharpByCoop.com photo)*

▶ **DOUG CAMPBELL:** Rings of curly koa ascend the handle of the damascus sub-hilt fighter. *(SharpByCoop. com photo)*

▲ **KEVIN CASEY:** Take a Tasmanian-burl handle, a tiger-eye-inlaid thumb stud, "feather"-damascus blade and titanium frame, and let 'er rip! *(SharpByCoop.com photo)*

▲ **JOSHUA STATES:** Buffalo horn and composite turquoise add black and blue to the partial-tang hunter that also parades a forged O1 blade and a stabilized box-elder-burl handle.

▼**JAMES SCROGGS:** Copper and walnut add a one-two punch to an already powerful pair of O1 fighters. (Ward photo)

▶**BILL LYONS:** Why inlay a curly maple handle with bird's-eye maple? Why not, asked the maker of the foxy 5160 fighter? (Ward photo)

▲**GARTH HINDMARCH:** The blue and brown grains interweave like the roots and soil from which they sprouted. The 440C drop-point hunter takes on a 416 stainless steel guard and mosaic pins.

▶**ROBERT BEATY:** Textured brass adds a touch of class to a stabilized-amboyna-burl, and zebra-leg-bone-handled woodsman fixed blade fashioned with file-worked **CPM-D2** steel. (BladeGallery.com photo)

▶**DANA HACKNEY:** An ivory-Micarta® spacer and end cap allow a spalted-maple handle to breathe, lending yet another aesthetic element to the drop-point hunter. (BladeGallery.com photo)

ALAN WARREN: The caramel lines of the mokumé bolsters feed into the brown amboyna wood handle opposite a 3-inch humpback blade. *(BladeGallery.com photo)*

ERIK FRITZ: Honduran rosewood is the hot handle choice for a hand-forged 52100 Santoku chef's knife, while African blackwood puts some space between blade and grip. *(BladeGallery.com photo)*

LLOYD R. HARNER III: Ironwood for Monday, redwood on Tuesday, black ash is for Wednesday … . *(SharpByCoop.com photo)*

JOHN DOYLE: A vest pocket bowie blends a smoky temper line with a smokin'-hot wood grip. *(BladeGallery.com photo)*

H.L. HOLBROOK: Handle slabs of stabilized box elder hug the tapered tang of a CPM-154 drop-point hunter. *(Hoffman photo)*

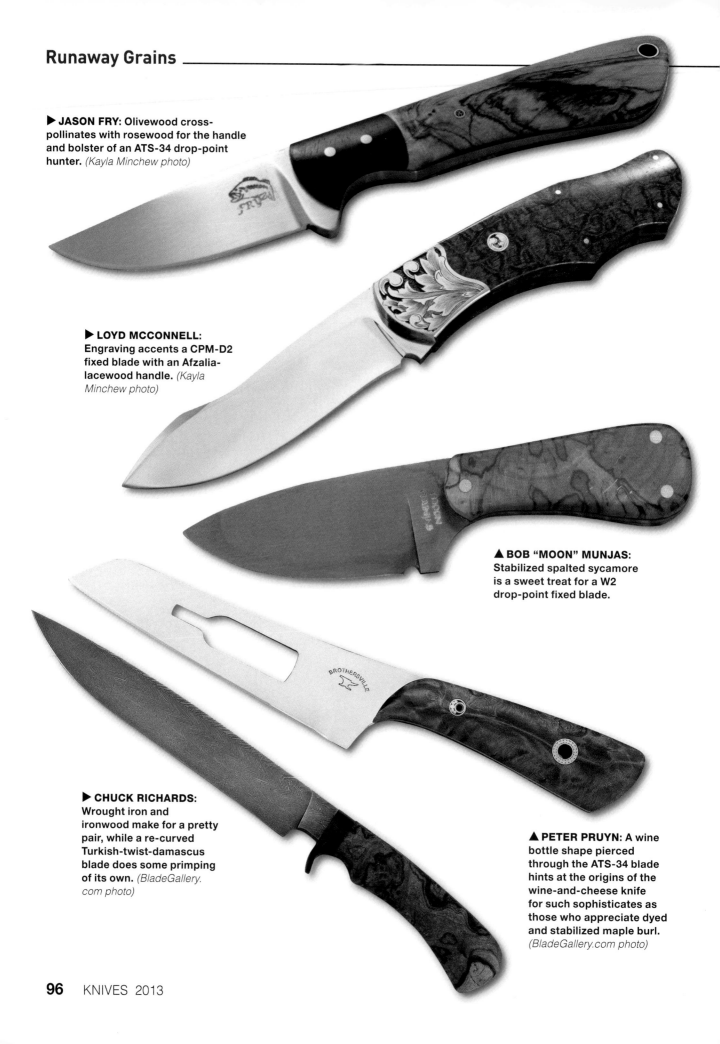

▶ **JASON FRY:** Olivewood cross-pollinates with rosewood for the handle and bolster of an ATS-34 drop-point hunter. *(Kayla Minchew photo)*

▶ **LOYD MCCONNELL:** Engraving accents a CPM-D2 fixed blade with an Afzalia-lacewood handle. *(Kayla Minchew photo)*

▲ **BOB "MOON" MUNJAS:** Stabilized spalted sycamore is a sweet treat for a W2 drop-point fixed blade.

▶ **CHUCK RICHARDS:** Wrought iron and ironwood make for a pretty pair, while a re-curved Turkish-twist-damascus blade does some primping of its own. *(BladeGallery. com photo)*

▲ **PETER PRUYN:** A wine bottle shape pierced through the ATS-34 blade hints at the origins of the wine-and-cheese knife for such sophisticates as those who appreciate dyed and stabilized maple burl. *(BladeGallery.com photo)*

Little Shavers

LEE FERGUSON: The mother-of-pearl grip, 2 3/8-inch 440C blade and titanium fittings are small in stature but not in demeanor. *(Ward photo)*

LARRY LUNN: The miniature katana includes a 2-inch twist-pattern-damascus blade, a mammoth-ivory handle and mokumé-gane fittings. *(Eric Eggly, PointSeven Studios photo)*

BILL DUFF: The miniature bowie is no duffer, but a 4-inch 440C cutting tool. *(Ward photo)*

RICK EATON: A classic Sheffield design, the half-horse/half-alligator, inlaid-silver pommel of the mini bowie leads into a fossil-ivory handle and a mosaic-damascus blade.

TOSHIAKI MICHINAKA: Two mini bowies lie on a full-size blade, with the little ones including ATS-34 steel, nickel-silver guards, and ebony and mother-of-pearl grips.

Channeling Loveless

Don't change that channel. No matter what you do, don't change that channel. There's not a greater knifemaker to channel than the late R.W. "Bob" Loveless, whose work took on legendary proportions long before he passed into another world. It was not only the innovations in knives that he brought to the table, and there were plenty of those, but also the persona behind the blades—the rainbow-colored painter's hat, chain smoking, occasional cussing, the once-over he'd give you whether you were young or old, eyes that looked through you, and possibly an eventual grin, though quite possibly not.

There was something about the style of a Loveless knife. You knew it when you saw it, and can still spot it from a hundred yards away. Yet there was substance behind the shine, a tapered tang, maybe a Micarta® or stacked-leather grip, red spacers, ATS-34 blade, dropped point or swedge along the spine, timeless tang stamp—whether the naked lady, Lawndale or Delaware Maid logo—heft and balance, proportion and useful design.

People respected Loveless, and not just those who were like him, but Japanese collectors, military men, hunters and trappers, artists and hard-working folks across the land. Whether you looked at him as an eccentric genius, someone who tinkered, a designer, curmudgeonly craftsman or godfather of knifemakers, he'd perhaps describe himself as an educated dirt farmer and leave it at that. His knives are as influential today as they were back when, and that's why channeling Loveless is not such a bad idea after all. It's a quite good one, and we'll leave it at that.

▼ **WILLIAM C. "BILL" JOHNSON:** It's not the stacked leather and CPM-154 steel but the way they're put together that counts them as a Loveless-style chute knife. *(Eric Eggly, PointSeven Studios photo)*

▶ **ALAN WARREN:** The only thing better than a Bob Loveless-style knife is a set of them, these with carbon fiber grips, stainless bolts, thong tubes and swedges along the blade spines. *(BladeGallery.com photo)*

▲ **MARCUS LIN:** Such attributes as a mirror-polished ATS-34 blade, green-canvas-Micarta® handle scales with red liners over a tapered tang and 416 stainless steel furniture define the Bob Loveless-style "Big Bear" sub-hilt bowie. *(SharpByCoop.com photo)*

▶ **JOHN YOUNG:** The maker's "Mini Wilderness" decked out in a double-ground ATS-34 blade and an amber-stag grip channel Loveless in a very real way. *(SharpByCoop. com photo)*

▼ **CHAD NELL:** The giraffe bone pretties up a Bob Loveless-style "New York Special" with tapered tang, red liners and 3.5-inch CPM-154 blade. *(SharpByCoop.com photo)*

▼ **I.R. BAILEY:** Not your standard drop-point hunter, this one screams "Loveless" in style and makeup.

▼ **THAD BUCHANAN:** In the style of a Loveless "Hideout," the double-ground CPM-154 fixed blade is treated to a pre-ban-ivory grip with a lot of character, much like its original inventor. *(SharpByCoop.com photo)*

▲ **STEVEN R. JOHNSON:** A small, petite version of a Bob Loveless Big Bear, the "Mama Bear" features an ATS-34 blade and a creamy interior-mammoth-ivory handle with a few surface nicks showing. It's slim and narrow with smaller-than-usual lugs, shorter than the original, and light and fast for its size. *(Hoffman photo)*

Blow-The-Door-Hinges-Off Bowies

What's more fitting for the knife culture than long blades, high-carbon steel, the American bowie knife pattern, barn door hinges, blacksmith shops, hammers, tongs and craftsmanship? Not a whole heck of a lot, that's what. The bowie knife, like its namesake Col. James Bowie, is ingrained in the culture of one of the world's youngest, most free, modern, advanced and diverse culture.

The clip point is as distinct and stylish as a Japanese tanto, Nepalese kukri, Persian fighter, Finnish puukko or Sikh dagger. The bowie not only evokes imagery of the Sandbar Fight and the Alamo, but also of cowboys, the Wild West, prairies, settlements, the gold rush and gamblers. They fit snugly in leather sheaths, swing low to the knee and rest comfortably on the hip.

Not many folk carry bowie knives anymore, but for those who traverse the ranches or desert flatlands of this land of plenty, and pull out long blades to cut rope, chop a branch, extract a cactus needle, notch a leather belt or carve a piece of wood. There's still a lot of barbed wire on the continent, and plenty of cattle and crops dotting the landscape from sea to shining sea.

Bowie knives have come a long way in material makeup, workmanship and overall aesthetics. They are no greenhorn knives, but sleek edged weapons and tools that will blow the door hinges off any old barn, if only to ride along on cattle drives or hitch a ride for Saturday visits into town.

▶ **LIN RHEA:** A bowie in ironwood, steel and bronze struts its stuff. *(Ward photo)*

▶ **WILLIAM TYC:** The Spanish notch bowie parades a pearl grip, ATS-34 blade, and a brass guard, pommel and pins. *(Kayla Minchew photo)*

▲ **JOHN HORRIGAN:** The laminated-steel bowie is one of high character and an ivory hilt that won't quit. *(Steve Woods photo)*

▶ **ADAM DESROSIERS:** A 1084-and-15N20-damascus blade and guard extend out from a carved walnut handle. *(SharpByCoop.com photo)*

▲ **JOHN WHITE:** By the time you've decided where to look first—the Turkish-twist-damascus blade, antique-walrus handle or carved guard—the bandits have taken over the stagecoach. This one comes with a takedown tool, spare assembly pins and a Paul Long sheath. *(Buddy Thomason photo)*

▲ **ALEX DANIELS:** It's a hunting bowie, and a hunting we shall go!

▶ **HALEY DESROSIERS:** The W2 blade is flat ground, the O1 guard blued, the spacer file worked, and the ivory of the walrus denomination. *(SharpByCoop.com photo)*

▲ **JERRY FISK:** Sometimes the stag is upstaged by the damascus steel and the browned-iron guard. *(Ward photo)*

Blow-The-Door-Hinges-Off Bowies

▶ **ARTHUR LYNN:** Sambar stag, an oval guard and a damascus blade made for inspired choices on the "Gladiator Bowie." Let the games begin. *(Buddy Thomason photo)*

▲ **GARY RODEWALD:** Three hundred and twenty layers of damascus keep pace with the wavy grains of stabilized Masur birch, as well as a nickel-silver guard and domed pins. *(BladeGallery.com photo)*

▶ **SHAYNE CARTER:** It took 52100 steel, walrus ivory and the skill of an ABS journeyman smith. *(Eric Eggly, PointSeven Studios photo)*

▲ **LARRY LUNN:** Coffin handles aren't only reserved for undertakers, though after the 16-inch stainless-and-ivory bowie gets done with the outlaws, they might need one. There are 10 large and eight small sapphires in the engraved guard, pommel and ferrule. *(Eric Eggly, PointSeven Studios photo)*

▲ **TOMMY GANN:** The blackwood dog-bone bowie is one of distinction and determination. *(Ward photo)*

▶ **RED ST. CYR:** The 52100 blade is 11 inches of pure steely glare, while the stag handle, and damascus guard and pommel are super additions. *(Eric Eggly, PointSeven Studios photo)*

◀ **JIM COFFEE:** The 6.5-inch Alabama damascus blade is a clip-point beauty with a solid stag grip, and a stainless steel guard, spacer and end cap. *(Eric Eggly, PointSeven Studios photo)*

▶ **ERIK FRITZ:** With 5160 and koa wood, the cowboy never has to say whoa to the horse or the intruder. *(Eric Eggly, PointSeven Studios photo)*

▲ **TONY HUGHES:** A clean rendition of the bowie knife pattern includes an oval guard and a black handle pinned in all the right places. *(Eric Eggly, PointSeven Studios photo)*

▲ **BRION TOMBERLIN:** Of the gent's bowie ilk is a stag and damascus example with silver spacers. *(Ward photo)*

▶ **GARY HOUSE:** Which has more character, the walrus ivory grip or clay-tempered, water-quenched 1095 blade with temper line? An African blackwood spacer makes for a nice segue. *(Eric Eggly, PointSeven Studios photo)*

▲ **JERRY VAN EIZENGA:** In ivory and 1084 steel the bowie has a nice palm swell, shapely guard and a blade that clips right along. *(Ward photo)*

▲ **J.R. COOK:** The 15-inch bowie sports a 5160 blade precision ground to the tip, a mammoth ivory handle and a heat colored guard. *(Ward photo)*

▲ **TERRY LEE RENNER:** The "Iron Duchess" showcases a 12-inch 1095 high-carbon steel blade deep-relief carved in an old German acorn pattern, fittings of melted bell bronze, and a "popcorn"-sambar-stag handle. *(SharpByCoop.com photo)*

▶ **BILL KIRKES:**
This nifty submarine commemorative bowie will float your boat, particularly the ivory grip, "S"-guard and embellished stainless steel handle shields. *(Ward photo)*

◀ **RALPH RICHARDS:** The attractive ringed gidgee of the handle might be native to Australia, but the bowie knife pattern is all American. *(Ward photo)*

▲ **DALE HUCKABEE:**
Some bowies with the most character are ground from old files, and outfitted with wrought-iron furniture and stag handles.

▲ **ALAN WARREN:**
The 8.375-inch blade of the blackwood-handle bowie will wield willingly during the melee. *(BladeGallery.com photo)*

▶ **RICK "BEAR BONE" SMITH:** A great field companion with classic looks, the bowie sports a 7-inch twist-pattern-damascus blade, a sambar-stag handle and a mild steel butt cap.

Blow-The-Door-Hinges-Off Bowies

▶ **JASON KNIGHT:** The bowie was wrought from ironwood and W2 steel. *(SharpByCoop.com photo)*

◀ **STEVEN KOSTER:** Where to start: how about with the 351-layer ladder-pattern-damascus blade and shell-file-worked guard, or the ebony grip and domed silver pins? *(Douglas Koster photo)*

◀ **JERRY MCCLURE:** Get a good hold of the fossil-walrus-ivory handle before falling into a trance over the damascus blade. *(Kayla Minchew photo)*

▶ **RON NEWTON:** The master smith fashioned a damascus and walrus-ivory camp bowie of take-down construction, complete with damascus takedown tools and a Paul Long sheath. *(SharpByCoop.com photo)*

▲ **RANDY GOLDEN:** A medium-build bowie is made up of CPM-154 blade steel with a false edge, an ancient-ivory handle, stainless steel guard, shell-shaped end cap, and nickel-silver pins and escutcheon plate. *(Bill Ingalls photo)*

Camp Grinds

▶ **JAMES LUCIE:** The spacers are neatly spaced, the crown stag making for a nice crown, and the steel giving a steely glare on the hand-forged William Scagel-style camp knife.

▶ **JAMES L. RODEBAUGH:** A curly-walnut handle and forge-finished 1084 blade lend character to the "Wind River Camp Knife." *(Eric Eggly, PointSeven Studios photo)*

◀ **MICHAEL O'MACHEARLEY and DOC WACHOLZ:** Mike and Doc made a bug-out blade in 52100 and Micarta®. *(Eric Eggly, PointSeven Studios photo)*

▲ **J.R. COOK:** To celebrate 25 years of knifemaking, Mr. Cook fashioned a camp set in 1084 steel and quilted maple with checkering. *(Ward photo)*

▼ **BUTCH DEVERAUX:** Sheep horn and she oak make beautiful bedfellows, or blade fellows, for the 52100 camp knife guarded in brass. *(SharpByCoop.com photo)*

Milky Mammoth & Mastodon Ivory

Creamy white can describe mastodon and mammoth ivory, but there is so much more there. Often the tusks of the ancient beasts look like spoiled milk with greens, blues and browns swirling among the otherwise chalky exterior of ancient ivory. Yellow, gold, orange and black—they all make appearances, like the rotted teeth of a witch or warlock. Only these are aesthetically superior, downright pleasing to the senses.

Permafrost never pushed up anything as delightful as the aged ivory tusks from behemoth mammals that roamed the earth anywhere between 25 million and 10,000 years ago. No wonder the ivory shows aged patina. Anything that old deserves to have developed character over time. And that's why knifemakers and collectors have fallen domed-head-over-elephant-toenails in love with mammoth and mastodon ivory.

It's not as simple as taking a tusk and slapping a slab of it on a knife frame, however. Like precious gems, it must be cut for quality and character, then finely fit and finished, bringing the colors and figuration to the forefront … palpable to the touch. The beasts have provided beauty, and it is up to knife artisans to ensure the offerings don't go unaccepted. They must make the best of their gifts, immortalizing the hairy beasts through inspired and ingenious use of milky mammoth and mastodon ivory.

◀ **JERRY MCCLURE:** A classically styled locking-liner folder combines elements like gold-wire inlay with a mustard-gold mammoth ivory handle, yellow-diamond thumb stud and twist-damascus blade. *(Ward photo)*

▲ **GUY STAINTHORP:** Nothing beats mammoth ivory for gripping a Bushcrafter blade.

▲ **DAN CHINNOCK:** Touches like a turquoise thumb stud and "leopard"-pattern-damascus blade bring out the colors of blue mammoth ivory. *(Ward photo)*

▶ **PETER CAREY:** If flipper folders are in your near future, why not a "Nitro Mini" in mammoth ivory, and a Gerome Weinand raindrop-damascus blade and bolsters.

◀ **JERRY MOEN:** Would you like some creamy mammoth ivory with your Carpenter steel blades? How about a pair with Nathan Dickenson-engraved bolsters and red spacers? *(Hoffman photo)*

▼ **GEORGE GARNER:** As the past meets the present, mammoth ivory is introduced to heat-blued Robert Eggerling leaf-pattern mosaic damascus and an opal thumb stud. *(Hoffman photo)*

▶ **DON HETHCOAT:** Don does a front-lock folder up in damascus and milky mammoth scales.

▲ **MEL FASSIO:** The lock-back folder embodies a soothing blend of milky mammoth ivory, mokumé and damascus blade steel.

▶ **DAVID LISCH:** The feather-damascus blade and D-guard protect the bark-mammoth-ivory handle like a downy pillow cradles a 10-carat diamond. *(Mitch Lum photo)*

▶ **BRION TOMBERLIN:** A 9.5-inch W2 blade with a wispy temper line combines with mammoth ivory on a convex-ground fighter. *(SharpByCoop.com photo)*

▶ **GARY MULKEY:** A blued wrought-iron guard separates the edge of the meteorite-and-W2 damascus blade from the mastodon-ivory grip of a "Campo de Cielo" bowie. *(Ward photo)*

▲ **LAMONT COOMBS:** If there's such a thing as presentation-grade mammoth ivory, this is it within the handle half of an ATS-34 fighter designed by Paul Rohaly of Rohaly Cutlery. *(SharpByCoop.com photo)*

◀ **DON HANSON III:** A sub-hilt fighter is distinguished by a 7.75-inch damascus blade and a North Sea mammoth ivory handle. *(SharpByCoop.com photo)*

Horseman's, Falconer's & Huntsmen's Swords

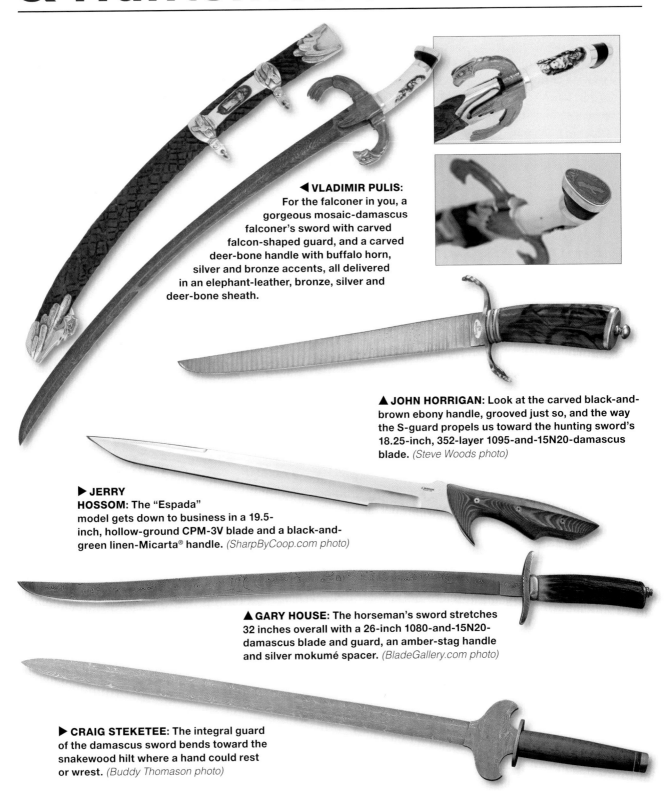

◄ VLADIMIR PULIS: For the falconer in you, a gorgeous mosaic-damascus falconer's sword with carved falcon-shaped guard, and a carved deer-bone handle with buffalo horn, silver and bronze accents, all delivered in an elephant-leather, bronze, silver and deer-bone sheath.

▲ JOHN HORRIGAN: Look at the carved black-and-brown ebony handle, grooved just so, and the way the S-guard propels us toward the hunting sword's 18.25-inch, 352-layer 1095-and-15N20-damascus blade. *(Steve Woods photo)*

► JERRY HOSSOM: The "Espada" model gets down to business in a 19.5-inch, hollow-ground CPM-3V blade and a black-and-green linen-Micarta® handle. *(SharpByCoop.com photo)*

▲ GARY HOUSE: The horseman's sword stretches 32 inches overall with a 26-inch 1080-and-15N20-damascus blade and guard, an amber-stag handle and silver mokumé spacer. *(BladeGallery.com photo)*

► CRAIG STEKETEE: The integral guard of the damascus sword bends toward the snakewood hilt where a hand could rest or wrest. *(Buddy Thomason photo)*

Tribal Warriors

No matter what god you pray to, you can appreciate the edged weapons on this and the following page. And if you had been a frontiersman, explorer, settler or Army lad, you would have prayed to the sun, moon, creator and stars when you saw a rawhide-wrapped tomahawk, war club, belt dagger, lance or spear. Yet, time has a way of softening the blows, allowing fears to subside, it lessons the pain, causing reflection and historical prospective. The United States is a young country with such a rich history, and it's not just the weapons of the White man that are remembered, remade, collected and regarded.

The edged tools and weapons of the Native Americans are instantly recognizable, admired and copied. Ethnically unique, there are no substitutes, nor were there alternatives at the time. The tools of man, no matter the color of their skin, ethnicity or religion, were vital to their survival, particularly knives and weapons. It was not only the West that was wild, nor the frontier that was untamed. The world was in constant flux, with cultures and people juxtaposing for land, power and riches.

Unsettling times called for weapons of defense and destruction. These were the peacekeepers of their time, the tools of the proud and fearless, those protecting their home and identity. They were and are the tribal warriors, and they continue to call their people home.

◀ **MARDI MESHEJIAN:** A wicked war hammer is done up in damascus and a lengthy carved-snakewood haft. *(Eric Eggly, PointSeven Studios photo)*

▶ **JOHN COHEA:** The bowie/fighter is wielded via a stag handle, outfitted with a heat-colored wrought-iron guard and protected by a Chad Nichols damascus blade. *(Ward photo)*

▲ **TOM BOYES:** Don't be distracted by the pearl handle, mosaic pins or damascus steel, bolsters and butt cap, the double-edged dagger is all tribal warrior.

► **TOMMY MCNABB:** From the maple haft to the bimetal, welded head, rawhide wrap, brass tacks, and bone and turquoise beads, the tomahawk displays the style of a native people.

▲ **TIM SCHOLL:** An L6-and-1095-damascus head with pipe make both war and peace possible, while the curly maple haft lends leverage. The pipe tomahawk also sports a gator-skin wrap.

▲ **MIKE WILLIAMS:** The Huron war club benefits from a rifle-stock-style maple haft with gorgeous grain lines and a fierce damascus double edge. *(Ward photo)*

▲ **WILLIAM LLOYD:** A carved bear-bone handle leads to a lapis lazuli spacer, jaw-bone guard and damascus dagger blade forged by Norm Schenk. *(Eric Eggly, PointSeven Studios photo)*

◄ **SHAWN SHROPSHIRE:** A reclaimed horseshoe rasp became the 5.25-inch blade of an elk-antler-handle Indian patch knife that also includes a rawhide wrap.

Easy-Handlin' Hunters

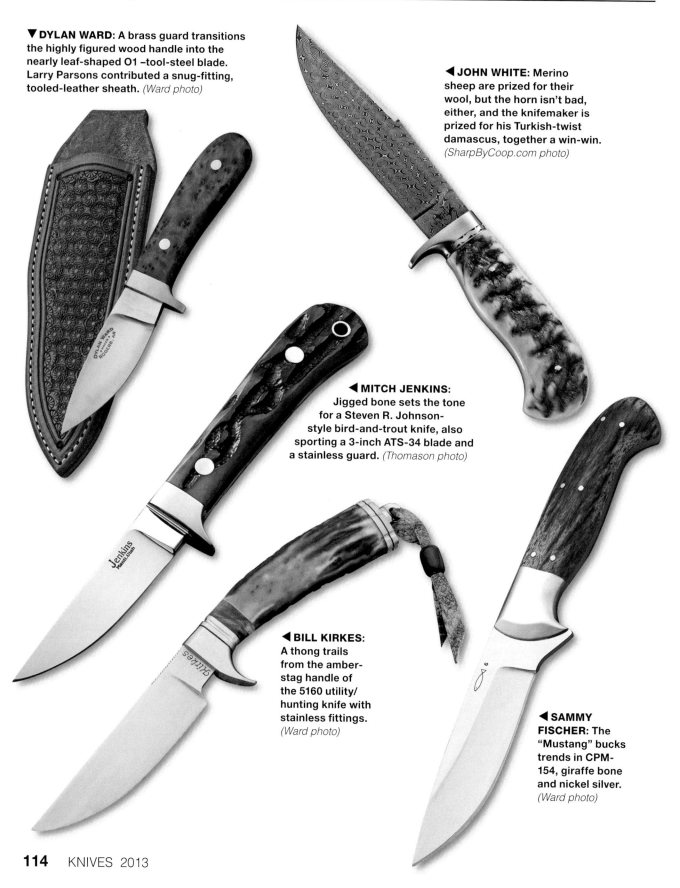

▼ **DYLAN WARD:** A brass guard transitions the highly figured wood handle into the nearly leaf-shaped O1 –tool-steel blade. Larry Parsons contributed a snug-fitting, tooled-leather sheath. *(Ward photo)*

◄ **JOHN WHITE:** Merino sheep are prized for their wool, but the horn isn't bad, either, and the knifemaker is prized for his Turkish-twist damascus, together a win-win. *(SharpByCoop.com photo)*

◄ **MITCH JENKINS:** Jigged bone sets the tone for a Steven R. Johnson-style bird-and-trout knife, also sporting a 3-inch ATS-34 blade and a stainless guard. *(Thomason photo)*

◄ **BILL KIRKES:** A thong trails from the amber-stag handle of the 5160 utility/ hunting knife with stainless fittings. *(Ward photo)*

◄ **SAMMY FISCHER:** The "Mustang" bucks trends in CPM-154, giraffe bone and nickel silver. *(Ward photo)*

▶ **HARVEY KING:** Only mosaic pins would stand out from the prettily patterned buckeye burl, with D2 steel proving an enlightened choice for the blade. *(Thomason photo)*

▼ **MIKE WILLIAMS:** Whether dressing the bird or filleting the trout, the drop-point 1084 blade and bone handle are up to the task. *(Ward photo)*

▲ **JOHN BARTLOW:** Bark elephant ivory lends age lines to the pristine ATS-34 elk hunter in the style of D'Alton Holder. *(Thomason photo)*

▶ **KEVIN LESSWING:** A couple ivories and some ironwood make up the handle of the W2 drop-point hunter with a differentially heat-treated blade. *(SharpByCoop. com photo)*

◀ **DAVID C. LEMOINE:** It's a rare big game drop-point hunter that has a heat-colored mosaic-damascus bolster planted between a stag handle and 4-inch CPM-S30V blade. Red liners set off the tapered tang. *(Ward photo)*

▼ **JERRY LAIRSON:** Cable damascus adds an edge to the 3.5-inch hunter in a walrus-ivory grip. *(Ward photo)*

▲ **ERIK FRITZ:** The maker gives the hunter a choice of G-10 and 52100 steel or ivory and damascus. *(Eric Eggly, PointSeven Studios photo)*

▲ **CHARLIE MAJORS:** Matching trailing-point hunters come in CPM-154 blades, Dwayne Dushane-engraved guards and sambar-stag handles. *(Johnny Stout Photography)*

▲ **DOUG CAMPBELL:** Which came first the damascus clip-point hunter or the antler handle? *(SharpByCoop. com photo)*

► **LIN RHEA:** Don't be sheepish about the sheep-horn hunter. It's OK to love it. *(Ward photo)*

DAN BURKE: Mr. Burke pays homage to Mr. R.W. Loveless by replicating a tapered-tang gut-hook hunter like only the late great could have made it. *(Eric Eggly, PointSeven Studios photo)*

MARCUS LIN: A nicely fit and finished tapered-tang hunter dons a 3.5-inch ATS-34 blade and sambar-stag handle scales. *(SharpByCoop. com photo)*

RUSSELL ROOSEVELT: You'll look svelte with a Roosevelt stag and damascus hunter on your belt. *(SharpByCoop.com photo)*

KEITH MURR: Yet another handle material rears its head—antique ivory Micarta®—and just in time for a D2 drop-point hunter/general purpose knife with mosaic pins. *(Ward photo)*

J.R. COOK: It's a shiver-me-timbers skinner in a 5-inch damascus blade, damascus finger guard and elephant-ivory handle. *(Ward photo)*

TRENDS **117**

▶ **SEAN O'HARE:** First he cut the silver vine with the upswept CPM-154 blade, then stabilized it for the handle and secured it with mosaic and stainless steel pins.

◀ **AARON WILBURN:** Oosic keeps the crown-stag grip a safe distance from the edge of the 4-inch, differentially heat-treated blade. *(BladeGallery. com photo)*

▶ **JOHN PARKS:** A slim hunter in 1095 and sambar stag may be all you need. *(SharpByCoop.com photo)*

▶ **JERRY FISK:** His "Gamemaster Hunter" is well outfitted in a 5-inch 1084 blade, an engraved guard and ironwood handle. *(Ward photo)*

◀ **T.K. STEINGASS:** The drop-point hunter and caper set leaves camp in spalted-maple handles and O1 blades. *(SharpByCoop.com photo)*

▶ **GEORGE TROUT:** One solid piece of 440C steel from point to butt, slabs of stag highlight the hunting knife. *(Hoffman photo)*

▶ **ANSSI RUUSUVUORI:** Who says hunters can't be pretty? This one struts its pink ivory, nickel silver, abalone, moose bone and damascus stuff. Hygel of Norway forged the blade steel.

▶ **DANIEL ZVONEK:** A mammoth-tooth-handle offering sports an ATS-34 blade, a 416 stainless steel finger guard and a stingray-skin sheath. *(Thomason photo)*

▶ **GARTH HINDMARCH:** The small drop-point hunter looks stylish in spalted maple, a leather thong and wooden bead.

▲ **ROB HUDSON:** Cued up and hued up for the hunt is a drop-point CPM-154 fixed blade in black ash, sambar stag, engraving and 24k-gold inlay.

▶ **CAL GANSHORN:** Using DC electrical current and salt water, Eugene Schreiner hand etched the ATS-34 blade in a howling wolf motif, and the knifemaker added touches like a spalted-maple handle and stainless steel bolster.

▲ **LARRY HOSTETLER:** If a drop-point hunter is in your future, none may be better than this one in ATS-34 blade steel, an Alabama damascus guard and desert ironwood handle. *(Hoffman photo)*

▶ **DICKIE ROBINSON:** Nothing less than ironwood and 1084 steel would suffice for the 4.5-inch drop-point hunter. *(Ward photo)*

◀ **KEITH BAGLEY:** Oosic and malachite make up the hot handle combo on a damascus hunter. *(Hoffman photo)*

▼ **JAMES LUCIE:** A small hand-forged William Scagel-style skinner, it is of the 1084 steel variety with an elk-horn handle and stacked spacers. *(Thomason photo)*

Amber Waves of Stag

▲ CHAD NELL: Red brick spacers and amber-stag handle scales put a little rouge on a CPM-154 sub-hilt fighter. *(SharpByCoop.com photo)*

▲ RICK "BEAR BONE" SMITH: The classic bowie-style fighting knife showcases a 9.5-inch satin-finished O1-tool-steel blade, a contoured guard, nickel silver ferrule and an aged, coffee-colored sambar stag handle.

▶ RADE HAWKINS: A fine-figured 154CM drop-point hunter parades nicely figured amber stag.

▶ J.P. JONES: Amber waves of stag wash over the handle of a D2 drop-point hunter. *(Ward photo)*

▲ CHARLES VESTAL: A Bob Loveless-style New York Special sports atypical amber stag handle scales and a CPM-154 blade. *(SharpByCoop.com photo)*

Fiery Fighters

That first knife a maker ever managed to put together—you've heard the story, he takes one of Dad's old file rasps, starts grinding it, shaping it and putting an edge on the already hardened, unforgiving steel. When semi-satisfied with the results, he fashions a handle and attaches it to the tang of the rasp, and then proceeds to sand, polish and buff until his arm detaches from its socket. And you know what? Few if any of those original works of primitive art were fighters. No, most were utility fixed blades, crude sheath knives or way too unwieldy daggers. Some could have passed for hunters and others as daily carry knives. Fighters, well, those are a few steps removed from the raspy knives of naiveté.

Though fighters are duty specific and recognizable in form, with shapes that are studied and purpose driven, they do vary from model to model. The blades are meant to slash, pierce and cut with equal aplomb, playing no favorites on the duty roster. It takes a trained eye to duplicate a fighting knife, to grind a fighter blade, usually taken on by those with police or military experience, where in their careers like with the knives they build, failure is not a viable option.

Each element of a fixed-blade fighter is essential. While the blade is designed for hard use and utilitarian applications, the guard is the protector, the handle an anchoring force, and whether a stick tang or tapered tang, what's beneath the grip is the backbone. It must be strong, truly unbreakable and light-weight, lightning quick, like the reflexes of a soldier … or at the very least, aspiring to those of a fiery fighter.

◀ **SAMMY FISCHER:** At first glance, one might not notice the sculpted nickel silver guard, the butt cap filed to match the exterior of the stag handle, or how the CPM-154 blade is shaped to perfection. *(Ward photo)*

▲ **JERRY HOSSOM:** In the "Vengeance Tanto" realm is a fiery CPM-3V fixed-blade fighter held in check by a black-canvas-Micarta® grip. *(SharpByCoop.com photo)*

◀ **ALAIN DESAULNIERS:** Winsome gold inlay and engraving by Martin Butler adorns the guard and sub-hilt of the fighter, complementing a mammoth-ivory grip, tapered tang, red liners and a CPM-154 blade. *(SharpByCoop.com photo)*

▶ **RON NEWTON:** The stag-handle sub-hilt fighter is built for speed and efficiency. *(Ward photo)*

▼ **BILL BUXTON:** If the damascus doesn't slay ya, the rest of the 10 1/8-inch fighter will. *(Ward photo)*

▶ **CHAD NELL:** The fixed-blade fighter and dagger combo, in carbon fiber and cold steel, will cut right through you. *(SharpByCoop.com photo)*

▼ **MIKE CRADDOCK:** There's smoke along the W-2 blade and fire within the stag-handle fighter. *(SharpByCoop.com photo)*

▲ **WADE COLTER:** From the Colter collection comes a stag-and-5160 fighter that disassembles so you can admire it inside and out, no doubt. *(Eric Eggly, PointSeven Studios photo)*

Fiery Fighters

▶ **E. SCOTT MCGHEE:** The big curly walnut handle meets a Cruforge V blade at a 416 stainless steel guard, where they all take time to assess the situation. *(SharpByCoop.com photo)*

◀ **MARCUS LIN:** A pair of ATS-34 fighters in canvas-Micarta® grips pays tribute to the late, great Bob Loveless who made them famous. *(SharpByCoop.com photo)*

▶ **DON HANSON III:** If you like the damascus and mammoth-ivory fighter, you'll have to put up some green. *(SharpByCoop.com photo)*

◀ **DAVID LISCH:** Damascus is reserved for either side of a stag grip, while W2 takes care of the fighting end of the knife. *(Mitch Lum photo)*

▶ **WILLIAM TYC:** Don't take too much of a liking to the D2 blade or bolted ivory-Micarta® handle, because with a tiger-snakeskin-overlaid sheath like that, you might not ever see the knife. *(Kayla Minchew photo)*

► **ZAC BUCHANAN:** Cape buffalo and ATS-34 pull double duty on an inviting fighting knife. *(Eric Eggly, PointSeven Studios photo)*

► **ERIK FRITZ:** The "Hell's Belle" makes its debut in an 11-inch 5160 blade, satin-finished mild-steel guard and ferrule, and a cocobolo handle complete with domed pins. *(BladeGallery.com photo)*

◄ **KYLE ROYER:** Mammoth ivory, file-worked spacers and the most dazzling of damascus let the long fighter rip and roar. *(SharpByCoop.com photo)*

▲ **RUSS ANDREWS II:** Lines run perpendicular to the edge of the damascus blade, anchored by equally stunning stag and some fancy file work. *(SharpByCoop.com photo)*

▲ **GEOFF KEYES:** Pointedly determined is the 10.5-inch damascus blade accompanied by ebony and sea cow bone. *(BladeGallery.com photo)*

Fiery Fighters

▶ **JASON KNIGHT:** This is no bloody-nosed, gashed and gassed fighter, but a gorgeous one with some punches left in him. *(SharpByCoop.com photo)*

▼ **GUY HIELSCHER:** By the looks of the tactical fighter, dressed in a camouflage Dura-Coat-finished O1-and-1018-damascus blade and Micarta® grip, it won't be a prototype for long. *(Buddy Thomason photo)*

◀ **NICK WHEELER:** Black G-10 gives the 15-inch fighter a good grip. *(SharpByCoop.com photo)*

▶ **DAVE RUANA:** The tapering clip point of the 1084 blade holds its own against a Montana elk horn grip and welded-brass guards. Micarta® acts as a spacer between the guards. *(Buddy Thomason photo)*

▲ **SHAWN KNOWLES:** Only stacked leather would suffice to balance the elongated CPM-154 fighter blade. *(SharpByCoop.com photo)*

▶ **R.J. MARTIN:** Creative grinding gives some cool to the cut of the 7.25-inch CTS-XHP blade of the canvas-Micarta®-handled fighter. *(Eric Eggly, PointSeven Studios photo)*

◀ **KEVIN CASEY:** Feather damascus and fossilized walrus tusk make up the 12.75-inch fixed-blade fighter. *(SharpByCoop.com photo)*

▲ **MICHAEL RUTH JR.:** Damascus and stag do a two-step along a 12-inch fighter. *(Ward photo)*

▼ **LAMONT COOMBS:** A stylish sub-hilt fighter, designed by Paul Rohaly, parades a 6.5-inch ATS-34 blade and a pre-ban elephant ivory handle. *(SharpByCoop.com photo)*

▶ **ALAN WARREN:** Preferring the term "tactical bowie," Alan's 12-inch fixed blade will do the job just the same. *(BladeGallery.com photo)*

▲ ANDERS HOGSTROM: Perhaps the most sculpted of the fighting class, the blue fossil-walrus-ivory handle of "The Corsican" is as alluring as the double-tempered 1050 blade. *(SharpByCoop.com photo)*

▶ J.R. REEVES: You might as well use blackwood on a stealth 5160 vest fighter with no flaws, many fans and maybe a few fiendish friends. *(Ward photo)*

◀ LARRY COX: Claro walnut makes an appearance on a 5160 fighter with a pronounced clip point. *(Ward photo)*

▲ JOEL WORLEY: Once he got started with files, Joel proceeded from the spine of the raindrop-pattern-damascus blade, along the guard and straight toward the sambar stag and spalted maple handle. *(PointSeven Studios photo)*

▶ DICKIE ROBINSON: An 11-inch 1084 fighter benefits from a giraffe-bone grip and proven design techniques. *(Ward photo)*

STATE OF THE ART

Eliminate any need for embellishment, and the knives in the *State Of The Art* section will cut. Most knife enthusiasts have heard it said, or have said themselves, that there are too many makers out there fashioning pieces that are purely aesthetic in nature, that they aren't practical utilitarian blades—they won't cut. That might be the case in some instances, but by-and-large knifemakers are a conscientious group who understand that a knife must first cut, and then look good.

Now, enter the embellishments, and life is indeed good on Edgy Street. You see, ingrained in its very being, knifemaking is a handcraft, an art form. Not everyone can build beautiful utilitarian knives that are finely fit and finished, with blades that bend but don't break, with crisp, clean edges, no gaps between bolsters and grips and that fit snuggly in leather sheaths. The guy typing this can't do that! He's about as mechanically and artistically inclined as the average bookkeeper, banker or, well, editor.

That's what makes scrimshaw, sculpting, engraving, carving, jewel and wire inlay, damascus pattern making, casting and etching so fascinating to the average guy or gal, why there are artists and art lovers, bladesmiths and sword enthusiasts, knifemakers and collectors. Sometimes it seems the people who can't create the art appreciate it the most. You'll find plenty to look at and enjoy in the *State Of The Art* section of *Knives 2013*.

Sharp Dress Folders

It's a name that evolved as knives evolved—dress folders. Like human, music or art evolution, knife evolution is as complicated as it is interesting. From pocketknives to one-hand folders, to tactical folding knives, high-tech folders, and finally dress folders, or dress tacticals, the progression included advances in opening mechanisms, locks, bushings, materials and blade steels.

Those who kept abreast of the advancements, and incorporated what worked into their own designs—who became innovators themselves—remained at the top of the knifemaking game. The top is where the collectors tend to congregate, looking for something that wows them, makes them stand up, take notice and eventually open the pocketbook for a few greens to leave on the table of an appreciative knife artisan.

We tease teenagers, or scoff at them, for wearing outlandish clothes, piercing their lips, noses and navels, and dying their heir. Yet, inevitably, middle America, Europe, the Far East and all places in-between adopt pieces of the fringe wear, and styles that they like best, stuff that won't get them laughed at too heartily by their neighbors. To innovate is to step outside the boundaries, try something new and be left wide open to ridicule. It is how reggae music, Capri pants and wrecked jeans occurred, as well as sharp dress folders.

◀ **MIKE PELLEGRIN:** The curved and curvaceous dress folder is adorned in Doug Ponzio Turkish-twist damascus, quartz, gold inlay and engraving. *(SharpByCoop.com photo)*

▶ **STEVE FECAS:** The white of the pearl, black of the carbon-fiber bolsters and gold fittings make coordinating an outfit to wear with the folder a breeze. *(SharpByCoop.com photo)*

▼ **RONALD BEST:** The carved and sculpted dress folder makes liberal use of Mike Norris damascus and black-lip pearl. *(SharpByCoop.com photo)*

▶ **GAIL LUNN:** Sapphires, damascus and black-lip pearl orbit this "Galaxy" folder. *(Eric Eggly, PointSeven Studios photo)*

▶ **STEVE JERNIGAN:** Two raised panels on the folding dagger showcase shapely black-lip-pearl inlays. *(Eric Eggly, PointSeven Studios photo)*

▲ **MIKE TYRE:** The gent's folder flaunts elephant ivory, silver-chain damascus, rope file work, blued titanium and 24k-gold screws. *(Eric Eggly, PointSeven Studios photo)*

▼ **KEN ERICKSON:** The swell-center hunter makes good use of sambar stag, CPM-154 blade steel and Nathan Dickinson engraving. *(SharpByCoop.com photo)*

▶ **REINHARD TSCHAGER:** If diamonds are a girl's best friend, then the 18k-gold folder engraved by Valerio Peli is a man's mate for life.

▲ GLENN E. WATERS: Golden flowers and butterflies flaunt their stuff on the mammoth-ivory handle and bolsters of a locking-liner folder. The engraved stainless-damascus blade depicts FuJin, the God of Wind, with a dragon holding a fireball on one side, and RaiJin, the God of Thunder, and a dragon on the opposite side.

▶ ALAIN and JORIS CHOMILIER: Gold pins and red sapphires highlight a pearl-handle dress folder in Chad Nichols damascus.

▶ KEVIN CASEY: Two dress locking folders parade feather-damascus blades and bolsters, and mammoth-ivory and wood handle slabs. What would be the shafts of the feathers run lengthwise down the centers of the blades, onto the bolsters, where feathery barbs flare out toward the sides and edges. *(SharpByCoop.com photo)*

◀ TERRY LEE RENNER: The "Deco Wing" folding art knife is a combination of Devin Thomas "dot matrix" damascus and black-lip mother-of-pearl. *(SharpByCoop.com photo)*

▶ **NORMAN E. SANDOW:** The handle of the locking-liner folder is titanium with the bolster area finished in pale gold, while the ATS-34 blade's opening dots are of the 18k-gold variety.

◀ **DON HANSON III:** A gift to his grandfather, Don's dress locking folder includes two sets of handle scales, one of his own damascus to complement the blade, and another in ivory. *(SharpByCoop.com photo)*

▼ **BILL BUXTON:** Gold-plated screws help hold the damascus and blue-mammoth-ivory folder together nicely. *(Ward photo)*

▲ **JOEL CHAMBLIN:** The addition of a gold handle shield and pins brings out colors in the black-lip pearl that would not otherwise be visible, and complements the blade steel of the doctor's knife nicely. *(Ward photo)*

Stone-Cold Steel Austenites

Stone is cold, and so is steel. Perhaps they were born bedfellows, and by the looks of stone-inlaid knives, combined with the keen eyes of those who excel at stone inlay, setting, beveling and cabochon cobbling, beauty is born from stone and steel. Stone-inlaid knives are some of the most collected, sought-after and revered. They can be jewel encrusted, often further embellished, and prized as symbols of wealth and prosperity.

They feel rich. And, being knives, they are symbols of strength and stability. These are knives often bestowed upon royalty, fashioned with wealthy clients in mind, and built with the precision of a watchmaker or jeweler. Many knifemakers possess jewelry making skills or backgrounds. They were jewelers, but became fascinated by the medium of a knife, the form, shape and function of the most beautiful of blades.

The title for this *State Of The Art* section is a takeoff on the name of the famous wrestler Stone Cold Steve Austin. He, too, rose to stardom as a result of his strength and prowess, and became the king jewel of the World Wrestling Federation. He owns and operates the Broken Skull Ranch in Tilden, Texas, where he hunts as often as possible, and likely pulls out a knife for cutting, skinning and field-dressing chores on occasion. It's doubtful any of the ranch blades are as stunning as these Stone-Cold Steel Austenites, but then not many of the makers had Steve Austin in mind when they inlaid quality stones into the handles of the fine art knives.

▶ **DES HORN:** The South African maker uses double-tempered, cryogenically treated, stain-resistant Damasteel, fine gold and lapis lazuli for his back-lock folding boot knife. *(Francesco Pachi photo)*

◀ **ALAIN and JORIS CHOMILIER:** Lapis lazuli, gold pins and meteorite combine to create a night sky on the grip of an upswept folder that also features Claude Schosseler damascus.

▲ **JAY FISHER:** Hand-engraved bolsters bookend the bright-orange/red brecciated-jasper handle of a custom ATS-34 drop-point hunter.

▶ **JOT SINGH KHALSA:** Natural gold quartz was quarried from the Sixteen to One Mine in California before being inlaid into the handle of a locking-liner folder, and married with 18-karat rose and yellow gold, diamonds and Mike Norris stainless damascus. Julie Warenski set the diamonds and engraved the piece.

◀ **LARRY NEWTON:** A fully engraved inter-frame folder parades blue lapis lazuli inlays, a 14k-gold release and double thumb studs, and a 30-turn black-etched and lacquered Damasteel blade. *(Eric Eggly, PointSeven Studios photo)*

▲ **BILL KELLER:** Malachite in matrix makes up the colorful handle of a "pool-and-eye"-damascus flipper folder with a raised clip point. The bolsters are Robert Eggerling damascus. *(Johnny Stout photo)*

▼ **T.R. OVEREYNDER:** Morrisonite jasper is a new country heard from—or at least it originates from the Owyhee Mountain area on the Idaho-Oregon border— and it does its part in prettying up a Carpenter Steel folding dagger engraved by Amayak Stepanyan. *(SharpByCoop.com photo)*

▲ **JOSHUA STATES:** Only the spacers are composite malachite and lapis, but they do their jobs in green and blue, complementing the black-ebony handle of the traditional twist-pattern-damascus Scottish dagger.

High-Art Handle Work

"Art is so subjective." It's an old cliché, so what does it mean exactly? It implies that what one views as creative, new, pleasing, shocking or a "statement," another could potentially consider unattractive, mundane, offensive or irrelevant. Maybe that last word is the key—relevance or irrelevance. In fashioning custom knives, just like in painting on canvas, it might be something a self-assessing craftsman should ask him or her self. Is what I am doing relevant? Does it hold meaning for others? Does it change things, make people view objects in a different manner, open their minds, enhance their experience?

The lists go on and on about how art affects people, and with knives there's yet another factor added into the mix, as if the bread batter needed any more ingredients. But knifemakers must ask themselves if what they're building is a functional, useful tool. Is it utilitarian? Will it hold up to hard use or abuse?

Perhaps art knives don't have to withstand prying, extreme cutting or hard use, but they should at the very least stay sharp, not break and be "user friendly," to the hand, the grip, the purchase, be easy to employ and maneuver. Therein lies the art—the combination of aesthetics and utility. The marriage elevates the craft to high art, and in this case, high-art handle work of the most cutting-edge form.

▲ **BILL KELLER:** A new way of looking at things could be what the composite mammoth-ivory handle, meteorite bolsters and Devin Thomas damascus blade provide. *(Johnny Stout photo)*

▶ **HANS WEINMUELLER:** Twisted gold wire doesn't wrap around the ironwood grip, but forms geometric shapes to embellish a neat Damasteel swing-blade folder with a frame that pivots and folds, as well. *(Buddy Thomason photo)*

▲ **RODRIGO SFREDDO:** It might seem like simple wire inlay on a carved-ebony grip, until you realize the gold-wire vine isn't perfectly symmetrical or smooth, but a natural-looking entity that enhances the lines of the damascus blade. *(Eric Eggly, PointSeven Studios photo)*

▶ **TAI GOO:** The cocobolo handle and sterling silver fittings send a single shockwave over the 1095 blade. *(Buddy Thomason photo)*

▲ **STEVE NOLTE:** The copper guard and pommel engraved by Billy Bates make a perfect frame for the copper-infused-quartz handle of the Alabama damascus fixed blade. *(Ward photo)*

▶ **WILLIAM C. "BILL" JOHNSON:** The spiral-fluted mammoth-tooth handle is wrapped in silver wire like the gift that it is. That's a 10-inch 440C dagger blade and a nicely shaped guard and pommel. *(Hoffman photo)*

◀ **WILLIAM LLOYD:** Who turned the whitetail deer antler into a dragon, its lair and a lot of skull-icious embellishments? William did. The sword cane comes with a K.C. Lund damascus blade and amethyst inlays. *(Eric Eggly, PointSeven Studios photo)*

◀ **STEVE HOEL:** Master gun engraver Barry Lee Hands contributes gold leaves and stems to the black bolsters and black-lip-pearl inlay of the inter-frame folder, which also features pink sapphires, green topaz and diamonds. *(SharpByCoop.com photo)*

▶ **JULIUS MOJZIS:** Sculpting a rhino scene from an ATS-34 integral drop-point hunter is akin to reshaping diamonds or plying platinum.

◀ **MATTHEW LERCH:** The double-action automatic shows off a "shark's-tooth"-damascus blade and handle frame, with 416 stainless steel overlays and a black-lip-pearl inlay for a layered effect. *(SharpByCoop.com photo)*

◀ **ARPAD BOJTOS:** Some of the finest artists in the world would have trouble achieving the mermaid scene carved and sculpted into a titanium grip, inlaid with gold, silver and mother-of-pearl, and attached to a Damasteel blade. *(SharpByCoop.com photo)*

▲ **AAD VAN RYSWYK:** Judicial placement of gold pins and rubies enhances the checked-ivory handle and mosaic-damascus bolsters of the locking-liner folder.

LARRY FUEGEN: Why not a "Smiling Red Dragon" gargoyle, carved from stag, mammoth ivory and gold, for the handle of a damascus folder? *(Chris Marchetti photo)*

▶ **ALAIN** and **JORIS CHOMILIER:** It makes one wonder if Chad Nichols had any idea his damascus could ever look as sculpted, carved and cool as this lock-back folder turned out to be. The handle and blade are carved to create a sense of continuity.

◀ **GLENN E. WATERS:** The "Shro Usagi" (white rabbit) folder, inspired by a Japanese story, is orchestrated in stainless damascus, yellow gold, 30 stainless steel inlays for the waves overtaking the rabbit, titanium and engraving.

◀ **TODD KOPP:** A hot-blued steel guard and pommel contrast nicely with the fluted pre-ban-elephant-ivory handle and 5160 dagger blade. *(Buddy Thomason photo)*

▲ **RICK EATON:** The step-down, side-lock, inter-frame folder of mosaic damascus features black-lip-pearl and gold inlays, as well as Arabesque engraving.

▶ **YASUTAKA WADA:** The all-integral ATS-34 fixed blade is sculpted in the form of a lotus leaf and root.

▶ **SERGE PANCHENKO:** The "Relic Wasp" body is antiqued copper and brass leading to a damascus stinger blade.

▲ **DARREL RALPH:** The frame of the "Gun Hammer 3D Alpha" assisted-opening folder is 3D-carved Chad Nichols "Moku-Ti" (two types of titanium forge-welded together), and the laminated blade is Nichols stainless damascus with a Stellite-6K core. (SharpByCoop.com photo)

◀ **EMMANUEL ESPOSITO:** The knifemaker turns cubist, inlaying black-lip pearl into a mosaic of cubes, adding a C-Lock system and an RWL-34 blade.

Cast Guards & Pommels

▶ **T.C. ROBERTS:** The cast-bronze and silver guard and pommel of the stag-handle damascus bowie are where the lions roar. *(Ward photo)*

▶ **J.D. SMITH:** The sterling-silver knife frame of "The Chimera" (a monstrous mythological creature) is embellished with gold panels, 320 sapphires, diamonds and emerald eyes. The 11-inch blade is herring bone damascus, the handle of Siberian black cherry, and the man credited for much of the art— Joseph Schnayder. *(SharpByCoop. com photo)*

▲ **REINHARD TSCHAGER:** The "Black Panther" jewel knife parades a black panther pommel in sterling silver, two diamond-inlaid gold bands, a black-coral handle and a Devin Thomas damascus blade.

▲ **KEVIN L. HOFFMAN:** "I Am The Walrus" includes a sterling silver lost-wax-cast, walrus-head guard that makes good use of a couple tusks, a fossil-walrus-oosic handle and a stainless-Damasteel blade.

Take it to Your Graver

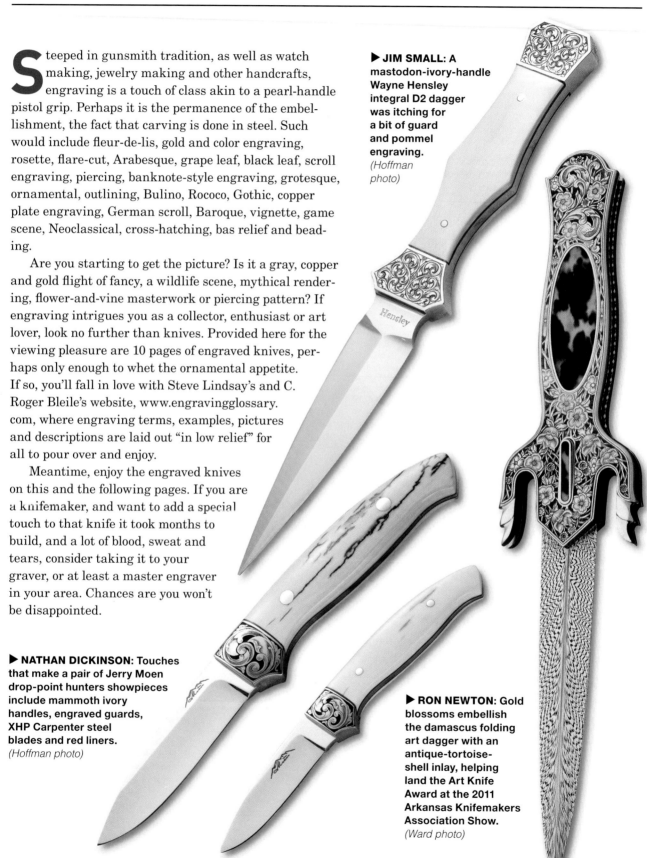

Steeped in gunsmith tradition, as well as watch making, jewelry making and other handcrafts, engraving is a touch of class akin to a pearl-handle pistol grip. Perhaps it is the permanence of the embellishment, the fact that carving is done in steel. Such would include fleur-de-lis, gold and color engraving, rosette, flare-cut, Arabesque, grape leaf, black leaf, scroll engraving, piercing, banknote-style engraving, grotesque, ornamental, outlining, Bulino, Rococo, Gothic, copper plate engraving, German scroll, Baroque, vignette, game scene, Neoclassical, cross-hatching, bas relief and beading.

Are you starting to get the picture? Is it a gray, copper and gold flight of fancy, a wildlife scene, mythical rendering, flower-and-vine masterwork or piercing pattern? If engraving intrigues you as a collector, enthusiast or art lover, look no further than knives. Provided here for the viewing pleasure are 10 pages of engraved knives, perhaps only enough to whet the ornamental appetite. If so, you'll fall in love with Steve Lindsay's and C. Roger Bleile's website, www.engravingglossary.com, where engraving terms, examples, pictures and descriptions are laid out "in low relief" for all to pour over and enjoy.

Meantime, enjoy the engraved knives on this and the following pages. If you are a knifemaker, and want to add a special touch to that knife it took months to build, and a lot of blood, sweat and tears, consider taking it to your graver, or at least a master engraver in your area. Chances are you won't be disappointed.

▶ **JIM SMALL:** A mastodon-ivory-handle Wayne Hensley integral D2 dagger was itching for a bit of guard and pommel engraving. *(Hoffman photo)*

▶ **NATHAN DICKINSON:** Touches that make a pair of Jerry Moen drop-point hunters showpieces include mammoth ivory handles, engraved guards, XHP Carpenter steel blades and red liners. *(Hoffman photo)*

▶ **RON NEWTON:** Gold blossoms embellish the damascus folding art dagger with an antique-tortoise-shell inlay, helping land the Art Knife Award at the 2011 Arkansas Knifemakers Association Show. *(Ward photo)*

▶ **JACOPO MARIUTTI:** A sea serpent with golden tongue swims on the steely surface of a blue coral sea.

▶ **BARRY LEE HANDS:** A tapered-tang S.R. Johnson ATS-34 fixed blade is handled in mother-of-pearl and crowned in gold leaves and vines. *(SharpByCoop.com photo)*

▲ **ROBERT KOVACIK:** Oak leaves make great steel scratching subjects for a deer-horn-handle hunter in RWL-34 steel.

▶ **RICK EATON:** Blending old styles with modern flair, the Mediterranean damascus dirk is treated to flare-cut engraving, Arabesque accents and banknote engraving, as well as an ancient ivory handle. *(Eric Eggly, PointSeven Studios photo)*

▶ **SIMONE DAINELLI:** The stainless steel handle of Leonardo Frizzi's folding dagger made a perfect palette for scroll engraving and other touches like a gold bale and pins.

▲ **ALICE CARTER:** A crowning achievement like Johnny Stout's two-blade trapper in 154CM steel and mammoth ivory is deserving of bolster and back-spacer engraving. *(Johnny Stout photo)*

STATE OF THE ART **143**

▶ **NATHAN DICKINSON:** Gold inlay and engraving blankets the red moss jasper handle of Mike Pellegrin's 440C folder that also showcases a carved blade. *(SharpByCoop.com photo)*

◀ **CHRIS BOOYSEN:** Do you start with the Picasso marble handle of Bertie Rietveld's bolster-tilt-lock folder, with the heat-colored "dragon-skin"-damascus blade or the gorgeous engraving? *(SharpByCoop.com photo)*

▶ **DAVID RICCARDO:** Front-to-back, top-to-bottom detailed engraving covers the titanium handle of Jeremy Marsh's "Chisel" in an Elmax stainless steel blade. *(SharpByCoop.com photo)*

◀ **JOE MASON:** Gold hints within floral engraving accent the fossilized walrus ivory handle of a Tom Ploppert CPM-154 single-blade folder. *(SharpByCoop.com photo)*

▲ **BRUCE SHAW:** In the "dress tactical" realm is a Keith Ouye flipper folder with a Devin Thomas damascus blade, jeweled liners and a fully-engraved 6AL-4V-titanium handle frame. *(SharpByCoop.com photo)*

▼ **JULIUS MOJZIS:** A tiger guards the integral N690 and buffalo-horn dagger.

◄ **JODY MULLER:** A Samurai emerges from the gold, copper and stainless steel bolsters of Michael Burch's 1095 folding tanto, remaining partially concealed by a crosshatching of mammoth ivory and the smoky temper line of the flipper folder blade.
(SharpByCoop.com photo)

▶ **TOM FERRY:** Can you really engrave a basket-weave pattern, transition it into tortured skulls and continue it on the other side? Apparently, yes.
(Eric Eggly, PointSeven Studios photo)

◄ **STEVE DUNN:** Etched, engraved and gold inlaid is the stag-handle coffin bowie in damascus blade steel.
(SharpByCoop.com photo)

▲ **MICHAEL HENNINGSSON:** The graver slipped on Michael as he embellished the RWL-34 handle of his "Odin's-eye"-damascus folder, and onto the mother-of-pearl handle where it left more amazing marks.

▶ **JERE DAVIDSON:** First the single piece of 1018 steel that makes up the handle frame of Bruce Bump's mosaic-damascus fixed blade was contoured and drilled, then gold inlaid and engraved, and complemented by an ancient-walrus-tusk inlay. *(SharpByCoop.com photo)*

▼ **MIKE "WHISKERS" ALLEN:** Gold-on-black with black-lip pearl was an inspired choice for the fully engraved 440C folder, and the gold skull bead on the leather lanyard is a nice touch, too. *(Buddy Thomason photo)*

◀ **PAUL MARKOW:** Engraving brings out the silver swirls within the mammoth-tooth inlays of a Murray Sterling damascus lock-back folder. *(Eric Eggly, PointSeven Studios photo)*

▲ **JOE MASON:** A take-down, D-guard, dog-bone bowie from the hands and mind of John White showcases a 10.25-inch multi-bar Turkish-twist-damascus blade, an antique-walrus-ivory handle, domed sterling silver pins, and gold inlay and engraving on the fat of the D-guard itself. *(SharpByCoop.com photo)*

▲ **NATHAN DICKINSON:** Ed Wallace's ivory-handle 154CM drop-point hunters are scrolled and inlaid for a fine-knife effect. *(Eric Eggly, PointSeven Studios photo)*

▶ **EDOUARD VOS:** What better to embellish the tiger-eye inlay of an Aad van Ryswyk inter-frame folder than 24k-gold tigers?

◀ **MARK WALDROP:** Gold inlay and engraving wends its way around the green-snail inserts of a damascus W.D. Pease inter-frame folder. *(Eric Eggly, PointSeven Studios photo)*

▲ **JULIE WARENSKI:** Where the gold inlay and engraving stops, the carved ivory begins and all is well with Curt Erickson's incredible fixed-blade art bowie. *(Eric Eggly, PointSeven Studios photo)*

▶ **C.J. KAI:** Athena The Huntress and Zeus make appearances on the gold-inlaid and engraved handle scene of a Joe Kious auto folder with a Jerry Rados Turkish-twist-damascus blade. *(SharpByCoop.com photo)*

◀ **JOT SINGH KHALSA:** The gold, engraved and jewel-inlaid kirpan sends an upswept Devin Thomas damascus blade into battle, anchored by a South African pietersite handle. *(SharpByCoop.com photo)*

STATE OF THE ART **147**

▲ **LISA TOMLIN:** An engraved gold horse adorns the antique-tortoise-shell handle of C. Gray Taylor's horse knife that showcases at least 18 implements, such as a hoof pick, bleeding blade, punches, etc., for horse care. *(Eric Eggly, PointSeven Studios photos)*

▶ **NATHAN DICKINSON:** With the trophy already engraved on the guard, everything else the Ed Wallace stag-handle 154CM hunter accomplishes simply fills more tags. *(Eric Eggly, PointSeven Studios photo)*

▲ **MICHAEL VAGNINO:** Amber-jigged-bone handle scales are married with bolster engraving as sharp as the CPM-154 blades of the folding trapper. The folder features "Ever Flush" springs that never protrude beyond the handle spine, even when opening the blades. *(SharpByCoop.com photo)*

▲ **KIRK REXROAT:** A leaf-shaped damascus blade is paid homage by leaf engraving on the bolsters of a snakewood-handle folder. *(Eric Eggly, PointSeven Studios photo)*

▶ **DWAYNE DUSHANE:** The flowing lines of a Charlie Majors trailing-point hunter include curved bolsters, scrollwork, Mike Norris "hornet's-nest" damascus and contoured mammoth ivory. *(Johnny Stout photo)*

▶ **MARIAN SAWBY:** The sea turtle theme with copper and 24k-gold inlays will turn heads, or bring them out of their shells, complemented by the black-jade handle and Mexican-fire-agate inlay of Scott Sawby's dress folder. *(SharpByCoop. com photo)*

▶ **VINCE EVANS:** The long, sloping damascus blade of the Turkish Kilij is highlighted by gold-wire inlay, engraving and an ivory hilt. *(Eric Eggly, PointSeven Studios photo)*

▶ **JULIE WARENSKI:** Don Lozier's dagger gets the royal engraving treatment, as well as a seven-bar Jerry Rados Turkish-twist-damascus blade. *(Eric Eggly, PointSeven Studios photo)*

▶ **SCOTT PILKINGTON:** The engraved S-7 blade and panels of Ron Appleton's "Multalock" folder must be seen under a microscope to be believed. The engraved scene portrays Jane Fonda's starring role in the 1968 movie *Barbarella*. *(Eric Eggly, PointSeven Studios photo)*

▶ **JON ROBYN:** Going by one of knifemaker Jack Levin's favorite paintings by Peter Breughel, Jon engraved and gold-inlaid the "Mysteria of the Hell" automatic folder that also parades a pop-up shield, carved pivots and fixtures, 24k-gold ring and Devin Thomas damascus blade. *(Francesco Pachi photo)*

◀ **JERRY FISK:** The gold inlay transcends the engraved pommel and guard, stretching onto the damascus blade of the ivory-handle "Arkansas Toothpick." *(Ward photo)*

◀ **DWIGHT TOWELL:** Just when you think you've seen it all, the maker pulls a plume agate out of his hat, complementing it with red, yellow and green floral engraving, and vine-and-leaf-type scrolls on the blade.

▲ **ALEXANDRA FEODOROW:** Guard and pommel engraving on a Richard Karl Hehn integral fixed blade depicts lions and water buffalo in their natural habitat, further highlighted by mammoth ivory earth tones.

▶ **SIMON LYTTON:** Most noticeable is the full, detailed handle engraving, as well as the twist-Damasteel blade and gold nail pulls, while less obvious amenities include file-worked screws, jeweled and anodized titanium liners, and a jeweled pivot system of rubies for the blade bearing. *(Kayla Minchew photo)*

▶ **JERE DAVIDSON:** The borderless, abstract floral-pattern engraving on the CPM-154 Bob Loveless-style integral fighter is just what knifemaker Edmund Davidson's client ordered as a gift for the Sultan of Johor. The Siberian mastodon ivory handle features Linda Karst Stone scrimshaw of the sultan's initials surrounded by the royal wreath and crown. *(Eric Eggly, PointSeven Studios photo)*

◀ **GIL RUDOLPH:** The bighorn-sheep-horn handle of Loyd McConnell's CPM-154 lock-back folder accompanies other big horns and big cats engraved on a backdrop of dense, golden underbrush. *(Eric Eggly, PointSeven Studios photo)*

◀ **MARCELLO PEDINI:** The engraved scene hints at the handle material of David Brodziak's 440C bowie—stegosaurus hip bone raised from the depths of extinction.

▲ **GORDON ALCORN:** From the textured African blackwood of John Doyle's 1080 hunter to the vine file work, wispy temper line and deep-cut bolster engraving, the eye candy never stops. *(BladeGallery.com photo)*

Rugged Steel Skins

▼ **DAVID BRODZIAK:** The "she devil" painted by Carol Ann O'Connor on the black-mulga-wood sheath is as attractive as the damascus art dagger itself. Jade and bronze also decorate the dagger.

◄ **DON HETHCOAT:** A painted bald eagle with carved-leather feathers is the perfect sheath décor for a damascus bowie forged from Harley-Davidson motorcycle chain.

► **LARRY PARSONS:** Snakeskin and tooled leather make nice slip cases for fixed blades. *(Kayla Minchew photo)*

▲ **STEVE POZNIKOFF:** The rugged steel skins are of the leather and belt-carry variety. *(Eric Eggly, PointSeven Studios photo)*

MARK NEVLING: A trio of leather neck-knife sheaths (leathernecks?) exhibits alligator, boa constrictor and alligator skin inlays.

RANDY GOLDEN: The cowhide sheath exhibits a silver flower medallion, tooling and an ostrich-skin wrap. *(Bill Ingalls photo)*

E. JAY HENDRICKSON: Engraved and inlaid fine silver not only embellishes the curly-maple sheath, but also spirals around the fluted handle of the damascus dagger. *(Eric Eggly, PointSeven Studios photo)*

J. NEILSON: The period sheath of the stag-handle W2 hunter was fashioned by John Cohea to include beads, cones and horsehair. *(Ward photo)*

DAVE KELLY: The deer-hide-lined pouch sheath is of basket-weave-pattern leather with a black-shark-hide drop loop.

Double-Take Damascus

JOHNNY STOUT: With elements as colorful as the blue-green, ancient-ivory handle slabs and blued mosaic damascus bolsters, it took a Bob Eggerling Turkish-twist-damascus blade to compete. *(Ward photo)*

DAVID LISCH: Dig the nickel-damascus blade, the smooth ivory handle, and the eye-popping damascus guard and pommel. *(SharpByCoop.com photo)*

GARY ROOT: It's an attractive package—the Bob Eggerling damascus blade of the bowie, ivory and Micarta® spacers, a bronze guard and butt cap, and a dyed-elk-horn handle. *(Kris Kandler photo)*

JOHN WHITE: As the blade grind of the Persian dagger swoops, so too does the pattern of the multi-bar Turkish-twist-damascus blade. Joe Mason gold-inlaid and engraved the guard and pommel, allowing the mammoth ivory between the two to breathe. *(Buddy Thomason photo)*

MIKE MOONEY: The tight pattern of the "diamondback"-stainless-damascus chef's knife blade would dazzle dinner guests, especially paired with the afzelia-lay-wood handle and mosaic pins.

▶ **RON NEWTON:** There are a lot of "rungs" on the 9.25-inch ladder-pattern-damascus blade of a spear-point bowie. The big boy also sports a fossil-walrus-ivory handle and a gold-inlaid and engraved damascus pommel cap. *(Ward photo)*

▶ **ADAM DESROSIERS:** The 1084-and-15N20 damascus of the "Keyhole Hunter" couples with the African blackwood handle like two puzzle pieces, or a key and matching keyhole. *(SharpByCoop.com photo)*

▶ **MICHAEL RUTH JR.:** Thirteen inches of damascus stretch out before an ancient-walrus-ivory handle and nickel-damascus guard and pommel. *(Ward photo)*

▲ **TERRY SCHREINER:** Rose-pattern Damasteel blooms on the blade, while mokumé bolsters and ironwood handle scales leave their own markings. *(Buddy Thomason photo)*

▼ **MARK NEVLING:** The "radial"-pattern damascus resembles a star that did its bursting on the blade. Fossil walrus ivory, ebony, amber and mokumé also burst onto the scene.

Double-Take Damascus

▶ **JERRY LAIRSON:** Damascus dips in all the right places along the blade, guard and pommel of a mammoth-ivory-handle dagger. *(Ward photo)*

▼ **DON HANSON III:** The 9.25-inch damascus blade sets a frenetic pace for a fighter with a grip of fossil walrus ivory. *(Ward photo)*

▲ **MICHAEL RUTH SR.:** Like shivers down a spine, the damascus dances its way across the bowie blade, with walrus ivory acting as a calming influence. *(Ward photo)*

▼ **JERRY HALFRICH:** Mike Norris "hornet's-nest" damascus makes for a nice stinger. *(SharpByCoop.com photo)*

▶ **ARTHUR LYNN:** Like legendary blades forged from meteorite, this 1084-15N20-and-meteorite-damascus piece takes its place in the annals of history. *(Buddy Thomason photo)*

▶ **TOMMY GANN:** Where the pattern dips the edge begins along the blade of a 15-inch bowie handled in stag. *(Ward photo)*

◀ **KEVIN CROSS:** The flat-ground damascus blade of the stag-handle skinner, forged by Robert Eggerling, showcases a consistent pattern left bare only where the knifemaker left his mark. *(SharpByCoop.com photo)*

▼ **LANDON ROBBINS:** The twist-damascus handle shield that matches the blade of the 11.5-inch hunter is a nice touch and perfect accoutrement for an ironwood grip. *(Ward photo)*

▶ **HARALD SELLEVOLD:** A stingray-skin grip secures the Dennis Fuglesang damascus blade nicely. The ferrule and butt cap are silver.

▲ **GARY HOUSE:** Ribbons of white snake through the damascus pattern of a Southwest bowie, handled in African blackwood, and built with a blued-mosaic-damascus guard. *(BladeGallery.com photo)*

Double-Take Damascus

▶ **JERRY McCLURE:** The "chaos"-damascus blade is controlled enough, and flourishes next to a wrought iron guard and fossil-walrus-ivory handle. *(Buddy Thomason photo)*

▶ **TERRY VANDEVENTER:** The "Resurrection Bowie" not only features a neatly-packed damascus pattern and matching cross handle shield, but the knifemaker also encourages enthusiasts to look into the pearl of the handle to see the mountains, clouds, sky and corona that he sees. Hallelujah! *(Buddy Thomason photo)*

▶ **KEVIN CASEY:** If the "feather" damascus doesn't tickle your fancy, perhaps the walrus ivory will. *(SharpByCoop. com photo)*

◀ **JERRY FISK:** The "Ram's Horn Sendero" will dazzle you with its "dog-star"-damascus blade and engraved guard. *(Buddy Thomason photo)*

▲ **REINHARD TSCHAGER:** Never seen anything like the Markus Becker damascus blade and bolsters of the classic drop-point bowie? Now you have, and complemented perfectly by giraffe bone, and gold and emerald inlays.

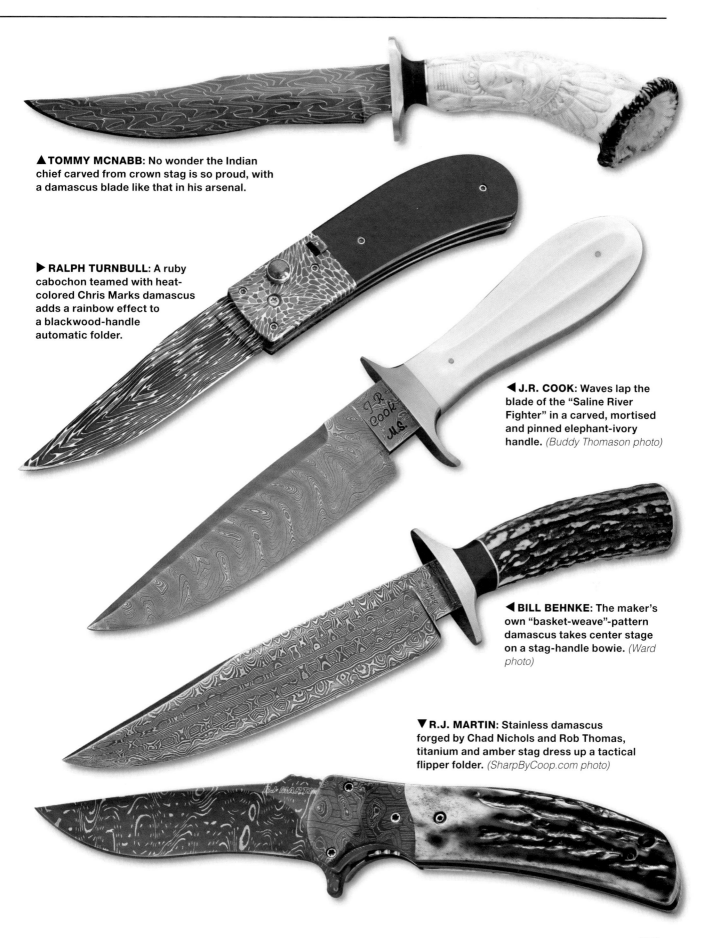

TOMMY MCNABB: No wonder the Indian chief carved from crown stag is so proud, with a damascus blade like that in his arsenal.

RALPH TURNBULL: A ruby cabochon teamed with heat-colored Chris Marks damascus adds a rainbow effect to a blackwood-handle automatic folder.

J.R. COOK: Waves lap the blade of the "Saline River Fighter" in a carved, mortised and pinned elephant-ivory handle. *(Buddy Thomason photo)*

BILL BEHNKE: The maker's own "basket-weave"-pattern damascus takes center stage on a stag-handle bowie. *(Ward photo)*

R.J. MARTIN: Stainless damascus forged by Chad Nichols and Rob Thomas, titanium and amber stag dress up a tactical flipper folder. *(SharpByCoop.com photo)*

▶ **STEVEN KOSTER:** Green jigged bone gives way to the 39-layer, ladder-pattern-damascus blade, guard and spacers of a spear-point bowie. *(Douglas Koster photo)*

▶ **LAURENT DOUSSOT:** Most people couldn't draw the pattern of the Devin Thomas stainless steel damascus, much less forge it. The blade of the "Ambi-Lock" folder is hollow ground. *(SharpByCoop.com photo)*

▼ **KEVIN LESSWING:** The thin knife profile is accentuated by the damascus blade and bolsters, and anchored by mammoth ivory handle scales. *(SharpByCoop.com photo)*

▲ **TERRY LEE RENNER:** The lively exterior of an Opinel-type barrel-lock folder includes heat-colored Bertie Reitveld "dragonskin" damascus, Devin Thomas "dot matrix" damascus and carved fossil walrus ivory. *(SharpByCoop.com photo)*

GEOFF KEYES: A damascus hunter's bowie blends a prettily-patterned blade with a blued "S"-guard and pommel, ebony and nickel-silver spacers, and a stellar-sea-cow-bone handle. *(BladeGallery.com photo)*

PHIL EVANS: Dizzying damascus does the 8.25-inch bowie blade proud. An amber-stag handle and stainless steel fittings complete the package. *(Ward photo)*

JOHN PERRY: Antique tortoise shell and "squirrel fur" damascus will make even the sanest of knife collectors bury all their nuts for the winter. It is a fine two-blade congress, isn't it? *(Ward photo)*

BILL MILLER: Composite damascus is a force to be reckoned with on a walrus-ivory-handle bowie. *(Ward photo)*

GARY MULKEY: The damascus blade pattern of the 14.5-inch bowie is just as pretty as the walrus-ivory grip. *(Ward photo)*

Stippling the Ivories

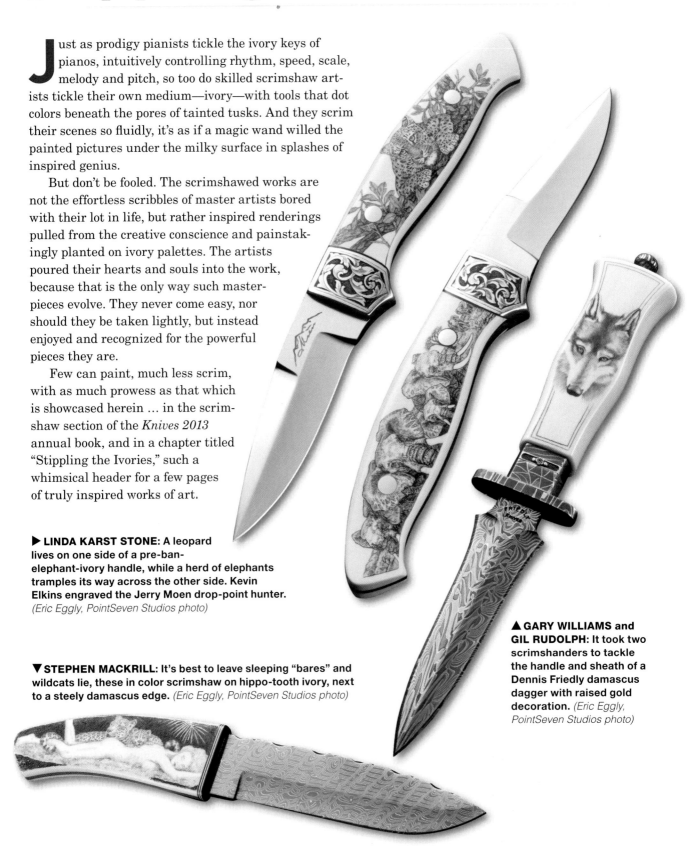

Just as prodigy pianists tickle the ivory keys of pianos, intuitively controlling rhythm, speed, scale, melody and pitch, so too do skilled scrimshaw artists tickle their own medium—ivory—with tools that dot colors beneath the pores of tainted tusks. And they scrim their scenes so fluidly, it's as if a magic wand willed the painted pictures under the milky surface in splashes of inspired genius.

But don't be fooled. The scrimshawed works are not the effortless scribbles of master artists bored with their lot in life, but rather inspired renderings pulled from the creative conscience and painstakingly planted on ivory palettes. The artists poured their hearts and souls into the work, because that is the only way such masterpieces evolve. They never come easy, nor should they be taken lightly, but instead enjoyed and recognized for the powerful pieces they are.

Few can paint, much less scrim, with as much prowess as that which is showcased herein … in the scrimshaw section of the *Knives 2013* annual book, and in a chapter titled "Stippling the Ivories," such a whimsical header for a few pages of truly inspired works of art.

▶ **LINDA KARST STONE:** A leopard lives on one side of a pre-ban-elephant-ivory handle, while a herd of elephants tramples its way across the other side. Kevin Elkins engraved the Jerry Moen drop-point hunter. *(Eric Eggly, PointSeven Studios photo)*

▼ **STEPHEN MACKRILL:** It's best to leave sleeping "bares" and wildcats lie, these in color scrimshaw on hippo-tooth ivory, next to a steely damascus edge. *(Eric Eggly, PointSeven Studios photo)*

▲ **GARY WILLIAMS** and **GIL RUDOLPH:** It took two scrimshanders to tackle the handle and sheath of a Dennis Friedly damascus dagger with raised gold decoration. *(Eric Eggly, PointSeven Studios photo)*

► **LINDA KARST STONE:** A riverboat and gamblers are depicted on one side of an Edmund Davidson ivory-handle bowie, and the Alamo and events that transpired there on the other side. Jere Davidson engraved most areas left untouched by the scrimshaw artist. *(Eric Eggly, PointSeven Studios photo)*

► **LINDA KARST STONE:** Osceola's Defiance of the Treaty of Payne's Landing in 1832 is immortalized in color scrimshaw on the ivory handle of an Ed Kalfayan sub-hilt fighter. *(Eric Eggly, PointSeven Studios photo)*

► **MATT STOTHART:** Scrimshaw of a panther and leopard is accompanied by Chris Meyer's engraving of the same subject matter on the bolsters of a Frank Potter old-school auto. *(SharpByCoop.com photo)*

◄ **DR. HANS PETER JENSEN:** A winged "Lilith of the 21st Century" lends innocent beauty to a Ludwig Fruhmann dagger that also features a Friedrich Schneider damascus blade.

▲ **GARY WILLIAMS:** When you can tell it's a wolf by the eyes, the scrimshaw succeeded in its mission, as does the whole of Barbara Baskett's wharncliffe locking-liner folder in a CPM-154 blade and Mike Sakmar mokumé bolsters. *(Eric Eggly, PointSeven Studios photo)*

▲ BARBARA CULLEN: To match up with scrimshaw on warthog tusk of a dog named Max, it took a group effort by Stuart Mason, Indian George and Gary Rua to forge a 4600EC-1084-and-nickel-damascus blade for Stuart Mason's hunter. *(SharpByCoop.com photo)*

▶ LINDA KARST STONE: Tigers take up residence of the fossil walrus ivory handle of a D' Holder 440C fixed blade engraved by Bruce Shaw. *(SharpByCoop.com photo)*

◀ LINDA KARST STONE: The hunted and the hunter share space on the walrus-ivory handle of a Mike Johnson fixed blade. *(Ward photo)*

▼ DR. HANS PETER JENSEN: Peregrine falcons are unusual but no less beautiful scrimshaw subjects, in this case on the ivory grip of a mosaic-damascus Johannes Ebner dagger.

◀ RON LUEBKE JR.: The sexy lines of a Loyd McConnell Jr. knife are all but overshadowed by steamy scrimshaw of a nude in ivory. *(Steve Woods photo)*

Fine Feather-Damascus Friends

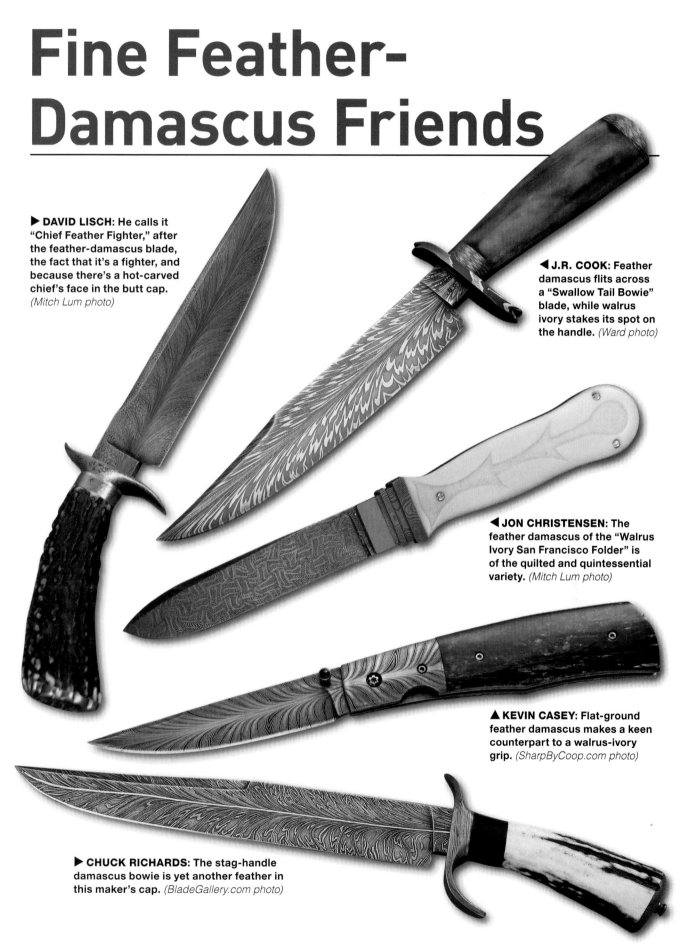

▶ **DAVID LISCH:** He calls it "Chief Feather Fighter," after the feather-damascus blade, the fact that it's a fighter, and because there's a hot-carved chief's face in the butt cap. *(Mitch Lum photo)*

◀ **J.R. COOK:** Feather damascus flits across a "Swallow Tail Bowie" blade, while walrus ivory stakes its spot on the handle. *(Ward photo)*

◀ **JON CHRISTENSEN:** The feather damascus of the "Walrus Ivory San Francisco Folder" is of the quilted and quintessential variety. *(Mitch Lum photo)*

▲ **KEVIN CASEY:** Flat-ground feather damascus makes a keen counterpart to a walrus-ivory grip. *(SharpByCoop.com photo)*

▶ **CHUCK RICHARDS:** The stag-handle damascus bowie is yet another feather in this maker's cap. *(BladeGallery.com photo)*

Mecca-Worthy Mosaics

There's one knife in this *State Of The Art* section with a blade the maker describes as "shop room floor" mosaic damascus. Now that's clever! What the maker—Mark Nevling—alludes to are famous mosaics throughout history, assemblages of small pieces of colored glass and stone used as decorative art in Cathedrals, palaces, courtyards and temples. Some of the glazed tiles consist of shells and ivory, arranged into patterns, pictures, depictions and other masterworks. Some are floor, and others wall or ceiling mosaics. So Nevling's "shop room floor" mosaic-damascus blade is likely one that reminds him of things he would see on the shop room floor, or perhaps he'd like the shop room floor to look like the mosaic-damascus blade.

Mosaic patterns in blades, much like those arranged with glazed tiles, are often repeated square or geometric shapes. Though there are several methods for forging mosaic damascus, they all involve multiple steel types or alloys that forge-weld together sufficiently. They are stacked, canned or pieced together like a puzzle, and then heated, pounded, folded, cut and stacked, and eventually ground, finished and honed.

It might sound like a lot of work for a pretty blade pattern, but then again the mosaics of the Basilica of San Lorenzo, the Great Palace of Constantinople or the Cathedral of Palermo didn't happen overnight. Add the fact that knife blades need to cut, not break, and hold an edge, and there we have it once again—utility and art combining in one form, the shape of a blade, and in an assemblage of Mecca-worthy mosaics, indeed.

▶ **MARK NEVLING:** No shop floor ever looked as good as the "shop-floor"-mosaic-damascus blade and bolsters of the mammoth-ivory-handle clip-point folder with gold screws and a blue-pau-shell thumb stud.

◀ **JERRY MOEN:** A mosaic of Robert Eggerling damascus dices up the blade and bolsters of an ivory-handle gent's folder. *(Ward photo)*

▲ **CLIFF PARKER:** A master of mosaic damascus does a blade and bolsters up in 1084 and 15N20 steels forged together to depict a trophy hunter's dream, and adds a stag handle and thumb-stud inlay to tie it all together. *(Eric Eggly, PointSeven Studios photo)*

▶ **DON HANSON III:** As shapely as the blade—with an incredible temper line—and antique-Westinghouse-Micarta® handle are, the mosaic-damascus bolsters attempt to steal their thunder. *(SharpByCoop. com photo)*

▼ **GARY HOUSE:** A blued butterfly-pattern mosaic-damascus blade is forged from 1080, 15N20, O1 and 4600E carbon steels, along with pure nickel. There is a matching butterfly-damascus guard, a mokumé-gane ferrule, and an ancient-baby-walrus-ivory-tip handle for one dynamic desk knife. *(BladeGallery. com photo)*

◀ **RICK DUNKERLEY:** One of the original "Montana mafia" forgers of mosaic damascus, Rick shows us how it's done on the blade and handle of an inter-frame folder, with only black-lip-pearl to interrupt the flow. *(Eric Eggly, PointSeven Studios photo)*

◀ **STEVE HILL:** So, you've never seen silver wire resembling a musical scale and notes inlaid into quilted maple before? Well, how about a heat-colored, guitar-pattern, mosaic-damascus blade forged by Joe Olson butted up against Robert Eggerling mosaic-damascus bolsters? Steve calls it "Purple Haze," what else? *(SharpByCoop.com photo)*

▲ **ANDERS HEDLUND:** The "Nordic Dream" folder doubles as a knife collector's dream, and includes a mosaic-damascus blade with three 18k-gold dots, a reindeer-pattern mosaic-damascus handle, pierced and engraved mammoth-ivory inlays and an engraved back spacer.

► **MIKE TYRE:** The stunning folder is dressed in a Larry Donnelly mosaic-damascus blade and bolsters, a mammoth-ivory handle and thumb stud inlay, and blue-anodized-titanium liners. The blade spine and back spacer are vine file-worked. *(Eric Eggly, PointSeven Studios photo)*

▲ **JON CHRISTENSEN:** A San Francisco-style fixed blade features a mosaic-tree-damascus blade, and a mosaic-damascus and fossil-walrus-ivory grip wrapped in nickel silver. *(Mitch Lum photo)*

▼ **ALAIN and JORIS CHOMILIER:** When Mattias Styrefors and Jonny Walker Nilsson combine their mosaic-damascus-forging skills the result is as hot as dragon's breath. The knife also sports a fossil-walrus-jaw grip.

◄ **TOBBE LUNDSTROM:** The "Prehistoric Pukko" gets its name from the dinosaurs roaming the blade and handle as if they had never become extinct. *(BladeGallery.com photo)*

► **JEFFREY E. DRISCOLL:** The "Wildflower" is winsomely wild, from the tip of the heat-blued Johan Gustafsson mosaic-damascus blade to the end of the carved African-blackwood handle. *(BladeGallery.com photo)*

Curly Wire & Maple Wood

▶ **STEVE NUCKELS:** The silver-wire-inlaid, stippled curly maple handle is only part of the package that also incorporates a forged 5160 blade and etched-wrought-iron guard. *(SharpByCoop.com photos)*

◀ **ALLEN NEWBERRY:** Silver wire forms an eight-point star on the curly maple handle of a 15-inch bowie. *(Ward photo)*

▶ **E. JAY HENDRICKSON:** The curly maple hilt of the "Jambia" is adorned in dogwood flowers and fine silver inlay, leading to a double-concave-ground 5160 blade. *(SharpByCoop.com photo)*

◀ **BILL BUXTON:** The fearsome foursome integrates a damascus spike tomahawk, bowie, drop-point hunter and folder, each anchored by a wire-inlaid tiger maple handle. *(SharpByCoop.com photo)*

Carved & Curvaceous

Some people like to think of carving as minimalist art, though the results are frequently monumental. Still, the act of carving—and often with knives, sculpting—is of material removal. Steel, ivory, pearl, wood and fine metals are carved away to create forms, beings, uninterrupted flowing figures or sculptures, those that cause reaction, feelings and emotion. A lack of emotion by the artist would be readily apparent.

The creative consciousness is awakened long before the carving tool hits its medium and curls of material peel off like layers of onion. It is the discovery of something alive within the medium, waiting to be uncovered and brought to life. If this sounds like hogwash, you'll have to take it up with the handle carvers and steel sculptors of the knife industry, those who fancy themselves enlightened messengers, or at least interpreters of an art form.

Regardless of interpretation, there is no argument that pleasantly palpable knives are far superior to square, boxy affairs, so the means isn't nearly as important as the ends. And to that end, perhaps all should sit back, relax and take in the knives that have lives of their own, the rounded, sculpted, carved and curvaceous kind.

▼**J.D. SMITH and JOSEPH SHNAYDER:** A comely "Kindjal" damascus dagger bears carved African blackwood, carved and sculpted silver, diamonds, rubies and further riches. *(SharpByCoop.com photo)*

▶ **DAVID BROADWELL:** The freeform dagger is the beneficiary of a carved-nephrite-jade handle, a lost-wax-cast-bronze guard, and a carved and double-ground Delbert Ealy damascus blade. *(Ward photo)*

▲ **LEONARDO FRIZZI:** Gold pins secure an antique-tortoise-shell gecko onto the mammoth-ivory grip of a locking-liner folder that also showcases a "hornet's-nest"-damascus blade.

◀ **TOMMY MCNABB:** A dragon born from carved stag enjoys the company of turquoise, brass and 5160 steel.

▲ **LUCAS BURNLEY:** The knifemaker had help from his colleague, Jens Anso, in applying a "modified Techno texture" to the handle scales and bolsters of a CPM-154 folder. The blade is treated to Lucas's "viral finish." *(Eric Eggly, PointSeven Studios photo)*

▶ **WILLIAM LLOYD:** Let's think about how much time and attention it takes to carve a leaf, much less a tree man of antler and ironwood, with garnet eyes and a damascus posterior. *(Eric Eggly, PointSeven Studios photo)*

▲ **VLADIMIR PULIS:** A rosewood panther with golden eyes wags a damascus tail. The jungle wilderness theme extends to the rosewood, carved-beef-bone, silver and alligator-leather sheath.

▶ **ARPAD BOJTOS:** In this honed Damasteel version of the Biblical story, Eve picks pure-gold apples.

Carved & Curvaceous

▶ **MIKE FELLOWS:** "Arothea" is a high-end art dagger made up of a three-bar-composite blade with a mosaic-damascus core, a carved and aged brass blade collar, heat-blued mild steel guard, and deep-relief-carved orca-tooth handle.

▼ **TERRY LEE RENNER:** The carved antique-tortoise-shell handle inlays give way to Delbert Ealy Turkish-damascus bolsters and "fish-pattern"-damascus blades. *(SharpByCoop.com photo)*

▶ **E. JAY HENDRICKSON:** Though the handle is curly maple, the carved leaves are oak and A-OK. *(SharpByCoop.com photo)*

▲ **ROBERT P. SMITH:** The hand-carved deer antler and ivory was one thing, but then the real work began with the carved stainless-damascus blade of the "Tibetan Spirit." What spirit it has! *(Ward photo)*

FACTORY TRENDS

I't's fitting that the *Knives* annual book wraps up with a *Factory Trends* section. With increasing frequency, production knife companies take their cues from custom knifemakers. There are more custom/factory knife collaborations than ever before in the history of the industry, and thus more handmade knife designs in production lines.

Countless locks, bearings, bushings, pocket clips, one-hand openers, spring assists and more, commonly incorporated into factory knife designs, had their beginnings in the custom market. They were originally designed by handmade knifemakers who then took their ideas to company representatives to have them mass-produced by the factories.

It is rare for an industry to share designs and implement innovations in such a way, and it is an exciting time to be involved in the knife arena. Large knives are here to stay, as evidenced in the "Some Blade Brawn" category herein, yet folders remain a mainstay—see "Lightning-Fast Folders." Tantos are proving popular, as are the ever-present brawny straight knives and skeletonized fixed blades with weight-reducing, aesthetic, palpable and utilitarian holes milled through the handles, blades and bolsters. They've all evolved from earlier designs, and taken on lives of their own, eventually becoming *Factory Trends.*

Miracle in New Hampshire

Dedicated activists did much more than just repeal New Hampshire's knife laws that banned switchblades, daggers, dirks and stilettos

By Evan F. Nappen, Attorney at Law

Imagine a state in America where any knife, regardless of blade length, design or operation, can be freely bought and sold, without sales tax, owned, possessed, carried open or concealed, transported, displayed, collected, made, manufactured, given, loaned, acquired, transferred, bequeathed or inherited under state law, with the only exception being possession in a courthouse and possession by felons.

Imagine further that such a state accomplished this feat by repealing its knife laws that had been on the books for over 50 years, and that had banned switchblades, daggers, dirks and stilettos. Now consider that not one of its 425 politicians in the state's democrat-controlled government (400 house members with democrat majority, 24 senators with democrat majority and one democrat governor) opposed the repeal. Then imagine that same government unanimously voting again to prohibit all local towns and municipalities from passing or enforcing any knife laws.

Believe it or not, on May 18, 2010, a unanimously passed bill (HB1665) was signed into law that repealed New Hampshire's knife laws, and on June 9, 2011, a unanimously passed bill (HB544) was signed into law which preempts New Hampshire cities, towns or political subdivisions from passing or enforcing any knife laws. This is the story of how a few dedicated activists helped make it happen, and how you can do the same in your state.

The above may sound politically impossible. When do 425 people agree on anything, no less agree twice? However, the above is 100 percent true, and it shows that reforming archaic knife laws can be done anywhere, and party affiliation is irrelevant. Now is the window of opportunity for knife rights. There is

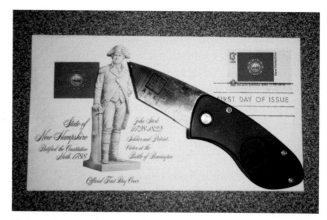

The author used his Al Mar Havana Clipper automatic knife/cigar cutter to cut the tip off a cigar he smoked in celebration of the passage of the New Hampshire knife rights bills. The knife is shown resting on a postal "First Day Cover" for the New Hampshire stamp.

An out-the-front automatic, the Microtech Combat Troodon rests on a New Hampshire state quarter display.

This is the beautiful New Hampshire Capitol where the knife rights bills passed.

no major national anti-knife movement or anti-knife groups in America. Although in the United Kingdom there is such a movement, it has not yet crossed the pond. I am sure it eventually will, because that is exactly what happened in Great Britain with their anti-gun push after World War I. There are important parallels between gun and knife rights issues. Knife owners must learn from the mistakes of gun owners so as not to repeat them.

The first national gun laws in the Untied States took place in the 1930s with the passage of the 1934 National Firearms Act (NFA). The NFA was passed largely due to media hype about gangland violence (Al Capone, Machine Gun Kelly, Bonnie and Clyde, etc.) The NFA was the only federal gun law until the passage of the 1968 Gun Control Act (68 GCA). During the 1950s America was extremely gun cultured and guns were no big deal. Having recently come out of World War II, most fathers were experienced and trained in the use of guns, including machine guns. Many schools had rifle teams and bringing your gun to school for hunting afterward was commonplace. This was the lost window of opportunity to repeal the 1934 NFA.

However, during the 1950s a new media hype arose making the switchblade its symbol, in the same way the sub-machine gun was the symbol of society's menace in the 1930s.

Rebel Without a Cause, West Side Story and similar movies and news stories constantly portrayed violent youths with switchblades. This helped lead to the passage of the federal 1958 Switchblade Act and many states passing their own knife bans as well.

Regain Lost Knife Rights

Now is our chance to regain lost knife rights. America is generally not anti-knife. Many of our returning soldiers have direct positive experience with knives including automatic folders. Although the public schools have a "zero tolerance" policy (I prefer to call it a "zero intelligence policy") for knives, just about every household has a knife. What the 1950s were to guns, the 2010s are to knives. Switchblades are no longer the symbol of youth violence that they were made out to be in the 1950s. As Second Amendment activist Jeff Knox, Director of Operations for The Firearms Coalition, said in support of the New Hampshire knife rights effort: "I think that the people of New Hampshire can safely lower their guard now that the youngest members of the Sharks and the Jets are in their 80s."

At the 2009 Gun Rights Policy Conference in St. Louis, Jeff Knox submitted Resolution 6 which stated:

Whereas: The banning of any personal tool or weapon has never resulted in increased public safety. Now therefore be it resolved by the delegates assembled at the Gun Rights Policy Conference in St. Louis, Missouri, this 27th day of September, 2009 that: We support the repeal of the Federal Switchblade Act and any other federal, state or local laws and regulations banning tools and weapons rather than addressing behavior.

Resolution adopted without discussion.

This was really a benchmark moment; it was the first time the repeal of all switchblade laws was unanimously supported by a national group of Second Amendment activists. Realizing that attitudes have changed from the 1950s regarding knives, I got together with a great New Hampshire legislator to fight for change in New Hampshire. That person was and is my dear friend Representative Jennifer Coffey. She is an EMT and a wonderful advocate for liberty. She has written a book about her legislative experiences titled *Knives, Lipstick and Liberty*. The book is an autobiography of Jenn. My purpose here is not to rehash the great story told by Jenn, but rather to focus on the mechanics of how the "Miracle in New Hampshire" occurred, and how you can make Resolution 6 a reality in your state.

Here are the steps to success:

1. Find a dedicated legislator who believes in the cause of knife rights to sponsor a bill. That person has to be committed and educated on the issue. New Hampshire was very fortunate to have Rep. Jennifer Coffey take on the issue.

2. Get groups and individuals to support it. Be aware that gun groups do not always support knives. In the past, knives have been banned to politically save guns from being banned. In New Hampshire we were able to get support from: Knife Rights, Inc.; Second Amendment Sisters; Abe Foote of Abe's Awesome Armaments; *BLADE® Magazine*; American Knife and Tool Institute; Benchmade Knives; Ralph Demicco of Riley's Sport Shop; Ed Fowler; Suzanna Hupp; Sandra Froman; Citizens Committee for the Right To Keep and Bear Arms; Jews for the Preservation Of Firearms Ownership; Pro-Gun NH; New Hampshire Wildlife Federation; Sword Forum; Firearms Coalition; Bikerbits; Cam and Company; Bloomfield Press; Americans for Tax Reform; NH Liberty Alliance; NH Arms Collectors Association; NH Firearms Dealers Association; *The New Gun Week*; *Guns Magazine*; *American Handgunner Magazine*; *BLADE* Blog; *Women & Guns Magazine*; *Knife World*; *Cutlery News*; Hannah Dustin League; USMilitaryKnives.com; Al Kulas; Smith & Wesson; Ethan Becker of Becker Knife and Tool Co.; Classic Cutlery; Capital Copy; House Republican Alliance; NH Chiefs of Police Assoc.; Dr. Katherine Albrecht; Brian "Bulldog" Tilton; Alisha Lekas; NH 912; and SurvivalTopics.com.

3. Create a dedicated website for the bill where you can publicize supporters, promote the bill and give news updates. This can be done very inexpensively. Buy your domain name for as little as $10

HANNAH DUSTIN
————1657~1737————
Famous symbol of frontier heroism. A victim of an Indian raid in 1697, on Haverhill, Massachusetts, whence she had been taken to a camp site on the nearby island in the river. After killing and later scalping ten Indians, she and the two other captives, Mary Neff and Samuel Lennardson, escaped down the river to safety.

Hannah Dustin was a pioneer woman kidnapped by Indians and had her baby killed by them. She fought, killed and scalped her captors using edged weapons—a tomahawk and a knife. The Hannah Dustin Defense League, dedicated to women defending themselves, supported the knife rights bills. It's the first statue ever built in the United States honoring a woman, and it is located on the spot on a small river island in Boscawen, N.H., where she defeated her kidnappers.

The monument honors Gen. John Stark who said the immortal words that are New Hampshire's state motto, "Live Free or Die."

from GoDaddy.com or a similar provider, and then get a free website from Weebly.com. This is exactly what we did. Our website was www.knifelawonline.com. The page headings on the website included the following, which anyone is free to copy:

a. Home: (This page gives an introduction to website)

b. News Updates New as of June 9, 2011:

c. What People Are Saying: (This page contains endorsements from famous supporters.)

d. Articles, Blogs and Radio

e. People to Know: (Information about Rep. Coffey and yours truly)

f. Resolution 6.

g. Contact: (Very important page so supporters can get involved)

h. 125 Honest Citizens Who Use A "Switchblade, Dirk, Dagger or Stiletto"

i. Knife Rights Raffle: (Our fund raiser that helped pay for our expenses)

j. The NEW LAW! (A celebration page after passage.)

4. Hire a lobbyist. Working with Knife Rights,

Inc., we were able to get a lobbyist to help with the bill's passage. Our lobbyist was former State Senator Bob Clegg, who was indispensable. We would not have succeeded without Bob's guidance and skill.

5. Prepare for the legislative committee hearings. This is a great chance to educate the public about knives. Bring in law-abiding folks who have suffered under the knife ban. For example, we had one gun dealer testify that he was arrested and all his knives seized because he sold a switchblade to a law enforcement officer, who he knew was a law enforcement officer, and he specifically sold him the knife because he was a law enforcement officer! Another dealer did a great job of showing the committee members the differences between various knives and how outdated and absurd the ban was.

6. Try to get law enforcement on your side. The New Hampshire Chief's of Police Association supported the New Hampshire Knife Rights Bill. The modern automatic knife is a valuable tool for law enforcement, EMT's, firefighters and honest citizens who have a job that needs a knife. Because of New Hampshire's knife ban, a dealer could not sell a prohibited knife even to a cop!

7. Be ready to challenge and deal with any opposition. It may come from unexpected sources. It may be based on emotion stemming from an anti-knife bias. It might come from personality issues. One person was so driven by envy of Rep. Coffey that this person tried to kill the New Hampshire Knife Rights Bill.

8. Get supporters to send letters, email and call their legislators. This can be done inexpensively by email blasts from the supporting groups to their members. Flyers at gun shows and shops are also effective. Grassroots support really helps make a difference.

New Hampshire leads the U.S. by having the first presidential primary in the nation. New Hampshire also leads the U.S. by being the first state to repeal all of its anti-knife laws. It is a wonderful experience to have total knife freedom. I love knowing that I can enjoy my knives without worrying about being turned into a criminal due to some outdated foolish law that makes an inanimate object a crime. The more states that reform their knife laws and have their own "miracles," the more protected our knives will be from an anti-knife push in the future. Total knife freedom is possible. The "Miracle in New Hampshire" proves it beyond any doubt.

Some Blade Brawn

▶ Designed by Darrel Ralph for piercing heavy materials, the Meyerco 18-XRAY Fixed Blade is a brawny straight-knife version of the company's 18-XRAY automatic.

▲ An Allen Elishewitz design, the Columbia River Knife & Tool full-tang F.T.W.S. stretches 11.63 inches overall, including a black-powder-coated spear-point blade with a sharpened top edge, a textured Zytel® handle and multi-carry sheath. *(Kris Kandler photo)*

◀ The Hogue Knives EX-F01 features a choice of a 5.5- or 7-inch swedge-ground blade in A2 tool steel, and a green or brown G-10 G-Mascus™ handle. Hidden cavities inside the handles store survival items, and the scales can be removed via a Torx™ wrench imbedded into one of the grips.

▶ The Browning "Shadowfax," designed by Russ Kommer, sports a 4 5/8-inch, full-tang, recurved 154CM blade, a G-10 handle, four finger grooves, a bird's-beak pommel, and a Blade-Tech Kydex® sheath with a Tek-Lok™ clip.

▶ According to SOG Specialty Knives & Tools, the company's Recon Bowie 2.0 is based on the original Recon, the first knife developed and procured by Military Assistance Command Vietnam-Studies and Observation Group (MACV-SOG) personnel in the Vietnam War.

Holed Up & Handy

▲ A hot little everyday-carry neck knife designed by Fred Perrin for Boker's International Collection, the chisel-ground Shark model, complete with large finger hole, weighs 1.5 ounces and stretches 3 5/8 inches.

◀ A collaborative effort between Ka-Bar Knives, Ethan Becker and ESEE Knives, the one-piece skeletonized Ka-Bar Eskabar is fashioned from black, epoxy-powder-coated 1095 high-carbon steel, and delivered in a molded plastic sheath with lanyard holes for multi-position carry.

▼ A small VG-10 integral fixed blade, the Nemesis Knives Hellion is delivered in a Kydex® sheath with a bead chain and accessories. *(Kris Kandler photos)*

▶ The all-154CM-steel TOPS Silver Bullet has a magnetic Micarta® sheath to keep it in handy places like on a refrigerator door. *(Kris Kandler photos)*

▶ A shower curtain ring is one place to hang the 420HC stainless steel Buck Smidgen via its molded-nylon sheath with hook clip. *(Kris Kandler photos)*

Lighting-Fast Folders

► Known for quick, quality out-the-front autos, Microtech offers the Ultratech in a 4.84-inch blade with finish options of black, satin, stonewashed and bead blasted.

◄ Among other amenities, Benchmade's 551 Griptilian and 556 Mini-Griptilian models incorporate 154CM blades, Axis® locks, dual thumb-stud openers and black, textured handles.

▲ When the blade of the Chris Reeve Knives Ti-Lock is opened, spring pressure forces the lock bar—mounted along the back of the blade—into a slot to lock the blade in place. *(Eric Eggly, PointSeven Studios photo)*

► Designed by Flavio Ikoma, each with his IKBS (Ikoma Korth Bearing System), the Columbia River Knife & Tool Sampa line is an example of non-assisted-opening but still lighting-quick flipper folders.

▲The Pro-Tech Knives TR-4 Shaw Skull 1 auto folder features a 4-inch, two-tone 154CM stainless steel blade, a 6061-T6-aluminum handle and a cast-sterling skull designed by Bruce Shaw and screwed into a pocket in the frame. The knife also includes a secondary safety switch, a stainless steel skull-crusher pommel, and a lanyard terminating in a skull dangler bead from the Schmuckatelli Company.

▶ Spyderco's Manix 2 folder incorporates the company's patented hole in the blade for quick, one-hand access, and a Ball Bearing Lock for security while in use.

▲ The Cold Steel Rajah III is one of several folders sporting the Tri-Ad lock designed by Andrew Demko.

A Trio Of Tantos

▲ The new, all-black Benchmade Nim Cub II features a 3.5-inch 154CM tanto blade, a textured Noryl GTC handle, and an extended pommel with lanyard hole.

▶ The black-powder-coated blade of the Ontario Ranger RD Tanto is a quarter-inch thick all the way to the chisel-ground tip. The knife also sports an olive drab Micarta® handle.

◀ This tanto version of the Hogue EX-01 button-lock folder (it also comes in a drop-point version) showcases a black G-10 G-Mascus handle and a stonewashed 154CM stainless steel blade.

Knives Marketplace

INTERESTING PRODUCT NEWS FOR BOTH THE CUTLER AND THE KNIFE ENTHUSIAST

The companies and individuals represented on the following pages will be happy to provide additional information — feel free to contact them.

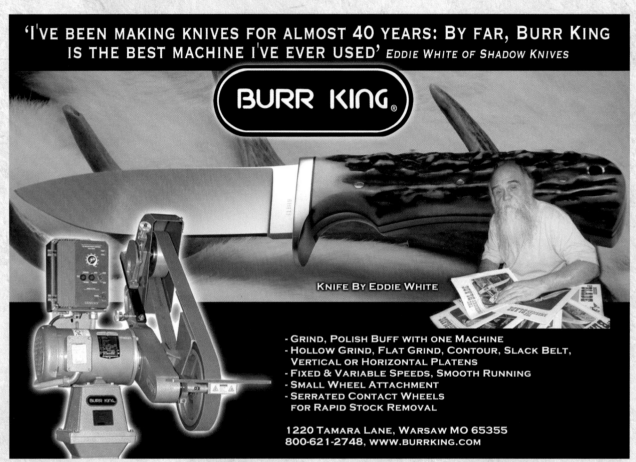

'I'VE BEEN MAKING KNIVES FOR ALMOST 40 YEARS: BY FAR, BURR KING IS THE BEST MACHINE I'VE EVER USED' *Eddie White of Shadow Knives*

BURR KING®

KNIFE BY EDDIE WHITE

- GRIND, POLISH BUFF WITH ONE MACHINE
- HOLLOW GRIND, FLAT GRIND, CONTOUR, SLACK BELT, VERTICAL OR HORIZONTAL PLATENS
- FIXED & VARIABLE SPEEDS, SMOOTH RUNNING
- SMALL WHEEL ATTACHMENT
- SERRATED CONTACT WHEELS FOR RAPID STOCK REMOVAL

1220 TAMARA LANE, WARSAW MO 65355
800-621-2748, WWW.BURRKING.COM

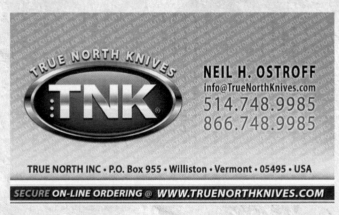

TRUE NORTH KNIVES

TNK®

NEIL H. OSTROFF
info@TrueNorthKnives.com
514.748.9985
866.748.9985

TRUE NORTH INC • P.O. Box 955 • Williston • Vermont • 05495 • USA

SECURE ON-LINE ORDERING @ WWW.TRUENORTHKNIVES.COM

BLADE

THE WORLD'S #1 KNIFE PUBLICATION

WWW.BLADEMAG.COM

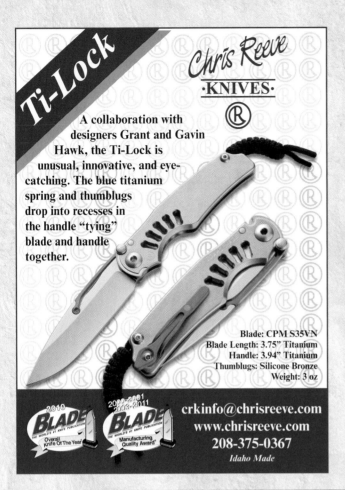
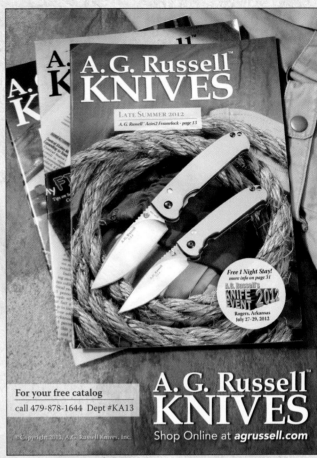

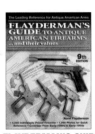

BUSSE COMBAT KNIFE COMPANY

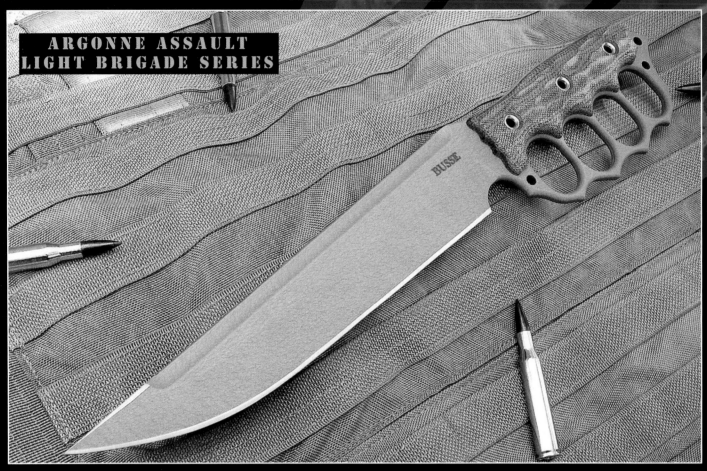

ARGONNE ASSAULT LIGHT BRIGADE SERIES

TEAM GEMINI LIGHT BRIGADE SERIES

SCRAP YARD KNIFE COMPANY

SWAMP RAT KNIFE WORKS

RODENT 9

RODENT 4

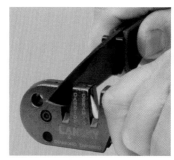

Retain your edge

UDDEHOLM PM STEEL FOR KNIVES

What is the best knife in the world? We all have different preferences, handling techniques and areas of use. No matter how and when you will use your knife, the blade steel is probably the single most important thing to consider. Uddeholm's superclean powder metallurgical steel grades are used in some of the toughest knives available on the market – knives that are put to extreme use in the hands of professionals. With Uddeholm Vanax or Elmax, a knife manufacturer can produce a blade that stays sharp, no matter what. Retain your edge – go for a better steel for your blade.

Introducing the all NEW

EXOTIC COLLECTION

SKINS
Elephant ~ Rhinoceros ~ Shark ~ Cape Buffalo ~ Hippopotamus
Snake ~ Frog ~ Crocodile ~ Ostrich ~ Stingray ~ Lizard ~ Ivory

Famars
USA ™

www.famarslama.com | www.famarsusa.com | 855.FAMARS1

Dealer Inquiries Welcome.

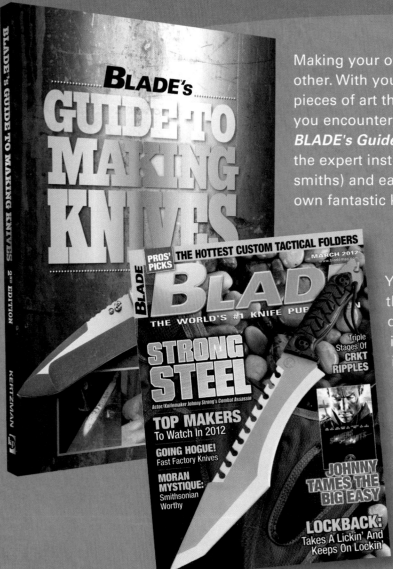

DIRECTORY

custom knifemakers

A

ABEGG, ARNIE,
5992 Kenwick Cr, Huntington Beach, CA 92648, Phone: 714-848-5697

ACCAWI, FUAD,
131 Bethel Rd, Clinton, TN 37716, Phone: 865-414-4836, gaccawi@comcast.net; Web: www.acremetalworks.com
Specialties: I create one of a kind pieces from small working knives to performance blades and swords. **Patterns:** Styles include, and not limited to hunters, Bowies, daggers, swords, folders and camp knives. **Technical:** I forge primarily 5160, produces own Damascus and does own heat treating. **Prices:** $150 to $3000. **Remarks:** I am a full-time bladesmith. I enjoy producing Persian and historically influenced work. **Mark:** My mark is an eight sided Middle Eastern star with initials in the center.

ACKERSON, ROBIN E,
119 W Smith St, Buchanan, MI 49107, Phone: 616-695-2911

ADAMS, JIM,
1648 Camille Way, Cordova, TN 38016, Phone: 901-326-0441, jim@JimAdamsKnives.com Web: www.jimadamsknives.com
Specialties: Fixed blades in classic design. **Patterns:** Hunters, fighters, and Bowies. **Technical:** Grinds Damascus, O1, others as requested. **Prices:** Starting at $150. **Remarks:** Full-time maker. **Mark:** J. Adams, Cordova, TN.

ADAMS, LES,
6413 NW 200 St, Hialeah, FL 33015, Phone: 305-625-1699
Specialties: Working straight knives of his design. **Patterns:** Fighters, tactical folders, law enforcing autos. **Technical:** Grinds ATS-34, 440C and D2. **Prices:** $100 to $500. **Remarks:** Part-time maker; first knife sold in 1989. **Mark:** First initial, last name, Custom Knives.

ADAMS, WILLIAM D,
PO Box 439, 405 Century Farms Rd, Burton, TX 77835, Phone: 979-289-0212, Fax: 979-289-6272, wd4adams@broadwaves.net
Specialties: Hunter scalpels and utility knives of his design. **Patterns:** Hunters and utility/camp knives. **Technical:** Grinds 1095, 440C and 440V. Uses stabilized wood and other stabilized materials. **Prices:** $100 to $200. **Remarks:** Part-time maker; first knife sold in 1994. **Mark:** Last name in script.

ADDISON, KYLE A,
588 Atkins Trail, Hazel, KY 42049-8629, Phone: 270-492-8120, kylest2@yahoo.com
Specialties: Hand forged blades including Bowies, fighters and hunters. **Patterns:** Custom leather sheaths. **Technical:** Forges 5160, 1084, and his own Damascus. **Prices:** $175 to $1500. **Remarks:** Part-time maker, first knife sold in 1996. ABS member. **Mark:** First and middle initial, last name under "Trident" with knife and hammer.

ADKINS, LARRY,
10714 East County Rd. 100S, Indianapolis, IN 46231, Phone: 317-838-7292
Specialties: Single blade slip joint folders. Bear Jaw Damascus hunters, Bowies, and fighters. Handles from stag, ossic, pearl, bone, mastodon-mammoth elephant. **Technical:** Forges own Damascus and all high carbon steels. Grinds 5160, 52100, 1095, O1 and L6. **Prices:** $150 and up. **Remarks:** Part-time maker, first knife sold in 2001. **Mark:** L. Adkins.

ADKINS, RICHARD L,
138 California Ct, Mission Viejo, CA 92692-4079

AIDA, YOSHIHITO,
26-7 Narimasu 2-chome, Itabashi-ku, Tokyo 175-0094, JAPAN, Phone: 81-3-3939-0052, Fax: 81-3-3939-0058, Web: http://riverside-land.com/
Specialties: High-tech working straight knives and folders of his design. **Patterns:** Bowies, lockbacks, hunters, fighters, fishing knives, boots. **Technical:** Grinds CV-134, ATS-34; buys Damascus; works in traditional Japanese fashion for some handles and sheaths. **Prices:** $700 to $1200; some higher. **Remarks:** Full-time maker; first knife sold in 1978. **Mark:** Initial logo and Riverside West.

ALBERICCI, EMILIO,
19 Via Masone, 24100, Bergamo, ITALY, Phone: 01139-35-215120
Specialties: Folders and Bowies. **Patterns:** Collector knives. **Technical:** Uses stock removal with extreme accuracy; offers exotic and high-tech materials. **Prices:** Not currently selling. **Remarks:** Part-time maker. **Mark:** None.

ALBERT, STEFAN,
U Lucenecka 434/4, Filakovo 98604, SLOVAK REPUBLIC, albert@albertknives.com Web: www.albertknives.com
Specialties: Art Knives, Miniatures, Scrimshaw, Bulino. **Prices:** From USD $500 to USD $25000. **Mark:** Albert

ALCORN, DOUGLAS A.,
14687 Fordney Rd., Chesaning, MI 48616, Phone: 989-845-6712, fortalcornknives@centurytel.net
Specialties: Gentleman style and presentation knives. **Patterns:** Hunters, miniatures, and military type fixed blade knives and axes. **Technical:** Blades are stock removal and forged using best quality stainless, carbon, and damascus steels. Handle materials are burls, ivory, pearl, leather and other exotics. **Prices:** $300 and up. **Motto:** Simple, Rugged, Elegant, Handcrafted **Remarks:** Knife maker since 1989 and full time since 1999, Knife Makers Guild (voting member), member of the Bladesmith Society. **Mark:** D.A. Alcorn (Loveless style mark), Maker, Chesaning, MI.

ALDERMAN, ROBERT,
2655 Jewel Lake Rd., Sagle, ID 83860, Phone: 208-263-5996
Specialties: Classic and traditional working straight knives in standard patterns or to customer specs and his design; period pieces. **Patterns:** Bowies, fighters, hunters and utility/camp knives. **Technical:** Casts, forges and grinds 1084; forges and grinds L6 and O1. Prefers an old appearance. **Prices:** $100 to $350; some to $700. **Remarks:** Full-time maker; first knife sold in 1975. Doing business as Trackers Forge. Knife-making school. Two-week course for beginners; covers forging, stock removal, hardening, tempering, case making. All materials supplied; $1250. **Mark:** Deer track.

ALEXANDER, DARREL,
Box 381, Ten Sleep, WY 82442, Phone: 307-366-2699, dalexwyo@tctwest.net
Specialties: Traditional working straight knives. **Patterns:** Hunters, boots and fishing knives. **Technical:** Grinds D2, 440C, ATS-34 and 154CM. **Prices:** $75 to $120; some to $250. **Remarks:** Full-time maker; first knife sold in 1983. **Mark:** Name, city, state.

ALEXANDER, EUGENE,
Box 540, Ganado, TX 77962-0540, Phone: 512-771-3727

ALEXANDER, OLEG, Cossack Blades,
15460 Stapleton Way, Wellington, FL 33414, Phone: 443-676-6111, Web: www.cossackblades.com
Technical: All knives are made from hand-forged Damascus (3-4 types of steel are used to create the Damascus) and have a HRC of 60-62. Handle materials are all natural, including various types of wood, horn, bone and leather. Embellishments include the use of precious metals and stones, including gold, silver, diamonds, rubies, sapphires and other unique materials. All knives include hand-made leather sheaths, and some models include wooden presentation boxes and display stands. **Prices:** $395 to over $10,000, depending on design and materials used. **Remarks:** Full-time maker, first knife sold in 1993. **Mark:** Rectangle enclosing a stylized Cyrillic letter "O" overlapping a stylized Cyrillic "K."

ALLEN, MIKE "WHISKERS",
12745 Fontenot Acres Rd, Malakoff, TX 75148, Phone: 903-489-1026, whiskersknives@aol.com; Web: www.whiskersknives.com
Specialties: Working and collector-quality lockbacks, liner locks, automatic folders and assisted openers of his own proprietary mechanisms. **Patterns:** Folders and fixed blades. **Technical:** Makes Damascus, 440C and ATS-34, engraves. **Prices:** $200 and up. **Remarks:** Full-time maker since 1984. **Mark:** Whiskers and month and year.

ALLRED, BRUCE F,
1764 N. Alder, Layton, UT 84041, Phone: 801-825-4612, allredbf@msn.com
Specialties: Custom hunting and utility knives. **Patterns:** Custom designs that include a unique grind line, thumb and mosaic pins. **Technical:** ATS-34, 154CM and 440C. **Remarks:** The handle material includes but not limited to Micarta (in various colors), natural woods and reconstituted stone.

ALLRED, ELVAN,
31 Spring Terrace Court, St. Charles, MO 63303, Phone: 636-936-8871, allredknives@yahoo.com; Web: www.allredcustomknives.com
Specialties: Innovative sculpted folding knives designed by Elvan's son Scott that are mostly one of a kind. **Patterns:** Mostly folders but some high-end straight knives. **Technical:** ATS-34 SS, 440C SS, stainless Damascus, S30V, 154cm; inlays are mostly natural materials such as pearl, coral, ivory, jade, lapis, and other precious stone. **Prices:** $500 to $4000, some higher. **Remarks:** Started making knives in the shop of Dr. Fred Carter in the early 1990s. Full-time maker since 2006, first knife sold in 1993. Take some orders but work mainly on one-of-a-kind art knives. **Mark:** Small oval with signature Eallred in the center and handmade above.

ALVERSON, TIM (R.V.),
622 Homestead St., Moscow, ID 83843, Phone: 208-874-2277, alvie35@yahoo.com Web: cwknives.blogspot.com
Specialties: Fancy working knives to customer specs; other types on request. **Patterns:** Bowies, daggers, folders and miniatures. **Technical:** Grinds 440C, ATS-34; buys some Damascus. **Prices:** Start at $100. **Remarks:** Full-time maker; first knife sold in 1981. **Mark:** R.V.A. around rosebud.

AMERI, MAURO,
Via Riaello No. 20, Trensasco St Olcese, 16010 Genova, ITALY, Phone: 010-8357077
Specialties: Working and using knives of his design. **Patterns:** Hunters, Bowies and camp knives. **Technical:** Grinds 440C, ATS-34 and 154CM. Handles in wood or Micarta; offers sheaths. **Prices:** $200 to $1200. **Remarks:** Spare-time maker; first knife sold in 1982. **Mark:** Last name, city.

AMMONS, DAVID C,
6225 N. Tucson Mtn. Dr, Tucson, AZ 85743, Phone: 520-307-3585
Specialties: Will build to suit. **Patterns:** Yours or his. **Prices:** $250 to $2000. **Mark:** AMMONS.

AMOUREUX, A W,
PO Box 776, Northport, WA 99157, Phone: 509-732-6292
Specialties: Heavy-duty working straight knives. **Patterns:** Bowies, fighters, camp knives and hunters for world-wide use. **Technical:** Grinds 440C, ATS-34 and 154CM. **Prices:** $80 to $2000. **Remarks:** Full-time maker; first knife sold in 1974. **Mark:** ALSTAR.

ANDERS, DAVID,
157 Barnes Dr, Center Ridge, AR 72027, Phone: 501-893-2294
Specialties: Working straight knives of his design. **Patterns:** Bowies, fighters and hunters. **Technical:** Forges 5160, 1080 and Damascus. **Prices:** $225 to

$3200. **Remarks:** Part-time maker; first knife sold in 1988. Doing business as Anders Knives. **Mark:** Last name/MS.

ANDERS, JEROME,
14560 SW 37th St, Miramar, FL 33027, Phone: 305-613-2990, web:www.andersknives.com
Specialties: Case handles and pin work. **Patterns:** Layered and mosaic steel. **Prices:** $275 and up. **Remarks:** All his knives are truly one-of-a-kind. **Mark:** J. Anders in half moon.

ANDERSEN, HENRIK LEFOLII,
Jagtvej 8, Groenholt, 3480, Fredensborg, DENMARK, Phone: 0011-45-48483026
Specialties: Hunters and matched pairs for the serious hunter. **Technical:** Grinds A2; uses materials native to Scandinavia. **Prices:** Start at $250. **Remarks:** Part-time maker; first knife sold in 1985. **Mark:** Initials with arrow.

ANDERSEN, KARL B.,
1699 N. Bluebell Bend Rd., Watseka, IL 60970, Phone: 815-644-0127, Karl@andersenforge.com Web: www.andersenforge.com
Specialties: Hunters, Bowies, Fighters, Camp knives forged from high carbon tool steels and Andersen Forge Damascus. **Technical:** All types of materials used. Exotic inlay materials and silver wire embellishments utilized. **Prices:** Starting at $450 and up. **Remarks:** Full-time maker. ABS Journeyman Smith. All knives sole authorship. Andersen Forge was instrumental in paving the way for take-down knife construction being more recognized and broadly accepted in knife making today. **Mark:** Andersen in script on obverse. J.S. on either side, depending on knife.

ANDERSON, GARY D.,
2816 Reservoir Rd, Spring Grove, PA 17362-9802, Phone: 717-229-2665
Specialties: From working knives to collectors quality blades, some folders. **Patterns:** Traditional and classic designs; customer patterns welcome. **Technical:** Forges Damascus carbon and stainless steels. Offers silver inlay, mokume, filework, checkering. **Prices:** $250 and up. **Remarks:** Part-time maker; first knife sold in 1985. Some engraving, scrimshaw and stone work. **Mark:** GAND, MS.

ANDERSON, MARK ALAN,
1176 Poplar St, Denver, CO 80220, mcantdrive95@comcast.net; Web: www.malancustomknives.com
Specialties: Stilettos. Automatics of several varieties and release mechanisms. **Patterns:** Drop point hunters, sub hilt fighters & drop point camp knives. **Technical:** Almost all my blades are hollow ground. **Prices:** $200 to $1800. **Remarks:** Focusing on fixed blade hunting, skinning & fighting knives now. **Mark:** Dragon head.

ANDERSON, MEL,
29505 P 50 Rd, Hotchkiss, CO 81419-8203, Phone: 970-872-4882, Fax: 970-872-4882, artnedge1@wmconnect.com
Specialties: Full-size, miniature and one-of-a-kind straight knives and folders of his design. **Patterns:** Tantos, Bowies, daggers, fighters, hunters and pressure folders. **Technical:** Grinds 440C, 5160, D2, 1095. **Prices:** Start at $145. **Remarks:** Knifemaker and sculptor, full-time maker; first knife sold in 1987. **Mark:** Scratchy Hand.

ANDERSON, TOM,
955 Canal Rd. Extd., Manchester, PA 17345, Phone: 717-266-6475, andersontech1@comcast.net Web: artistryintitanium.com
Specialties: Battle maces and war hammers.

ANDREWS, ERIC,
132 Halbert Street, Grand Ledge, MI 48837, Phone: 517-627-7304
Specialties: Traditional working and using straight knives of his design. **Patterns:** Full-tang hunters, skinners and utility knives. **Technical:** Forges carbon steel; heat-treats. All knives come with sheath; most handles are of wood. **Prices:** $80 to $160. **Remarks:** Part-time maker; first knife sold in 1990. Doing business as The Tinkers Bench.

ANDREWS, RUSS,
PO Box 7732, Sugar Creek, MO 64054, Phone: 816-252-3344, russandrews@sbcglobal.net; Web:wwwrussandrewsknives.com
Specialties: Hand forged bowies & hunters. **Mark:** E. R. Andrews II. ERAII.

ANGELL, JON,
22516 East CR1474, Hawthorne, FL 32640, Phone: 352-475-5380, syrjon@aol.com

ANKROM, W.E.,
14 Marquette Dr, Cody, WY 82414, Phone: 307-587-3017, weankrom@hotmail.com
Specialties: Best quality folding knives of his design. Bowies, fighters, chute knives, boots and hunters. **Patterns:** Lock backs, liner locks, single high art. **Technical:** ATS-34 commercial Damascus, CPM 154 steel. **Prices:** $500 and up. **Remarks:** Full-time maker; first knife sold in 1975. **Mark:** Name or name, city, state.

ANSO, JENS,
GL. Skanderborgvej, 116, 8472 Sporup, DENMARK, Phone: 45 86968826, info@ansoknives.com; Web: www.ansoknives.com
Specialties: Working knives of his own design. **Patterns:** Balisongs, swords, folders, drop-points, sheepsfoots, hawkbill, tanto, recurve. **Technical:** Grinds RWL-34 Damasteel S30V, CPM 154CM. Handrubbed or beadblasted finish. **Price:** $400 to $1200, some up to $3500. **Remarks:** Full-time maker since January 2002. First knife sold 1997. Doing business as ANSOKNIVES. **Mark:** ANSO and/or ANSO with logo.

APELT, STACY E,
8076 Moose Ave, Norfolk, VA 23518, Phone: 757-583-5872, sapelt@cox.net
Specialties: Exotic wood and burls, ivories, Bowies, custom made knives to order. **Patterns:** Bowies, hunters, fillet, professional cutlery and Japanese style blades and swords. **Technical:** Hand forging, stock removal, scrimshaw, carbon, stainless and Damascus steels. **Prices:** $65 to $5000. **Remarks:** Professional Goldsmith. **Mark:** Stacy E. Apelt - Norfolk VA.

APPLEBY, ROBERT,
746 Municipal Rd, Shickshinny, PA 18655, Phone: 570-864-0879, applebyknives@yahoo.com; Web: www.applebyknives.com
Specialties: Working using straight knives and folders of his own and popular and historical designs. **Patterns:** Variety of straight knives and folders. **Technical:** Hand forged or grinds O1, 1084, 5160, 440C, ATS-34, commercial Damascus, makes own sheaths. **Prices:** Starting at $75. **Remarks:** Part-time maker, first knife sold in 1995. **Mark:** APPLEBY over SHICKSHINNY, PA.

APPLETON, RON,
315 Glenn St, Bluff Dale, TX 76433, Phone: 254-728-3039, ron@helovesher.com or ronappleton@hotmail.com; Web: http://community.webshots.com/user/angelic574
Specialties: One-of-a-kind folding knives. **Patterns:** Unique folding multi-locks and high-tech patterns. **Technical:** All parts machined, D2, S7, 416, 440C, 6A14V et.al. **Prices:** Start at $12000. **Remarks:** Full-time maker; first knife sold in 1996. **Mark:** Initials with anvil or initials within arrowhead, signed and dated. Usually only shows at the Art Knife Invitational every 2 years in San Diego, CA.

ARBUCKLE, JAMES M,
114 Jonathan Jct, Yorktown, VA 23693, Phone: 757-867-9578, a_r_buckle@hotmail.com
Specialties: One-of-a-kind of his design; working knives. **Patterns:** Mostly chef's knives and hunters. **Technical:** Forged and stock removal blades using exotic hardwoods, natural materials, Micarta and stabilized woods. Forge 5160 and 1084; stock removal D2, ATS-34, 440C and 154CM. Makes own pattern welded steel. **Prices:** $195 to $700. **Remarks:** Forge, grind, heat-treat, finish and embellish all knives himself. Does own leatherwork. Part-time maker. ABS Journeyman smith 2007; ASM member. **Mark:** J. Arbuckle or J. ARBUCKLE MAKER.

ARCHER, RAY AND TERRI,
4207 South 28 St., Omaha, NE 68107, Phone: 402-505-3084, archerr@cox.net Web: www.archersknives.com
Specialties: Back to basics high finish working knives and upscale. **Patterns:** Hunters/skinners, camping. **Technical:** Flat grinds ATS-34, 440C, S30V. Buys Damascus. **Price:** $100 to $500, some higher. **Remarks:** Full time makers. Make own sheaths; first knife sold 1994. Member of PKA & OK CA (Oregon Knife Collector Assoc.). **Mark:** Last name over knives.

ARDWIN, COREY,
4700 North Cedar, North Little Rock, AR 72116, Phone: 501-791-0301, Fax: 501-791-2974, Boog@hotmail.com

ARM-KO KNIVES,
PO Box 76280, Marble Ray 4035 KZN, SOUTH AFRICA, Phone: 27 31 5771451, arm-koknives.co.za; Web: www.arm-koknives.co.za
Specialties: They will make what your fastidious taste desires. Be it cool collector or tenacious tactical with handles of mother-of-pearl, fossil & local ivories. Exotic dye/stabilized burls, giraffe bone, horns, carbon fiber, g10, and titanium etc. **Technical:** Via stock removal, grinding Damasteel, carbon & mosaic. Damascus, ATS-34, N690, 440A, 440B, 12C27, RWL34 and high carbon EN 8, 5160 all heat treated in house. **Prices:** From $200 and up. **Remarks:** Father a part-time maker for well over 10 years and member of Knifemakers Guild in SA. Son full-time maker over 3 years. **Mark:** Logo of initials A R M and H A R M "Edged Tools."

ARMS, ERIC,
11153 7 Mile Road, Tustin, MI 49688, Phone: 231-829-3726, ericarms@netonecom.net
Specialties: Working hunters, high performance straight knives. **Patterns:** Variety of hunters, scagel style, Ed Fowler design and drop point. **Technical:** Forge 52100, 5160, 1084 hand grind, heat treat, natural handle, stag horn, elk, big horn, flat grind, convex, all leather sheath work. **Prices:** Starting at $150 **Remarks:** Part-time maker **Mark:** Eric Arms

ARNOLD, JOE,
47 Patience Cres, London, Ont., CANADA N6E 2K7, Phone: 519-686-2623, arnoldknivesandforge@bell.net
Specialties: Traditional working and using straight knives of his design and to customer specs. **Patterns:** Fighters, hunters and Bowies. **Technical:** Grinds 440C, ATS-34, 5160, and Forges 1084-1085 **Prices:** $75 to $500; some to $2500. **Remarks:** Full-time maker; first knife sold in 1988. **Mark:** Last name, country.

ARROWOOD, DALE,
556 Lassetter Rd, Sharpsburg, GA 30277, Phone: 404-253-9672
Specialties: Fancy and traditional straight knives of his design and to customer specs. **Patterns:** Bowies, fighters and hunters. **Technical:** Grinds ATS-34 and 440C; forges high-carbon steel. Engraves and scrimshaws. **Prices:** $125 to $200; some to $245. **Remarks:** Part-time maker; first knife sold in 1989. **Mark:** Anvil with an arrow through it; Old English "Arrowood Knives."

ASHBY, DOUGLAS,
10123 Deermont Trail, Dallas, TX 75243, Phone: 214-929-7531, doug@ashbycustomknives.com Web: ashbycustomknives.com
Specialties: Traditional and fancy straight knives and folders of his design or to customer specs. **Patterns:** Skinners, hunters, utility/camp knives, locking liner folders. **Technical:** Grinds ATS-34, commercial Damascus, and other steels on request. **Prices:** $125 to $1000. **Remarks:** Part-time maker; first knife sold in 1990. **Mark:** Name, city.

custom knifemakers

ASHWORTH, BOYD,
1510 Bullard Place, Powder Springs, GA 30127, Phone: 770-422-9826, boydashworth@comcast.net; Web: www.boydashworthknives.com
Specialties: Turtle folders. Fancy Damascus locking folders. **Patterns:** Fighters, hunters and gents. **Technical:** Forges own Damascus; offers filework; uses exotic handle materials. **Prices:** $500 to $2500. **Remarks:** Part-time maker; first knife sold in 1993. **Mark:** Last name.

ATHEY, STEVE,
3153 Danube Way, Riverside, CA 92503, Phone: 951-850-8612, stevelonnie@yahoo.com
Specialties: Stock removal. **Patterns:** Hunters & Bowies. **Prices:** $100 to $500. **Remarks:** Part-time maker. **Mark:** Last name with number on blade.

ATKINS, JIM,
758 270th Ave, Frederic, WI 54837, Phone: 715-472-8510, jubjub223@gmail.com
Specialties: Hardworking combat and hunting knives. Military utility knives and other hard working knives **Patterns:** Tapered tang **Technical:** Forging recycled 5160. Stock removal with O1. Handles of Micarta and natural materials. Some 5160. Differential quench. **Remarks:** Part-time maker since 2000. Funtionalm indestructable and elegant **Mark:** Stylized initials.

ATKINSON, DICK,
General Delivery, Wausau, FL 32463, Phone: 850-638-8524
Specialties: Working straight knives and folders of his design; some fancy. **Patterns:** Hunters, fighters, boots; locking folders in interframes. **Technical:** Grinds A2, 440C and 154CM. Likes filework. **Prices:** $85 to $300; some exceptional knives. **Remarks:** Full-time maker; first knife sold in 1977. **Mark:** Name, city, state.

AYARRAGARAY, CRISTIAN L.,
Buenos Aires 250, (3100) Parana-Entre Rios, ARGENTINA, Phone: 043-231753
Specialties: Traditional working straight knives of his design. **Patterns:** Fishing and hunting knives. **Technical:** Grinds and forges carbon steel. Uses native Argentine woods and deer antler. **Prices:** $150 to $250; some to $400. **Remarks:** Full-time maker; first knife sold in 1980. **Mark:** Last name, signature.

B

BAARTMAN, GEORGE,
PO Box 1116, Bela-Bela 0480, Limpopo, SOUTH AFRICA, Phone: 27 14 736 4036, Fax: 086 636 3408, thabathipa@gmail.com
Specialties: Fancy and working LinerLock® folders of own design and to customers specs. Specialize in pattern filework on liners. **Patterns:** LinerLock® folders. **Technical:** Grinds 12C27, ATS-34, and Damascus, prefer working with stainless damasteel. Hollow grinds to hand-rubbed and polished satin finish. Enjoys working with mammoth, warthog tusk and pearls. **Prices:** Folders from $380 to $1000. **Remarks:** Part-time maker. Member of the Knifemakers Guild of South Africa since 1993. **Mark:** BAARTMAN.

BACHE-WIIG, TOM,
N-5966, Eivindvik, NORWAY, Phone: 475-778-4290, Fax: 475-778-1099, tom.bache-wiig@enivest.net; Web: tombachewiig.com
Specialties: High-art and working knives of his design. **Patterns:** Hunters, utility knives, hatchets, axes and art knives. **Technical:** Grinds Uddeholm Elmax, powder metallurgy tool stainless steel. Handles made of rear burls of Nordic woods stabilized with vacuum/high-pressure technique. **Prices:** $430 to $900; some to $2300. **Remarks:** Part-time maker; first knife sold 1988. **Mark:** Etched name and eagle head.

BACON, DAVID R.,
906 136th St E, Bradenton, FL 34202-9694, Phone: 813-996-4289

BAGLEY, R. KEITH,
OLD PINE FORGE, 4415 Hope Acres Dr, White Plains, MD 20695, Phone: 301-932-0990, oldpineforge@hotmail.com
Specialties: Hand-made Damascus hunters, skinners, Bowies. **Technical:** Use ATS-34, 5160, O1, 1085, 1095. **Patterns:** Ladder-wave lightning bolt. **Price:** $275 to 750. **Remarks:** Farrier for 25 years, blacksmith for 25 years, knifemaker for 10 years. **Mark:** KB inside horseshoe and anvil.

BAILEY, I.R.,
Lamorna Cottage, Common End, Colkirk, ENGLAND NR 21 7JD, Phone: 01-328-856-183, irbailey1975@tiscali.co.uk Web: irbailey.co.uk
Specialties: Hunters, utilities, Bowies, camp knives, fighters. Mainly influenced by Moran, Loveless and Lile. **Technical:** Primarily stock removal using flat ground 1095, 1075, and 80CrV2. Occasionally forges including own basic Damascus. Uses both native and exotic hardwoods, stag, Leather, Micarta and other synthetic handle materials, with brass or 301 stainless fittings. Does some filework and leather tooling. Does own heat treating. **Remarks:** Part-time maker since 2005. All knives and sheaths are sole authorship. **Mark:** Last name stamped.

BAILEY, JOSEPH D.,
3213 Jonesboro Dr, Nashville, TN 37214, Phone: 615-889-3172, jbknfemkr@aol.com
Specialties: Working and using straight knives; collector pieces. **Patterns:** Bowies, hunters, tactical, folders. **Technical:** 440C, ATS-34, Damascus and wire Damascus. Offers scrimshaw. **Prices:** $85 to $1200. **Remarks:** Part-time maker; first knife sold in 1988. **Mark:** Joseph D Bailey Nashville Tennessee.

BAKER, HERB,
14104 NC 87 N, Eden, NC 27288, Phone: 336-627-0338

BAKER, RAY,
PO Box 303, Sapulpa, OK 74067, Phone: 918-224-8013
Specialties: High-tech working straight knives. **Patterns:** Hunters, fighters, Bowies, skinners and boots of his design and to customer specs. **Technical:** Grinds 440C, 1095 spring steel or customer request; heat-treats. Custom-made scabbards for any knife. **Prices:** $125 to $500; some to $1000. **Remarks:** Full-time maker; first knife sold in 1981. **Mark:** First initial, last name.

BAKER, TONY,
707 Lake Highlands Dr, Allen, TX 75002, Phone: 214-543-1001, tonybakerknives@yahoo.com
Specialties: Hunting knives, integral made **Technical:** 154cm, S30V, and S90V **Prices:** Starting at $500. **Prices:** $200-$1200 **Remarks:** First knife made in 2001

BAKER, WILD BILL,
Box 361, Boiceville, NY 12412, Phone: 914-657-8646
Specialties: Primitive knives, buckskinners. **Patterns:** Skinners, camp knives and Bowies. **Technical:** Works with L6, files and rasps. **Prices:** $100 to $350. **Remarks:** Part-time maker; first knife sold in 1989. **Mark:** Wild Bill Baker, Oak Leaf Forge, or both.

BALBACH, MARKUS,
Heinrich - Worner - Str 3, 35789 Weilmunster-Laubuseschbach/Ts., GERMANY 06475-8911, Fax: 912986, Web: www.schmiede-balbach.de
Specialties: High-art knives and working/using straight knives and folders of his design and to customer specs. **Patterns:** Hunters and daggers. **Technical:** Stainless steel, one of Germany's greatest Smithies. Supplier for the forges of Solingen. **Remarks:** Full-time maker; first knife sold in 1984. Doing business as Schmiedewerkstatte M. Balbach. **Mark:** Initials stamped inside the handle.

BALL, BUTCH,
2161 Reedsville Rd., Floyd, VA 24091, Phone: 540-392-3485, ballknives@yahoo.com
Specialties: Fancy and Tactical Folders and Automatics. **Patterns:** Fixed and folders. **Technical:** Use various Damascus and ATS34, 154cm. **Prices:** $300 - $1500. **Remarks:** Part-time maker. Sold first knife in 1990. **Mark:** Ball or BCK with crossed knives.

BALL, KEN,
127 Sundown Manor, Mooresville, IN 46158, Phone: 317-834-4803
Specialties: Classic working/using straight knives of his design and to customer specs. **Patterns:** Hunters and utility/camp knives. **Technical:** Flat-grinds ATS-34. Offers filework. **Prices:** $150 to $400. **Remarks:** Part-time maker; first knife sold in 1994. Doing business as Ball Custom Knives. **Mark:** Last name.

BALLESTRA, SANTINO,
via D. Tempesta 11/17, 18039 Ventimiglia (IM), ITALY 0184-215228, ladasin@libero.it
Specialties: Using and collecting straight knives. **Patterns:** Hunting, fighting, skinners, Bowies, medieval daggers and knives. **Technical:** Forges ATS-34, D2, O2, 1060 and his own Damascus. Uses ivory and silver. **Prices:** $500 to $2000; some higher. **Remarks:** Full-time maker; first knife sold in 1979. **Mark:** First initial, last name.

BALLEW, DALE,
PO Box 1277, Bowling Green, VA 22427, Phone: 804-633-5701
Specialties: Miniatures only to customer specs. **Patterns:** Bowies, daggers and fighters. **Technical:** Files 440C stainless; uses ivory, abalone, exotic woods and some precious stones. **Prices:** $100 to $800. **Remarks:** Part-time maker; first knife sold in 1988. **Mark:** Initials and last name.

BANAITIS, ROMAS,
84 Winthrop St., Medway, MA 02053, Phone: 774-248-5851, rbanaitis@verizon.net
Specialties: Designing art and fantasy knives. **Patterns:** Folders, daggers and fixed blades. **Technical:** Hand-carved blades, handles and fittings in stainless steel, sterling silver and titanium. **Prices:** Moderate to upscale. **Remarks:** First knife sold in 1996. **Mark:** Romas Banaitis.

BANKS, DAVID L.,
99 Blackfoot Ave, Riverton, WY 82501, Phone: 307-856-3154/Cell: 307-851-5599
Specialties: Heavy-duty working straight knives. **Patterns:** Hunters, Bowies and camp knives. **Technical:** Forges Damascus 1084-15N20, L6-W1 pure nickel, 5160, 52100 and his own Damascus; differential heat treat and tempers. Handles made of horn, antlers and exotic wood. Hand-stitched harness leather sheaths. **Prices:** $300 to $2000. **Remarks:** Part-time maker. **Mark:** Banks Blackfoot forged Dave Banks and initials connected.

BAREFOOT, JOE W.,
1654 Honey Hill, Wilmington, NC 28442, Phone: 910-641-1143
Specialties: Working straight knives of his design. **Patterns:** Hunters, fighters and boots; tantos and survival knives. **Technical:** Grinds D2, 440C and ATS-34. Mirror finishes. Uses ivory and stag on customer request only. **Prices:** $50 to $160; some to $500. **Remarks:** Part-time maker; first knife sold in 1980. **Mark:** Bare footprint.

BARKER, JOHN,
5725 Boulder Bluff Dr., Cumming, GA 30040, Phone: 678-357-8586, barkerknives@bellsouth.net Web: www.barkerknives.com
Specialties: Tactical fixed blades and folders. **Technical:** Stock removal method and CPM and Carpenter powdered technology steels. **Prices:** $150 and up. **Remarks:** First knife made 2006. **Mark:** Snarling dog with "Barker" over the top of its head and "Knives" below.

BARKER, REGGIE,
603 S Park Dr, Springhill, LA 71075, Phone: 318-539-2958, wrbarker@cmaaccess.com; Web: www.reggiebarkerknives.com
Specialties: Camp knives and hatchets. **Patterns:** Bowie, skinning, hunting, camping, fighters, kitchen or customer design. **Technical:** Forges carbon steel and own pattern welded steels. **Prices:** $225 to $2000. **Remarks:** Full-time maker. Winner of 1999 and 2000 Spring Hammering Cutting contest. Winner of Best Value of Show 2001; Arkansas Knife Show and Journeyman Smith. Border Guard Forge. **Mark:** Barker JS.

BARKER, ROBERT G.,
2311 Branch Rd, Bishop, GA 30621, Phone: 706-769-7827
Specialties: Traditional working/using straight knives of his design. Patterns: Bowies, hunters and utility knives, ABS Journeyman Smith. Technical: Hand forged carbon and Damascus. Forges to shape high-carbon 5160, cable and chain. Differentially heat-treats. Prices: $200 to $500; some to $1000. Remarks: Spare-time maker; first knife sold in 1987. Mark: BARKER/J.S.

BARKER, STUART,
14 Belvoir Close, Oadby, Leicester, England LE2 4SG, Phone: +447887585411, sc_barker@hotmail.com Web: www.barkerknives.co.uk
Specialties: Fixed blade working knives of his design. Patterns: Kitchen, hunter, utility/camp knives. Technical: Grinds O1, Rw134 & Damasteel, hand rubbed or shot blast finishes. Prices: $150 - $500 Remarks: Part-time maker, first knife sold 2006. Mark: Last initial

BARKES, TERRY,
14844 N. Bluff Rd., Edinburgh, IN 46124, Phone: 812-526-6390, knifenpocket@sbcglobal.net; Web:http:// my.hsonline.net/wizard/TerryBarkesKnives.htm
Specialties: Traditional working straight knives of his designs. Patterns: Drop point hunters, boot knives, skinning, fighter, utility, all purpose, camp, and grill knives. Technical: Grinds 1095 - 1084 - 52100 - 01, Hollow grinds and flat grinds. Hand rubbed finish from 400 to 2000 grit or High polish buff. Hard edge and soft back, heat treat by maker. Likes File work, natural handle material, bone, stag, water buffalo horn, wildbeast bone, ironwood. Prices: $200 and up Remarks: Full-time maker, first knifge sold in 2005. Doing business as Barkes Knife Shop. Marks: Barkes - USA, Barkes Double Arrow - USA

BARLOW, JANA POIRIER,
3820 Borland Cir, Anchorage, AK 99517, Phone: 907-243-4581

BARNES, AUBREY G.,
11341 Rock Hill Rd, Hagerstown, MD 21740, Phone: 301-223-4587, a.barnes@myactv.net
Specialties: Classic Moran style reproductions and using knives of his own design. Patterns: Bowies, hunters, fighters, daggers and utility/camping knives. Technical: Forges 5160, 1085, L6 and Damascus, Silver wire inlays. Prices: $500 to $5000. Remarks: Full-time maker; first knife sold in 1992. Doing business as Falling Waters Forge. Mark: First and middle initials, last name, M.S.

BARNES, GARY L.,
Box 138, New Windsor, MD 21776-0138, Phone: 410-635-6243, Fax: 410-635-6243, mail@glbarnes.com; Web: www.glbarnes.com or www.barnespneumatic.com
Specialties: Ornate button lock Damascus folders. Patterns: Barnes original. Technical: Forges own Damascus. Prices: Average $2500. Remarks: ABS Master Smith since 1983. Mark: Hand engraved logo of letter B pierced by dagger.

BARNES, GREGORY,
266 W Calaveras St, Altadena, CA 91001, Phone: 626-398-0053, snake@annex.com

BARNES, JACK,
PO Box 1315, Whitefish, MT 59937-1315, Phone: 406-862-6078

BARNES, JIM,
PO BOX 50, Christoval, TX 76935, Phone: 325-896-7819
Specialties: Traditional and working straight and folder knives of all designs. Standard or customer request specialties.
Technical: Grinds ATS-34, 440C, and D2 heat treats. All folders have filework.
Prices: Start at $175 for straight and start at $275 for folders.
Remarks: Full-time maker first knife sold in 1984. DBA Jim Barnes Custom Knives
Mark: Logo with Name City and State

BARNES, MARLEN R.,
904 Crestview Dr S, Atlanta, TX 75551-1854, Phone: 903-796-3668, MRBlives@worldnet.att.net
Specialties: Hammer forges random and mosaic Damascus. Patterns: Hatchets, straight and folding knives. Technical: Hammer forges carbon steel using 5160, 1084 and 52100 with 15N20 and 203E nickel. Prices: $150 and up. Remarks: Part-time maker; first knife sold 1999. Mark: Script M.R.B., other side J.S.

BARNES, WENDELL,
PO Box 272, Clinton, MT 59825, Phone: 406-825-0908
Specialties: Working straight knives. Patterns: Hunters, folders, neck knives. Technical: Grinds 440C, ATS-34, D2 and Damascus. Prices: Start at $75. Remarks: Spare-time maker; first knife sold in 1996. Mark: First initial, split heart, last name.

BARNES JR., CECIL C.,
141 Barnes Dr, Center Ridge, AR 72027, Phone: 501-893-2567

BARNETT, BRUCE,
PO Box 447, Mundaring 6073, Western Australia, Phone: 61-4-19243855, bruce@barnettcustomknives.com; web: www.barnettcustomknives.com
Specialties: Most types of fixed blades, folders, carving sets. Patterns: Hunters, Bowies, Camp Knives, Fighters, Lockback and Slipjoint Folders. Prices: $200 up Remarks: Part time maker. Member Australian Knifemakers Guild and American Bladesmith Society. Mark: Barnett

BARNETT, VAN,
BARNETT INT'L INC, 1135 Terminal Way Ste #209, Reno, NV 89502, Phone: 304-727-5512; 775-513-6969; 775-686-9084, ImATimeMachine@gmail.com & illusionknives@gmail.com; Web: www.VanBarnett.com
Specialties: Collector grade one-of-a-kind / embellished high art daggers and art folders. Patterns: Art daggers and folders. Technical: Forges and grinds own Damascus. Prices: Upscale. Remarks: Designs and makes one-of-a-kind highly embellished art knives using high karat gold, diamonds and other gemstones, pearls, stone and fossil ivories, carved steel guards and blades, all knives are carved and or engraved, does own engraving, carving and other embellishments, sole authorship; full-time maker since 1981. Does one high art collaboration a year with Dellana. Member of ABS. Member Art Knife Invitational Group (AKI) Mark: VBARNETT

BARR, JUDSON C.,
1905 Pickwick Circle, Irving, TX 75060, Phone: 214-724-0564, judsonbarrknives@yahoo.com
Specialties: Bowies. Patterns: Sheffield and Early American. Technical: Forged carbon steel and Damascus. Also stock removal. Remarks: Journeyman member of ABS. Mark: Barr.

BARRETT, RICK L. (TOSHI HISA),
18943 CR 18, Goshen, IN 46528, Phone: 574-533-4297, barrettrick@hotmail.com
Specialties: Japanese-style blades from sushi knives to katana and fantasy pieces. Patterns: Swords, axes, spears/lances, hunter and utility knives. Technical: Forges and grinds Damascus and carbon steels, occasionally uses stainless. Prices: $250 to $4000+. Remarks: Full-time bladesmith, jeweler. Mark: Japanese mei on Japanese pieces and stylized initials.

BARRON, BRIAN,
123 12th Ave, San Mateo, CA 94402, Phone: 650-341-2683
Specialties: Traditional straight knives. Patterns: Daggers, hunters and swords. Technical: Grinds 440C, ATS-34 and 1095. Sculpts bolsters using an S-curve. Prices: $130 to $270; some to $1500. Remarks: Part-time maker; first knife sold in 1993. Mark: Diamond Drag "Barron."

BARRY, SCOTT,
Box 354, Laramie, WY 82073, Phone: 307-721-8038, scottyb@uwyo.edu
Specialties: Currently producing mostly folders, also make fixed blade hunters & fillet knives. Technical: Steels used are 440/C, ATS/34, 154/CM, S30V, Damasteel & Mike Norris stainless Damascus. Prices: Range from $300 $1000. Remarks: Part-time maker. First knife sold in 1972. Mark: DSBarry, etched on blade.

BARRY III, JAMES J.,
115 Flagler Promenade No., West Palm Beach, FL 33405, Phone: 561-832-4197
Specialties: High-art working straight knives of his design also high art tomahawks. Patterns: Hunters, daggers and fishing knives. Technical: Grinds 440C only. Prefers exotic materials for handles. Most knives embellished with filework, carving and scrimshaw. Many pieces designed to stand unassisted. Prices: $500 to $10,000. Remarks: Part-time maker; first knife sold in 1975. Guild member (Knifemakers) since 1991. Mark: Branded initials as a J and B together.

BARTH, J.D.,
101 4th St, PO Box 186, Alberton, MT 59820, Phone: 406-722-4557, mtdeerhunter@blackfoot.net; Web: www.jdbarthcustomknives.com
Specialties: Working and fancy straight knives of his design. LinerLock® folders, stainless and Damascus, fully file worked, nitre bluing. Technical: Grinds ATS-34, 440-C, stainless and carbon Damascus. Uses variety of natural handle materials and Micarta. Likes dovetailed bolsters. Filework on most knives, full and tapered tangs. Makes custom fit sheaths for each knife. Mark: Name over maker, city and state.

BARTLOW, JOHN,
5078 Coffeen Ave, Sheridan, WY 82801, Phone: 307 673-4941, bartlow@bresnan.net
Specialties: Working hunters, greenriver skinners, classic capers and bird & trouts. Technical: ATS-34, CPM154, Damascus available on all linerlocks. Prices: Full-time maker, guild member from 1988. Mark: Bartlow, Sheridan WYO.

BASKETT, BARBARA,
427 Sutzer Ck Rd, Eastview, KY 42732, Phone: 270-862-5019, baskettknives@windstream.net
Specialties: Hunters and LinerLocks. Technical: 440-C, CPM 154, S30V. Prices: $250 and up. Mark: B. Baskett.

BASKETT, LEE GENE,
427 Sutzer Ck. Rd., Eastview, KY 42732, Phone: 270-862-5019, Fax: Cell: 270-766-8724, baskettknives@hotmail.com Web: www.baskettknives.com
Specialties: Fancy working knives and fancy art pieces, often set up in fancy desk stands. Patterns: Fighters, Bowies, and Survial Knives; lockback folders and liner locks along with traditional styles. Cutting competition knives. Technical: Grinds O1, 440-c, S30V, power CPM154, CPM 4, D2, buys Damascus. Filework provided on most knives. Prices: $250 and up. Remarks: Part-time maker, first knife sold in 1980. Mark: Baskett

BASSETT, DAVID J.,
P.O. Box 69-102, Glendene, Auckland 0645, NEW ZEALAND, Phone: 64 9 818 9083, Fax: 64 9 818 9013, david@customknifemaking.co.nz; Web: www.customknifemaking.co.nz
Specialties: Working/using knives. Patterns: Hunters, fighters, boot, skinners, tanto. Technical: Grinds 440C, 12C27, D2 and some Damascus via stock removal method. Prices: $150 to $500. Remarks: Part-time maker, first knife sold in 2006. Also carries range of natural and synthetic handle material, pin stock etc. for sale. Mark: Name over country in semi-circular design.

BATLEY, MARK S.,
PO Box 217, Wake, VA 23176, Phone: 804 776-7794

BATSON, JAMES,
176 Brentwood Lane, Madison, AL 35758
Specialties: Forged Damascus blades and fittings in collectible period pieces. Patterns: Integral art knives, Bowies, folders, American-styled blades and miniatures. Technical: Forges carbon steel and his Damascus. Prices: $150 to

custom knifemakers

$1800; some to $4500. **Remarks:** Semi retired full-time maker; first knife sold in 1978. **Mark:** Name, bladesmith with horse's head.

BATSON, RICHARD G.,
6591 Waterford Rd, Rixeyville, VA 22737, Phone: 540-937-2318
Specialties: Military, utility and fighting knives in working and presentation grade. **Patterns:** Daggers, combat and utility knives. **Technical:** Grinds O1, 1095 and 440C. Etches and scrimshaws; offers polished, Parkerized finishes. **Prices:** $350 to $1500. **Remarks:** Semi-retired, limit production. First knife sold in 1958. **Mark:** Bat in circle, hand-signed and serial numbered.

BATTS, KEITH,
500 Manning Rd, Hooks, TX 75561, Phone: 903-277-8466, kbatts@cableone.net
Specialties: Working straight knives of his design or to customer specs. **Patterns:** Bowies, hunters, skinners, camp knives and others. **Technical:** Forges 5160 and his Damascus; offers filework. **Prices:** $245 to $895. **Remarks:** Part-time maker; first knife sold in 1988. **Mark:** Last name.

BAUCHOP, ROBERT,
PO Box 330, Munster, Kwazulu-Natal 4278, SOUTH AFRICA, Phone: +27 39 3192449
Specialties: Fantasy knives; working and using knives of his design and to customer specs. **Patterns:** Hunters, swords, utility/camp knives, diver's knives and large swords. **Technical:** Grinds Sandvick 12C27, D2, 440C. Uses South African hardwoods red ivory, wild olive, African blackwood, etc. on handles. **Prices:** $200 to $800; some to $2000. **Remarks:** Full-time maker; first knife sold in 1986. Doing business as Bauchop Custom Knives and Swords. **Mark:** Viking helmet with Bauchop (bow and chopper) crest.

BAXTER, DALE,
291 County Rd 547, Trinity, AL 35673, Phone: 256-355-3626, dale@baxterknives.com
Specialties: Bowies, fighters, and hunters. **Patterns:** No patterns: all unique true customs. **Technical:** Hand forge and hand finish. Steels: 1095 and L6 for carbon blades, 1095/L6 for Damascus. **Remarks:** Full-time bladesmith and sold first knife in 1998. **Mark:** Dale Baxter (script) and J.S. on reverse.

BEAM, JOHN R.,
1310 Foothills Rd, Kalispell, MT 59901, Phone: 406-755-2593
Specialties: Classic, high-art and working straight knives of his design. **Patterns:** Bowies and hunters. **Technical:** Grinds 440C, Damascus and scrap. **Prices:** $175 to $600; some to $3000. **Remarks:** Part-time maker; first knife sold in 1950. Doing business as Beam's Knives. **Mark:** Beam's Knives.

BEASLEY, GENEO,
PO Box 339, Wadsworth, NV 89442, Phone: 775-575-2584

BEATTY, GORDON H.,
121 Petty Rd, Seneca, SC 29672, Phone: 864-882-6278
Specialties: Working straight knives, some fancy. **Patterns:** Traditional patterns, mini-skinners and letter openers. **Technical:** Grinds 440C, D2 and ATS-34; makes knives one-at-a-time. **Prices:** $75 to $450. **Remarks:** Part-time maker; first knife sold in 1982. **Mark:** Name.

BEATY, ROBERT B.,
CUTLER, 1995 Big Flat Rd, Missoula, MT 59804, Phone: 406-549-1818
Specialties: Plain and fancy working knives and collector pieces; will accept custom orders. **Patterns:** Hunters, Bowies, utility, kitchen and camp knives; locking folders. **Technical:** Grinds D-2, ATS-34, Dendrite D-2, makes all tool steel Damascus, forges 1095, 5160, 52100. **Prices:** $150 to $600, some to $1100. **Remarks:** Full-time maker; first knife sold 1995. **Mark:** Stainless: First name, middle initial, last name, city and state. Carbon: Last name stamped on Ricasso.

BEAUCHAMP, GAETAN,
125 de la Rivire, Stoneham, PQ, CANADA G3C 0P6, Phone: 418-848-1914, Fax: 418-848-6859, knives@gbeauchamp.ca; Web: www.gbeauchamp.ca
Specialties: Working knives and folders of his design and to customer specs. **Patterns:** Hunters, fighters, fantasy knives. **Technical:** Grinds ATS-34, 440C, Damascus. Scrimshaws on ivory; specializes in buffalo horn and black backgrounds. Offers a variety of handle materials. **Prices:** Start at $250. **Remarks:** Full-time maker; first knife sold in 1992. **Mark:** Signature etched on blade.

BECKER, FRANZ,
AM Kreuzberg 2, 84533, Marktl/Inn, GERMANY 08678-8020
Specialties: Stainless steel knives in working sizes. **Patterns:** Semi- and full-integral knives; interframe folders. **Technical:** Grinds stainless steels; likes natural handle materials. **Prices:** $200 to $2000. **Mark:** Name, country.

BEERS, RAY,
2501 Lakefront Dr, Lake Wales, FL 33898, Phone: 443-841-4143, rbknives@copper.net

BEETS, MARTY,
390 N 5th Ave, Williams Lake, BC, CANADA V2G 2G4, Phone: 250-392-7199
Specialties: Working and collectable straight knives of his own design. **Patterns:** Hunter, skinners, Bowies and utility knives. **Technical:** Grinds various steels-does all his own work including heat treating. Uses a variety of handle material specializing in exotic hardwoods, antler and horn. **Price:** $125 to $400. **Remarks:** Wife, Sandy does handmade/hand stitched sheaths. First knife sold in 1988. Business name Beets Handmade Knives.

BEGG, TODD M.,
420 169 St S, Spanaway, WA 98387, Phone: 253-531-2113, tntbegg@comcast.net Web: www.beggknives.com
Specialties: High-grade tacticle folders and fixed blades. **Patterns:** Folders, integrals, fighters. **Technical:** Specializes in flipper folders using "IK135" bearing system. **Price:** $400 - $15,000. **Remarks:** Uses modern designs and materials.

BEHNKE, WILLIAM,
8478 Dell Rd, Kingsley, MI 49649, Phone: 231-263-7447, bill@billbehnkeknives.com Web: www.billbehnkeknives.com
Specialties: Hunters, belt knives, folders, hatchets and tomahawks. **Patterns:** Traditional styling in moderate-sized straight and folding knives. **Technical:** Forges own Damascus, W-2 and CRU Forge V. **Prices:** $150 to $2000. **Remarks:** Part-time maker. **Mark:** Bill Behnke Knives.

BELL, DON,
Box 98, Lincoln, MT 59639, Phone: 406-362-3208, dlb@linctel.net
Patterns: Folders, hunters and custom orders. **Technical:** Carbon steel 52100, 5160, 1095, 1084. Making own Damascus. Flat grinds. Natural handle material including fossil. ivory, pearl, & ironwork. **Remarks:** Full-time maker. First knife sold in 1999. **Mark:** Last name.

BELL, DONALD,
2 Division St, Bedford, Nova Scotia, CANADA B4A 1Y8, Phone: 902-835-2623, donbell@accesswave.ca; Web: www.bellknives.com
Specialties: Fancy knives: carved and pierced folders of his own design. **Patterns:** Locking folders, pendant knives, jewelry knives. **Technical:** Grinds Damascus, pierces and carves blades. **Prices:** $500 to $2000, some to $3000. **Remarks:** Spare-time maker; first knife sold in 1993. **Mark:** Bell symbol with first initial inside.

BELL, GABRIEL,
88321 North Bank Lane, Coquille, OR 97423, Phone: 541-396-3605, gabriel@dragonflyforge.com; Web: www.dragonflyforge.com & tomboyama.com
Specialties: Full line of combat quality Japanese swords. **Patterns:** Traditional tanto to katana. **Technical:** Handmade steel and welded cable. **Prices:** Swords from bare blades to complete high art $1500 to $28,000. **Remarks:** Studied with father Michael Bell. Instruction in sword crafts. Working in partnership with Michael Bell. **Mark:** Dragonfly in shield or kunitoshi.

BELL, MICHAEL,
88321 N Bank Lane, Coquille, OR 97423, Phone: 541-396-3605, michael@dragonflyforge.com; Web: www. Dragonflyforge.com & tomboyama.com
Specialties: Full line of combat quality Japanese swords. **Patterns:** Traditional tanto to katana. **Technical:** Handmade steel and welded cable. **Prices:** Swords from bare blades to complete high art $1500 to $28,000. **Remarks:** Studied with Japanese master Nakajima Muneyoshi. Instruction in sword crafts. Working in partnership with son, Gabriel. **Mark:** Dragonfly in shield or tombo kunimitsu.

BELL, TONY,
PO Box 24, Woodland, AL 36280, Phone: 256-449-2655, tbell905@aol.com
Specialties: Hand forged period knives and tomahawks. Art knives and knives made for everyday use. **Technical:** Makes own Damascus. Forges 1095, 5160, 1080, L6 steels. Does own heat treating. **Prices:** $75-$1200. **Remarks:** Full time maker. **Mark:** Bell symbol with initial T in the middle.

BENDIK, JOHN,
7076 Fitch Rd, Olmsted Falls, OH 44138

BENJAMIN JR., GEORGE,
3001 Foxy Ln, Kissimmee, FL 34746, Phone: 407-846-7259
Specialties: Fighters in various styles to include Persian, Moro and military. **Patterns:** Daggers, skinners and one-of-a-kind grinds. **Technical:** Forges O1, D2, A2, 5160 and Damascus. Favors Pakkawood, Micarta, and mirror or Parkerized finishes. Makes unique para-military leather sheaths. **Prices:** $150 to $600; some to $1200. **Remarks:** Doing business as The Leather Box. **Mark:** Southern Pride Knives.

BENNETT, BRETT C,
4717 Sullivan St, Cheyenne, WY 82009, Phone: 307-220-3919, brett@bennettknives.com; Web: www.bennettknives.com
Specialties: Hand-rubbed finish on all blades. **Patterns:** Most fixed blade patterns. **Technical:** ATS-34, D-2, 1084/15N20 Damascus, 1084 forged. **Prices:** $100 and up. **Mark:** "B.C. Bennett" in script or "Bennett" stamped in script.

BENNETT, GLEN C,
5821 S Stewart Blvd, Tucson, AZ 85706

BENNETT, PETER,
PO Box 143, Engadine N.S.W. 2233, AUSTRALIA, Phone: 02-520-4975 (home), Fax: 02-528-8219 (work)
Specialties: Fancy and embellished working and using straight knives to customer specs and in standard patterns. **Patterns:** Fighters, hunters, bird/trout and fillet knives. **Technical:** Grinds 440C, ATS-34 and Damascus. Uses rare Australian desert timbers for handles. **Prices:** $90 to $500; some to $1500. **Remarks:** Full-time maker; first knife sold in 1985. **Mark:** First and middle initials, last name; country.

BENNICA, CHARLES,
11 Chemin du Salet, 34190 Moules et Baucels, FRANCE, Phone: +33 4 67 73 42 40, cbennica@bennica-knives.com; Web: www.bennica-knives.com
Specialties: Fixed blades and folding knives; the latter with slick closing mechanisms with push buttons to unlock blades. Unique handle shapes, signature to the maker. **Technical:** 416 stainless steel frames for folders and ATS-34 blades. Also specializes in Damascus.

BENSINGER, J. W.,
583 Jug Brook Rd., Marshfield, VT 05658, Phone: 802-917-1789, jwbensinger@gmail.com Web: www.vermontbladesmith.com
Specialties: Working hunters, bowies for work and defense, and Finnish patterns. Occasional folders. **Technical:** High performance handforged knives in 5160, 52100, 1080, and in-house damascus. **Prices:** Range from $130 for simple bushcraft knives to $500 for larger knives. Damascus prices on request.

Remarks: First knife made in 1980 or so. Full-time maker. Customer designs welcome. **Mark:** "JWB" and year in cursive.

BENSON, DON,
2505 Jackson St #112, Escalon, CA 95320, Phone: 209-838-7921
Specialties: Working straight knives of his design. **Patterns:** Axes, Bowies, tantos and hunters. **Technical:** Grinds 440C. **Prices:** $100 to $150; some to $400. **Remarks:** Spare-time maker; first knife sold in 1980. **Mark:** Name.

BENTLEY, C L,
2405 Hilltop Dr, Albany, GA 31707, Phone: 912-432-6656

BER, DAVE,
656 Miller Rd, San Juan Island, WA 98250, Phone: 206-378-7230
Specialties: Working straight and folding knives for the sportsman; welcomes customer designs. **Patterns:** Hunters, skinners, Bowies, kitchen and fishing knives. **Technical:** Forges and grinds saw blade steel, wire Damascus, O1, L6, 5160 and 440C. **Prices:** $100 to $300; some to $500. **Remarks:** Full-time maker; first knife sold in 1985. **Mark:** Last name.

BERG, LOTHAR,
37 Hillcrest Ln, Kitchener ON, CANADA N2K 1S9, Phone: 519-745-3260; 519-745-3260

BERGER, MAX A.,
5716 John Richard Ct, Carmichael, CA 95608, Phone: 916-972-9229, bergerknives@aol.com
Specialties: Fantasy and working/using straight knives of his design. **Patterns:** Fighters, hunters and utility/camp knives. **Technical:** Grinds ATS-34 and 440C. Offers fileworks and combinations of mirror polish and satin finish blades. **Prices:** $200 to $600; some to $2500. **Remarks:** Part-time maker; first knife sold in 1992. **Mark:** Last name.

BERGH, ROGER,
Dalkarlsa 291, 91598 Bygdea, SWEDEN, Phone: 469-343-0061, knivroger@hotmail.com; Web: www.rogerbergh.com
Specialties: Collectible all-purpose straight-blade knives. Damascus steel blades, carving and artistic design knives are heavily influenced by nature and have an organic hand crafted feel.

BERGLIN, BRUCE,
17441 Lake Terrace Place, Mount Vernon, WA 98274, Phone: 360-422-8603, bruce@berglins.com
Specialties: Working and using fixed blades and folders of his own design. **Patterns:** Hunters, boots, bowies, utility, liner locks and slip joints some with vintage finish. **Technical:** Forges carbon steel, grinds carbon steel. Prefers natural handle material. **Prices:** Start at $300. **Remarks:** Part-time maker since 1998. **Mark:** (2 marks) Last name; First initial. Second initial & Last name, surrounded with an oval.

BERTOLAMI, JUAN CARLOS,
Av San Juan 575, Neuquen, ARGENTINA 8300, fliabertolami@infovia.com.ar
Specialties: Hunting and country labor knives. All of them unique high quality pieces and supplies collectors too. **Technical:** Austrian stainless steel and elephant, hippopotamus and orca ivory, as well as ebony and other fine woods for the handles.

BERTUZZI, ETTORE,
Via Partigiani 3, 24068 Seriate (Bergamo), ITALY, Phone: 035-294262, Fax: 035-294262
Specialties: Classic straight knives and folders of his design, to customer specs and in standard patterns. **Patterns:** Bowies, hunters and locking folders. **Technical:** Grinds ATS-34, D3, D2 and various Damascus. **Prices:** $300 to $500. **Remarks:** Part-time maker; first knife sold in 1993. **Mark:** Name etched on ricasso.

BESEDICK, FRANK E,
1257 Country Club Road, Monongahela, PA 15063-1057, Phone: 724-292-8016, bxtr.bez3@verizon.net
Specialties: Traditional working and using straight knives of his design. **Patterns:** Hunters, utility/camp knives and miniatures; buckskinner blades and tomahawks. **Technical:** Forges and grinds 5160, O1 and Damascus. Offers filework and scrimshaw. **Prices:** $75 to $300; some to $750. **Remarks:** Part-time maker; first knife sold in 1990. **Mark:** Name or initials.

BESHARA, BRENT (BESH),
PO BOX 557, Holyrood, NL, CANADA A0A 2R0, Phone: 705-428-3152, BESH@beshknives.com Web: www.beshknives.com
Specialties: Fixed blade tools and knives. **Patterns:** BESH Wedge tools and knives. **Technical:** Custom design work, grinds 0-1, D-2, 440C, 154cm. Offers kydex sheathing **Prices:** Start at $250. **Remarks:** Inventor of BESH Wedge geometry, custom maker and designer since 2000. Retired (24yrs) Special Forces, Special Operations Navy bomb disposal diver. Lifelong martial artist. **Mark:** "BESH" stamped.

BEST, RON,
1489 Adams Lane, Stokes, NC 27884, Phone: 252-714-1264, ronbestknives@msn.com; Web: www.ronbestknives.com
Specialties: All integral fixed blades, interframe. **Patterns:** Bowies, hunters, fighters, fantasy, daggers & swords. **Technical:** Grinds 440C, D-2 and ATS-34. **Prices:** $600 to $8000.

BETANCOURT, ANTONIO L.,
5718 Beefwood Ct., St. Louis, MO 63129, Phone: 314-306-1869, bet2001@charter.net
Specialties: One-of-a-kind fixed blades and art knives. **Patterns:** Hunters and Bowies with embellished handles. **Technical:** Uses cast sterling silver and lapidary with fine gemstones, fossil ivory, and scrimshaw. Grinds Damascus

and 440C. **Prices:** $100 to $800. **Remarks:** Part-time maker, first knife sold in 1974. **Mark:** Initials in cursive.

BEUKES, TINUS,
83 Henry St, Risiville, Vereeniging 1939, SOUTH AFRICA, Phone: 27 16 423 2053
Specialties: Working straight knives. **Patterns:** Hunters, skinners and kitchen knives. **Technical:** Grinds D2, 440C and chain, cable and stainless Damascus. **Prices:** $80 to $180. **Remarks:** Part-time maker; first knife sold in 1993. **Mark:** Full name, city, logo.

BEVERLY II, LARRY H,
PO Box 741, Spotsylvania, VA 22553, Phone: 540-898-3951
Specialties: Working straight knives, slip-joints and liner locks. Welcomes customer designs. **Patterns:** Bowies, hunters, guardless fighters and miniatures. **Technical:** Grinds 440C, A2 and O1. **Prices:** $125 to $1000. **Remarks:** Part-time maker; first knife sold in 1986. **Mark:** Initials or last name in script.

BEZUIDENHOUT, BUZZ,
PO BOX 28284, Malvern, KZN, SOUTH AFRICA 4055, Phone: 031-4632827, Fax: 031-4632827, buzzbee@mweb.co.za
Specialties: Working and Fancy Folders, my or customer design. **Patterns:** Boots, hunters, kitchen knives and utility/camp knives. **Technical:** Use 12-C-27 + stainless damascus, some carbon damascus. Uses local hardwoods, horn: kudu, impala, buffalo, giraffe bone and ivory for handles. **Prices:** $250 to upscale. **Remarks:** Part-time maker; first knife sold in 1985. Member S.A. Knife Makers Guild **Mark:** First name with a bee emblem.

BIGGERS, GARY,
VENTURA KNIVES, 1278 Colina Vista, Ventura, CA 93003, Phone: 805-658-6610, Fax: 805-658-6610
Specialties: Fixed blade knives of his design. **Patterns:** Hunters, boots/fighters, Bowies and utility knives. **Technical:** Grinds ATS-34, O1 and commercial Damascus. **Prices:** $150 to $550. **Remarks:** Part-time maker: first knife sold in 1996. Doing business as Ventura Knives. **Mark:** First and last name, city and state.

BILLGREN, PER,
Stallgatan 9, S815 76 Soderfors, SWEDEN, Phone: +46 293 30600, Fax: +46 293 30124, mail@damasteel.se Web:www.damasteel.se
Specialties: Damasteel, stainless Damascus steels. **Patterns:** Bluetongue, Heimskringla, Muhammad's ladder, Rose, Twist, Odin's eye, Vinland, Hakkapelliitta. **Technical:** Modern Damascus steel made by patented powder metallurgy method. **Prices:** $80 to $180. **Remarks:** Damasteel is available through distributors around the globe.

BINGENHEIMER, BRUCE,
553 Tiffany Dr., Spring Creek, NV 89815, Phone: 775-934-6295, mbing@citlink.net
Specialties: Forging fixed blade hunters, bowies, fighters. **Technical:** Forges own Damascus. Steel choices 5160, 1084. Damascus steels 15N20, 1080. **Prices:** $300 and up. **Remarks:** ABS Journeyman Smith 2010. Member of Montana Knife Makers Association and Oregon Knife Collector's Association. **Mark:** Bingenheimer (arched over) M B.

BIRDWELL, IRA LEE,
PO Box 1448, Congress, AZ 85332, Phone: 928-925-3258, heli.ira@gmail.com
Specialties: Special orders. **Mark:** Engraved signature.

BISH, HAL,
9347 Sweetbriar Trace, Jonesboro, GA 30236, Phone: 770-477-2422, hal-bish@hp.com

BISHER, WILLIAM (BILL),
1015 Beck Road, Denton, NC 27239, Phone: 336-859-4686, blackturtleforge@wildblue.net;Web: www.blackturtleforge.com
Specialties: Period pieces, also contemporary belt knives, friction folders. **Patterns:** Own design, hunters, camp/utility, Bowies, belt axes, neck knives, carving sets. **Technical:** Forges straight high carbon steels, and own Damascus, grinds ATS34 and 154CM. Uses natural handle materials (wood, bone, stag horn), micarta and stabilized wood. **Prices:** Starting at $75 - $2500. **Remarks:** Past president of North Carolina Custom Knifemakers Guild, member ABS, Full-time maker as of 2007, first knife made 1989, all work in house, blades and sheaths **Mark:** Last name under crown and turtle

BIZZELL, ROBERT,
145 Missoula Ave, Butte, MT 59701, Phone: 406-782-4403, patternweld@yahoo.com
Specialties: Damascus Bowies. **Patterns:** Composite, mosaic and traditional. **Technical:** Fixed blades & LinerLock® folders. **Prices:** Fixed blades start at $275. Folders start at $500. **Remarks:** Currently not taking orders. **Mark:** Hand signed.

BLACK, EARL,
3466 South, 700 East, Salt Lake City, UT 84106, Phone: 801-466-8395
Specialties: High-art straight knives and folders; period pieces. **Patterns:** Boots, Bowies and daggers; lockers and gents. **Technical:** Grinds 440C and 154CM. Buys some Damascus. Scrimshaws and engraves. **Prices:** $200 to $1800; some to $2500 and higher. **Remarks:** Full-time maker; first knife sold in 1980. **Mark:** Name, city, state.

BLACK, SCOTT,
27100 Leetown Rd, Picayune, MS 39466, Phone: 601-799-5939, copperheadforge@telepak.net
Specialties: Friction folders; fighters. **Patterns:** Bowies, fighters, hunters, smoke hawks, friction folders, daggers. **Technical:** All forged, all work done by him, own hand-stitched leather work; own heat-treating. **Prices:** $100 to $2200. **Remarks:** ABS Journeyman Smith. Cabel / Damascus/ High Carbone.

BLACK—BOOCO

Mark: Hot Mark - Copperhead Snake.

BLACK, TOM,
921 Grecian NW, Albuquerque, NM 87107, Phone: 505-344-2549, blackknives@comcast.net
Specialties: Working knives to fancy straight knives of his design. **Patterns:** Drop-point skinners, folders, using knives, Bowies and daggers. **Technical:** Grinds 440C, 154CM, ATS-34, A2, D2 and Damascus. Offers engraving and scrimshaw. **Prices:** $250 and up; some over $8500. **Remarks:** Full-time maker; first knife sold in 1970. **Mark:** Name, city.

BLACKWELL, ZANE,
PO BOX 234, Eden, TX 76837, Phone: 325-869-8821, blackwellknives@hotmail.com
Specialties: Hunters and slipjoint folders. **Patterns:** Drop point fixed-blade hunter and classic slipjoint patterns. **Prices:** Hunters start at $200, folders at $250. **Mark:** Name and Eden, Texas.

BLACKWOOD, NEIL,
617 East Carter Rd, Lakeland, FL 33813, Phone: 863-701-4305, nblackwood4@gmail.com; Web: www.blackwoodcustomknives.blogspot.com
Specialties: Fixed blades and tactical folders. **Technical:** Blade steels D2 Talonite, Stellite, CPM S30V and RWL 34. Handle materials: G-10 carbon fiber and Micarta in the synthetics: giraffe bone and exotic woods on the natural side. **Prices:** $1000 to $1500. **Remarks:** Makes everything from the frames to the stop pins, pivot pins: everything but the stainless screws; one factory/custom collaboration (the Hybrid Hunter) with Outdoor Edge is in place and negotiations are under way for one with Benchmade. Collaborations with Boker. **Mark:** Blackwood

BLANCHARD, G R (GARY),
PO BOX 292, Dandridge, TN 37725, Phone: 865-397-9515, blanchardcustomknives@yahoo.com; Web: www.blanchardcustomknives.com
Specialties: Fancy folders with patented button blade release and high-art straight knives of his design. **Patterns:** Boots, daggers and locking folders. **Technical:** Grinds 440C and ATS-34 and Damascus. Engraves his knives. **Prices:** $1000 to $15,000 or more. **Remarks:** Full-time maker; first knife sold in 1989. **Mark:** First and middle initials, last name or last name only.

BLAUM, ROY,
319 N Columbia St, Covington, LA 70433, Phone: 985-893-1060
Specialties: Working straight knives and folders of his design; lightweight easy-open folders. **Patterns:** Hunters, boots, fishing and woodcarving/whittling knives. **Technical:** Grinds A2, D2, O1, 154CM and ATS-34. Offers leatherwork. **Prices:** $40 to $800; some higher. **Remarks:** Full-time maker; first knife sold in 1976. **Mark:** Engraved signature or etched logo.

BLOODWORTH CUSTOM KNIVES,
3502 W. Angelica Dr., Meridian, ID 83646, Phone: 208-888-7778
Patterns: Working straight knives, hunters, skinners, bowies, utility knives of his designs or customer specs. Scagel knives. Period knives and traditional frontier knives and sheaths. **Technical:** Grinds D2, ATS34, 154CM, 5160, 01, Damascus, Heat treats, natural and composite handle materials. **Prices:** $185.00 to $1,500. **Remarks:** Roger Smith knife maker. Full-time maker; first knife sold in 1978 **Mark:** Sword over BLOODWORTH.

BLOOMER, ALAN T,
PO Box 154, 116 E 6th St, Maquon, IL 61458, Phone: 309-875-3583 Cell: 309-371-8520, alant.bloomer@winco.net
Specialties: Folders & straight knives & custom pen maker. **Patterns:** All kinds. **Technical:** Does own heat treating. **Prices:** $400 to $1000. **Remarks:** Part-time maker. No orders. **Mark:** Stamp Bloomer.

BLUM, KENNETH,
1729 Burleson, Brenham, TX 77833, Phone: 979-836-9577
Specialties: Traditional working straight knives of his design. **Patterns:** Camp knives, hunters and Bowies. **Technical:** Forges 5160; grinds 440C and D2. Uses exotic woods and Micarta for handles. **Prices:** $150 to $300. **Remarks:** Part-time maker; first knife sold in 1978. **Mark:** Last name on ricasso.

BLYSTONE, RONALD L.,
231 Bailey Road, Creekside, PA 15732, Phone: 724-397-2671, taxibly@hotmail.com
Specialties: Traditional forged working knives. **Patterns:** Hunting utility and skinners of his own design. **Technical:** Forges his own pattern welded Damascus using carbon steel. **Prices:** Starting at $150. **Remarks:** Spare-time maker. **Mark:** Initials - upsidedown R against the B, inside a circle, over the word FORGE

BOARDMAN, GUY,
39 Mountain Ridge R, New Germany 3619, SOUTH AFRICA, Phone: 031-726-921
Specialties: American and South African-styles. **Patterns:** Bowies, American and South African hunters, plus more. **Technical:** Grinds Bohler steels, some ATS-34. **Prices:** $100 to $600. **Remarks:** Part-time maker; first knife sold in 1986. **Mark:** Name, city, country.

BOCHMAN, BRUCE,
183 Howard Place, Grants Pass, OR 97526, Phone: 541-471-1985, 183bab@gmail.com
Specialties: Hunting, fishing, bird and tactical knives. **Patterns:** Hunters, fishing and bird knives. **Technical:** ATS34, 154CM, mirror or satin finish. Damascus. **Prices:** $250 to $350; some to $750. **Remarks:** Part-time maker; first knife sold in 1977. **Mark:** Custom Knives by B. Bochman

BODEN, HARRY,
Via Gellia Mill, Bonsall Matlock, Derbyshire DE4 2AJ, ENGLAND, Phone: 0629-825176
Specialties: Traditional working straight knives and folders of his design. **Patterns:** Hunters, locking folders and utility/camp knives. **Technical:** Grinds Sandvik 12C27, D2 and O1. **Prices:** £70 to £150; some to £300. **Remarks:** Full-time maker; first knife sold in 1986. **Mark:** Full name.

BODNER, GERALD "JERRY",
4102 Spyglass Ct, Louisville, KY 40229, Phone: 502-968-5946
Specialties: Fantasy straight knives in standard patterns. **Patterns:** Bowies, fighters, hunters and micro-miniature knives. **Technical:** Grinds Damascus, 440C and D2. Offers filework. **Prices:** $35 to $180. **Remarks:** Part-time maker; first knife sold in 1993. **Mark:** Last name in script and JAB in oval above knives.

BODOLAY, ANTAL,
Rua Wilson Soares Fernandes #31, Planalto, Belo Horizonte MG-31730-700, BRAZIL, Phone: 031-494-1885
Specialties: Working folders and fixed blades of his design or to customer specs; some art daggers and period pieces. **Patterns:** Daggers, hunters, locking folders, utility knives and Khukris. **Technical:** Grinds D6, high-carbon steels and 420 stainless. Forges files on request. **Prices:** $30 to $350. **Remarks:** Full-time maker; first knife sold in 1965. **Mark:** Last name in script.

BOEHLKE, GUENTER,
Parkstrasse 2, 56412 Grossholbach, GERMANY 2602-5440, Boehlke-Messer@t-online.de; Web: www.boehlke-messer.de
Specialties: Classic working/using straight knives of his design. **Patterns:** Hunters, utility/camp knives and ancient remakes. **Technical:** Grinds Damascus, CPM-T-440V and 440C. Inlays gemstones and ivory. **Prices:** $220 to $700; some to $2000. **Remarks:** Spare-time maker; first knife sold in 1985. **Mark:** Name, address and bow and arrow.

BOGUSZEWSKI, PHIL,
PO Box 99329, Lakewood, WA 98499, Phone: 253-581-7096, knives01@aol.com
Specialties: Working folders—some fancy—mostly of his design. **Patterns:** Folders, slip-joints and lockers; also makes anodized titanium frame folders. **Technical:** Grinds BG42 and Damascus; offers filework. **Prices:** $550 to $3000. **Remarks:** Full-time maker; first knife sold in 1979. **Mark:** Name, city and state.

BOHRMANN, BRUCE,
61 Portland St, Yarmouth, ME 04096, Phone: 207-846-3385, bbohr@maine.rr.com; Web: Bohrmannknives.com
Specialties: Fixed blade sporting, camping, hunting knives. **Technical:** 440c. Stock removal. Hardened to 58-60 rockwell. **Prices:** Swords from bare blades to complete high art $1500 to $28,000. ALSO special "Heritage" production using historic certified woods (from washintons', Jeffersons', Madisons', Henry Plantations; 45,000-50,000 year old Kauri wood from New Zealand - $1250. **Remarks:** Full-time maker. First knife made in 1955. **Mark:** The letter "B" connected to and lying beneath deer antlers.

BOJTOS, ARPAD,
Dobsinskeho 10, 98403 Lucenec, SLOVAKIA, Phone: 00421-47 4333512; Cell: 00421-91 5875066, botjos@stonline.sk; Web: www.arpadbojtos.sk
Specialties: Art knives. **Patterns:** Daggers, fighters and hunters. **Technical:** Grinds ATS-34. Carves on steel, handle materials and sheaths. **Prices:** $5000 to $10,000; some over. **Remarks:** Full-time maker; first knife sold in 1990. **Mark:** AB.

BOLEWARE, DAVID,
PO Box 96, Carson, MS 39427, Phone: 601-943-5372
Specialties: Traditional and working/using straight knives of his design, to customer specs and in standard patterns. **Patterns:** Bowies, hunters and utility/camp knives. **Technical:** Grinds ATS-34, 440C and Damascus. **Prices:** $85 to $350; some to $600. **Remarks:** Part-time maker; first knife sold in 1989. **Mark:** First and last name, city, state.

BOLEY, JAMIE,
PO Box 477, Parker, SD 57053, Phone: 605-297-0014, jamie@polarbearforge.com
Specialties: Working knives and historical influenced reproductions. **Patterns:** Hunters, skinners, scramasaxes, and others. **Technical:** Forges 5160, O1, L6, 52100, W1, W2 makes own Damascus. **Prices:** Starts at $125. **Remarks:** Part-time maker. **Mark:** Polar bear paw print with name on the left side and Polar Bear Forge on the right.

BONASSI, FRANCO,
Via Nicoletta 4, Pordenone 33170, ITALY, Phone: 0434-550821, frank.bonassi@alice.it
Specialties: Fancy and working one-of-a-kind folder knives of his design. **Patterns:** Folders, linerlocks and back locks. **Technical:** Grinds CPM, ATS-34, 154CM and commercial Damascus. Uses only titanium foreguards and pommels. **Prices:** Start at $350. **Remarks:** Spare-time maker; first knife sold in 1988. Has made cutlery for several celebrities; Gen. Schwarzkopf, Fuzzy Zoeller, etc. **Mark:** FRANK.

BOOCO, GORDON,
175 Ash St, PO Box 174, Hayden, CO 81639, Phone: 970-276-3195
Specialties: Fancy working straight knives of his design and to customer specs. **Patterns:** Hunters and Bowies. **Technical:** Grinds 440C, D2 and A2. Heat-treats. **Prices:** $150 to $350; some $600 and higher. **Remarks:** Part-time maker; first knife sold in 1984. **Mark:** Last name with push dagger artwork.

BOOS, RALPH,
6018-37A Avenue NW, Edmonton, Alberta, CANADA T6L 1H4, Phone: 780-463-7094
Specialties: Classic, fancy and fantasy miniature knives and swords of his design or to customer specs. **Patterns:** Bowies, daggers and swords. **Technical:** Hand files O1, stainless and Damascus. Engraves and carves. Does heat bluing and acid etching. **Prices:** $125 to $350; some to $1000. **Remarks:** Part-time maker; first knife sold in 1982. **Mark:** First initials back to back.

BOOTH, PHILIP W,
301 S Jeffery Ave, Ithaca, MI 48847, Phone: 989-875-2844, Web: wwwphilipbooth.com
Specialties: Folding knives of his design using various mechanisms. **Patterns:** "Minnow" folding knives, a series of small folding knives started in 1996 and changing yearly. One of a kind hot-rod car themed folding knives. **Technical:** Grinds ATS-34, 1095 and commercial Damascus. Offers gun blue finishes and file work. **Prices:** $200 and up. **Remarks:** Part-time maker, first knife sold in 1991. **Mark:** Last name or name with city and map logo.

BORGER, WOLF,
Benzstrasse 8, 76676 Graben-Neudorf, GERMANY, Phone: 07255-72303, Fax: 07255-72304, wolf@messerschmied.de; Web: www.messerschmied.de
Specialties: High-tech working and using straight knives and folders, many with corkscrews or other tools, of his design. **Patterns:** Hunters, Bowies and folders with various locking systems. **Technical:** Grinds 440C, ATS-34 and CPM. Uses stainless Damascus. **Prices:** $250 to $900; some to $1500. **Remarks:** Full-time maker; first knife sold in 1975. **Mark:** Howling wolf and name; first name on Damascus blades.

BOSE, REESE,
PO Box 61, Shelburn, IN 47879, Phone: 812-397-5114
Specialties: Traditional working and using knives in standard patterns and multi-blade folders. **Patterns:** Multi-blade slip-joints. **Technical:** ATS-34, D2 and CPM 440V. **Prices:** $275 to $1500. **Remarks:** Full-time maker; first knife sold in 1992. Photos by Jack Busfield. **Mark:** R. Bose.

BOSE, TONY,
7252 N. County Rd, 300 E., Shelburn, IN 47879-9778, Phone: 812-397-5114
Specialties: Traditional working and using knives in standard patterns; multi-blade folders. **Patterns:** Multi-blade slip-joints. **Technical:** Grinds commercial Damascus, ATS-34 and D2. **Prices:** $400 to $1200. **Remarks:** Full-time maker; first knife sold in 1972. **Mark:** First initial, last name, city, state.

BOSSAERTS, CARL,
Rua Albert Einstein 906, 14051-110, Ribeirao Preto, S.P., BRAZIL, Phone: 016 633 7063
Specialties: Working and using straight knives of his design, to customer specs and in standard patterns. **Patterns:** Hunters, fighters and utility/camp knives. **Technical:** Grinds ATS-34, 440V and 440C; does filework. **Prices:** 60 to $400. **Remarks:** Part-time maker; first knife sold in 1992. **Mark:** Initials joined together.

BOST, ROGER E,
30511 Cartier Dr, Palos Verdes, CA 90275-5629, Phone: 310- 541-6833, rogerbost@cox.net
Specialties: Hunters, fighters, boot, utility. **Patterns:** Loveless-style. **Technical:** ATS-34, 60-61RC, stock removal and forge. **Prices:** $300 and up. **Remarks:** First knife sold in 1990. Cal. Knifemakers Assn., ABS. **Mark:** Diamond with initials inside and Palos Verdes California around outside.

BOSWORTH, DEAN,
329 Mahogany Dr, Key Largo, FL 33037, Phone: 305-451-1564, DLBOZ@bellsouth.net
Specialties: Free hand hollow ground working knives with hand rubbed satin finish, filework and inlays. **Patterns:** Bird and Trout, hunters, skinners, fillet, Bowies, miniatures. **Technical:** Using 440C, ATS-34, D2, Meier Damascus, custom wet formed sheaths. **Prices:** $250 and up. **Remarks:** Part-time maker; first knife made in 1985. Member Florida Knifemakers Assoc. **Mark:** BOZ stamped in block letters.

BOURBEAU, JEAN YVES,
15 Rue Remillard, Notre Dame, Ile Perrot, Quebec, CANADA J7V 8M9, Phone: 514-453-1069
Specialties: Fancy/embellished and fantasy folders of his design. **Patterns:** Bowies, fighters and locking folders. **Technical:** Grinds 440C, ATS-34 and Damascus. Carves precious wood for handles. **Prices:** $150 to $1000. **Remarks:** Part-time maker; first knife sold in 1994. **Mark:** Interlaced initials.

BOWLES, CHRIS,
PO Box 985, Reform, AL 35481, Phone: 205-375-6162
Specialties: Working/using straight knives, and period pieces. **Patterns:** Utility, tactical, hunting, neck knives, machetes, and swords. **Grinds:** 0-1, 154 cm, BG-42, 440V. **Prices:** $50 to $400 some higher. **Remarks:** Full-time maker. **Mark:** Bowles stamped or Bowles etched in script.

BOXER, BO,
LEGEND FORGE, 6477 Hwy 93 S #134, Whitefish, MT 59937, Phone: 505-799-0173, legendforge@aol.com; Web: www.legendforgesknives.com
Specialties: Handmade hunting knives, Damascus hunters. Most are antler handled. Also, hand forged Damascus steel. **Patterns:** Hunters and Bowies. **Prices:** $125 to $2500 on some very exceptional Damascus knives. Remarks: Makes his own custom leather sheath stamped with maker stamp. His knives are used by the outdoorsman of the Smoky Mountains, North Carolina, and the Rockies of Montana and New Mexico. Spends one-half of the year in Montana and the other part of the year in Taos, New Mexico. **Mark:** The name "Legend Forge" hand engraved on every blade.

BOYD, FRANCIS,
1811 Prince St, Berkeley, CA 94703, Phone: 510-841-7210
Specialties: Folders and kitchen knives, Japanese swords. **Patterns:** Push-button sturdy locking folders; San Francisco-style chef's knives. **Technical:** Forges and grinds; mostly uses high-carbon steels. **Prices:** Moderate to heavy. **Remarks:** Designer. **Mark:** Name.

BOYE, DAVID,
PO Box 1238, Dolan Springs, AZ 86441, Phone: 800-853-1617, Fax: 928-767-4273, boye@cltlink.net; Web: www.boyeknives.com
Specialties: Folders and Boye Basics. Forerunner in the use of dendritic steel and dendritic cobalt for blades. **Patterns:** Lockback folders and fixed blade sheath knives in cobalt. **Technical:** Casts blades in cobalt. **Prices:** From $129 to $360. **Remarks:** Part-time maker; author of Step-by-Step Knifemaking. **Mark:** Name.

BOYES, TOM,
2505 Wallace Lake Rd., West Bend, WI 53090, Phone: 262-391-2172
Specialties: Hunters, working knives. **Technical:** Grinds ATS-34, 440C, O1 tool steel and Damascus. **Prices:** $60 to $1000. **Remarks:** First knife sold in 1998. Doing business as R. Boyes Knives.

BOYSEN, RAYMOND A,
125 E St Patrick, Rapid Ciy, SD 57701, Phone: 605-341-7752
Specialties: Hunters and Bowies. **Technical:** High performance blades forged from 52100 and 5160. **Prices:** $200 and up. **Remarks:** American Bladesmith Society Journeyman Smith. Part-time bladesmith. **Mark:** BOYSEN.

BRACKETT, JAMIN,
PO Box 387, Fallston, NC 28042, Phone: 704-718-3304, jaminbrackett@bellsouth.net; Web: brackettknives.com
Specialties: Hunting, camp, fishing, tactical, and general outdoor use. Handmade of my own design or to customer specs. **Patterns:** Drop point, tanto, fillet, and small EDC the "Tadpole", as well as large camp and tactical knives. **Technical:** Stock removal method, ATS-34 steel cryogenically treated to HRC 59-6. Mirror polish and bead blasted finishes. Handle materials include exotic woods, stag, buffalo horn, colored laminates, Micarta, and G-10. Come hand stitched 8-9 OZ leather sheaths treated in beeswax saddle oil mixture. Tactical models include reinforced tactical nylon sheaths Mollie system compatible. **Prices:** Standard models $150-$325. Personalized engraving available, for gifts and special occasions. **Remarks:** Part-time maker. First knife made in 2009. Member of NC Custom Knifemakers Guild. **Mark:** "Brackett", in bold. Each knife and sheath numbered.

BRADBURN, GARY,
BRADBURN CUSTOM CUTLERY, 1714 Park Place, Wichita, KS 67203, Phone: 316-640-5684, gary@bradburnknives.com; Web: www.bradburnknives.com
Specialties: Specialize in clay-tempered Japanese-style knives and swords. **Patterns:** Also Bowies and fighters. **Technical:** Forge and/or grind carbon steel only. **Prices:** $150 to $1200. **Mark:** Initials GB stylized to look like Japanese character.

BRADFORD, GARRICK,
582 Guelph St, Kitchener ON, CANADA N2H-5Y4, Phone: 519-576-9863

BRADLEY, DENNIS,
178 Bradley Acres Rd, Blairsville, GA 30512, Phone: 706-745-4364, bzbtaz@brmemc.net Web: www.dennisbradleyknives.com
Specialties: Working straight knives and folders, some high-art. **Patterns:** Hunters, boots and daggers; slip-joints and two-blades. **Technical:** Grinds ATS-34, D2, 440C and commercial Damascus. **Prices:** $100 to $500; some to $2000. **Remarks:** Part-time maker; first knife sold in 1973. **Mark:** BRADLEY KNIVES in double heart logo.

BRADLEY, JOHN,
PO Box 33, Pomona Park, FL 32181, Phone: 386-649-4739, johnbradleyknives@yahoo.com
Specialties: Fixed-blade using and art knives; primitive folders. **Patterns:** Skinners, Bowies, camp knives and primitive knives. **Technical:** Forged and ground 52100, 1095, O1 and Damascus. **Prices:** $250 to $2000. **Remarks:** Full-time maker; first knife sold in 1988. **Mark:** Last name.

BRANDSEY, EDWARD P,
4441 Hawkridge Ct, Janesville, WI 53546, Phone: 608-868-9010, ebrandsey@centurytel.net
Patterns: Large bowies, hunters, neck knives and buckskinner-styles. Native American influence on some. An occasional tanto, art piece. Does own scrimshaw. See Egnath's second book. Now making locking liner folders. **Technical:** ATS-34, CPM154, 440-C, O-1, and some Damascus. Paul Bos treating past 20 years. **Prices:** $350 to $800; some to $4000. **Remarks:** Full-time maker. First knife sold in 1973. **Mark:** Initials connected - registered Wisc. Trademark since March 1983.

BRANDT, MARTIN W,
833 Kelly Blvd, Springfield, OR 97477, Phone: 541-747-5422, oubob747@aol.com

BRANTON, ROBERT,
PO BOX 807, Awendaw, SC 29429, Phone: 843-928-3624, www.brantonknives.com
Specialties: Working straight knives of his design or to customer specs; throwing knives. **Patterns:** Hunters, fighters and some miniatures. **Technical:** Grinds ATS-34, A2 and 1050; forges 5160, O1. Offers hollow- or convex-grinds. **Prices:** $25 to $400. **Remarks:** Part-time maker; first knife sold in 1985. Doing business as Pro-Flyte, Inc. **Mark:** Last name; or first and last name, city, state.

BRASCHLER, CRAIG W.,
HC4 Box 667, Doniphan, MO 63935, Phone: 573-996-5058
Specialties: Art knives, Bowies, utility hunters, slip joints, miniatures, engraving. **Technical:** Flat grinds. Does own selective heat treating. Does own engraving. **Prices:** Starting at $200. **Remarks:** Full-time maker since 2003. **Mark:** Braschler over Martin Oval stamped.

BRATCHER, BRETT,
11816 County Rd 302, Plantersville, TX 77363, Phone: 936-894-3788, Fax: (936) 894-3790, brett_bratcher@msn.com
Specialties: Hunting and skinning knives. **Patterns:** Clip and drop point. Hand forged. **Technical:** Material 5160, D2, 1095 and Damascus. **Price:** $200 to $500. **Mark:** Bratcher.

BRAY JR., W LOWELL,
6931 Manor Beach Rd, New Port Richey, FL 34652, Phone: 727-846-0830, brayknives@aol.com Web: www.brayknives.com
Specialties: Traditional working and using straight knives and collector pieces. **Patterns:** One of a kind pieces, hunters, fighters and utility knives. **Technical:** Grinds 440C and ATS-34; forges 52100 and Damascus. **Prices:** $125 to $800. **Remarks:** Spare-time maker; first knife sold in 1992. **Mark:** Lowell Bray Knives in shield or Bray Primative in shield.

BREED, KIM,
733 Jace Dr, Clarksville, TN 37040, Phone: 931-980-4956, sfbreed@yahoo.com
Specialties: High end through working folders and straight knives. **Patterns:** Hunters, fighters, daggers, Bowies. His design or customers. Likes one-of-a-kind designs. **Technical:** Makes own Mosaic and regular Damascus, but will use stainless steels. Offers filework and sculpted material. **Prices:** $150 to $2000. **Remarks:** Full-time maker. First knife sold in 1990. **Mark:** Last name.

BREND, WALTER,
4094 Columbia Hwy., Ridge Springs, SC 29129, Phone: 256-736-3520, walterbrend@hotmail.com Web: www.brendknives.com
Specialties: Tactical-style knives, fighters, automatics. **Technical:** Grinds D-Z and 440C blade steels, 154CM steel. **Prices:** Micarta handles, titanium handles.

BRENNAN, JUDSON,
PO Box 1165, Delta Junction, AK 99737, Phone: 907-895-5153, Fax: 907-895-5404
Specialties: Period pieces. **Patterns:** All kinds of Bowies, rifle knives, daggers. **Technical:** Forges miscellaneous steels. **Prices:** Upscale, good value. **Remarks:** Muzzle-loading gunsmith; first knife sold in 1978. **Mark:** Name.

BRESHEARS, CLINT,
1261 Keats, Manhattan Beach, CA 90266, Phone: 310-372-0739, Fax: 310-372-0739, breshears1@verizon.net; Web: www.clintknives.com
Specialties: Working straight knives and folders. **Patterns:** Hunters, Bowies and survival knives. Folders are mostly hunters. **Technical:** Grinds 440C, 154CM and ATS-34; prefers mirror finishes. **Prices:** $125 to $750; some to $1800. **Remarks:** Part-time maker; first knife sold in 1978. **Mark:** First name.

BREUER, LONNIE,
PO Box 877384, Wasilla, AK 99687-7384
Specialties: Fancy working straight knives. **Patterns:** Hunters, camp knives and axes, folders and Bowies. **Technical:** Grinds 440C, AEB-L and D2; likes wire inlay, scrimshaw, decorative filing. **Prices:** $60 to $150; some to $300. **Remarks:** Part-time maker; first knife sold in 1977. **Mark:** Signature.

BREWER, CRAIG,
425 White Cedar, Killeen, TX 76542, Phone: 254-634-6934, craig6@embargmail.com
Specialties: Folders; slip joints, some lock backs and an occasional liner lock. **Patterns:** I like the old traditional patterns. **Technical:** Grinds CPM steels most being CPM-154, 1095 for carbon and some Damascus. **Prices:** $350 and up. **Remarks:** Full-time maker, first knife sold in 2005. **Mark:** BREWER.

BRITTON, TIM,
PO Box 71, Bethania, NC 27010, Phone: 366-923-2062, timbritton@yahoo.com; Web: www.timbritton.com
Specialties: Small and simple working knives, sgian dubhs, slip joint folders and special tactical designs. **Technical:** Forges and grinds stainless steel. **Prices:** $165 to ???. **Remarks:** Veteran knifemaker. **Mark:** Etched signature.

BROADWELL, DAVID,
PO Box 4314, Wichita Falls, TX 76308, Phone: 940-782-4442, david@broadwellstudios.com; Web: www.broadwellstudios.com
Specialties: Sculpted high-art straight and folding knives. **Patterns:** Daggers, sub-hilted fighters, folders, sculpted art knives and some Bowies. **Technical:** Grinds mostly Damascus; carves; prefers natural handle materials, including stone. Some embellishment. **Prices:** $500 to $4000; some higher. **Remarks:** Full-time maker since 1989; first knife sold in 1981. **Mark:** Stylized emblem bisecting "B"/with last name below.

BROCK, KENNETH L,
PO Box 375, 207 N Skinner Rd, Allenspark, CO 80510, Phone: 303-747-2547, brockknives@nedernet.net
Specialties: Custom designs, full-tang working knives and button lock folders of his design. **Patterns:** Hunters, miniatures and minis. **Technical:** Flat-grinds D2 and 440C; makes own sheaths; heat-treats. **Prices:** $75 to $800. **Remarks:** Full-time maker; first knife sold in 1978. **Mark:** Last name, city, state and serial number.

BRODZIAK, DAVID,
27 Stewart St, PO Box 1130, Albany, West Australia, AUSTRALIA 6331, Phone: 61 8 9841 3314, Fax: 61898115065, brodziakomninet.net.au; Web: www.brodziakcustomknives.com

BROMLEY, PETER,
BROMLEY KNIVES, 1408 S Bettman, Spokane, WA 99212, Phone: 509-534-4235, Fax: 509-536-2666
Specialties: Period Bowies, folder, hunting knives; all sizes and shapes. **Patterns:** Bowies, boot knives, hunters, utility, folder, working knives. **Technical:** High-carbon steel (1084, 1095 and 5160). Stock removal and forge. **Prices:** $85 to $750. **Remarks:** Almost full-time, first knife sold in 1987. A.B.S. Journeyman Smith. **Mark:** Bromley, Spokane, WA.

BROOKER, DENNIS,
55858 260th Ave., Chariton, IA 50049, Phone: 641-862-3263, dbrooker@dbrooker.com Web: www.dbrooker.com
Specialties: Fancy straight knives and folders of his design. Obsidian and glass knives. **Patterns:** Hunters, folders and boots. **Technical:** Forges and grinds. Full-time engraver and designer; instruction available. **Prices:** Moderate to upscale. **Remarks:** Part-time maker. Takes no orders; sells only completed work. **Mark:** Name.

BROOKS, BUZZ,
2345 Yosemite Dr, Los Angles, CA 90041, Phone: 323-256-2892

BROOKS, MICHAEL,
2811 64th St, Lubbock, TX 79413, Phone: 806-438-3862, chiang@clearwire.net
Specialties: Working straight knives of his design or to customer specs. **Patterns:** Martial art, Bowies, hunters, and fighters. **Technical:** Grinds 440C, D2 and ATS-34; offers wide variety of handle materials. **Prices:** $75 & up. **Remarks:** Part-time maker; first knife sold in 1985. **Mark:** Initials.

BROOKS, STEVE R,
1610 Dunn Ave, Walkerville, MT 59701, Phone: 406-782-5114, Fax: 406-782-5114, steve@brooksmoulds.com; Web: brooksmoulds.com
Specialties: Working straight knives and folders; period pieces. **Patterns:** Hunters, Bowies and camp knives; folding lockers; axes, tomahawks and buckskinner knives; swords and stilettos. **Technical:** Damascus and mosaic Damascus. Some knives come embellished. **Prices:** $400 to $2000. **Remarks:** Full-time maker; first knife sold in 1982. **Mark:** Lazy initials.

BROOME, THOMAS A,
1212 E. Aliak Ave, Kenai, AK 99611-8205, Phone: 907-283-9128, tomlei@ptialaska.ent; Web: www.alaskanknives.com
Specialties: Working hunters and folders **Patterns:** Traditional and custom orders. **Technical:** Grinds ATS-34, BG-42, CPM-S30V. **Prices:** $175 to $350. **Remarks:** Full-time maker; first knife sold in 1979. Doing business as Thom's Custom Knives, Alaskan Man O; Steel Knives. **Mark:** Full name, city, state.

BROTHERS, DENNIS L.,
2007 Kent Rd., Oneonta, AL 35121, Phone: 205-466-3276, blademan@brothersblades.com Web: www.brothersblades.com
Specialties: Fixed blade hunting/working knives of maker's deigns. Works with customer designed specifications. **Patterns:** Hunters, camp knives, kitchen/utility, bird, and trout. Standard patterns and customer designed. **Technical:** Stock removal. Works with stainless and tool steels. SS cryo-treatment. Hollow and flat grinds. **Prices:** $200 - $400. **Remarks:** Sole authorship knives and customer leather sheaths. Part-time maker. Find on facebook "Brothers Blades by D.L. Brothers" **Mark:** "D.L. Brothers, 4B, Oneonta, AL" on obverse side of blade.

BROTHERS, ROBERT L,
989 Philpott Rd, Colville, WA 99114, Phone: 509-684-8922
Specialties: Traditional working and using straight knives and folders of his design and to customer specs. **Patterns:** Bowies, fighters and hunters. **Technical:** Grinds D2; forges Damascus. Makes own Damascus from saw steel wire rope and chain; part-time goldsmith and stone-setter. **Prices:** $100 to $400; some higher. **Remarks:** Part-time maker; first knife sold in 1986. **Mark:** Initials and year made.

BROUS, JASON,
5940 Matthews St., Goleta, CA 93110, Phone: 805-717-7192, contact@brousblades.com Web: www.brousblades.com
Patterns: Mostly fixed blades. **Technical:** Stock removal method using D2, CPM 154, 440c, ATS-34 or 1095 steels. **Prices:** $100 - $400. **Remarks:** Started May 2010.

BROWER, MAX,
2016 Story St, Boone, IA 50036, Phone: 515-432-2938, mbrower@mchsi.com
Specialties: Hunters. Working/using straight knives. **Patterns:** Bowies, hunters and boots. **Technical:** Grinds 440C and ATS-34. **Prices:** $250 and up. **Remarks:** Spare-time maker; first knife sold in 1981. **Mark:** Last name.

BROWN, DENNIS G,
1633 N 197th Pl, Shoreline, WA 98133, Phone: 206-542-3997, denjilbro@msn.com

BROWN, DOUGLAS,
1500 Lincolnshire Way, Fort Worth, TX 76134, www.debrownphotography.com

BROWN, HAROLD E,
3654 NW Hwy 72, Arcadia, FL 34266, Phone: 863-494-7514, brknives@strato.net
Specialties: Fancy and exotic working knives. **Patterns:** Folders, slip-lock, locking several kinds. **Technical:** Grinds D2 and ATS-34. Embellishment available. **Prices:** $175 to $1000. **Remarks:** Part-time maker; first knife sold in 1976. **Mark:** Name and city with logo.

BROWN, JIM,
1097 Fernleigh Cove, Little Rock, AR 72210

BROWN, ROB E,
PO Box 15107, Emerald Hill 6011, Port Elizabeth, SOUTH AFRICA, Phone: 27-41-3661086, Fax: 27-41-4511731, rbknives@global.co.za
Specialties: Contemporary-designed straight knives and period pieces. Patterns: Utility knives, hunters, boots, fighters and daggers. Technical: Grinds 440C, D2, ATS-34 and commercial Damascus. Knives mostly mirror finished; African handle materials. Prices: $100 to $1500. Remarks: Full-time maker; first knife sold in 1985. Mark: Name and country.

BROWNE, RICK,
980 West 13th St, Upland, CA 91786, Phone: 909-985-1728
Specialties: Sheffield pattern pocket knives. Patterns: Hunters, fighters and daggers. No heavy-duty knives. Technical: Grinds ATS-34. Prices: Start at $450. Remarks: Part-time maker; first knife sold in 1975. Mark: R.E. Browne, Upland, CA.

BROWNING, STEVEN W,
3400 Harrison Rd, Benton, AR 72015, Phone: 501-316-2450

BRUCE, RICHARD L.,
13174 Surcease Mine Road, Yankee Hill, CA 95965, Phone: 530-532-0880, Richardkarenbruce@yahoo.com
RL Bruce Custom Knives

BRUCE, RICHARD L.,
13174 Surcease Mine Road, Yankee Hill, CA 95965, Phone: 530-532-0880, richardkarenbruce@yahoo.com
Specialties: Working straight knives. Prefers natural handle material; stag bone and woods. Admires the classic straight knife look. Patterns: Hunters, Fighters, Fishing Knives. Technical: Uses 01, 1095, L6, W2 steel. Stock removal method, flat grind, heat treats and tempers own knives. Builds own sheaths; simple but sturdy. Prices: $150-$400. Remarks: Sold first knife in 2006; part-time maker. Mark: RL Bruce.

BRUNCKHORST, LYLE,
COUNTRY VILLAGE, 23706 7th Ave SE Ste B, Bothell, WA 98021, Phone: 425-402-3484, bronks@bronksknifeworks.com; Web: www.bronksknifeworks.com
Specialties: Forges own Damascus with 1084 and 15N20, forges 5160, 52100. Grinds CPM 154 CM, ATS-34, S30V. Hosts Biannual Northwest School of Knifemaking and Northwest Hammer In. Offers online and in-house sharpening services and knife sharpeners. Maker of the Double L Hoofknife. Traditional working and using knives, the new patent pending Xross-Bar Lock folders, tomahawks and irridescent RR spike knives. Patterns: Damascus Bowies, hunters, locking folders and featuring the ultra strong locking tactical folding knives. Prices: $185 to $1500; some to $3750. Remarks: Full-time maker; first knife made in 1976. Mark: Bucking horse or bronk.

BRUNER JR., FRED BRUNER BLADES,
E10910 W Hilldale Dr, Fall Creek, WI 54742, Phone: 715-877-2496, brunerblades@msn.com
Specialties: Pipe tomahawks, swords, makes his own. Patterns: Drop point hunters. Prices: $65 to $1500. Remarks: Voting member of the Knifemakers Guild. Mark: Fred Bruner.

BRYAN, TOM,
PO Box 1271, Gilbert, AZ 85299, Phone: 480-812-8529
Specialties: Straight and folding knives. Patterns: Drop-point hunter fighters. Technical: ATS-34, 154CM, 440C and A2. Prices: $150 to $800. Remarks: Part-time maker; sold first knife in 1994. DBA as T. Bryan Knives. Mark: T. Bryan.

BUCHANAN, THAD,
THAD BUCHANAN CUSTOM KNIVES, 915 NW Perennial Way, Prineville, OR 97754, Phone: 541-416-2556, knives@crestviewcable.com; Web: www.buchananblades.com
Specialties: Fixed blades. Patterns: Various hunters, trout, bird, utility, boots & fighters, including most Loveless patterns. Technical: Stock removal, high polish, variety handle materials. Prices: $450 to $2000. Remarks: 2005 and 2008 Blade Magazine handmade award for hunter/utility. 2006 Blade West best fixed blade award; 2008 Blade West best hunter/utility. 2010 and 2011 Best Fixed Blade at Plaza Cutlery Show. Mark: Thad Buchanan - maker

BUCHNER, BILL,
PO Box 73, Idleyld Park, OR 97447, Phone: 541-498-2247, blazinhammer@earthlink.net; Web: www.home.earthlink.net/~blazinghammer
Specialties: Working straight knives, kitchen knives and high-art knives of his design. Technical: Uses W1, L6 and his own Damascus. Invented "spectrum metal" for letter openers, folder handles and jewelry. Likes sculpturing and carving in Damascus. Prices: $40 to $3000; some higher. Remarks: Full-time maker; first knife sold in 1978. Mark: Signature.

BUCKBEE, DONALD M,
243 South Jackson Trail, Grayling, MI 49738, Phone: 517-348-1386
Specialties: Working straight knives, some fancy, in standard patterns; concentrating on kitchen knives. Patterns: Kitchen knives, hunters, Bowies. Technical: Grinds D2, 440C, ATS-34. Makes ultra-lights in hunter patterns. Prices: $100 to $250; some to $350. Remarks: Part-time maker; first knife sold in 1984. Mark: Antlered bee—a buck bee.

BUCKNER, JIMMIE H,
PO Box 162, Putney, GA 31782, Phone: 229-436-4182
Specialties: Camp knives, Bowies (one-of-a-kind), liner-lock folders, tomahawks, camp axes, neck knives for law enforcement and hide-out knives for body guards and professional people. Patterns: Hunters, camp knives,

Bowies. Technical: Forges 1084, 5160 and Damascus (own), own heat treats. Prices: $195 to $795 and up. Remarks: Full-time maker; first knife sold in 1980, ABS Master Smith. Mark: Name over spade.

BUDELL, MICHAEL,
1100-A South Market St, Brenham, TX 77833, Phone: 979-836-0098, mbbudell@att.net
Specialties: Slip Joint Folders. Technical: Grinds 01, 440C. File work springs, blades and liners. Natural material scales giraffe, mastadon ivory, elephant ivory, and jigged bone. Prices: $175 - $350. Remarks: Part-time maker; first knife sold 2006. Mark: XA

BUEBENDORF, ROBERT E,
108 Lazybrooke Rd, Monroe, CT 06468, Phone: 203-452-1769
Specialties: Traditional and fancy straight knives of his design. Patterns: Hand-makes and embellishes belt buckle knives. Technical: Forges and grinds 440C, O1, W2, 1095, his own Damascus and 154CM. Prices: $200 to $500. Remarks: Full-time maker; first knife sold in 1978. Mark: First and middle initials, last name and MAKER.

BULLARD, BENONI,
4416 Jackson 4, Bradford, AR 72020, Phone: 501-344-2672, benandbren@earthlink.net
Specialties: Bowies and hunters. Patterns: Camp knives, bowies, hunters, slip joints, folders, lock blades, miniatures, Hawks Tech. Technical: Makes own Damascus. Forges 5160, 1085, 15 N 20. Favorite is 5160. Prices: $150 - $1500. Remarks: Part-time maker. Sold first knife in 2006. Mark: Benoni with a star over the letter i.

BULLARD, RANDALL,
7 Mesa Dr., Canyon, TX 79015, Phone: 806-655-0590
Specialties: Working/using straight knives and folders of his design or to customer specs. Patterns: Hunters, locking folders and slip-joint folders. Technical: Grinds O1, ATS-34 and 440C. Does file work. Prices: $125 to $300; some to $500. Remarks: Part-time maker; first knife sold in 1993. Doing business as Bullard Custom Knives. Mark: First and middle initials, last name, maker, city and state.

BULLARD, TOM,
117 MC 8068, Flippin, AR 72634, Phone: 870-453-3421, tbullard@southshore.com; Web: www.southshore.com/~tombullard
Specialties: Traditional folders and hunters. Patterns: Bowies, hunters, single and 2-blade trappers, lockback folders. Technical: Grinds 440-C, ATS-34, 0-1, commercial Damascus. Prices: $150 and up. Remarks: Offers filework and engraving by Norvell Foster and Terry Thies. Does not make screw-together knives. Mark: T Bullard.

BUMP, BRUCE D.,
1103 Rex Ln, Walla Walla, WA 99362, Phone: 509 522-2219, brucebump1@gmail.com; Web: www.brucebumpknives.com
Specialties: "One-of-a-kind" folders to cut and shoots. Patterns: Damascus patterns including feather patterns. Technical: Dual threat weapons of his own design. Prices: Call for prices. Remarks: Full-time maker ABS mastersmith 2003. Mark: Bruce D. Bump "Custom", Bruce D. Bump "MS".

BURDEN, JAMES,
405 Kelly St, Burkburnett, TX 76354

BURGER, FRED,
Box 436, Munster 4278, Kwa-Zulu Natal, SOUTH AFRICA, Phone: 27 39 3192316, info@swordcane.com; Web: www.swordcane.com
Specialties: Sword canes, folders, and fixed blades. Patterns: 440C and carbon steel blades. Technical: Double hollow ground and Poniard-style blades. Prices: $300 to $3000. Remarks: Full-time maker with son, Barry, since 1987. Member South African Guild. Mark: Last name in oval pierced by a dagger.

BURGER, PON,
12 Glenwood Ave, Woodlands, Bulawayo, ZIMBABWE 75514
Specialties: Collector's items. Patterns: Fighters, locking folders of traditional styles, buckles. Technical: Scrimshaws 440C blade. Uses polished buffalo horn with brass fittings. Cased in buffalo hide book. Prices: $450 to $1100. Remarks: Full-time maker; first knife sold in 1973. Doing business as Burger Products. Mark: Spirit of Africa.

BURGER, TIAAN,
69 Annie Botha Ave, Riviera, Pretoria, South Africa, tiaan_burger@hotmail.com
Specialties: Sliplock and multi-blade folder. Technical: High carbon or stainless with African handle materials Remarks: Occasional fixed blade knives.

BURKE, BILL,
12 Chapman Lane, Boise, ID 83716, Phone: 208-336-3792, billburke@bladegallery.com
Specialties: Hand-forged working knives. Patterns: Fowler pronghorn, clip point and drop point hunters. Technical: Forges 52100 and 5160. Makes own Damascus from 15N20 and 1084. Prices: $450 and up. Remarks: Dedicated to fixed-blade high-performance knives. ABS Journeyman. Also makes "Ed Fowler" miniatures. Mark: Initials connected.

BURKE, DAN,
29 Circular Rd., Springdale, NL Canada A0J 1T0, Phone: 708-867-2026, dansknives@eastlink.ca
Specialties: Slip joint folders. Patterns: Traditional folders. Technical: Grinds D2 and BG-42. Prefers natural handle materials; heat-treats. Prices: $440 to $1900. Remarks: Full-time maker; first knife sold in 1976. Mark: First initial and last name.

BURNLEY, LUCAS,
1005 La Font Rd. SW, Albuquerque, NM 87105, Phone: 505-265-4297, burnleyknives@comcast.net
Specialties: Contemporary tactical fixed blade, and folder designs, some art knives. **Patterns:** Hybrids, neo Japanese, defensive, utility and field knives. **Technical:** Grinds CPM154, A2, D2, BG42, Stainless Damascus as well as titanium and aerospace composites. **Prices:** Most models $150 - $1000. Some specialty pieces higher. **Remarks:** Full-time maker, first knife sold in 2003. **Mark:** Last name, Burnley Knives, or Burnley Design.

BURRIS, PATRICK R,
11078 Crystal Lynn Ct, Jacksonville, FL 32226, Phone: 904-757-3938, keenedge@comcast.net
Specialties: Traditional straight knives. **Patterns:** Hunters, Bowies, locking liner folders. **Technical:** Flat grinds CPM stainless and Damascus. **Remarks:** Offers filework, embellishment, exotic materials and Damascus **Mark:** Last name in script.

BURROWS, CHUCK,
WILD ROSE TRADING CO, 289 La Posta Canyon Rd, Durango, CO 81303, Phone: 970-259-8396, chuck@wrtcleather.com; Web: www.wrtcleather.com
Specialties: Presentation knives, hawks, and sheaths based on the styles of the American frontier incorporating carving, beadwork, rawhide, braintan, and other period correct materials. Also makes other period style knives such as Scottish Dirks and Moorish jambiyahs. **Patterns:** Bowies, Dags, tomahawks, war clubs, and all other 18th and 19th century frontier style edged weapons and tools. **Technical:** Carbon steel only: 5160, 1080/1084, 1095, O1, Damascus-Our Frontier Shear Steel, plus other styles available on request. Forged knives, hawks, etc. are made in collaborations with bladesmiths. Gib Guignard (under the name of Cactus Rose) and Mark Williams (under the name UB Forged). Blades are usually forge finished and all items are given an aged period look. **Prices:** $500 plus. **Remarks:** Full-time maker, first knife sold in 1973. 40+ years experience working leather. **Mark:** A lazy eight or lazy eight with a capital T at the center. On leather either the lazy eight with T or a WRTC makers stamp.

BURROWS, STEPHEN R,
1020 Osage St, Humboldt, KS 66748, Phone: 816-921-1573
Specialties: Fantasy straight knives of his design, to customer specs and in standard patterns; period pieces. **Patterns:** Fantasy, bird and trout knives, daggers, fighters and hunters. **Technical:** Forges 5160 and 1095 high-carbon steel, O1 and his Damascus. Offers lost wax casting in bronze or silver of cross guards and pommels. **Prices:** $65 to $600; some to $2000. **Remarks:** Full-time maker; first knife sold in 1983. Doing business as Gypsy Silk. **Mark:** Etched name.

BUSCH, STEVE,
1989 Old Town Loop, Oakland, OR 97462, Phone: 541-459-2833, steve@buschcustomknives.com; Web: wwwbuschcustomknives.blademakers.com
Specialties: D/A automatic right and left handed, folders, fixed blade working mainly in Damascus file work, functional art knives, nitrate bluing, heat bluing most all scale materials. **Prices:** $150 to $2000. **Remarks:** Trained under Vallotton family 3 1/2 years on own since 2002. **Mark:** Signature and date of completion on all knives.

BUSFIELD, JOHN,
153 Devonshire Circle, Roanoke Rapids, NC 27870, Phone: 252-537-3949, Fax: 252-537-8704, busfield@charter.net; Web: www.busfieldknives.com
Specialties: Investor-grade folders; high-grade working straight knives. **Patterns:** Original price-style and trailing-point interframe and sculpted-frame folders, drop-point hunters and semi-skinners. **Technical:** Grinds 154CM and ATS-34. Offers interframes, gold frames and inlays; uses jade, agate and lapis. **Prices:** $275 to $2000. **Remarks:** Full-time maker; first knife sold in 1979. **Mark:** Last name and address.

BUSSE, JERRY,
11651 Co Rd 12, Wauseon, OH 43567, Phone: 419-923-6471
Specialties: Working straight knives. **Patterns:** Heavy combat knives and camp knives. **Technical:** Grinds D2, A2, INFI. **Prices:** $1100 to $3500. **Remarks:** Full-time maker; first knife sold in 1983. **Mark:** Last name in logo.

BUTLER, BART,
822 Seventh St, Ramona, CA 92065, Phone: 760-789-6431

BUTLER, JOHN,
777 Tyre Rd, Havana, FL 32333, Phone: 850-539-5742
Specialties: Hunters, Bowies, period. **Technical:** Damascus, 52100, 5160, L6 steels. **Prices:** $80 and up. **Remarks:** Making knives since 1986. Journeyman (ABS). **Mark:** JB.

BUTLER, JOHN R,
20162 6th Ave N E, Shoreline, WA 98155, Phone: 206-362-3847, rjjjrb@sprynet.com

BUXTON, BILL,
155 Oak Bend Rd, Kaiser, MO 65047, Phone: 573-348-3577, camper@yhti.net; Web: www.billbuxtonknives.com
Specialties: Forged fancy and working straight knives and folders. Mostly one-of-a-kind pieces. **Patterns:** Fighters, daggers, Bowies, hunters, linerlock folders, axes and tomahawks. **Technical:** Forges 52100, 0-1, 1080. Makes own Damascus (mosaic and random patterns) from 1080, 1095, 15n20, and powdered metals 1084 and 4800a. Offers sterling silver inlay, n/s pin patterning and pewter pouring on axe and hawk handles. **Prices:** $300 to $1500. **Remarks:** Full-time maker, sold first knife in 1998. **Mark:** First and last name.

BYBEE, BARRY J,
795 Lock Rd. E, Cadiz, KY 42211-8615
Specialties: Working straight knives of his design. **Patterns:** Hunters, fighters, boot knives, tantos and Bowies. **Technical:** Grinds ATS-34, 440C. Likes stag and Micarta for handle materials. **Prices:** $125 to $200; some to $1000. **Remarks:** Part-time maker; first knife sold in 1968. **Mark:** Arrowhead logo with name, city and state.

BYRD, WESLEY L,
189 Countryside Dr, Evensville, TN 37332, Phone: 423-775-3826, w.l.byrd@worldnet.att.net
Specialties: Hunters, fighters, Bowies, dirks, sgian dubh, utility, and camp knives. **Patterns:** Wire rope, random patterns. Twists, W's, Ladder, Kite Tail. **Technical:** Uses 52100, 1084, 5160, L6, and 15n20. **Prices:** Starting at $180. **Remarks:** Prefer to work with customer for their design preferences. ABS Journeyman Smith. **Mark:** BYRD, WB <X.

C

C. DEBRAGA, JOSE,
1341 9e Rue, Trois Rivieres, Quebec, CANADA G8Y 2Z2, Phone: 418-948-5864, josecdebraga@cgocable.ca; Web: www.togiarts.com/CSC/Home.html
Specialties: Art knives, fantasy pieces and working knives of his design or to customer specs. **Patterns:** Knives with sculptured or carved handles, from miniatures to full-size working knives. **Technical:** Grinds and hand-files 440C and ATS-34. A variety of steels and handle materials available. Offers lost wax casting. **Prices:** Start at $300. **Remarks:** Full-time maker; wax modeler, sculptor and knifemaker; first knife sold in 1984. **Mark:** Initials in stylized script and serial number.

CABE, JERRY (BUDDY),
62 McClaren Ln, Hattieville, AR 72063, Phone: 501-354-3581

CABRERA, SERGIO B,
24500 Broad Ave, Wilmington, CA 90744

CAFFREY, EDWARD J,
2608 Central Ave West, Great Falls, MT 59404, Phone: 406-727-9102, caffreyknives@gmail.com; Web: www.caffreyknives.net
Specialties: One-of-a-kind using and collector quality pieces. Will accept some customer designs. **Patterns:** Bowies, folders, hunters, fighters, camp/utility, tomahawks and hatchets. **Technical:** Forges all types of Damascus, specializing in Mosaic Damascus, 52100, 5160, 1080/1084 and most other commonly forged steels. **Prices:** Starting at $185; typical hunters start at $400; collector pieces can range into the thousands. **Remarks:** Offers one-on-one basic and advanced bladesmithing classes. ABS Mastersmith. Full-time maker. **Mark:** Stamped last name and MS on straight knives. Etched last name with MS on folders.

CALDWELL, BILL,
255 Rebecca, West Monroe, LA 71292, Phone: 318-323-3025
Specialties: Straight knives and folders with machined bolsters and liners. **Patterns:** Fighters, Bowies, survival knives, tomahawks, razors and push knives. **Technical:** Owns and operates a very large, well-equipped blacksmith and bladesmith shop with six large forges and eight power hammers. **Prices:** $400 to $3500; some to $10,000. **Remarks:** Full-time maker and self-styled blacksmith; first knife sold in 1962. **Mark:** Wild Bill and Sons.

CALLAHAN, F TERRY,
PO Box 880, Boerne, TX 78006, Phone: 830-981-8274, Fax: 830-981-8279, ftclaw@gvtc.com
Specialties: Custom hand-forged edged knives, collectible and functional. **Patterns:** Bowies, folders, daggers, hunters & camp knives . **Technical:** Forges 5160, 1095 and his own Damascus. Offers filework and handmade sheaths. **Prices:** $125 to $2000. **Remarks:** First knife sold in 1990. ABS/Journeyman Bladesmith. **Mark:** Initials inside a keystone symbol.

CALVERT JR., ROBERT W (BOB),
911 Julia, Rayville, LA 71269, Phone: 318-728-4113 ext. 2, Fax: (318) 728-0000, rcalvert1@gmail.com
Specialties: Using and hunting knives; your design or his. Since 1990. **Patterns:** Forges own Damascus; all patterns. **Technical:** 5160, D2, 52100, 1084. Prefers natural handle material. **Prices:** $250 and up. **Remarks:** TOMB Member, ABS. Journeyman Smith. ABS Board of directors **Mark:** Calvert (Block) J S.

CAMERER, CRAIG,
3766 Rockbridge Rd, Chesterfield, IL 62630, Phone: 618-753-2147, craig@camererknives.com; Web: www.camererknives.com
Specialties: Everyday carry knives, hunters and Bowies. **Patterns:** D-guard, historical recreations and fighters. **Technical:** Most of his knives are forged to shape. **Prices:** $100 and up. **Remarks:** Member of the ABS and PKA. Journeymen Smith ABS.

CAMERON, RON G,
PO Box 183, Logandale, NV 89021, Phone: 702-398-3356, rntcameron@mvdsl.com
Specialties: Fancy and embellished working/using straight knives and folders of his design. **Patterns:** Bowies, hunters and utility/camp knives. **Technical:** Grinds ATS-34, AEB-L and Devin Thomas Damascus or own Damascus from 1084 and 15N20. Does filework, fancy pins, mokume fittings. Uses exotic hardwoods, stag and Micarta for handles. Pearl & mammoth ivory. **Prices:** $175 to $850 some to $1000. **Remarks:** Part-time maker; first knife sold in 1994. Doing business as Cameron Handmade Knives. **Mark:** Last name, town, state or last name.

CAMPBELL, DICK,
196 Graham Rd, Colville, WA 99114, Phone: 509-684-6080, dicksknives@aol.com
Specialties: Working straight knives, folders & period pieces. **Patterns:** Hunters, fighters, boots: 19th century Bowies, Japanese swords and daggers. **Technical:** Grinds 440C, 154CM. **Prices:** $200 to $2500. **Remarks:** Full-time maker. First knife sold in 1975. **Mark:** Name.

CAMPBELL, DOUG,
46 W Boulder Rd., McLeod, MT 59052, Phone: 406-222-8153, dkcampbl@yahoo.com
Specialties: Sole authorship of most any fixed blade knife. **Patterns:** Capers, hunters, camp knives, bowies, fighters. **Technical:** Forged from 1084, 5160, 52100, and self forged pattern-welded Damascus. **Prices:** $150-$750. **Remarks:** Part-time knifesmith. Built first knife in 1987, tried to make every knife since better than the one before. ABS JourneymanSmith . **Mark:** Grizzly track surrounded by a C.

CAMPOS, IVAN,
R.XI de Agosto 107, Tatui, SP, BRAZIL 18270-000, Phone: 00-55-15-2518092, Fax: 00-55-15-2594368, ivan@ivancampos.com; Web: www.ivancompos.com
Specialties: Brazilian handmade and antique knives.

CANDRELLA, JOE,
1219 Barness Dr, Warminster, PA 18974, Phone: 215-675-0143
Specialties: Working straight knives, some fancy. **Patterns:** Daggers, boots, Bowies. **Technical:** Grinds 440C and 154CM. **Prices:** $100 to $200; some to $1000. **Remarks:** Part-time maker; first knife sold in 1985. Does business as Franjo. **Mark:** FRANJO with knife as J.

CANNADY, DANIEL L,
Box 301, 358 Parkwood Terrace, Allendale, SC 29810, Phone: 803-584-2813, Fax: 803-584-2813
Specialties: Working straight knives and folders in standard patterns. **Patterns:** Drop-point hunters, Bowies, skinners, fishing knives with concave grind, steak knives and kitchen cutlery. **Technical:** Grinds D2, 440C and ATS-34. **Prices:** $65 to $325; some to $1000. **Remarks:** Full-time maker; first knife sold in 1980. **Mark:** Last name above Allendale, S.C.

CANTER, RONALD E,
96 Bon Air Circle, Jackson, TN 38305, Phone: 731-668-1780, canterr@charter.net
Specialties: Traditional working knives to customer specs. **Patterns:** Beavertail skinners, Bowies, hand axes and folding lockers. **Technical:** Grinds 440C, Micarta & deer antler. **Prices:** $75 and up. **Remarks:** Spare-time maker; first knife sold in 1973. **Mark:** Three last initials intertwined.

CANTRELL, KITTY D,
19720 Hwy 78, Ramona, CA 92076, Phone: 760-788-8304

CAPDEPON, RANDY,
553 Joli Rd, Carencro, LA 70520, Phone: 318-896-4113, Fax: 318-896-8753
Specialties: Straight knives and folders of his design. **Patterns:** Hunters and locking folders. **Technical:** Grinds ATS-34, 440C and D2. **Prices:** $200 to $600. **Remarks:** Part-time maker; first knife made in 1992. Doing business as Capdepon Knives. **Mark:** Last name.

CAPDEPON, ROBERT,
829 Vatican Rd, Carencro, LA 70520, Phone: 337-896-8753, Fax: 318-896-8753
Specialties: Traditional straight knives and folders of his design. **Patterns:** Boots, hunters and locking folders. **Technical:** Grinds ATS-34, 440C and D2. Hand-rubbed finish on blades. Likes natural horn materials for handles, including ivory. Offers engraving. **Prices:** $250 to $750. **Remarks:** Full-time maker; first knife made in 1992. **Mark:** Last name.

CAREY, PETER,
P.O. Box 4712, Lago Vista, TX 78645, Phone: 512-358-4839, Web: www.careyblade.com
Specialties: Tactical folders, Every Day Carry to presentation grade. Working straight knives, hunters, and tactical. **Patterns:** High-tech patterns of his own design, Linerlocks, Framelocks, Flippers. **Technical:** Hollow grinds CPM154, 535VN, stainless Damascus, Stellite. Uses titanium, carbon fiber, G10, and select natural handle materials. **Prices:** Starting at $450. **Remarks:** Full-time maker, first knife sold in 2002. **Mark:** Last name in diamond.

CARLISLE, JEFF,
PO Box 282 12753 Hwy 200, Simms, MT 59477, Phone: 406-264-5693

CARPENTER, RONALD W,
Rt. 4 Box 323, Jasper, TX 75951, Phone: 409-384-4087

CARR, JOSEPH E.,
W183 N8974 Maryhill Drive, Menomonee Falls, WI 53051, Phone: 920-625-3607, carsmith1@SBCGlobal.net; Web: Hembrook3607@charter.net
Specialties: JC knives. **Patterns:** Hunters, Bowies, fighting knives, every day carries. **Technical:** Grinds ATS-34 and Damascus. **Prices:** $200 to $750. **Remarks:** Full-time maker for 2 years, being taught by Ron Hembrook.

CARR, TIM,
3660 Pillon Rd, Muskegon, MI 49445, Phone: 231-766-3582, tim@blackbearforgemi.com Web:www.blackbearforgemi.com
Specialties: Hunters, camp knives. **Patterns:** His or yours. **Technical:** Hand forges 5160, 52100 and Damascus. **Prices:** $125 to $700. **Remarks:** Part-time maker. **Mark:** The letter combined from maker's initials TRC.

CARRILLO, DWAINE,
C/O AIRKAT KNIVES, 1021 SW 15th St, Moore, OK 73160, Phone: 405-503-5879, Web: www.airkatknives.com

CARROLL, CHAD,
12182 McClelland, Grant, MI 49327, Phone: 231-834-9183, CHAD724@msn.com
Specialties: Hunters, Bowies, folders, swords, tomahawks. **Patterns:** Fixed blades, folders. **Prices:** $100 to $2000. **Remarks:** ABS Journeyman May 2002. **Mark:** A backwards C next to a forward C, maker's initials.

CARSON, HAROLD J "KIT",
1076 Brizendine Lane, Vine Grove, KY 40175, Phone: 270 877-6300, Fax: 270 877 6338, KCKnives@bbtel.com; Web: www.kitcarsonknives.com/album
Specialties: Military fixed blades and folders; art pieces. **Patterns:** Fighters, D handles, daggers, combat folders and Crosslock-styles, tactical folders, tactical fixed blades. **Technical:** Grinds Stellite 6K, Talonite, CPM steels, Damascus. **Prices:** $400 to $750; some to $5000. **Remarks:** Full-time maker; first knife sold in 1973. **Mark:** Name stamped or engraved.

CARTER, FRED,
5219 Deer Creek Rd, Wichita Falls, TX 76302, Phone: 904-723-4020
Specialties: High-art investor-class straight knives; some working hunters and fighters. **Patterns:** Classic daggers, Bowies; interframe, stainless and blued steel folders with gold inlay. **Technical:** Grinds a variety of steels. Uses no glue or solder. Engraves and inlays. **Prices:** Generally upscale. **Remarks:** Full-time maker. **Mark:** Signature in oval logo.

CARTER, MIKE,
2522 Frankfort Ave, Louisville, KY 40206, Phone: 502-387-4844, mike@cartercrafts.com Web: www.cartercrafts.com
Remarks: Voting Member Knifemakers Guild.

CARTER, MURRAY M,
22097 NW West Union Rd, Hillsboro, OR 97124, Phone: 503-447-1029, murray@cartercutlery.com; Web: www.cartercutlery.com
Specialties: Traditional Japanese cutlery, utilizing San soh ko (three layer) or Kata-ha (two layer) blade construction. Laminated neck knives, traditional Japanese etc. **Patterns:** Works from over 200 standard Japanese and North American designs. **Technical:** Hot forges and cold forges Hitachi white steel #1, Hitachi blue super steel exclusively. **Prices:** $800 to $10,000. **Remarks:** Owns and operates North America's most exclusive traditional Japanese bladesmithing school; web site available at which viewers can subscribe to 10 free knife sharpening and maintenance reports. **Mark:** Name in cursive, often appearing with Japanese characters. **Other:** Very interestng and informative monthly newsletter.

CASEY, KEVIN,
10583 N. 42nd St., Hickory Corners, MI 49060, Phone: 269-719-7412, kevincasey@tds.net; Web: www.kevincaseycustomknives.com
Specialties: Fixed blades and folders. **Patterns:** Liner lock folders and feather Damascus pattern, mammoth ivory. **Technical:** Forges Damascus and carbon steels. **Prices:** Starting at $500 - $2500. **Remarks:** Member ABS, Knifemakers Guild, Custom Knifemakers Collectors Association.

CASHEN, KEVIN R,
5615 Tyler St, Hubbardston, MI 48845, Phone: 989-981-6780, kevin@cashenblades.com; Web: www.cashenblades.com
Specialties: Working straight knives, high art pattern welded swords, traditional renaissance and ethnic pieces. **Patterns:** Hunters, Bowies, utility knives, swords, daggers. **Technical:** Forges 1095, 1084 and his own O1/L6 Damascus. **Prices:** $100 to $4000+. **Remarks:** Full-time maker; first knife sold in 1985. Doing business as Matherton Forge. **Mark:** Black letter Old English initials and Master Smith stamp.

CASTEEL, DIANNA,
PO Box 63, Monteagle, TN 37356, Phone: 931-212-4341, ddcasteel@charter.net; Web: www.casteelcustomknives.com
Specialties: Small, delicate daggers and miniatures; most knives one-of-a-kind. **Patterns:** Daggers, boot knives, fighters and miniatures. **Technical:** Grinds 440C. Offers stainless Damascus. **Prices:** Start at $350; miniatures start at $250. **Remarks:** Full-time maker. **Mark:** Di in script.

CASTEEL, DOUGLAS,
PO Box 63, Monteagle, TN 37356, Phone: 931-212-4341, Fax: 931-723-1856, ddcasteel@charter.net; Web: www.casteelcustomknives.com
Specialties: One-of-a-kind collector-class period pieces. **Patterns:** Daggers, Bowies, swords and folders. **Technical:** Grinds 440C. Offers gold and silver castings.Offers stainless Damascus **Prices:** Upscale. **Remarks:** Full-time maker; first knife sold in 1982. **Mark:** Last name.

CASTELLUCIO, RICH,
220 Stairs Rd, Amsterdam, NY 12010, Phone: 518-843-5540, rcastellucio@nycap.rr.com
Patterns: Bowies, push daggers, and fantasy knives. **Technical:** Uses ATS-34, 440C, 154CM. I use stabilized wood, bone for the handles. Guards are made of copper, brass, stainless, nickle, and mokume.

CASTON, DARRIEL,
125 Ashcat Way, Folsom, CA 95630, Phone: 916-539-0744, darrielc@gmail.com

CASWELL, JOE,
173 S Ventu Park Rd, Newbury, CA 91320, Phone: 805-499-0707, Web:www.caswellknives.com
Specialties: Historic pattern welded knives and swords, hand forged. Also high precision folding and fixed blade "gentleman" and "tactical" knives of

his design, period firearms. Inventor of the "In-Line" retractable pocket clip for folding knives. **Patterns:**Hunters, tactical/utility, fighters, bowies, daggers, pattern welded medieval swords, precision folders. **Technical:**Forges own Damascus especially historic forms. Sometimes uses modern stainless steels and Damascus of other makers. Makes some pieces entirely by hand, others using the latest CNC techniques and by hand. Makes sheaths too. **Prices:**$100-$5,500. **Remarks:**Full time makers since 1995. Making mostly historic recreations for exclusive clientele. Recently moving into folding knives and 'modern' designs. **Mark:**CASWELL or CASWELL USA Accompanied by a mounted knight logo.

CATOE, DAVID R,
4024 Heutte Dr, Norfolk, VA 23518, Phone: 757-480-3191
Technical: Does own forging, Damascus and heat treatments. **Price:** $200 to $500; some higher. **Remarks:** Part-time maker; trained by Dan Maragni 1985-1988; first knife sold 1989. **Mark:** Leaf of a camellia.

CAWTHORNE, CHRISTOPHER A,
PO Box 604, Wrangell, AK 99929, Phone: 661-902-3724, chriscawthorne@hotmail.com
Specialties: High-carbon steel, cable wire rope, silver wire inlay. **Patterns:** Forge welded Damascus and wire rope, random pattern. **Technical:** Hand forged, 50 lb. little giant power hammer, W-2, 0-1, L6, 1095. **Prices:** $650 to $2500. **Remarks:** School ABS 1985 w/Bill Moran, hand forged, heat treat. **Mark:** Cawthorne, forged in stamp.

CECCHINI, GUSTAVO T.,
R. XV Novembro 2841, Sao Jose Rio Preto, SPAIN 15015110, Phone: 55 1732224267, tomaki@terra.com.be Web: www.gtcknives.com
Specialties: Tactical and HiTech folders. **Technical:** Stock removal. Stainless steel fixed blades. S30V, S35Vn, S90V, CowryX, Damasteel, Chad Nichols SS damascus, RWL 34, CPM 154 CM, BG 42. **Prices:** $500 - $1500. **Remarks:** Full-time since 2004. **Mark:** Tang Stamp "GTC"

CEPRANO, PETER J.,
213 Townsend Brooke Rd., Auburn, ME 04210, Phone: 207-786-5322, bpknives@gmail.com
Specialties: Traditional working/using straight knives; tactical/defense straight knives. Own designs or to a customer's specs. **Patterns:** Hunters, skinners, utility, Bowies, fighters, camp and survival, neck knives. **Technical:** Forges 1095, 5160, W2, 52100 and old files; grinds CPM154cm, ATS-34, 440C, D2, CPMs30v, Damascus from other makes and other tool steels. Hand-sewn and tooled leather and Kydex sheaths. **Prices:** Starting at $125. **Remarks:** Full-time maker, first knife sold in 2001. Doing business as Big Pete Knives. **Mark:** Bold BPK over small BigPeteKnivesUSA.

CHAFFEE, JEFF L,
14314 N. Washington St, PO Box 1, Morris, IN 47033, Phone: 812-212-6188
Specialties: Fancy working and utility folders and straight knives. **Patterns:** Fighters, dagger, hunter and locking folders. **Technical:** Grinds commercial Damascus, 440C, ATS-34, D2 and O1. Prefers natural handle materials. **Prices:** $350 to $2000. **Remarks:** Part-time maker; first knife sold in 1988. **Mark:** Last name.

CHAMBERLAIN, CHARLES R,
PO Box 156, Barren Springs, VA 24313-0156, Phone: 703-381-5137

CHAMBERLAIN, JON A,
15 S. Lombard, E. Wenatchee, WA 98802, Phone: 509-884-6591
Specialties: Working and kitchen knives to customer specs; exotics on special order. **Patterns:** Over 100 patterns in stock. **Technical:** Prefers ATS-34, D2, L6 and Damascus. **Prices:** Start at $50. **Remarks:** First knife sold in 1986. Doing business as Johnny Custom Knifemakers. **Mark:** Name in oval with city and state enclosing.

CHAMBERLIN, JOHN A,
11535 Our Rd., Anchorage, AK 99516, Phone: 907-346-1524, Fax: 907-562-4583
Specialties: Art and working knives. **Patterns:** Daggers and hunters; some folders;. **Technical:** Grinds ATS-34, 440C, A2, D2 and Damascus. Uses Alaskan handle materials such as oosic, jade, whale jawbone, fossil ivory. **Prices:** Start at $200. **Remarks:** Favorite knives to make are double-edged. Does own heat treating and cryogenic deep freeze. Full-time maker; first knife sold in 1984. **Mark:** Name over English shield and dagger.

CHAMBLIN, JOEL,
960 New Hebron Church Rd, Concord, GA 30206, Phone: 678-588-6769, chamblinknives@yahoo.com Web: chamblinknives.com
Specialties: Fancy and working folders. **Patterns:** Fancy locking folders, traditional, multi-blades and utility. **Technical:** Uses ATS-34, CPM 154, and commercial Damascus. Offers filework. **Prices:** Start at $400. **Remarks:** Full-time maker; first knife sold in 1989. **Mark:** Last name.

CHAMPION, ROBERT,
7001 Red Rock Rd., Amarillo, TX 79118, Phone: 806-622-3970
Specialties: Traditional working straight knives. **Patterns:** Hunters, skinners, camp knives, Bowies, daggers. **Technical:** Grinds 440C and D2. **Prices:** $100 to $600. **Remarks:** Part-time maker; first knife sold in 1979. Stream-line hunters. **Mark:** Last name with dagger logo, city and state.

CHAPO, WILLIAM G,
45 Wildridge Rd, Wilton, CT 06897, Phone: 203-544-9424
Specialties: Classic straight knives and folders of his design and to customer specs; period pieces. **Patterns:** Boots, Bowies and locking folders. **Technical:** Forges stainless Damascus. Offers filework. **Prices:** $750 and up. **Remarks:** Full-time

maker; first knife sold in 1989. **Mark:** First and middle initials, last name, city, state.

CHARD, GORDON R,
104 S. Holiday Lane, Iola, KS 66749, Phone: 620-365-2311, Fax: 620-365-2311, gchard@cox.net
Specialties: High tech folding knives in one-of-a-kind styles. **Patterns:** Liner locking folders of own design. Also fixed blade Art Knives. **Technical:** Clean work with attention to fit and finish. Blade steel mostly ATS-34 and 154CM, some CPM440V Vaso Wear and Damascus. **Prices:** $150 to $2500. **Remarks:** First knife sold in 1983. **Mark:** Name, city and state surrounded by wheat on each side.

CHASE, ALEX,
208 E. Pennsylvania Ave., DeLand, FL 32724, Phone: 386-734-9918, chase8578@bellsouth.net
Specialties: Historical steels, classic and traditional straight knives of his design and to customer specs. **Patterns:** Art, fighters, hunters and Japanese style. **Technical:** Forges O1-L6 Damascus, meteoric Damascus, 52100, 5160; uses fossil walrus and mastodon ivory etc. **Prices:** $150 to $1000; some to $3500. **Remarks:** Full-time maker; Guild member since 1996. Doing business as Confederate Forge. **Mark:** Stylized initials-A.C.

CHASE, JOHN E,
217 Walnut, Aledo, TX 76008, Phone: 817-441-8331, jchaseknives@sbcglobal.net
Specialties: Straight high-tech working knives in standard patterns or to customer specs. **Patterns:** Hunters, fighters, daggers and Bowies. **Technical:** Grinds D2, O1, 440C; offers mostly satin finishes. **Prices:** Start at $265. **Remarks:** Part-time maker; first knife sold in 1974. **Mark:** Last name in logo.

CHAUVIN, JOHN,
200 Anna St, Scott, LA 70583, Phone: 337-237-6138, Fax: 337-230-7980
Specialties: Traditional working and using straight knives of his design, to customer specs and in standard patterns. **Patterns:** Bowies, fighters, and hunters. **Technical:** Grinds ATS-34, 440C and O1 high-carbon. Paul Bos heat treating. Uses ivory, stag, oosic and stabilized Louisiana swamp maple for handle materials. Makes sheaths using alligator and ostrich. **Prices:** $200 and up. Bowies start at $500. **Remarks:** Part-time maker; first knife sold in 1995. **Mark:** Full name, city, state.

CHAUZY, ALAIN,
1 Rue de Paris, 21140 Seur-en-Auxios, FRANCE, Phone: 03-80-97-03-30, Fax: 03-80-97-34-14
Specialties: Fixed blades, folders, hunters, Bowies-scagel-style. **Technical:** Forged blades only. Steels used XC65, 07C, and own Damascus. **Prices:** Contact maker for quote. **Remarks:** Part-time maker. **Mark:** Number 2 crossed by an arrow and name.

CHEATHAM, BILL,
PO Box 636, Laveen, AZ 85339, Phone: 602-237-2786, blademan76@aol.com
Specialties: Working straight knives and folders. **Patterns:** Hunters, fighters, boots and axes; locking folders. **Technical:** Grinds 440C. **Prices:** $150 to $350; exceptional knives to $600. **Remarks:** Full-time maker; first knife sold in 1976. **Mark:** Name, city, state.

CHERRY, FRANK J,
3412 Tiley N.E., Albuquerque, NM 87110, Phone: 505-883-8643

CHEW, LARRY,
3025 De leon Dr., Weatherford, TX 76087, Phone: 817-573-8035, chewman@swbell.net; Web: www.voodooinside.com
Specialties: High-tech folding knives. **Patterns:** Double action automatic and manual folding patterns of his design. **Technical:** CAD designed folders utilizing roller bearing pivot design known as "VooDoo." Double action automatic folders with a variety of obvious and disguised release mechanisms, some with lock-outs. **Prices:** Manual folders start at $475, double action autos start at $750. **Remarks:** Made and sold first knife in 1988, first folder in 1989. Full-time maker since 1997. **Mark:** Name and location etched in blade, Damascus autos marked on spring inside frame. Earliest knives stamped LC.

CHILDERS, DAVID,
4106 Mossy Oaks, W. Spring, TX 77389, Phone: 281-353-4113, Web: www.davidchildersknives.com

CHINNOCK, DANIEL T.,
380 River Ridge Dr., Union, MO 63084, Phone: 314-276-6936, Web: www.DanChinnock.com; email: Sueanddanc@cs.com
Specialties: One of a kind folders in Damascus and Mammoth Ivory. Performs intricate pearl inlays into snake wood and giraffe bone. Makes matching ivory pistol grips for colt 1911's and Colt SAA. **Patterns:** New folder designs each year, thin ground and delicate gentleman's folders, large "hunting" folders in stainless Damascus and CPM154. Several standard models carried by Internet dealers. **Prices:** $500-$1500 **Remarks:** Full-time maker in 2005 and a voting member of the Knifemakers Guild. Performs intricate file work on all areas of knife. **Mark:** Signature on inside of backbar, starting in 2009 blades are stamped with a large "C" and "Dan" buried inside the "C".

CHOATE, MILTON,
1665 W. County 17-1/2, Somerton, AZ 85350, Phone: 928-627-7251, mccustom@juno.com
Specialties: Classic working and using straight knives of his design, to customer specs and in standard patterns. **Patterns:** Bowies, hunters and utility/camp knives. **Technical:** Grinds 440C; grinds and forges 1095 and 5160. Does filework on top and guards on request. **Prices:** $200 to $800. **Remarks:** Full-time maker, first knife made in 1990. All knives come with handmade sheaths by Judy Choate. **Mark:** Knives marked "Choate."

CHOMILIER, ALAIN AND JORIS,
20 rue des Hauts de Chanturgue, 63100 Clermont-Ferrand, France, Phone: + 33 4 73 25 64 41, jo_chomilier@yahoo.fr
Specialties: One-of-a-kind knives; exclusive designs; art knives in carved patinated bronze, mainly folders, some straight knives and art daggers. **Patterns:** Liner-lock, side-lock, button-lock, lockback folders. **Technical:** Grind carbon and stainless damascus; also carve and patinate bronze. **Prices:** $400 to $3000, some to $4000. **Remarks:** Spare-time makers; first knife sold in 1995; Use fossil stone and ivory, mother-of-pearl, (fossil) coral, meteorite, bronze, gemstones, high karat gold. **Mark:** A. J. Chomilier in italics.

CHRISTENSEN, JON P,
516 Blue Grouse, Stevensville, MT 59870, Phone: 406-697-8377, jpcknives@gmail.com; Web: www.jonchristensenknives.com
Specialties: Hunting/utility knives, folders, art knives. **Patterns:** Mosaic damascus **Technical:** Sole authorship, forges 01, 1084, 52100, 5160, Damascus from 1084/15N20. **Prices:** $220 and up. **Remarks:** ABS Mastersmith, first knife sold in 1999. **Mark:** First and middle initial surrounded by last initial.

CHURCHMAN, T W (TIM),
475 Saddle Horn Drive, Bandera, TX 78003, Phone: 830-796-8350
Specialties: Fancy and traditional straight knives. Bird/trout knives of his design and to customer specs. **Patterns:** Bird/trout knives, Bowies, daggers, fighters, boot knives, some miniatures. **Technical:** Grinds 440C, D2 and 154CM. Offers stainless fittings, fancy filework, exotic and stabilized woods, elk and other antler, and hand sewed lined sheaths. Also flower pins as a style. **Prices:** $350 to $450; some to $2,250. **Remarks:** Part-time maker; first knife made in 1981 after reading *"KNIVES '81."* Doing business as "Custom Knives Churchman Made." **Mark:** "Churchman" over Texas outline, "Bandera" under.

CLAIBORNE, JEFF,
1470 Roberts Rd, Franklin, IN 46131, Phone: 317-736-7443, jeff@claiborneknives.com; Web: www.claiborneknives.com
Specialties: Multi blade slip joint folders. All one-of-a-kind by hand, no jigs or fixtures, swords, straight knives, period pieces, camp knives, hunters, fighters, ethnic swords all periods. Handle: uses stag, pearl, oosic, bone ivory, mastadon-mammoth, elephant or exotic woods. **Technical:** Forges high-carbon steel, makes Damascus, forges cable grinds, O1, 1095, 5160, 52100, L6. **Prices:** $250 and up. **Remarks:** Part-time maker; first knife sold in 1989. **Mark:** Stylized initials in an oval.

CLAIBORNE, RON,
2918 Ellistown Rd, Knox, TN 37924, Phone: 615-524-2054, Bowie@icy.net
Specialties: Multi-blade slip joints, swords, straight knives. **Patterns:** Hunters, daggers, folders. **Technical:** Forges Damascus: mosaic, powder mosaic. Prefers bone and natural handle materials; some exotic woods. **Prices:** $125 to $2500. **Remarks:** Part-time maker; first knife sold in 1979. Doing business as Thunder Mountain Forge Claiborne Knives. **Mark:** Claiborne.

CLARK, D E (LUCKY),
413 Lyman Lane, Johnstown, PA 15909-1409
Specialties: Working straight knives and folders to customer specs. **Patterns:** Customer designs. **Technical:** Grinds D2, 440C, 154CM. **Prices:** $100 to $200; some higher. **Remarks:** Part-time maker; first knife sold in 1975. **Mark:** Name on one side; "Lucky" on other.

CLARK, HOWARD F,
115 35th Pl, Runnells, IA 50237, Phone: 515-966-2126, howard@mvforge.com; Web: mvforge.com
Specialties: Currently Japanese-style swords. **Patterns:** Katana. **Technical:** Forges L6 and 1086. **Prices:** $1200 to 5000. **Remarks:** Full-time maker; first knife sold in 1979. Doing business as Morgan Valley Forge. **Prior Mark:** Block letters and serial number on folders; anvil/initials logo on straight knives. **Current Mark:** Two character kanji "Big Ear."

CLARK, NATE,
604 Baird Dr, Yoncalla, OR 97499, nateclarkknives@hotmail.com; Web: www.nateclarkknives.com
Specialties: Automatics (push button and hidden release) ATS-34 mirror polish or satin finish, Damascus, pearl, ivory, abalone, woods, bone, Micarta, G-10, filework and carving and sheath knives. **Prices:** $100 to $2500. **Remarks:** Full-time knifemaker since 1996. **Mark:** Nate Clark on spring, spacer or blade.

CLARK, R W,
R.W. CLARK CUSTOM KNIVES, 17602 W. Eugene Terrace, Surprise, AZ 85388-5047, Phone: 909-279-3494, info@rwclarkknives.com
Specialties: Military field knives and Asian hybrids. Hand carved leather sheaths. **Patterns:** Fixed blade hunters, field utility and military. Also presentation and collector grade knives. **Technical:** First maker to use liquid metals LM1 material in knives. Other materials include S30V, O1, stainless and carbon Damascus. **Prices:** $75 to $2000. Average price $300. **Remarks:** Started knifemaking in 1990, full-time in 2000. **Mark:** R.W. Clark, Custom, Corona, CA in standard football shape. Also uses three Japanese characters, spelling Clark, on Asian Hybrids.

CLAY, WAYNE,
Box 125B, Pelham, TN 37366, Phone: 931-467-3472, Fax: 931-467-3076
Specialties: Working straight knives and folders in standard patterns. **Patterns:** Hunters and kitchen knives; gents and hunter patterns. **Technical:** Grinds ATS-34. **Prices:** $125 to $500; some to $1000. **Remarks:** Full-time maker; first knife sold in 1978. **Mark:** Name.

CLINCO, MARCUS,
821 Appelby Street, Venice, CA 90291, Phone: 818-610-9640, marcus@clincoknives.com
Specialties: I make mostly fixed blade knives with an emphasis on everyday working and tactical models. Most of my knives are stock removal with the exception of my sole authored damascus blades. I have several integral models including a one piece tactical model named the viper. **Technical:** Most working knife models in ATS 34. Integrals in O-1, D-2 and 440 C. Damascus in 1080 and 15 N 20. Large camp and Bowie models in 5160 and D-2. Handle materials used include micarta, stabilized wood, G-10 and occasionally stag and ivory. **Prices:** $200 - $600.

COATS, KEN,
317 5th Ave, Stevens Point, WI 54481, Phone: 715-544-0115, kandk_c@charter.net
Specialties: Does own jigged bone scales **Patterns:** Traditional slip joints - shadow patterns **Technical:** ATS-34 Blades and springs. Milled frames. Grinds ATS-34, 440C. Stainless blades and backsprings. Does all own heat treating and freeze cycle. Blades are drawn to 60RC. Nickel silver or brass bolsters on folders are soldered, neutralized and pinned. Handles are jigged bone, hardwoods antler, and Micarta. Cuts and jigs own bone, usually shades of brown or green. **Prices:** $300 and up

COCKERHAM, LLOYD,
1717 Carolyn Ave, Denham Springs, IA 70726, Phone: 225-665-1565

COFFEE, JIM,
2785 Rush Rd., Norton, OH 44203, Phone: 330-631-3355, jcoffee735@aol.com; Web: jcoffeecustomknives.com
Specialties: Stock Removal, hunters, skinners, fighters. **Technical:** Bowie handle material - stabilized wood, micarta, mammoth ivory, stag. Full tang and hidden tang. Steels - 0-1, d-2, 5160, damascus **Prices:** $150 to $500 and up. **Remarks:** Part-time maker since 2008. **Mark:** full name in a football etch.

COFFEY, BILL,
68 Joshua Ave, Clovis, CA 93611, Phone: 559-299-4259
Specialties: Working and fancy straight knives and folders of his design. **Patterns:** Hunters, fighters, utility, LinerLock® folders and fantasy knives. **Technical:** Grinds 440C, ATS-34, A-Z and commercial Damascus. **Prices:** $250 to $1000; some to $2500. **Remarks:** Full-time maker. First knife sold in 1993. **Mark:** First and last name, city, state.

COFFMAN, DANNY,
541 Angel Dr S, Jacksonville, AL 36265-5787, Phone: 256-435-1619
Specialties: Straight knives and folders of his design. Now making liner locks for $650 to $1200 with natural handles and contrasting Damascus blades and bolsters. **Patterns:** Hunters, locking and slip-joint folders. **Technical:** Grinds Damascus, 440C and D2. Offers filework and engraving. **Prices:** $100 to $400; some to $800. **Remarks:** Spare-time maker; first knife sold in 1992. Doing business as Customs by Coffman. **Mark:** Last name stamped or engraved.

COHEA, JOHN M,
114 Rogers Dr., Nettleton, MS 38855, Phone: 662-322-5916, jhncohea@hotmail.com; Web: http://jmcknives.blademakers.com
Specialties: Frontier style knives, hawks, and leather. **Patterns:** Bowies, hunters, patch/neck knives, tomahawks, and friction folders. **Technical:** Makes both forged and stock removal knives using high carbon steels and damascus. Uses natural handle materials that include antler, bone, ivory, horn, and figured hardwoods. Also makes rawhide covered sheaths that include fringe, tacks, antique trade beads, and other period correct materials. **Prices:** $100 - $1500, some higher. **Remarks:** Part-time maker, first knife sold in 1999. **Mark:** COHEA stamped on riccasso.

COHEN, N J (NORM),
2408 Sugarcone Rd, Baltimore, MD 21209, Phone: 410-484-3841, inquiry@njknives.com; Web: www.njcknives.com
Specialties: Working class knives. **Patterns:** Hunters, skinners, bird knives, push daggers, boots, kitchen and practical customer designs. **Technical:** Stock removal 440C, ATS-34. Uses Micarta, Corian. Some woods and stabilized woods in handles. **Prices:** $50 to $250. **Remarks:** Part-time maker; first knife sold in 1982. **Mark:** NJC engraved.

COIL, JIMMIE J,
2936 Asbury Pl, Owensboro, KY 42303, Phone: 270-684-7827
Specialties: Traditional working and straight knives of his design. **Patterns:** Hunters, Bowies and fighters. **Technical:** Grinds 440C, ATS-34 and D2. Blades are flat-ground with brush finish; most have tapered tang. Offers filework. **Prices:** $65 to $250; some to $750. **Remarks:** Spare-time maker; first knife sold in 1974. **Mark:** Name.

COLE, DAVE,
620 Poinsetta Dr, Satellite Beach, FL 32937, Phone: 321-773-1687, Web: http://dcknivesandleather.blademakers.com
Specialties: Fixed blades and friction folders of his design or customers. **Patterns:** Utility, hunters, and Bowies. **Technical:** Grinds O1, 1095, 1080, Damascus; prefers natural handle materials. Full custom sheathmaker specializing in inlays, exotics, lacing. **Prices:** $100 and up. **Remarks:** Part-time maker, custom sheath services for others; first knife sold in 1991. **Mark:** D Cole.

COLE, JAMES M,
505 Stonewood Blvd, Bartonville, TX 76226, Phone: 817-430-0302, dogcole@swbell.net

COLE, WELBORN I,
365 Crystal Ct, Athens, GA 30606, Phone: 404-261-3977
Specialties: Traditional straight knives of his design. **Patterns:** Hunters. **Technical:** Grinds 440C, ATS-34 and D2. Good wood scales. **Prices:** NA. **Remarks:** Full-time maker; first knife sold in 1983. **Mark:** Script initials.

COLEMAN, JOHN A,
7325 Bonita Way, Citrus Heights, CA 95610-3003, Phone: 916-335-1568, slimsknifes@yahoo.com
Specialties: Minis, hunters, bowies of his design or yours. **Patterns:** Plain to fancy file back working knives. **Technical:** Grinds 440C, ATS-34, 145CM, D2, 1095, 5160, 01. Some hand-forged blades. Exotic woods bone, antler and some ivory. **Prices:** $100 to $500. **Remarks:** Does some carving in handles. Part-time maker. First knife sold in 1989. OKCA 2010 Award winner for best mini of show. **Mark:** Cowboy setting on log whittling Slim's Custom Knives above cowboy and name and state under cowboy.

COLLINS, LYNN M,
138 Berkley Dr, Elyria, OH 44035, Phone: 440-366-7101
Specialties: Working straight knives. **Patterns:** Field knives, boots and fighters. **Technical:** Grinds D2, 154CM and 440C. **Prices:** Start at $200. **Remarks:** Spare-time maker; first knife sold in 1980. **Mark:** Initials, asterisks.

COLTER, WADE,
PO Box 2340, Colstrip, MT 59323, Phone: 406-748-4573; Shop: 406-748-2010; Cell: 406-740-15
Specialties: Fancy and embellished straight knives, folders and swords of his design; historical and period pieces. **Patterns:** Bowies, swords and folders. **Technical:** Hand forges 52100 ball bearing steel and L6, 1090, cable and chain Damascus from 5N20 and 1084. Carves and makes sheaths. **Prices:** $250 to $3500. **Remarks:** SemiRetired; first knife sold in 1990. Doing business as "Colter's Hell" Forge. **Mark:** Initials on left side ricasso.

CONKLIN, GEORGE L,
Box 902, Ft. Benton, MT 59442, Phone: 406-622-3268, Fax: 406-622-3410, 7bbgrus@3rivers.net
Specialties: Designer and manufacturer of the "Brisket Breaker." **Patterns:** Hunters, utility/camp knives and hatchets. **Technical:** Grinds 440C, ATS-34, D2, 1095, 154CM and 5160. Offers some forging and heat-treats for others. Offers some jewelling. **Prices:** $65 to $200; some to $1000. **Remarks:** Full-time maker. Doing business as Rocky Mountain Knives. **Mark:** Last name in script.

CONLEY, BOB,
1013 Creasy Rd, Jonesboro, TN 37659, Phone: 423-753-3302
Specialties: Working straight knives and folders. **Patterns:** Lockers, two-blades, gents, hunters, traditional-styles, straight hunters. **Technical:** Grinds 440C, 154CM and ATS-34. Engraves. **Prices:** $250 to $450; some to $600. **Remarks:** Full-time maker; first knife sold in 1979. **Mark:** Full name, city, state.

CONN JR., C T,
206 Highland Ave, Attalla, AL 35954, Phone: 205-538-7688
Specialties: Working folders, some fancy. **Patterns:** Full range of folding knives. **Technical:** Grinds O2, 440C and 154CM. **Prices:** $125 to $300; some to $600. **Remarks:** Part-time maker; first knife sold in 1982. **Mark:** Name.

CONNOLLY, JAMES,
2486 Oro-Quincy Hwy, Oroville, CA 95966, Phone: 530-534-5363, rjconnolly@sbcglobal.net
Specialties: Classic working and using knives of his design. **Patterns:** Boots, Bowies, daggers and swords. **Technical:** Grinds ATS-34, BG42, A2, O1. **Prices:** $100 to $500; some to $1500. **Remarks:** Part-time maker; first knife sold in 1980. Doing business as Gold Rush Designs. **Mark:** First initial, last name, Handmade.

CONNOR, JOHN W,
PO Box 12981, Odessa, TX 79768-2981, Phone: 915-362-6901

CONNOR, MICHAEL,
Box 502, Winters, TX 79567, Phone: 915-754-5602
Specialties: Straight knives, period pieces, some folders. **Patterns:** Hunters to camp knives to traditional locking folders to Bowies. **Technical:** Forges 5160, O1, 1084 steels and his own Damascus. **Prices:** Moderate to upscale. **Remarks:** Spare-time maker; first knife sold in 1974. ABS Master Smith 1983. **Mark:** Last name, M.S.

CONTI, JEFFREY D,
21104 75th St E, Bonney Lake, WA 98390, Phone: 253-447-4660, Fax: 253-512-8629
Specialties: Working straight knives. **Patterns:** Fighters and survival knives; hunters, camp knives and fishing knives. **Technical:** Grinds D2, 154CM and O1. Engraves. **Prices:** Start at $80. **Remarks:** Part-time maker; first knife sold in 1980. Does own heat treating. **Mark:** Initials, year, steel type, name and number of knife.

CONWAY, JOHN,
13301 100th Place NE, Kirkland, WA 98034, Phone: 425-823-2821, jcknives@Frontier.com
Specialties: Folders; working and Damascus. Straight knives, camp, utility and fighting knives. **Patterns:** LinerLock® folders of own design. Hidden tang straight knives of own design. **Technical:** Flat grinds forged carbon steels and own Damascus steel, including mosaic. **Prices:** $300 to $850. **Remarks:** Part-

time maker since 1999. **Mark:** Oval with stylized initials J C inset.

COOGAN, ROBERT,
1560 Craft Center Dr, Smithville, TN 37166, Phone: 615-597-6801, http://iweb.tntech.edu/rcoogan/
Specialties: One-of-a-kind knives. **Patterns:** Unique items like ulu-style Appalachian herb knives. **Technical:** Forges; his Damascus is made from nickel steel and W1. **Prices:** Start at $100. **Remarks:** Part-time maker; first knife sold in 1979. **Mark:** Initials or last name in script.

COOK, JAMES R,
455 Anderson Rd, Nashville, AR 71852, Phone: 870 845 5173, jr@jrcookknives.com; Web: www.jrcookknives.com
Specialties: Working straight knives and folders of his design or to customer specs. **Patterns:** Bowies, hunters and camp knives. **Technical:** Forges 1084 and high-carbon Damascus. **Prices:** $500 to $10000. **Remarks:** Full-time maker; first knife sold in 1986. **Mark:** First and middle initials, last name.

COOK, LOUISE,
475 Robinson Ln, Ozark, IL 62972, Phone: 618-777-2932
Specialties: Working and using straight knives of her design and to customer specs; period pieces. **Patterns:** Bowies, hunters and utility/camp knives. **Technical:** Forges 5160. Filework; pin work; silver wire inlay. **Prices:** Start at $50/inch. **Remarks:** Part-time maker; first knife sold in 1990. Doing business as Panther Creek Forge. **Mark:** First name and Journeyman stamp on one side; panther head on the other.

COOK, MIKE,
475 Robinson Ln, Ozark, IL 62972, Phone: 618-777-2932
Specialties: Traditional working and using straight knives of his design and to customer specs. **Patterns:** Bowies, hunters and utility/camp knives. **Technical:** Forges 5160. Filework; pin work. **Prices:** Start at $50/inch. **Remarks:** Spare-time maker; first knife sold in 1991. **Mark:** First initial, last name and Journeyman stamp on one side; panther head on the other.

COOK, MIKE A,
10927 Shilton Rd, Portland, MI 48875, Phone: 517-242-1352, macook@hughes.net Web: www.artofishi.com
Specialties: Fancy/embellished and period pieces of his design. **Patterns:** Daggers, fighters and hunters. **Technical:** Stone bladed knives in agate, obsidian and jasper. Scrimshaws; opal inlays. **Prices:** $60 to $300; some to $800. **Remarks:** Part-time maker; first knife sold in 1988. Doing business as Art of Ishi. **Mark:** Initials and year.

COOMBS JR., LAMONT,
546 State Rt 46, Bucksport, ME 04416, Phone: 207-469-3057, Fax: 207-469-3057, theknifemaker@hotmail.com; Web: www.knivesby.com/coomb-knives.html
Specialties: Classic fancy and embellished straight knives; traditional working and using straight knives. Knives of his design and to customer specs. **Patterns:** Hunters, folders and utility/camp knives. **Technical:** Hollow- and flat-grinds ATS-34, 440C, A2, D2 and O1; grinds Damascus from other makers. **Prices:** $100 to $500; some to $3500. **Remarks:** Full-time maker; first knife sold in 1988. **Mark:** Last name on banner, handmade underneath.

COON, RAYMOND C,
21135 S.E. Tillstrom Rd, Damascus, OR 97089, Phone: 503-658-2252, Raymond@damascusknife.com; Web: Damascusknife.com
Specialties: Working straight knives in standard patterns. **Patterns:** Hunters, Bowies, daggers, boots and axes. **Technical:** Forges high-carbon steel and Damascus or 97089. **Prices:** Start at $235. **Remarks:** Full-time maker; does own leatherwork, makes own Damascus, daggers; first knife sold in 1995. **Mark:** First initial, last name.

COOPER, PAUL,
9 Woods St., Woburn, MA 01801, Phone: 781-938-0519, byksm@yahoo.com
Specialties: Forged, embellished, hand finished fixed-blade knives. **Patterns:** One of a kind designs, often inspired by traditional and historic pieces. **Technical:** Works in tool steel, damascus and natural materials. **Prices:** $500 - $2000. **Remarks:** Part-time maker, formally apprenticed under J.D. Smith. Sold first piece in 2006. **Mark:** Letter C inside bleeding heart.

COPELAND, THOM,
171 Country Line Rd S, Nashville, AR 71852, tcope@cswnet.com
Specialties: Hand forged fixed blades; hunters, Bowies and camp knives. **Remarks:** Member of ABS and AKA (Arkansas Knifemakers Association). **Mark:** Copeland.

COPPINS, DANIEL,
7303 Sherrard Rd, Cambridge, OH 43725, Phone: 740-439-4199
Specialties: Grinds 440 C, D-2. Antler handles. **Patterns:** Drop point hunters, fighters, Bowies, bird and trout daggers. **Prices:** $40 to $800. **Remarks:** Sold first knife in 2002. **Mark:** DC.

CORBY, HAROLD,
218 Brandonwood Dr, Johnson City, TN 37604, Phone: 423-926-9781
Specialties: Large fighters and Bowies; self-protection knives; art knives. Along with art knives and combat knives, Corby now has a all new automatic MO.PB1, also side lock MO LL-1 with titanium liners G-10 handles. **Patterns:** Sub-hilt fighters and hunters. **Technical:** Grinds 154CM, ATS-34 and 440C. **Prices:** $200 to $6000. **Remarks:** Full-time maker; first knife sold in 1969. Doing business as Knives by Corby. **Mark:** Last name.

CORDOVA, JOSEPH G,
1450 Lillie Dr, Bosque Farms, NM 87068, Phone: 505-869-3912, kcordova@rt66.com
Specialties: One-of-a-kind designs, some to customer specs. **Patterns:** Fighter called the 'Gladiator', hunters, boots and cutlery. **Technical:** Forges 1095, 5160; grinds ATS-34, 440C and 154CM. **Prices:** Moderate to upscale. **Remarks:** Full-time maker; first knife sold in 1953. Past chairman of American Bladesmith Society. **Mark:** Cordova made.

CORKUM, STEVE,
34 Basehoar School Rd, Littlestown, PA 17340, Phone: 717-359-9563, sco7129849@aol.com; Web: www.hawkknives.com

COSTA, SCOTT,
409 Coventry Rd, Spicewood, TX 78669, Phone: 830-693-3431
Specialties: Working straight knives. **Patterns:** Hunters, skinners, axes, trophy sets, custom boxed steak sets, carving sets and bar sets. **Technical:** Grinds D2, ATS-34, 440 and Damascus. Heat-treats. **Prices:** $225 to $2000. **Remarks:** Full-time maker; first knife sold in 1985. **Mark:** Initials connected.

COTTRILL, JAMES I,
1776 Ransburg Ave, Columbus, OH 43223, Phone: 614-274-0020
Specialties: Working straight knives of his design. **Patterns:** Caters to the boating and hunting crowd; cutlery. **Technical:** Grinds O1, D2 and 440C. Likes filework. **Prices:** $95 to $250; some to $500. **Remarks:** Full-time maker; first knife sold in 1977. **Mark:** Name, city, state, in oval logo.

COUSINO, GEORGE,
7818 Norfolk, Onsted, MI 49265, Phone: 517-467-4911, cousinoknives@yahoo.com; Web: www.cousinoknives.com
Specialties: Hunters, Bowies using knives. **Patterns:** Hunters, Bowies, buckskinners, folders and daggers. **Technical:** Grinds 440C. **Prices:** $95 to $300. **Remarks:** Part-time maker; first knife sold in 1981. **Mark:** Last name.

COVER, JEFF,
11355 Allen Rd, Potosi, MO 63664, Phone: 573-749-0008, jeffcovercustomknives@hotmail.com
Specialties: Folders and straight knives. **Patterns: Technical: Various** knife steels and handle materials. **Prices:** $70 to $500. **Mark:** Jeff Cover J.C. Custom Knives.

COVER, RAYMOND A,
1206 N Third St, Festus, MO 63028-1628, Phone: 636-937-5955
Specialties: High-tech working straight knives and folders in standard patterns. **Patterns:** Slip joint folders, two-bladed folders. **Technical:** Grinds D2, and ATS-34. **Prices:** $165 to $250; some to $400. **Remarks:** Part-time maker; first knife sold in 1974. **Mark:** Name.

COVER, RAYMOND A,
16235 State Hwy U, Mineral Point, MO 63660, Phone: 573-749-3783
Specialties: High tech working straight knives and folders in working patterns. Slip joints, lock backs, multi bladed folders **Technical:** Various knife steels and handle materials. **Prices:** Swords from bare blades to complete high art $200 to $600. **Mark:** "R Cover"

COWLES, DON,
1026 Lawndale Dr, Royal Oak, MI 48067, Phone: 248-541-4619, don@cowlesknives.com; Web: www.cowlesknives.com
Specialties: Straight, non-folding pocket knives of his design. **Patterns:** Gentlemen's pocket knives. **Technical:** Grinds CPM154, S30V, Damascus, Talonite. Engraves; pearl inlays in some handles. **Prices:** Start at $300. **Remarks:** Full-time maker; first knife sold in 1994. **Mark:** Full name with oak leaf.

COX, COLIN J,
107 N. Oxford Dr, Raymore, MO 64083, Phone: 816-352-2122, Colin4knives@aol.com; Web: www.colincoxknives.com
Specialties: Working straight knives and folders of his design; period pieces. **Patterns:** Hunters, fighters and survival knives. Folders, two-blades, gents and hunters. **Technical:** Grinds D2, 440C, 154CM and ATS-34. **Prices:** $125 to $750; some to $4000. **Remarks:** Full-time maker; first knife sold in 1981. **Mark:** Full name, city and state.

COX, LARRY,
701 W. 13th St, Murfreesboro, AR 71958, Phone: 870-258-2429, Fax: Cell: 870-557-8062
Patterns: Hunters, camp knives, Bowies, and skinners. **Technical:** Forges carbon steel 1084, 1080, 15N29, 5160 and Damascus. Forges own pattern welded Damascus as well as doing own heat treat. **Prices:** $150 and up. **Remarks:** Sole ownership; knives and sheaths. Part-time maker; first knife sold in 2007. Member ABS and Arkansas Knifemakers Association. **Mark:** COX.

COX, SAM,
1756 Love Springs Rd, Gaffney, SC 29341, Phone: 864-489-1892
Remarks: Started making knives in 1981 for another maker. 1st knife sold under own name in 1983. Full-time maker 1985-2009. Retired in 2010. Now part time. **Mark:** Different logo each year.

COYE, BILL,
PO Box 470684, Tulsa, OK 74147, Phone: 918-232-5721, info@coyeknives.com; Web: www.coyeknives.com
Specialties: Tactical and utility knives. **Patterns:** Fighters and utility. **Technical:** Grinds CPM154CM, 154CM, CTS-XHP and Elmax stainless steels. **Prices:** $210 to $320. **Remarks:** Part-time maker. First knife sold in 2009. **Mark:** COYE.

CRAIG, ROGER L,
2617 SW Seabrook Ave, Topeka, KS 66614, Phone: 785-249-4109
Specialties: Working and camp knives, some fantasy; all his design. **Patterns:** Fighters, hunter. **Technical:** Grinds 1095 and 5160. Most knives have file work. **Prices:** $50 to $250. **Remarks:** Part-time maker; first knife sold in 1991. Doing business as Craig Knives. **Mark:** Last name-Craig.

CRAIN, JACK W,
PO Box 212, Granbury, TX 76048, jack@jackcrainknives.com Web: www.jackcrainknives.com
Specialties: Fantasy and period knives; combat and survival knives. **Patterns:** One-of-a-kind art or fantasy daggers, swords and Bowies; survival knives. **Technical:** Forges Damascus; grinds stainless steel. Carves. **Prices:** $350 to $2500; some to $20,000. **Remarks:** Full-time maker; first knife sold in 1969. Designer and maker of the knives seen in the films *Dracula 2000*, *Executive Decision*, *Demolition Man*, *Predator I* and *II*, *Commando*, *Die Hard I* and *II*, *Road House*, *Ford Fairlane* and *Action Jackson*, and television shows *War of the Worlds*, *Air Wolf*, *Kung Fu: The Legend Cont.* and *Tales of the Crypt*. **Mark:** Stylized crane.

CRAMER, BRENT,
PO BOX 99, Wheatland, IN 47597, Phone: 812-881-9961, Bdcramer@juno.com Web: BDCramerKnives.com
Specialties: Traditional and custom working and using knives. **Patterns:** Traditional single blade slip-joint folders and standard fixed blades. **Technical:** Stock removal only. Pivot bushing construction on folders. Steel: D-2, 154 CM, ATS-34, CPM-D2, CPM-154CM, 0-1, 52100, A-2. All steels heat treated in shop with LN Cryo. Handle Material: Stag, Bone, Wood, Ivory, and Micarta. **Prices:** $150 - $550. **Remarks:** Part-time maker. First fixed blade sold in 2003. First folder sold in 2007. **Mark:** BDC and B.D.Cramer.

CRAWFORD, PAT AND WES,
205 N. Center, West Memphis, AR 72301, Phone: 870-732-2452, patcrawford1@earthlink.com; Web: www.crawfordknives.com
Specialties: Stainless steel Damascus. High-tech working self-defense and combat types and folders. **Patterns:** Tactical-more fancy knives now. **Technical:** Grinds S30V. **Prices:** $400 to $2000; first knife sold in 1973. **Mark:** Last name.

CRAWLEY, BRUCE R,
16 Binbrook Dr, Croydon 3136 Victoria, AUSTRALIA
Specialties: Folders. **Patterns:** Hunters, lockback folders and Bowies. **Technical:** Grinds 440C, ATS-34 and commercial Damascus. Offers filework and mirror polish. **Prices:** $160 to $3500. **Remarks:** Part-time maker; first knife sold in 1990. **Mark:** Initials.

CRENSHAW, AL,
Rt 1 Box 717, Eufaula, OK 74432, Phone: 918-452-2128
Specialties: Folders of his design and in standard patterns. **Patterns:** Hunters, locking folders, slip-joint folders, multi blade folders. **Technical:** Grinds 440C, D2 and ATS-34. Does filework on back springs and blades; offers scrimshaw on some handles. **Prices:** $150 to $300; some higher. **Remarks:** Part-time maker; first knife sold in 1981. Doing business as A. Crenshaw Knives. **Mark:** First initial, last name, Lake Eufaula, state stamped; first initial last name in rainbow; Lake Eufaula across bottom with Okla. in middle.

CRIST, ZOE,
2274 Deep Gap Rd., Flat Rock, NC 28731, Phone: 828-685-0147, zoe@zoecristknives.com Web: www.zoecristknives.com
Specialties: Mosaic and classic pattern Damascus. Custom Damascus and traditional Damascus working and art knives. Also makes Mokume. Works to customer specs. **Patterns:** All Damascus knives, bowies, fighters, neck, boot, and high-end art knives. **Technical:** Makes all his own Damascus Steel from 1095, L6, 15n20. Forges all knives, heat treats, filework, differential heat treating. **Prices:** $150 - $2500. **Remarks:** Full-time maker, has been making knives since 1988, went full-time 2009. Also makes own leather sheaths. **Mark:** Small "z" with long tail on left side of blade at ricasso.

CROCKFORD, JACK,
1859 Harts Mill Rd, Chamblee, GA 30341, Phone: 770-457-4680
Specialties: Lockback folders. **Patterns:** Hunters, fishing and camp knives, traditional folders. **Technical:** Grinds A2, D2, ATS-34 and 440C. Engraves and scrimshaws. **Prices:** Start at $175. **Remarks:** Part-time maker; first knife sold in 1975. **Mark:** Name.

CROSS, KEVIN,
PO Box 38, Higganum, CT 06441, Phone: 860-345-3949, kevincross@comcast.net
Specialties: Working/using and presentation grade fixed-blade knives. Also, kitchen knives with custom handles. **Patterns:** Hunters, skinners, fighters. Bowies, camp knives. **Technical:** Stock removal maker. Uses O1, 1095, 154 CPM as well as Damascus from Eggerling, Ealy, Donnelly, Nichols, Barr and others. Most handles are natural materials such as burled and spalted woods, stag and ancient ivory. **Prices:** $200 - $1,200. **Remarks:** Part-time maker. First knife sold around 1997. **Mark:** Name, city and state.

CROSS, ROBERT,
RMB 200B, Manilla Rd, Tamworth 2340, NSW, AUSTRALIA, Phone: 067-618385

CROTTS, DAN,
PO Box 68, Elm Springs, AR 72728, Phone: 479-248-7116, dancrottsknives@yahoo.com Web: www.facebook.com/dancrottsknives
Specialties: User grade, hunting, tactical and folders. **Technical:** High-end tool steel. **Prices:** $2200. **Remarks:** Specializes in making performance blades. **Mark:** Crotts.

CROWDER, GARY L,
HC61 Box 364, Sallisaw, OK 74955, Phone: 918-775-9009, gcrowder99@yahoo.com
Specialties: Folders, multi-blades. **Patterns:** Traditional with a few sheath knives. **Technical:** Flat grinds ATS-34, D2 and others, as well as Damascus via stock-removal. **Prices:** $150 to $600. **Remarks:** Retired, part-time maker. First knife sold in 1994. **Mark:** small acid-etched "Crowder" on blade.

CROWDER, ROBERT,
Box 1374, Thompson Falls, MT 59873, Phone: 406-827-4754
Specialties: Traditional working knives to customer specs. **Patterns:** Hunters, Bowies, fighters and fillets. **Technical:** Grinds ATS-34, 154CM, 440C, Vascowear and commercial Damascus. **Prices:** $225 to $500; some to $2500. **Remarks:** Full-time maker; first knife sold in 1985. **Mark:** R Crowder signature & Montana.

CROWELL, JAMES L,
PO Box 822, 676 Newnata Cutoff, Mtn. View, AR 72560, Phone: 870-746-4215, crowellknives@yahoo.com; Web: www.crowellknives.com
Specialties: Bowie knives; fighters and working knives. **Patterns:** Hunters, fighters, Bowies, daggers and folders. Period pieces: War hammers, Japanese and European. **Technical:** Forges 10 series carbon steels as well as O1, L6 and his own Damascus. **Prices:** $425 to $4500; some to $7500. **Remarks:** Full-time maker; first knife sold in 1980. Earned ABS Master Bladesmith in 1986. 2011 Marked 25 years as an ABS Mastersmith. **Mark:** A shooting star.

CROWL, PETER,
5786 County Road 10, Waterloo, IN 46793, Phone: 260-488-2532, pete@petecrowlknives.com; Web: www.petecrowlknives.com
Specialties: Bowie, hunters. **Technical:** Forges 5160, 1080, W2, 52100. **Prices:** $200 and up. **Remarks:** ABS Journeyman smith. **Mark:** Last name in script.

CROWNER, JEFF,
1565 Samuel Drive, Cottage Grove, OR 97424, Phone: 541-201-3182, Fax: 541-579-3762
Specialties: Custom knife maker. I make some of the following: wilderness survival blades, martial art weapons, hunting blades. **Technical:** I differentially heat treat every knife. I use various steels like 5160, L-6, Cable Damascus, 52100, 6150, and some stainless types. I use the following for handle materials: TeroTuf by Columbia Industrial products and exotic hardwoods and horn. I make my own custom sheaths as well with either kydex or leather.

CROWTHERS, MARK F,
PO Box 4641, Rolling Bay, WA 98061-0641, Phone: 206-842-7501

CUCCHIARA, MATT,
387 W. Hagler, Fresno, CA 93711, Phone: 559-917-2328, matt@cucchiaraknives.com Web: www.cucchiaraknives.com
Specialties: I make large and small, plain or hand carved Ti handled Tactical framelock folders. All decoration and carving work done by maker. Also known for my hand carved Ti pocket clips. **Prices:** Start at around $400 and go as high as $1500 or so.

CULVER, STEVE,
5682 94th St, Meriden, KS 66512, Phone: 785-484-0146, Web: www.culverart.com
Specialties: Edged tools and weapons, collectible and functional. **Patterns:** Bowies, daggers, swords, hunters, folders and edged tools. **Technical:** Forges carbon steels and his own pattern welded steels. **Prices:** $500 to $5,000. **Remarks:** Full-time maker; first knife sold in 1989. **Mark:** Last name, M. S.

CUMMING, BOB,
CUMMING KNIVES, 35 Manana Dr, Cedar Crest, NM 87008, Phone: 505-286-0509, cumming@comcast.net; Web: www.cummingknives.com
Specialties: One-of-a-kind exhibition grade custom Bowie knives, exhibition grade and working hunters, bird & trout knives, salt and fresh water fillet knives. Low country oyster knives, custom tanto's plains Indian style sheaths & custom leather, all types of exotic handle materials, scrimshaw and engraving. Added folders in 2006. Custom oyster knives. **Prices:** $95 to $3500 and up. **Remarks:** Mentored by the late Jim Nolen, sold first knife in 1978 in Denmark. Retired U.S. Foreign Service Officer. Member NCCKG. **Mark:** Stylized CUMMING.

CURTISS, STEVE L,
PO Box 448, Eureka, MT 59914, Phone: 406-889-5510, Fax: 406-889-5510, slc@bladerigger.com; Web: http://www.bladerigger.com
Specialties: True custom and semi-custom production (SCP), specialized concealment blades; advanced sheaths and tailored body harnessing systems. **Patterns:** Tactical/personal defense fighters, swords, utility and custom patterns. **Technical:** Grinds A2 and Talonite®; heat-treats. Sheaths: Kydex or Kydex-lined leather laminated or Kydex-lined with Rigger Coat™. Exotic materials available. **Prices:** $50 to $10,000. **Remarks:** Full-time maker. Doing business as Blade Rigger L.L.C. Martial artist and unique defense industry tools and equipment. **Mark:** For true custom: Initials and for SCP: Blade Rigger.

D

DAILEY, G E,
577 Lincoln St, Seekonk, MA 02771, Phone: 508-336-5088, gedailey@msn.com; Web: www.gedailey.com
Specialties: One-of-a-kind exotic designed edged weapons. **Patterns:** Folders, daggers and swords. **Technical:** Reforges and grinds Damascus; prefers hollow-grinding. Engraves, carves, offers filework and sets stones and uses exotic gems and gold. **Prices:** Start at $1100. **Remarks:** Full-time maker. First knife sold in 1982. **Mark:** Last name or stylized initialed logo.

DAKE, C M,
19759 Chef Menteur Hwy, New Orleans, LA 70129-9602, Phone: 504-254-0357, Fax: 504-254-9501
Specialties: Fancy working folders. **Patterns:** Front-lock lockbacks, button-lock folders. **Technical:** Grinds ATS-34 and Damascus. **Prices:** $500 to $2500; some higher. **Remarks:** Full-time maker; first knife sold in 1988. Doing business as Bayou Custom Cutlery. **Mark:** Last name.

DAKE, MARY H,
Rt 5 Box 287A, New Orleans, LA 70129, Phone: 504-254-0357

DALLYN, KELLY,
124 Deerbrook Place S.E., Calgary, AB, CANADA T2J 6J5, Phone: 403-475-3056, info@dallyn-knives.com Web: dallyn-knives.com
Specialties: Kitchen, utility, and hunting knives

DAMASTEEL STAINLESS DAMASCUS,
3052 Isim Rd., Norman, OK 73026, Phone: 888-804-0683; 405-321-3614, damascus@newmex.com; Web: www.ssdamacus.com
Patterns: Rose, Odin's eye, 5, 20, 30 twists Hakkapelitta, TNT, and infinity, Big Rose, Mumin

DAMLOVAC, SAVA,
10292 Bradbury Dr, Indianapolis, IN 46231, Phone: 317-839-4952
Specialties: Period pieces, fantasy, Viking, Moran type all Damascus daggers. **Patterns:** Bowies, fighters, daggers, Persian-style knives. **Technical:** Uses own Damascus, some stainless, mostly hand forges. **Prices:** $150 to $2500; some higher. **Remarks:** Full-time maker; first knife sold in 1993. Specialty, Bill Moran all Damascus dagger sets, in Moran-style wood case. **Mark:** "Sava" stamped in Damascus or etched in stainless.

D'ANDREA, JOHN,
8517 N Linwood Loop, Citrus Springs, FL 34433-5045, Phone: 352-489-2803, jpda@optonline.net
Specialties: Fancy working straight knives and folders with filework and distinctive leatherwork. **Patterns:** Hunters, fighters, daggers, folders and an occasional sword. **Technical:** Grinds ATS-34, 154CM, 440C and D2. **Prices:** $220 to $1000. **Remarks:** Part-time maker; first knife sold in 1986. **Mark:** First name, last initial imposed on samurai sword.

D'ANGELO, LAURENCE,
14703 NE 17th Ave, Vancouver, WA 98686, Phone: 360-573-0546
Specialties: Straight knives of his design. **Patterns:** Bowies, hunters and locking folders. **Technical:** Grinds D2, ATS-34 and 440C. Hand makes all sheaths. **Prices:** $100 to $200. **Remarks:** Full-time maker; first knife sold in 1987. **Mark:** Football logo—first and middle initials, last name, city, state, Maker.

DANIEL, TRAVIS E,
PO Box 1223, Thomaston, GA 30286, Phone: 252-362-1229, tedsknives@mail.com
Specialties: Traditional working straight knives of his design or to customer specs. **Patterns:** Hunters, fighters and utility/camp knives. **Technical:** Grinds ATS-34, 440-C, 154CM, forges his own Damascus. Stock removal. **Prices:** $90 to $1200. **Remarks:** Full-time maker; first knife sold in 1976. **Mark:** TED.

DANIELS, ALEX,
1416 County Rd 415, Town Creek, AL 35672, Phone: 256-685-0943, akdknives@gmail.com; Web: http://alexdanielscustomknives.com
Specialties: Working and using straight knives and folders; period pieces, reproduction Bowies. **Patterns:** Mostly reproduction Bowies but offers full line of knives. **Technical:** BG-42, 440C, 1095, 52100 forged blades. **Prices:** $350 to $5500. **Remarks:** Full-time maker; first knife sold in 1963. **Mark:** First and middle initials, last name, city and state.

DANNEMANN, RANDY,
RIM RANCH, 27752 P25 Rd, Hotchkiss, CO 81419
Specialties: Hunting knives. **Patterns:** Utility hunters, trout. **Technical:** 440C and D2. **Price:** $95 to $450. **Remarks:** First knife sold 1974. **Mark:** R. Dannemann Colorado or stamped Dannemann.

DARBY, DAVID T,
30652 S 533 Rd, Cookson, OK 74427, Phone: 918-457-4868, knfmkr@fullnet.net
Specialties: Forged blades only, all styles. **Prices:** $350 and up. **Remarks:** ABS Journeyman Smith. **Mark:** Stylized quillion dagger incorporates last name (Darby).

DARBY, JED,
7878 E Co Rd 50 N, Greensburg, IN 47240, Phone: 812-663-2696
Specialties: Traditional working/using straight knives of his design and to customer specs. **Patterns:** Bowies, hunters and utility/camp knives. **Technical:** Grinds 440C, ATS-34 and Damascus. **Prices:** $70 to $550; some to $1000. **Remarks:** Full-time maker; first knife sold in 1992. Doing business as Darby Knives. **Mark:** Last name and year.

DARBY, RICK,
71 Nestingrock Ln, Levittown, PA 19054
Specialties: Working straight knives. **Patterns:** Boots, fighters and hunters with mirror finish. **Technical:** Grinds 440C and CPM440V. **Prices:** $125 to $300. **Remarks:** Part-time maker; first knife sold in 1974. **Mark:** First and middle initials, last name.

DARCEY, CHESTER L,
1608 Dominik Dr, College Station, TX 77840, Phone: 979-696-1656, DarceyKnives@yahoo.com
Specialties: Lockback, LinerLock® and scale release folders. **Patterns:** Bowies, hunters and utilities. **Technical:** Stock removal on carbon and stainless steels, forge own Damascus. **Prices:** $200 to $1000. **Remarks:**

Part-time maker, first knife sold in 1999. **Mark:** Last name in script.

DARK, ROBERT,
2218 Huntington Court, Oxford, AL 36203, Phone: 256-831-4645, dark@darkknives.com; Web: www.darkknives.com
Specialties: Fixed blade working knives of maker's designs. Works with customer designed specifications. **Patterns:** Hunters, Bowies, camp knives, kitchen/utility, bird and trout. Standard patterns and customer designed. **Technical:** Forged and stock removal. Works with high carbon, stainless and Damascus steels. Hollow and flat grinds. **Prices:** $175 to $750. **Remarks:** Sole authorship knives and custom leather sheaths. Full-time maker. **Mark:** "R Dark" on left side of blade.

DARPINIAN, DAVE,
PO Box 2643, Olathe, KS 66063, Phone: 913-244-7114, darpo1956@yahoo.com Web: www.kansasknives.org
Specialties: Hunters, fighters, utilities, lock back folders. **Patterns:** Full range of straight knives including art daggers. **Technical:** Art grinds, Damascus, 1095, Clay temper hammon, Stock removal and forging. **Prices:** $300 to $1000. **Remarks:** First knife sold in 1986, part-time maker. **Mark:** Last name.

DAVIDSON, EDMUND,
3345 Virginia Ave, Goshen, VA 24439, Phone: 540-997-5651, Web: www.edmunddavidson.com
Specialties: High class art integrals. **Patterns:** Many hunters and art models. **Technical:** CPM 154-CM. **Prices:** $100 to infinity. **Remarks:** Full-time maker; first knife sold in 1986. **Mark:** Name in deer head or custom logos.

DAVIDSON, LARRY,
14249 River Rd., New Braunfels, TX 78132, Phone: 830-214-5144, lazza@davidsonknives.com; Web: www.davidsonknives.com

DAVIS, BARRY L,
4262 US 20, Castleton, NY 12033, Phone: 518-477-5036, daviscustomknives@yahoo.com
Specialties: Collector grade Damascus folders. Traditional designs with focus on turn-of-the-century techniques employed. Sole authorship. Forges own Damascus, does all carving, filework, gold work and piquet. Uses only natural handle material. Enjoys doing multi-blade as well as single blade folders and daggers. **Prices:** Prices range from $2000 to $7000. **Remarks:** First knife sold in 1980.

DAVIS, CHARLIE,
ANZA KNIVES, PO Box 710806, Santee, CA 92072, Phone: 619-561-9445, Fax: 619-390-6283, sales@anzaknives.com; Web: www.anzaknives.com
Specialties: Fancy and embellished working straight knives of his design. **Patterns:** Hunters, camp and utility knives. **Technical:** Grinds high-carbon files. **Prices:** $20 to $185, custom depends. **Remarks:** Full-time maker; first knife sold in 1980. Now offers custom. **Mark:** ANZA U.S.A.

DAVIS, DON,
8415 Coyote Run, Loveland, CO 80537-9665, Phone: 970-669-9016, Fax: 970-669-8072
Specialties: Working straight knives in standard patterns or to customer specs. **Patterns:** Hunters, utility knives, skinners and survival knives. **Technical:** Grinds 440C, ATS-34. **Prices:** $75 to $250. **Remarks:** Full-time maker; first knife sold in 1985. **Mark:** Signature, city and state.

DAVIS, JESSE W,
7398A Hwy 3, Sarah, MS 38665, Phone: 662-613-1644, jandddvais1@earthlink.net
Specialties: Working straight knives and boots in standard patterns and to customer specs. **Patterns:** Boot knives, daggers, fighters, subhilts & Bowies. **Technical:** Grinds A2, D2, 440C and commercial Damascus. **Prices:** $125 to $1000. **Remarks:** Full-time maker; first knife sold in 1977. Former member Knifemakers Guild (in good standing). **Mark:** Name or initials.

DAVIS, JOEL,
74538 165th, Albert Lea, MN 56007, Phone: 507-377-0808, joelknives@yahoo.com
Specialties: Complete sole authorship presentation grade highly complex pattern-welded mosaic Damascus blade and bolster stock. **Patterns:** To date Joel has executed over 900 different mosaic Damascus patterns in the past four years. Anything conceived by maker's imagination. **Technical:** Uses various heat colorable "high vibrancy" steels, nickel 200 and some powdered metal for bolster stock only. Uses 1095, 1075 and 15N20. High carbon steels for cutting edge blade stock only. **Prices:** 15 to $50 per square inch and up depending on complexity of pattern. **Remarks:** Full-time mosaic Damascus metal smith focusing strictly on never-before-seen mosaic patterns. Most of maker's work is used for art knives ranging between $1500 to $4500.

DAVIS, JOHN,
235 Lampe Rd, Selah, WA 98942, Phone: 509-697-3845, 509-945-4570, jdwelds@charter.net
Specialties: Damascus and mosaic Damascus, working knives, working folders, art knives and art folders. **Technical:** Some ATS-34 and stainless Damascus. Embellishes with fancy stabilized wood, mammoth and walrus ivory. **Prices:** Start at $150. **Remarks:** Part-time maker; first knife sold in 1996. **Mark:** Name and state on Damascus stamp initials; name inside back RFR.

DAVIS, STEVE,
3370 Chatsworth Way, Powder Springs, GA 30127, Phone: 770-427-5740, bsdavis@bellsouth.net
Specialties: Gents and ladies folders. **Patterns:** Straight knives, slip-joint folders, locking-liner folders. **Technical:** Grinds ATS-34 forges own Damascus. Offers filework; prefers hand-rubbed finishes and natural handle materials. Uses pearl, ivory, stag and exotic woods. **Prices:** $250 to $800; some to $1500.

Remarks: Full-time maker; first knife sold in 1988. Doing business as Custom Knives by Steve Davis. **Mark:** Name engraved on blade.

DAVIS, TERRY,
Box 111, Sumpter, OR 97877, Phone: 541-894-2307
Specialties: Traditional and contemporary folders. **Patterns:** Multi-blade folders, whittlers and interframe multiblades; sunfish patterns. **Technical:** Flatgrinds ATS-34. **Prices:** $400 to $1000; some higher. **Remarks:** Full-time maker; first knife sold in 1985. **Mark:** Name in logo.

DAVIS, VERNON M,
2020 Behrens Circle, Waco, TX 76705, Phone: 254-799-7671
Specialties: Presentation-grade straight knives. **Patterns:** Bowies, daggers, boots, fighters, hunters and utility knives. **Technical:** Hollow-grinds 440C, ATS-34 and D2. Grinds an aesthetic grind line near choil. **Prices:** $125 to $550; some to $5000. **Remarks:** Part-time maker; first knife sold in 1980. **Mark:** Last name and city inside outline of state.

DAVIS, W C,
1955 S 1251 Rd, El Dorado Springs, MO 64744, Phone: 417-876-1259
Specialties: Fancy working straight knives and folders. **Patterns:** Folding lockers and slip-joints; straight hunters, fighters and Bowies. **Technical:** Grinds A2, ATS-34, 154, CPM T490V and CPM 530V. **Prices:** $100 to $300; some to $1000. **Remarks:** Full-time maker; first knife sold in 1972. **Mark:** Name.

DAVIS JR., JIM,
5129 Ridge St, Zephyrhills, FL 33541, Phone: 813-779-9213 813-469-4241 Cell, jimdavisknives@aol.com
Specialties: Presentation-grade fixed blade knives w/composite hidden tang handles. Employs a variety of ancient and contemporary ivories. **Patterns:** One-of-a-kind gents, personal, and executive knives and hunters w/unique cam-lock pouch sheaths and display stands. **Technical:** Flat grinds ATS-34 and stainless Damascus w/most work by hand w/assorted files. **Prices:** $300 and up. **Remarks:** Full-time maker, first knives sold in 2000. **Mark:** Signature w/printed name over "HANDCRAFTED."

DAVISON, TODD A.,
415 So. Reed, Lyons, KS 67554, Phone: 620-894-0402, todd@tadscustomknives.com; Web: www.tadscustomknives.com
Specialties: Making working/using and collector folders of his design. All knives are truly made one of a kind. Each knife has a serial number inside the liner. **Patterns:** Single and double blade traditional slip-joint pocket knives. **Technical:** Free hand hollow ground blades, hand finished. Using only the very best materials possible. Holding the highest standards to fit & finish and detail. Does his own heat treating. ATS34 and D2 steel. **Prices:** $450 to $900, some higher. **Remarks:** Full time maker, first knife sold in 1981. **Mark:** T.A. DAVISON stamped.

DAWKINS, DUDLEY L,
221 NW Broadmoor Ave., Topeka, KS 66606-1254, Phone: 785-235-0468, dawkind@sbcglobal.net
Specialties: Stylized old or "Dawkins Forged" with anvil in center. New tang stamps. **Patterns:** Straight knives. **Technical:** Mostly carbon steel; some Damascus-all knives forged. **Prices:** Knives: $275 and up; Sheaths: $95 and up. **Remarks:** All knives supplied with wood-lined sheaths. Also make custom wood-lined sheaths $55 and up. ABS Member, sole authorship. **Mark:** Stylized "DLD or Dawkins Forged with anvil in center.

DAWSON, BARRY,
7760 E Hwy 69, Prescott Valley, AZ 86314, Phone: 928-255-9830, dawsonknives@yahoo.com; Web: www.dawsonknives.com
Specialties: Samurai swords, combat knives, collector daggers, tactical, folding and hunting knives. **Patterns:** Offers over 60 different models. **Technical:** Grinds 440C, ATS-34, own heat-treatment. **Prices:** $75 to $1500; some to $5000. **Remarks:** Full-time maker; first knife sold in 1975. **Mark:** Last name, USA in print or last name in script.

DAWSON, LYNN,
7760 E Hwy 69 #C-5 157, Prescott Valley, AZ 86314, Phone: 928-713-2812, lynnknives@yahoo.com; Web: www.lynnknives.com
Specialties: Swords, hunters, utility, and art pieces. **Patterns:** Over 25 patterns to choose from. **Technical:** Grinds 440C, ATS-34, own heat treating. **Prices:** $80 to $1000. **Remarks:** Custom work and her own designs. **Mark:** The name "Lynn" in print or script.

DE MARIA JR., ANGELO,
12 Boronda Rd, Carmel Valley, CA 93924, Phone: 831-659-3381, Fax: 831-659-1315, angelodemaria1@mac.com
Specialties: Damascus, fixed and folders, sheaths. **Patterns:** Mosaic and random. **Technical:** Forging 5160, 1084 and 15N20. **Prices:** $200+. **Remarks:** Part-time maker. **Mark:** Angelo de Maria Carmel Valley, CA etch or AdM stamp.

DE MESA, JOHN,
1565 W. Main St., STE. 208 #229, Lewisville, TX 75057, Phone: 972-310-3877, TogiArts@me.com; Web: http://togiarts.com/ and http://togiarts.com/CSC/index.html
Specialties: Japanese sword polishing. **Technical:** Traditional sword polishing of Japanese swords made by sword makers in Japan and U.S. **Prices:** Starting at $75 per inch. **Remarks:** Custom Swords Collaborations IN collaboration with Jose De Braga, we can mount Japanese style sword with custom carved handles, sword fittings and scabbards to customer specs.

DEAN, HARVEY J,
3266 CR 232, Rockdale, TX 76567, Phone: 512-446-3111, Fax: 512-446-5060, dean@tex1.net; Web: www.harveydean.com
Specialties: Collectible, functional knives. **Patterns:** Bowies, hunters, folders,

daggers, swords, battle axes, camp and combat knives. **Technical:** Forges 1095, O1 and his Damascus. **Prices:** $350 to $10,000. **Remarks:** Full-time maker; first knife sold in 1981. **Mark:** Last name and MS.

DEBAUD, JAKE,
2403 Springvale Lane, Dallas, TX 75234, Phone: 214-916-1891, jake.debaud@ gmail.com Web: www.debaudknives.com
Specialties: Custom damascus art knives, hunting knives and tactical knives. **Technical:** A2, D2, 01, 1095 and some stainless if requested ATS-34 or 154CM and S30V. **Remarks:** Full-time maker. Have been making knives for three years.

DEBRAGA, JOVAN,
141 Notre Dame des Victoir, Quebec, CANADA G2G 1J3, Phone: 418-997-0819/418-877-1915, jovancdebraga@msn.com
Specialties: Art knives, fantasy pieces and working knives of his design or to customer specs. **Patterns:** Knives with sculptured or carved handles, from miniatures to full-sized working knives. **Technical:** Grinds and hand-files 440C, and ATS-34. A variety of steels and handle materials available. **Prices:** Start at $300. **Remarks:** Full time maker. Sculptor and knifemaker. First knife sold in 2003. **Mark:** Initials in stylized script and serial number.

DEL RASO, PETER,
28 Mayfield Dr, Mt. Waverly, Victoria, 3149, AUSTRALIA, Phone: 613 98060644, delraso@optusnet.com.au
Specialties: Fixed blades, some folders, art knives. **Patterns:** Daggers, Bowies, tactical, boot, personal and working knives. **Technical:** Grinds ATS-34, commercial Damascus and any other type of steel on request. **Prices:** $100 to $1500. **Remarks:** Part-time maker, first show in 1993. **Mark:** Maker's surname stamped.

DELAROSA, JIM,
2116 N Pontiac Dr, Janesville, WI 53545, Phone: 262-422-8604, D-knife@ hotmail.com
Specialties: Working straight knives and folders of his design or customer specs. **Patterns:** Hunters, skinners, fillets, utility and locking folders. **Technical:** Grinds ATS-34, 440-C, D2, O1 and commercial Damascus. **Prices:** $100 to $500; some higher. **Remarks:** Part-time maker. **Mark:** First and last name.

DELL, WOLFGANG,
Am Alten Berg 9, D-73277 Owen-Teck, GERMANY, Phone: 49-7021-81802, wolfgang@dell-knives.de; Web: www.dell-knives.de
Specialties: Fancy high-art straight of his design and to customer specs. **Patterns:** Fighters, hunters, Bowies and utility/camp knives. **Technical:** Grinds ATS-34, RWL-34, Elmax, Damascus (Fritz Schneider). Offers high gloss finish and engraving. **Prices:** $500 to $1000; some to $1600. **Remarks:** Full-time maker; first knife sold in 1992. **Mark:** Hopi hand of peace.

DELLANA,
STARLANI INT'L INC, 1135 Terminal Way Ste #209, Reno, NV 89502, Phone: 304-727-5512; 702-569-7827, 1dellana@gmail.com; Web: www.dellana.cc
Specialties: Collector grade fancy/embellished high art folders and art daggers. **Patterns:** Locking folders and art daggers. **Technical:** Forges her own Damascus and W-2. Engraves, does stone setting, filework, carving and gold/platinum fabrication. Prefers exotic, high karat gold, platinum, silver, gemstone and mother-of-pearl handle materials. **Price:** Upscale. **Remarks:** Sole authorship, full-time maker, first knife sold in 1994. Also does one high art collaboration a year with Van Barnett. Member: Art Knife Invitational and ABS. **Mark:** First name.

DELONG, DICK,
PO Box 1024, Centerville, TX 75833-1024, Phone: 903-536-1454
Specialties: Fancy working knives and fantasy pieces. **Patterns:** Hunters and small skinners. **Technical:** Grinds and files O1, D2, 440C and Damascus. Offers cocobolo and Osage orange for handles. **Prices:** Start at $50. **Remarks:** Part-time maker. Member of Art Knife Invitational. Voting member of Knifemakers Guild. Member of ABS. **Mark:** Last name; some unmarked.

DEMENT, LARRY,
PO Box 1807, Prince Fredrick, MD 20678, Phone: 410-586-9011
Specialties: Fixed blades. **Technical:** Forged and stock removal. **Prices:** $75 to $200. **Remarks:** Affordable, good feelin', quality knives. Part-time maker.

DEMPSEY, GORDON S,
PO Box 7497, N. Kenai, AK 99635, Phone: 907-776-8425
Specialties: Working straight knives. **Patterns:** Pattern welded Damascus and carbon steel blades. **Technical:** Pattern welded Damascus and carbon steel. **Prices:** $80 to $250. **Remarks:** Part-time maker; first knife sold in 1974. **Mark:** Name.

DENNEHY, JOHN D,
2959 Zachary Drive, Loveland, CO 80537, Phone: 970-218-7128, www.thewildirishrose.com
Specialties: Working straight knives, throwers, and leatherworker's knives. **Technical:** 440C, & O1, heat treats own blades, part-time maker, first knife sold in 1989. **Patterns:** Small hunting to presentation Bowies, leatherworks round and head knives. **Prices:** $200 and up. **Remarks:** Custom sheath maker, sheath making seminars at the Blade Show.

DENNING, GENO,
CAVEMAN ENGINEERING, 135 Allenvalley Rd, Gaston, SC 29053, Phone: 803-794-6067, cden101656@aol.com; Web: www.cavemanengineering.com
Specialties: Mirror finish. **Patterns:** Hunters, fighters, folders. **Technical:** ATS-34, 440V, S-30-V D2. **Prices:** $100 and up. **Remarks:** Full-time maker since 1996. Sole income since 1999. Instructor at Montgomery Community College (Grinding Blades). A director of SCAK: South Carolina Association of

Knifemakers. **Mark:** Troy NC.

DERESPINA, RICHARD,
, Willow Grove, PA, Phone: 917-843-7627, derespinaknives@yahoo.com Web: www.derespinaknives.com
Specialties: Custom fixed blades and folders, Kris and Karambit. **Technical:** I use the stock removal method. Steels I use are S30V, 154CM, D2, 440C, BG42. Handles made of G10 particularly Micarta, etc. **Prices:** $150 to $550 depending on model. **Remarks:** Full-time maker. **Mark:** My etched logos are two, my last name and Brooklyn NY mark as well as the Star/Yin Yang logo. The star being both representative of various angles of attack common in combat as well as being three triangles, each points to levels of metaphysical understanding. The Yin and Yang have my company initials on each side D & K. Yin and Yang shows the ever present physics of life.

DERESPINA, RICHARD,
20 Woodhill Rd, Willow Grove, PA 19090, Phone: 917-843-7627, info@ derespinaknives.com; Web: www.derespinaknives.com
Specialties: Karambit, Kris, tactical knives, fixed blades and folders. **Prices:** $150 to $800 each. **Remarks:** 14 years in knife making. **Mark:** Derespina Knives U.S.A. 2. Star with Yin/Yang symbol in the center with D in white and K in black.

DERINGER, CHRISTOPH,
625 Chemin Lower, Cookshire, Quebec, CANADA J0B 1M0, Phone: 819-345-4260, cdsab@sympatico.ca
Specialties: Traditional working/using straight knives and folders of his design and to customer specs. **Patterns:** Boots, hunters, folders, art knives, kitchen knives and utility/camp knives. **Technical:** Forges 5160, O1 and Damascus. Offers a variety of filework. **Prices:** Start at $250. **Remarks:** Full-time maker; first knife sold in 1989. **Mark:** Last name stamped/engraved.

DERR, HERBERT,
413 Woodland Dr, St. Albans, WV 25177, Phone: 304-727-3866
Specialties: Damascus one-of-a-kind knives, carbon steels also. **Patterns:** Birdseye, ladder back, mosaics. **Technical:** All styles functional as well as artistically pleasing. **Prices:** $90 to $175 carbon, Damascus $250 to $800. **Remarks:** All Damascus made by maker. **Mark:** H.K. Derr.

DESAULNIERS, ALAIN,
100 Pope Street, Cookshire, Quebec, Canada J0B 1M0, pinklaperez@ sympatico.ca Web: www.desoknives.com
Specialties: Mostly Loveless style knives. **Patterns:** Double grind fighters, hunters, daggers, etc. **Technical:** Stock removal, ATS-34, CPM. High-polished blades, tapered tangs, high-quality handles. **Remarks:** Full-time. Collaboration with John Young. **Prices:** $425 and up. **Mark:** Name and city in logo.

DESROSIERS, ADAM,
PO Box 1954, Petersburg, AK 99833, Phone: 907-518-4570, adam@ alaskablades.com Web: www.alaskablades.com
Specialties: High performance, forged, carbon steel and damascus camp choppers, and hunting knives. Hidden tang, full tang, and full integral construction. High performance heat treating. Knife designs inspired by life in Alaskan bush. **Technical:** Hand forges tool steels and damascus. Sole authorship. Full range of handle materials, micarta to Ivory. Preferred steels: W-2, O-1, L-6, 15n20, 1095. **Prices:** $200 - $3000. **Remarks:** ABS member. Has trained with Masters around the world. **Mark:** DrsRosiers over Alaska, underlined with a rose.

DESROSIERS, HALEY,
PO Box 1954, Petersburg, AK 99833, Phone: 907-518-1416, haley@ alaskablades.com Web: www.alaskablades.com
Specialties: Hunting knives, integrals and a few choppers, high performance. **Technical:** Hand forged blades designed for hard use, exotic wood, antler and ivory handles. **Prices:** $300 - $1500. **Remarks:** Forged first knife in 2001. Part-time bladesmith all year except for commercial fishing season. **Mark:** Capital HD.

DETMER, PHILLIP,
14140 Bluff Rd, Breese, IL 62230, Phone: 618-526-4834, jpdetmer@att.net
Specialties: Working knives. **Patterns:** Bowies, daggers and hunters. **Technical:** Grinds ATS-34 and D2. **Prices:** $60 to $400. **Remarks:** Part-time maker; first knife sold in 1977. **Mark:** Last name with dagger.

DEUBEL, CHESTER J.,
6211 N. Van Ark Rd., Tucson, AZ 85743, Phone: 520-444-5246, cjdeubel@ yahoo.com; Web: www.cjdeubel.com
Specialties: Fancy working straight knives and folders of his or customer design, with intricate file work. **Patterns:** Fighters, Bowies, daggers, hunters, camp knives, and cowboy. **Technical:** Flat guard, hollow grind, antiqued, all types Damascus, 154cpm Stainsteel, high carbon steel, 440c Stainsteel. **Prices:** From $250 to $3500. **Remarks:** Started making part-time in 1980; went to full-time in 2000. Don Patch is my engraver. **Mark:** C.J. Deubel.

DI MARZO, RICHARD,
1417 10th St S, Birmingham, AL 35205, Phone: 205-252-3331
Specialties: Handle artist. Scrimshaw carvings.

DIAZ, JOSE,
409 W. 12th Ave, Ellensburg, WA 98926, jose@diaztools.com Web: www.diaztools.com
Specialties: Affordable custom user-grade utility and camp knives. Also makes competition cutting knives. **Patterns:** Mas. **Technical:** Blade materials range from high carbon steels and Damascus to high performance tool and stainless steels. Uses both forge and stock removal methods in shaping the

steel. Handle materials include Tero Tuf, Black Butyl Burl, Micarta, natural woods and G10. **Prices:** $65-$700. **Remarks:** Part-time knife maker; made first knife in 2008. **Mark:** Reclining tree frog with a smile, and "Diaz Tools."

DICK, DAN,
P.O. Box 2303, Hutchinson, KS 67504-2303, Phone: 620-669-6805, Dan@DanDickKnives.com; Web: www.dandickknives.com
Specialties: Traditional working/using fixed bladed knives of maker's design. **Patterns:** Hunters, Skinners, Utility, Kitchen, Tactical, Bowies. **Technical:** Stock removal maker using D2. Prefers such materials as exotic and fancy burl woods. Makes his own sheaths, all leather with tooling. **Prices:** $110 and up. **Remarks:** Part-time maker since 2006. **Marks:** Name in outline border of Kansas.

DICKERSON, GAVIN,
PO Box 7672, Petit 1512, SOUTH AFRICA, Phone: +27 011-965-0988, Fax: +27 011-965-0988
Specialties: Straight knives of his design or to customer specs. **Patterns:** Hunters, skinners, fighters and Bowies. **Technical:** Hollow-grinds D2, 440C, ATS-34, 12C27 and Damascus upon request. Prefers natural handle materials; offers synthetic handle materials. **Prices:** $190 to $2500. **Remarks:** Part-time maker; first knife sold in 1982. **Mark:** Name in full.

DICKISON, SCOTT S,
179 Taylor Rd, Portsmouth, RI 02871, Phone: 401-847-7398, squared22@cox.net; Web: http://sqauredknives.com
Specialties: Straight knives, locking folders and slip joints of his design. **Patterns:** Sgain dubh, bird and trout knives. **Technical:** Forges and grinds commercial Damascus, D2, O1 and sandvik stainless. **Prices:** $400 to $1000; some higher. **Remarks:** Part-time maker; first knife sold in 1989. **Mark:** Stylized initials.

DICRISTOFANO, ANTHONY P,
PO Box 2369, Northlake, IL 60164, Phone: 847-845-9598, sukemitsu@sbcglobal.net Web: www.namahagesword.com
Specialties: Japanese-style swords. **Patterns:** Katana, Wakizashi, Otanto, Kozuka. **Technical:** Tradition and some modern steels. All clay tempered and traditionally hand polished using Japanese wet stones. **Remarks:** Part-time maker. **Prices:** Varied, available on request. **Mark:** Blade tang signed in "SUKEMITSU."

DIETZ, HOWARD,
421 Range Rd, New Braunfels, TX 78132, Phone: 830-885-4662
Specialties: Lock-back folders, working straight knives. **Patterns:** Folding hunters, high-grade pocket knives. ATS-34, 440C, CPM 440V, D2 and stainless Damascus. **Prices:** $300 to $1000. **Remarks:** Full-time gun and knifemaker; first knife sold in 1995. **Mark:** Name, city, and state.

DIETZEL, BILL,
PO Box 1613, Middleburg, FL 32068, Phone: 904-282-1091
Specialties: Forged straight knives and folders. **Patterns:** His interpretations. **Technical:** Forges his Damascus and other steels. **Prices:** Middle ranges. **Remarks:** Likes natural materials; uses titanium in folder liners. Master Smith (1997). **Mark:** Name.

DIGANGI, JOSEPH M,
Box 950, Santa Cruz, NM 87567, Phone: 505-753-6414, Fax: 505-753-8144, Web: www.digangidesigns.com
Specialties: Kitchen and table cutlery. **Patterns:** French chef's knives, carving knives, steak knife sets, some camp knives and hunters. Holds patents and trademarks for "System II" kitchen cutlery set. **Technical:** Grinds ATS-34. **Prices:** $150 to $595; some to $1200. **Remarks:** Full-time maker; first knife sold in 1983. **Mark:** DiGangi Designs.

DILL, DAVE,
7404 NW 30th St, Bethany, OK 73008, Phone: 405-789-0750
Specialties: Folders of his design. **Patterns:** Various patterns. **Technical:** Hand-grinds 440C, ATS-34. Offers engraving and filework on all folders. **Prices:** Starting at $450. **Remarks:** Full-time maker; first knife sold in 1987. **Mark:** First initial, last name.

DILL, ROBERT,
1812 Van Buren, Loveland, CO 80538, Phone: 970-667-5144, Fax: 970-667-5144, dillcustomknives@msn.com
Specialties: Fancy and working knives of his design. **Patterns:** Hunters, Bowies and fighters. **Technical:** Grinds 440C and D2. **Prices:** $100 to $800. **Remarks:** Full-time maker; first knife sold in 1984. **Mark:** Logo stamped into blade.

DILLUVIO, FRANK J,
311 Whitetail Dr., Prudenville, MI 48651, Phone: 989-202-4051, fjdknives@hotmail.com; Web: www.fdilluviocustomknives.com
Specialties: Folders, fixed blades. **Patterns:** Many. **Technical:** Grinds 440-c, D-2. Precision fits. **Prices:** $225 and up. **Remarks:** Full-time maker; first knife sold in 1984. **Mark:** Name and state.

DINTRUFF, CHUCK,
1708 E. Martin Luther King Blvd., Seffner, FL 33584, Phone: 813-381-6916, DINTRUFFKNIVES@aol.com; Web: dintruffknives.com and spinwellfab.com

DION, GREG,
3032 S Jackson St, Oxnard, CA 93033, Phone: 519-981-1033
Specialties: Working straight knives, some fancy. Welcomes special orders. **Patterns:** Hunters, fighters, camp knives, Bowies and tantos. **Technical:** Grinds ATS-34, 154CM and 440C. **Prices:** $85 to $300; some to $600. **Remarks:** Part-time maker; first knife sold in 1985. **Mark:** Name.

DIOTTE, JEFF,
DIOTTE KNIVES, 159 Laurier Dr, LaSalle Ontario, CANADA N9J 1L4, Phone: 519-978-2764

DIPPOLD, AL,
90 Damascus Ln, Perryville, MO 63775, Phone: 573-547-1119, adippold@midwest.net
Specialties: Fancy one-of-a-kind locking folders. **Patterns:** Locking folders. **Technical:** Forges and grinds mosaic and pattern welded Damascus. Offers filework on all folders. **Prices:** $500 to $3500; some higher. **Remarks:** Full-time maker; first knife sold in 1980. **Mark:** Last name in logo inside of liner.

DISKIN, MATT,
PO Box 653, Freeland, WA 98249, Phone: 360-730-0451
Specialties: Damascus autos. **Patterns:** Dirks and daggers. **Technical:** Forges mosaic Damascus using 15N20, 1084, 02, 06, L6; pure nickel. **Prices:** Start at $500. Remarks; Full-time maker. **Mark:** Last name.

DIXON JR., IRA E,
PO Box 2581, Ventura, CA 93002-2581, irasknives@yahoo.com
Specialties: Straight knives of his design. **Patterns:** All patterns include art knives. **Technical:** Grinds CPM materials, Damascus and some tool steels. **Prices:** $275 to $2000. **Remarks:** Full-time maker; first knife sold in 1993. **Mark:** First name, Handmade.

DOBRATZ, ERIC,
25371 Hillary Lane, Laguna Hills, CA 92653, Phone: 949-233-5170, knifesmith@gmail.com
Specialties: Differentially quenched blades with Hamon of his design or with customer input. **Patterns:** Hunting, camp, kitchen, fighters, bowies, traditional tanto, and unique fixed blade designs. **Technical:** Hand-forged high carbon and damascus. Prefers natural material for handles; rare/exotic woods and stag, but also uses micarta and homemade synthetic materials. **Prices:** $150 - $1500. **Remarks:** Part-time maker; first knife made in 1995. **Mark:** Stylized Scarab beetle.

DODD, ROBERT F,
4340 E Canyon Dr, Camp Verde, AZ 86322, Phone: 928-567-3333, rfdknives@commspeed.net; Web: www.rfdoddknives.com
Specialties: Folders, fixed blade hunter/skinners, Bowies, daggers. **Patterns:** Drop point. **Technical:** ATS-34 and Damascus. **Prices:** $250 and up. **Remarks:** Hand tooled leather sheaths. **Mark:** R. F. Dodd, Camp Verde AZ.

DOGGETT, BOB,
1310 Vinetree Rd, Brandon, FL 33510, Phone: 813-205-5503, dogman@tampabay.rr.com; Web: www.doggettcustomknives.com
Specialties: Clean, functional working knives. **Patterns:** Classic-styled hunter, fighter and utility fixed blades; liner locking folders. **Technical:** Uses stainless steel and commercial Damascus, 416 stainless for bolsters and hardware, hand-rubbed satin finish, top quality handle materials and titanium liners on folders. **Prices:** Start at $175. **Remarks:** Part-time maker. **Mark:** Last name.

DOIRON, DONALD,
6 Chemin Petit Lac des Ced, Messines, PQ, CANADA J0X-2J0, Phone: 819-465-2489

DOMINY, CHUCK,
PO Box 593, Colleyville, TX 76034, Phone: 817-498-4527
Specialties: Titanium LinerLock® folders. **Patterns:** Hunters, utility/camp knives and LinerLock® folders. **Technical:** Grinds 440C and ATS-34. **Prices:** $250 to $3000. **Remarks:** Full-time maker; first knife sold in 1976. **Mark:** Last name.

DOOLITTLE, MIKE,
13 Denise Ct, Novato, CA 94947, Phone: 415-897-3246
Specialties: Working straight knives in standard patterns. **Patterns:** Hunters and fishing knives. **Technical:** Grinds 440C, 154CM and ATS-34. **Prices:** $125 to $200; some to $750. **Remarks:** Part-time maker; first knife sold in 1981. **Mark:** Name, city and state.

DORNELES, LUCIANO OLIVERIRA,
Rua 15 De Novembro 2222, Nova Petropolis, RS, BRAZIL 95150-000, Phone: 011-55-54-303-303-90, tchebufalo@hotmail.com
Specialties: Traditional "true" Brazilian-style working knives and to customer specs. **Patterns:** Brazilian hunters, utility and camp knives, Bowies, Dirk. A master at the making of the true "Faca Campeira Gaucha," the true camp knife of the famous Brazilian Gauchos. A Dorneles knife is 100 percent hand-forged with sledge hammers only. Can make spectacular Damascus hunters/daggers. **Technical:** Forges only 52100 and his own Damascus, can put silver wire inlay on customer design handles on special orders; uses only natural handle materials. **Prices:** $250 to $1000. **Mark:** Symbol with L. Dorneles.

DOTSON, TRACY,
1280 Hwy C-4A, Baker, FL 32531, Phone: 850-537-2407
Specialties: Folding fighters and small folders. **Patterns:** LinerLock® and lockback folders. **Technical:** Hollow-grinds ATS-34 and commercial Damascus. **Prices:** Start at $250. **Remarks:** Part-time maker; first knife sold in 1995. **Mark:** Last name.

DOUCETTE, R,
CUSTOM KNIVES, 112 Memorial Dr, Brantford, Ont., CANADA N3R 5S3, Phone: 519-756-9040, randy@randydoucetteknives.com; Web: www.randydoucetteknives.com
Specialties: Filework, tactical designs, multiple grinds. **Patterns:** Tactical folders, fancy folders, daggers, tantos, karambits. **Technical:** All knives are handmade. The only outsourcing is heat treatment. **Prices:** $500 to $2,500. **Remarks:** Full-time knifemaker; 2-year waiting list. **Mark:** R. Doucette

DOUGLAS, JOHN J,
506 Powell Rd, Lynch Station, VA 24571, Phone: 804-369-7196
Specialties: Fancy and traditional straight knives and folders of his design and to customer specs. **Patterns:** Locking folders, swords and sgian dubhs. **Technical:** Grinds 440C stainless, ATS-34 stainless and customer's choice. Offers newly designed non-pivot uni-lock folders. Prefers highly polished finish. **Prices:** $160 to $1400. **Remarks:** Full-time maker; first knife sold in 1975. Doing business as Douglas Keltic. **Mark:** Stylized initial. Folders are numbered; customs are dated.

DOURSIN, GERARD,
Chemin des Croutoules, F 84210, Pernes les Fontaines, FRANCE
Specialties: Period pieces. **Patterns:** Liner locks and daggers. **Technical:** Forges mosaic Damascus. **Prices:** $600 to $4000. **Remarks:** First knife sold in 1983. **Mark:** First initial, last name and I stop the lion.

DOUSSOT, LAURENT,
1008 Montarville, St. Bruno, Quebec, CANADA J3V 3T1, Phone: 450-441-3298, doussot@skalja.com; Web: www.skalja.com, www.doussot-knives.com
Specialties: Fancy and embellished folders and fantasy knives. **Patterns:** Fighters and locking folders. **Technical:** Grinds ATS-34 and commercial Damascus. Scale carvings on all knives; most bolsters are carved titanium. **Prices:** $350 to $3000. **Remarks:** Part-time maker; first knife was sold in 1992. **Mark:** Stylized initials inside circle.

DOWELL, T M,
139 NW St Helen's Pl, Bend, OR 97701, Phone: 541-382-8924, Fax: 541-382-8924, tmdknives@webtv.net
Specialties: Integral construction in hunting knives. **Patterns:** Limited to featherweights, lightweights, integral hilt and caps. **Technical:** Grinds D-2, BG-42 and Vasco wear. **Prices:** $275 and up. **Remarks:** Full-time maker; first knife sold in 1967. **Mark:** Initials logo.

DOWNIE, JAMES T,
1295 - 906 Sandy Lane, Sarnia, Ontario, CANADA N7V 4K5, Phone: 519-491-8234, Web: www.ckg.org (click on members page)
Specialties: Serviceable straight knives and folders; period pieces. **Patterns:** Hunters, Bowies, camp knives, fillet and miniatures. **Technical:** Grinds D2, 440C and ATS-34, Damasteel, stainless steel Damascus. **Prices:** $150 and up. **Remarks:** Full-time maker, first knife sold in 1978. **Mark:** Signature of first and middle initials, last name.

DOWNING, LARRY,
12268 State Route 181 N, Bremen, KY 42325, Phone: 270-525-3523, larrydowning@bellsouth.net; Web: www.downingknives.com
Specialties: Working straight knives and folders. **Patterns:** From mini-knives to daggers, folding lockers to interframes. **Technical:** Forges and grinds 154CM, ATS-34 and his own Damascus. **Prices:** $195 to $950; some higher. **Remarks:** Part-time maker; first knife sold in 1979. **Mark:** Name in arrowhead.

DOWNING, TOM,
2675 12th St, Cuyahoga Falls, OH 44223, Phone: 330-923-7464
Specialties: Working straight knives; period pieces. **Patterns:** Hunters, fighters and tantos. **Technical:** Grinds 440C, ATS-34 and CPM-T-440V. Prefers natural handle materials. **Prices:** $150 to $900, some to $1500. **Remarks:** Part-time maker; first knife sold in 1979. **Mark:** First and middle initials, last name.

DOWNS, JAMES F,
2247 Summit View Rd, Powell, OH 43065, Phone: 614-766-5350, jfdowns1@yahoo.com
Specialties: Working straight knives of his design or to customer specs. **Patterns:** Folders, Bowies, boot, hunters, utility. **Technical:** Grinds 440C and other steels. Prefers mastodon ivory, all pearls, stabilized wood and elephant ivory. **Prices:** $75 to $1200. **Remarks:** Full-time maker; first knife sold in 1980. **Mark:** Last name.

DOX, JAN,
Zwanebloemlaan 27, B 2900 Schoten, BELGIUM, Phone: 32 3 658 77 43, jan.dox@scarlet.be; Web: doxblades.weebly.com
Specialties: Working/using knives, from kitchen to battlefield. **Patterns:** Own designs, some based on traditional ethnic patterns (Scots, Celtic, Scandinavian and Japanese) or to customer specs. **Technical:** Grinds D2/A2 and stainless, forges carbon steels, convex edges. Handles: Wrapped in modern or traditional patterns, resin impregnated if desired. Natural or synthetic materials, some carved. **Prices:** $50 and up. **Remarks:** Spare-time maker, first knife sold 2001. **Mark:** Name or stylized initials.

DOZIER, BOB,
PO Box 1941, Springdale, AR 72765, Phone: 888-823-0023/479-756-0023, Fax: 479-756-9139, info@dozierknives.com; Web www.dozierknives.com
Specialties: Using knives (fixed blades and folders). **Patterns:** Some fine collector-grade knives. **Technical:** Uses D2. Prefers Micarta handle material. **Prices:** Using knives: $195 to $700. **Remarks:** Full-time maker; first knife sold in 1965. No longer doing semi-handmade line. **Mark:** State, made, last name in a circle (for fixed blades); Last name with arrow through 'D' and year over name (for folders).

DRAPER, AUDRA,
#10 Creek Dr, Riverton, WY 82501, Phone: 307-856-6807 or 307-851-0426 cell, adraper@wyoming.com; Web: www.draperknives.com
Specialties: One-of-a-kind straight and folding knives. Also pendants, earring and bracelets of Damascus. **Patterns:** Design custom knives, using, Bowies, and minis. **Technical:** Forge Damascus; heat-treats all knives. **Prices:** Vary depending on item. **Remarks:** Full-time maker; master bladesmith in the ABS. Member of the PKA; first knife sold in 1995. **Mark:** Audra.

DRAPER, MIKE,
#10 Creek Dr, Riverton, WY 82501, Phone: 307-856-6807, adraper@wyoming.com
Specialties: Mainly folding knives in tactical fashion, occasonal fixed blade. **Patterns:** Hunters, Bowies and camp knives, tactical survival. **Technical:** Grinds S30V stainless steel. **Prices:** Starting at $250+. **Remarks:** Full-time maker; first knife sold in 1996. **Mark:** Initials M.J.D. or name, city and state.

DREW, GERALD,
213 Hawk Ridge Dr, Mill Spring, NC 28756, Phone: 828-713-4762
Specialties: Blade ATS-34 blades. Straight knives. **Patterns:** Hunters, camp knives, some Bowies and tactical. **Technical:** ATS-34 preferred. **Price:** $65 to $400. **Mark:** GL DREW.

DRISCOLL, MARK,
4115 Avoyer Pl, La Mesa, CA 91941, Phone: 619-670-0695, markdriscoll91941@yahoo.com
Specialties: High-art, period pieces and working/using knives of his design or to customer specs; some fancy. **Patterns:** Swords, Bowies, fighters, daggers, hunters and primitive (mountain man-styles). **Technical:** Forges 52100, 5160, O1, L6, 1095, 15n20, W-2 steel and makes his own Damascus and mokume; also does multiple quench heat treating. Uses exotic hardwoods, ivory and horn, offers fancy file work, carving, scrimshaws. **Prices:** $150 to $550; some to $1500. **Remarks:** Part-time maker; first knife sold in 1986. Doing business as Mountain Man Knives. **Mark:** Double "M."

DROST, JASON D,
Rt 2 Box 49, French Creek, WV 26218, Phone: 304-472-7901
Specialties: Working/using straight knives of his design. **Patterns:** Hunters and utility/camp knives. **Technical:** Grinds 154CM and D2. **Prices:** $125 to $5000. **Remarks:** Spare-time maker; first knife sold in 1995. **Mark:** First and middle initials, last name, maker, city and state.

DROST, MICHAEL B,
Rt 2 Box 49, French Creek, WV 26218, Phone: 304-472-7901
Specialties: Working/using straight knives and folders of all designs. **Patterns:** Hunters, some Bowies and utility/camp knives. **Technical:** Grinds ATS-34, D2 and CPM-T-440V. Offers dove-tailed bolsters and spacers, filework and scrimshaw. **Prices:** $125 to $400; some to $740. **Remarks:** Full-time maker; first knife sold in 1990. Doing business as Drost Custom Knives. **Mark:** Name, city and state.

DRUMM, ARMIN,
Lichtensteinstrasse 33, D-89160 Dornstadt, GERMANY, Phone: 49-163-632-2842, armin@drumm-knives.de; Web: www.drumm-knives.de
Specialties: One-of-a-kind forged and Damascus fixed blade knives and folders. **Patterns:** Classic Bowie knives, daggers, fighters, hunters, folders, swords. **Technical:** Forges own Damascus and carbon steels, filework, carved handles. **Prices:** $250 to $800, some higher. **Remarks:** First knife sold in 2001, member of the German Knifemakers Guild. **Mark:** First initial, last name.

DUFF, BILL,
2801 Ash St, Poteau, OK 74953, Phone: 918-647-4458
Specialties: Straight knives and folders, some fancy. **Patterns:** Hunters, folders and miniatures. **Technical:** Grinds 440-C and commercial Damascus. **Prices:** $200 to $1000 some higher. **Remarks:** First knife some in 1976. **Mark:** Bill Duff.

DUFOUR, ARTHUR J,
8120 De Armoun Rd, Anchorage, AK 99516, Phone: 907-345-1701
Specialties: Working straight knives from standard patterns. **Patterns:** Hunters, Bowies, camp and fishing knives—grinded thin and pointed. **Technical:** Grinds 440C, ATS-34, AEB-L. Tempers 57-58R; hollow-grinds. **Prices:** $135; some to $250. **Remarks:** Part-time maker; first knife sold in 1970. **Mark:** Prospector logo.

DUGDALE, DANIEL J.,
11 Eleanor Road, Walpole, MA 02081, Phone: 508-668-3528, dlpdugdale@comcast.net
Specialties: Button-lock and straight knives of his design. **Patterns:** Utilities, hunters, skinners, and tactical. **Technical:** Falt grinds D-2 and 440C, aluminum handles with anodized finishes. **Prices:** $150 to $500. **Remarks:** Part-time maker since 1977. **Mark:** Deer track with last name, town and state.

DUNCAN, RON,
1462 County Road 1635, Cairo, MO 65239, Phone: 660-263-8949, www.duncanmadeknives.com
Remarks: Duncan Made Knives

DUNKERLEY, RICK,
PO Box 601, Lincoln, MT 59639, Phone: 406-210-4101, dunkerleyknives@gmail.com Web: www.dunkerleyknives.com
Specialties: Mosaic Damascus folders and carbon steel utility knives. **Patterns:** One-of-a-kind folders, standard hunters and utility designs. **Technical:** Forges 52100, Damascus and mosaic Damascus. Prefers natural handle materials. **Prices:** $200 and up. **Remarks:** Full-time maker; first knife sold in 1984, ABS Master Smith. Doing business as Dunkerley Custom Knives. Dunkerley handmade knives, sole authorship. **Mark:** Dunkerley, MS.

DUNN, CHARLES K,
17740 GA Hwy 116, Shiloh, GA 31826, Phone: 706-846-2666
Specialties: Fancy and working straight knives and folders of his design and to customer specs. **Patterns:** Bowies, hunters and locking folders. **Technical:** Grinds 440C and ATS-34. Engraves; filework offered. **Prices:** $75 to $300. **Remarks:** Part-time maker; first knife sold in 1988. **Mark:** First initial, last

name, city, state.

DUNN, STEVE,
376 Biggerstaff Rd, Smiths Grove, KY 42171, Phone: 270-563-9830, dunndeal@verizon.net; Web: www.stevedunnknives.com
Specialties: Working and using straight knives of his design; period pieces. Also offer engraving & gold inlays. **Patterns:** Hunters, skinners, Bowies, fighters, camp knives, folders, swords and battle axes. **Technical:** Forges own Damascus, 1075, 15N20, 52100, 1084, L6. **Prices:** Moderate to upscale. **Remarks:** Full-time maker; first knife sold in 1990. **Mark:** Last name and MS.

DURAN, JERRY T,
PO Box 80692, Albuquerque, NM 87198-0692, Phone: 505-873-4676, jtdknives@hotmail.com; Web: www.kmg.org/jtdknives
Specialties: Tactical folders, Bowies, fighters, liner locks, autopsy and hunters. **Patterns:** Folders, Bowies, hunters and tactical knives. **Technical:** Forges own Damascus and forges carbon steel. **Prices:** Moderate to upscale. **Remarks:** Full-time maker; first knife sold in 1978. **Mark:** Initials in elk rack logo.

DURHAM, KENNETH,
BUZZARD ROOST FORGE, 10495 White Pike, Cherokee, AL 35616, Phone: 256-359-4287, www.home.hiwaay.net/~jamesd/
Specialties: Bowies, dirks, hunters. **Patterns:** Traditional patterns. **Technical:** Forges 1095, 5160, 52100 and makes own Damascus. **Prices:** $85 to $1600. **Remarks:** Began making knives about 1995. Received Journeyman stamp 1999. Got Master Smith stamp in 2004. **Mark:** Bull's head with Ken Durham above and Cherokee AL below.

DURIO, FRED,
144 Gulino St, Opelousas, LA 70570, Phone: 337-948-4831/cell 337-351-2652, fdurio@yahoo.com
Specialties: Folders. **Patterns:** Liner locks; plain and fancy. **Technical:** Makes own Damascus. **Prices:** Moderate to upscale. **Remarks:** Full-time maker. **Mark:** Last name-Durio.

DUVALL, FRED,
10715 Hwy 190, Benton, AR 72015, Phone: 501-778-9360
Specialties: Working straight knives and folders. **Patterns:** Locking folders, slip joints, hunters, fighters and Bowies. **Technical:** Grinds D2 and CPM440V; forges 5160. **Prices:** $100 to $400; some to $800. **Remarks:** Part-time maker; first knife sold in 1973. **Mark:** Last name.

DWYER, DUANE,
120 N. Pacific St., L7, San Marcos, CA 92069, Phone: 760-471-8275, striderknives@aol.com Web: www.striderknives.com
Specialties: Primarily tactical. **Patterns:** Fixed and folders. **Technical:** Primarily stock removal specializing in highly technical materials. **Prices:** $100 and up, based on the obvious variables. **Remarks:** Full-time maker since 1996.

DYER, DAVID,
4531 Hunters Glen, Granbury, TX 76048, Phone: 817-573-1198
Specialties: Working skinners and early period knives. **Patterns:** Customer designs, his own patterns. **Technical:** Coal forged blades; 5160 and 52100 steels. Grinds D2, 1095, L6. **Prices:** $150 for neck knives and small (3" to 3-1/2"). To $600 for large blades and specialty blades. **Mark:** Last name DYER electro etched.

DYESS, EDDIE,
1005 Hamilton, Roswell, NM 88201, Phone: 505-623-5599, eddyess@msn.com
Specialties: Working and using straight knives in standard patterns. **Patterns:** Hunters and fighters. **Technical:** Grinds 440C, 154CM and D2 on request. **Prices:** $150 to $300, some higher. **Remarks:** Spare-time maker; first knife sold in 1980. **Mark:** Last name.

E

EAKER, ALLEN L,
416 Clinton Ave Dept KI, Paris, IL 61944, Phone: 217-466-5160
Specialties: Traditional straight knives and folders of his design. **Patterns:** Hunters, locking folders and slip-joint folders. **Technical:** Grinds 440C; inlays. **Prices:** $125 to $325; some to $500. **Remarks:** Spare-time maker; first knife sold in 1994. **Mark:** Initials in tankard logo stamped on tang, serial number on back side.

EALY, DELBERT,
PO Box 121, Indian River, MI 49749, Phone: 231-238-4705

EATON, FRANK L JR,
41 Vista Woods Rd, Stafford, VA 22556, Phone: 540-657-6160, FEton2@aol.com
Specialties: Full tang/hidden tang fixed working and art knives of his own design. **Patterns:** Hunters, skinners, fighters, Bowies, tacticals and daggers. **Technical:** Stock removal maker, prefer using natural materials. **Prices:** $175 to $400. **Remarks:** Part-time maker - Active Duty Airborn Ranger-Making 4 years. **Mark:** Name over 75th Ranger Regimental Crest.

EATON, RICK,
313 Dailey Rd, Broadview, MT 59015, Phone: 406-667-2405, rick@eatonknives.com; Web: www.eatonknives.com
Specialties: Interframe folders and one-hand-opening side locks. **Patterns:** Bowies, daggers, fighters and folders. **Technical:** Grinds 154CM, ATS-34, 440C and other maker's Damascus. Makes own mosaic Damascus. Offers high-quality hand engraving, Bulino and gold inlay. **Prices:** Upscale. **Remarks:** Full-time maker; first knife sold in 1982. **Mark:** Full name or full name and address.

EBISU, HIDESAKU,
3-39-7 Koi Osako Nishi Ku, Hiroshima City, JAPAN 733 0816

ECHOLS, RODGER,
2853 Highway 371 W, Nashville, AR 71852-7577, Phone: 870-845-9173 or 870-845-0400, blademanechols@aol.com; Web: www.echolsknives.com
Specialties: Liner locks, auto-scale release, lock backs. **Patterns:** His or yours. **Technical:** Autos. **Prices:** $500 to $1700. **Remarks:** Likes to use pearl, ivory and Damascus the most. Made first knife in 1984. Part-time maker; tool and die maker by trade. **Mark:** Name.

EDDY, HUGH E,
211 E Oak St, Caldwell, ID 83605, Phone: 208-459-0536

EDEN, THOMAS,
PO Box 57, Cranbury, NJ 08512, Phone: 609-371-0774, njirrigation@msn.com
Specialties: Chef's knives. **Patterns:** Fixed blade, working patterns, hand forged. **Technical:** Damascus. **Remarks:** ABS Smith. **Mark:** Eden (script).

EDGE, TOMMY,
1244 County Road 157, Cash, AR 72421, Phone: 501-477-5210, tedge@tex.net
Specialties: Fancy/embellished working knives of his design. **Patterns:** Bowies, hunters and utility/camping knives. **Technical:** Grinds 440C, ATS-34 and D2. Makes own cable Damascus; offers filework. **Prices:** $70 to $250; some to $1500. **Remarks:** Part-time maker; first knife sold in 1973. **Mark:** Stamped first initial, last name and stenciled name, city and state in oval shape.

EDMONDS, WARRICK,
, Adelaide Hills, South Australia, Phone: 61-8-83900339, warrick@riflebirdknives.com Web: www.riflebirdknives.com
Specialties: Fixed blade knives with select and highly figured exotic or unique Australian wood handles. Themed collectors knives to individually designed working knives from Damascus, RWL34, 440C or high carbon steels. **Patterns:** Hunters, utilities and workshop knives, cooks knives with a Deco to Modern flavour. Hand sewn individual leather sheaths. **Technical:** Stock removal using only steel from well known and reliable sources. **Prices:** $250Aust to $1000Aust. **Remarks:** Part-time maker since 2004. **Mark:** Name stamped into sheath.

EDWARDS, FAIN E,
PO Box 280, Topton, NC 28781, Phone: 828-321-3127

EDWARDS, MITCH,
303 New Salem Rd, Glasgow, KY 42141, Phone: 270-404-0758 / 270-404-0758, medwards@glasgow-ky.com; Web: www.traditionalknives.com
Specialties: Period pieces. **Patterns:** Neck knives, camp, rifleman and Bowie knives. **Technical:** All hand forged, forges own Damascus O1, 1084, 1095, L6, 15N20. **Prices:** $200 to $1000. **Remarks:** Journeyman Smith. **Mark:** Broken heart.

EHRENBERGER, DANIEL ROBERT,
1213 S Washington St, Mexico, MO 65265, Phone: 573-633-2010
Specialties: Affordable working/using straight knives of his design and to custom specs. **Patterns:** 10" western Bowie, fighters, hunting and skinning knives. **Technical:** Forges 1085, 1095, his own Damascus and cable Damascus. **Prices:** $80 to $500. **Remarks:** Full-time maker, first knife sold 1994. **Mark:** Ehrenberger JS.

EIRICH, WILLIAM,
61535 S. Hwy 97, Ste. 9-163, Bend, OR 97702, Phone: 541-280-8373, tapejet@live.com
Specialties: Hunting, folders, other. **Technical:** Stock removal. 154CM, 1050, M390, 5160, 01, 52100, ATS-34, and D2 steel. **Prices:** $200 and up. **Remarks:** First knife made 2004. **Mark:** Circle with an "E" in the center and a wing to the right of the circle with the name "Eirich" below framed by dots.

EKLUND, MAIHKEL,
Fone Stam V9, S-820 41 Farila, SWEDEN, info@art-knives.com; Web: www.art-knives.com
Specialties: Collector-grade working straight knives. **Patterns:** Hunters, Bowies and fighters. **Technical:** Grinds ATS-34, Uddeholm and Dama steel. Engraves and scrimshaws. **Prices:** $200 to $2000. **Remarks:** Full-time maker; first knife sold in 1983. **Mark:** Initials or name.

ELDRIDGE, ALLAN,
7731 Four Winds Dr, Ft. Worth, TX 76133, Phone: 817-370-7778; Cell: 817-296-3528
Specialties: Fancy classic straight knives in standard patterns. **Patterns:** Hunters, Bowies, fighters, folders and miniatures. **Technical:** Grinds O1 and Damascus. Engraves silver-wire inlays, pearl inlays, scrimshaws and offers filework. **Prices:** $50 to $500; some to $1200. **Remarks:** Spare-time maker; first knife sold in 1965. **Mark:** Initials.

ELISHEWITZ, ALLEN,
3960 Lariat Ridge, New Braunfels, TX 78132, Phone: 830-899-5356, allen@elishewitzknives.com; Web: elishewitzknives.com
Specialties: Collectible high-tech working straight knives and folders of his design. **Patterns:** Working, utility and tactical knives. **Technical:** Designs and uses innovative locking mechanisms. All designs drafted and field-tested. **Prices:** $600 to $1000. **Remarks:** Full-time maker; first knife sold in 1989. **Mark:** Gold medallion inlaid in blade.

ELLEFSON, JOEL,
PO Box 1016, 310 S 1st St, Manhattan, MT 59741, Phone: 406-284-3111
Specialties: Working straight knives, fancy daggers and one-of-a-kinds. **Patterns:** Hunters, daggers and some folders. **Technical:** Grinds A2, 440C and ATS-34. Makes own mokume in bronze, brass, silver and shibuishi; makes brass/steel blades. **Prices:** $100 to $500; some to $2000. **Remarks:** Part-time

maker; first knife sold in 1978. **Mark:** Stylized last initial.

ELLERBE, W B,

3871 Osceola Rd, Geneva, FL 32732, Phone: 407-349-5818
Specialties: Period and primitive knives and sheaths. **Patterns:** Bowies to patch knives, some tomahawks. **Technical:** Grinds Sheffield O1 and files. **Prices:** Start at $35. **Remarks:** Full-time maker; first knife sold in 1971. Doing business as Cypress Bend Custom Knives. **Mark:** Last name or initials.

ELLIOTT, JERRY,

4507 Kanawha Ave, Charleston, WV 25304, Phone: 304-925-5045, elliottknives@verizon.net
Specialties: Classic and traditional straight knives and folders of his design and to customer specs. **Patterns:** Hunters, locking folders and Bowies. **Technical:** Grinds ATS-34, 154CM, O1, D2 and T-440-V. All guards silver-soldered; bolsters are pinned on straight knives, spot-welded on folders. **Prices:** $80 to $265; some to $1000. **Remarks:** Full-time maker; first knife sold in 1972. **Mark:** First and middle initials, last name, knife maker, city, state.

ELLIS, DAVE/ABS MASTERSMITH,

770 Sycamore Ave., Suite 122 Box 451, Vista, CA 92083, Phone: 760-945-7177, www.exquisiteknives.com
Specialties: Bowies, utility and combat knives. **Patterns:** Using knives to art quality pieces. **Technical:** Forges 5160, L6, 52100, cable and his own Damascus steels. **Prices:** $300 to $4000. **Remarks:** Part-time maker. California's first ABS Master Smith. **Mark:** Dagger-Rose with name and M.S. mark.

ELLIS, WILLIAM DEAN,

2767 Edgar Ave, Sanger, CA 93657, Phone: 559-314-4459, urleebird@comcast.net; Web: www.billysblades.com
Specialties: Classic and fancy knives of his design. **Patterns:** Boots, fighters and utility knives. **Technical:** Grinds ATS-34, D2 and Damascus. Offers tapered tangs and six patterns of filework; tooled multi-colored sheaths. **Prices:** $250 to $1500 **Remarks:** Part-time maker; first knife sold in 1991. Doing business as Billy's Blades. Also make shave-ready straight razors for actual use. **Mark:** "B" in a five-point star next to "Billy," city and state within a rounded-corner rectangle.

ELLIS, WILLY B,

4941 Cardinal Trail, Palm Harbor, FL 34683, Phone: 727-942-6420, Web: www.willyb.com
Specialties: One-of-a-kind high art and fantasy knives of his design. Occasional customs full size and miniatures. **Patterns:** Bowies, fighters, hunters and others. **Technical:** Grinds 440C, ATS-34, 1095, carbon Damascus, ivory bone, stone and metal carving. **Prices:** $175 to $15,000. **Remarks:** Full-time maker, first knife made in 1973. Member Knifemakers Guild. Jewel setting inlays. **Mark:** Willy B. or WB'S C etched or carved.

ELROD, ROGER R,

58 Dale Ave, Enterprise, AL 36330, Phone: 334-347-1863

EMBRETSEN, KAJ,

FALUVAGEN 67, S-82830 Edsbyn, SWEDEN, Phone: 46-271-21057, Fax: 46-271-22961, kay.embretsen@telia.com Web:www.embretsenknives.com
Specialties: Damascus folding knives. **Patterns:** Uses mammoth ivory and some pearl. **Technical:** Uses own Damascus steel. **Remarks:** Full time since 1983. **Prices:** $2500 to $8000. **Mark:** Name inside the folder.

EMERSON, ERNEST R,

PO Box 4180, Torrance, CA 90510-4180, Phone: 310-212-7455, info@emersonknives.com; Web: www.emersonknives.com
Specialties: High-tech folders and combat fighters. **Patterns:** Fighters, LinerLock® combat folders and SPECWAR combat knives. **Technical:** Grinds 154CM and Damascus. Makes folders with titanium fittings, liners and locks. Chisel grind specialist. **Prices:** $550 to $850; some to $10,000. **Remarks:** Full-time maker; first knife sold in 1983. **Mark:** Last name and Specwar knives.

ENCE, JIM,

145 S 200 East, Richfield, UT 84701, Phone: 435-896-6206
Specialties: High-art period pieces (spec in California knives) art knives. **Patterns:** Art, boot knives, fighters, Bowies and occasional folders. **Technical:** Grinds 440C for polish and beauty boys; makes own Damascus. **Prices:** Upscale. **Remarks:** Full-time maker; first knife sold in 1977. Does own engraving, gold work and stone work. Guild member since 1977. Founding member of the AKI. **Mark:** Ence, usually engraved.

ENGLAND, VIRGIL,

1340 Birchwood St, Anchorage, AK 99508, Phone: 907-274-9494, WEB:www.virgilengland.com
Specialties: Edged weapons and equipage, one-of-a-kind only. **Patterns:** Axes, swords, lances and body armor. **Technical:** Forges and grinds as pieces dictate. Offers stainless and Damascus. **Prices:** Upscale. **Remarks:** A veteran knifemaker. No commissions. **Mark:** Stylized initials.

ENGLE, WILLIAM,

16608 Oak Ridge Rd, Boonville, MO 65233, Phone: 816-882-6277
Specialties: Traditional working and using straight knives of his design. **Patterns:** Hunters, Bowies and fighters. **Technical:** Grinds 440C, ATS-34 and 154 CM. **Prices:** $250 to $500; some higher. **Remarks:** Part-time maker; first knife sold in 1982. All knives come with certificate of authenticity. **Mark:** Last name in block lettering.

ENGLISH, JIM,

14586 Olive Vista Dr., Jamul, CA 91935, Phone: 619-669-0833
Specialties: High-quality working straight knives. **Patterns:** Hunters, fighters, skinners, tantos, utility and fillet knives, Bowies and *san-mai* Damascus Bowies. **Technical:** Hollow-grind 440C by hand. Feature linen Micarta handles, desert ironwood, many different woods, stabilized woods, nickel-silver handle bolts and handmade sheaths. **Prices:** $125 to $600. **Remarks:** Company name is Mountain Home Knives. **Mark:** Mountain Home Knives.

ENGLISH, JIM,

14586 Olive Vista Dr, Jamul, CA 91935, Phone: 619-669-0833
Specialties: Traditional working straight knives to customer specs. **Patterns:** Hunters, Bowies, fighters, tantos, daggers, boot and utility/camp knives. **Technical:** Grinds 440C, ATS-34, commercial Damascus and customer choice. **Prices:** $130 to $350. **Remarks:** Part-time maker; first knife sold in 1985. In addition to custom line, also does business as Mountain Home Knives. **Mark:** Double "A," Double "J" logo.

ENNIS, RAY,

1220S 775E, Ogden, UT 84404, Phone: 800-410-7603, Fax: 501-621-2683, nifmakr@hotmail.com; Web:www.ennis-entrekusa.com

ENOS III, THOMAS M,

12302 State Rd 535, Orlando, FL 32836, Phone: 407-239-6205, tmenos3@att.net
Specialties: Heavy-duty working straight knives; unusual designs. **Patterns:** Swords, machetes, daggers, skinners, filleting, period pieces. **Technical:** Grinds 440C, D2, 154CM. **Prices:** $75 to $1500. **Remarks:** Full-time maker; first knife sold in 1972. No longer accepting custom requests. Will be making his own designs. Send SASE for listing of items for sale. **Mark:** Name in knife logo and year, type of steel and serial number.

ENTIN, ROBERT,

127 Pembroke St 1, Boston, MA 02118

EPTING, RICHARD,

4021 Cody Dr, College Station, TX 77845, Phone: 979-690-6496, rgeknives@hotmail.com; Web: www.eptingknives.com
Specialties: Folders and working straight knives. **Patterns:** Hunters, Bowies, and locking folders. **Technical:** Forges high-carbon steel and his own Damascus. **Prices:** $200 to $800; some to $1800. **Remarks:** Part-time maker, first knife sold 1996. **Mark:** Name in arch logo.

ERICKSON, L.M.,

1379 Black Mountain Cir, Ogden, UT 84404, Phone: 801-737-1930
Specialties: Straight knives; period pieces. **Patterns:** Bowies, fighters, boots and hunters. **Technical:** Grinds 440C, 154CM and commercial Damascus. **Prices:** $200 to $900; some to $5000. **Remarks:** Part-time maker; first knife sold in 1981. **Mark:** Name, city, state.

ERICKSON, WALTER E.,

22280 Shelton Tr, Atlanta, MI 49709, Phone: 989-785-5262, wberic@racc2000.com
Specialties: Unusual survival knives and high-tech working knives. **Patterns:** Butterflies, hunters, tantos. **Technical:** Grinds ATS-34 or customer choice. **Prices:** $150 to $500; some to $1500. **Remarks:** Full-time maker; first knife sold in 1981. **Mark:** Using pantograph with assorted fonts (no longer stamping).

ERIKSEN, JAMES THORLIEF,

dba VIKING KNIVES, 3830 Dividend Dr, Garland, TX 75042, Phone: 972-494-3667, Fax: 972-235-4932, VikingKnives@aol.com
Specialties: Heavy-duty working and using straight knives and folders utilizing traditional, Viking original and customer specification patterns. Some high-tech and fancy/embellished knives available. **Patterns:** Bowies, hunters, skinners, boot and belt knives, utility/camp knives, fighters, daggers, locking folders, slip-joint folders and kitchen knives. **Technical:** Hollow-grinds 440C, D2, ASP-23, ATS-34, 154CM, Vascowear. **Prices:** $150 to $300; some to $600. **Remarks:** Full-time maker; first knife sold in 1985. Doing business as Viking Knives. For a color catalog showing 50 different models, mail $5 to above address. **Mark:** VIKING or VIKING USA for export.

ERNEST, PHIL (PJ),

PO Box 5240, Whittier, CA 90607-5240, Phone: 562-556-2324, hugger883562@yahoo.com; Web:www.ernestcustomknives.com
Specialties: Fixed blades. **Patterns:** Wide range. Many original as well as hunters, camp, fighters, daggers, bowies and tactical. Specialzin in Wharncliff's of all sizes. **Technical:** Grinds commercial Damascus, Mosaid Damascus. ATS-34, and 440C. Full Tangs with bolsters. Handle material includes all types of exotic hardwood, abalone, peal mammoth tooth, mammoth ivory, Damascus steel and Mosaic Damascus. **Remarks:** Full time maker. First knife sold in 1999. **Prices:** $200 to $1800. Some to $2500. **Mark:** Owl logo with PJ Ernest Whittier CA or PJ Ernest.

ESPOSITO, EMMANUEL,

Via Reano 70, Buttigliera Alta TO, ITALY 10090, Phone: 39-011932-16-21, www.emmanuelmaker.it
Specialties: Folding knife with his patent system lock mechanism with mosaic inlay.

ESSEGIAN, RICHARD,

7387 E Tulare St, Fresno, CA 93727, Phone: 309-255-5950
Specialties: Fancy working knives of his design; art knives. **Patterns:** Bowies and some small hunters. **Technical:** Grinds A2, D2, 440C and 154CM. Engraves and inlays. **Prices:** Start at $600. **Remarks:** Part-time maker; first knife sold in 1986. **Mark:** Last name, city and state.

ETZLER, JOHN,
11200 N Island, Grafton, OH 44044, Phone: 440-748-2460, jetzler@bright.net; Web: members.tripod.com/~etzlerknives/
Specialties: High-art and fantasy straight knives and folders of his design and to customer specs. **Patterns:** Folders, daggers, fighters, utility knives. **Technical:** Forges and grinds nickel Damascus and tool steel; grinds stainless steels. Prefers exotic, natural materials. **Prices:** $250 to $1200; some $6500. **Remarks:** Full-time maker; first knife sold in 1992. **Mark:** Name or initials.

EVANS, BRUCE A,
409 CR 1371, Booneville, MS 38829, Phone: 662-720-0193, beknives@avsia.com; Web: www.bruceevans.homestead.com/open.html
Specialties: Forges blades. **Patterns:** Hunters, Bowies, or will work with customer. **Technical:** 5160, cable Damascus, pattern welded Damascus. **Prices:** $200 and up. **Mark:** Bruce A. Evans Same with JS on reverse of blade.

EVANS, CARLTON,
PO Box 46, Gainesville, TX 76241, Phone: 817-886-9231, carlton@carltonevans.com; Web: www.carltonevans.com
Specialties: High end folders and fixed blades. **Technical:** Uses the stock removal methods. The materials used are of the highest quality. **Remarks:** Full-time knifemaker, voting member of Knifemakers Guild, member of the Texas Knifemakers and Collectors Association.

EVANS, PHIL,
594 SE 40th, Columbus, KS 66725, Phone: 620-249-0639, phil@glenviewforge.com Web: www.glenviewforge.com
Specialties: Working knives, hunters, skinners, also enjoys making Bowies and fighters, high carbon or Damascus. **Technical:** Forges own blades and makes own Damascus. Uses all kinds of ancient Ivory and bone. Stabilizes own native hardwoods. **Prices:** $150 - $1,500. **Remarks:** Part-time maker. Made first knife in 1995. **Mark:** EVANS.

EVANS, RONALD B,
209 Hoffer St, Middleton, PA 17057-2723, Phone: 717-944-5464

EVANS, VINCENT K AND GRACE,
HC 1 Box 5275, Keaau, HI 96749-9517, Phone: 808-966-8978, evansvk@gmail.com Web: www.picturetrail.com/vevans
Specialties: Period pieces; swords. **Patterns:** Scottish, Viking, central Asian. **Technical:** Forges 5160 and his own Damascus. **Prices:** $700 to $4000; some to $8000. **Remarks:** Full-time maker; first knife sold in 1983. **Mark:** Last initial with fish logo.

EWING, JOHN H,
3276 Dutch Valley Rd, Clinton, TN 37716, Phone: 865-457-5757, johnja@comcast.net
Specialties: Working straight knives, hunters, camp knives. **Patterns:** Hunters. **Technical:** Grinds 440-D2. Forges 5160, 1095 prefers forging. **Prices:** $150 and up. **Remarks:** Part-time maker; first knife sold in 1985. **Mark:** First initial, last name, some embellishing done on knives.

F

FAIRLY, DANIEL,
2209 Bear Creek Canyon Rd, Bayfield, CO 81122, danielfairlyknives@gmail.com; Web: www.danielfairlyknives.com
Specialties: One of a kind handmade knives made for hard use. **Patterns:** Heavy duty choppers, every day carry and neck knives, Japanese influenced designs, ultra light titanium utilities. **Technical:** Grinds mostly tool steel and carbidized titanium in .050" to .360" thick material. Uses heavy duty handle materials and flared test tube fasteners or epoxy soaked wrapped handles. Most grinds are chisel; flat convex and hollow grinds used. **Prices:** $75 to $700. **Remarks:** Full-time maker since first knife sold in Feb. 2011. **Mark:** Fairly written in all capitals with larger F.

FANT JR., GEORGE,
1983 CR 3214, Atlanta, TX 75551-6515, Phone: (903) 846-2938

FARID R, MEHR,
8 Sidney Close, Tunbridge Wells, Kent, ENGLAND TN2 5QQ, Phone: 011-44-1892 520345, farid@faridknives.com; Web: www.faridknives.com
Specialties: Hollow handle survival knives. High tech folders. **Patterns:** Flat grind blades & chisel ground LinerLock® folders. **Technical:** Grinds 440C, CPMT-440V, CPM-420V, CPM-15V, CPM5125V, and T-1 high speed steel. **Prices:** $550 to $5000. **Remarks:** Full-time maker; first knife sold in 1991. **Mark:** First name stamped.

FARR, DAN,
285 Glen Ellyn Way, Rochester, NY 14618, Phone: 585-721-1388
Specialties: Hunting, camping, fighting and utility. **Patterns:** Fixed blades. **Technical:** Forged or stock removal. **Prices:** $150 to $750.

FASSIO, MELVIN G,
420 Tyler Way, Lolo, MT 59847, Phone: 406-273-9143
Specialties: Working folders to customer specs. **Patterns:** Locking folders, hunters and traditional-style knives. **Technical:** Grinds 440C. **Prices:** $125 to $350. **Remarks:** Part-time maker; first knife sold in 1975. **Mark:** Name and city, dove logo.

FAUCHEAUX, HOWARD J,
PO Box 206, Loreauville, LA 70552, Phone: 318-229-6467
Specialties: Working straight knives and folders; period pieces. Also a hatchet with capping knife in the handle. **Patterns:** Traditional locking folders, hunters, fighters and Bowies. **Technical:** Forges W2, 1095 and his own Damascus;

stock removal D2. **Prices:** Start at $200. **Remarks:** Full-time maker; first knife sold in 1969. **Mark:** Last name.

FAUST, DICK,
624 Kings Hwy N, Rochester, NY 14617, Phone: 585-544-1948, dickfaustknives@mac.com
Specialties: High-performance working straight knives. **Patterns:** Hunters and utility/camp knives. **Technical:** Hollow grinds 154CM full tang. Exotic woods, stag and Micarta handles. Provides a custom leather sheath with each knife. **Prices:** From $200 to $600, some higher. **Remarks:** Full-time maker. **Mark:** Signature.

FAUST, JOACHIM,
Kirchgasse 10, 95497 Goldkronach, GERMANY

FECAS, STEPHEN J,
1312 Shadow Lane, Anderson, SC 29625, Phone: 864-287-4834, Fax: 864-287-4834
Specialties: Front release lock backs, liner locks. Folders only. **Patterns:** Gents folders. **Technical:** Grinds ATS-34, Damascus-Ivories and pearl handles. **Prices:** $650 to $1200. **Remarks:** Full-time maker since 1980. First knife sold in 1977. All knives hand finished to 1500 grit. **Mark:** Last name signature.

FELIX, ALEXANDER,
PO Box 4036, Torrance, CA 90510, Phone: 310-320-1836, sgiandubh@dslextreme.com
Specialties: Straight working knives, fancy ethnic designs. **Patterns:** Hunters, Bowies, daggers, period pieces. **Technical:** Forges carbon steel and Damascus; forged stainless and titanium jewelry, gold and silver casting. **Prices:** $110 and up. **Remarks:** Jeweler, ABS Journeyman Smith. **Mark:** Last name.

FELLOWS, MIKE,
PO Box 162, Mosselbay 6500, SOUTH AFRICA, Phone: 27 82 960 3868, karatshin@gmail.com
Specialties: Miniatures, art knives and folders with occasionally hunters and skinners. **Patterns:** Own designs. **Technical:** Uses own Damascus. **Prices:** Upon request. **Remarks:** Use only indigenous materials. Exotic hard woods, horn & ivory. Does all own embellishments. **Mark:** "SHIN" letter from Hebrew alphabet over Hebrew word "Karat." **Other:** Member of knifemakers guild of Southern Africa.

FERGUSON, JIM,
32131 Via Bande, Temecula, CA 92592, Phone: 951-302-0267, Web: www.twistednickel.com www.howtomakeaknife.net
Specialties: Nickel Damascus, Bowies, daggers, push blades. Also makes swords, battle axes and utilities. **Patterns:** All styles. **Technical:** Sells in U.S. and Canada. **Prices:** $350 to $600, some to $1000. **Mark:** Jim Ferguson/USA. Also make swords, battle axes and utilities.

FERGUSON, JIM,
3543 Shadyhill Dr, San Angelo, TX 76904, Phone: 325-655-1061
Specialties: Straight working knives and folders. **Patterns:** Working belt knives, hunters, Bowies and some folders. **Technical:** Grinds ATS-34, D2 and Vascowear. Flat-grinds hunting knives. **Prices:** $200 to $600; some to $1000. **Remarks:** Full-time maker; first knife sold in 1987. **Mark:** First and middle initials, last name.

FERGUSON, LEE,
1993 Madison 7580, Hindsville, AR 72738, Phone: 479-443-0084, info@fergusonknives.com; Web: www.fergusonknives.com
Specialties: Straight working knives and folders, some fancy. **Patterns:** Hunters, daggers, working folders and slip-joints. **Technical:** Grinds D2, 440C and ATS-34; heat-treats. **Prices:** $50 to $600; some to $4000. **Remarks:** Full-time maker; first knife sold in 1977. **Mark:** Full name.

FERGUSON, LINDA,
1993 Madison 7580, Hindsville, AR 72738, Phone: 479-443-0084, info@fergusonknives.com; Web: www.fergusonknives.com
Specialties: Mini knives. **Patterns:** Daggers & hunters. **Technical:** Hollow ground, stainless steel or Damascus. **Prices:** $65 to $250. **Remarks:** 2004 member Knifemakers Guild, Miniature Knifemakers Society. **Mark:** LF inside a Roman numeral 2.

FERRARA, THOMAS,
122 Madison Dr, Naples, FL 33942, Phone: 813-597-3363, Fax: 813-597-3363
Specialties: High-art, traditional and working straight knives and folders of all designs. **Patterns:** Boots, Bowies, daggers, fighters and hunters. **Technical:** Grinds 440C, D2 and ATS-34; heat-treats. **Prices:** $100 to $700; some to $1300. **Remarks:** Part-time maker; first knife sold in 1983. **Mark:** Last name.

FERRIER, GREGORY K,
3119 Simpson Dr, Rapid City, SD 57702, Phone: 605-342-9280

FERRY, TOM,
16005 SE 322nd St, Auburn, WA 98092, Phone: 253-939-4468, tomferryknives@Q.com; Web: tomferryknives.com
Specialties: Presentation grade knives. **Patterns:** Folders and fixed blades. **Technical:** Specialize in Damascus and engraving. **Prices:** $500 and up. **Remarks:** DBA: Soos Creek Ironworks. ABS Master Smith. **Mark:** Combined T and F in a circle and/or last name.

FILIPPOU, IOANNIS-MINAS,
7 Krinis Str Nea Smyrni, Athens 17122, GREECE, Phone: (1) 935-2093

FINCH, RICKY D,
1179 Hwy 844, West Liberty, KY 41472, Phone: 606-743-7151, finchknives@mrtc.com; Web: www.finchknives.com
   Specialties: Traditional working/using straight knives of his design or to customer spec. **Patterns:** Hunters, skinners and utility/camp knives. LinerLock® of his design. **Technical:** Grinds 440C, ATS-34 and CPM154, hand rubbed stain finish, use Micarta, stabilized wood, natural and exotic. **Prices:** $85 to $225. **Remarks:** Part-time maker, first knife made 1994. Doing business as Finch Knives. **Mark:** Last name inside outline of state of Kentucky.

FIORINI, BILL,
703 W. North St., Grayville, IL 62844, Phone: 618-375-7191, smallflowerlonchura@yahoo.com
   Specialties: Fancy working knives. **Patterns:** Hunters, boots, Japanese-style knives and kitchen/utility knives and folders. **Technical:** Forges own Damascus, mosaic and mokune-gane. **Prices:** Full range. **Remarks:** Full-time metal smith researching pattern materials. **Mark:** Orchid crest with name KOKA in Japanese.

FISHER, JAY,
1405 Edwards, Clovis, NM 88101, jayfisher@jayfisher.com Web: www.JayFisher.com
   Specialties: High-art, working and collector's knives of his design and client's designs. Military working and commemoratives. Gemstone handles, Locking combat sheaths. **Patterns:** Hunters, daggers, folding knives, museum pieces and high-art sculptures. **Technical:** 440C, ATS-34, CPMS30V, D2, O1, CPM154CM, CPMS35VN. Prolific maker of stone-handled knives and swords. **Prices:** $850 to $150,000. **Remarks:** Full-time maker; first knife sold in 1980. High resolution etching, computer and manual engraving. **Mark:** Signature "JaFisher"

FISHER, LANCE,
9 Woodlawn Ave., Pompton Lakes, NJ 07442, Phone: 973-248-8447, lance.fisher@sandvik.com
   Specialties: Wedding cake knives and servers, forks, etc. Including velvet lined wood display cases. **Patterns:** Drop points, upswept skinners, Bowies, daggers, fantasy, medieval, San Francisco style, chef or kitchen cutlery. **Technical:** Stock removal method only. Steels include but are not limited to CPM 154, D2, CPM S35VN, CPM S90V and Sandvik 13C26. Handle materials include stag, sheep horn, exotic woods, micarta, and G10 as well as reconstituted stone. **Prices:** $350 - $2000. **Remarks:** Part-time maker, will become full-time on retirement. Made and sold first knife in 1981 and has never looked back. **Mark:** Tang stamp.

FISK, JERRY,
10095 Hwy 278 W, Nashville, AR 71852, Phone: 870-845-4456, jerry@fisk-knives.com; Web: wwwfisk-knives.com
   Specialties: Edged weapons, collectible and functional. **Patterns:** Bowies, daggers, swords, hunters, camp knives and others. **Technical:** Forges carbon steels and his own pattern welded steels. **Prices:** $1100 to $20,000. **Remarks:** National living treasure. **Mark:** Name, MS.

FISTER, JIM,
PO Box 307, Simpsonville, KY 40067
   Specialties: One-of-a-kind collectibles and period pieces. **Patterns:** Bowies, camp knives, hunters, buckskinners, and daggers. **Technical:** Forges, 1085, 5160, 52100, his own Damascus, pattern and turkish. **Prices:** $150 to $2500. **Remarks:** Part-time maker; first knife sold in 1982. **Mark:** Name and MS.

FITCH, JOHN S,
45 Halbrook Rd, Clinton, AR 72031-8910, Phone: 501-893-2020

FITZGERALD, DENNIS M,
4219 Alverado Dr, Fort Wayne, IN 46816-2847, Phone: 219-447-1081
   Specialties: One-of-a-kind collectibles and period pieces. **Patterns:** Skinners, fighters, camp and utility knives; period pieces. **Technical:** Forges 1085, 1095, L6, 5160, 52100, his own pattern and Turkish Damascus. **Prices:** $100 to $500. **Remarks:** Part-time maker; first knife sold in 1985. Doing business as The Ringing Circle. **Mark:** Name and circle logo.

FLINT, ROBERT,
2902 Aspen, Anchorage, AK 99517, Phone: 907-243-6706
   Specialties: Working straight knives and folders. **Patterns:** Utility, hunters, fighters and gents. **Technical:** Grinds ATS-34, BG-42, D2 and Damascus. **Prices:** $150 and up. **Remarks:** Part-time maker, first knife sold in 1998. **Mark:** Last name; stylized initials.

FLOURNOY, JOE,
5750 Lisbon Rd, El Dorado, AR 71730, Phone: 870-863-7208, flournoy@ipa.net
   Specialties: Working straight knives and folders. **Patterns:** Hunters, Bowies, camp knives, folders and daggers. **Technical:** Forges only high-carbon steel, steel cable and his own Damascus. **Prices:** $350 Plus. **Remarks:** First knife sold in 1977. **Mark:** Last name and MS in script.

FLYNT, ROBERT G,
15173 Christy Lane, Gulfport, MS 39503, Phone: 228-265-0410, flyntstoneknives@bellsouth.net Web: www.flyntstoneknifeworks.com
   Specialties:
   All types of fixed blades: Drop point, clip point, trailing point, bull nose hunters, tactical, fighters and Bowies. Folders I've made include liner lock, slip joint and lock back styles.

Technical: Using 154 cm, cpm154, ats34, 440c, cpm3v and 52100 steel, most of my blades are made by stock removal, hollow and flat grind methods. I do forge some cable Damascus and use numerous types of Damascus that is purchased in billets from various makers. All file work and bluing is done by me.
I have made handles from a variety of wood, bone and horn materials, including some with wire inlay and other embellishments.
Most knives are sold with custom fit leather sheaves most include exotic skin inlay when appropriate.
   Prices: $150 and up depending on embellishments on blade and sheath. **Remarks:** Full time maker. First knife made in 1966. **Mark:** Last name in cursive letters or a knife striking a flint stone.

FOGARIZZU, BOITEDDU,
via Crispi 6, 07016 Pattada, ITALY
   Specialties: Traditional Italian straight knives and folders. **Patterns:** Collectible folders. **Technical:** forges and grinds 12C27, ATS-34 and his Damascus. **Prices:** $200 to $3000. **Remarks:** Full-time maker; first knife sold in 1958. **Mark:** Full name and registered logo.

FOGG, DON,
98 Lake St., Auburn, ME 04210, Phone: 205-483-0822, dfogg@dfoggknives.com; Web: www.dfoggknives.com
   Specialties: Swords, daggers, Bowies and hunting knives. **Patterns:** Collectible folders. **Technical:** Hand-forged high-carbon and Damascus steel. **Prices:** $200 to $5000. **Remarks:** Full-time maker; first knife sold in 1976. **Mark:** 24K gold cherry blossom.

FONTENOT, GERALD J,
901 Maple Ave, Mamou, LA 70554, Phone: 318-468-3180

FORREST, BRIAN,
FORREST KNIVES, PO Box 611, Descanso, CA 91916, Phone: 619-445-6343, forrestforge@gmail.com; Web: www.forrestforge.biz
   Specialties: Forged tomahawks, working knives, big Bowies. **Patterns:** Traditional and extra large Bowies. **Technical:** Hollow grinds: 440C, 1095, S160 Damascus. **Prices:**" $125 and up. **Remarks:** Member of California Knifemakers Association. Full-time maker. First knife sold in 1971. **Mark:** Forrest USA/Tomahawks marked FF (Forrest Forge).

FORTHOFER, PETE,
5535 Hwy 93S, Whitefish, MT 59937, Phone: 406-862-2674
   Specialties: Interframes with checkered wood inlays; working straight knives. **Patterns:** Interframe folders and traditional-style knives; hunters, fighters and Bowies. **Technical:** Grinds D2, 440C, 154CM and ATS-34. **Prices:** $350 to $2500; some to $1500. **Remarks:** Part-time maker; full-time gunsmith. First knife sold in 1979. **Mark:** Name and logo.

FORTUNE PRODUCTS, INC.,
205 Hickory Creek Rd, Marble Falls, TX 78654, Phone: 830-693-6111, Fax: 830-693-6394, Web: www.accusharp.com
   Specialties: Knife sharpeners.

FOSTER, AL,
118 Woodway Dr, Magnolia, TX 77355, Phone: 936-372-9297
   Specialties: Straight knives and folders. **Patterns:** Hunting, fishing, folders and Bowies. **Technical:** Grinds 440-C, ATS-34 and D2. **Prices:** $100 to $1000. **Remarks:** Full-time maker; first knife sold in 1981. **Mark:** Scorpion logo and name.

FOSTER, BURT,
23697 Archery Range Rd, Bristol, VA 24202, Phone: 276-669-0121, burt@burtfoster.com; Web:www.burtfoster.com
   Specialties: Working straight knives, laminated blades, and some art knives of his design. **Patterns:** Bowies, hunters, daggers. **Technical:** Forges 52100, W-2 and makes own Damascus. Does own heat treating. **Remarks:** ABS MasterSmith. Full-time maker, believes in sole authorship. **Mark:** Signed "BF" initials.

FOSTER, NORVELL C,
7945 Youngsford Rd, Marion, TX 78124-1713, Phone: 830-914-2078
   Specialties: Engraving; ivory handle carving. **Patterns:** American-large and small scroll-oak leaf and acorns. **Prices:** $25 to $400. **Remarks:** Have been engraving since 1957. **Mark:** N.C. Foster - Marion - Tex and current year.

FOSTER, RONNIE E,
95 Riverview Rd., Morrilton, AR 72110, Phone: 501-354-5389
   Specialties: Working, using knives, some period pieces, work with customer specs. **Patterns:** Hunters, fighters, Bowies, liner-lock folders, camp knives. **Technical:** Forge-5160, 1084, O1, 15N20-makes own Damascus. **Prices:** $200 (start). **Remarks:** Part-time maker. First knife sold 1994. **Mark:** Ronnie Foster MS.

FOSTER, TIMOTHY L,
723 Sweet Gum Acres Rd, El Dorado, AR 71730, Phone: 870-863-6188

FOWLER, CHARLES R,
226 National Forest Rd 48, Ft McCoy, FL 32134-9624, Phone: 904-467-3215

FOWLER, ED A.,
Willow Bow Ranch, PO Box 1519, Riverton, WY 82501, Phone: 307-856-9815
   Specialties: High-performance working and using straight knives. **Patterns:** Hunter, camp, bird, and trout knives and Bowies. New model, the gentleman's Pronghorn. **Technical:** Low temperature forged 52100 from virgin 5-1/2 round bars, multiple quench heat treating, engraves all knives, all handles domestic sheep horn processed and aged at least 5 years. Makes heavy duty hand-stitched waxed harness leather pouch type sheathes. **Prices:** $800 to $7000. **Remarks:** Full-time maker. First knife sold in 1962. **Mark:** Initials connected.

FOWLER, JERRY,
610 FM 1660 N, Hutto, TX 78634, Phone: 512-846-2860, fowler@inetport.com
Specialties: Using straight knives of his design. **Patterns:** A variety of hunting and camp knives, combat knives. Custom designs considered. **Technical:** Forges 5160, his own Damascus and cable Damascus. Makes sheaths. Prefers natural handle materials. **Prices:** Start at $150. **Remarks:** Part-time maker; first knife sold in 1986. Doing business as Fowler Forge Knife Works. **Mark:** First initial, last name, date and J.S.

FOX, PAUL,
4721 Rock Barn Rd, Claremont, NC 28610, Phone: 828-459-2000, jessepfox@gmail.com
Specialties: Unique locking mechanisms. **Patterns:** Pen knives, one-of-a-kind tactical knives. **Technical:** All locking mechanisms are his. **Prices:** $350 and up. **Remarks:** First knife sold in 1976. Guild member since 1977. **Mark:** Fox, P Fox, Paul Fox. Cuts out all parts of knives in shop.

FRALEY, D B,
1355 Fairbanks Ct, Dixon, CA 95620, Phone: 707-678-0393, dbtfnives@sbcglobal.net; Web:www.dbfraleyknives.com
Specialties Usable gentleman's fixed blades and folders. **Patterns:** Foure folders in four different sizes in liner lock and frame lock. **Technical:** Grinds CPMS30V, 154, 6K stellite. **Prices:** $250 and up. **Remarks:** Part time maker. First knife sold in 1990. **Mark:** First and middle initials, last name over a buffalo.

FRAMSKI, WALTER P,
24 Rek Ln, Prospect, CT 06712, Phone: 203-758-5634

FRANCE, DAN,
Box 218, Cawood, KY 40815, Phone: 606-573-6104
Specialties: Traditional working and using straight knives of his design. **Patterns:** Hunters, Bowies and utility/camp knives. **Technical:** Forges and grinds O1, 5160 and L6. **Prices:** $35 to $125; some to $350. **Remarks:** Spare-time maker; first knife sold in 1985. **Mark:** First name.

FRANCIS, JOHN D,
FRANCIS KNIVES, 18 Miami St., Ft. Loramie, OH 45845, Phone: 937-295-3941, jdfrancis72@gmail.com
Specialties: Utility and hunting-style fixed bladed knives of 440 C and ATS-34 steel; Micarta, exotic woods, and other types of handle materials. **Prices:** $90 to $150 range. **Remarks:** Exceptional quality and value at factory prices. **Mark:** Francis-Ft. Loramie, OH stamped on tang.

FRANK, HEINRICH H,
1147 SW Bryson St, Dallas, OR 97338, Phone: 503-831-1489, Fax: 503-831-1489
Specialties: High-art investor-class folders, handmade and engraved. **Patterns:** Folding daggers, hunter-size folders and gents. **Technical:** Grinds 07 and O1. **Prices:** $4800 to $16,000. **Remarks:** Full-time maker; first knife sold in 1965. Doing business as H.H. Frank Knives. **Mark:** Name, address and date.

FRANKLIN, MIKE,
9878 Big Run Rd, Aberdeen, OH 45101, Phone: 937-549-2598, Web: www.mikefranklinknives.com, hawgcustomknives.com
Specialties: High-tech tactical folders. **Patterns:** Tactical folders. **Technical:** Grinds CPM-T-440V, 440-C, ATS-34; titanium liners and bolsters; carbon fiber scales. Uses radical grinds and severe serrations. **Prices:** $100 to $1000. **Remarks:** Full-time maker; first knife sold in 1969. All knives made one at a time, 100% by the maker. **Mark:** Stylized boar with HAWG.

FRAPS, JOHN R,
3810 Wyandotte Tr, Indianapolis, IN 46240-3422, Phone: 317-849-9419, jfraps@att.net; Web: www.frapsknives.com
Specialties: Working and collector grade LinerLock® and slip joint folders. **Patterns:** One-of-a kind linerlocks and traditional slip joints. **Technical:** Flat and hollow grinds ATS-34, Damascus, Talonite, CPM S30V, 154Cm, Stellite 6K; hand rubbed or mirror finish. **Prices:** $200 to $1500, some higher. **Remarks:** Voting member of the Knifemaker's Guild; Full-time maker; first knife sold in 1997. **Mark:** Cougar Creek Knives and/or name.

FRAZIER, JIM,
6315 Wagener Rd., Wagener, SC 29164, Phone: 803-564-6467, jbfrazierknives@hotmail.com Web: www.jbfrazierknives.com
Specialties: Hunters, semi skinners, bird and trout, folders, many patterns of own design with George Herron/Geno Denning influence. **Technical:** Stock removal maker using CPM-154, ATS-34, S30-V, D2. Hollow grind, mainly mirror finish, some satin finish. Prefer to use natural handle material such as stag, horn, mammoth ivory, highly figured woods, some micarta, others on request. Makes own leather sheaths on 1958 straight needle stitcher. **Prices:** $300. **Remarks:** Part-time maker since 1989. **Mark:** JB Frazier in arch with Knives under it.Stamp on sheath is outline of state of SC, JB Frazier Knives Wagener SC inside outline.

FRED, REED WYLE,
3149 X S, Sacramento, CA 95817, Phone: 916-739-0237
Specialties: Working straight knives of his design. **Patterns:** Hunting and camp knives. **Technical:** Forges any 10 series, old files and carbon steels. Offers initialing upon request; prefers natural handle materials. **Prices:** $30 to $300. **Remarks:** Part-time maker; first knife sold in 1994. Doing business as R.W. Fred Knifemaker. **Mark:** Engraved first and last initials.

FREDEEN, GRAHAM,
5121 Finadene Ct., Colorado Springs, CO 80916, Phone: 719-331-5665, fredeenblades@hotmail.com Web: www.fredeenblades.com
Specialties: Working class knives to high-end custom knives. Traditional pattern welding and mosaic Damascus blades. **Patterns:** All types: Bowies, fighters, hunters, skinners, bird and trout, camp knives, utility knives, daggers, etc. Occasionally swords, both European and Asian. **Technical:** Differential heat treatment and Hamon. Damascus steel rings and jewelry. Hand forged blades and Damascus steel. High carbon blade steels: 1050, 1075/1080, 1084, 1095, 5160, 52100, W1, W2, O1, 15n20 **Prices:** $100 - $2,000. **Remarks:** Sole authorship. Part-time maker. First blade produced in 2005. Member of American Bladesmith Society and Professional Knifemaker's Association **Mark:** "Fredeen" etched on the ricasso or on/along the spine of the blade.

FREDERICK, AARON,
459 Brooks Ln, West Liberty, KY 41472-8961, Phone: 606-7432015, aaronf@mrtc.com; Web: www.frederickknives.com
Specialties: Makes most types of knives, but as for now specializes in the Damascus folder. Does all own Damascus and forging of the steel. Also prefers natural handle material such as ivory and pearl. Prefers 14k gold screws in most of the knives he do. Also offer several types of file work on blades, spacers, and liners. Has just recently started doing carving and can do a limited amount of engraving.

FREER, RALPH,
114 12th St, Seal Beach, CA 90740, Phone: 562-493-4925, Fax: same, ralphfreer@adelphia.net
Specialties: Exotic folders, liner locks, folding daggers, fixed blades. **Patters:** All original. **Technical:** Lots of Damascus, ivory, pearl, jeweled, thumb studs, carving ATS-34, 420V, 530V. **Prices:** $400 to $2500 and up. **Mark:** Freer in German-style text, also Freer shield.

FREY JR., W FREDERICK,
305 Walnut St, Milton, PA 17847, Phone: 570-742-9576, wffrey@ptd.net
Specialties: Working straight knives and folders, some fancy. **Patterns:** Wide range miniatures, boot knives and lock back folders. **Technical:** Grinds A2, O1 and D2; vaseo wear, cru-wear and CPM S90V. **Prices:** $100 to $250; some to $1200. **Remarks:** Spare-time maker; first knife sold in 1983. All knives include quality hand stitched leather sheaths. **Mark:** Last name in script.

FRIEDLY, DENNIS E,
12 Cottontail Lane E, Cody, WY 82414, Phone: 307-527-6811, friedlyknives@hotmail.com Web: www.friedlyknives.com
Specialties: Fancy working straight knives and daggers, lock back folders and liner locks. Also embellished bowies. **Patterns:** Hunters, fighters, short swords, minis and miniatures; new line of full-tang hunters/boots. **Technical:** Grinds 440C, commercial Damascus, mosaic Damascus and ATS-34 blades; prefers hidden tangs and full tangs. Both flat and hollow grinds. **Prices:** $350 to $2500. Some to $10,000. **Remarks:** Full-time maker; first knife sold in 1972. **Mark:** D.E. Friedly-Cody, WY. Friedly Knives

FRIGAULT, RICK,
1189 Royal Pines Rd, Golden Lake, Ont, CANADA K0J 1X0, Phone: 613-401-2869, Web: www.rfrigaultknives.ca
Specialties: Fixed blades. **Patterns:** Hunting, tactical and large Bowies. **Technical:** Grinds ATS-34, 440-C, D-2, CPMS30V, CPMS60V, CPMS90V, BG42 and Damascus. Use G-10, Micarta, ivory, antler, ironwood and other stabilized woods for carbon fiber handle material. Makes leather sheaths by hand. Tactical blades include a Concealex sheath made by "On Scene Tactical." **Remarks:** Sold first knife in 1997. Member of Canadian Knifemakers Guild. **Mark:** RFRIGAULT.

FRITZ, ERIK L,
837 River St Box 1203, Forsyth, MT 59327, Phone: 406-351-1101, tacmedic45@yahoo.com
Specialties: Forges carbon steel 1084, 5160, 52100 and Damascus. **Patterns:** Hunters, camp knives, bowies and folders as well as forged tactical. **Technical:** Forges own Mosaic and pattern welded Damascus as well as doing own heat treat. **Prices:** A$200 and up. **Remarks:** Sole authorship knives and sheaths. Part time maker first knife sold in 2004. ABS member. **Mark:** E. Fritz in arc on left side ricasso.

FRITZ, JESSE,
900 S. 13th St, Slaton, TX 79364, Phone: 806-828-5083
Specialties: Working and using straight knives in standard patterns. **Patterns:** Hunters, utility/camp knives and skinners with gut hook, Bowie knives, kitchen carving sets by request. **Technical:** Grinds 440C, O1 and 1095. Uses 1095 steel. Fline-napped steel design, blued blades, filework and machine jewelling. Inlays handles with turquoise, coral and mother-of-pearl. Makes sheaths. **Prices:** $85 to $275; some to $500. **Mark:** Last name only (FRITZ).

FRIZZELL, TED,
14056 Low Gap Rd, West Fork, AR 72774, Phone: 501-839-2516, mmhwaxes@aol.com Web: www.mineralmountain.com
Specialties: Swords, axes and self-defense weapons. **Patterns:** Small skeleton knives to large swords. **Technical:** Grinds 5160 almost exclusively—1/4" to 1/2"—bars some O1 and A2 on request. All knives come with Kydex sheaths. **Prices:** $45 to $1200. **Remarks:** Full-time maker; first knife sold in 1984. Doing business as Mineral Mountain Hatchet Works. Wholesale orders welcome. **Mark:** A circle with line in the middle; MM and HW within the circle.

FRIZZI, LEONARDO,
Via Kyoto 31, Firenze, ITALY 50126, Phone: 335-344750, postmaster@frizzi-knives.com; Web: www.frizzi-knives.com
Specialties: Fancy handmade one-of a kind folders of his own design, some fixed blade and dagger. **Patterns:** Folders liner loch and back locks. **Technical:** Grinds rwl 34, cpm 154, cpm s30v, stainless damascus and the best craft damascus, own heat treating. I usually prefer satin finish the flat of the blade

and mirror polish the hollow grind; special 18k gold, filework. **Prices:** $450 to $1500. **Remarks:** Part-time maker, first knife sold in 2003. **Mark:** Full name, city, country, or initial, last name and city, or initial in square logo.

FRONEFIELD, DANIEL,
20270 Warriors Path, Peyton, CO 80831, Phone: 719-749-0226, dfronfld@hiwaay.com
Specialties: Fixed and folding knives featuring meteorites and other exotic materials. **Patterns:** San-mai Damascus, custom Damascus. **Prices:** $500 to $3000.

FROST, DEWAYNE,
1016 Van Buren Rd, Barnesville, GA 30204, Phone: 770-358-1426, lbrtyhill@aol.com
Specialties: Working straight knives and period knives. **Patterns:** Hunters, Bowies and utility knives. **Technical:** Forges own Damascus, cable, etc. as well as stock removal. **Prices:** $150 to $500. **Remarks:** Part-time maker ABS Journeyman Smith. **Mark:** Liberty Hill Forge Dewayne Frost w/liberty bell.

FRUHMANN, LUDWIG,
Stegerwaldstr 8, 84489 Burghausen, GERMANY
Specialties: High-tech and working straight knives of his design. **Patterns:** Hunters, fighters and boots. **Technical:** Grinds ATS-34, CPM-T-440V and Schneider Damascus. Prefers natural handle materials. **Prices:** $200 to $1500. **Remarks:** Spare-time maker; first knife sold in 1990. **Mark:** First initial and last name.

FRY, JASON,
1701 North Willis, Abilene, TX 79603, Phone: 325-669-4805, frycustomknives@gmail.com; Web: www.frycustomknives.com
Specialties: Prefer drop points, both with or without bolsters. Prefer native Texas woods and often do contrasting wood bolsters. Also does own leather work. **Patterns:** Primarily EDC and hunting/skinning knives under 8 inches. Also slipjoint folders, primarily single blade trappers and jacks. **Technical:** 1080 carbon steel, D2 tool steel, and 154CM stainless. Make knives by stock removal and does own heat treating in a digitally controlled kiln. **Prices:** $150 to $400. **Remarks:** Part-time maker since July 2008. **Mark:** FRY placed on blade underneath jumping largemouth bass to reflect other interests.

FUEGEN, LARRY,
617 N Coulter Circle, Prescott, AZ 86303, Phone: 928-776-8777, fuegen@cableone.net; Web: www.larryfuegen.com
Specialties: High-art folders and classic and working straight knives. **Patterns:** Forged scroll folders, lockback folders and classic straight knives. **Technical:** Forges 5160, 1095 and his own Damascus. Works in exotic leather; offers elaborate filework and carving; likes natural handle materials, now offers own engraving. **Prices:** $600 to $12,000. **Remarks:** Full-time maker; first knife sold in 1975. Sole authorship on all knives. ABS Mastersmith. **Mark:** Initials connected.

FUJIKAWA, SHUN,
Sawa 1157 Kaizuka, Osaka 597 0062, JAPAN, Phone: 81-724-23-4032, Fax: 81-726-23-9229
Specialties: Folders of his design and to customer specs. **Patterns:** Locking folders. **Technical:** Grinds his own steel. **Prices:** $450 to $2500; some to $3000. **Remarks:** Part-time maker.

FUJISAKA, STANLEY,
45-004 Holowai St, Kaneohe, HI 96744, Phone: 808-247-0017, s.fuj@earthlink.net
Specialties: Fancy working straight knives and folders. **Patterns:** Hunters, boots, personal knives, daggers, collectible art knives. **Technical:** Grinds 440C, 154CM and ATS-34; clean lines, inlays. **Prices:** $400 to $2000; some to $6000. **Remarks:** Full-time maker; first knife sold in 1984. **Mark:** Name, city, state.

FUKUTA, TAK,
38-Umeagae-cho, Seki-City, Gifu-Pref, JAPAN, Phone: 0575-22-0264
Specialties: Bench-made fancy straight knives and folders. **Patterns:** Sheffield-type folders, Bowies and fighters. **Technical:** Grinds commercial Damascus. **Prices:** Start at $300. **Remarks:** Full-time maker. **Mark:** Name in knife logo.

FULLER, BRUCE A,
1305 Airhart Dr, Baytown, TX 77520, Phone: 281-427-1848, fullcoforg@aol.com
Specialties: One-of-a-kind working/using straight knives and folders of his designs. **Patterns:** Bowies, hunters, folders, and utility/camp knives. **Technical:** Forges high-carbon steel and his own Damascus. Prefers El Solo Mesquite and natural materials. Offers filework. **Prices:** $200 to $500; some to $1800. **Remarks:** Spare-time maker; first knife sold in 1991. Doing business as Fullco Forge. **Mark:** Fullco, M.S.

FULLER, JACK A,
7103 Stretch Ct, New Market, MD 21774, Phone: 301-798-0119
Specialties: Straight working knives of his design and to customer specs. **Patterns:** Fighters, camp knives, hunters, tomahawks and art knives. **Technical:** Forges 5160, O1, W2 and his own Damascus. Does silver wire inlay and own leather work, wood lined sheaths for big camp knives. **Prices:** $400 and up. **Remarks:** Part-time maker. Master Smith in ABS; first knife sold in 1979. **Mark:** Fuller's Forge, MS.

FULTON, MICKEY,
406 S Shasta St, Willows, CA 95988, Phone: 530-934-5780
Specialties: Working straight knives and folders of his design. **Patterns:**

Hunters, Bowies, lockback folders and steak knife sets. **Technical:** Hand-filed, sanded, buffed ATS-34, 440C and A2. **Prices:** $65 to $600; some to $1200. **Remarks:** Full-time maker; first knife sold in 1979. **Mark:** Signature.

G

GADBERRY, EMMET,
82 Purple Plum Dr, Hattieville, AR 72063, Phone: 501-354-4842

GADDY, GARY LEE,
205 Ridgewood Lane, Washington, NC 27889, Phone: 252-946-4359
Specialties: Working/using straight knives of his design; period pieces. **Patterns:** Bowies, hunters, utility/camp knives, oyster knives. **Technical:** Grinds ATS-34, O1; forges 1095. **Prices:** $175+ **Remarks:** Spare-time maker; first knife sold in 1991. No longer accepts orders. **Mark:** Quarter moon stamp.

GAETA, ANGELO,
R. Saldanha Marinho, 1295 Centro Jau, SP-17201-310, BRAZIL, Phone: 0146-224543, Fax: 0146-224543
Specialties: Straight using knives to customer specs. **Patterns:** Hunters, fighting, daggers, belt push dagger. **Technical:** Grinds D6, ATS-34 and 440C stainless. Titanium nitride golden finish upon request. **Prices:** $60 to $300. **Remarks:** Full-time maker; first knife sold in 1992. **Mark:** First initial, last name.

GAETA, ROBERTO,
Rua Mandissununga 41, Sao Paulo, BRAZIL 05619-010, Phone: 11-37684626, karlaseno@uol.com.br
Specialties: Wide range of using knives. **Patterns:** Brazilian and North American hunting and fighting knives. **Technical:** Grinds stainless steel; likes natural handle materials. **Prices:** $500 to $800. **Remarks:** Full-time maker; first knife sold in 1979. **Mark:** BOB'G.

GAINES, BUDDY,
GAINES KNIVES, 155 Red Hill Rd., Commerce, GA 30530, Web: www.gainesknives.com
Specialties: Collectible and working folders and straight knives. **Patterns:** Folders, hunters, Bowies, tactical knives. **Technical:** Forges own Damascus, grinds ATS-34, D2, commercial Damascus. Prefers mother-of-pearl and stag. **Prices:** Start at $200. **Remarks:** Part-time maker, sold first knife in 1985. **Mark:** Last name.

GAINEY, HAL,
904 Bucklevel Rd, Greenwood, SC 29649, Phone: 864-223-0225, Web: www.scak.org
Specialties: Traditional working and using straight knives and folders. **Patterns:** Hunters, slip-joint folders and utility/camp knives. **Technical:** Hollow-grinds ATS-34 and D2; makes sheaths. **Prices:** $95 to $145; some to $500. **Remarks:** Full-time maker; first knife sold in 1975. **Mark:** Eagle head and last name.

GALLAGHER, BARRY,
135 Park St, Lewistown, MT 59457, Phone: 406-538-7056, Web: www.gallagherknives.com
Specialties: One-of-a-kind Damascus folders. **Patterns:** Folders, utility to high art, some straight knives, hunter, Bowies, and art pieces. **Technical:** Forges own mosaic Damascus and carbon steel, some stainless. **Prices:** $400 to $5000+. **Remarks:** Full-time maker; first knife sold in 1993. Doing business as Gallagher Custom Knives. **Mark:** Last name.

GAMBLE, FRANK,
4676 Commercial St SE #26, Salem, OR 97302, Phone: 503-581-7993, gamble6831@comcast.net
Specialties: Fantasy and high-art straight knives and folders of his design. **Patterns:** Daggers, fighters, hunters and special locking folders. **Technical:** Grinds 440C and ATS-34; forges Damascus. Inlays; offers jewelling. **Prices** $150 to $10,000. **Remarks:** Full-time maker; first knife sold in 1976. **Mark:** First initial, last name.

GAMBLE, ROGER,
18515 N.W. 28th Pl., Newberry, FL 32669, ROGERLGAMBLE@COX.NET
Specialties: Traditional working/using straight knives and folders of his design. **Patterns:** Liner locks and hunters. **Technical:** Grinds ATS-34 and Damascus. **Prices:** $150 to $2000. **Remarks:** Part-time maker; first knife sold in 1982. Doing business as Gamble Knives. **Mark:** First name in a fan of cards over last name.

GANN, TOMMY,
2876 State Hwy. 198, Canton, TX 75103, Phone: 903-848-9375
Specialties: Art and working straight knives of my design or customer preferences/design. **Patterns:** Bowie, fighters, hunters, daggers. **Technical:** Forges Damascus 52100 and grinds ATS-34 and D2. **Prices:** $200 to $2500. **Remarks:** Full-time knifemaker, first knife sold in 2002. ABS journey bladesmith. **Mark:** TGANN.

GANSHORN, CAL,
123 Rogers Rd., Regina, Saskatchewan, CANADA S4S 6T7, Phone: 306-584-0524
Specialties: Working and fancy fixed blade knives. **Patterns:** Bowies, hunters, daggers, and filleting. **Technical:** Makes own forged Damascus billets, ATS, salt heat treating, and custom forges and burners. **Prices:** $250 to $1500. **Remarks:** Part-time maker. **Mark:** Last name etched in ricasso area.

GARAU, MARCELLO,
Via Alagon 42, 09170, Oristano, Italy, Phone: 00393479073454, marcellogarau@libero.it Web: www.knifecreator.com
Specialties: Mostly lock back folders with interframe. **Technical:** Forges own

damascus for both blades and frames. **Prices:** 200 - 1800 Euro. **Remarks:** Full-time maker; first knife made in 1995. Attends Milano Knife Show and ECCKSHOW yearly. **Mark:** M.Garau inside handle.

GARCIA, MARIO EIRAS,
R. Edmundo Scanapieco, 300 Caxingui, Sao Paulo SP-05516-070, BRAZIL, Fax: 011-37214528
    Specialties: Fantasy knives of his design; one-of-a-kind only. **Patterns:** Fighters, daggers, boots and two-bladed knives. **Technical:** Forges car leaf springs. Uses only natural handle material. **Prices:** $100 to $200. **Remarks:** Part-time maker; first knife sold in 1976. **Mark:** Two "B"s, one opposite the other.

GARNER, GEORGE,
7527 Calhoun Dr. NE, Albuquerque, NM 87109, Phone: 505-797-9317, razorbackblades@msn.com Web: www.razorbackblades.com
    Specialties: High art locking liner folders and Daggers of his own design. Working and high art straight knives. **Patterns:** Bowies, daggers, fighters and locking liner folders. **Technical:** Grinds 440C, CPM-154, ATS34 and others. Damascus, Mosaic Damascus and Mokume. Makes own custom leather sheaths. **Prices:** $150 - $2,500. **Remarks:** Part-time maker since 1993. Full-time maker as of 2011. Company name is Razorback Blades. **Mark:** GEORGE GARNER.

GARNER, LARRY W,
13069 FM 14, Tyler, TX 75706, Phone: 903-597-6045, lwgarner@classicnet.net
    Specialties: Fixed blade hunters and Bowies. **Patterns:** His designs or yours. **Technical:** Hand forges 5160. **Prices:** $200 to $500. **Remarks:** Apprentice bladesmith. **Mark:** Last name.

GARVOCK, MARK W,
RR 1, Balderson, Ont., CANADA K1G 1A0, Phone: 613-833-2545, Fax: 613-833-2208, garvock@travel-net.com
    Specialties: Hunters, Bowies, Japanese, daggers and swords. **Patterns:** Cable Damascus, random pattern welded or to suit. **Technical:** Forged blades; hi-carbon. **Prices:** $250 to $900. **Remarks:** CKG member and ABS member. Shipping and taxes extra. **Mark:** Big G with M in middle.

GAUDETTE, LINDEN L,
5 Hitchcock Rd, Wilbraham, MA 01095, Phone: 413-596-4896
    Specialties: Traditional working knives in standard patterns. **Patterns:** Broad-bladed hunters, Bowies and camp knives; wood carver knives; locking folders. **Technical:** Grinds ATS-34, 440C and 154CM. **Prices:** $150 to $400; some higher. **Remarks:** Full-time maker; first knife sold in 1975. **Mark:** Last name in Gothic logo; used to be initials in circle.

GEDRAITIS, CHARLES J,
GEDRAITIS HAND CRAFTED KNIVES, 444 Shrewsbury St, Holden, MA 01520, Phone: 508-963-1861, gedraitisknives@yahoo.com; Web: www.gedraitisknives.com
    Specialties: One-of-a-kind folders & automatics of his own design. **Patterns:** One-of-a-kind. **Technical:** Forges to shape mostly stock removal. **Prices:** $300 to $2500. **Remarks:** Full-time maker. **Mark:** 3 scallop shells with an initial inside each one: CJG.

GEISLER, GARY R,
PO Box 294, Clarksville, OH 45113, Phone: 937-383-4055, ggeisler@in-touch.net
    Specialties: Period Bowies and such; flat ground. **Patterns:** Working knives usually modeled close after an existing antique. **Technical:** Flat grinds 440C, A2 and ATS-34. **Prices:** $300 and up. **Remarks:** Part-time maker; first knife sold in 1982. **Mark:** G.R. Geisler Maker; usually in script on reverse side because maker is left-handed.

GEORGE, HARRY,
3137 Old Camp Long Rd, Aiken, SC 29805, Phone: 803-649-1963, hdkk-george@scescape.net
    Specialties: Working straight knives of his design or to customer specs. **Patterns:** Hunters, skinners and utility knives. **Technical:** Grinds ATS-34. Prefers natural handle materials, hollow-grinds and mirror finishes. **Prices:** Start at $70. **Remarks:** Part-time maker; first knife sold in 1985. Trained under George Herron. Member SCAK. Member Knifemakers Guild. **Mark:** Name, city, state.

GEORGE, LES,
6521 Fenwick Dr., Corpus Christi, TX 78414, Phone: 361-288-9777, les@georgeknives.com; Web: www.georgeknives.com
    Specialties: Tactical frame locks and fixed blades. **Patterns:** Folders, balisongs, and fixed blades. **Technical:** CPM154, S30V, Chad Nichols Damascus. **Prices:** $200 to $800. **Remarks:** Full-time maker, first knife sold in 1992. Doing business as www.georgeknives.com. **Mark:** Last name over logo.

GEORGE, TOM,
550 Aldbury Dr, Henderson, NV 89014, tagmaker@aol.com
    Specialties: Working straight knives, display knives, custom meat cleavers, and folders of his design. **Patterns:** Hunters, Bowies, daggers, buckskinners, swords and folders. **Technical:** Uses D2, 440C, ATS-34 and 154CM. **Prices:** $500 to $13,500. **Remarks:** Custom orders not accepted "at this time". Full-time maker. First knife1982; first 350 knives were numbered; after that no numbers. Almost all his knives today are Bowies and swords. Creator and maker of the "Past Glories" series of knives. **Mark:** Tom George maker.

GEPNER, DON,
2615 E Tecumseh, Norman, OK 73071, Phone: 405-364-2750
    Specialties: Traditional working and using straight knives of his design. **Patterns:** Bowies and daggers. **Technical:** Forges his Damascus, 1095 and 5160. **Prices:** $100 to $400; some to $1000. **Remarks:** Spare-time maker; first knife sold in 1991. Has been forging since 1954; first edged weapon made at 9 years old. **Mark:** Last initial.

GERNER, THOMAS,
PO Box 301 Walpole, Western Australia, AUSTRALIA 6398, gerner@bordernet.com.au; Web: www.deepriverforge.com
    Specialties: Forged working knives; plain steel and pattern welded. **Patterns:** Tries most patterns heard or read about. **Technical:** 5160, L6, O1, 52100 steels; Australian hardwood handles. **Prices:** $220 and up. **Remarks:** Achieved ABS Master Smith rating in 2001. **Mark:** Like a standing arrow and a leaning cross, T.G. in the Runic (Viking) alphabet.

GIAGU, SALVATORE AND DEROMA MARIA ROSARIA,
Via V Emanuele 64, 07016 Pattada (SS), ITALY, Phone: 079-755918, Fax: 079-755918, coltelligiagupattada@tiscali.it Web: www.culterpattada.it
    Specialties: Using and collecting traditional and new folders from Sardegna. **Patterns:** Folding, hunting, utility, skinners and kitchen knives. **Technical:** Forges ATS-34, 440, D2 and Damascus. **Prices:** $200 to $2000; some higher. **Mark:** First initial, last name and name of town and muflon's head.

GIBERT, PEDRO,
Los Alamos 410, 8370 San Martin de los Andes Neuquen, ARGENTINA, Phone: 054-2972-410868, rosademayo@infovia.com.ar
    Specialties: Hand forges: Stock removal and integral. High quality artistic knives of his design and to customer specifications. **Patterns:** Country (Argentine gaucho-style), knives, folders, Bowies, daggers, hunters. Others upon request. **Technical:** Blade: Bohler k110 Austrian steel (high resistance to waste). Handles: (Natural materials) ivory elephant, killer whale, hippo, walrus tooth, deer antler, goat, ram, buffalo horn, bone, rhea, sheep, cow, exotic woods (South America native woods) hand carved and engraved guards and blades. Stainless steel guards, finely polished: semi-matte or shiny finish. Sheaths: Raw or tanned leather, hand-stitched; rawhide or cotton yarn embroidered. Box: One wood piece, hand carved. Wooden hinges and locks. **Prices:** $600 and up. **Remarks:** Full-time maker. Made first knife in 1987. **Mark:** Only a rose logo. Buyers initials upon request.

GIBO, GEORGE,
PO Box 4304, Hilo, HI 96720, Phone: 808-987-7002, geogibo@hilo808.net
    Specialties: Straight knives and folders. **Patterns:** Hunters, bird and trout, utility, gentlemen and tactical folders. **Technical:** Grinds ATS-34, BG-42, Talonite, Stainless Steel Damascus. **Prices:** $250 to $1000. **Remarks:** Spare-time maker; first knife sold in 1995. **Mark:** Name, city and state around Hawaiian "Shaka" sign.

GIBSON SR., JAMES HOOT,
90 Park Place Ave., Bunnell, FL 32110, Phone: 386-437-4383, hootsknives.aol.com
    Specialties: Bowies, folders, daggers, and hunters. **Patterns:** Most all. **Technical:** ATS-440C hand cut and grind. Also traditional old fashioned folders. **Prices:** $250 to $3000. **Remarks:** 100 percent handmade. **Mark:** HOOT

GILBERT, CHANTAL,
291 Rue Christophe-Colomb est #105, Quebec City Quebec, CANADA G1K 3T1, Phone: 418-525-6961, Fax: 418-525-4666, gilbertc@medion.qc.ca; Web:www.chantalgilbert.com
    Specialties: Straight art knives that may resemble creatures, often with wings, shells and antennae, always with a beak of some sort, fixed blades in a feminine style. **Technical:** ATS-34 and Damascus. Handle materials usually silver that she forms to shape via special molds and a press; ebony and fossil ivory. **Prices:** Range from $500 to $4000. **Remarks:** Often embellishes her art knives with rubies, meteorite, 18k gold and similar elements.

GILBREATH, RANDALL,
55 Crauswell Rd, Dora, AL 35062, Phone: 205-648-3902
    Specialties: Damascus folders and fighters. **Patterns:** Folders and fixed blades. **Technical:** Forges Damascus and high-carbon; stock removal stainless steel. **Prices:** $300 to $1500. **Remarks:** Full-time maker; first knife sold in 1979. **Mark:** Name in ribbon.

GILJEVIC, BRANKO,
35 Hayley Crescent, Queanbeyan 2620, N.S.W., AUSTRALIA 0262977613
    Specialties: Classic working straight knives and folders of his design. **Patterns:** Hunters, Bowies, skinners and locking folders. **Technical:** Grinds 440C. Offers acid etching, scrimshaw and leather carving. **Prices:** $150 to $1500. **Remarks:** Part-time maker; first knife sold in 1987. Doing business as Sambar Custom Knives. **Mark:** Company name in logo.

GINGRICH, JUSTIN,
325 North Linton Street, Blue Earth, MN 56013, Phone: 507-230-0398, justin@rangerknives.com Web: www.rangerknives.com
    Specialties: Anything from bushcraft to tactical, heavy on the tactical. **Patterns:** Fixed blades and folders. **Technical:** Uses all types of steel and handle material, method is stock-removal. **Prices:** $30 - $1000. **Remarks:** Full-time maker. **Mark:** Tang stamp is the old Ranger Knives logo.

GIRAFFEBONE INC.,
3052 Isim Road, Norman, OK 73026, Phone: 888-804-0683; 405-321-3614, sandy@giraffebone.com; Web: www.giraffebone.com
    Specialties: Giraffebone, horns, African hardwoods, and mosaic Damascus

GIRTNER, JOE,
409 Catalpa Ave, Brea, CA 92821, Phone: 714-529-2388, conceptsinknives@aol.com
    Specialties: Art knives and miniatures. **Patterns:** Mainly Damascus (some carved). **Technical:** Many techniques and materials combined. Wood carving knives and tools, hunters, custom orders. **Prices:** $55 to $3000. **Mark:** Name.

GITTINGER, RAYMOND,
6940 S Rt 100, Tiffin, OH 44883, Phone: 419-397-2517

GLOVER, RON,
100 West Church St., Mason, OH 45040, Phone: 513-404-7107, r.glover@zoomtown.com
Specialties: High-tech working straight knives and folders. **Patterns:** Hunters to Bowies; some interchangeable blade models; unique locking mechanisms. **Technical:** Grinds 440C, 154CM; buys Damascus. **Prices:** $70 to $500; some to $800. **Remarks:** Part-time maker; first knife sold in 1981. **Mark:** Name in script.

GLOVER, WARREN D,
dba BUBBA KNIVES, PO Box 475, Cleveland, GA 30528, Phone: 706-865-3998, Fax: 706-348-7176, warren@bubbaknives.net; Web: www.bubbaknives.net
Specialties: Traditional and custom working and using straight knives of his design and to customer request. **Patterns:** Hunters, skinners, bird and fish, utility and kitchen knives. **Technical:** Grinds 440, ATS-34 and stainless steel Damascus. **Prices:** $75 to $400 and up. **Remarks:** Full-time maker; sold first knife in 1995. **Mark:** Bubba, year, name, state.

GODDARD, WAYNE,
473 Durham Ave, Eugene, OR 97404, Phone: 541-689-8098, wgoddard44@comcast.net
Specialties: Working/using straight knives and folders. **Patterns:** Hunters and folders. **Technical:** Works exclusively with wire Damascus and his own-pattern welded material. **Prices:** $250 to $4000. **Remarks:** Full-time maker; first knife sold in 1963. **Mark:** Blocked initials on forged blades; regular capital initials on stock removal.

GODLESKY, BRUCE F.,
1002 School Rd., Apollo, PA 15613, Phone: 724-840-5786, brucegodlesky@yahoo.com; Web: www.birdforge.com
Specialties: Working/using straight knives and tomahawks, mostly forged. **Patterns:** Hunters, birds and trout, fighters and tomahawks. **Technical:** Most forged, some stock removal. Carbon steel only. 5160, O-1, W2, 10xx series. Makes own Damascus and welded cable. **Prices:** Starting at $75. **Mark:** BIRDOG FORGE.

GOERS, BRUCE,
3423 Royal Ct S, Lakeland, FL 33813, Phone: 941-646-0984
Specialties: Fancy working and using straight knives of his design and to customer specs. **Patterns:** Hunters, fighters, Bowies and fantasy knives. **Technical:** Grinds ATS-34, some Damascus. **Prices:** $195 to $600; some to $1300. **Remarks:** Part-time maker; first knife sold in 1990. Doing business as Vulture Cutlery. **Mark:** Buzzard with initials.

GOFOURTH, JIM,
3776 Aliso Cyn Rd, Santa Paula, CA 93060, Phone: 805-659-3814
Specialties: Period pieces and working knives. **Patterns:** Bowies, locking folders, patent lockers and others. **Technical:** Grinds A2 and 154CM. **Prices:** Moderate. **Remarks:** Spare-time maker. **Mark:** Initials interconnected.

GOLDBERG, DAVID,
321 Morris Rd, Ft Washington, PA 19034, Phone: 215-654-7117, david@goldmountainforge.com; Web: www.goldmountainforge.com
Specialties: Japanese-style designs, will work with special themes in Japanese genre. **Patterns:** Kozuka, Tanto, Wakazashi, Katana, Tachi, Sword canes, Yari and Naginata. **Technical:** Forges his own Damascus and makes his own handmade tamehagane steel from straw ash, iron, carbon and clay. Uses traditional materials, carves fittings handles and cases. Hardens all blades in traditional Japanese clay differential technique. **Remarks:** Full-time maker; first knife sold in 1987. Japanese swordsmanship teacher (jaido) and Japanese self-defense teach (aikido). **Mark:** Name (kinzan) in Japanese Kanji on Tang under handle.

GOLDEN, RANDY,
6492 Eastwood Glen Dr, Montgomery, AL 36117, Phone: 334-271-6429, rgolden1@mindspring.com
Specialties: Collectable quality hand rubbed finish, hunter, camp, Bowie straight knives, custom leather sheaths with exotic skin inlays and tooling. **Technical:** Stock removal ATS-34, CPM154, S30V and BG-42. Natural handle materials primarily stag and ivory. **Prices:** $500 to $1500. **Remarks:** Full-time maker, member Knifemakers Guild, first knife sold in 2000. **Mark:** R. R. Golden Montgomery, AL.

GONZALEZ, LEONARDO WILLIAMS,
Ituzaingo 473, Maldonado, CP 20000, URUGUAY, Phone: 598 4222 1617, Fax: 598 4222 1617, willyknives@hotmail.com
Specialties: Classic high-art and fantasy straight knives; traditional working and using knives of his design, in standard patterns or to customer specs. **Patterns:** Hunters, Bowies, daggers, fighters, boots, swords and utility/camp knives. **Technical:** Forges and grinds high-carbon and stainless Bohler steels. **Prices:** $100 to $2500. **Remarks:** Full-time maker; first knife sold in 1985. **Mark:** Willy, whale, R.O.U.

GOO, TAI,
5920 W Windy Lou Ln, Tucson, AZ 85742, Phone: 520-744-9777, taigoo@msn.com; Web: www.taigoo.com
Specialties: High art, neo-tribal, bush and fantasy. **Technical:** Hand forges, does own heat treating, makes own Damascus. **Prices:** $150 to $500 some to $10,000. **Remarks:** Full-time maker; first knife sold in 1978. **Mark:** Chiseled signature.

GOOD, D.R.,
D.R. Good Custom Knives and Weaponry, 6125 W. 100 S., Tipton, IN 46072, Phone: 765-963-6971, drntammigood@bluemarble.net
Specialties: Working knives, own design, Scagel style, "critter" knives, carved handles. **Patterns:** Bowies, large and small, neck knives and miniatures. Offers carved handles, snakeheads, eagles, wolves, bear, skulls. **Technical:** Damascus, some stelite, 6K, pearl, ivory, moose. **Prices:** $150 - $1500. **Remarks:** Full-time maker. First knife was Bowie made from a 2-1/2 truck bumper in military. **Mark:** D.R. Good in oval and for minis, DR with a buffalo skull.

GOODE, BEAR,
PO Box 6474, Navajo Dam, NM 87419, Phone: 505-632-8184
Specialties: Working/using straight knives of his design and in standard patterns. **Patterns:** Bowies, hunters and utility/camp knives. **Technical:** Grinds 440C, ATS-34, 154-CM; forges and grinds 1095, 5160 and other steels on request; uses Damascus. **Prices:** $60 to $225; some to $500 and up. **Remarks:** Part-time maker; first knife sold in 1993. Doing business as Bear Knives. **Mark:** First and last name with a three-toed paw print.

GOODE, BRIAN,
203 Gordon Ave, Shelby, NC 28152, Phone: 704-434-6496, web:www.bgoodeknives.com
Specialties: Flat ground working knives with etched/antique or brushed finish. **Patterns:** Field, camp, hunters, skinners, survival, kitchen, maker's design or yours. Currently full tang only with supplied leather sheath. **Technical:** 0-1, D2 and other ground flat stock. Stock removal and differential heat treat preferred. Etched antique/etched satin working finish preferred. Micarta and hardwoods for strength. **Prices:** $150 to $700. **Remarks:** Part-time maker and full-time knife lover. First knife sold in 2004. **Mark:** B. Goode with NC separated by a feather.

GOODPASTURE, TOM,
13432 Farrington Road, Ashland, VA 23005, Phone: 804-752-8363, rtg007@aol.com; web: goodpastureknives.com
Specialties: Working/using straight knives of his own design, or customer specs. File knives and primative reproductions. **Patterns:** Hunters, bowies, small double-edge daggers, kitchen, custom miniatures and camp/utility. **Technical:** Stock removal, D-2, 0-1, 12C27, 420 HC, 52100. Forged blades of W-2, 1084, and 1095. Flat grinds only. **Prices:** $60 - $300. **Remarks:** Part-time maker, first knife sold at Blade Show 2005. Lifetime guarantee and sharpening. **Mark:** Early mark were initials RTG, current mark: Goodpasture.

GORDON, LARRY B,
23555 Newell Cir W, Farmington Hills, MI 48336, Phone: 248-477-5483, lbgordon1@aol.com
Specialties: Folders, small fixed blades. New design rotating scale release automatic. **Patterns:** Rotating handle locker. Ambidextrous fire (R&L) **Prices:** $450 minimum. **Remarks:** High line materials preferred. **Mark:** Gordon.

GORENFLO, JAMES T (JT),
9145 Sullivan Rd, Baton Rouge, LA 70818, Phone: 225-261-5868
Specialties: Traditional working and using straight knives of his design. **Patterns:** Bowies, hunters and utility/camp knives. **Technical:** Forges 5160, 1095, 52100 and his own Damascus. **Prices:** Start at $200. **Remarks:** Part-time maker; first knife sold in 1992. **Mark:** Last name or initials, J.S. on reverse.

GOSSMAN, SCOTT,
PO Box 41, Whiteford, MD 21160, Phone: 443-617-2444, scogos@peoplepc.com; Web:www.gossmanknives.com
Specialties: Heavy duty knives for big game hunting and survival. **Patterns:** Modified clip point/spear point blades, bowies, hunters, and bushcraft. **Technical:** Grinds D-2, A2, O1, CPM154, CPM535VN and 57 convex grinds and edges. **Price:** $65 to $500. **Remarks:** Full time maker does business as Gossman Knives. **Mark:** Gossman and steel type.

GOTTAGE, DANTE,
43227 Brooks Dr, Clinton Twp., MI 48038-5323, Phone: 810-286-7275
Specialties: Working knives of his design or to customer specs. **Patterns:** Large and small skinners, fighters, Bowies and fillet knives. **Technical:** Grinds O1, 440C and 154CM and ATS-34. **Prices:** $150 to $600. **Remarks:** Part-time maker; first knife sold in 1975. **Mark:** Full name in script letters.

GOTTAGE, JUDY,
43227 Brooks Dr, Clinton Twp., MI 48038-5323, Phone: 586-286-7275, jgottage@remaxmetropolitan.com
Specialties: Custom folders of her design or to customer specs. **Patterns:** Interframes or integral. **Technical:** Stock removal. **Prices:** $300 to $3000. **Remarks:** Full-time maker; first knife sold in 1980. **Mark:** Full name, maker in script.

GOTTSCHALK, GREGORY J,
12 First St. (Ft. Pitt), Carnegie, PA 15106, Phone: 412-279-6692
Specialties: Fancy working straight knives and folders to customer specs. **Patterns:** Hunters to tantos, locking folders to minis. **Technical:** Grinds 440C, 154CM, ATS-34. Now making own Damascus. Most knives have mirror finishes. **Prices:** Start at $150. **Remarks:** Part-time maker; first knife sold in 1977. **Mark:** Full name in crescent.

GOUKER, GARY B,
PO Box 955, Sitka, AK 99835, Phone: 907-747-3476
Specialties: Hunting knives for hard use. **Patterns:** Skinners, semi-skinners, and such. **Technical:** Likes natural materials, inlays, stainless steel. **Prices:** Moderate. **Remarks:** New Alaskan maker. **Mark:** Name.

GRAHAM, GORDON,
3145 CR 4008, New Boston, TX 75570, Phone: 903-293-2610, Web: www.grahamknives.com
Prices: $325 to $850. **Mark:** Graham.

GRANGER, PAUL J,
704 13th Ct. SW, Largo, FL 33770-4471, Phone: 727-953-3249, grangerknives@live.com Web: http://palehorsefighters.blogspot.com
Specialties: Working straight knives of his own design and a few folders. **Patterns:** 2.75" to 4" work knives, tactical knives and Bowies from 5"-9." **Technical:** Grinds CPM154-CM, ATS-34 and forges 52100 and 1084. Offers filework. **Prices:** $95 to $500. **Remarks:** Part-time maker since 1997. Sold first knife in 1997. Doing business as Granger Knives and Pale Horse Fighters. Member of ABS and Florida Knifemakers Association. **Mark:** "Granger" or "Palehorse Fighters."

GRAVELINE, PASCAL AND ISABELLE,
38, Rue de Kerbrezillic, 29350 Moelan-sur-Mer, FRANCE, Phone: 33 2 98 39 73 33, atelier.graveline@wanadoo.fr; Web: www.graveline-couteliers.com
Specialties: French replicas from the 17th, 18th and 19th centuries. **Patterns:** Traditional folders and multi-blade pocket knives; traveling knives, fruit knives and fork sets; puzzle knives and friend's knives; rivet less knives. **Technical:** Grind 12C27, ATS-34, Damascus and carbon steel. **Prices:** $500 to $5000. **Remarks:** Full-time makers; first knife sold in 1992. **Mark:** Last name over head of ram.

GRAVES, DAN,
4887 Dixie Garden Loop, Shreveport, LA 71105, Phone: 318-865-8166, Web: wwwtheknifemaker.com
Specialties: Traditional forged blades and Damascus. **Patterns:** Bowies (D guard also), fighters, hunters, large and small daggers. **Remarks:** Full-time maker. **Mark:** Initials with circle around them.

GRAY, BOB,
8206 N Lucia Court, Spokane, WA 99208, Phone: 509-468-3924
Specialties: Straight working knives of his own design or to customer specs. **Patterns:** Hunter, fillet and carving knives. **Technical:** Forges 5160, L6 and some 52100; grinds 440C. **Prices:** $100 to $600. **Remarks:** Part-time knifemaker; first knife sold in 1991. Doing business as Hi-Land Knives. **Mark:** HI-L.

GRAY, DANIEL,
GRAY KNIVES, 686 Main Rd., Brownville, ME 04414, Phone: 207-965-2191, mail@grayknives.com; Web: www.grayknives.com
Specialties: Straight knives, fantasy, folders, automatics and traditional of his own design. **Patterns:** Automatics, fighters, hunters. **Technical:** Grinds O1, 154CM and D2. **Prices:** From $155 to $750. **Remarks:** Full-time maker; first knife sold in 1974. **Mark:** Gray Knives.

GREBE, GORDON S,
PO Box 296, Anchor Point, AK 99556-0296, Phone: 907-235-8242
Specialties: Working straight knives and folders, some fancy. **Patterns:** Tantos, Bowies, boot fighter sets, locking folders. **Technical:** Grinds stainless steels; likes 1/4" inch stock and glass-bead finishes. **Prices:** $75 to $250; some to $2000. **Remarks:** Full-time maker; first knife sold in 1968. **Mark:** Initials in lightning logo.

GRECO, JOHN,
100 Mattie Jones Rd, Greensburg, KY 42743, Phone: 270-932-3335, johngreco@grecoknives.com; Web: www.grecoknives.com
Specialties: Folders. **Patterns:** Tactical, fighters, camp knives, short swords. **Technical:** Stock removal carbon steel. **Prices:** Affordable. **Remarks:** Full-time maker since 1979. First knife sold in 1979. **Mark:** GRECO

GREEN, BILL,
6621 Eastview Dr, Sachse, TX 75048, Phone: 972-463-3147
Specialties: High-art and working straight knives and folders of his design and to customer specs. **Patterns:** Bowies, hunters, kitchen knives and locking folders. **Technical:** Grinds ATS-34, D2 and 440V. Hand-tooled custom sheaths. **Prices:** $70 to $350; some to $750. **Remarks:** Part-time maker; first knife sold in 1990. **Mark:** Last name.

GREEN, WILLIAM (BILL),
46 Warren Rd, View Bank Vic., AUSTRALIA 3084, Fax: 03-9459-1529
Specialties: Traditional high-tech straight knives and folders. **Patterns:** Japanese-influenced designs, hunters, Bowies, folders and miniatures. **Technical:** Forges O1, D2 and his own Damascus. Offers lost wax castings for bolsters and pommels. Likes natural handle materials, gems, silver and gold. **Prices:** $400 to $750; some to $1200. **Remarks:** Full-time maker. **Mark:** Initials.

GREENAWAY, DON,
3325 Dinsmore Tr, Fayetteville, AR 72704, Phone: 501-521-0323
Specialties: Liner locks and bowies. **Prices:** $150 to $1500. **Remarks:** 20 years experience. **Mark:** Greenaway over Fayetteville, Ark.

GREENE, CHRIS,
707 Cherry Lane, Shelby, NC 28150, Phone: 704-434-5620

GREENE, DAVID,
570 Malcom Rd, Covington, GA 30209, Phone: 770-784-0657
Specialties: Straight working using knives. **Patterns:** Hunters. **Technical:** Forges mosaic and twist Damascus. Prefers stag and desert ironwood for handle material.

GREENE, STEVE,
DUNN KNIVES INC, PO Box 307 1449 Nocatee St., Intercession City, FL 33848, Phone: 800-245-6483, steve.greene@dunnknives.com; Web: www.dunnknives.com
Specialties: Skinning & fillet knives. **Patterns:** Skinners, drop points, clip points and fillets. **Technical:** S60V, S90V and 20 CV powdered metal steel. **Prices:** $90 to $250. **Mark:** Dunn by Greene and year. **Remarks:** Full-time knifemaker. First knife sold in 1972.

GREENFIELD, G O,
2605 15th St #310, Everett, WA 98201, garyg1946@yahoo.com
Specialties: High-tech and working straight knives and folders of his design. **Patterns:** Boots, daggers, hunters and one-of-a-kinds. **Technical:** Grinds ATS-34, D2, 440C and T-440V. Makes sheaths for each knife. **Prices:** $100 to $800; some to $10,000. **Remarks:** Part-time maker; first knife sold in 1978. **Mark:** Springfield®, serial number.

GREGORY, MICHAEL,
211 Calhoun Rd, Belton, SC 29627, Phone: 864-338-8898, gregom.123@charter.net
Specialties: Interframe folding knives, working hunters and period pieces. Hand rubbed finish. **Patterns:** Hunters, bowies, daggers, and folding knives. **Technical:** Grinds ATS-34 and other makers damascus. **Prices:** $150 and up. **Remarks:** Full-time maker; first knife sold in 1980. **Mark:** Name, city in logo.

GREINER, RICHARD,
1073 E County Rd 32, Green Springs, OH 44836

GREISS, JOCKL,
Herrenwald 15, D 77773 Schenkenzell, GERMANY, Phone: +49 7836 95 71 69 or +49 7836 95 55 76, www.jocklgreiss@yahoo.com
Specialties: Classic and working using straight knives of his design. **Patterns:** Bowies, daggers and hunters. **Technical:** Uses only Jerry Rados Damascus. All knives are one-of-a-kind made by hand; no machines are used. **Prices:** $700 to $2000; some to $3000. **Remarks:** Full-time maker; first knife sold in 1984. **Mark:** An "X" with a long vertical line through it.

GREY, PIET,
PO Box 363, Naboomspruit 0560, SOUTH AFRICA, Phone: 014-743-3613
Specialties: Fancy working and using straight knives of his design. **Patterns:** Fighters, hunters and utility/camp knives. **Technical:** Grinds ATS-34 and AEB-L; forges and grinds Damascus. Solder less fitting of guards. Engraves and scrimshaws. **Prices:** $125 to $750; some to $1500. **Remarks:** Part-time maker; first knife sold in 1970. **Mark:** Last name.

GRIFFIN, RENDON AND MARK,
9706 Cedardale, Houston, TX 77055, Phone: 713-468-0436
Specialties: Working folders and automatics of their designs. **Patterns:** Standard lockers and slip-joints. **Technical:** Most blade steels; stock removal. **Prices:** Start at $350. **Remarks:** Rendon's first knife sold in 1966; Mark's in 1974. **Mark:** Last name logo.

GRIFFIN JR., HOWARD A,
14299 SW 31st Ct, Davie, FL 33330, Phone: 954-474-5406, mgriffin18@aol.com
Specialties: Working straight knives and folders. **Patterns:** Hunters, Bowies, locking folders with his own push-button lock design. **Technical:** Grinds 440C. **Prices:** $100 to $200; some to $500. **Remarks:** Part-time maker; first knife sold in 1983. **Mark:** Initials.

GRIMES, MARK,
PO BOX 1293, Bedford, TX 76095, Phone: 817-416-7507
Specialties: Qs. **Patterns:** Hunters, fighters, bowies. **Technical:** Custom hand forged 1084 steel blades full and hidden tang, heat treating, sheathes. **Prices:** $150-$400. **Remarks:** Part-time maker, first knife sold in 2009. **Mark:** Last name.

GRIZZARD, JIM,
3802 Mary Dr, Oxford, AL 36203, Phone: 256-403-1232, grizzardforgiven@aol.com
Specialties: Hand carved art knives inspired by sole authorship. **Patterns:** Fixedblades, folders, and swords. **Technical:** Carving handles, artgrinding, forged and stock removal. **Prices:** Vary. **Remarks:** Uses knives mostly as a ministry to bless others. **Mark:** FOR HIS GLORY CUSTOM KNIVES OR j grizzard in a grizzly bear.

GROSPITCH, ERNIE,
18440 Amityville Dr, Orlando, FL 32820, Phone: 407-568-5438, shrpknife@aol.com; Web: www.erniesknives.com
Specialties: Bowies, hunting, fishing, kitchen, lockback folders, leather craft. **Patterns:** His design or customer. **Technical:** Stock removal using most available steels. **Prices:** $140 and up. **Remarks:** Full-time maker, sold first knife in 1990. **Mark:** Etched name/maker city and state.

GROSS, W W,
109 Dylan Scott Dr, Archdale, NC 27263-3858
Specialties: Working knives. **Patterns:** Hunters, boots, fighters. **Technical:** Grinds. **Prices:** Moderate. **Remarks:** Full-time maker. **Mark:** Name.

GROSSMAN, STEWART,
24 Water St #419, Clinton, MA 01510, Phone: 508-365-2291; 800-mysword
Specialties: Miniatures and full-size knives and swords. **Patterns:** One-of-a-kind miniatures—jewelry, replicas—and wire-wrapped figures. Full-size art, fantasy and combat knives, daggers and modular sculpture. **Technical:** Forges and grinds most metals and Damascus. Uses gems, crystals, electronics and motorized mechanisms. **Prices:** $20 to $300; some to $4500 and higher. **Remarks:** Full-time maker; first knife sold in 1985. **Mark:** G1.

GRUSSENMEYER, PAUL G,
310 Kresson Rd, Cherry Hill, NJ 08034, Phone: 856-428-1088, pgrussentne@comcast.net; Web: www.pgcarvings.com
Specialties: Assembling fancy and fantasy straight knives with his own carved handles. **Patterns:** Bowies, daggers, folders, swords, hunters and miniatures. **Technical:** Uses forged steel and Damascus, stock removal and knapped obsidian blades. **Prices:** $250 to $4000. **Remarks:** Spare-time maker; first knife sold in 1991. **Mark:** First and last initial hooked together on handle.

GUARNERA, ANTHONY R,
42034 Quail Creek Dr, Quartzhill, CA 93536, Phone: 661-722-4032
Patterns: Hunters, camp, Bowies, kitchen, fighter knives. **Technical:** Forged and stock removal. **Prices:** $100 and up.

GUINN, TERRY,
13026 Hwy 6 South, Eastland, TX 76448, Phone: 254-629-8603, Web: www.terryguinn.com
Specialties: Working fixed blades and balisongs. **Patterns:** Almost all types of folding and fixed blades, from patterns and "one of a kind". **Technical:** Stock removal all types of blade steel with preference for air hardening steel. Does own heat treating, all knives Rockwell tested in shop. **Prices:** $200 to $2,000. **Remarks:** Part time maker since 1982, sold first knife 1990. **Mark:** Full name with cross in the middle.

GUNTER, BRAD,
13 Imnaha Rd., Tijeras, NM 87059, Phone: 505-281-8080

GUNTHER, EDDIE,
11 Nedlands Pl Burswood, 2013 Auckland, NEW ZEALAND, Phone: 006492722373, eddit.gunther49@gmail.com
Specialties: Drop point hunters, boot, Bowies. All mirror finished. **Technical:** Grinds D2, 440C, 12c27. **Prices:** $250 to $800. **Remarks:** Part-time maker, first knife sold in 1986. **Mark:** Name, city, country.

GURGANUS, CAROL,
2553 NC 45 South, Colerain, NC 27924, Phone: 252-356-4831, Fax: 252-356-4650
Specialties: Working and using straight knives. **Patterns:** Fighters, hunters and kitchen knives. **Technical:** Grinds D2, ATS-34 and Damascus steel. Uses stag, and exotic wood handles. **Prices:** $100 to $300. **Remarks:** Part-time maker; first knife sold in 1992. **Mark:** Female symbol, last name, city, state.

GURGANUS, MELVIN H,
2553 NC 45 South, Colerain, NC 27924, Phone: 252-356-4831, Fax: 252-356-4650
Specialties: High-tech working folders. **Patterns:** Leaf-lock and back-lock designs, bolstered and interframe. **Technical:** D2 and 440C; Heat-treats, carves and offers lost wax casting. **Prices:** $300 to $3000. **Remarks:** Part-time maker; first knife sold in 1983. **Mark:** First initial, last name and maker.

H

HACKNEY, DANA A.,
33 Washington St., Monument, CO 80132, Phone: 719-481-3940; Cell: 719-651-5634, shacknee@peoplepc.com and dshackney@Q.com
Specialties: Hunters, bowies, and everyday carry knives, and some kitchen cutlery. **Technical:** Forges 1080 series, 5160, 0-1, W-2, and his own damascus. Uses CPM154 mostly for stainless knives. **Prices:** $100 and up. **Remarks:** Sole ownership knives and sheaths. Full-time maker as of July 2012. Sold first knife in 2005. ABS, MKA, and PKA member. **Mark:** Last name, HACKNEY on left-side ricasso.

HAGEN, DOC,
PO Box 58, 41780 Kansas Point Ln, Pelican Rapids, MN 56572, Phone: 218-863-8503, dochagen@gmail.com; Web: www.dochagencustomknives.com
Specialties: Folders. Autos:bolster release-dual action. Slipjoint folders**Patterns:** Defense-related straight knives; wide variety of folders. **Technical:** Dual action release, bolster release autos. **Prices:** $300 to $800; some to $3000. **Remarks:** Full-time maker; first knife sold in 1975. Makes his own Damascus. **Mark:** DOC HAGEN in shield, knife, banner logo; or DOC.

HAGGERTY, GEORGE S,
PO Box 88, Jacksonville, VT 05342, Phone: 802-368-7437, swewater@sover.net
Specialties: Working straight knives and folders. **Patterns:** Hunters, claws, camp and fishing knives, locking folders and backpackers. **Technical:** Forges and grinds W2, 440C and 154CM. **Prices:** $85 to $300. **Remarks:** Part-time maker; first knife sold in 1981. **Mark:** Initials or last name.

HAGUE, GEOFF,
Unit 5, Project Workshops, Laines Farm, Quarley, SP11 8PX, UK, Phone: (+44) 01672-870212, Fax: (+44) 01672 870212, geoff@hagueknives.com; Web: www.hagueknives.com
Specialties: Quality folding knives. **Patterns:** Back lock, locking liner, slip joint, and friction folders. **Technical:** RWL34, D2, titanium, and some gold decoraqtion. Mainly natural handle materials. **Prices:** $900 to $2,000. **Remarks:** Full-time maker. **Mark:** Last name.

HAINES, JEFF HAINES CUSTOM KNIVES,
901 A E. Third St., Wauzeka, WI 53826, Phone: 608-875-5325, jeffhaines@centurytel.net
Patterns: Hunters, skinners, camp knives, customer designs welcome. **Technical:** Forges 1095, 5160, and Damascus, grinds A2. **Prices:** $50 and up. **Remarks:** Part-time maker since 1995. **Mark:** Last name.

HALFRICH, JERRY,
340 Briarwood, San Marcos, TX 78666, Phone: 512-353-2582, Fax: 512-392-3659, jerryhalfrich@grandecom.net; Web: www.halfrichknives.com
Specialties: Working knives and specialty utility knives for the professional and serious hunter. Uses proven designs in both straight and folding knives. Plays close attention to fit and finish. Art knives on special request. **Patterns:** Hunters, skinners, lock back liner lock. **Technical:** Grinds both flat and hollow D2, damasteel, BG42 makes high precision folders. **Prices:** $300 to $600, sometimes $1000. **Remarks:** Full-time maker since 2000. DBA Halfrich Custom Knives. **Mark:** Halfrich, San Marcos, TX in a football shape.

HALL, JEFF,
179 Niblick Rd, # 180, Paso Robles, CA 93446, Phone: 562-594-4740, info@nemesis-knives.com; Web: nemisis-knives.com
Specialties: Collectible and working folders of his design. **Technical:** Grinds S30V, 154CM, and various makers' Damascus. **Patterns:** Fighters, gentleman's, hunters and utility knives. **Prices:** $400 to $600; some to $1000. **Remarks:** Full-time maker. First knife sold 1998. **Mark:** Last name.

HALLIGAN, ED,
3434 Sun Lit Grove, San Antonio, TX 78247, Phone: 210-912-8167, beano101010@yahoo.com
Specialties: Working straight knives and folders, some fancy. **Patterns:** Liner locks, hunters, skinners, boots, fighters and swords. **Technical:** Grinds ATS-34; forges 5160; makes cable and pattern Damascus. **Prices:** $160 to $2500. **Remarks:** Full-time maker; first knife sold in 1985. Doing business as Halligan Knives. **Mark:** Last name, city, state and USA.

HAMLET JR., JOHNNY,
300 Billington, Clute, TX 77531, Phone: 979-265-6929, nifeman@swbell.net; Web: www.hamlets-handmade-knives.com
Specialties: Working straight knives and folders. **Patterns:** Hunters, fighters, fillet and kitchen knives, locking folders. Likes upswept knives and trailing-points. **Technical:** Grinds 440C, D2, ATS-34. Makes sheaths. **Prices:** $125 and up. **Remarks:** Full-time maker; sold first knife in 1988. **Mark:** Hamlet's Handmade in script.

HAMMOND, HANK,
189 Springlake Dr, Leesburg, GA 31763, Phone: 229-434-1295, godogs57@bellsouth.net
Specialties: Traditional hunting and utility knives of his design. Will also design and produce knives to customer's specifications. **Patterns:** Straight or sheath knives, hunters skinners as well as Bowies and fighters. **Technical:** Grinds (hollow and flat grinds) CPM 154CM, ATS-34. Also uses Damascus and forges 52100. Offers filework on blades. Handle materials include all exotic woods, red stag, sambar stag, deer, elk, oosic, bone, fossil ivory, Micarta, etc. All knives come with sheath handmade for that individual knife. **Prices:** $100 up to $500. **Remarks:** Part-time maker. Sold first knife in 1981. Doing business as Double H Knives. **Mark:** "HH" inside 8 point deer rack.

HAMMOND, JIM,
PO Box 486, Arab, AL 35016, Phone: 256-586-0270, jim@jimhammondknives.com; Web: www.jimhammondknives.com
Specialties: High-tech fighters and folders. **Patterns:** Proven-design fighters. **Technical:** Grinds 440C, 440V, S30V and other specialty steels. **Prices:** $385 to $1200; some to $9200. **Remarks:** Full-time maker; first knife sold in 1977. Designer for Columbia River Knife and Tool. **Mark:** Full name, city, state in shield logo.

HANCOCK, TIM,
10805 N. 83rd St, Scottsdale, AZ 85260, Phone: 480-998-8849
Specialties: High-art and working straight knives and folders of his design and to customer preferences. **Patterns:** Bowies, fighters, daggers, tantos, swords, folders. **Technical:** Forges Damascus and 52100; grinds ATS-34. Makes Damascus. Silver-wire inlays; offers carved fittings and file work. **Prices:** $500 to $10,000. **Remarks:** Full-time maker; first knife sold in 1988. Master Smith ABS. **Mark:** Last name or heart.

HAND, BILL,
PO Box 717, 1103 W. 7th St., Spearman, TX 79081, Phone: 806-659-2967, Fax: 806-659-5139, klinker43@yahoo.com
Specialties: Traditional working and using straight knives and folders of his design or to customer specs. **Patterns:** Hunters, Bowies, folders and fighters. **Technical:** Forges 5160, 52100 and Damascus. **Prices:** Start at $150. **Remarks:** Part-time maker; Journeyman Smith. Current delivery time 12 to 16 months. **Mark:** Stylized initials.

HANSEN, LONNIE,
PO Box 4956, Spanaway, WA 98387, Phone: 253-847-4632, lonniehansen@msn.com; Web: lchansen.com
Specialties: Working straight knives of his design. **Patterns:** Tomahawks, tantos, hunters, fillet. **Technical:** Forges 1086, 52100, grinds 440V, BG-42. **Prices:** Starting at $300. **Remarks:** Part-time maker since 1989. **Mark:** First initial and last name. Also first and last initial.

HANSEN, ROBERT W,
35701 University Ave NE, Cambridge, MN 55008, Phone: 763-689-3242
Specialties: Working straight knives, folders and integrals. **Patterns:** From hunters to minis, camp knives to miniatures; folding lockers and slip-joints in original styles. **Technical:** Grinds O1, 440C and 154CM; likes filework. **Prices:** $100 to $450; some to $600. **Remarks:** Part-time maker; first knife sold in 1983. **Mark:** Fish w/h inside surrounded by Bob Hansen maker.

HANSON III, DON L.,
PO Box 13, Success, MO 65570-0013, Phone: 573-674-3045, Web: www.sunfishforge.com; Web: www.donhansonknives.com
Specialties: One-of-a-kind Damascus folders and forged fixed blades. **Patterns:** Small, fancy pocket knives, large folding fighters and Bowies. **Technical:** Forges own pattern welded Damascus, file work and carving also carbon steel blades with hamons. **Prices:** $800 and up. **Remarks:** Full-time maker, first knife sold in 1984. ABS mastersmith. **Mark:** Sunfish.

HARA, KOUJI,
292-2 Osugi, Seki-City, Gifu-Pref. 501-3922, JAPAN, Phone: 0575-24-7569, Fax: 0575-24-7569, info@knifehousehara.com; Web: www.knifehousehara.com
Specialties: High-tech and working straight knives of his design; some folders. **Patterns:** Hunters, locking folders and utility/camp knives. **Technical:** Grinds Cowry X, Cowry Y and ATS-34. Prefers high mirror polish; pearl handle inlay. **Prices:** $400 to $2500. **Remarks:** Full-time maker; first knife sold in 1980. Doing business as Knife House "Hara." **Mark:** First initial, last name in fish.

HARDING, CHAD,
12365 Richland Ln, Solsberry, IN 47459, hardingknivs@yahoo.com; Web: http://hardingknives.weeby.com
Specialties: hunters and camp knives, ocaasional fighters or bowies. **Technical:** Hand forge 90% of work. Prefer 10XX steels and tool steels. Makes own Damascus and cable and chainsaw chain Damascus. 100% sole authorship on knives and sheaths. Mostly natural handle material, prefer wood and stag. **Prices:** $150 to $1000. **Remarks:** Part-time maker, member of ABS. First knife sold in 2005. **Mark:** Last name, city and state; folders, last name with stars inside folding knife.

HARDY, DOUGLAS E,
114 Cypress Rd, Franklin, GA 30217, Phone: 706-675-6305

HARDY, SCOTT,
639 Myrtle Ave, Placerville, CA 95667, Phone: 530-622-5780, Web: www.innercite.com/~shardy
Specialties: Traditional working and using straight knives of his design. **Patterns:** Most anything with an edge. **Technical:** Forges carbon steels. Japanese stone polish. Offers mirror finish; differentially tempers. **Prices:** $100 to $1000. **Remarks:** Part-time maker; first knife sold in 1982. **Mark:** First initial, last name and Handmade with bird logo.

HARKINS, J A,
PO Box 218, Conner, MT 59827, Phone: 406-821-1060, kutter@customknives.net; Web: customknives.net
Specialties: OTFs. **Patterns:** OTFs, Automatics, Folders. **Technical:** Grinds ATS-34. Engraves; offers gem work. **Prices:** $1500 and up. **Remarks:** Celebrating 20th year as full-time maker . **Mark:** First and middle initials, last name.

HARLEY, LARRY W,
348 Deerfield Dr, Bristol, TN 37620, Phone: 423-878-5368 (shop)/Cell 423-571-0638, Fax: 276-466-6771, Web: www.lonesomepineknives.com
Specialties: One-of-a-kind Persian in one-of-a-kind Damascus. Working knives, period pieces. **Technical:** Forges and grinds ATS-34, 440c, L6, 15, 20, 1084, and 52100. **Patterns:** Full range of straight knives, tomahawks, razors, buck skinners and hog spears. **Prices:** $200 and up. **Mark:** Pine tree.

HARLEY, RICHARD,
348 Deerfield Dr, Bristol, TN 37620, Phone: 423-878-5368/423-571-0638
Specialties: Hunting knives, Bowies, friction folders, one-of-a-kind. **Technical:** Forges 1084, S160, 52100, Lg. **Prices:** $150 to $1000. **Mark:** Pine tree with name.

HARM, PAUL W,
818 Young Rd, Attica, MI 48412, Phone: 810-724-5582, harm@blclinks.net
Specialties: Early American working knives. **Patterns:** Hunters, skinners, patch knives, fighters, folders. **Technical:** Forges and grinds 1084, O1, 52100 and own Damascus. **Prices:** $75 to $1000. **Remarks:** First knife sold in 1990. **Mark:** Connected initials.

HARNER, LLOYD R. "BUTCH",
4865 Hanover Rd., Hanover, PA 17331, harnerknives@gmail.com; Web: harnerknives.com
Specialties: Kitchen knives and razors. **Technical:** CPM3V, CPM154, and crucible super-alloy blade steels. **Remarks:** Full-time maker since 2007. **Mark:** Maker's name, "L R Harner."

HARRINGTON, ROGER,
P.O. Box 157, Battle, East Sussex, ENGLAND TN 33 3 DD, Phone: 0854-838-7062, info@bisonbushcraft.co.uk; Web: www.bisonbushcraft.co.uk
Specialties: Working straight knives to his or customer's designs, flat saber Scandinavia-style grinds on full tang knives, also hollow and convex grinds. **Technical:** Grinds O1, D2, Damascus. **Prices:** $200 to $800. **Remarks:** First knife made by hand in 1997 whilst traveling around the world. **Mark:** Bison with bison written under.

HARRIS, CASS,
19855 Fraiser Hill Ln, Bluemont, VA 20135, Phone: 540-554-8774, Web: www.tdogforge.com
Prices: $160 to $500.

HARRIS, JAY,
991 Johnson St, Redwood City, CA 94061, Phone: 415-366-6077
Specialties: Traditional high-tech straight knives and folders of his design. **Patterns:** Daggers, fighters and locking folders. **Technical:** Uses 440C, ATS-34 and CPM. **Prices:** $250 to $850. **Remarks:** Spare-time maker; first knife sold in 1980.

HARRIS, JEFFERY A,
214 Glen Cove Dr, Chesterfield, MO 63017, Phone: 314-469-6317, Fax: 314-469-6374, jeffro135@aol.com
Remarks: Purveyor and collector of handmade knives.

HARRIS, JOHN,
14131 Calle Vista, Riverside, CA 92508, Phone: 951-653-2755, johnharrisknives@yahoo.com
Specialties: Hunters, daggers, Bowies, bird and trout, period pieces, Damascus and carbon steel knives, forged and stock removal. **Prices:** $200 to $1000.

HARRIS, RALPH DEWEY,
2607 Bell Shoals Rd, Brandon, FL 33511, Phone: 813-681-5293, Fax: 813-654-8175
Specialties: Collector quality interframe folders. **Patterns:** High tech locking folders of his own design with various mechanisms. **Technical:** Grinds 440C, ATS-34 and commercial Damascus. Offers various frame materials including 416ss, and titanium; file worked frames and his own engraving. **Prices:** $400 to $3000. **Remarks:** Full-time maker; first knife sold in 1978. **Mark:** Last name, or name and city.

HARRISON, BRIAN,
BFH KNIVES, 2359 E Swede Rd, Cedarville, MI 49719, Phone: 906-484-2011, bfhknives@easternup.net; Web: www.bfhknives.com
Specialties: High grade fixed blade knives. **Patterns:** Many sizes & variety of patterns from small pocket carries to large combat and camp knives. Mirror and bead blast finishes. All handles of high grade materials from ivory to highly figured stabilized woods to stag, deer & moose horn and Micarta. Hand sewn fancy sheaths for pocket or belt. **Technical:** Flat & hollow grinds usually ATS-34 but some O1, L6 and stellite 6K. **Prices:** $150 to $1200. **Remarks:** Full-time maker, sole authorship. Made first knife in 1980, sold first knife in 1999. Received much knowledge from the following makers: George Young, Eric Erickson, Webster Wood, Ed Kalfayan who are all generous men. **Mark:** Engraved blade outline w/BFH Knives over the top edge, signature across middle & Cedarville, MI underneath.

HARRISON, JIM (SEAMUS),
721 Fairington View Dr, St. Louis, MO 63129, Phone: 314-894-2525, jrh@seamusknives.com; Web: www.seamusknives.com
Specialties: "Crossover" folders, liner-locks and frame-locks. **Patterns:** Uber, Author, Skyyy Folders, Grant Survivor, Fixed blade. **Technical:** Use CPM S30V and 154, Stellite 6k and S.S. Damascus by Norris, Thomas and Damasteel. **Prices:** Folders $375 to $1,000. **Remarks:** Full-time maker since 2008, Maker since 1999. **Mark:** Seamus

HARSEY, WILLIAM H,
82710 N. Howe Ln, Creswell, OR 97426, Phone: 519-895-4941, harseyjr@cs.com
Specialties: High-tech kitchen and outdoor knives. **Patterns:** Folding hunters, trout and bird folders; straight hunters, camp knives and axes. **Technical:** Grinds; etches. **Prices:** $125 to $300; some to $1500. Folders start at $350. **Remarks:** Full-time maker; first knife sold in 1979. **Mark:** Full name, state, U.S.A.

HART, BILL,
647 Cedar Dr, Pasadena, MD 21122, Phone: 410-255-4981
Specialties: Fur-trade era working straight knives and folders. **Patterns:** Springback folders, skinners, Bowies and patch knives. **Technical:** Forges and stock removes 1095 and 5160 wire Damascus. **Prices:** $100 to $600. **Remarks:** Part-time maker; first knife sold in 1986. **Mark:** Name.

HARTMAN, ARLAN (LANNY),
6102 S Hamlin Cir, Baldwin, MI 49304, Phone: 231-745-4029
Specialties: Working straight knives and folders. **Patterns:** Drop-point hunters, coil spring lockers, slip-joints. **Technical:** Flat-grinds D2, 440C and ATS-34. **Prices:** $300 to $2000. **Remarks:** Part-time maker; first knife sold in 1982. **Mark:** Last name.

HARTMAN, TIM,
3812 Pedroncelli Rd NW, Albuquerque, NM 87107, Phone: 505-385-6924, tbonz1@comcast.net
Specialties: Exotic wood scales, sambar stag, filework, hunters. **Patterns:** Fixed blade hunters, skinners, utility and hiking. **Technical:** 154CM, Ats-34 and D2. Mirror finish and contoured scales. **Prices:** Start at $200-$450. **Remarks:** Started making knives in 2004. **Mark:** 3 lines Ti Hartman, Maker, Albuquerque NM

HARVEY, HEATHER,
HEAVIN FORGE, PO Box 768, Belfast 1100, SOUTH AFRICA, Phone: 27-13-253-0914, heather@heavinforge.co.za; Web: www.heavinforge.co.za
Specialties: Integral hand forged knives, traditional African weapons, primitive folders and by-gone forged-styles. **Patterns:** All forged knives, war axes, spears, arrows, forks, spoons, and swords. **Technical:** Own carbon Damascus and mokume. Also forges stainless, brass, copper and titanium. Traditional forging and heat-treatment methods used. **Prices:** $300 to $5000, average $1000. **Remarks:** Full-time maker and knifemaking instructor. Master bladesmith with ABS. First Damascus sold in 1995, first knife sold in 1998. Often collaborate with husband, Kevin (ABS MS) using the logo "Heavin." **Mark:** First name and sur name, oval shape with "M S" in middle.

custom knifemakers

HARVEY, KEVIN,
HEAVIN FORGE, PO Box 768, Belfast 1100, SOUTH AFRICA, Phone: 27-13-253-0914, info@heavinforge.co.za Web: www.heavinforge.co.za
Specialties: Large knives of presentation quality and creative art knives. Patterns: Fixed blades of Bowie, dagger and fighter-styles, occasionally folders and swords. Technical: Stock removal of stainless and forging of carbon steel and own Damascus. Indigenous African handle materials preferred. Own engraving Often collaborate with wife, Heather (ABS MS) under the logo "Heavin." Prices: $500 to $5000 average $1500. Remarks: Full-time maker and knifemaking instructor. Master bladesmith with ABS. First knife sold in 1984. Mark: First name and surname, oval with "M S" in the middle.

HARVEY, MAX,
14 Bass Rd, Bull Creek, Perth 6155, Western Australia, AUSTRALIA, Phone: 09-332-7585
Specialties: Daggers, Bowies, fighters and fantasy knives. Patterns: Hunters, Bowies, tantos and skinners. Technical: Hollow-and flat-grinds 440C, ATS-34, 154CM and Damascus. Offers gem work. Prices: $250 to $4000. Remarks: Part-time maker; first knife sold in 1981. Mark: First and middle initials, last name.

HARVEY, MEL,
P.O. Box 176, Nenana, AK 99760, Phone: 907-832-5660, tinker1@nenana.net
Specialties: Fixed blade knives for hunting and fishing. Patterns: Hunters, skinners. Technical: Stock removal on ATS-34, 440C, 01, 1095; Damascus blades using 1095 and 15N20. Prices: Starting at $350. Remarks: New maker. Mark: Mel Harvey.

HASLINGER, THOMAS,
164 Fairview Dr SE, Calgary, AB, CANADA T2H 1B3, Phone: 403-253-9628, Web: www.haslinger-knives.com; www.haslinger-culinary.com
Specialties: One-of-a-kind using, working and art knives HCK signature sweeping grind lines. Maker of New Generation and Evolution Chef series. Differential heat treated stainless steel. Patterns: Likes to work with customers on design. Technical: Grinds various specialty alloys, including Damascus, High end satin finish. Prefers natural handle materials e.g. ancient ivory stag, pearl, abalone, stone and exotic woods. Does inlay work with stone, some sterling silver, niobium and gold wire work. Custom sheaths using matching woods or hand stitched with unique leather. Offers engraving. Prices: $300 and up. Remarks: Full-time maker; first knife sold in 1994. Doing business as Haslinger Custom Knives. Mark: Two marks used, high end work uses stylized initials, other uses elk antler with Thomas Haslinger, Canada, handcrafted above.

HAWES, CHUCK,
HAWES FORGE, PO Box 176, Weldon, IL 61882, Phone: 217-736-2479
Specialties: 95 percent of all work in own Damascus. Patterns: Slip-joints liner locks, hunters, Bowie's, swords, anything in between. Technical: Forges everything, uses all high-carbon steels, no stainless. Prices: $150 to $4000. Remarks: Like to do custom orders, his style or yours. Sells Damascus. Full-time maker since 1995. Mark: Small football shape. Chuck Hawes maker Weldon, IL.

HAWK, GRANT AND GAVIN,
Box 401, Idaho City, ID 83631, Phone: 208-392-4911, Web: www.9-hawkknives.com
Specialties: Large folders with unique locking systems D.O.G. lock, toad lock. Technical: Grinds ATS-34, titanium folder parts. Prices: $450 and up. Remarks: Full-time maker. Mark: First initials and last names.

HAWKINS, BUDDY,
PO Box 5969, Texarkana, TX 75505-5969, Phone: 903-838-7917, buddyhawkins@cableone.net

HAWKINS, RADE,
110 Buckeye Rd, Fayetteville, GA 30214, Phone: 770-964-1177, radeh@bellsouth.net; Web: wwwhawkinscustomknives.com
Specialties: All styles. Patterns: All styles. Technical: Grinds and forges. Makes own Damascus Prices: Start at $190. Remarks: Full-time maker; first knife sold in 1972. Member knifemakers guild, ABS Journeyman Smith. Mark: Rade Hawkins Custom Knives.

HAYES, SCOTTY,
Texarkana College, 2500 N Robinson Rd., Tesarkana, TX 75501, Phone: 903-838-4541, ext. 3236, Fax: 903-832-5030, shayes@texakanacollege.edu; Web: www.americanbladesmith.com/2005ABSo/o20schedule.htm
Specialties: ABS School of Bladesmithing.

HAYES, WALLY,
9960, 9th Concession, RR#1, Essex, Ont., CANADA N8M-2X5, Phone: 519-776-1284, Web: www.hayesknives.com
Specialties: Classic and fancy straight knives and folders. Patterns: Daggers, Bowies, fighters, tantos. Technical: Forges own Damascus and O1; engraves. Prices: $150 to $14,000. Mark: Last name, M.S. and serial number.

HAYNES, JERRY,
260 Forest Meadow Dr, Gunter, TX 75058, Phone: 903-433-1424, jhaynes@arrow-head.com; Web: http://www.arrow-head.com
Specialties: Working straight knives and folders of his design, also historical blades. Patterns: Hunters, skinners, carving knives, fighters, renaissance daggers, locking folders and kitchen knives. Technical: Grinds ATS-34, CPM, Stellite 6K, D2 and acquired Damascus. Prefers exotic handle materials. Has B.A. in design. Studied with R. Buckminster Fuller. Prices: $200 to $1200. Remarks: Part-time maker. First knife sold in 1953. Mark: Arrowhead and last name.

HAYS, MARK,
HAYS HANDMADE KNIVES, 1008 Kavanagh Dr., Austin, TX 78748, Phone: 512-292-4410, markhays@austin.rr.com
Specialties: Working straight knives and folders. Patterns inspired by Randall and Stone. Patterns: Bowies, hunters and slip-joint folders. Technical: 440C stock removal. Repairs and restores Stone knives. Prices: Start at $200. Remarks: Part-time maker, brochure available, with Stone knives 1974-1983, 1990-1991. Mark: First initial, last name, state and serial number.

HEADRICK, GARY,
122 Wilson Blvd, Juan Les Pins, FRANCE 06160, Phone: 033 610282885, headrick-gary@wanadoo.fr; Web: couteaux-scrimshaw.com
Specialties: Hi-tech folders with natural furnishings. Back lock & back spring. Patterns: Damascus and mokumes. Technical: Self made Damascus all steel (no nickel). All chassis titanium. Prices: $500 to $2000. Remarks: Full-time maker for last 7 years. German Guild-French Federation. 10 years active. Mark: HEADRICK on ricosso is new marking.

HEANEY, JOHN D,
9 Lefe Court, Haines City, FL 33844, Phone: 863-422-5823, jdh199@msn.com; Web: www.heaneyknives.com
Specialties: Forged 5160, O1 and Damascus. Prefers using natural handle material such as bone, stag and oosic. Plans on using some of the various ivories on future knives. Prices: $250 and up. Remarks: ABS member. Received journeyman smith stamp in June. Mark: Heaney JS.

HEASMAN, H G,
28 St Mary's Rd, Llandudno, N. Wales, UNITED KINGDOM LL302UB, Phone: (UK)0492-876351
Specialties: Miniatures only. Patterns: Bowies, daggers and swords. Technical: Files from stock high-carbon and stainless steel. Prices: $400 to $600. Remarks: Part-time maker; first knife sold in 1975. Doing business as Reduced Reality. Mark: NA.

HEATH, WILLIAM,
PO Box 131, Bondville, IL 61815, Phone: 217-863-2576
Specialties: Classic and working straight knives, folders. Patterns: Hunters and Bowies LinerLock® folders. Technical: Grinds ATS-34, 440C, 154CM, Damascus, handle materials Micarta, woods to exotic materials snake skins cobra, rattle snake, African flower snake. Does own heat treating. Prices: $75 to $300 some $1000. Remarks: Full-time maker. First knife sold in 1979. Mark: W. D. HEATH.

HEBEISEN, JEFF,
310 19th Ave N, Hopkins, MN 55343, Phone: 952-935-4506, jhebeisen@peoplepc.com
Specialties: One of a kind fixed blade of any size up to 16". Patterns: Miniature, Hunters, Skinners, Daggers, Bowies, Fighters and Neck knives. Technical: Stock removal using CPM-154, D2, 440C. Handle mterial varies depending on intended use, mostly natural materials such as bone, horn, antler, and wood. Filework on many. Heavy duty sheaths made to fit. Prices: From $100 to $750. Remarks: Full-time maker. First knife sold in 2007. Mark: Arched name over buffalo skull.

HEDGES, DEE,
192 Carradine Rd., Bedfordale, WA Australia 6112, dark_woods_forge@yahoo.com.au; Web: www.darkwoodforge.com
Patterns: Makes any and all patterns and style of blades from working blades to swords to Japanese inspired. Favors exotic and artistic variations and unique one-off pieces. Technical: Forges all blades from a range of steels, favoring 1084, W2, 52100, 5160 and Damascus blends make from a 1084/15n20 mix. Prices: Start at $200. Remarks: Full-time bladesmith and jeweller. Started making blades professionally in 1999, earning my Journeyman Smith rating in 2010. Mark: "Dark Woods" atop an ivy leaf, with "Forge" underneath.

HEDLUND, ANDERS,
Samstad 400, 454 91, Brastad, SWEDEN, Phone: 46-523-139 48, anderskniv@passagen.se; Web: http://hem.passagen.se/anderskniv
Specialties: Fancy high-end collectible folders, high-end collectible Nordic hunters with leather carvings on the sheath. Carvings combine traditional designs with own designs. Patterns: Own designs. Technical: Grinds most steels, but prefers mosaic Damascus and RWL-34. Prefers mother-of-pearl, mammoth, and mosaic steel for folders. Prefers desert ironwood, mammoth, stabilized arctic birch, willow burl, and Damascus steel or RWL-34 for stick tang knives. Prices: Starting at $750 for stick tang knives and staring at $1500 for folders. Remarks: Part-time maker, first knife sold in 1988. Nordic champion (five countries) several times and Swedish champion 20 times in different classes. Mark: Stylized initials or last name.

HEDRICK, DON,
131 Beechwood Hills, Newport News, VA 23608, Phone: 757-877-8100, donaldhedrick@cox.net
Specialties: Working straight knives; period pieces and fantasy knives. Patterns: Hunters, boots, Bowies and miniatures. Technical: Grinds 440C and commercial Damascus. Also makes micro-mini Randall replicas. Prices: $150 to $550; some to $1200. Remarks: Part-time maker; first knife sold in 1982. Mark: First initial, last name in oval logo.

HEFLIN, CHRISTOPHER M,
6013 Jocely Hollow Rd, Nashville, TN 37205, Phone: 615-352-3909, blix@bellsouth.net

HEGWALD, J L,
1106 Charles, Humboldt, KS 66748, Phone: 316-473-3523
Specialties: Working straight knives, some fancy. **Patterns:** Makes Bowies, miniatures. **Technical:** Forges or grinds O1, L6, 440C; mixes materials in handles. **Prices:** $35 to $200; some higher. **Remarks:** Part-time maker; first knife sold in 1983. **Mark:** First and middle initials.

HEHN, RICHARD KARL,
Lehnmuehler Str 1, 55444 Dorrebach, GERMANY, Phone: 06724 3152
Specialties: High-tech, full integral working knives. **Patterns:** Hunters, fighters and daggers. **Technical:** Grinds CPM T-440V, CPM T-420V, forges his own stainless Damascus. **Prices:** $1000 to $10,000. **Remarks:** Full-time maker; first knife sold in 1963. **Mark:** Runic last initial in logo.

HEIMDALE, J E,
7749 E 28 CT, Tulsa, OK 74129, Phone: 918-640-0784, heimdale@sbcglobal.net
Specialties: Art knives **Patterns:** Bowies, daggers **Technical:** Makes all components and handles - exotic woods and sheaths. Uses Damascus blades by other Blademakers, notably R.W. Wilson. **Prices:** $300 and up. **Remarks:** Part-time maker. First knife sold in 1999. **Marks:** JEHCO

HEINZ, JOHN,
611 Cafferty Rd, Upper Black Eddy, PA 18972, Phone: 610-847-8535, Web: www.herugrim.com
Specialties: Historical pieces / copies. **Technical:** Makes his own steel. **Prices:** $150 to $800. **Mark:** "H."

HEITLER, HENRY,
8106 N Albany, Tampa, FL 33604, Phone: 813-933-1645
Specialties: Traditional working and using straight knives of his design and to customer specs. **Patterns:** Fighters, hunters, utility/camp knives and fillet knives. **Technical:** Flat-grinds ATS-34; offers tapered tangs. **Prices:** $135 to $450; some to $600. **Remarks:** Part-time maker; first knife sold in 1990. **Mark:** First initial, last name, city, state circling double H's.

HELSCHER, JOHN W,
2645 Highway 1, Washington, IA 52353, Phone: 319-653-7310

HELTON, ROY,
HELTON KNIVES, 2941 Comstock St., San Diego, CA 92111, Phone: 858-277-5024

HEMPERLEY, GLEN,
13322 Country Run Rd, Willis, TX 77318, Phone: 936-228-5048, hemperley.com
Specialties: Specializes in hunting knives, does fixed and folding knives.

HENDRICKS, SAMUEL J,
2162 Van Buren Rd, Maurertown, VA 22644, Phone: 703-436-3305
Specialties: Integral hunters and skinners of thin design. **Patterns:** Boots, hunters and locking folders. **Technical:** Grinds ATS-34, 440C and D2. Integral liners and bolsters of N-S and 7075 T6 aircraft aluminum. Does leatherwork. **Prices:** $50 to $250; some to $500. **Remarks:** Full-time maker; first knife sold in 1992. **Mark:** First and middle initials, last name, city and state in football-style logo.

HENDRICKSON, E JAY,
4204 Ballenger Creek Pike, Frederick, MD 21703, Phone: 301-663-6923, Fax: 301-663-6923, ejayhendrickson@comcast.net
Specialties: Specializes in silver wire inlay. **Patterns:** Bowies, Kukri's, camp, hunters, and fighters. **Technical:** Forges 06, 1084, 5160, 52100, D2, L6 and W2; makes Damascus. Moran-styles on order. **Prices:** $400 to $5000. **Remarks:** Full-time maker; first knife sold in 1975. **Mark:** Last name, M.S.

HENDRICKSON, SHAWN,
2327 Kaetzel Rd, Knoxville, MD 21758, Phone: 301-432-4306
Specialties: Hunting knives. **Patterns:** Clip points, drop points and trailing point hunters. **Technical:** Forges 5160, 1084 and L6. **Prices:** $175 to $400.

HENDRIX, JERRY,
HENDRIX CUSTOM KNIVES, 175 Skyland Dr. Ext., Clinton, SC 29325, Phone: 864-833-2659, jhendrix@backroads.net
Specialties: Traditional working straight knives of all designs. **Patterns:** Hunters, utility, boot, bird and fishing. **Technical:** Grinds ATS-34 and 440C. **Prices:** $85 to $275. **Remarks:** Full-time maker. Hand stitched, waxed leather sheaths. **Mark:** Last name in shape of knife.

HENDRIX, WAYNE,
9636 Burton's Ferry Hwy, Allendale, SC 29810, Phone: 803-584-3825, Fax: 803-584-3825, w.hendrixknives@gmail.com Web: www.hendrixknives.com
Specialties: Working/using knives of his design. **Patterns:** Hunters and fillet knives. **Technical:** Grinds ATS-34, D2 and 440C. **Prices:** $100 and up. **Remarks:** Full-time maker; first knife sold in 1985. **Mark:** Last name.

HENNINGSSON, MICHAEL,
Tralsvagen 1, Vastra Frolunda (Gothenburg), SWEDEN, Phone: 46 31-471073; Cell:46702555745,michael.henningsson@gmail.com;Web:henningssonknives.wordpress.com
Specialties: Handmade folding knives, mostly tactical linerlocks and framelocks. **Patterns:** Own design in both engravings and knife models. **Technical:** All kinds of stee; such as Damascus, but prefer clean RWL-43. Tweaking a lot with hand engraving and therefore likes clean steel mostly. Work a lot with inlays of various materials. **Prices:** Starting at $1200 and up, depending on decoration and engravings. **Remarks:** Part-time maker, first knife sold in 2010. **Mark:** Hand engraved name or a Viking sail with initials in runes

HENRIKSEN, HANS J,
Birkegaardsvej 24, DK 3200 Helsinge, DENMARK, Fax: 45 4879 4899
Specialties: Zirconia ceramic blades. **Patterns:** Customer designs. **Technical:** Slip-cast zirconia-water mix in plaster mould; offers hidden or full tang. **Prices:** White blades start at $10cm; colored +50 percent. **Remarks:** Part-time maker; first ceramic blade sold in 1989. **Mark:** Initial logo.

HENSLEY, WAYNE,
PO Box 904, Conyers, GA 30012, Phone: 770-483-8938
Specialties: Period pieces and fancy working knives. **Patterns:** Boots to Bowies, locking folders to miniatures. Large variety of straight knives. **Technical:** Grinds ATS-34, 440C, D2 and commercial Damascus. **Prices:** $85 and up. **Remarks:** Full-time maker; first knife sold in 1974. **Mark:** Last name.

HERB, MARTIN,
2500 Starwood Dr, Richmond, VA 23229

HERBST, GAWIE,
PO Box 59158, Karenpark 0118, Akasia, South Africa, Phone: +27 72 060 3687, Fax: +27 12 549 1876, gawie@herbst.co.za Web: www.herbst.co.za
Specialties: Hunters, Utility knives, Art knives and Liner lock folders.

HERBST, PETER,
Komotauer Strasse 26, 91207 Lauf a.d. Pegn., GERMANY, Phone: 09123-13315, Fax: 09123-13379
Specialties: Working/using knives and folders of his design. **Patterns:** Hunters, fighters and daggers; interframe and integral. **Technical:** Grinds CPM-T-440V, UHB-Elmax, ATS-34 and stainless Damascus. **Prices:** $300 to $3000; some to $8000. **Remarks:** Full-time maker; first knife sold in 1981. **Mark:** First initial, last name.

HERBST, THINUS,
PO Box 59158, Karenpark 0118, Akasia, South Africa, Phone: +27 82 254 8016, thinus@herbst.co.za; Web: www.herbst.co.za
Specialties: Plain and fancy working straight knives of own design and liner lock folders. **Patterns:** Hunters, utility knives, art knives, and liner lock folders. **Technical:** Prefer exotic materials for handles. Most knives embellished with file work, carving and scrimshaw. **Prices:** $200 to $2000. **Remarks:** Full-time maker, member of the Knifemakers Guild of South Africa.

HERMAN, TIM,
517 E. 126 Terrace, Olathe, KS 66061-2731, Phone: 913-839-1924, HermanKnives@comcast.net
Specialties: Investment-grade folders of his design; interframes and bolster frames. **Patterns:** Interframes and new designs in carved stainless. **Technical:** Grinds ATS-34 and damasteel Damascus. Engraves and gold inlays with pearl, jade, lapis and Australian opal. **Prices:** $1500 to $20,000 and up. **Remarks:** Full-time maker; first knife sold in 1978. Inventor of full-color bulino engraving since 1993. **Mark:** Etched signature.

HERNDON, WM R "BILL",
32520 Michigan St, Acton, CA 93510, Phone: 661-269-5860, Fax: 661-269-4568, bherndons1@roadrunner.com
Specialties: Straight knives, plain and fancy. **Technical:** Carbon steel (white and blued), Damascus, stainless steels. **Prices:** Start at $175. **Remarks:** Full-time maker; first knife sold in 1976. American Bladesmith Society journeyman smith. **Mark:** Signature and/or helm logo.

HERRING, MORRIS,
Box 85 721 W Line St, Dyer, AR 72935, Phone: 501-997-8861, morrish@ipa.com

HETHCOAT, DON,
Box 1764, Clovis, NM 88101, Phone: 575-762-5721, dhethcoat@plateautel.net; Web: www.donhethcoat.com
Specialties: Liner locks, lock backs and multi-blade folder patterns. **Patterns:** Hunters, Bowies. **Technical:** Grinds stainless; forges Damascus. **Prices:** Moderate to upscale. **Remarks:** Full-time maker; first knife sold in 1969. **Mark:** Last name on all.

HIBBEN, DARYL,
PO Box 172, LaGrange, KY 40031-0172, Phone: 502-222-0983, dhibben1@bellsouth.net
Specialties: Working straight knives, some fancy to customer specs. **Patterns:** Hunters, fighters, Bowies, short sword, art and fantasy. **Technical:** Grinds 440C, ATS-34, 154CM, Damascus; prefers hollow-grinds. **Prices:** $275 and up. **Remarks:** Full-time maker; first knife sold in 1979. **Mark:** Etched full name in script.

HIBBEN, GIL,
PO Box 13, LaGrange, KY 40031, Phone: 502-222-1397, Fax: 502-222-2676, gil@hibbenknives.com Web: www.hibbenknives.com
Specialties: Working knives and fantasy pieces to customer specs. **Patterns:** Full range of straight knives, including swords, axes and miniatures; some locking folders. **Technical:** Grinds ATS-34, 440C and D2. **Prices:** $300 to $2000; some to $10,000. **Remarks:** Full-time maker; first knife sold in 1957. Maker and designer of *Rambo III* knife; made swords for movie *Marked for Death* and throwing knife for movie *Under Seige*; made belt buckle knife and knives for movie *Perfect Weapon*; made knives featured in movie *Star Trek the Next Generation*, *Star Trek Nemesis*. 1990 inductee Cutlery Hall of Fame; designer for United Cutlery. Official klingon armourer for Star Trek. Knives also for movies of the Expendables and the Expendables sequel. Over 37 movies and TV productions. President of the Knifemakers Guild. Celebrating 55 years since first knife sold. **Mark:** Hibben Knives. City and state, or signature.

HIBBEN, JOLEEN,
PO Box 172, LaGrange, KY 40031, Phone: 502-222-0983, dhibben1@bellsouth.net
Specialties: Miniature straight knives of her design; period pieces. **Patterns:**

HIBBEN—HOFFMAN

Hunters, axes and fantasy knives. **Technical:** Grinds Damascus, 1095 tool steel and stainless 440C or ATS-34. Uses wood, ivory, bone, feathers and claws on/for handles. **Prices:** $60 to $600. **Remarks:** Spare-time maker; first knife sold in 1991. Design knives, make & tool leather sheaths. Produced first inlaid handle in 2005, used by Daryl on a dagger. **Mark:** Initials or first name.

HIBBEN, WESTLEY G,
14101 Sunview Dr, Anchorage, AK 99515
Specialties: Working straight knives of his design or to customer specs. **Patterns:** Hunters, fighters, daggers, combat knives and some fantasy pieces. **Technical:** Grinds 440C mostly. Filework available. **Prices:** $200 to $400; some to $3000. **Remarks:** Part-time maker; first knife sold in 1988. **Mark:** Signature.

HICKS, GARY,
341 CR 275, Tuscola, TX 79562, Phone: 325-554-9762

HIELSCHER, GUY,
PO Box 992, 6550 Otoe Rd., Alliance, NE 69301, Phone: 308-762-4318, g-hielsc@bbcwb.net Web: www.ghknives.com
Specialties: Working Damascus fixed blade knives. **Patterns:** Hunters, fighters, capers, skinners, bowie, drop point. **Technical:** Forges own Damascus using 1018 and 0-1 tool steels. **Prices:** $285 and up. **Remarks:** Member of PKA. Part-time maker; sold first knife in 1988. **Mark:** Arrowhead with GH inside.

HIGH, TOM,
5474 S 1128 Rd, Alamosa, CO 81101, Phone: 719-589-2108, www.rockymountainscrimshaw.com
Specialties: Hunters, some fancy. **Patterns:** Drop-points in several shapes; some semi-skinners. Knives designed by and for top outfitters and guides. **Technical:** Grinds ATS-34; likes hollow-grinds, mirror finishes; prefers scrimable handles. **Prices:** $300 to $8000.. **Remarks:** Full-time maker; first knife sold in 1965. Limited edition wildlife series knives. **Mark:** Initials connected; arrow through last name.

HILKER, THOMAS N,
PO Box 409, Williams, OR 97544, Phone: 541-846-6461
Specialties: Traditional working straight knives and folders. **Patterns:** Folding skinner in two sizes, Bowies, fork and knife sets, camp knives and interchangeable. **Technical:** Grinds D2, 440C and ATS-34. Heat-treats. **Prices:** $50 to $350; some to $400. Doing business as Thunderbolt Artisans. Only limited production models available; not currently taking orders. **Remarks:** Full-time maker; first knife sold in 1983. **Mark:** Last name.

HILL, HOWARD E,
41785 Mission Lane, Polson, MT 59860, Phone: 406-883-3405, Fax: 406-883-3486, knifeman@bigsky.net
Specialties: Autos, complete new design, legal in Montana (with permit). **Patterns:** Bowies, daggers, skinners and lockback folders. **Technical:** Grinds 440C; uses micro and satin finish. **Prices:** $150 to $1000. **Remarks:** Full-time maker; first knife sold in 1981. **Mark:** Persuader.

HILL, RICK,
20 Nassau, Maryville, IL 62062-5618, Phone: 618-288-4370
Specialties: Working knives and period pieces to customer specs. **Patterns:** Hunters, locking folders, fighters and daggers. **Technical:** Grinds D2, 440C and 154CM; forges his own Damascus. **Prices:** $75 to $500; some to $3000. **Remarks:** Part-time maker; first knife sold in 1983. **Mark:** Full name in hill shape logo.

HILL, STEVE E,
40 Rand Pond Rd, Goshen, NH 03752, Phone: 603-863-4762, Fax: 603-863-4762, kingpirateboy2@juno.com; Web: www.stevehillknives.com
Specialties: Fancy manual and automatic LinerLock® folders, small fixed blades and classic Bowie knives. **Patterns:** Classic to cool folding and fixed blade designs. **Technical:** Grinds Damascus and occasional 440C, D2. Prefers natural handle materials; offers elaborate filework, carving, and inlays. **Prices:** $400 to $6000, some higher. **Remarks:** Full-time maker; first knife sold in 1978. Google search: Steve Hill custom knives. **Mark:** First initial, last name and handmade. (4400, D2). Damascus folders: mark inside handle.

HILLMAN, CHARLES,
225 Waldoboro Rd, Friendship, ME 04547, Phone: 207-832-4634
Specialties: Working knives of his own or custom design. Heavy Scagel influence. **Patterns:** Hunters, fishing, camp and general utility. Occasional folders. **Technical:** Grinds D2 and 440C. File work, blade and handle carving, engraving. Natural handle materials-antler, bone, leather, wood, horn. Sheaths made to order. **Prices:** $60 to $500. **Remarks:** Part-time maker; first knife sold 1986. **Mark:** Last name in oak leaf.

HINDERER, RICK,
5373 Columbus Rd., Shreve, OH 44676, Phone: 330-263-0962, Fax: 330-263-0962, rhind64@earthlink.net; Web: www.rickhindererknives.com
Specialties: Working tactical knives, and some one-of-a kind. **Patterns:** Makes his own. **Technical:** Grinds Duratech 20 CV and CPM S30V. **Prices:** $150 to $4000. **Remarks:** Full-time maker doing business as Rick Hinderer Knives, first knife sold in 1988. **Mark:** R. Hinderer.

HINDMARCH, GARTH,
PO Box 135, Carlyle SK S0C 0R0, CANADA, Phone: 306-453-2568
Specialties: Working and fancy straight knives, Bowies. **Patterns:** Hunters, skinners, Bowies. **Technical:** Grind 440C, ATS-34, some Damascus. **Prices:** $175 - $700. **Remarks:** Part-time maker; first knife sold 1994. All knives satin finish. Does file work, offers engraving, stabilized wood, Giraffe bone, some Micarta. **Mark:** First initial last name, city, province.

HINK III, LES,
1599 Aptos Lane, Stockton, CA 95206, Phone: 209-547-1292
Specialties: Working straight knives and traditional folders in standard patterns or to customer specs. **Patterns:** Hunting and utility/camp knives; others on request. **Technical:** Grinds carbon and stainless steels. **Prices:** $80 to $200; some higher. **Remarks:** Part-time maker; first knife sold in 1980. **Mark:** Last name, or last name 3.

HINMAN, THEODORE,
186 Petty Plain Road, Greenfield, MA 01301, Phone: 413-773-0448, armenemargosian@verizon.net
Specialties: Tomahawks and axes. Offers classes in bladesmithing and toolmaking.

HINSON AND SON, R,
2419 Edgewood Rd, Columbus, GA 31906, Phone: 706-327-6801
Specialties: Working straight knives and folders. **Patterns:** Locking folders, liner locks, combat knives and swords. **Technical:** Grinds 440C and commercial Damascus. **Prices:** $200 to $450; some to $1500. **Remarks:** Part-time maker; first knife sold in 1983. Son Bob is co-worker. **Mark:** HINSON, city and state.

HINTZ, GERALD M,
5402 Sahara Ct, Helena, MT 59602, Phone: 406-458-5412
Specialties: Fancy, high-art, working/using knives of his design. **Patterns:** Bowies, hunters, daggers, fish fillet and utility/camp knives. **Technical:** Forges ATS-34, 440C and D2. Animal art in horn handles or in the blade. **Prices:** $75 to $400; some to $1500. **Remarks:** Part-time maker; first knife sold in 1980. Doing business as Big Joe's Custom Knives. Will take custom orders. **Mark:** F.S. or W.S. with first and middle initials and last name.

HIRAYAMA, HARUMI,
4-5-13 Kitamachi, Warabi City, Saitama Pref. 335-0001, JAPAN, Phone: 048-443-2248, Fax: 048-443-2248, Web: www.ne.jp/asahi/harumi/knives
Specialties: High-tech working knives of her design. **Patterns:** Locking folders, interframes, straight gents and slip-joints. **Technical:** Grinds 440C or equivalent; uses natural handle materials and gold. **Prices:** Start at $2500. **Remarks:** Part-time maker; first knife sold in 1985. **Mark:** First initial, last name.

HIROTO, FUJIHARA,
2-34-7 Koioosako Nishi-ku Hiroshima-city, Hiroshima, JAPAN, Phone: 082-271-8389, fjhr8363@crest.ocn.ne.jp

HITCHMOUGH, HOWARD,
95 Old Street Rd, Peterborough, NH 03458-1637, Phone: 603-924-9646, Fax: 603-924-9595, hhrlm@comcast.net; Web: www.hitchmoughknives.com
Specialties: High class folding knives. **Patterns:** Lockback folders, liner locks, pocket knives. **Technical:** Uses ATS-34, stainless Damascus, titanium, gold and gemstones. Prefers hand-rubbed finishes and natural handle materials. **Prices:** $2500 - $7500. **Remarks:** Full-time maker; first knife sold in 1967. **Mark:** Last name.

HOBART, GENE,
100 Shedd Rd, Windsor, NY 13865, Phone: 607-655-1345

HOCKENSMITH, DAN,
104 North Country Rd 23, Berthoud, CO 80513, Phone: 970-231-6506, blademan@skybeam.com; Web: www.dhockensmithknives.com
Specialties: Traditional working and using straight knives of his design. **Patterns:** Hunters, Bowies, folders and utility/camp knives. **Technical:** Uses his Damascus, 5160, carbon steel, 52100 steel and 1084 steel. Hand forged. **Prices:** $250 to $1500. **Remarks:** Part-time maker; first knife sold in 1987. **Mark:** Last name or stylized "D" with H inside.

HODGE III, JOHN,
422 S 15th St, Palatka, FL 32177, Phone: 904-328-3897
Specialties: Fancy straight knives and folders. **Patterns:** Various. **Technical:** Pattern-welded Damascus—"Southern-style." **Prices:** To $1000. **Remarks:** Part-time maker; first knife sold in 1981. **Mark:** JH3 logo.

HOEL, STEVE,
PO Box 283, Pine, AZ 85544, Phone: 602-476-4278
Specialties: Investor-class folders, straight knives and period pieces of his design. **Patterns:** Folding interframes lockers and slip-joints; straight Bowies, boots and daggers. **Technical:** Grinds 154CM, ATS-34 and commercial Damascus. **Prices:** $600 to $1200; some to $7500. **Remarks:** Full-time maker. **Mark:** Initial logo with name and address.

HOFER, LOUIS,
BOX 125, Rose Prairie, B.C., CANADA V0C 2H0, Phone: 250-827-3999, ldhofer@xplornet.com
Specialties: Damascus knives, working knives, fixed blade bowies, daggers. **Patterns:** Hunting, skinning, custom. **Technical:** Wild damascus, random damascus. **Prices:** $450 and up. **Remarks:** Part-time maker since 1995. **Mark:** Logo of initials.

HOFFMAN, JAY,
Hoffman Haus Knives, 911 W Superior St., Munising, MI 49862, Phone: 906-387-3440, hoffmanhaus1@yahoo.com Web: www.hoffmanhausknives.com
Technical: Scrimshaw, metal carving, own casting of hilts and pommels, etc. Most if not all leather work for sheaths. **Remarks:** Has been making knives for 50 + years. Professionally since 1991. **Mark:** Early knives marked "Hoffman Haus" and year. Now marks "Hoffman Haus Knives" on the blades. Starting in 2010 uses heraldic device. Will build to your specs. Lag time 1-2 months.

HOFFMAN, KEVIN L,
28 Hopeland Dr, Savannah, GA 31419, Phone: 912-920-3579, Fax: 912-920-3579, kevh052475@aol.com; Web: www.KLHoffman.com
Specialties: Distinctive folders and fixed blades. **Patterns:** Titanium frame lock folders. **Technical:** Sculpted guards and fittings cast in sterling silver and 14k gold. Grinds ATS-34, CPM S30V Damascus. Makes kydex sheaths for his fixed blade working knives. **Prices:** $400 and up. **Remarks:** Full-time maker since 1981. **Mark:** KLH.

HOGAN, THOMAS R,
2802 S. Heritage Ave, Boise, ID 83709, Phone: 208-362-7848

HOGSTROM, ANDERS T,
Halmstadsvagen 36, 121 53, Johanneshov, SWEDEN, Phone: 46 702 674 574, andershogstrom@hotmail.com or info@andershogstrom.com; Web: www.andershogstrom.com
Specialties: Short and long daggers, fighters and swords For select pieces makes wooden display stands. **Patterns:** Daggers, fighters, short knives and swords and an occasional sword. **Technical:** Grinds 1050 High Carbon, Damascus and stainless, forges own Damasus on occasion, fossil ivories. Does clay tempering and uses exotic hardwoods. **Prices:** Start at $850. **Marks:** Last name in maker's own signature.

HOKE, THOMAS M,
3103 Smith Ln, LaGrange, KY 40031, Phone: 502-222-0350
Specialties: Working/using knives, straight knives. Own designs and customer specs. **Patterns:** Daggers, Bowies, hunters, fighters, short swords. **Technical:** Grind 440C, Damascus and ATS-34. Filework on all knives. Tooling on sheaths (custom fit on all knives). Any handle material, mostly exotic. **Prices:** $100 to $700; some to $1500. **Remarks:** Full-time maker, first knife sold in 1986. **Mark:** Dragon on banner which says T.M. Hoke.

HOLBROOK, H L,
PO Box 483, Sandy Hook, KY 41171, Phone: Home: 606-738-9922 Cell: 606-794-1497, hhknives@mrtc.com
Specialties: Traditional working using straight knives of his design, to customer specs and in standard patterns. Stabilized wood. **Patterns:** Hunters, mild tacticals and neck knives with kydex sheaths. **Technical:** Grinds CPM154CM, 154CM. Blades have hand-rubbed satin finish. Uses exotic woods, stag and Micarta. Hand-sewn sheath with each straight knife. **Prices:** $125 - $400. **Remarks:** Part-time maker; first knife sold in 1983. Doing business as Holbrook Knives. **Mark:** Name, city, state.

HOLDER, D'ALTON,
18910 McNeil Rd., Wickenburg, AZ 85390, Phone: 928-684-2025, Fax: 623-878-3964, dholderknives@cox.net; Web: d'holder.com
Specialties: Deluxe working knives and high-art hunters. **Patterns:** Drop-point hunters, fighters, Bowies. **Technical:** Grinds ATS-34; uses amber and other materials in combination on stick tangs. **Prices:** $400 to $1000; some to $2000. **Remarks:** Full-time maker; first knife sold in 1966. **Mark:** D'HOLDER, city and state.

HOLLOWAY, PAUL,
714 Burksdale Rd, Norfolk, VA 23518, Phone: 757-547-6025, houdini969@yahoo.com
Specialties: Working straight knives and folders to customer specs. **Patterns:** Lockers and slip-joints; fighters and boots; fishing and push knives, from swords to miniatures. **Technical:** Grinds A2, D2, 154CM, 440C and ATS-34. **Prices:** $210 to $1500; some to $1200. **Remarks:** Part-time maker; semi-retired; first knife sold in 1981. **Mark:** Name and city in logo.

HOOK, BOB,
3247 Wyatt Rd, North Pole, AK 99705, Phone: 907-488-8886, grayling@alaska.net; Web: www.alaskaknifeandforge.com
Specialties: Forged carbon steel. Damascus blades. **Patterns:** Pronghorns, bowies, drop point hunters and knives for the kitchen. **Technical:** 5160, 52100, carbon steel and 1084 and 15N20 pattern welded steel blades are hand forged. Heat treated and ground by maker. Handles are natural materials from Alaska. I favor sole authorship of each piece. **Prices:** $300-$1000. **Remarks:** Journeyman smith with ABS. I have attended the Bill Moran School of Bladesmithing. Knife maker since 2000. **Mark:** Hook.

HORN, DES,
PO Box 322, Onrusrivier 7201, SOUTH AFRICA, Phone: 27283161795, Fax: +27866280824, deshorn@usa.net
Specialties: Folding knives. **Patterns:** Ball release side lock mechanism and interframe automatics. **Technical:** Prefers working in totally stainless materials. **Prices:** $800 to $7500. **Remarks:** Full-time maker. Enjoys working in gold, titanium, meteorite, pearl and mammoth. **Mark:** Des Horn.

HORN, JESS,
2526 Lansdown Rd, Eugene, OR 97404, Phone: 541-463-1510, jandahorn@earthlink.net
Specialties: Investor-class working folders; period pieces; collectibles. **Patterns:** High-tech design and finish in folders; liner locks, traditional slip-joints and featherweight models. **Technical:** Grinds ATS-34, 154CM. **Prices:** Start at $1000. **Remarks:** Full-time maker; first knife sold in 1968. **Mark:** Full name or last name.

HORNE, GRACE,
The Old Public Convenience, 469 Fulwood Road, Sheffield, UNITED KINGDOM S10 3QA, gracehorne@hotmail.co.uk Web: www.gracehorn.co.uk
Specialties: Knives of own design, mainly slip-joint folders. **Technical:** Grinds RWL34, Damasteel and own Damascus for blades. Scale materials vary from traditional (coral, wood, precious metals, etc) to unusual (wool, fabric, felt, etc). **Prices:** $500 - $1500 **Remarks:** Part-time maker. **Mark:** 'gH' and 'Sheffield'.

HORRIGAN, JOHN,
433 C.R. 200 D, Burnet, TX 78611, Phone: 512-756-7545, jhorrigan@yahoo.com Web: www.eliteknives.com
Specialties: High-end custom knives. **Prices:** $200 - $6500. **Remarks:** Part-time maker. Obtained Mastersmith stamp 2005. First knife made in 1982. **Mark:** Horrigan M.S.

HORTON, SCOT,
PO Box 451, Buhl, ID 83316, Phone: 208-543-4222
Specialties: Traditional working stiff knives and folders. **Patterns:** Hunters, skinners, utility, hatchets and show knives. **Technical:** Grinds ATS-34 and D-2 tool steel. **Prices:** $400 to $2500. **Remarks:** First knife sold in 1990. **Mark:** Full name in arch underlined with arrow, city, state.

HOSSOM, JERRY,
3585 Schilling Ridge, Duluth, GA 30096, Phone: 770-449-7809, jerry@hossom.com; Web: www.hossom.com
Specialties: Working straight knives of his own design. **Patterns:** Fighters, combat knives, modern Bowies and daggers, modern swords, concealment knives for military and LE uses. **Technical:** Grinds 154CM, S30V, CPM-3V, CPM-154 and stainless Damascus. Uses natural and synthetic handle materials. **Prices:** $350-1500, some higher. **Remarks:** Full-time maker since 1997. First knife sold in 1983. **Mark:** First initial and last name, includes city and state since 2002.

HOSTETLER, LARRY,
10626 Pine Needle Dr., Fort Pierce, FL 34945, Phone: 772-465-8352, hossknives@bellsouth.net Web: www.hoss-knives.com
Specialties: EDC working knives and custom collector knives. Utilizing own designs and customer designed creations. Maker uses a wide variety of exotic materials. **Technical:** Stock removal, grinds ATS-34, carbon and stainless Damascus, embellishes most pieces with file work. **Prices:** $200 - $1500. Some custom orders higher. **Remarks:** Motto: "EDC doesn't have to be ugly." First knife made in 2001, part-time maker, voting member in the Knife Maker's Guild. Doing business as "Hoss Knives." **Mark:** "Hoss" etched into blade with a turn of the century fused bomb in place of the "O" in Hoss.

HOUSE, CAMERON,
2001 Delaney Rd Se, Salem, OR 97306, Phone: 503-585-3286, chouse357@aol.com
Specialties: Working straight knives. **Patterns:** Hunters, Bowies, fighters. **Technical:** Grinds ATS-34, 530V, 154CM. **Remarks:** Part-time maker, first knife sold in 1993. **Prices:** $150 and up. **Mark:** HOUSE.

HOUSE, GARY,
2851 Pierce Rd, Ephrata, WA 98823, Phone: 509-754-3272, spindry101@aol.com
Specialties: Mosaic Damascus bar stock. Forged blades. **Patterns:** Unlimited, SW Indian designs, geometric patterns, using 1084, 15N20 and some nickel. Bowies, hunters and daggers. **Technical:** Forged company logos and customer designs in mosaic damascus. **Prices:** $500 & up. **Remarks:** Some of the finest and most unique patterns available. ABS Journeyman Smith. **Marks:** Initials GTH, G hanging T, H.

HOUSE, NATHAN,
4 East HaneKamp St., Lonaconing, MD 21539, Phone: 301-463-3613, poppyhouse@verizon.net Web: www.houseknives.com
Specialties: User style knives that are wicked sharp and are meant to cut. **Technical:** Stock removal and favorite steel D2. **Prices:** $185 - $250. **Remarks:** Full-time maker. **Mark:** "House Knives" in a circle.

HOWARD, DURVYN M,
4220 McLain St S, Hokes Bluff, AL 35903, Phone: 256-492-5720, Fax: Cell: 256-504-1853
Specialties: Collectible upscale folders; one-of-a-kind, gentlemen's folders. Multiple patents. **Patterns:** Conceptual designs; each unique and different. **Technical:** Uses natural and exotic materials and precious metals. **Prices:** $5000 to $25,000. **Remarks:** Full-time maker; by commission or available work. Work displayed at select shows, K.G. Show etc. **Mark:** Howard: new for 2000; Howard in Garamond Narrow "etched."

HOWE, TORI,
30020 N Stampede Rd, Athol, ID 83801, Phone: 208-449-1509, wapiti@knifescales.com; Web:www.knifescales.com
Specialties: Custom knives, knife scales & Damascus blades. **Remarks:** Carry James Luman polymer clay knife scales.

HOWELL, JASON G,
1112 Sycamore, Lake Jackson, TX 77566, Phone: 979-297-9454, tinyknives@yahoo.com; Web:www.howellbladesmith.com
Specialties: Fixed blades and LinerLock® folders. Makes own Damascus. **Patterns:** Clip and drop point. **Prices:** $150 to $750. **Remarks:** Likes making Mosaic Damascus out of the ordinary stuff. Member of TX Knifemakers and Collectors Association; apprentice in ABS; working towards Journeyman Stamp. **Mark:** Name, city, state.

HOWELL, LEN,
550 Lee Rd 169, Opelika, AL 36804, Phone: 334-749-1942
Specialties: Traditional and working knives of his design and to customer specs. **Patterns:** Buckskinner, hunters and utility/camp knives. **Technical:** Forges cable Damascus, 1085 and 5160; makes own Damascus. **Mark:** Engraved last name.

HOWELL, TED,
1294 Wilson Rd, Wetumpka, AL 36092, Phone: 205-569-2281, Fax: 205-569-1764
Specialties: Working/using straight knives and folders of his design; period pieces. **Patterns:** Bowies, fighters, hunters. **Technical:** Forges 5160, 1085 and cable. Offers light engraving and scrimshaw; filework. **Prices:** $75 to $250; some to $450. **Remarks:** Part-time maker; first knife sold in 1991. Doing business as Howell Co. **Mark:** Last name, Slapout AL.

HOWSER, JOHN C,
54 Bell Ln, Frankfort, KY 40601, Phone: 502-875-3678, howsercustomknives@fewpb.net
Specialties: Slip joint folders (old patterns-multi blades). **Patterns:** Traditional slip joint folders, lockbacks, hunters and fillet knives. **Technical:** Steel S30V, CPM154, ATS-34 and D2. **Prices:** $200 to $600 some to $800. **Remarks:** Full-time maker; first knife sold in 1974. **Mark:** Signature or stamp.

HOY, KEN,
54744 Pinchot Dr, North Fork, CA 93643, Phone: 209-877-7805

HRISOULAS, JIM,
SALAMANDER ARMOURY, 284-C Lake Mead Pkwy #157, Henderson, NV 89105, Phone: 702-566-8551, www.atar.com
Specialties: Working straight knives; period pieces. **Patterns:** Swords, daggers and sgian dubhs. **Technical:** Double-edged differential heat treating. **Prices:** $85 to $175; some to $600 and higher. **Remarks:** Full-time maker; first knife sold in 1973. Author of *The Complete Bladesmith, The Pattern Welded Blade* and *The Master Bladesmith.* Doing business as Salamander Armory. **Mark:** 8R logo and sword and salamander.

HUCKABEE, DALE,
254 Hwy 260, Maylene, AL 35114, Phone: 205-664-2544, dalehuckabee@hotmail.com
Specialties: Fixed blade hunter and Bowies of his design. **Technical:** Steel used: 5160, 1084, and Damascus. **Prices:** $225 and up, depending on materials used. **Remarks:** Hand forged. Journeyman Smith. Part-time maker. **Mark:** Stamped Huckabee J.S.

HUCKS, JERRY,
KNIVES BY HUCKS, 1807 Perch Road, Moncks Corner, SC 29461, Phone: 843-761-6481, knivesbyhucks@netrockets.com
Specialties: Oyster knives, hunters, Bowies, fillets. Bowies are the maker's favorite with stag & ivory. **Patterns:** Yours and his. **Technical:** ATS-34, BG-42, CPM-154, maker's cable Damascus, also 1084 & 15N20. **Prices:** $125 and up. **Remarks:** Full-time maker, retired as a machinist in 1990. Makes sheaths sewn by hand with some carving. **Mark:** Robin Hood hat with moncke corner, S.C. in oval.

HUDSON, ANTHONY B,
PO Box 368, Amanda, OH 43102, Phone: 740-969-4200, abhudsonknives@yahoo.com; Web: abhudsonknives.com
Specialties: Hunting knives, fighters, survival, period pieces (U.S.) **Remarks:** ABS Journeyman Smith. **Mark:** A.B. HUDSON (except for period pieces).

HUDSON, C ROBBIN,
497 Groton Hollow Rd, Rummney, NH 03266, Phone: 603-786-9944, bladesmith8@gmail.com
Specialties: High-art working knives. **Patterns:** Hunters, Bowies, fighters and kitchen knives. **Technical:** Forges W2, nickel steel, pure nickel steel, composite and mosaic Damascus; makes knives one-at-a-time. **Prices:** 500 to $1200; some to $5000. **Remarks:** Full-time maker; first knife sold in 1970. **Mark:** Last name and MS.

HUDSON, ROB,
340 Roush Rd, Northumberland, PA 17857, Phone: 570-473-9588, robscustknives@aol.com Web:www.robscustomknives.com
Specialties: Presentation hunters and Bowies. **Technical:** Hollow grinds CPM-154 stainless and stainless Damascus. **Prices:** $400 to $2000. **Remarks:** Full-time maker. Does business as Rob's Custom Knives. **Mark:** Capital R, Capital H in script.

HUDSON, ROBERT,
3802 Black Cricket Ct, Humble, TX 77396, Phone: 713-454-7207
Specialties: Working straight knives of his design. **Patterns:** Bowies, hunters, skinners, fighters and utility knives. **Technical:** Grinds D2, 440C, 154CM and commercial Damascus. **Prices:** $85 to $350; some to $1500. **Remarks:** Part-time maker; first knife sold in 1980. **Mark:** Full name, handmade, city and state.

HUGHES, DAN,
301 Grandview Bluff Rd, Spencer, TN 38585, Phone: 931-946-3044
Specialties: Working straight knives to customer specs. **Patterns:** Hunters, fighters, fillet knives. **Technical:** Grinds 440C and ATS-34. **Prices:** $55 to $175; some to $300. **Remarks:** Part-time maker; first knife sold in 1984. **Mark:** Initials.

HUGHES, DARYLE,
10979 Leonard, Nunica, MI 49448, Phone: 616-837-6623, hughes.builders@verizon.net
Specialties: Working knives. **Patterns:** Buckskinners, hunters, camp knives, kitchen and fishing knives. **Technical:** Forges and grinds 52100 and Damascus. **Prices:** $125 to $1000. **Remarks:** Part-time maker; first knife sold in 1979. **Mark:** Name and city in logo.

HUGHES, ED,
280 1/2 Holly Lane, Grand Junction, CO 81503, Phone: 970-243-8547, edhughes26@msn.com
Specialties: Working and art folders. **Patterns:** Buys Damascus. **Technical:** Grinds stainless steels. Engraves. **Prices:** $300 and up. **Remarks:** Full-time maker; first knife sold in 1978. **Mark:** Name or initials.

HUGHES, LAWRENCE,
207 W Crestway, Plainview, TX 79072, Phone: 806-293-5406
Specialties: Working and display knives. **Patterns:** Bowies, daggers, hunters, buckskinners. **Technical:** Grinds D2, 440C and 154CM. **Prices:** $125 to $300; some to $2000. **Remarks:** Full-time maker; first knife sold in 1979. **Mark:** Name with buffalo skull in center.

HULETT, STEVE,
115 Yellowstone Ave, West Yellowstone, MT 59758-0131, Phone: 406-646-4116, Web: www.seldomseenknives.com
Specialties: Classic, working/using knives, straight knives, folders. Your design, custom specs. **Patterns:** Utility/camp knives, hunters, and LinerLock folders, lock back pocket knives. **Technical:** Grinds 440C stainless steel, O1 Carbon, 1095. Shop is retail and knife shop; people watch their knives being made. We do everything in house: "all but smelt the ore, or tan the hide." **Prices:** Strarting $250 to $7000. **Remarks:** Full-time maker; first knife sold in 1994. **Mark:** Seldom seen knives/West Yellowstone Montana.

HULSEY, HOYT,
379 Shiloh, Attalla, AL 35954, Phone: 256-538-6765
Specialties: Traditional working straight knives and folders of his design. **Patterns:** Hunters and utility/camp knives. **Technical:** Grinds 440C, ATS-34, O1 and A2. **Prices:** $75 to $250. **Remarks:** Part-time maker; first knife sold in 1989. **Mark:** Hoyt Hulsey Attalla AL.

HUME, DON,
2731 Tramway Circle NE, Albuquerque, NM 87122, Phone: 505-796-9451

HUMENICK, ROY,
PO Box 55, Rescue, CA 95672, rhknives@gmail.com; Web: www.humenick.com
Specialties: Traditional multiblades and tactical slipjoints. **Patterns:** Original folder and fixed blade designs, also traditional patterns. **Technical:** Grinds premium steels and Damascus. **Prices:** $350 and up; some to $1500. **Remarks:** First knife sold in 1984. **Mark:** Last name in ARC.

HUMPHREY, LON,
83 Wilwood Ave., Newark, OH 43055, Phone: 740-644-1137, ironcrossforge@hotmail.com
Specialties: Hunters, tacticals, and bowie knives. **Prices:** I make knives that start in the $150 range and go up to $1000 for a large bowie. **Remarks:** Has been blacksmithing since age 13 and progressed to the forged blade.

HUMPHREYS, JOEL,
90 Boots Rd, Lake Placid, FL 33852, Phone: 863-773-0439
Specialties: Traditional working/using straight knives and folders of his design and in standard patterns. **Patterns:** Hunters, folders and utility/camp knives. **Technical:** Grinds ATS-34, D2, 440C. All knives have tapered tangs, mitered bolster/handle joints, handles of horn or bone fitted sheaths. **Prices:** $135 to $225; some to $350. **Remarks:** Part-time maker; first knife sold in 1990. Doing business as Sovereign Knives. **Mark:** First name or "H" pierced by arrow.

HUNT, MAURICE,
10510NCR650E, Brownsburg, IN 46112, Phone: 317-892-2982, mdhuntknives@juno.com
Patterns: Bowies, hunters, fighters. **Prices:** $200 to $800. **Remarks:** Part-time maker. Journeyman Smith.

HUNTER, HYRUM,
285 N 300 W, PO Box 179, Aurora, UT 84620, Phone: 435-529-7244
Specialties: Working straight knives of his design or to customer specs. **Patterns:** Drop and clip, fighters dagger, some folders. **Technical:** Forged from two-piece Damascus. **Prices:** Prices are adjusted according to size, complexity and material used. **Remarks:** Will consider any design you have. Part-time maker; first knife sold in 1990. **Mark:** Initials encircled with first initial and last name and city, then state. Some patterns are numbered.

HUNTER, RICHARD D,
7230 NW 200th Ter, Alachua, FL 32615, Phone: 386-462-3150
Specialties: Traditional working/using knives of his design or customer suggestions; filework. **Patterns:** Folders of various types, Bowies, hunters, daggers. **Technical:** Traditional blacksmith; hand forges high-carbon steel (5160, 1084, 52100) and makes own Damascus; grinds 440C and ATS-34. **Prices:** $200 and up. **Remarks:** Part-time maker; first knife sold in 1992. **Mark:** Last name in capital letters.

HURST, COLE,
1583 Tedford, E. Wenatchee, WA 98802, Phone: 509-884-9206
Specialties: Fantasy, high-art and traditional straight knives. **Patterns:** Bowies, daggers and hunters. **Technical:** Blades are made of stone; handles are made of stone, wood or ivory and embellished with fancy woods, ivory or antlers. **Prices:** $100 to $300; some to $2000. **Remarks:** Spare-time maker; first knife sold in 1985. **Mark:** Name and year.

HURST, JEFF,
PO Box 247, Rutledge, TN 37861, Phone: 865-828-5729, jhurst@esper.com
  Specialties: Working straight knives and folders of his design. **Patterns:** Tomahawks, hunters, boots, folders and fighters. **Technical:** Forges W2, O1 and his own Damascus. Makes mokume. **Prices:** $250 to $600. **Remarks:** Full-time maker; first knife sold in 1984. Doing business as Buzzard's Knob Forge. **Mark:** Last name; partnered knives are marked with Newman L. Smith, handle artisan, and SH in script.

HUSIAK, MYRON,
PO Box 238, Altona 3018, Victoria, AUSTRALIA, Phone: 03-315-6752
  Specialties: Straight knives and folders of his design or to customer specs. **Patterns:** Hunters, fighters, lock-back folders, skinners and boots. **Technical:** Forges and grinds his own Damascus, 440C and ATS-34. **Prices:** $200 to $900. **Remarks:** Part-time maker; first knife sold in 1974. **Mark:** First initial, last name in logo and serial number.

HUTCHESON, JOHN,
SURSUM KNIFE WORKS, 1237 Brown's Ferry Rd., Chattanooga, TN 37419, Phone: 423-667-6193, sursum5071@aol.com; Web: www.sursumknife.com
  Specialties: Straight working knives, hunters. **Patterns:** Customer designs, hunting, speciality working knives. **Technical:** Grinds D2, S7, O1 and 5160, ATS-34 on request. **Prices:** $100 to $300, some to $600. **Remarks:** First knife sold 1985, also produces a mid-tech line. Doing business as Sursum Knife Works. **Mark:** Family crest boar's head over 3 arrows.

HUTCHINSON, ALAN,
315 Scenic Hill Road, Conway, AR 72034, Phone: 501-470-9653, mama_wolfie@yahoo.com
  Specialties: Bowie knives, fighters and working/hunter knives. **Technical:** Forges 10 series carbon steels as well as 5160 and 01. **Prices:** Range from $150 and up. **Remarks:** Prefers natural handle materials, full-time maker, first forged blade in 1970. **Mark:** Last name.

HYTOVICK, JOE "HY",
14872 SW 111th St, Dunnellon, FL 34432, Phone: 800-749-5339, Fax: 352-489-3732, hyclassknives@aol.com
  Specialties: Straight, folder and miniature. **Technical:** Blades from Wootz, Damascus and Alloy steel. **Prices:** To $5000. **Mark:** HY.

I

IAMES, GARY,
PO Box 8493, South Lake, Tahoe, CA 96158, Phone: 530-541-2250, iames@charter.net
  Specialties: Working and fancy straight knives and folders. **Patterns:** Bowies, hunters, wedding sets and liner locking folders. **Technical:** Grinds 440C, ATS-34, forges 5160 and 1080, makes Damascus. **Prices:** $300 and up. **Mark:** Initials and last name, city or last name.

IKOMA, FLAVIO,
R Manoel Rainho Teixeira 108-Pres, Prudonte SP19031-220, BRAZIL, Phone: 0182-22-0115, fikoma@itelesonica.com.br
  Specialties: Tactical fixed blade knives, LinerLock® folders and balisongs. **Patterns:** Utility and defense tactical knives built with hi-tech materials. **Technical:** Grinds S30V and Damasteel. **Prices:** $500 to $1000. **Mark:** Ikoma hand made beside Samurai

IMBODEN II, HOWARD L.,
620 Deauville Dr, Dayton, OH 45429, Phone: 513-439-1536
  Specialties: One-of-a-kind hunting, flint, steel and art knives. **Technical:** Forges and grinds stainless, high-carbon and Damascus. Uses obsidian, cast sterling silver, 14K and 18K gold guards. Carves ivory animals and more. **Prices:** $65 to $25,000. **Remarks:** Full-time maker; first knife sold in 1986. Doing business as Hill Originals. **Mark:** First and last initials, II.

IMEL, BILLY MACE,
1616 Bundy Ave, New Castle, IN 47362, Phone: 765-529-1651
  Specialties: High-art working knives, period pieces and personal cutlery. **Patterns:** Daggers, fighters, hunters; locking folders and slip-joints with interframes. **Technical:** Grinds D2, 440C and 154CM. **Prices:** $300 to $2000; some to $6000. **Remarks:** Part-time maker; first knife sold in 1973. **Mark:** Name in monogram.

IRIE, MICHAEL L,
MIKE IRIE HANDCRAFT, 1606 Auburn Dr., Colorado Springs, CO 80909, Phone: 719-572-5330, mikeirie@aol.com
  Specialties: Working fixed blade knives and handcrafted blades for the do-it-yourselfer. **Patterns:** Twenty standard designs along with custom. **Technical:** Blades are ATS-34, BG-43, 440C with some outside Damascus. **Prices:** Fixed blades $95 and up, blade work $45 and up. **Remarks:** Formerly dba Wood, Irie and Co. with Barry Wood. Full-time maker since 1991. **Mark:** Name.

ISAO, OHBUCHI,
702-1 Nouso Yame-City, Fukuoka, JAPAN, Phone: 0943-23-4439, www.5d.biglobe.ne.jp/~ohisao/

ISHIHARA, HANK,
86-18 Motomachi, Sakura City, Chiba Pref., JAPAN, Phone: 043-485-3208, Fax: 043-485-3208
  Specialties: Fantasy working straight knives and folders of his design. **Patterns:** Boots, Bowies, daggers, fighters, hunters, fishing, locking folders and utility camp knives. **Technical:** Grinds ATS-34, 440C, D2, 440V, CV-134, COS25 and Damascus. Engraves. **Prices:** $250 to $1000; some to $10,000. **Remarks:** Full-time maker; first knife sold in 1987. **Mark:** HANK.

J

JACKS, JIM,
344 S. Hollenbeck Ave, Covina, CA 91723-2513, Phone: 626-331-5665
  Specialties: Working straight knives in standard patterns. **Patterns:** Bowies, hunters, fighters, fishing and camp knives, miniatures. **Technical:** Grinds Stellite 6K, 440C and ATS-34. **Prices:** Start at $100. **Remarks:** Spare-time maker; first knife sold in 1980. **Mark:** Initials in diamond logo.

JACKSON, CHARLTON R,
6811 Leyland Dr, San Antonio, TX 78239, Phone: 210-601-5112

JACKSON, DAVID,
214 Oleander Ave, Lemoore, CA 93245, Phone: 559-925-8547, jnbcrea@lemoorenet.com
  Specialties: Forged steel. **Patterns:** Hunters, camp knives, Bowies. **Prices:** $150 and up. **Mark:** G.D. Jackson - Maker - Lemoore CA.

JACKSON, JIM,
1 Jesus Hospital, High St. Bray, ENGLAND SL6 2AN, Phone: 01628-620026, jlandsejackson@btconnect.com
  Specialties: Large Bowies, concentrating on form and balance; collector quality Damascus daggers. **Patterns:** With fancy filework and engraving available. **Technical:** Forges O1, 5160 and 1084 and 15N20 Damascus. **Remarks:** Part-time maker. All knives come with a custom tooled leather swivel sheath of exotic material. No orders currently undertaken. **Mark:** Jackson England with in a circle M.S.

JACQUES, ALEX,
10 Exchange St., Apt 1, East Greenwich, RI 02818, Phone: 617-771-4441, customrazors@gmail.com Web: www.customrazors.com
  Specialties: Functional art. One of a kind, heirloom quality straight razors. **Technical:** Damascus, 01, CPM154, and various other high carbon and stainless steels using the stock removal method. **Prices:** $450 and up. **Remarks:** Slowly transitioning to full-time maker; first knife made in 2008. **Mark:** Jack-O-Lantern logo with "A. Jacques" underneath.

JAKSIK JR., MICHAEL,
427 Marschall Creek Rd, Fredericksburg, TX 78624, Phone: 830-997-1119
  Mark: MJ or M. Jaksik.

JARVIS, PAUL M,
30 Chalk St, Cambridge, MA 02139, Phone: 617-547-4355 or 617-661-3015
  Specialties: High-art knives and period pieces of his design. **Patterns:** Japanese and Mid-Eastern knives. **Technical:** Grinds Myer Damascus, ATS-34, D2 and O1. Specializes in height-relief Japanese-style carving. Works with silver, gold and gems. **Prices:** $200 to $17,000. **Remarks:** Part-time maker; first knife sold in 1978.

JEAN, GERRY,
25B Cliffside Dr, Manchester, CT 06040, Phone: 860-649-6449
  Specialties: Historic replicas. **Patterns:** Survival and camp knives. **Technical:** Grinds A2, 440C and 154CM. Handle slabs applied in unique tongue-and-groove method. **Prices:** $125 to $250; some to $1000. **Remarks:** Spare-time maker; first knife sold in 1973. **Mark:** Initials and serial number.

JEFFRIES, ROBERT W,
Route 2 Box 227, Red House, WV 25168, Phone: 304-586-9780, wvknifeman@hotmail.com; Web: www.jeffriesknieswv.tripod.com
  Specialties: Hunters, Bowies, daggers, lockback folders and LinerLock push buttons. **Patterns:** Skinning types, drop points, typical working hunters, folders one-of-a-kind. **Technical:** Grinds all types of steel. Makes his own Damascus. **Prices:** $125 to $600. Private collector pieces to $3000. **Remarks:** Starting engraving. Custom folders of his design. Part-time maker since 1988. **Mark:** Name etched or on plate pinned to blade.

JENKINS, MITCH,
194 East 500 South, Manti, Utah 84642, Phone: 435-813-2532, mitch.jenkins@gmail.com Web: MitchJenkinsKnives.com
  Specialties: Hunters, working knives. **Patterns:** Johnson and Loveless Style. Drop points, skinners and semi-skinners, Capers and utilities. **Technical:** 154CM and ATS-34. Experimenting with S30V and love working with Damascus on occasion. **Prices:** $150 and up. **Remarks:** Slowly transitioning to full-time maker; first knife made in 2008. **Mark:** Jenkins Manti, Utah and M. Jenkins, Utah.

JENSEN, JOHN LEWIS,
JENSEN KNIVES, PO Box 50041, Pasadena, CA 91116, Phone: 323-559-7454, Fax: 626-449-1148, john@jensenknives.com; Web: www.jensenknives.com
  Specialties: Designer and fabricator of modern, original one-of-a-kind, hand crafted, custom ornamental edged weaponry. Combines skill, precision, distinction and the finest materials, geared toward the discriminating art collector. **Patterns:** Folding knives and fixed blades, daggers, fighters and swords. **Technical:** High embellishment, BFA 96 Rhode Island School of Design: jewelry and metalsmithing. Grinds 440C, ATS-34, Damascus. Works with custom made Damascus to his specs. Uses gold, silver, gemstones, pearl, titanium, fossil mastodon and walrus ivories. Carving, file work, soldering, deep etches Damascus, engraving, layers, bevels, blood grooves. Also forges his own Damascus. **Prices:** Start at $10,000. **Remarks:** Available on a first come basis and via commission based on his designs. Knifemakers Guild voting member and ABS apprenticesmith and member of the Society of North American Goldsmiths. **Mark:** Maltese cross/butterfly shield.

JERNIGAN, STEVE,
3082 Tunnel Rd., Milton, FL 32571, Phone: 850-994-0802, Fax: 850-994-0802, jerniganknives@mchsi.com
Specialties: Investor-class folders and various theme pieces. **Patterns:** Array of models and sizes in side plate locking interframes and conventional liner construction. **Technical:** Grinds ATS-34, CPM-T-440V and Damascus. Inlays mokume (and minerals) in blades and sculpts marble cases. **Prices:** $650 to $1800; some to $6000. **Remarks:** Full-time maker, first knife sold in 1982. **Mark:** Last name.

JIM, KRAUSE,
3272 Hwy H, Farmington, MO 63640, Phone: 573-756-7388, james_krause@sbcglobal.net
Specialties: Folders, fixed blades, neck knives. **Patterns:** Stock removal. **Technical:** S35VN, most CPM steel, 1095, stainless and corbon Damascus from the best makers. **Remarks:** Full-time maker, first knife made in 2000. **Mark:** Krause Handmade with Christian Fish

JOBIN, JACQUES,
46 St Dominique, Levis Quebec, CANADA G6V 2M7, Phone: 418-833-0283, Fax: 418-833-8378
Specialties: Fancy and working straight knives and folders; miniatures. **Patterns:** Minis, fantasy knives, fighters and some hunters. **Technical:** ATS-34, some Damascus and titanium. Likes native snake wood. Heat-treats. **Prices:** Start at $250. **Remarks:** Full-time maker; first knife sold in 1986. **Mark:** Signature on blade.

JOEHNK, BERND,
Posadowskystrasse 22, 24148 Kiel, GERMANY, Phone: 0431-7297705, Fax: 0431-7297705
Specialties: One-of-a-kind fancy/embellished and traditional straight knives of his design and from customer drawing. **Patterns:** Daggers, fighters, hunters and letter openers. **Technical:** Grinds and file 440C, ATS-34, powder metal orgical, commercial Damascus and various stainless and corrosion-resistant steels. **Prices:** Upscale. **Remarks:** Likes filework. Leather sheaths. Offers engraving. Part-time maker; first knife sold in1990. Doing business as metal design kiel. All knives made by hand. **Mark:** From 2005 full name and city, with certificate.

JOHANNING CUSTOM KNIVES, TOM,
1735 Apex Rd, Sarasota, FL 34240 9386, Phone: 941-371-2104, Fax: 941-378-9427, Web: www.survivalknives.com
Specialties: Survival knives. **Prices:** $375 to $775.

JOHANSSON, ANDERS,
Konstvartarevagen 9, S-772 40 Grangesberg, SWEDEN, Phone: 46 240 23204, Fax: +46 21 358778, www.scrimart.u.se
Specialties: Scandinavian traditional and modern straight knives. **Patterns:** Hunters, fighters and fantasy knives. **Technical:** Grinds stainless steel and makes own Damascus. Prefers water buffalo and mammoth for handle material. **Prices:** Start at $100. **Remarks:** Spare-time maker; first knife sold in 1994. Works together with scrimshander Viveca Sahlin. **Mark:** Stylized initials.

JOHNS, ROB,
1423 S. Second, Enid, OK 73701, Phone: 405-242-2707
Specialties: Classic and fantasy straight knives of his design or to customer specs; fighters for use at Medieval fairs. **Patterns:** Bowies, daggers and swords. **Technical:** Forges and grinds 440C, D2 and 5160. Handles of nylon, walnut or wire-wrap. **Prices:** $150 to $350; some to $2500. **Remarks:** Full-time maker; first knife sold in 1980. **Mark:** Medieval Customs, initials.

JOHNSON, C E GENE,
1240 Coan Street, Chesterton, IN 46304, Phone: 219-787-8324, ddjlady55@aol.com
Specialties: Lock-back folders and springers of his design or to customer specs. **Patterns:** Hunters, Bowies, survival lock-back folders. **Technical:** Grinds D2, 440C, A18, O1, Damascus; likes filework. **Prices:** $100 to $2000. **Remarks:** Full-time maker; first knife sold in 1975. **Mark:** Gene.

JOHNSON, DAVID A,
1791 Defeated Creek Rd, Pleasant Shade, TN 37145, Phone: 615-774-3596, artsmith@mwsi.net

JOHNSON, GORDON A.,
981 New Hope Rd, Choudrant, LA 71227, Phone: 318-768-2613
Specialties: Using straight knives and folders of my design, or customers. Offering filework and hand stitched sheaths. **Patterns:** Hunters, bowies, folders and miniatures. **Technical:** Forges 5160, 1084, 52100 and my own Damascus. Some stock removal on working knives and miniatures. **Prices:** Mid range. **Remarks:** First knife sold in 1990. ABS apprentice smith. **Mark:** Interlocking initials G.J. or G. A. J.

JOHNSON, JERRY,
PO Box 491, Spring City, Utah 84662, Phone: 435-851-3604, Web: sanpetesilver.com
Specialties: Hunter, fighters, camp. **Patterns:** Multiple. **Prices:** $225 - $3000. **Mark:** Jerry E. Johnson Spring City, UT in several fonts.

JOHNSON, JERRY L,
29847 260th St, Worthington, MN 56187, Phone: 507-376-9253; Cell: 507-370-3523, Web: jljknives.com
Specialties: Straight knives, hunters, bowies, and fighting knives. **Patterns:** Drop points, trailing points, bowies, and some favorite Loveless patterns. **Technical:** Grinds ATS 34, 440C, S30V, forges own damascus, mirror finish, satin finish, file work and engraving done by self. **Prices:** $250 to $1500. **Remarks:** Part-time maker since 1991, member of knifemakers guild since 2009. **Mark:** Name over a sheep head or elk head with custom knives under the head.

JOHNSON, JOHN R,
PO Box 246, New Buffalo, PA 17069, Phone: 717-834-6265, jrj@jrjknives.com; Web: www.jrjknives.com
Specialties: Working hunting and tactical fixed blade sheath knives. **Patterns:** Hunters, tacticals, Bowies, daggers, neck knives and primitives. **Technical:** Flat, convex and hollow grinds. ATS-34, CPM154CM, L6, O1, D2, 5160, 1095 and Damascus. **Prices:** $60 to $700. **Remarks:** Full-time maker, first knife sold in 1996. Doing business as JRJ Knives. Custom sheath made by maker for every knife, **Mark:** Initials connected.

JOHNSON, JOHN R,
5535 Bob Smith Ave, Plant City, FL 33565, Phone: 813-986-4478, rottyjohn@msn.com
Specialties: Hand forged and stock removal. **Technical:** High tech. Folders. **Mark:** J.R. Johnson Plant City, FL.

JOHNSON, MIKE,
38200 Main Rd, Orient, NY 11957, Phone: 631-323-3509, mjohnsoncustomknives@hotmail.com
Specialties: Large Bowie knives and cutters, fighters and working knives to customer specs. **Technical:** Forges 5160, O1. **Prices:** $325 to $1200. **Remarks:** Full-time bladesmith. **Mark:** Johnson.

JOHNSON, R B,
Box 11, Clearwater, MN 55320, Phone: 320-558-6128, Fax: 320-558-6128, rbjohnson@mywdo.com or rb@rbjohnsonknives.com; Web: rbjohnsonknives.com
Specialties: Liner locks with titanium, mosaic Damascus. **Patterns:** LinerLock® folders, skeleton hunters, frontier Bowies. **Technical:** Damascus, mosaic Damascus, A-2, O1, 1095. **Prices:** $200 and up. **Remarks:** Full-time maker since 1973. Not accepting orders. **Mark:** R B Johnson (signature).

JOHNSON, RANDY,
2575 E Canal Dr, Turlock, CA 95380, Phone: 209-632-5401
Specialties: Folders. **Patterns:** Locking folders. **Technical:** Grinds Damascus. **Prices:** $200 to $400. **Remarks:** Spare-time maker; first knife sold in 1989. Doing business as Puedo Knifeworks. **Mark:** PUEDO.

JOHNSON, RICHARD,
W165 N10196 Wagon Trail, Germantown, WI 53022, Phone: 262-251-5772, rlj@execpc.com; Web: http://www.execpc.com/~rlj/index.html
Specialties: Custom knives and knife repair.

JOHNSON, RUFFIN,
215 LaFonda Dr, Houston, TX 77060, Phone: 281-448-4407
Specialties: Working straight knives and folders. **Patterns:** Hunters, fighters and locking folders. **Technical:** Grinds 440C and 154CM; hidden tangs and fancy handles. **Prices:** $450 to $650; some to $1350. **Remarks:** Full-time maker; first knife sold in 1972. **Mark:** Wolf head logo and signature.

JOHNSON, RYAN M,
3103 Excelsior Ave., Signal Mountain, TN 37377, Phone: 866-779-6922, rmjtactical@gmail.com Web: www.rmjforge.com www.rmjtactical.com
Specialties: Historical and Tactical Tomahawks. Some period knives and folders. **Technical:** Forges a variety of steels including own Damascus. **Prices:** $500 - $1200 **Remarks:** Full-time maker began forging in 1986. **Mark:** Sledgehammer with halo.

JOHNSON, STEVEN R,
202 E 200 N, PO Box 5, Manti, UT 84642, Phone: 435-835-7941, Fax: 435-835-7941, srj@mail.manti.com; Web: www.srjknives.com
Specialties: Investor-class working knives. **Patterns:** Hunters, fighters, boots. **Technical:** Grinds CPM 154-CM and CTS 40-CP. **Prices:** $1,500 to $20,000. **Remarks:** Full-time maker; first knife sold in 1972. Also see SR Johnson forum on www.knifenetwork.com. **Mark:** Registered trademark, including name, city, state, and optional signature mark.

JOHNSON, TOMMY,
144 Poole Rd., Troy, NC 27371, Phone: 910-975-1817, tommy@tjohnsonknives.com Web: www.tjohnsonknives.com
Specialties: Straight knives for hunting, fishing, utility, and linerlock and slip joint folders since 1982.

JOHNSON, WM. C. "BILL",
225 Fairfield Pike, Enon, OH 45323, Phone: 937-864-7802, wjohnson64@woh.RR.com
Patterns: From hunters to art knives as well as custom canes, some with blades. **Technical:** Stock removal method utilizing 440C, ATS34, 154CPM, and custom Damascus. **Prices:** $175 to over $2500, depending on design, materials, and embellishments. **Remarks:** Full-time maker. First knife made in 1978. Member of the Knifemakers Guild since 1982. **Mark:** Crescent shaped WM. C. "BILL" JOHNSON, ENON OHIO. Also uses an engraved or electro signature on some art knives and on Damascus blades.

JOHNSTON, DR. ROBT,
PO Box 9887 1 Lomb Mem Dr, Rochester, NY 14623

JOKERST, CHARLES,
9312 Spaulding, Omaha, NE 68134, Phone: 402-571-2536
Specialties: Working knives in standard patterns. **Patterns:** Hunters, fighters and pocketknives. **Technical:** Grinds 440C, ATS-34. **Prices:** $90 to $170.

Remarks: Spare-time maker; first knife sold in 1984. **Mark:** Early work marked RCJ; current work marked with last name and city.

JONES, BARRY M AND PHILLIP G,
221 North Ave, Danville, VA 24540, Phone: 804-793-5282
Specialties: Working and using straight knives and folders of their design and to customer specs; combat and self-defense knives. **Patterns:** Bowies, fighters, daggers, swords, hunters and LinerLock® folders. **Technical:** Grinds 440C, ATS-34 and D2; flat-grinds only. All blades hand polished. **Prices:** $100 to $1000, some higher. **Remarks:** Part-time makers; first knife sold in 1989. **Mark:** Jones Knives, city, state.

JONES, CURTIS J,
210 Springfield Ave, Washington, PA 15301-5244, Phone: 724-225-8829
Specialties: Big Bowies, daggers, his own style of hunters. **Patterns:** Bowies, daggers, hunters, swords, boots and miniatures. **Technical:** Grinds 440C, ATS-34 and D2. Fitted guards only; does not solder. Heat-treats. Custom sheaths: hand-tooled and stitched. **Prices:** $125 to $1500; some to $3000. **Remarks:** Full-time maker; first knife sold in 1975. Mail orders accepted. **Mark:** Stylized initials on either side of three triangles interconnected.

JONES, ENOCH,
7278 Moss Ln, Warrenton, VA 20187, Phone: 540-341-0292
Specialties: Fancy working straight knives. **Patterns:** Hunters, fighters, boots and Bowies. **Technical:** Forges and grinds O1, W2, 440C and Damascus. **Prices:** $100 to $350; some to $1000. **Remarks:** Part-time maker; first knife sold in 1982. **Mark:** First name.

JONES, FRANKLIN (FRANK) W,
6030 Old Dominion Rd, Columbus, GA 31909, Phone: 706-563-6051, frankscuba@bellsouth.net
Specialties: Traditional/working/tactical/period straight knives of his or your design. **Patterns:** Hunters, skinners, utility/camp, fighters, kitchen, neck knives, Harley chains. **Technical:** Forges using 5160, O1, 52100, 1084 1095 and Damascus. Also stock removal of stainless steel. **Prices:** $150 to $1000. **Remarks:** Full-time, American Bladesmith Society Journeyman Smith. **Mark:** F.W. Jones, Columbus, GA.

JONES, JACK P.,
17670 Hwy. 2 East, Ripley, MS 38663, Phone: 662-837-3882, jacjones@ripleycable.net
Specialties: Working knives in classic design. **Patterns:** Hunters, fighters, and Bowies. **Technical:** Grinds ATS-34, D2, A2, CPM-154 CM. **Prices:** $200 and up. **Remarks:** Full-time maker since retirement in 2005, first knife sold in 1976. **Mark:** J.P. Jones, Ripley, MS.

JONES, JOHN A,
779 SW 131 Hwy, Holden, MO 64040, Phone: 816-682-0238
Specialties: Working, using knives. Hunters, skinners and fighters. **Technical:** Grinds D2, O1, 440C, 1095. Prefers forging; creates own Damascus. File working on most blades. **Prices:** $50 to $500. **Remarks:** Part-time maker; first knife sold in 1996. Doing business as Old John Knives. **Mark:** OLD JOHN and serial number.

JONES, ROGER MUDBONE,
GREENMAN WORKSHOP, 320 Prussia Rd, Waverly, OH 45690, Phone: 740-739-4562, greenmanworkshop@yahoo.com
Specialties: Working in cutlery to suit working woodsman and fine collector. **Patterns:** Bowies, hunters, folders, hatchets in both period and modern style, scale miniatures a specialty. **Technical:** All cutlery hand forged to shape with traditional methods; multiple quench and draws, limited Damascus production hand carves wildlife and historic themes in stag/antler/ivory, full line of functional and high art leather. All work sole authorship. **Prices:** $50 to $5000 **Remarks:** Full-time maker/first knife sold in 1979. **Mark:** Stamped R. Jones hand made or hand engraved sig. W/Bowie knife mark.

JORGENSEN, CARSON,
1805 W Hwy 116, Mt Pleasant, UT 84647, tcjorgensenknife@gmail.com; Web: tcjknives.com
Specialties: Stock removal, Loveless Johnson and young styles. **Prices:** Most $100 to $800.

K

K B S, KNIVES,
RSD 181, North Castlemaine, Vic 3450, AUSTRALIA, Phone: 0011 61 3 54 705864, Fax: 0011 61 3 54 706233
Specialties: Bowies, daggers and miniatures. **Patterns:** Art daggers, traditional Bowies, fancy folders and miniatures. **Technical:** Hollow or flat grind, most steels. **Prices:** $200 to $600+. **Remarks:** Full-time maker; first knife sold in 1983. **Mark:** Initials and address in Southern Cross motif.

KACZOR, TOM,
375 Wharncliffe Rd N, Upper London, Ont., CANADA N6G 1E4, Phone: 519-645-7640

KAGAWA, KOICHI,
1556 Horiyamashita, Hatano-Shi, Kanagawa, JAPAN
Specialties: Fancy high-tech straight knives and folders to customer specs. **Patterns:** Hunters, locking folders and slip-joints. **Technical:** Uses 440C and ATS-34. **Prices:** $500 to $2000; some to $20,000. **Remarks:** Part-time maker; first knife sold in 1986. **Mark:** First initial, last name-YOKOHAMA.

KAIN, CHARLES,
KAIN DESIGNS, 1736 E. Maynard Dr., Indianapolis, IN 46227, Phone: 317-781-9549, Fax: 317-781-8521, charles@kaincustomknives.com; Web: www.kaincustomknives.com
Specialties: Unique Damascus art folders. **Patterns:** Any. **Technical:** Specialized & patented mechanisms. **Remarks:** Unique knife & knife mechanism design. **Mark:** Kain and Signet stamp for unique pieces.

KAJIN, AL,
PO Box 1047, 342 South 6th Ave, Forsyth, MT 59327, Phone: 406-346-2442, kajinknives@cablemt.net
Specialties: Utility/working knives, hunters, kitchen cutlery. Produces own Damascus steel from 15N20 and 1084 and cable. Forges 52100, 5160, 1084, 15N20 and O1. Stock removal ATS-34, D2, O1, and L6. **Patterns:** All types, especially like to work with customer on their designs. **Technical:** Maker since 1989. ABS member since 1995. Does own differential heat treating, cryogenic soaking when appropriate. Does all leather work. **Prices:** Stock removal starts at $250. Forged blades and Damascus starts at $300. Kitchen cutlery starts at $100. **Remarks:** Likes to use exotic woods. **Mark:** Interlocked AK on forged blades, etched stylized Kajin in outline of Montana on stock removal knives.

KANKI, IWAO,
691-2 Tenjincho, Ono-City, Hyogo, JAPAN 675-1316, Phone: 07948-3-2555, Web: www.chiyozurusadahide.jp
Specialties: Plane, knife. **Prices:** Not determined yet. **Remarks:** Masters of traditional crafts designated by the Minister of International Trade and Industry (Japan). **Mark:** Chiyozuru Sadahide.

KANSEI, MATSUNO,
109-8 Uenomachi Nishikaiden, Gitu-city, JAPAN 501-1168, Phone: 81-58-234-8643
Specialties: Folders of original design. **Patterns:** LinerLock® folder. **Technical:** Grinds VG-10, Damascus. **Prices:** $350 to $2000. **Remarks:** Full-time maker. First knife sold in 1993. **Mark:** Name.

KANTER, MICHAEL,
ADAM MICHAEL KNIVES, 14550 West Honey Ln., New Berlin, WI 53151, Phone: 262-860-1136, mike@adammichaelknives.com; Web: www.adammichaelknives.com
Specialties: Fixed blades and folders. **Patterns:** Drop point hunters, Bowies and fighters. **Technical:** Jerry Rados Damascus, BG42, CPM, S60V and S30V. **Prices:** $375 and up. **Remarks:** Ivory, mammoth ivory, stabilized woods, and pearl handles. **Mark:** Engraved Adam Michael.

KARP, BOB,
PO Box 47304, Phoenix, AZ 85068, Phone: 602 870-1234
602 870-1234, Fax: 602-331-0283
Remarks: Bob Karp "Master of the Blade."

KATO, SHINICHI,
Rainbow Amalke 402, Ohoragnchi, Nakashidami, Moriyama-ku Nagoya, JAPAN 463-0002, Phone: 81-52-736-6032, skato-402@u0l.gate01.com
Specialties: Flat grind and hand finish. **Patterns:** Bowie, fighter. Hunting and folding knives. **Technical:** Hand forged, flat grind. **Prices:** $100 to $2000. **Remarks:** Part-time maker. **Mark:** Name.

KATSUMARO, SHISHIDO,
2-6-11 Kamiseno Aki-ku, Hiroshima, JAPAN, Phone: 090-3634-9054, Fax: 082-227-4438, shishido@d8.dion.ne.jp

KAUFFMAN, DAVE,
4 Clark Creek Loop, Montana City, MT 59634, Phone: 406-442-9328
Specialties: Field grade and exhibition grade hunting knives and ultra light folders. **Patterns:** Fighters, Bowies and drop-point hunters. **Technical:** S30V and SS Damascus. **Prices:** $155 to $1200. **Remarks:** Full-time maker; first knife sold in 1989. On the cover of *Knives '94*. **Mark:** First and last name, city and state.

KAWASAKI, AKIHISA,
11-8-9 Chome Minamiamachi, Suzurandai Kita-Ku, Kobe, JAPAN, Phone: 078-593-0418, Fax: 078-593-0418
Specialties: Working/using knives of his design. **Patterns:** Hunters, kit camp knives. **Technical:** Forges and grinds Molybdenum Panadium. Grinds ATS-34 and stainless steel. Uses Chinese Quince wood, desert ironwood and cow leather. **Prices:** $300 to $800; some to $1000. **Remarks:** Full-time maker. **Mark:** A.K.

KAY, J WALLACE,
332 Slab Bridge Rd, Liberty, SC 29657

KAZSUK, DAVID,
PO Box 39, Perris, CA 92572-0039, Phone: 909-780-2288, ddkaz@hotmail.com
Specialties: Hand forged. **Prices:** $150+. **Mark:** Last name.

KEARNEY, JAROD,
1505 Parkersburg Turnpike, Swoope, VA 24479, jarodkearney@gmail.com Web: www.jarodkearney.com
Patterns: Bowies, skinners, hunters, Japanese blades, Sgian Dubhs

KEESLAR, JOSEPH F,
391 Radio Rd, Almo, KY 42020, Phone: 270-753-7919, Fax: 270-753-7919, sjkees@apex.net
Specialties: Classic and contemporary Bowies, combat, hunters, daggers and folders. **Patterns:** Decorative filework, engraving and custom leather sheaths available. **Technical:** Forges 5160, 52100 and his own Damascus steel. **Prices:** $300 to $3000. **Remarks:** Full-time maker; first knife sold in 1976. ABS Master Smith. **Mark:** First and middle initials, last name in hammer, knife and anvil logo, M.S.

KEESLAR, STEVEN C,
115 Lane 216 Hamilton Lake, Hamilton, IN 46742, Phone: 260-488-3161, sskeeslar@hotmail.com
Specialties: Traditional working/using straight knives of his design and to customer specs. **Patterns:** Bowies, hunters, utility/camp knives. **Technical:** Forges 5160, files 52100 Damascus. **Prices:** $100 to $600; some to $1500. **Remarks:** Part-time maker; first knife sold in 1976. ABS member. **Mark:** Fox head in flames over Steven C. Keeslar.

KEETON, WILLIAM L,
6095 Rehobeth Rd SE, Laconia, IN 47135-9550, Phone: 812-969-2836, wlkeeton@hughes.net; Web: www.keetoncustomknives.com
Specialties: Plain and fancy working knives. **Patterns:** Hunters and fighters; locking folders and slip-joints. Names patterns after Kentucky Derby winners. **Technical:** Grinds any of the popular alloy steels. **Prices:** $185 to $8000. **Remarks:** Full-time maker; first knife sold in 1971. **Mark:** Logo of key.

KEHIAYAN, ALFREDO,
Cuzco 1455 Ing. Maschwitz, CP B1623GXU Buenos Aires, ARGENTINA, Phone: 54-03488-442212, Fax: 54-077-75-4493-5359, alfredo@kehiayan.com.ar; Web: www.kehiayan.com.ar
Specialties: Functional straight knives. **Patterns:** Utility knives, skinners, hunters and boots. **Technical:** Forges and grinds SAE 52.100, SAE 6180, SAE 9260, SAE 5160, 440C and ATS-34, titanium with nitride. All blades mirror-polished; makes leather sheath and wood cases. **Prices:** $70 to $800; some to $6000. **Remarks:** Full-time maker; first knife sold in 1983. Some knives are satin finish (utility knives). **Mark:** Name.

KEISUKE, GOTOH,
105 Cosumo-City, Otozu 202 Ohita-city, Ohita, JAPAN, Phone: 097-523-0750, k-u-an@ki.rim.or.jp

KELLER, BILL,
12211 Las Nubes, San Antonio, TX 78233, Phone: 210-653-6609
Specialties: Primarily folders, some fixed blades. **Patterns:** Autos, liner locks and hunters. **Technical:** Grinds stainless and Damascus. **Prices:** $400 to $1000, some to $4000. **Remarks:** Part-time maker, first knife sold 1995. **Mark:** Last name inside outline of Alamo.

KELLEY, GARY,
17485 SW Pheasant Lane, Aloha, OR 97006, Phone: 503-649-7867, garykelley@thebladmaker.com; Web: wwwthebladmaker.com
Specialties: Primitive knives and blades. **Patterns:** Fur trade era rifleman's knives, tomahawks, and hunting knives. **Technical:** Hand-forges and precision investment casts. **Prices:** $35 to $125. **Remarks:** Family business. Doing business as The Blademaker. **Mark:** Fir tree logo.

KELLY, DAVE,
865 S. Shenandoah St., Los Angeles, CA 90035, Phone: 310-657-7121, dakcon@sbcglobal.net
Specialties: Collector and user one-of-a-kind (his design) fixed blades, liner lock folders, and leather sheaths. **Patterns:** Utility and hunting fixed blade knives with hand-sewn leather sheaths, Gentleman liner lock folders. **Technical:** Grinds carbon steels, hollow, convex, and flat. Offers clay differentially hardened blades, etched and polished. Uses Sambar stag, mammoth ivory, and high-grade burl woods. Hand-sewn leather sheaths for fixed blades and leather pouch sheaths for folders. **Prices:** $250 to $750, some higher. **Remarks:** Full-time maker, first knife made in 2003. **Mark:** First initial, last name with large K.

KELLY, STEVEN,
11407 Spotted Fawn Ln., Bigfork, MT 59911, Phone: 406-837-1489, www.skknives.com
Technical: Damascus from 1084 or 1080 and 15n20. 52100.

KELSEY, NATE,
3401 Cherry St, Anchorage, AK 99504, Phone: 907-360-4469, edgealaska@mac.com; Web: www.edgealaska.com
Specialties: Hand forges or stock removal traditional working knives of own or customer design. Forges own Damascus, makes custom leather sheaths, does fine engraving and scrimshaw. **Technical:** Forges 52100, 1084/15N20, 5160. Grinds ATS-34, 154CM. Prefers natural handle materials. **Prices:** $300 to $1500. **Remarks:** Part-time maker since 1990. Member ABS, Arkansas Knifemakers Assoc. **Mark:** Name and city.

KELSO, JIM,
577 Collar Hill Rd, Worcester, VT 05682, Phone: 802-229-4254, Fax: 802-229-0595, kelsonmaker@gmail.com; Web:www.jimkelso.com
Specialties: Fancy high-art straight knives and folders that mix Eastern and Western influences. Only uses own designs. **Patterns:** Daggers, swords and locking folders. **Technical:** Grinds only custom Damascus. Works with top Damascus bladesmiths. **Prices:** $6000 to $20,000 . **Remarks:** Full-time maker; first knife sold in 1980. **Mark:** Stylized initials.

KEMP, LAWRENCE,
8503 Water Tower Rd, Ooltewah, TN 37363, Phone: 423-344-2357, larry@kempknives.com Web: www.kempknives.com
Specialties: Bowies, hunters and working knives. **Patterns:** Bowies, camp knives, hunters and skinners. **Technical:** Forges carbon steel, and his own Damascus. **Prices:** $250 to $1500. **Remarks:** Part-time maker, first knife sold in 1991. ABS Journeyman Smith since 2006. **Mark:** L.A. Kemp.

KENNEDY JR., BILL,
PO Box 850431, Yukon, OK 73085, Phone: 405-354-9150
Specialties: Working straight knives and folders. **Patterns:** Hunters, minis, fishing, and pocket knives. **Technical:** Grinds D2, 440C, ATS-34, BG42. **Prices:** $110 and up. **Remarks:** Part-time maker; first knife sold in 1980. **Mark:** Last name and year made.

KERANEN, PAUL,
4122 S. E. Shiloh Ct., Tacumseh, KS 66542, Phone: 785-220-2141, paul@pkknives.com Web: www.pkknives.com
Specialties: Specializes in Japanese style knives and swords. Most clay tempered with hamon. **Patterns:** Does bowies, fighters and hunters. **Technical:** Forges and grinds carbons steel only. Make my own Damascus. **Prices:** $75 to $800. **Mark:** PK etched.

KERN, R W,
20824 Texas Trail W, San Antonio, TX 78257-1602, Phone: 210-698-2549, rkern@ev1.net
Specialties: Damascus, straight and folders. **Patterns:** Hunters, Bowies and folders. **Technical:** Grinds ATS-34, 440C and BG42. Forges own Damascus. **Prices:** $200 and up. **Remarks:** First knives 1980; retired; work as time permits. Member ABS, Texas Knifemaker and Collectors Association. **Mark:** Outline of Alamo with kern over outline.

KEYES, DAN,
6688 King St, Chino, CA 91710, Phone: 909-628-8329

KEYES, GEOFF P.,
13027 Odell Rd NE, Duvall, WA 98019, Phone: 425-844-0758, 5ef@polarisfarm.com; Web: www5elementsforge.com
Specialties: Working grade fixed blades, 19th century style gents knives. **Patterns:** Fixed blades, your design or mine. **Technical:** Hnad-forged 5160, 1084, and own Damascus. **Prices:** $200 and up. **Remarks:** Geoff Keyes DBA 5 Elements Forge, ABS Journeyman Smith. **Mark:** Early mark KEYES etched in script. New mark as of 2009: pressed GPKeyes.

KHALSA, JOT SINGH,
368 Village St, Millis, MA 02054, Phone: 508-376-8162, Fax: 508-532-0517, jotkhalsa@comcast.net; Web: www.khalsakirpans.com, www.lifeknives.com, and www.thekhalsaraj.com
Specialties: Liner locks, one-of-a-kind daggers, swords, and kirpans (Sikh daggers) all original designs. **Technical:** Forges own Damascus, uses others high quality Damascus including stainless, and grinds stainless steels. Uses natural handle materials frequently unusual minerals. Pieces are frequently engraved and more recently carved. **Prices:** Start at $700.

KHARLAMOV, YURI,
Oboronnay 46, 2, Tula, 300007, RUSSIA
Specialties: Classic, fancy and traditional knives of his design. **Patterns:** Daggers and hunters. **Technical:** Forges only Damascus with nickel. Uses natural handle materials; engraves on metal, carves on nut-tree; silver and pearl inlays. **Prices:** $600 to $2380; some to $4000. **Remarks:** Full-time maker; first knife sold in 1988. **Mark:** Initials.

KI, SHIVA,
5222 Ritterman Ave, Baton Rouge, LA 70805, Phone: 225-356-7274, shivakicustomknives@netzero.net; Web: www.shivakicustomknives.com
Specialties: Working straight knives and folders. **Patterns:** Emphasis on personal defense knives, martial arts weapons. **Technical:** Forges and grinds; makes own Damascus; prefers natural handle materials. **Prices:** $550 to $10,000. **Remarks:** Full-time maker; first knife sold in 1981. **Mark:** Name with logo.

KIEFER, TONY,
112 Chateaugay Dr, Pataskala, OH 43062, Phone: 740-927-6910
Specialties: Traditional working and using straight knives in standard patterns. **Patterns:** Bowies, fighters and hunters. **Technical:** Grinds 440C and D2; forges D2. Flat-grinds Bowies; hollow-grinds drop-point and trailing-point hunters. **Prices:** $110 to $300; some to $200. **Remarks:** Spare-time maker; first knife sold in 1988. **Mark:** Last name.

KILBY, KEITH,
1902 29th St, Cody, WY 82414, Phone: 307-587-2732
Specialties: Works with all designs. **Patterns:** Mostly Bowies, camp knives and hunters of his design. **Technical:** Forges 52100, 5160, 1095, Damascus and mosaic Damascus. **Prices:** $250 to $3500. **Remarks:** Part-time maker; first knife sold in 1974. Doing business as Foxwood Forge. **Mark:** Name.

KILEY, MIKE AND JANDY,
ROCKING K KNIVES, 1325 Florida, Chino Valley, AZ 86323, Phone: 928-910-2647
Specialties: Period knives for cowboy action shooters and mountain men. **Patterns:** Bowies, drop-point hunters, skinners, sheepsfoot blades and spear points. **Technical:** Steels are 1095, 0-1, Damascus and others upon request. Handles include all types of wood, with cocobolo, ironwood, rosewood, maple and bacote being favorites as well as buffalo horn, stag, elk antler, mammoth ivory, giraffe boon, sheep horn and camel bone. **Prices:** $100 to $500 depending on style and materials. Hand-tooled leather sheaths by Jan and Mike. **Mark:** Stylized K on one side; Kiley on the other.

KILPATRICK, CHRISTIAN A,
6925 Mitchell Ct, Citrus Hieghts, CA 95610, Phone: 916-729-0733, crimsonkil@gmail.com; Web:www.crimsonknives.com
Specialties: All forged weapons (no firearms) from ancient to modern. All

blades produced are first and foremost useable tools, and secondly but no less importantly, artistic expressions. **Patterns:** Hunters, bowies, daggers, swords, axes, spears, boot knives, bird knives, ethnic blades and historical reproductions. Customer designs welcome. **Technical:** Forges and grinds, makes own Damascus. Does file work. **Prices:** $125 to $3200. **Remarks:** 26 year part time maker. First knife sold in 2002.

KIMBERLEY, RICHARD L.,
86-B Arroyo Hondo Rd, Santa Fe, NM 87508, Phone: 505-820-2727
    Specialties: Fixed-blade and period knives. **Technical:** O1, 52100, 9260 steels. **Remarks:** Member ABS. Marketed under "Kimberleys of Santa Fe." **Mark:** "By D. KIMBERLEY SANTA FE NM."

KIMSEY, KEVIN,
198 Cass White Rd. NW, Cartersville, GA 30121, Phone: 770-387-0779 and 770-655-8879
    Specialties: Tactical fixed blades and folders. **Patterns:** Fighters, folders, hunters and utility knives. **Technical:** Grinds 440C, ATS-34 and D2 carbon. **Prices:** $100 to $400; some to $600. **Remarks:** Three-time *Blade* magazine award winner, knifemaker since 1983. **Mark:** Rafter and stylized KK.

KING, BILL,
14830 Shaw Rd, Tampa, FL 33625, Phone: 813-961-3455, billkingknives@yahoo.com
    Specialties: Folders, lockbacks, liner locks, automatics and stud openers. **Patterns:** Wide varieties; folders. **Technical:** ATS-34 and some Damascus; single and double grinds. Offers filework and jewel embellishment; nickel-silver Damascus and mokume bolsters. **Prices:** $150 to $475; some to $850. **Remarks:** Full-time maker; first knife sold in 1976. All titanium fitting on liner-locks; screw or rivet construction on lock-backs. **Mark:** Last name in crown.

KING, FRED,
430 Grassdale Rd, Cartersville, GA 30120, Phone: 770-382-8478, Web: http://www.fking83264@aol.com
    Specialties: Fancy and embellished working straight knives and folders. **Patterns:** Hunters, Bowies and fighters. **Technical:** Grinds ATS-34 and D2; forges 5160 and Damascus. Offers filework. **Prices:** $100 to $3500. **Remarks:** Spare-time maker; first knife sold in 1984. **Mark:** Kings Edge.

KING, JASON M,
PO Box 151, Eskridge, KS 66423, Phone: 785-449-2638, jason@jasonkingknives.com; Web: www.jasonmkingknives.com
    Specialties: Working and using straight knives of his design and sometimes to customer specs. Some slip joint and lockback folders. **Patterns:** Hunters, Bowies, tacticals, fighters; some miniatures. **Technical:** Grinds D2, 440C and other Damascus. **Prices:** $75 to $200; some up to $500. **Remarks:** First knife sold in 1998. Likes to use height quality stabilized wood. **Mark:** JMK.

KING JR., HARVEY G,
32170 Hwy K4, Alta Vista, KS 66834, Phone: 785-499-5207, Web: www.harveykingknives.com
    Specialties: Traditional working and using straight knives of his design and to customer specs. **Patterns:** Hunters, Bowies and fillet knives. **Technical:** Grinds O1, A2 and D2. Prefers natural handle materials; offers leatherwork. **Prices:** Start at $125. **Remarks:** Full-time maker; first knife sold in 1988. **Mark:** Name, city, state, and serial number.

KINKER, MIKE,
8755 E County Rd 50 N, Greensburg, IN 47240, Phone: 812-663-5277, kinkercustomknives@gmail.com
    Specialties: Working/using knives, straight knives. Starting to make folders. Your design. **Patterns:** Boots, daggers, hunters, skinners, hatchets. **Technical:** Grind 440C and ATS-34, others if required. Damascus, dovetail bolsters, jeweled blade. **Prices:** $125 to 375; some to $1000. **Remarks:** Part-time maker; first knife sold in 1991. Doing business as Kinker Custom Knives. **Mark:** Kinker

KINNIKIN, TODD,
EUREKA FORGE, 7 Capper Dr., Pacific, MO 63069-3603, Phone: 314-938-6248
    Specialties: Mosaic Damascus. **Patterns:** Hunters, fighters, folders and automatics. **Technical:** Forges own mosaic Damascus with tool steel Damascus edge. Prefers natural, fossil and artifact handle materials. **Prices:** $1200 to $2400. **Remarks:** Full-time maker; first knife sold in 1994. **Mark:** Initials connected.

KIOUS, JOE,
1015 Ridge Pointe Rd, Kerrville, TX 78028, Phone: 830-367-2277, kious@hctc.net
    Specialties: Investment-quality interframe and bolstered folders. **Patterns:** Folder specialist, all types. **Technical:** Both stainless and non-stainless Damascus. Also uses CPM 154CM, M4, and CPM D2. **Prices:** $1300 to $5000; some to $10,000. **Remarks:** Full-time maker; first knife sold in 1969. **Mark:** Last name, city and state or last name only.

KIRK, RAY,
PO Box 1445, Tahlequah, OK 74465, Phone: 918-456-1519, ray@rakerknives.com; Web: www.rakerknives.com
    Specialties: Folders, skinners fighters, and Bowies. **Patterns:** Neck knives and small hunters and skinners. **Technical:** Forges all knives from 52100 and own Damascus. **Prices:** $65 to $3000. **Remarks:** Started forging in 1989; makes own Damascus. Does custom steel rolling. Has some 52100 and Damascus in custom flat bar 52100 for sale **Mark:** Stamped "Raker" on blade.

KITSMILLER, JERRY,
67277 Las Vegas Dr, Montrose, CO 81401, Phone: 970-249-4290
    Specialties: Working straight knives in standard patterns. **Patterns:** Hunters, boots. **Technical:** Grinds ATS-34 and 440C only. **Prices:** $75 to $200; some to $300. **Remarks:** Spare-time maker; first knife sold in 1984. **Mark:** JandS Knives.

KLAASEE, TINUS,
PO Box 10221, George 6530, SOUTH AFRICA
    Specialties: Hunters, skinners and utility knives. **Patterns:** Uses own designs and client specs. **Technical:** N690 stainless steel 440C Damascus. **Prices:** $700 and up. **Remarks:** Use only indigenous materials. Hardwood, horns and ivory. Makes his own sheaths and boxes. **Mark:** Initials and sur name over warthog.

KNAPP, MARK,
Mark Knapp Custom Knives, 1971 Fox Ave, Fairbanks, AK 99701, Phone: 907-452-7477, info@markknappcustomknives.com; Web: www.markknappcustomknives.com
    Specialties: Mosaic handles of exotic natural materials from Alaska and around the world. Folders, fixed blades, full and hidden tangs. **Patterns:** Folders, hunters, skinners, and camp knives. **Technical:** Forges own Damascus, uses both forging and stock removal with ATS-34, 154CM, stainless Damascus, carbon steel and carbon Damascus. **Prices:** $800-$3000. **Remarks:** Full time maker, sold first knife in 2000. **Mark:** Mark Knapp Custom Knives Fairbanks, AK.

KNAPTON, CHRIS C.,
76 Summerland Dr., Henderson, Auckland, New Zealand, Phone: 098-353-598, knappo@xtra.co.nz
    Specialties: Working and fancy straight knives of his own design. **Patterns:** Utility, hunters, skinners, Persian, all full tang. **Technical:** Predominate knife steel 12C27, also in use CPM154. High class natural and synthetic handle materials used. All blades made via the stock removal method and flat ground. **Prices:** $180 - $450; some higher. **Remarks:** Part-time maker. **Mark:** Stylized letter K and country name.

KNICKMEYER, HANK,
6300 Crosscreek, Cedar Hill, MO 63016, Phone: 636-285-3210
    Specialties: Complex mosaic Damascus constructions. **Patterns:** Fixed blades, swords, folders and automatics. **Technical:** Mosaic Damascus with all tool steel Damascus edges. **Prices:** $500 to $2000; some $3000 and higher. **Remarks:** Part-time maker; first knife sold in 1989. Doing business as Dutch Creek Forge and Foundry. **Mark:** Initials connected.

KNICKMEYER, KURT,
6344 Crosscreek, Cedar Hill, MO 63016, Phone: 314-274-0481

KNIGHT, JASON,
110 Paradise Pond Ln, Harleyville, SC 29448, Phone: 843-452-1163, jasonknightknives.com
    Specialties: Bowies. **Patterns:** Bowies and anything from history or his own design. **Technical:** 1084, 5160, O1, 52102, Damascus/forged blades. **Prices:** $200 and up. **Remarks:** Bladesmith. **Mark:** KNIGHT.

KNIPSCHIELD, TERRY,
808 12th Ave NE, Rochester, MN 55906, Phone: 507-288-7829, terry@knipknives.com; Web: www.knipknives.com
    Specialties: Folders and fixed blades and leather working knives. **Patterns:** Variations of traditional patterns and his own new designs. **Technical:** Stock removal. Grinds CPM-154CM, ATS-34, stainless Damascus, 01.**Prices:** $60 to $1200 and higher for upscale folders. **Mark:** Etchd logo on blade, KNIP with shield image.

KNIPSTEIN, R C (JOE),
731 N Fielder, Arlington, TX 76012, Phone: 817-265-0573;817-265-2021, Fax: 817-265-3410
    Specialties: Traditional pattern folders along with custom designs. **Patterns:** Hunters, Bowies, folders, fighters, utility knives. **Technical:** Grinds 440C, D2, 154CM and ATS-34. Natural handle materials and full tangs are standard. **Prices:** Start at $300. **Remarks:** Part-time maker; first knife sold in 1989. **Mark:** Last name.

KNOTT, STEVE,
KNOTT KNIVES, 203 Wild Rose, Guyton, GA 31312, Phone: 912-772-7655
    Technical: Uses ATS-34/440C and some commercial Damascus, single and double grinds with mirror or satin finishes. **Patterns:** Hunters, boot knives, Bowies, and tantos, slip joint and lock-back folders. Uses a wide variety of handle materials to include ironwood, coca-bola and colored stabilized wood, also horn, bone and ivory upon customer request. **Remarks:** First knife sold in 1991. Part-time maker.

KNOWLES, SHAWN,
750 Townsbury Rd, Great Meadows, NJ 07838, Phone: 973-670-3307, skcustomknives@gmail.com Web: shawnknowlescustomknives.com

KNUTH, JOSEPH E,
3307 Lookout Dr, Rockford, IL 61109, Phone: 815-874-9597
    Specialties: High-art working straight knives of his design or to customer specs. **Patterns:** Daggers, fighters and swords. **Technical:** Grinds 440C, ATS-34 and D2. **Prices:** $150 to $1500; some to $15,000. **Remarks:** Full-time maker; first knife sold in 1989. **Mark:** Initials on bolster face.

KOHLS, JERRY,
N4725 Oak Rd, Princeton, WI 54968, Phone: 920-295-3648
    Specialties: Working knives and period pieces. **Patterns:** Hunters-boots and Bowies, your designs or his. **Technical:** Grinds, ATS-34 440c 154CM and 1095 and commercial Damascus. **Remarks:** Part-time maker. **Mark:** Last name.

KOJETIN, W,
20 Bapaume Rd Delville, Germiston 1401, SOUTH AFRICA, Phone: 27118733305/ mobile 27836256208
    Specialties: High-art and working straight knives of all designs. **Patterns:** Daggers, hunters and his own Man hunter Bowie. **Technical:** Grinds D2 and

ATS-34; forges and grinds 440B/C. Offers "wrap-around" pava and abalone handles, scrolled wood or ivory, stacked filework and setting of faceted semi-precious stones. **Prices:** $185 to $600; some to $11,000. **Remarks:** Spare-time maker; first knife sold in 1962. **Mark:** Billy K.

KOLITZ, ROBERT,
W9342 Canary Rd, Beaver Dam, WI 53916, Phone: 920-887-1287
   Specialties: Working straight knives to customer specs. **Patterns:** Bowies, hunters, bird and trout knives, boots. **Technical:** Grinds O1, 440C; commercial Damascus. **Prices:** $50 to $100; some to $500. **Remarks:** Spare-time maker; first knife sold in 1979. **Mark:** Last initial.

KOMMER, RUSS,
4609 35th Ave N, Fargo, ND 58102, Phone: 701-281-1826, russkommer@yahoo.com Web: www.russkommerknives.com
   Specialties: Working straight knives with the outdoorsman in mind. **Patterns:** Hunters, semi-skinners, fighters, folders and utility knives, art knives. **Technical:** Hollow-grinds ATS-34, 440C and 440V. **Prices:** $125 to $850; some to $3000. **Remarks:** Full-time maker; first knife sold in 1995. **Mark:** Bear paw—full name, city and state or full name and state.

KOPP, TODD M,
PO Box 3474, Apache Jct., AZ 85217, Phone: 480-983-6143, tmkopp@msn.com
   Specialties: Classic and traditional straight knives. Fluted handled daggers. **Patterns:** Bowies, boots, daggers, fighters, hunters, swords and folders. **Technical:** Grinds 5160, 440C, ATS-34. All Damascus steels, or customers choice. Some engraving and filework. **Prices:** $200 to $1200; some to $4000. **Remarks:** Part-time maker; first knife sold in 1989. **Mark:** Last name in Old English, some others name, city and state.

KOSTER, STEVEN C,
16261 Gentry Ln, Huntington Beach, CA 92647, kosterknives@verizon.net Web: www.kosterhandforgedknives.com
   Specialties: Walking sticks, hand axes, tomahawks, Damascus. **Patterns:** Ladder, twists, round horn. **Technical:** Use 5160, 52100, 1084, 1095 steels. Ladder, twists. **Prices:** $200 to $1000. **Remarks:** Wood and leather sheaths with silver furniture. ABS Journeyman 2003. California knifemakers member. **Mark:** Koster squeezed between lines.

KOVACIK, ROBERT,
Erenburgova 23, 98401 Lucenec, SLOVAKIA, Phone: Mobil:00421907644800, kovacikart@gmail.com Web: www.robertkovacik.com
   Specialties: Engraved hunting knives, guns engraved; Knifemakers. **Technical:** Fixed blades, folder knives, miniatures. **Prices:** $350 to $10,000 U.S. **Mark:** R.

KOVAR, EUGENE,
2626 W 98th St., Evergreen Park, IL 60642, Phone: 708-636-3724/708-790-4115, baldemaster333@aol.com
   Specialties: One-of-a-kind miniature knives only. **Patterns:** Fancy to fantasy miniature knives; knife pendants and tie tacks. **Technical:** Files and grinds nails, nickel-silver and sterling silver. **Prices:** $5 to $35; some to $100. **Mark:** GK.

KOYAMA, CAPTAIN BUNSHICHI,
3-23 Shirako-cho, Nakamura-ku, Nagoya City 453-0817, JAPAN, Phone: 052-461-7070, Fax: 052-461-7070
   Specialties: Innovative folding knife. **Patterns:** General purpose one hand. **Technical:** Grinds ATS-34 and Damascus. **Prices:** $400 to $900; some to $1500. **Remarks:** Part-time maker; first knife sold in 1994. **Mark:** Captain B. Koyama and the shoulder straps of CAPTAIN.

KRAFT, STEVE,
408 NE 11th St, Abilene, KS 67410, Phone: 785-263-1411
   Specialties: Folders, lockbacks, scale release auto, push button auto. **Patterns:** Hunters, boot knives and fighters. **Technical:** Grinds ATS-34, Damascus; uses titanium, pearl, ivory etc. **Prices:** $500 to $2500. **Remarks:** Part-time maker; first knife sold in 1984. **Mark:** Kraft.

KRAPP, DENNY,
1826 Windsor Oak Dr, Apopka, FL 32703, Phone: 407-880-7115
   Specialties: Fantasy and working straight knives of his design. **Patterns:** Hunters, fighters and utility/camp knives. **Technical:** Grinds ATS-34 and 440C. **Prices:** $85 to $300; some to $800. **Remarks:** Spare-time maker; first knife sold in 1988. **Mark:** Last name.

KRAUSE, ROY W,
22412 Corteville, St. Clair Shores, MI 48081, Phone: 810-296-3995, Fax: 810-296-2663
   Specialties: Military and law enforcement/Japanese-style knives and swords. **Patterns:** Combat and back-up, Bowies, fighters, boot knives, daggers, tantos, wakazashis and katanas. **Technical:** Grinds ATS-34, A2, D2, 1045, O1 and commercial Damascus; differentially hardened Japanese-style blades. **Prices:** Moderate to upscale. **Remarks:** Full-time maker. **Mark:** Last name on traditional knives; initials in Japanese characters on Japanese-style knives.

KREGER, THOMAS,
1996 Dry Branch Rd., Lugoff, SC 29078, Phone: 803-438-4221, tdkreger@bellsouth.net
   Specialties: South Carolina/George Herron style working/using knives. Customer designs considered. **Patterns:** Hunters, skinners, fillet, liner lock folders, kitchen, and camp knives. **Technical:** Hollow and flat grinds of ATS-34, CPM154CM, and 5160. **Prices:** $100 and up. **Remarks:** Full-time maker. President of the South Carolina Association of Knifemakers 2002-06. **Mark:** TDKreger.

KREH, LEFTY,
210 Wichersham Way, "Cockeysville", MD 21030

KREIBICH, DONALD L.,
1638 Commonwealth Circle, Reno, NV 89503, Phone: 775-746-0533, dmkreno@sbcglobal.net
   Specialties: Working straight knives in standard patterns. **Patterns:** Bowies, boots and daggers; camp and fishing knives. **Technical:** Grinds 440C, 154CM and ATS-34; likes integrals. **Prices:** $100 to $200; some to $500. **Remarks:** Part-time maker; first knife sold in 1980. **Mark:** First and middle initials, last name.

KRESSLER, D F,
Mittelweg 31 i, D-28832 Achim, GERMANY, Phone: 49-4202765742, Fax: 49-042 02/7657 41, info@kresslerknives.com; Web: www.kresslerknives.com
   Specialties: High-tech integral and interframe knives. **Patterns:** Hunters, fighters, daggers. **Technical:** Grinds new state-of-the-art steels; prefers natural handle materials. **Prices:** Upscale. **Mark:** Name in logo.

KUBASEK, JOHN A,
74 Northhampton St, Easthampton, MA 01027, Phone: 413-527-7917, jaknife01@verizon.net
   Specialties: Left- and right-handed LinerLock® folders of his design or to customer specs. Also new knives made with Ripcord patent. **Patterns:** Fighters, tantos, drop points, survival knives, neck knives and belt buckle knives. **Technical:** Grinds 154CM, S30 and Damascus. **Prices:** $395 to $1500. **Remarks:** Part-time maker; first knife sold in 1985. **Mark:** Name and address etched.

KUKULKA, WOLFGANG,
Golf Tower 2, Apt. 107, Greens, PO BOX 126229, Dubai, United Arab Emirates, Phone: 00971-50-2201047, wolfgang.kukulka@hotmail.com
   Specialties: Fully handmade from various steels: Damascus Steel, Japanese Steel, 1.2842, 1.2379, K110, K360, M390 microclean **Patterns:** Handles made from stabilized wood, different hard woods, horn and various materials **Technical:** Hardness of blades: 58-67 HRC.

L

LADD, JIM S,
1120 Helen, Deer Park, TX 77536, Phone: 713-479-7286
   Specialties: Working knives and period pieces. **Patterns:** Hunters, boots and Bowies plus other straight knives. **Technical:** Grinds D2, 440C and 154CM. **Prices:** $125 to $225; some to $550. **Remarks:** Part-time maker; first knife sold in 1965. Doing business as The Tinker. **Mark:** First and middle initials, last name.

LADD, JIMMIE LEE,
1120 Helen, Deer Park, TX 77536, Phone: 713-479-7186
   Specialties: Working straight knives. **Patterns:** Hunters, skinners and utility knives. **Technical:** Grinds 440C and D2. **Prices:** $75 to $225. **Remarks:** First knife sold in 1979. **Mark:** First and middle initials, last name.

LAINSON, TONY,
114 Park Ave, Council Bluffs, IA 51503, Phone: 712-322-5222
   Specialties: Working straight knives, liner locking folders. **Technical:** Grinds 154CM, ATS-34, 440C buys Damascus. Handle materials include Micarta, carbon fiber G-10 ivory pearl and bone. **Prices:** $95 to $600. **Remarks:** Part-time maker; first knife sold in 1987. **Mark:** Name and state.

LAIRSON SR., JERRY,
HC 68 Box 970, Ringold, OK 74754, Phone: 580-876-3426, bladesmt@brightok.net; Web: www.lairson-custom-knives.net
   Specialties: Damascus collector grade knives & high performance field grade hunters & cutting competition knives. **Patterns:** Damascus, random, raindrop, ladder, twist and others. **Technical:** All knives hammer forged. Mar Tempering **Prices:** Field grade knives $300. Collector grade $400 & up. **Mark:** Lairson. **Remarks:** Makes any style knife but prefer fighters and hunters. ABS Mastersmith, AKA member, KGA member. Cutting competition competitor.

LAKE, RON,
3360 Bendix Ave, Eugene, OR 97401, Phone: 541-484-2683
   Specialties: High-tech working knives; inventor of the modern interframe folder. **Patterns:** Hunters, boots, etc.; locking folders. **Technical:** Grinds 154CM and ATS-34. Patented interframe with special lock release tab. **Prices:** $2200 to $3000; some higher. **Remarks:** Full-time maker; first knife sold in 1966. **Mark:** Last name.

LALA, PAULO RICARDO P AND LALA, ROBERTO P.,
R Daniel Martins 636, Centro, Presidente Prudente, SP-19031-260, BRAZIL, Phone: 0182-210125, Web: http://www.orbita.starmedia/~korth
   Specialties: Straight knives and folders of all designs to customer specs. **Patterns:** Bowies, daggers fighters, hunters and utility knives. **Technical:** Grinds and forges D6, 440C, high-carbon steels and Damascus. **Prices:** $60 to $400; some higher. **Remarks:** Full-time makers; first knife sold in 1991. All stainless steel blades are ultra sub-zero quenched. **Mark:** Sword carved on top of anvil under KORTH.

LAMB, CURTIS J,
3336 Louisiana Ter, Ottawa, KS 66067-8996, Phone: 785-242-6657

LAMBERT, JARRELL D,
2321 FM 2982, Granado, TX 77962, Phone: 512-771-3744
Specialties: Traditional working and using straight knives of his design and to customer specs. **Patterns:** Bowies, hunters, tantos and utility/camp knives. **Technical:** Grinds ATS-34; forges W2 and his own Damascus. Makes own sheaths. **Prices:** $80 to $600; some to $1000. **Remarks:** Part-time maker; first knife sold in 1982. **Mark:** Etched first and middle initials, last name; or stamped last name.

LAMBERT, KIRBY,
536 College Ave, Regina Saskatchewan S4N X3, CANADA, kirby@ lambertknives.com; Web: www.lambertknives.com
Specialties: Tactical/utility folders. Tactical/utility Japanese style fixed blades. **Prices:** $200 to $1500 U.S. **Remarks:** Full-time maker since 2002. **Mark:** Black widow spider and last name Lambert.

LAMEY, ROBERT M,
15800 Lamey Dr, Biloxi, MS 39532, Phone: 228-396-9066, Fax: 228-396-9022, rmlamey@ametro.net; Web: www.lameyknives.com
Specialties: Bowies, fighters, hard use knives. **Patterns:** Bowies, fighters, hunters and camp knives. **Technical:** Forged and stock removal. **Prices:** $125 to $350. **Remarks:** Lifetime reconditioning; will build to customer designs, specializing in hard use, affordable knives. **Mark:** LAMEY.

LAMPSON, FRANK G,
3215 Saddle Bag Circle, Rimrock, AZ 86335, Phone: 928-567-7395, fglampson@ yahoo.com
Specialties: Working folders; one-of-a-kinds. **Patterns:** Folders, hunters, utility knives, fillet knives and Bowies. **Technical:** Grinds ATS-34, 440C and 154CM. **Prices:** $100 to $750; some to $3500. **Remarks:** Full-time maker; first knife sold in 1971. **Mark:** Name in fish logo.

LANCASTER, C G,
No 2 Schoonwinkel St, Parys, Free State, SOUTH AFRICA, Phone: 0568112090
Specialties: High-tech working and using knives of his design and to customer specs. **Patterns:** Hunters, locking folders and utility/camp knives. **Technical:** Grinds Sandvik 12C27, 440C and D2. Offers anodized titanium bolsters. **Prices:** $450 to $750; some to $1500. **Remarks:** Part-time maker; first knife sold in 1990. **Mark:** Etched logo.

LANCE, BILL,
PO Box 4427, Eagle River, AK 99577, Phone: 907-694-1487
Specialties: Ooloos and working straight knives; limited issue sets. **Patterns:** Several ulu patterns, drop-point skinners. **Technical:** Uses ATS-34, Vascomax 350; ivory, horn and high-class wood handles. **Prices:** $85 to $300; art sets to $3000. **Remarks:** First knife sold in 1981. **Mark:** Last name over a lance.

LANDERS, JOHN,
758 Welcome Rd, Newnan, GA 30263, Phone: 404-253-5719
Specialties: High-art working straight knives and folders of his design. **Patterns:** Hunters, fighters and slip-joint folders. **Technical:** Grinds 440C, ATS-34, 154CM and commercial Damascus. **Prices:** $85 to $250; some to $500. **Remarks:** Part-time maker; first knife sold in 1989. **Mark:** Last name.

LANG, DAVID,
6153 Cumulus Circle, Kearns, UT 84118, Phone: 801-809-1241, dknifeguy@ msn.com
Specialties: Hunters, Fighters, Push Daggers, Upscale Art Knives, Folders. **Technical:** Flat grind, hollow grind, hand carving, casting. **Remarks:** Will work from my designs or to your specifications. I have been making knives 10 years and have gleaned help from Jerry Johnson, Steven Rapp, Earl Black, Steven Johnson, and many others. **Prices:** $225 - $3000. **Mark:** Dland over UTAH.

LANGLEY, GENE H,
1022 N. Price Rd, Florence, SC 29506, Phone: 843-669-3150
Specialties: Working knives in standard patterns. **Patterns:** Hunters, boots, fighters, locking folders and slip-joints. **Technical:** Grinds 440C, 154CM and ATS-34. **Prices:** $125 to $450; some to $1000. **Remarks:** Part-time maker; first knife sold in 1979. **Mark:** Name.

LANGLEY, MICK,
1015 Centre Crescent, Qualicum Beach, B.C., CANADA V9K 2G6, Phone: 250-752-4261
Specialties: Period pieces and working knives. **Patterns:** Bowies, push daggers, fighters, boots. Some folding lockers. **Technical:** Forges 5160, 1084, W2 and his own Damascus. **Prices:** $250 to $2500; some to $4500. **Remarks:** Full-time maker, first knife sold in 1977. **Mark:** Langley with M.S. (for ABS Master Smith)

LANKTON, SCOTT,
8065 Jackson Rd. R-11, Ann Arbor, MI 48103, Phone: 313-426-3735
Specialties: Pattern welded swords, krisses and Viking period pieces. **Patterns:** One-of-a-kind. **Technical:** Forges W2, L6 nickel and other steels. **Prices:** $600 to $12,000. **Remarks:** Part-time bladesmith, full-time smith; first knife sold in 1976. **Mark:** Last name logo.

LAOISLAV, SANTA-LASKY,
Hrochot 264, 976 37 Hrochot, Okres Banska Bystrica, Slovensko (Slovakia), Phone: +421-905-544-280, santa.ladislav@pobox.sk; Web: www.lasky.sk
Specialties: Damascus hunters, daggers and swords. **Patterns:** Carious Damascus patterns. **Prices:** $300 to $6000 U.S. **Mark:** L or Lasky.

LAPEN, CHARLES,
Box 529, W. Brookfield, MA 01585
Specialties: Chef's knives for the culinary artist. **Patterns:** Camp knives, Japanese-style swords and wood working tools, hunters. **Technical:** Forges 1075, car spring and his own Damascus. Favors narrow and Japanese tangs. **Prices:** $200 to $400; some to $2000. **Remarks:** Part-time maker; first knife sold in 1972. **Mark:** Last name.

LAPLANTE, BRETT,
4545 CR412, McKinney, TX 75071, Phone: 972-838-9191, blap007@aol.com
Specialties: Working straight knives and folders to customer specs. **Patterns:** Survival knives, Bowies, skinners, hunters. **Technical:** Grinds D2 and 440C. Heat-treats. **Prices:** $200 to $800. **Remarks:** Part-time maker; first knife sold in 1987. **Mark:** Last name in Canadian maple leaf logo.

LARAMIE, MARK,
301 McCain St., Raeford, NC 28376, Phone: 978-502-2726, mark@malknives. com; Web: www.malknives.com
Specialties: Traditional fancy & art knives. **Patterns:** Slips, back-lock L/L, automatics, single and multi blades. **Technical:** Free hand ground blades of D2, 440, and Damascus. **Mark:** M.A.L. Knives w/fish logo.

LARGIN, KEN,
KELGIN KNIVES, 104 Knife Works Ln, Sevierville, TN 37876, Phone: 765-969-5012, kelginfinecutlery@hotmail.com; Web: wwwkelgin.com
Specialties: Retired from general knife making. Only take limited orders in meteorite Damascus or solid meteorite blades. **Patterns:** Any. **Technical:** Stock removal or forged. **Prices:** $500 & up. **Remarks:** Runs the Kelgin Knife Makers Co-op at Smoky Mtn. Knife Works. **Mark:** K.C. Largin (Kelgin mark retired in 2004).

LARK, DAVID,
6641 Schneider Rd., Kingsley, MI 49649, Phone: 231-342-1076, dblark58@ yahoo.com
Specialties: Traditional straight knives, art knives, folders. **Patterns:** All types. **Technical:** Grinds all types of knife making steel and makes damascus. **Prices:** $600 and up. **Remarks:** Full-time maker, custom riflemaker, and engraver. **Mark:** Lark in script and DBL on engraving.

LARSON, RICHARD,
549 E Hawkeye Ave, Turlock, CA 95380, Phone: 209-668-1615, lebatardknives@ aol.com
Specialties: Sound working knives, lightweight folders, practical tactical knives. **Patterns:** Hunters, trout and bird knives, fish fillet knives, Bowies, tactical sheath knives, one- and two-blade folders. **Technical:** Grinds ATS-34, A2, D2, CPM 3V and commercial. Damascus; forges and grinds 52100, O1 and 1095. Machines folder frames from aircraft aluminum. **Prices:** $40 to $650. **Remarks:** Full-time maker. First knife made in 1974. Offers knife repair, restoration and sharpening. All knives are serial numbered and registered in the name of original purchaser. **Mark:** Stamped last name or etched logo of last name, city, and state.

LARY, ED,
951 Rangeline Rd, Mosinee, WI 54455, laryblades@hotmail.com
Specialties: Upscale hunters and art knives with display presentations. **Patterns:** Hunters, period pieces. **Technical:** Grinds all steels, heat treats, fancy file work and engraving. **Prices:** Upscale. **Remarks:** Full-time maker since 1974. **Mark:** Hand engraved "Ed Lary" in script.

LAURENT, KERMIT,
1812 Acadia Dr, LaPlace, LA 70068, Phone: 504-652-5629
Specialties: Traditional and working straight knives and folders of his design. **Patterns:** Bowies, hunters, utilities and folders. **Technical:** Forges own Damascus, plus uses most tool steels and stainless. Specializes in altering cable patterns. Uses stabilized handle materials, especially select exotic woods. **Prices:** $100 to $2500; some to $50,000. **Remarks:** Full-time maker; first knife sold in 1982. Doing business as Kermit's Knife Works. Favorite material is meteorite Damascus. **Mark:** First name.

LAWRENCE, ALTON,
201 W Stillwell, De Queen, AR 71832, Phone: 870-642-7643, Fax: 870-642-4023, uncle21@riversidemachine.net; Web: riversidemachine.net
Specialties: Classic straight knives and folders to customer specs. **Patterns:** Bowies, hunters, folders and utility/camp knives. **Technical:** Forges 5160, 1095, 1084, Damascus and railroad spikes. **Prices:** Start at $100. **Remarks:** Part-time maker; first knife sold in 1988. **Mark:** Last name inside fish symbol.

LAY, L J,
602 Mimosa Dr, Burkburnett, TX 76354, Phone: 940-569-1329
Specialties: Working straight knives in standard patterns; some period pieces. **Patterns:** Drop-point hunters, Bowies and fighters. **Technical:** Grinds ATS-34 to mirror finish; likes Micarta handles. **Prices:** Moderate. **Remarks:** Full-time maker; first knife sold in 1985. **Mark:** Name or name with ram head and city or stamp L J Lay.

LAY, R J (BOB),
Box 1225, Logan Lake, B.C., CANADA V0K 1W0, Phone: 250-523-9923, Fax: SAME, rjlay@telus.net
Specialties: Traditional-styled, fancy straight knifes of his design. Specializing in hunters. **Patterns:** Bowies, fighters and hunters. **Technical:** Grinds 440C, ATS-34, S30V, CPM-154CM. Uses exotic handle and spacer material. File cut, prefers narrow tang. Sheaths available. **Price:** $200 to $500, some to $5000. **Remarks:** Full-time maker, first knife sold in 1976. Doing business as Lay's Custom Knives. **Mark:** Signature acid etched.

LEACH, MIKE J,
5377 W Grand Blanc Rd., Swartz Creek, MI 48473, Phone: 810-655-4850
Specialties: Fancy working knives. **Patterns:** Hunters, fighters, Bowies and heavy-duty knives; slip-joint folders and integral straight patterns. **Technical:** Grinds D2, 440C and 154CM; buys Damascus. **Prices:** Start at $300. **Remarks:** Full-time maker; first knife sold in 1952. **Mark:** First initial, last name.

LEAVITT JR., EARL F,
Pleasant Cove Rd Box 306, E. Boothbay, ME 04544, Phone: 207-633-3210
Specialties: 1500-1870 working straight knives and fighters; pole arms. **Patterns:** Historically significant knives, classic/modern custom designs. **Technical:** Flat-grinds O1; heat-treats. Filework available. **Prices:** $90 to $350; some to $1000. **Remarks:** Full-time maker; first knife sold in 1981. Doing business as Old Colony Manufactory. **Mark:** Initials in oval.

LEBATARD, PAUL M,
14700 Old River Rd, Vancleave, MS 39565, Phone: 228-826-4137, Fax: Cell phone: 228-238-7461, lebatardknives@aol.com
Specialties: Sound working hunting and fillet knives, folding knives, practical tactical knives. **Patterns:** Hunters, trout and bird knives, fish fillet knives, kitchen knives, Bowies, tactical sheath knives, one- and two-blade folders. **Technical:** Grinds ATS-34, D-2, CPM 3-V, CPM-154CM, and commercial Damascus; forges and grinds 1095, 01, and 52100. **Prices:** $75 to $650; some to $1200. **Remarks:** Full-time maker, first knife made in 1974. Charter member Gulf Coast Custom Knifemakers; Voting member Knifemaker's Guild. **Mark:** Stamped last name, or etched logo of last name, city, and state. **Other:** All knives are serial numbered and registered in the name of the original purchaser.

LEBER, HEINZ,
Box 446, Hudson's Hope, B.C., CANADA V0C 1V0, Phone: 250-783-5304
Specialties: Working straight knives of his design. **Patterns:** 20 models, from capers to Bowies. **Technical:** Hollow-grinds D2 and M2 steel; mirror-finishes and full tang only. Likes moose, elk, stone sheep for handles. **Prices:** $175 to $1000. **Remarks:** Full-time maker; first knife sold in 1975. **Mark:** Initials connected.

LEBLANC, GARY E,
7342 145th Ave, Royalton, MN 56373, Phone: 320-232-0245, butternutcove@hotmail.com
Specialties: Hunting and fishing, some kitchen knives and the Air Assualt tactical knife. Does own leather and Kydex work. **Patterns:** Stock removal. **Technical:** Mostly ATS34 for spec knives--orders, whatever the customer desires. **Prices:** Full range: $85 for parring knife, up $4000 plus fro collector grade hunter and fillet set. **Remarks:** First knife in 1998. **Mark:** Circular with star in center and LEBLANC on upper curve and KNIFEWORKS on lower curve.

LECK, DAL,
Box 1054, Hayden, CO 81639, Phone: 970-276-3663
Specialties: Classic, traditional and working knives of his design and in standard patterns; period pieces. **Patterns:** Boots, daggers, fighters, hunters and push daggers. **Technical:** Forges O1 and 5160; makes his own Damascus. **Prices:** $175 to $700; some to $1500. **Remarks:** Part-time maker; first knife sold in 1990. Doing business as The Moonlight Smithy. **Mark:** Stamped: hammer and anvil with initials.

LEE, RANDY,
PO Box 1873, St. Johns, AZ 85936, Phone: 928-337-2594, Fax: 928-337-5002, randyleeknives@yahoo.com; Web.www.randyleeknives.com
Specialties: Traditional working and using straight knives of his design. **Patterns:** Bowies, fighters, hunters, daggers. **Technical:** Grinds ATS-34, 440C Damascus, and 154CPM. Offers sheaths. **Prices:** $325 to $2500. **Remarks:** Full-time maker; first knife sold in 1979. **Mark:** Full name, city, state.

LELAND, STEVE,
2300 Sir Francis Drake Blvd, Fairfax, CA 94930-1118, Phone: 415-457-0318, Fax: 415-457-0995, Web: www.stephenleland@comcast.net
Specialties: Traditional and working straight knives and folders of his design. **Patterns:** Hunters, fighters, Bowies, chefs. **Technical:** Grinds O1, ATS-34 and 440C. Does own heat treat. Makes nickel silver sheaths. **Prices:** $150 to $750; some to $1500. **Remarks:** Part-time maker; first knife sold in 1987. Doing business as Leland Handmade Knives. **Mark:** Last name.

LEMCKE, JIM L,
10649 Haddington Ste 180, Houston, TX 77043, Phone: 888-461-8632, Fax: 713-461-8221, jimll@hal-pc.org; Web: www.texasknife.com
Specialties: Large supply of custom ground and factory finished blades; knife kits; leather sheaths; in-house heat treating and cryogenic tempering; exotic handle material (wood, ivory, oosik, horn, stabilized woods); machines and supplies for knifemaking; polishing and finishing supplies; heat treat ovens; etching equipment; bar, sheet and rod material (brass, stainless steel, nickel silver); titanium sheet material. Catalog. $4.

LEMOINE, DAVID C,
1037 S College St, Mountain Home, AR 72653, Phone: 870-656-4730, dlemoine@davidlemoineknives.com; Web: davidlemoineknives.com
Specialties: Superior edge geometry on high performance custom classic and tactical straight blades and liner lock folders. **Patterns:** Hunters, skinners, bird and trout, fillet, camp, tactical, and military knives. Some miniatures. **Technical:** Flat and hollow grinds, CPMS90V, CPMS35V, CPMS30V, D2, A2, O1, 440C, ATS34, 154cm, Damasteel, Chad Nichols, Devin Thomas, and Robert Eggerling Damascus. Hidden and full tapered tangs, ultra-smooth folding mechanisms. File work, will use most all handle materials, does own professional in-house heat treatment and Rockwell testing. Hot blueing. **Prices:** $250 and up. **Remarks:**

Part-time maker, giving and selling knives since 1986. Each patron receives a NIV Sportsman's Field Bible. **Mark:** Name, city and state in full oval with cross in the center. Reverse image on other side. The cross never changes.

LENNON, DALE,
459 County Rd 1554, Alba, TX 75410, Phone: 903-765-2392, devildaddy1@netzero.net
Specialties: Working / using knives. **Patterns:** Hunters, fighters and Bowies. **Technical:** Grinds high carbon steels, ATS-34, forges some. **Prices:** Starts at $120. **Remarks:** Part-time maker, first knife sold in 2000. **Mark:** Last name.

LEONARD, RANDY JOE,
188 Newton Rd, Sarepta, LA 71071, Phone: 318-994-2712

LEONE, NICK,
9 Georgetown Dr, Pontoon Beach, IL 62040, Phone: 618-792-0734, nickleone@sbcglobal.net
Specialties: 18th century period straight knives. **Patterns:** Fighters, daggers, bowies. Besides period pieces makes modern designs. **Technical:** Forges 5160, W2, O1, 1098, 52100 and his own Damascus. **Prices:** $100 to $1000; some to $3500. **Remarks:** Full-time maker; first knife sold in 1987. Doing business as Anvil Head Forge. **Mark:** AHF, Leone, NL

LERCH, MATTHEW,
N88 W23462 North Lisbon Rd, Sussex, WI 53089, Phone: 262-246-6362, Web: www.lerchcustomknives.com
Specialties: Folders and folders with special mechanisms. **Patterns:** Interframe and integral folders; lock backs, assisted openers, side locks, button locks and liner locks. **Technical:** Grinds ATS-34, 1095, 440 and Damascus. Offers filework and embellished bolsters. **Prices:** $900 and up. **Remarks:** Part-time maker; first knife sold in 1992. **Mark:** Last name.

LESSWING, KEVIN,
29A East 34th St, Bayonne, NJ 07002, Phone: 551-221-1841, klesswing@excite.com
Specialties: Traditonal working and using straight knives of his design or to customer specs. A few folders. Makes own leather sheaths. **Patterns:** Hunters, daggers, bowies, bird and trout. **Technical:** Forges high carbon and tool steels, makes own Damascus, grinds CPM154CM, Damasteel, and other stainless steels. Does own heat treating. **Remarks:** Voting member of Knifemakers Guild, part-time maker. **Mark:** KL on early knives, LESSWING on Current knives.

LEU, POHAN,
PO BOX 15423, Rio Rancho, NM 87174, Phone: 949-300-6412, pohanleu@hotmail.com Web: www.leucustom.com
Specialties: Japanese influenced fixed blades made to your custom specifications. Knives and swords. A2 tool steel, Stock Removal. **Prices:** $180 and up. **Remarks:** Full-time; first knife sold in 2003. **Mark:** LEU or PL.

LEVENGOOD, BILL,
15011 Otto Rd, Tampa, FL 33624, Phone: 813-961-5688, bill.levengood@verison.net; Web: www.levengoodknives.com
Specialties: Working straight knives and folders. **Patterns:** Hunters, Bowies, folders and collector pieces. **Technical:** Grinds ATS-34, S-30V, CPM-154 and Damascus. **Prices:** $175 to $1500. **Remarks:** Full time maker; first knife sold in 1983. **Mark:** Last name, city, state.

LEVIN, JACK,
201 Brighton 1st Road, Suite 3R, Brooklyn, NY 11235, Phone: 718-415-7911, jacklevin1@yahoo.com
Specialties: Folders with mechanisms.

LEVINE, BOB,
101 Westwood Dr, Tullahoma, TN 37388, Phone: 931-454-9943, levineknives@msn.com
Specialties: Working left- and right-handed LinerLock® folders. **Patterns:** Hunters and folders. **Technical:** Grinds ATS-34, 440C, D2, O1 and some Damascus; hollow and some flat grinds. Uses fossil ivory, Micarta and exotic woods. Provides custom leather sheath with each fixed knife. **Prices:** Starting at $275. **Remarks:** Full-time maker; first knife sold in 1984. Voting member Knifemakers Guild, German Messermaher Guild. **Mark:** Name and logo.

LEWIS, BILL,
PO Box 63, Riverside, IA 52327, Phone: 319-629-5574, wildbill37@geticonnect.com
Specialties: Folders of all kinds including those made from one-piece of white tail antler with or without the crown. **Patterns:** Hunters, folding hunters, fillet, Bowies, push daggers, etc. **Prices:** $20 to $200. **Remarks:** Full-time maker; first knife sold in 1978. **Mark:** W.E.L.

LEWIS, MIKE,
21 Pleasant Hill Dr, DeBary, FL 32713, Phone: 386-753-0936, dragonsteel@prodigy.net
Specialties: Traditional straight knives. **Patterns:** Swords and daggers. **Technical:** Grinds 440C, ATS-34 and 5160. Frequently uses cast bronze and cast nickel guards and pommels. **Prices:** $100 to $750. **Remarks:** Part-time maker; first knife sold in 1988. **Mark:** Dragon Steel and serial number.

LEWIS, TOM R,
1613 Standpipe Rd, Carlsbad, NM 88220, Phone: 575-885-3616, lewisknives@carlsbadnm.com; Web: www.cavemen.net/lewisknives/
Specialties: Traditional working straight knives. **Patterns:** Outdoor knives, hunting knives and Bowies. **Technical:** Grinds ATS-34 forges 5168 and O1. Makes wire, pattern welded and chainsaw Damascus. **Prices:** $140 to $1500.

Remarks: Part-time maker; first knife sold in 1980. Doing business as TR Lewis Handmade Knives. **Mark:** Lewis family crest.

LICATA, STEVEN,
LICATA CUSTOM KNIVES, 146 Wilson St. 1st Floor, Boonton, NJ 07005, Phone: 973-588-4909, kniveslicata@aol.com; Web: www.licataknives.com
Specialties: Fantasy swords and knives. One-of-a-kind sculptures in steel. **Prices:** $200 to $25,000.

LIEBENBERG, ANDRE,
8 Hilma Rd, Bordeauxrandburg 2196, SOUTH AFRICA, Phone: 011-787-2303
Specialties: High-art straight knives of his design. **Patterns:** Daggers, fighters and swords. **Technical:** Grinds 440C and 12C27. **Prices:** $250 to $500; some $4000 and higher. Giraffe bone handles with semi-precious stones. **Remarks:** Spare-time maker; first knife sold in 1990. **Mark:** Initials.

LIEGEY, KENNETH R,
288 Carney Dr, Millwood, WV 25262, Phone: 304-273-9545
Specialties: Traditional working/using straight knives of his design and to customer specs. **Patterns:** Hunters, utility/camp knives, miniatures. **Technical:** Grinds 440C. **Prices:** $75 to $150; some to $300. **Remarks:** Spare-time maker; first knife sold in 1977. **Mark:** First and middle initials, last name.

LIGHTFOOT, GREG,
RR #2, Kitscoty, AB, CANADA T0B 2P0, Phone: 780-846-2812; 780-800-1061, Pitbull@lightfootknives.com; Web: www.lightfootknives.com
Specialties: Stainless steel and Damascus. **Patterns:** Boots, fighters and locking folders. **Technical:** Grinds BG-42, 440C, D2, CPM steels, Stellite 6K. Offers engraving. **Prices:** $500 to $2000. **Remarks:** Full-time maker; first knife sold in 1988. Doing business as Lightfoot Knives. **Mark:** Shark with Lightfoot Knives below.

LIN, MARCUS,
1109 W 190th St, Unit G, Los Angeles, CA 90248, Phone: 808-636-0977, marcuslin7@gmail.com; Web: www.linknives.com
Specialties: Working knives. **Patterns:** Original patterns from the Loveless Shop designed by R.W. Loveless, and maker's own patterns. **Technical:** Main blade material is ATS34/154CM. Experience with many other alloys, Stellite 6K, Damasteel, and tool steels. **Prices:** $150 to $1650. **Remarks:** Part-time maker since 2004. Mentored by: R.W. Loveless and Jim Merritt. Sole authorship work, except for heat treat which is done by Paul Bos Heat Treating. **Mark:** Two used: "Marcus Lin, maker, Loveless Design" and "LIN, CALIFORNIA" (with Chinese characters on left side for "Forest.")

LINKLATER, STEVE,
8 Cossar Dr, Aurora, Ont., CANADA L4G 3N8, Phone: 905-727-8929, knifman@sympatico.ca
Specialties: Traditional working/using straight knives and folders of his design. **Patterns:** Fighters, hunters and locking folders. **Technical:** Grinds ATS-34, 440V and D2. **Prices:** $125 to $350; some to $600. **Remarks:** Part-time maker; first knife sold in 1987. Doing business as Links Knives. **Mark:** LINKS.

LISCH, DAVID K,
9239 8th Ave. SW, Seattle, WA 98106, Phone: 206-919-5431, Web: www.davidlisch.com
Specialties: One-of-a-kind collectibles, straight knives of own design and to customer specs. **Patterns:** Hunters, skinners, Bowies, and fighters. **Technical:** Forges all his own Damascus under 360-pound air hammer. Forges and chisels wrought iron, pure iron, and bronze butt caps. **Prices:** Starting at $800. **Remarks:** Full-time blacksmith, part-time bladesmith. **Mark:** D. Lisch J.S.

LISTER JR., WELDON E,
116 Juniper Ln, Boerne, TX 78006, Phone: 210-269-0102, wlister@grtc.com; Web: www.weldonlister.com
Specialties: One-of-a-kind fancy and embellished folders. **Patterns:** Locking and slip-joint folders. **Technical:** Commercial Damascus and O1. All knives embellished. Engraves, inlays, carves and scrimshaws. **Prices:** Upscale. **Remarks:** Spare-time maker; first knife sold in 1991. **Mark:** Last name.

LITTLE, GARY M,
94716 Conklin Meadows Ln, PO Box 156, Broadbent, OR 97414, Phone: 503-572-2656
Specialties: Fancy working knives. **Patterns:** Hunters, tantos, Bowies, axes and buckskinners; locking folders and interframes. **Technical:** Forges and grinds O1, L6m, 1095, and 15N20; makes his own Damascus; bronze fittings. **Prices:** $120 to $1500. **Remarks:** Full-time maker; first knife sold in 1979. Doing business as Conklin Meadows Forge. **Mark:** Name, city and state.

LITTLE, LARRY,
1A Cranberry Ln, Spencer, MA 01562, Phone: 508-885-2301, littcran@aol.com
Specialties: Working straight knives of his design or to customer specs. Likes Scagel-style. **Patterns:** Hunters, fighters, Bowies, folders. **Technical:** Grinds and forges L6, O1, 5160, 1095, 1080. Prefers natural handle material especially antler. Uses nickel silver. Makes own heavy duty leather sheath. **Prices:** Start at $125. **Remarks:** Part-time maker. First knife sold in 1985. Offers knife repairs. **Mark:** Little on one side, LL brand on the other.

LIVELY, TIM AND MARIAN,
PO Box 1172, Marble Falls, TX 78654, Web: www.livelyknives.com
Specialties: Multi-cultural primitive knives of their design on speculation. **Patterns:** Old world designs. **Technical:** Hand forges using ancient techniques without electricity; hammer finish. **Prices:** High. **Remarks:** Retired 2009. Offers knifemaking DVD online. **Mark:** Last name.

LIVESAY, NEWT,
3306 S. Dogwood St, Siloam Springs, AR 72761, Phone: 479-549-3356, Fax: 479-549-3357, newt@newtlivesay.com; Web:www.newtlivesay.com
Specialties: Combat utility knives, hunting knives, titanium knives, swords, axes, KYDWX sheaths for knives and pistols, custom orders.

LIVINGSTON, ROBERT C,
PO Box 6, Murphy, NC 28906, Phone: 704-837-4155
Specialties: Art letter openers to working straight knives. **Patterns:** Minis to machetes. **Technical:** Forges and grinds most steels. **Prices:** Start at $20. **Remarks:** Full-time maker; first knife sold in 1988. Doing business as Mystik Knifeworks. **Mark:** MYSTIK.

LOCKETT, STERLING,
527 E Amherst Dr, Burbank, CA 91504, Phone: 818-846-5799
Specialties: Working straight knives and folders to customer specs. **Patterns:** Hunters and fighters. **Technical:** Grinds. **Prices:** Moderate. **Remarks:** Spare-time maker. **Mark:** Name, city with hearts.

LOERCHNER, WOLFGANG,
WOLFE FINE KNIVES, PO Box 255, Bayfield, Ont., CANADA N0M 1G0, Phone: 519-565-2196
Specialties: Traditional straight knives, mostly ornate. **Patterns:** Small swords, daggers and stilettos; locking folders and miniatures. **Technical:** Grinds D2, 440C and 154CM; all knives hand-filed and flat-ground. **Prices:** Vary. **Remarks:** Part-time maker; first knife sold in 1983. Doing business as Wolfe Fine Knives. **Mark:** WOLFE.

LONEWOLF, J AGUIRRE,
481 Hwy 105, Demorest, GA 30535, Phone: 706-754-4660, Fax: 706-754-8470, lonewolfandsons@windstream.net, Web: www.knivesbylonewolf.com www.eagleswinggallery.com
Specialties: High-art working and using straight knives of his design. **Patterns:** Bowies, hunters, utility/camp knives and fine steel blades. **Technical:** Forges Damascus and high-carbon steel. Most knives have hand-carved moose antler handles. **Prices:** $55 to $500; some to $2000. **Remarks:** Full-time maker; first knife sold in 1989. Doing business as Lonewolf and Sons LLC. **Mark:** Stamp.

LONG, GLENN A,
10090 SW 186th Ave, Dunnellon, FL 34432, Phone: 352-489-4272, galong99@att.net
Specialties: Classic working and using straight knives of his design and to customer specs. **Patterns:** Hunters, Bowies, utility. **Technical:** Grinds 440C D2 and 440V. **Prices:** $85 to $300; some to $800. **Remarks:** Part-time maker; first knife sold in 1990. **Mark:** Last name inside diamond.

LONGWORTH, DAVE,
PO Box 222, Neville, OH 45156, Phone: 513-876-2372
Specialties: High-tech working knives. **Patterns:** Locking folders, hunters, fighters and elaborate daggers. **Technical:** Grinds O1, ATS-34, 440C; buys Damascus. **Prices:** $125 to $600; some higher. **Remarks:** Part-time maker; first knife sold in 1980. **Mark:** Last name.

LOOS, HENRY C,
210 Ingraham, New Hyde Park, NY 11040, Phone: 516-354-1943, hcloos@optonline.net
Specialties: Miniature fancy knives and period pieces of his design. **Patterns:** Bowies, daggers and swords. **Technical:** Grinds O1 and 440C. Uses sterling, 18K, rubies and emeralds. All knives come with handmade hardwood cases. **Prices:** $90 to $195; some to $250. **Remarks:** Spare-time maker; first knife sold in 1990. **Mark:** Script last initial.

LORO, GENE,
2457 State Route 93 NE, Crooksville, OH 43731, Phone: 740-982-4521, Fax: 740-982-1249, geney@aol.com
Specialties: Hand forged knives. **Patterns:** Damascus, Random, Ladder, Twist, etc. **Technical:** ABS Journeyman Smith. **Prices:** $200 and up. **Remarks:** Loro and hand forged by Gene Loro. **Mark:** Loro. Retired engineer.

LOTT, SHERRY,
1100 Legion Park Rd, Greensburg, KY 42743, Phone: 270-932-2212, info@greenriverleather.com
Specialties: One-of-a-kind, usually carved handles. **Patterns:** Art. **Technical:** Carbon steel, stock removal. **Prices:** Moderate. **Mark:** Sherry Lott. **Remarks:** First knife sold in 1994.

LOUKIDES, DAVID E,
76 Crescent Circle, Cheshire, CT 06410, Phone: 203-271-3023, Lousharp1@sbcglobal.net; Web: www.prayerknives.com
Specialties: Hand forged working blades and collectible pieces. **Patterns:** Chef knives, bowies, and hunting knives. . **Technical:** Uses 1084, 1095, 5160, W2, and O1.**Prices:** Normally $175 to $800. **Remarks:** part-time maker, Journeyman Bladesmith, Full-time Journeyman Toolmaker. **Mark:** LOUKIDES, or previously on older knives, initial DEL

LOVE, ED,
19443 Mill Oak, San Antonio, TX 78258, Phone: 210-497-1021, Fax: 210-497-1021, annaedlove@sbcglobal.net
Specialties: Hunting, working knives and some art pieces. **Technical:** Grinds ATS-34, and 440C. **Prices:** $150 and up. **Remarks:** Part-time maker. First knife sold in 1980. **Mark:** Name in a weeping heart.

LOVESTRAND, SCHUYLER,
1136 19th St SW, Vero Beach, FL 32962, Phone: 772-778-0282, Fax: 772-466-1126, lovestranded@aol.com
Specialties: Fancy working straight knives of his design and to customer specs; unusual fossil ivories. **Patterns:** Hunters, fighters, Bowies and fishing knives. **Technical:** Grinds stainless steel. **Prices:** $450 and up. **Remarks:** Part-time maker; first knife sold in 1982. **Mark:** Name in logo.

LOVETT, MICHAEL,
PO Box 121, Mound, TX 76558, Phone: 254-865-9956, michaellovett@embarqmail.com
Specialties: The Loveless Connection Knives as per R.W. Loveless-Jim Merritt. **Patterns:** All Loveless Patterns and Original Lovett Patterns. **Technical:** Complicated double grinds and premium fit and finish. **Prices:** $1000 and up. **Remarks:** High degree of fit and finish - Authorized collection by R. W. Loveless. **Mark:** Loveless Authorized football or double nude.

LOZIER, DON,
5394 SE 168th Ave, Ocklawaha, FL 32179, Phone: 352-625-3576
Specialties: Fancy and working straight knives of his design and in standard patterns. **Patterns:** Daggers, fighters, boot knives, and hunters. **Technical:** Grinds ATS-34, 440C and Damascus. Most pieces are highly embellished by notable artisans. Taking limited number of orders per annum. **Prices:** Start at $250; most are $1250 to $3000; some to $12,000. **Remarks:** Full-time maker. **Mark:** Name.

LUCHAK, BOB,
15705 Woodforest Blvd, Channelview, TX 77530, Phone: 281-452-1779
Specialties: Presentation knives; start of The Survivor series. **Patterns:** Skinners, Bowies, camp axes, steak knife sets and fillet knives. **Technical:** Grinds 440C. Offers electronic etching; filework. **Prices:** $50 to $1500. **Remarks:** Full-time maker; first knife sold in 1983. Doing business as Teddybear Knives. **Mark:** Full name, city and state with Teddybear logo.

LUCHINI, BOB,
1220 Dana Ave, Palo Alto, CA 94301, Phone: 650-321-8095, rwluchin@bechtel.com

LUCIE, JAMES R,
4191 E. Fruitport Rd., Fruitport, MI 49415, Phone: 231-865-6390, scagel@netonecom.net
Specialties: Hand-forges William Scagel-style knives. **Patterns:** Authentic scagel-style knives and miniatures. **Technical:** Forges 5160, 52100 and 1084 and forges his own pattern welded Damascus steel. **Prices:** Start at $750. **Remarks:** Full-time maker; first knife sold in 1975. Believes in sole authorship of his work. ABS Journeyman Smith. **Mark:** Scagel Kris with maker's name and address.

LUCKETT, BILL,
108 Amantes Ln, Weatherford, TX 76088, Phone: 817-594-9288, bill_luckett@hotmail.com Web: www.billluckettcustomknives.com
Specialties: Uniquely patterned robust straight knives. **Patterns:** Fighters, Bowies, hunters. **Technical:** 154CM stainless. **Prices:** $550 to $1500. **Remarks:** Part-time maker; first knife sold in 1975. Knifemakers Guild Member. **Mark:** Last name over Bowie logo.

LUDWIG, RICHARD O,
57-63 65 St, Maspeth, NY 11378, Phone: 718-497-5969
Specialties: Traditional working/using knives. **Patterns:** Boots, hunters and utility/camp knives folders. **Technical:** Grinds 440C, ATS-34 and BG42. File work on guards and handles; silver spacers. Offers scrimshaw. **Prices:** $325 to $400; some to $2000. **Remarks:** Full-time maker. **Mark:** Stamped first initial, last name, state.

LUI, RONALD M,
4042 Harding Ave, Honolulu, HI 96816, Phone: 808-734-7746
Specialties: Working straight knives and folders in standard patterns. **Patterns:** Hunters, boots and liner locks. **Technical:** Grinds 440C and ATS-34. **Prices:** $100 to $700. **Remarks:** Spare-time maker; first knife sold in 1988. **Mark:** Initials connected.

LUMAN, JAMES R,
Clear Creek Trail, Anaconda, MT 59711, Phone: 406-560-1461
Specialties: San Mai and composite end patterns. **Patterns:** Pool and eye Spirograph southwest composite patterns. **Technical:** All patterns with blued steel; all made by him. **Prices:** $200 to $800. **Mark:** Stock blade removal. Pattern welded steel. Bottom ricasso JRL.

LUNDSTROM, JAN-AKE,
Mastmostigen 8, 66010 Dals-Langed, SWEDEN, Phone: 0531-40270
Specialties: Viking swords, axes and knives in cooperation with handle makers. **Patterns:** All traditional-styles, especially swords and inlaid blades. **Technical:** Forges his own Damascus and laminated steel. **Prices:** $200 to $1000. **Remarks:** Full-time maker; first knife sold in 1985; collaborates with museums. **Mark:** Runic.

LUNDSTROM, TORBJORN (TOBBE),
Norrskenet 4, 830 13 ARE, Sweden, 9lundstrm@telia.com Web: http://tobbeiare.se/site/
Specialties: Hunters and collectible knives. **Patterns:** Nordic-style hunters and art knives with unique materials such as mammoth and fossil walrus ivory. **Technical:** Uses forged blades by other makers, particularly Mattias Styrefors who mostly uses 15N20 and 20C steels and is a mosaic blacksmith. **Remarks:** First knife made in 1986.

LUNN, GAIL,
434 CR 1422, Mountain Home, AR 72653, Phone: 870-424-2662, gail@lunnknives.com; Web: www.lunnknives.com
Specialties: Fancy folders and double action autos, some straight blades. **Patterns:** One-of-a-kind, all types. **Technical:** Stock removal, hand made. **Prices:** $300 and up. **Remarks:** Fancy file work, exotic materials, inlays, stone etc. **Mark:** Name in script.

LUNN, LARRY A,
434 CR 1422, Mountain Home, AR 72653, Phone: 870-424-2662, larry@lunnknives.com; Web: www.lunnknives.com
Specialties: Fancy folders and double action autos; some straight blades. **Patterns:** All types; his own designs. **Technical:** Stock removal; commercial Damascus. **Prices:** $125 and up. **Remarks:** File work inlays and exotic materials. **Mark:** Name in script.

LUPOLE, JAMIE G,
KUMA KNIVES, 285 Main St., Kirkwood, NY 13795, Phone: 607-775-9368, jlupole@stny.rr.com
Specialties: Working and collector grade fixed blades, ethnic-styled blades. **Patterns:** Fighters, Bowies, tacticals, hunters, camp, utility, personal carry knives, some swords. **Technical:** Forges and grinds 10XX series and other high-carbon steels, grinds ATS-34 and 440C, will use just about every handle material available. **Prices:** $80 to $500 and up. **Remarks:** Part-time maker since 1999. **Marks:** "KUMA" hot stamped, name, city and state-etched, or "Daiguma saku" in kanji.

LUTZ, GREG,
127 Crescent Rd, Greenwood, SC 29646, Phone: 864-229-7340
Specialties: Working and using knives and period pieces of his design and to customer specs. **Patterns:** Fighters, hunters and swords. **Technical:** Forges 1095 and O1; grinds ATS-34. Differentially heat-treats forged blades; uses cryogenic treatment on ATS-34. **Prices:** $50 to $350; some to $1200. **Remarks:** Part-time maker; first knife sold in 1986. Doing business as Scorpion Forge. **Mark:** First initial, last name.

LYLE III, ERNEST L,
LYLE KNIVES, PO Box 1755, Chiefland, FL 32644, Phone: 352-490-6693, ernestlyle@msn.com
Specialties: Fancy period pieces; one-of-a-kind and limited editions. **Patterns:** Arabian/Persian influenced fighters, military knives, Bowies and Roman short swords; several styles of hunters. **Technical:** Grinds 440C, D2 and 154 CM. Engraves. **Prices:** $200 - $7500. **Remarks:** Full-time maker; first knife sold in 1972. **Mark:** Lyle Knives over Chiefland, Fla.

LYNCH, TAD,
140 Timberline Dr., Beebe, AR 72012, Phone: 501-626-1647, lynchknives@yahoo.com Web: lynchknives.com
Specialties: Forged fixed blades. **Patterns:** Bowies, choppers, fighters, hunters. **Technical:** Hand-forged W-2, 1084, 1095 clay quenched 52100, 5160. **Prices:** Starting at $250. **Remarks:** Part-time maker, also offers custom leather work via wife Amy Lynch. **Mark:** T.D. Lynch over anvil.

LYNN, ARTHUR,
29 Camino San Cristobal, Galisteo, NM 87540, Phone: 505-466-3541, lynnknives@aol.com
Specialties: Handforged Damascus knives. **Patterns:** Folders, hunters, Bowies, fighters, kitchen. **Technical:** Forges own Damascus. **Prices:** Moderate.

LYTTLE, BRIAN,
Box 5697, High River, AB, CANADA T1V 1M7, Phone: 403-558-3638, brian@lyttleknives.com; Web: www.lyttleknives.com
Specialties: Fancy working straight knives and folders; art knives. **Patterns:** Bowies, daggers, dirks, sgian dubhs, folders, dress knives, tantos, short swords. **Technical:** Forges Damascus steel; engraving; scrimshaw; heat-treating; classes. **Prices:** $450 to $15,000. **Remarks:** Full-time maker; first knife sold in 1983. **Mark:** Last name, country.

M

MACDONALD, DAVID,
2824 Hwy 47, Los Lunas, NM 87031, Phone: 505-866-5866

MACDONALD, JOHN,
310 Rte 27, Apt 18, Raymond, NH 03077, Phone: 603-244-2988
Specialties: Working/using straight knives of his design and to customer specs. **Patterns:** Japanese cutlery, Bowies, hunters and working knives. **Technical:** Grinds O1, L6 and ATS-34. Swords have matching handles and scabbards with Japanese flair. **Prices:** $70 to $250; some to $500. **Remarks:** Part-time maker; first knife sold in 1988. Custom knife cases made from pine and exotic hardwoods for table display or wall hanging. Doing business as Mac the Knife. **Mark:** Initials.

MACKIE, JOHN,
13653 Lanning, Whittier, CA 90605, Phone: 562-945-6104
Specialties: Forged. **Patterns:** Bowie and camp knives. **Technical:** Attended ABS Bladesmith School. **Prices:** $75 to $500. **Mark:** JSM in a triangle.

MACKRILL, STEPHEN,
PO Box 1580, Pinegowrie, JHB 2123, SOUTH AFRICA, Phone: 27-11-474-7139, Fax: 27-11-474-7139, info@mackrill.co.za; Web: www.mackrill.net
Specialties: Art fancy, historical, collectors and corporate gifts cutlery. **Patterns:** Fighters, hunters, camp, custom lock back and LinerLock® folders. **Technical:** N690, 12C27, ATS-34, silver and gold inlay on handles; wooden and

silver sheaths. **Prices:** $330 and upwards. **Remarks:** First knife sold in 1978. **Mark:** Mackrill fish with country of origin.

MADRULLI, MME JOELLE,
Residence Ste Catherine B1, Salon De Provence, FRANCE 13330

MAE, TAKAO,
1-119 1-4 Uenohigashi, Toyonaka, Osaka, JAPAN 560-0013, Phone: 81-6-6852-2758, Fax: 81-6-6481-1649, takamae@nifty.com
Remarks: Distinction stylish in art-forged blades, with lacquered ergonomic handles.

MAESTRI, PETER A,
S11251 Fairview Rd, Spring Green, WI 53588, Phone: 608-546-4481
Specialties: Working straight knives in standard patterns. **Patterns:** Camp and fishing knives, utility green-river-styled. **Technical:** Grinds 440C, 154CM and 440A. **Prices:** $15 to $45; some to $150. **Remarks:** Full-time maker; first knife sold in 1981. Provides professional cutler service to professional cutters. **Mark:** CARISOLO, MAESTRI BROS., or signature.

MAGEE, JIM,
741 S. Ohio St., Salina, KS 67401, Phone: 785-820-6928, jimmagee@cox.net
Specialties: Working and fancy folding knives. **Patterns:** Liner locking folders, favorite is his Persian. **Technical:** Grinds ATS-34, Devin Thomas & Eggerling Damascus, titanium. Liners Prefer mother-of-pearl handles. **Prices:** Start at $225 to $1200. **Remarks:** Part-time maker, first knife sold in 2001. Purveyor since 1982. Past president of the Professional Knifemakers Association **Mark:** Last name.

MAGRUDER, JASON,
460 Arnos Rd, Unit 66, Talent, OR 97540, Phone: 719-210-1579, belstain@hotmail.com; jason@magruderknives.com; web: MagruderKnives.com
Specialties: Unique and innovative designs combining the latest modern materials with traditional hand craftsmanship. **Patterns:** Fancy neck knives. Tactical gents folders. Working straight knives. **Technical:** Flats grinds CPM3v, CPM154, ATS34, 1080, and his own forged damascus. Hand carves carbon fiber, titanium, wood, ivory, and pearl handles. Filework and carving on blades. **Prices:** $150 and up. **Remarks:** Part-time maker; first knife sold in 2000. **Mark:** Last name.

MAHOMEDY, A R,
PO Box 76280, Marble Ray KZN, 4035, SOUTH AFRICA, Phone: +27 31 577 1451, arm-koknives@mweb.co.za; Web: www.arm-koknives.co.za
Specialties: Daggers and elegant folders of own design finished with finest exotic materials currently available. **Technical:** Via stock removal, grinds Damasteel, Damascus and the famous hardenable stainless steels. **Prices:** U.S. $650 and up. **Remarks:** Part-time maker. First knife sold in 1995. Voting member knifemakers guild of SA, FEGA member starting out Engraving. **Mark:** Initials A R M crowned with a "Minaret."

MAHOMEDY, HUMAYD A.R.,
PO BOX 76280, Marble Ray 4035, KZN, South Africa, Phone: +27 31 577 1451, arm-koknives@mweb.co.za
Specialties: Tactical folding and fixed blade knives. **Patterns:** Fighters, utilities, tacticals, folders and fixed blades, daggers, modern interpretation of Bowies. **Technical:** Stock-removal knives of Bohler N690, Bohler K110, Bohler K460, Sandvik 12C27, Sandvik RWL 34. Handle materials used are G10, Micarta, Cape Buffalo horn, Water Buffalo horn, Kudu horn, Gemsbok horn, Giraffe bone, Elephant ivory, Mammoth ivory, Arizona desert ironwood, stabilised and dyed burls. **Prices:** $250 - $1000. **Remarks:** First knife sold in 2002. Full-time knifemaker since 2002. First person of color making knives full-time in South Africa. Doing business as HARM EDGED TOOLS. **Mark:** HARM and arrow over EDGED TOOLS.

MAIENKNECHT, STANLEY,
38648 S R 800, Sardis, OH 43946

MAINES, JAY,
SUNRISE RIVER CUSTOM KNIVES, 5584 266th St., Wyoming, MN 55092, Phone: 651-462-5301, jaymaines@fronternet.net; Web: http://www.sunrisecustomknives.com
Specialties: Heavy duty working, classic and traditional fixed blades. Some high-tech and fancy embellished knives available. **Patterns:** Hunters, skinners, fillet, bowies tantos, boot daggers etc. etc. **Technical:** Hollow ground, stock removal blades of 440C, ATS-34 and CPM S-90V. Prefers natural handle materials, exotic hard woods, and stag, rams and buffalo horns. Offers dovetailed bolsters in brass, stainless steel and nickel silver. Custom sheaths from matching wood or hand-stitched from heavy duty water buffalo hide. **Prices:** Moderate to up-scale. **Remarks:** Part-time maker; first knife sold in 1992. Doing business as Sunrise River Custom Knives. Offers fixed blade knives repair and handle conversions. **Mark:** Full name under a Rising Sun logo.

MAISEY, ALAN,
PO Box 197, Vincentia 2540, NSW, AUSTRALIA, Phone: 2-4443 7829, tosanaji@excite.com
Specialties: Daggers, especially krisses; period pieces. **Technical:** Offers knives and finished blades in Damascus and nickel Damascus. **Prices:** $75 to $2000; some higher. **Remarks:** Part-time maker; provides complete restoration service for krisses. Trained by a Japanese Kris smith. **Mark:** None, triangle in a box, or three peaks.

MAJORS, CHARLIE,
1911 King Richards Ct, Montgomery, TX 77316, Phone: 713-826-3135, charliemajors@sbcglobal.net
Specialties: Fixed-blade hunters and slip-joint and lock-back folders. **Technical:** Practices stock removal method, preferring CPM154 steel and natural handle materials such as ironwood, stag, and mammoth ivory. Also takes customer requests. Does own heat treating and cryogenic quenching. **Remarks:** First knife made in 1980.

MAKOTO, KUNITOMO,
3-3-18 Imazu-cho, Fukuyama-city, Hiroshima, JAPAN, Phone: 084-933-5874, kunitomo@po.iijnet.or.jp

MALABY, RAYMOND J,
835 Calhoun Ave, Juneau, AK 99801, Phone: 907-586-6981, Fax: 907-523-8031, malaby@gci.net
Specialties: Straight working knives. **Patterns:** Hunters, skiners, Bowies, and camp knives. **Technical:** Hand forged 1084, 5160, O1 and grinds ATS-34 stainless. **Prices:** $195 to $400. **Remarks:** First knife sold in 1994. **Mark:** First initial, last name, city, and state.

MALLETT, J.P.,
3952 San Felipe Rd., Santa Fe, NM 87507, Phone: 505-577-3355
Specialties: Deep hollow grinds with nice lines and file worked spines. **Patterns:** Makes own damascus. Raindrop, ladder, random, etc. **Technical:** Has been a grinder for many years. **Prices:** $100 - $2000. **Remarks:** Teaching bladesmithing classes beginning January, 2011. **Mark:** Mallett. Older models stamped M only.

MALLOY, JOE,
1039 Schwabe St, Freeland, PA 18224, Phone: 570-436-6416, jdmalloy@msn.com
Specialties: Working straight knives and lock back folders—plain and fancy—of his design. **Patterns:** Hunters, utility, Bowie, survival knives, folders. **Technical:** Grinds ATS-34, 440C, D2 and A2 and Damascus. Makes own leather and kydex sheaths. **Prices:** $100 to $1800. **Remarks:** Part-time maker; first knife sold in 1982. **Mark:** First and middle initials, last name, city and state.

MANARO, SAL,
10 Peri Ave., Holbrook, NY 11741, Phone: 631-737-1180, maker@manaroknives.com
Specialties: Tactical folders, bolstered titanium LinerLocks, handmade folders, and fixed blades with hand-checkered components. **Technical:** Compound grinds, hidden fasteners and welded components, with blade steels including CPM-154, damascus, Stellite, D2, S30V and O-1 by the stock-removal method of blade making. **Prices:** $500 and up. **Remarks:** Part-time maker, made first knife in 2001. **Mark:** Last name with arrowhead underline.

MANDT, JOE,
3735 Overlook Dr. NE, St. Petersburg, FL 33703, Phone: 813-244-3816, jmforge@mac.com
Specialties: Forged Bowies, camp knives, hunters, skinners, fighters, boot knives, military style field knives. **Technical:** Forges plain carbon steel and high carbon tool steels, including W2, 1084, 5160, O1, 9260, 15N20, cable Damascus, pattern welded Damascus, flat and convex grinds. Prefers natural handle materials, hand-rubbed finishes, and stainless low carbon steel, Damascus and wright iron fittings. Does own heat treat. **Prices:** $150 to $750. **Remarks:** Part-time maker, first knife sold in 206. **Mark:** "MANDT".

MANEKER, KENNETH,
RR 2, Galiano Island, B.C., CANADA V0N 1P0, Phone: 604-539-2084
Specialties: Working straight knives; period pieces. **Patterns:** Camp knives and hunters; French chef knives. **Technical:** Grinds 440C, 154CM and Vascowear. **Prices:** $50 to $200; some to $300. **Remarks:** Part-time maker; first knife sold in 1981. Doing business as Water Mountain Knives. **Mark:** Japanese Kanji of initials, plus glyph.

MANKEL, KENNETH,
7836 Cannonsburg Rd, PO Box 35, Cannonsburg, MI 49317, Phone: 616-874-6955, Fax: 616-8744-4053

MANLEY, DAVID W,
3270 Six Mile Hwy, Central, SC 29630, Phone: 864-654-1125, dmanleyknives@wmconnect.com
Specialties: Working straight knives of his design or to custom specs. **Patterns:** Hunters, boot and fighters. **Technical:** Grinds 440C and ATS-34. **Prices:** $60 to $250. **Remarks:** Part-time maker; first knife sold in 1994. **Mark:** First initial, last name, year and serial number.

MANN, MICHAEL L,
IDAHO KNIFE WORKS, PO Box 144, Spirit Lake, ID 83869, Phone: 509 994-9394, Web: www.idahoknifeworks.com
Specialties: Good working blades-historical reproduction, modern or custom design. **Patterns:** Cowboy Bowies, Mountain Man period blades, old-style folders, designer and maker of "The Cliff Knife", hunter knives, hand ax and fish fillet. **Technical:** High-carbon steel blades-hand forged 5160. Stock removed 15N20 steel. Also Damascus. **Prices:** $130 to $670+. **Remarks:** Made first knife in 1965. Full-time making knives as Idaho Knife Works since 1986. Functional as well as collectible. Each knife truly unique! **Mark:** Four mountain peaks are his initials MM.

MANN, TIM,
BLADEWORKS, PO Box 1196, Honokaa, HI 96727, Phone: 808-775-0949, Fax: 808-775-0949, birdman@shaka.com
Specialties: Hand-forged knives and swords. **Patterns:** Bowies, tantos, pesh kabz, daggers. **Technical:** Use 5160, 1050, 1075, 1095 and ATS-34 steels, cable Damascus. **Prices:** $200 to $800. **Remarks:** Just learning to forge Damascus. **Mark:** None yet.

MARAGNI, DAN,
RD 1 Box 106, Georgetown, NY 13072, Phone: 315-662-7490
Specialties: Heavy-duty working knives, some investor class. **Patterns:** Hunters, fighters and camp knives, some Scottish types. **Technical:** Forges W2 and his own Damascus; toughness and edge-holding a high priority. **Prices:** $125 to $500; some to $1000. **Remarks:** Full-time maker; first knife sold in 1975. **Mark:** Celtic initials in circle.

MARCHAND, RICK,
Wildertools, 681 Middleton Lane, Wheatley, Ontario N0P 2P0, Phone: 519-825-9726, rickmarchand@wildertools.com
Specialties: Specializing in multicultural, period stylized blades and accoutrements. **Technical:** Hand forged from 1070/84 and 5160 steel. **Prices:** $175 - $900. **Remarks:** 3 years full-time maker. ABS Apprentice Smith. **Mark:** Tang stamp: "MARCHAND" along with two Japanese-style characters resembling "W" and "M."

MARINGER, TOM,
2692 Powell St., Springdale, AR 72764, maringer@arkansas.net; Web: shirepost.com/cutlery.
Specialties: Working straight and curved blades with stainless steel furniture and wire-wrapped handles. **Patterns:** Subhilts, daggers, boots, swords. **Technical:** Grinds D-2, A-2, ATS-34. May be safely disassembled by the owner via pommel screw or pegged construction. **Prices:** $2000 to $3000, some to $20,000. **Remarks:** Former full-time maker, now part-time. First knife sold in 1975. **Mark:** Full name, year, and serial number etched on tang under handle.

MARKLEY, KEN,
7651 Cabin Creek Lane, Sparta, IL 62286, Phone: 618-443-5284
Specialties: Traditional working and using knives of his design and to customer specs. **Patterns:** Fighters, hunters and utility/camp knives. **Technical:** Forges 5160, 1095 and L6; makes his own Damascus; does file work. **Prices:** $150 to $800; some to $2000. **Remarks:** Part-time maker; first knife sold in 1991. Doing business as Cabin Creek Forge. **Mark:** Last name, JS.

MARLOWE, CHARLES,
10822 Poppleton Ave, Omaha, NE 68144, Phone: 402-933-5065, cmarlowe1@cox.net; Web: www.marloweknives.com
Specialties: Folding knives and balisong. **Patterns:** Tactical pattern folders. **Technical:** Grind ATS-34, S30V, CPM154, 154CM, Damasteel, others on request. Forges/grinds 1095 on occasion. **Prices:** Start at $450. **Remarks:** First knife sold in 1993. Full-time since 1999. **Mark:** Turtle logo with Marlowe above, year below.

MARLOWE, DONALD,
2554 Oakland Rd, Dover, PA 17315, Phone: 717-764-6055
Specialties: Working straight knives in standard patterns. **Patterns:** Bowies, fighters, boots and utility knives. **Technical:** Grinds D2 and 440C. Integral design hunter models. **Prices:** $130 to $850. **Remarks:** Spare-time maker; first knife sold in 1977. **Mark:** Last name.

MARSH, JEREMY,
6169 3 Mile NE, Ada, MI 49301, Phone: 616-889-1945, steelbean@hotmail.com; Web: www.marshcustomknives.com
Specialties: Locking liner folders, dressed-up gents knives, tactical knives, and dress tacticals. **Technical:** CPM S30V stainless and Damascus blade steels using the stock-removal method of bladesmithing. **Prices:** $450 to $1500. **Remarks:** Self-taught, part-time knifemaker; first knife sold in 2004. **Mark:** Maker's last name and large, stylized M.

MARSHALL, STEPHEN R,
975 Harkreader Rd, Mt. Juliet, TN 37122

MARTIN, BRUCE E,
Rt. 6, Box 164-B, Prescott, AR 71857, Phone: 501-887-2023
Specialties: Fancy working straight knives of his design. **Patterns:** Bowies, camp knives, skinners and fighters. **Technical:** Forges 5160, 1095 and his own Damascus. Uses natural handle materials; filework available. **Prices:** $75 to $350; some to $500. **Remarks:** Full-time maker; first knife sold in 1979. **Mark:** Name in arch.

MARTIN, GENE,
PO Box 396, Williams, OR 97544, Phone: 541-846-6755, bladesmith@customknife.com
Specialties: Straight knives and folders. **Patterns:** Fighters, hunters, skinners, boot knives, spring back and lock back folders. **Technical:** Grinds ATS-34, 440C, Damascus and 154CM. Forges; makes own Damascus; scrimshaws. **Prices:** $150 to $2500. **Remarks:** Full-time maker; first knife sold in 1993. Doing business as Provision Forge. **Mark:** Name and/or crossed staff and sword.

MARTIN, HAL W,
781 Hwy 95, Morrilton, AR 72110, Phone: 501-354-1682, hal.martin@sbcglobal.net
Specialties: Hunters, Bowies and fighters. **Prices:** $250 and up. **Mark:** MARTIN.

MARTIN, HERB,
2500 Starwood Dr, Richmond, VA 23229, Phone: 804-747-1675, hamjlm@hotmail.com
Specialties: Working straight knives. **Patterns:** Skinners, hunters and utility. **Technical:** Hollow grinds ATS-34, and Micarta handles. **Prices:** $85 to $125. **Remarks:** Part-time Maker. First knife sold in 2001. **Mark:** HA MARTIN.

MARTIN, MICHAEL W,
Box 572, Jefferson St, Beckville, TX 75631, Phone: 903-678-2161
Specialties: Classic working/using straight knives of his design and in standard patterns. **Patterns:** Hunters. **Technical:** Grinds ATS-34, 440C, O1 and A2. Bead blasted, Parkerized, high polish and satin finishes. Sheaths are handmade. Also hand forges cable Damascus. **Prices:** $185 to $280 some higher. **Remarks:** Part-time maker; first knife sold in 1995. Doing business as Michael W. Martin Knives. **Mark:** Name and city, state in arch.

MARTIN, PETER,
28220 N. Lake Dr, Waterford, WI 53185, Phone: 262-706-3076, Web: www.petermartinknives.com
Specialties: Fancy, fantasy and working straight knives and folders of his design and in standard patterns. **Patterns:** Bowies, fighters, hunters, locking folders and liner locks. **Technical:** Forges own Mosaic Damascus, powdered steel and his own Damascus. Prefers natural handle material; offers file work and carved handles. **Prices:** Moderate. **Remarks:** Full-time maker; first knife sold in 1988. Doing business as Martin Custom Products. **Mark:** Martin Knives.

MARTIN, RANDALL J,
51 Bramblewood St, Bridgewater, MA 02324, Phone: 508-279-0682
Specialties: High tech folding and fixed blade tactical knives employing the latest blade steels and exotic materials. Employs a unique combination of 3d-CNC machining and hand work on both blades and handles. All knives are designed for hard use. Clean, radical grinds and ergonomic handles are hallmarks of RJ's work, as is his reputation for producing "Scary Sharp" knives. **Technical:** Grinds CPM30V, CPM 3V, CPM154CM, A2 and stainless Damascus. Other CPM alloys used on request. Performs all heat treating and cryogenic processing in-house. **Remarks:** Full-time maker since 2001 and materials engineer. Former helicopter designer. First knife sold in 1976.

MARTIN, TONY,
PO Box 10, Arcadia, MO 63621, Phone: 573-546-2254, arcadian@charter.net; Web: www.arcadianforge.com
Specialties: Specializes in historical designs, esp. puukko, skean dhu. **Remarks:** Premium quality blades, exotic wood handles, unmatched fit and finish. **Mark:** AF.

MARTIN, WALTER E,
570 Cedar Flat Rd, Williams, OR 97544, Phone: 541-846-6755

MARTIN

MARTIN, JOHN ALEXANDER,
821 N Grand Ave, Okmulgee, OK 74447, Phone: 918-758-1099, jam@jamblades.com; Web: www.jamblades.com
Specialties: Inlaid and engraved handles. **Patterns:** Bowies, fighters, hunters and traditional patterns. Swords, fixed blade knives, folders and axes. **Technical:** Forges 5160, 1084, 10XX, O1, L6 and his own Damascus. **Prices:** Start at $300. **Remarks:** Part-time maker. **Mark:** Two initials with last name and MS or 5 pointed star.

MARZITELLI, PETER,
19929 35A Ave, Langley, B.C., CANADA V3A 2R1, Phone: 604-532-8899, marzitelli@shaw.ca
Specialties: Specializes in unique functional knife shapes and designs using natural and synthetic handle materials. **Patterns:** Mostly folders, some daggers and art knives. **Technical:** Grinds ATS-34, S/S Damascus and others. **Prices:** $220 to $1000 (average $375). **Remarks:** Full-time maker; first knife sold in 1984. **Mark:** Stylized logo reads "Marz."

MASON, BILL,
1114 St Louis #33, Excelsior Springs, MO 64024, Phone: 816-637-7335
Specialties: Combat knives; some folders. **Patterns:** Fighters to match knife types in book *Cold Steel*. **Technical:** Grinds O1, 440C and ATS-34. **Prices:** $115 to $250; some to $350. **Remarks:** Spare-time maker; first knife sold in 1979. **Mark:** Initials connected.

MASSEY, AL,
Box 14 Site 15 RR#2, Mount Uniacke, Nova Scotia, CANADA B0N 1Z0, Phone: 902-866-4754, armjan@eastlink.ca
Specialties: Working knives and period pieces. **Patterns:** Swords and daggers of Celtic to medieval design, Bowies. **Technical:** Forges 5160, 1084 and 1095. Makes own Damascus. **Prices:** $200 to $500, damascus $300-$1000. **Remarks:** Part-time maker, first blade sold in 1988. **Mark:** Initials and JS on Ricasso.

MASSEY, ROGER,
4928 Union Rd, Texarkana, AR 71854, Phone: 870-779-1018
Specialties: Traditional and working straight knives and folders of his design and to customer specs. **Patterns:** Bowies, hunters, daggers and utility knives. **Technical:** Forges 1084 and 52100, makes his own Damascus. Offers filework and silver wire inlay in handles. **Prices:** $200 to $1500; some to $2500. **Remarks:** Part-time maker; first knife sold in 1991. **Mark:** Last name, M.S.

MASSEY, RON,
61638 El Reposo St., Joshua Tree, CA 92252, Phone: 760-366-9239 after 5 p.m., Fax: 763-366-4620
   Specialties: Classic, traditional, fancy/embellished, high art, period pieces, working/using knives, straight knives, folders, and automatics. Your design, customer specs, about 175 standard patterns. **Patterns:** Automatics, hunters and fighters. All folders are side-locking folders. Unless requested as lock books slip joint he specializes or custom designs. **Technical:** ATS-34, 440C, D-2 upon request. Engraving, filework, scrimshaw, most of the exotic handle materials. All aspects are performed by him: inlay work in pearls or stone, handmade Pem' work. **Prices:** $110 to $2500; some to $6000. **Remarks:** Part-time maker; first knife sold in 1976.

MATA, LEONARD,
3583 Arruza St, San Diego, CA 92154, Phone: 619-690-6935

MATHEWS, CHARLIE AND HARRY,
TWIN BLADES, 121 Mt Pisgah Church Rd., Statesboro, GA 30458, Phone: 912-865-9098, twinblades@bulloch.net; Web: www.twinxblades.com
   Specialties: Working straight knives, carved stag handles. **Patterns:** Hunters, fighters, Bowies and period pieces. **Technical:** Grinds D2, CPMS30V, CPM3V, ATS-34 and commercial Damascus; handmade sheaths some with exotic leather, file work. Forges 1095, 1084, and 5160. **Prices:** Starting at $125. **Remarks:** Twin brothers making knives full-time under the label of Twin Blades. Charter members Georgia Custom Knifemakers Guild. Members of The Knifemakers Guild. **Mark:** Twin Blades over crossed knives, reverse side steel type.

MATSUNO, KANSEI,
109-8 Uenomachi Nishikaiden, Gifu-City 501-1168, JAPAN, Phone: 81 58 234 8643

MATSUOKA, SCOT,
94-415 Ukalialii Place, Mililani, HI 96789, Phone: 808-625-6658, Fax: 808-625-6658, scottym@hawaii.rr.com; Web: www.matsuokaknives.com
   Specialties: Folders, fixed blades with custom hand-stitched sheaths. **Patterns:** Gentleman's knives, hunters, tactical folders. **Technical:** CPM 154CM, 440C, 154, BG42, bolsters, file work, and engraving. **Prices:** Starting price $350. **Remarks:** Part-time maker, first knife sold in 2002. **Mark:** Logo, name and state.

MATSUSAKI, TAKESHI,
MATSUSAKI KNIVES, 151 Ono-Cho Sasebo-shi, Nagasaki, JAPAN, Phone: 0956-47-2938, Fax: 0956-47-2938
   Specialties: Working and collector grade front look and slip joint. **Patterns:** Sheffierd type folders. **Technical:** Grinds ATS-34 k-120. **Price:** $250 to $1000, some to $8000. **Remarks:** Part-time maker, first knife sold in 1990. **Mark:** Name and initials.

MAXEN, MICK,
2 Huggins Welham Green, "Hatfield, Herts", UNITED KINGDOM AL97LR, Phone: 01707 261213, mmaxen@aol.com
   Specialties: Damascus and Mosaic. **Patterns:** Medieval-style daggers and Bowies. **Technical:** Forges CS75 and 15N20 / nickel Damascus. **Mark:** Last name with axe above.

MAXFIELD, LYNN,
382 Colonial Ave, Layton, UT 84041, Phone: 801-544-4176, lcmaxfield@msn.com
   Specialties: Sporting knives, some fancy. **Patterns:** Hunters, fishing, fillet, special purpose: some locking folders. **Technical:** Grinds 440-C, 154-CM, CPM154, D2, CPM S30V, and Damascus. **Prices:** $125 to $400; some to $900. **Remarks:** Part-time maker; first knife sold in 1979. **Mark:** Name, city and state.

MAXWELL, DON,
1484 Celeste Ave, Clovis, CA 93611, Phone: 559-299-2197, maxwellknives@aol.com; Web: maxwellknives.com
   Specialties: Fancy folding knives and fixed blades of his design. **Patterns:** Hunters, fighters, utility/camp knives, LinerLock® folders, flippers and fantasy knives. **Technical:** Grinds 440C, ATS-34, D2, CPM 154, and commercial Damascus. **Prices:** $250 to $1000; some to $2500. **Remarks:** Full-time maker; first knife sold in 1987. **Mark:** Last name only or Maxwell MAX-TAC.

MAY, CHARLES,
10024 McDonald Rd., Aberdeen, MS 39730, Phone: 662-369-0404, charlesmayknives@yahoo.com; Web: charlesmayknives.blademakers.com
   Specialties: Fixed-blade sheath knives. **Patterns:** Hunters and fillet knives. **Technical:** Scandinavian-ground D2 and S30V blades, black micarta and wood handles, nickel steel pins with maker's own pocket carry or belt-loop pouches. **Prices:** $215 to $495. **Mark:** "Charles May Knives" and a knife in a circle.

MAYNARD, LARRY JOE,
PO Box 493, Crab Orchard, WV 25827
   Specialties: Fancy and fantasy straight knives. **Patterns:** Big knives; a Bowie with a full false edge; fighting knives. **Technical:** Grinds standard steels. **Prices:** $350 to $500; some to $1000. **Remarks:** Full-time maker; first knife sold in 1986. **Mark:** Middle and last initials.

MAYNARD, WILLIAM N.,
2677 John Smith Rd, Fayetteville, NC 28306, Phone: 910-425-1615
   Specialties: Traditional and working straight knives of all designs. **Patterns:** Combat, Bowies, fighters, hunters and utility knives. **Technical:** Grinds 440C, ATS-34 and commercial Damascus. Offers fancy filework; handmade sheaths. **Prices:** $100 to $300; some to $750. **Remarks:** Full-time maker; first knife sold in 1988. **Mark:** Last name.

MAYO JR., HOMER,
18036 Three Rivers Rd., Biloxi, MS 39532, Phone: 228-326-8298
   Specialties: Traditional working straight knives, folders and tactical. **Patterns:** Hunters, fighters, tactical, bird, Bowles, fish fillet knives and lightweight folders. **Technical:** Grinds 440C, ATS-34, D-2, Damascus, forges and grinds 52100 and custom makes sheaths. **Prices:** $100 to $1000. **Remarks:** Part-time maker **Mark:** All knives are serial number and registered in the name of the original purchaser, stamped last name or etched.

MAYO JR., TOM,
67 412 Alahaka St, Waialua, HI 96791, Phone: 808-637-6560, mayot001@hawaii.rr.com; Web: www.mayoknives.com
   Specialties: Framelocks/tactical knives. **Patterns:** Combat knives, hunters, Bowies and folders. **Technical:** Titanium/stellite/S30V. **Prices:** $500 to $1000. **Remarks:** Full-time maker; first knife sold in 1982. **Mark:** Volcano logo with name and state.

MAYVILLE, OSCAR L,
2130 E. County Rd 910S, Marengo, IN 47140, Phone: 812-338-4159
   Specialties: Working straight knives; period pieces. **Patterns:** Kitchen cutlery, Bowies, camp knives and hunters. **Technical:** Grinds A2, O1 and 440C. **Prices:** $50 to $350; some to $500. **Remarks:** Full-time maker; first knife sold in 1984. **Mark:** Initials over knife logo.

MCABEE, WILLIAM,
27275 Norton Grade, Colfax, CA 95713, Phone: 530-389-8163
   Specialties: Working/using knives. **Patterns:** Fighters, Bowies, Hunters. **Technical:** Grinds ATS-34. **Prices:** $75 to $200; some to $350. **Remarks:** Part-time maker; first knife sold in 1990. **Mark:** Stylized WM stamped.

MCCALLEN JR., HOWARD H,
110 Anchor Dr, So Seaside Park, NJ 08752

MCCARLEY, JOHN,
4165 Harney Rd, Taneytown, MD 21787
   Specialties: Working straight knives; period pieces. **Patterns:** Hunters, Bowies, camp knives, miniatures, throwing knives. **Technical:** Forges W2, O1 and his own Damascus. **Prices:** $150 to $300; some to $1000. **Remarks:** Part-time maker; first knife sold in 1977. **Mark:** Initials in script.

MCCARTY, HARRY,
1479 Indian Ridge Rd, Blaine, TN 37709, harry@indianridgeforge.com; Web: www.indianridgeforge.com
   Specialties: Period pieces. **Patterns:** Trade knives, Bowies, 18th and 19th century folders and hunting swords. **Technical:** Forges and grinds high-carbon steel. **Prices:** $75 to $1300. **Remarks:** Full-time maker; first knife sold in 1977. Doing business as Indian Ridge Forge. **Mark:** Stylized initials inside a shamrock.

MCCLURE, JERRY,
3052 Isim Rd, Norman, OK 73026, Phone: 405-321-3614, jerry@jmccclureknives.net; Web: www.jmcclureknives.net
   Specialties: Gentleman's folder, linerlock with my jeweled pivot system of eight rubies, forged one-of-a-kind Damascus Bowies, and a line of hunting/camp knives. **Patterns:** Folders, Bowie, and hunting/camp **Technical** Forges own Damascus, also uses Damasteel and does own heat treating. **Prices** $500 to $3,000 and up **Remarks** Full-time maker, made first knife in 1965. **Mark** J.MCCLURE

MCCLURE, MICHAEL,
803 17th Ave, Menlo Park, CA 94025, Phone: 650-323-2596, mikesknives@att.net
   Specialties: Working/using straight knives of his design and to customer specs. **Patterns:** Bowies, hunters, skinners, utility/camp, tantos, fillets and boot knives. **Technical:** Forges high-carbon and Damascus; also grinds stainless, all grades. **Prices:** Start at $200. **Remarks:** Part-time maker; first knife sold in 1991. ABS Journeyman Smith. **Mark:** Mike McClure.

MCCONNELL JR., LOYD A,
309 County Road 144-B, Marble Falls, TX 78654, Phone: 830-798-8087, cckknives@cckknives.com; Web: www.cckknives.com
   Specialties: Working straight knives and folders, some fancy. **Patterns:** Hunters, boots, Bowies, locking folders and slip-joints. **Technical:** Grinds CPM Steels, ATS-34 and BG-42 and commercial Damascus. **Prices:** $450 to $10,000. **Remarks:** Full-time maker; first knife sold in 1975. Doing business as Cactus Custom Knives. Markets product knives under name: Lone Star Knives. **Mark:** Name, city and state in cactus logo.

MCCORNOCK, CRAIG,
MCC MTN OUTFITTERS, 4775 Rt. 212/PO 162, Willow, NY 12495, Phone: 845-679-9758, Mccmtn@aol.com; Web: www.mccmtn.com
   Specialties: Carry, utility, hunters, defense type knives and functional swords. **Patterns:** Drop points, hawkbills, tantos, waklzashis, katanas **Technical:** Stock removal, forged and Damascus, (yes, he still flints knap). **Prices:** $200 to $2000. **Mark:** McM.

MCCOUN—MCNABB

MCCOUN, MARK,
14212 Pine Dr, DeWitt, VA 23840, Phone: 804-469-7631, mccounandsons@live.com
Specialties: Working/using straight knives of his design and in standard patterns; custom miniatures. **Patterns:** Locking liners, integrals. **Technical:** Grinds Damascus, ATS-34 and 440C. **Prices:** $150 to $500. **Remarks:** Part-time maker; first knife sold in 1989. **Mark:** Name, city and state.

MCCRACKIN, KEVIN,
3720 Hess Rd, House Spings, MO 63051, Phone: 636-677-6066

MCCRACKIN AND SON, V J,
3720 Hess Rd, House Springs, MO 63051, Phone: 636-677-6066
Specialties: Working straight knives in standard patterns. **Patterns:** Hunters, Bowies and camp knives. **Technical:** Forges L6, 5160, his own Damascus, cable Damascus. **Prices:** $125 to $700; some to $1500. **Remarks:** Part-time maker; first knife sold in 1983. Son Kevin helps make the knives. **Mark:** Last name, M.S.

MCCULLOUGH, JERRY,
274 West Pettibone Rd, Georgiana, AL 36033, Phone: 334-382-7644, ke4er@alaweb.com
Specialties: Standard patterns or custom designs. **Technical:** Forge and grind scrap-tool and Damascus steels. Use natural handle materials and turquoise trim on some. Filework on others. **Prices:** $65 to $250 and up. **Remarks:** Part-time maker. **Mark:** Initials (JM) combined.

MCDONALD, RICH,
5010 Carmel Rd., Hillboro, OH 45133, Phone: 937-466-2071, rmclongknives@aol.com; Web; www.longknivesandleather.com
Specialties: Traditional working/using and art knives of his design. **Patterns:** Bowies, hunters, folders, primitives and tomahawks. **Technical:** Forges 5160, 1084, 1095, 52100 and his own Damascus. Fancy filework. **Prices:** $200 to $1500. **Remarks:** Full-time maker; first knife sold in 1994. **Mark:** First and last initials connected.

MCDONALD, ROBERT J,
14730 61 Court N, Loxahatchee, FL 33470, Phone: 561-790-1470
Specialties: Traditional working straight knives to customer specs. **Patterns:** Fighters, swords and folders. **Technical:** Grinds 440C, ATS-34 and forges own Damascus. **Prices:** $150 to $1000. **Remarks:** Part-time maker; first knife sold in 1988. **Mark:** Electro-etched name.

MCDONALD, ROBIN J,
7300 Tolleson Ave NW, Albuquerque, NM 87114-3546
Specialties: Working knives of maker's design. **Patterns:** Bowies, hunters, camp knives and fighters. **Technical:** Forges primarily 5160. **Prices:** $100 to $500. **Remarks:** Part-time maker; first knife sold in 1999. **Mark:** Initials RJM.

MCDONALD, W J "JERRY",
7173 Wickshire Cove E, Germantown, TN 38138, Phone: 901-756-9924, wjmcdonaldknives@email.msn.com; Web: www.mcdonaldknives.com
Specialties: Classic and working/using straight knives of his design and in standard patterns. **Patterns:** Bowies, hunters kitchen and traditional spring back pocket knives. **Technical:** Grinds ATS-34, 154CM, D2, 440V, BG42 and 440C. **Prices:** $125 to $1000. **Remarks:** Full-time maker; first knife sold in 1989. **Mark:** First and middle initials, last name, maker, city and state. Some of his knives are stamped McDonald in script.

MCFALL, KEN,
PO Box 458, Lakeside, AZ 85929, Phone: 928-537-2026, Fax: 928-537-8066, knives@citlink.net
Specialties: Fancy working straight knives and some folders. **Patterns:** Daggers, boots, tantos, Bowies; some miniatures. **Technical:** Grinds D2, ATS-34 and 440C. Forges his own Damascus. **Prices:** $200 to $1200. **Remarks:** Part-time maker; first knife sold in 1984. **Mark:** Name, city and state.

MCFARLIN, ERIC E,
PO Box 2188, Kodiak, AK 99615, Phone: 907-486-4799
Specialties: Working knives of his design. **Patterns:** Bowies, skinners, camp knives and hunters. **Technical:** Flat and convex grinds 440C, A2 and AEB-L. **Prices:** Start at $200. **Remarks:** Part-time maker; first knife sold in 1989. **Mark:** Name and city in rectangular logo.

MCFARLIN, J W,
3331 Pocohantas Dr, Lake Havasu City, AZ 86404, Phone: 928-453-7612, Fax: 928-453-7612, aztheedge@NPGcable.com
Technical: Flat grinds, D2, ATS-34, 440C, Thomas and Peterson Damascus. **Remarks:** From working knives to investment. Customer designs always welcome. 100 percent handmade. Made first knife in 1972. **Prices:** $150 to $3000. **Mark:** Hand written in the blade.

MCGILL, JOHN,
PO Box 302, Blairsville, GA 30512, Phone: 404-745-4686
Specialties: Working knives. **Patterns:** Traditional patterns; camp knives. **Technical:** Forges L6 and 9260; makes Damascus. **Prices:** $50 to $250; some to $500. **Remarks:** Full-time maker; first knife sold in 1982. **Mark:** XYLO.

MCGOWAN, FRANK E,
2023 Robin Ct, Winter address, Sebring, FL 33870, Phone: 443-745-2611, fmcgowan11@verizon.net
Specialties: Fancy working knives and folders to customer specs. **Patterns:** Survivor knives, fighters, fishing knives, folders and hunters. **Technical:** Grinds and forges O1, 440C, 5160, ATS-34, 52100 or customer choice. **Prices:** $100 to $1000, some more. **Remarks:** Full-time maker. First knife sold in 1986. **Mark:** Last name.

MCGOWAN, FRANK E,
12629 Howard Lodge Dr, Summer address, Sykesville, MD 21784, Phone: 410-489-4323, fmcgowan11@verizon.net
Specialties: Fancy working knives and folders to customer specs. **Patterns:** Survivor knives, fighters, fishing knives, folders and hunters. **Technical:** Grinds and forges O1, 440C, 5160, ATS-34, 52100, or customer choice. **Prices:** $100 to $1000; some more. **Remarks:** Full-time maker; first knife sold in 1986. **Mark:** Last name.

MCGRATH, PATRICK T,
8343 Kenyon Ave, Westchester, CA 90045, Phone: 310-338-8764, hidinginLA@excite.com

MCGRODER, PATRICK J,
5725 Chapin Rd, Madison, OH 44057, Phone: 216-298-3405, Fax: 216-298-3405
Specialties: Traditional working/using knives of his design. **Patterns:** Bowies, hunters and utility/camp knives. **Technical:** Grinds ATS-34, D2 and customer requests. Does reverse etching; heat-treats; prefers natural handle materials; custom made sheath with each knife. **Prices:** $125 to $250. **Remarks:** Part-time maker. **Mark:** First and middle initials, last name, maker, city and state.

MCGUANE IV, THOMAS F,
410 South 3rd Ave, Bozeman, MT 59715, Phone: 406-586-0248, Web: http://www.thomasmcguane.com
Specialties: Multi metal inlaid knives of handmade steel. **Patterns:** Lock back and LinerLock® folders, fancy straight knives. **Technical:** 1084/1SN20 Damascus and Mosaic steel by maker. **Prices:** $1000 and up. **Mark:** Surname or name and city, state.

MCHENRY, WILLIAM JAMES,
Box 67, Wyoming, RI 02898, Phone: 401-539-8353
Specialties: Fancy high-tech folders of his design. **Patterns:** Locking folders with various mechanisms. **Technical:** One-of-a-kind only, no duplicates. Inventor of the Axis Lock. Most pieces disassemble and feature top-shelf materials including gold, silver and gems. **Prices:** Upscale. **Remarks:** Full-time maker; first knife sold in 1988. Former goldsmith. **Mark:** Last name or first and last initials.

MCINTYRE, SHAWN,
71 Leura Grove, Hawthorn East Victoria, AUSTRALIA 3123, Phone: 61 3 9813 2049/Cell 61 412 041 062, macpower@netspace.net.au; Web: www.mcintyreknives.com
Specialties: Damascus & CS fixed blades and art knives. **Patterns:** Bowies, hunters, fighters, kukris, integrals. **Technical:** Forges, makes own Damascus including pattern weld, mosaic, and composite multi-bars form O1 & 15N20 Also uses 1084, W2, and 52100. **Prices:** $275 to $2000. **Remarks:** Full-time maker since 1999. **Mark:** Mcintyre in script.

MCKEE, NEIL,
674 Porter Hill Rd., Stevensville, MT 59870, Phone: 406-777-3507, mckeenh@peoplepc.com
Specialties: Early American. **Patterns:** Nessmuk, DeWeese, French folders, art pieces. **Technical:** Engraver. **Prices:** $150 to $1000. **Mark:** Oval with initials.

MCKENZIE, DAVID BRIAN,
2311 B Ida Rd, Campbell River B, CANADA V9W-4V7

MCKIERNAN, STAN,
11751 300th St, Lamoni, IA 50140, Phone: 641-784-6873/641-781-0368, slmck@hotmailc.com
Specialties: Self-sheathed knives and miniatures. **Patterns:** Daggers, ethnic designs and individual styles. **Technical:** Grinds Damascus and 440C. **Prices:** $200 to $500, some to $1500. **Mark:** "River's Bend" inside two concentric circles.

MCLENDON, HUBERT W,
125 Thomas Rd, Waco, GA 30182, Phone: 770-574-9796
Specialties: Using knives; his design or customer's. **Patterns:** Bowies and hunters. **Technical:** Hand ground or forged ATS-34, 440C and D2. **Prices:** $100 to $300. **Remarks:** First knife sold in 1978. **Mark:** McLendon or Mc.

MCLUIN, TOM,
36 Fourth St, Dracut, MA 01826, Phone: 978-957-4899, tmcluin@comcast.net; Web: www.mcluinknives.com
Specialties: Working straight knives and folders of his design. **Patterns:** Boots, hunters and folders. **Technical:** Grinds ATS-34, 440C, O1 and Damascus; makes his own mokume. **Prices:** $100 to $400; some to $700. **Remarks:** Part-time maker; first knife sold in 1991. **Mark:** Last name.

MCLURKIN, ANDREW,
2112 Windy Woods Dr, Raleigh, NC 27607, Phone: 919-834-4693, mclurkincustomknives.com
Specialties: Collector grade folders, working folders, fixed blades, and miniatures. Knives made to order and to his design. **Patterns:** Locking liner and lock back folders, hunter, working and tactical designs. **Technical:** Using patterned Damascus, Mosaic Damascus, ATS-34, BG-42, and CPM steels. Prefers natural handle materials such as pearl, ancient ivory and stabilized wood. Also using synthetic materials such as carbon fiber, titanium, and G10. **Prices:** $250 and up. **Mark:** Last name. Mark is often on inside of folders.

MCNABB, TOMMY,
CAROLINA CUSTOM KNIVES, PO Box 327, Bethania, NC 27010, Phone: 336-924-6053, Fax: 336-924-4854, tommy@tmcnabb.com; Web: carolinaknives.com
Specialties: Classic and working knives of his own design or to customer's specs. **Patterns:** Traditional bowies. Tomahawks, hunters and customer

designs. **Technical:** Forges his own Damascus steel, hand forges or grinds ATS-34 and other hi-tech steels. Prefers mirror finish or satin finish on working knives. Uses exotic or natural handle material and stabilized woods. **Price:** $300-$3500. **Remarks:** Full time maker. Made first knife in 1982. **Mark**""Carolina Custom Knives" on stock removal blades "T. McNabb" on custom orders and Damascus knives.

MCNEES, JONATHAN,
15203 Starboard Pl, Northport, AL 35475, Phone: 205-391-8383, jmackusmc@yahoo.com; Web: www.mcneescustomknives.com
   Specialties: Tactical, outdoors, utility. **Technical:** Stock removal method utilizing carbon and stainless steels to include 1095, cpm154, A2, cpms35v. **Remarks:** Part-time maker, first knife made in 2007. **Mark:** Jmcnees

MCRAE, J MICHAEL,
6100 Lake Rd, Mint Hill, NC 28227, Phone: 704-545-2929, scotia@carolina.rr.com; Web: www.scotiametalwork.com
   Specialties: Scottish dirks, sgian dubhs, broadswords. **Patterns:** Traditional blade styles with traditional and slightly non-traditional handle treatments. **Technical:** Forges 5160 and his own Damascus. Prefers stag and exotic hardwoods for handles, many intricately carved. **Prices:** Starting at $125, some to $3500. **Remarks:** Journeyman Smith in ABS, member of North Carolina Custom Knifemakers Guild and ABANA. Full-time maker, first knife sold in 1982. Doing business as Scotia Metalwork. **Mark:** Last name underlined with a claymore.

MEERDINK, KURT,
248 Yulan Barryville Rd., Barryville, NY 12719-5305, Phone: 845-557-0783
   Specialties: Working straight knives. **Patterns:** Hunters, Bowies, tactical and neck knives. **Technical:** Grinds ATS-34, 440C, D2, Damascus. **Prices:** $95 to $1100. **Remarks:** Full-time maker, first knife sold in 1994. **Mark:** Meerdink Maker, Rio NY.

MEERS, ANDREW,
1100 N Normal Ave., Allyn Bldg MC 4301, Carbondale, IL 62901, Phone: 774-217-3574, namsuechool@gmail.com
   Specialties: Pattern welded blades, in the New England style. **Patterns:** Can do open or closed welding and fancies middle eastern style blades. **Technical:** 1095, 1084, 15n20, 5160, w1, w2 steels **Remarks:** Part-time maker attending graduate school at SIUC; looking to become full-time in the future as well as earn ABS Journeyman status. **Mark:** Korean character for south.

MEIER, DARYL,
75 Forge Rd, Carbondale, IL 62901, Phone: 618-549-3234, Web: www.meiersteel.com
   Specialties: One-of-a-kind knives and swords. **Patterns:** Collaborates on blades. **Technical:** Forges his own Damascus, W1 and A203E, 440C, 431, nickel 200 and clad steel. **Prices:** $250 to $450; some to $6000. **Remarks:** Full-time smith and researcher since 1974; first knife sold in 1974. **Mark:** Name or circle/arrow symbol or SHAWNEE.

MELIN, GORDON C,
14207 Coolbank Dr, La Mirada, CA 90638, Phone: 562-946-5753

MELOY, SEAN,
7148 Rosemary Lane, Lemon Grove, CA 91945-2105, Phone: 619-465-7173
   Specialties: Traditional working straight knives of his design. **Patterns:** Bowies, fighters and utility/camp knives. **Technical:** Grinds 440C, ATS-34 and D2. **Prices:** $125 to $300. **Remarks:** Part-time maker; first knife sold in 1985. **Mark:** Broz Knives.

MENEFEE, RICKY BOB,
2440 County Road 1322, Blawchard, OK 73010, rmenefee@pldi.net
   Specialties: Working straight knives and pocket knives. **Patterns:** Hunters, fighters, minis & Bowies. **Technical:** Grinds ATS-34, 440C, D2, BG42 and S30V. **Price:** $130 to $1000. **Remarks:** Part-time maker, first knife sold in 2001. Member of KGA of Oklahoma, also Knifemakers Guild. **Mark:** Menefee made or Menefee stamped in blade.

MENSCH, LARRY C,
Larry's Knife Shop, 578 Madison Ave, Milton, PA 17847, Phone: 570-742-9554
   Specialties: Custom orders. **Patterns:** Bowies, daggers, hunters, tantos, short swords and miniatures. **Technical:** Grinds ATS-34, stainless steel Damascus; blade grinds hollow, flat and slack. Filework; bending guards and fluting handles with finger grooves. **Prices:** $200 and up. **Remarks:** Full-time maker; first knife sold in 1993. Doing business as Larry's Knife Shop. **Mark:** Connected capital "L" and small "m" in script.

MERCER, MIKE,
149 N. Waynesville Rd, Lebanon, OH 45036, Phone: 513-932-2837, mmercer08445@roadrunner.com
   Specialties: Miniatures and autos. **Patterns:** All folder patterns. **Technical:** Diamonds and gold, one-of-a-kind, Damascus, O1, stainless steel blades. **Prices:** $500 to $5000. **Remarks:** Carved wax - lost wax casting. **Mark:** Stamp - Mercer.

MERCHANT, TED,
7 Old Garrett Ct, White Hall, MD 21161, Phone: 410-343-0380
   Specialties: Traditional and classic working knives. **Patterns:** Bowies, hunters, camp knives, fighters, daggers and skinners. **Technical:** Forges W2 and 5160; makes own Damascus. Makes handles with wood, stag, horn, silver and gem stone inlay; fancy filework. **Prices:** $125 to $600; some to $1500. **Remarks:** Full-time maker; first knife sold in 1985. **Mark:** Last name.

MERZ III, ROBERT L,
1447 Winding Canyon, Katy, TX 77493, Phone: 281-391-2897, bobmerz@consolidated.net; Web: www.merzknives.com
   Specialties: Folders. **Prices:** $350 to $1,400. **Remarks:** Full time maker; first knife sold in 1974. **Mark:** MERZ.

MESHEJIAN, MARDI,
5 Bisbee Court 109 PMB 230, Santa Fe, NM 87508, Phone: 505-310-7441, toothandnail13@yahoo.com
   Specialties: One-of-a-kind fantasy and high art straight knives & folders. **Patterns:** Swords, daggers, folders and other weapons. **Technical:** Forged steel Damascus and titanium Damascus. **Prices:** $300 to $5000 some to $7000. **Mark:** Stamped stylized "M."

MESSER, DAVID T,
134 S Torrence St, Dayton, OH 45403-2044, Phone: 513-228-6561
   Specialties: Fantasy period pieces, straight and folding, of his design. **Patterns:** Bowies, daggers and swords. **Technical:** Grinds 440C, O1, 06 and commercial Damascus. Likes fancy guards and exotic handle materials. **Prices:** $100 to $225; some to $375. **Remarks:** Spare-time maker; first knife sold in 1991. **Mark:** Name stamp.

METHENY, H A "WHITEY",
7750 Waterford Dr, Spotsylvania, VA 22551, Phone: 540842-1440, Fax: 540-582-3095, hametheny@aol.com; Web: www.methenyknives.com
   Specialties: Working and using straight knives of his design and to customer specs. **Patterns:** Hunters and kitchen knives. **Technical:** Grinds 440C and ATS-34. Offers filework; tooled custom sheaths. **Prices:** $350 to $450. **Remarks:** Spare-time maker; first knife sold in 1990. **Mark:** Initials/full name football logo.

METSALA, ANTHONY,
30557 103rd St. NW, Princeton, MN 55371, Phone: 763-389-2628, acmetsala@izoom.net; Web: www.metsalacustomknives.com
   Specialties: Sole authorship one-off mosaic Damascus liner locking folders, sales of makers finished one-off mosaic Damascus blades. **Patterns:** Except for a couple EDC folding knives, maker does not use patterns. **Technical:** Forges own mosaic Damascus carbon blade and bolster material. All stainless steel blades are heat treated by Paul Bos. **Prices:** $250 to $1500. **Remarks:** Full-time knifemaker and Damascus steel maker, first knife sold in 2005. **Mark:** A.C. Metsala or Metsala.

METZ, GREG T,
c/o Yellow Pine Bar HC 83, BOX 8080, Cascade, ID 83611, Phone: 208-382-4336, metzenterprise@yahoo.com
   Specialties: Hunting and utility knives. **Prices:** $350 and up. **Remarks:** Natural handle materials; hand forged blades; 1084 and 1095. **Mark:** METZ (last name).

MEYER, CHRISTOPHER J,
737 Shenipsit Lake Rd, Tolland, CT 06084, Phone: 860-875-1826, shenipsitforge.cjm@gmail.com
   Specialties: Hand forged tool steels. **Patterns:** Bowies, fighters, hunters, razors and camp knives. **Technical:** Forges O1, 1084, W2, Grinds ATS-34, O1, D2, CPM154CM. **Remarks:** Spare-time maker, sold first knife in 2003. **Mark:** Name or "Shenipsit forge, Meyer".

MICHINAKA, TOSHIAKI,
I-679 Koyamacho-nishi Tottori-shi, Tottori 680-0947, JAPAN, Phone: 0857-28-5911
   Specialties: Art miniature knives. **Patterns:** Bowies, hunters, fishing, camp knives & miniatures. **Technical:** Grinds ATS-34 and 440C. **Prices:** $300 to $900 some higher. **Remarks:** Part-time maker. First knife sold in 1982. **Mark:** First initial, last name.

MICKLEY, TRACY,
42112 Kerns Dr, North Mankato, MN 56003, Phone: 507-947-3760, tracy@mickleyknives.com; Web: www.mickleyknives.com
   Specialties: Working and collectable straight knives using mammoth ivory or burl woods, LinerLock® folders. **Patterns:** Custom and classic hunters, utility, fighters and Bowies. **Technical:** Grinding 154-CM, BG-42 forging O1 and 52100. **Prices:** Starting at $325 **Remarks:** Part-time since 1999. **Mark:** Last name.

MIDGELY, BEN,
, Phone: 918-655-6701, mauricemidgely@windstrem.net
   Specialties: Multi-blade folders, slip-joints, some lock-backs and hunters. File work, engraving and scrimshaw. **Patterns:** Reproduce old patterns, trappers, muskrats, stockman, whittlers, lockbacks an hunters. **Technical:** Grinds ATS-34, 440C, 12-C-27, CPM-154, some carbon steel, and commercial Damascus. **Prices:** $385 to $1875. **Remarks:** Full-time maker, first knife sold in 2002. **Mark:** Name, city, and state stamped on blade.

MIKOLAJCZYK, GLEN,
4650 W. 7 Mile Rd., Caledonia, WI 53108, Phone: 414-791-0424, Fax: 262-835-9697, glenmikol@aol.com Web: www.customtomahawk.com
   Specialties: Pipe hawks, fancy folders, bowies, long blades, hunting knives, all of his own design. **Technical:** Sole-author, forges own Damascus and powdered steel. Works with ivory, bone, tortoise, horn and antlers, tiger maple, pearl for handle materials. Designs and does intricate file work and custom sheaths. Enjoys exotic handle materials. **Prices:** Moderate. **Remarks:** Founded Weg Von Wennig Forge in 2003, first knife sold in 2004. Also, designs and builds mini-forges. Will build upon request. International sales accepted. **Mark:** Tomahawk and name.

MILES JR., C R "IRON DOCTOR",
1541 Porter Crossroad, Lugoff, SC 29078, Phone: 803-438-5816
Specialties: Traditional working straight knives of his design or made to custom specs. **Patterns:** Hunters, fighters, utility camp knives and hatches. **Technical:** Grinds O1, D2, ATS-34, 440C, 1095, and 154 CPM. Forges 18th century style cutlery of high carbon steels. Also forges and grinds old files and farrier's rasps to make knives. Custom leather sheaths. **Prices:** $100 and up. **Remarks:** Part-time maker, first knife sold in 1997. Member of South Carolina Association of Knifemakers since 1997. **Mark:** Iron doctor plus name and serial number.

MILITANO, TOM,
CUSTOM KNIVES, 77 Jason Rd., Jacksonville, AL 36265-6655, Phone: 256-435-7132, jeffkin57@aol.com
Specialties: Fixed blade, one-of-a-kind knives. **Patterns:** Bowies, fighters, hunters and tactical knives. **Technical:** Grinds 440C, CPM 154CM, A2, and Damascus. Hollow grinds, flat grinds, and decorative filework. **Prices:** $150 plus. **Remarks:** Part-time maker. Sold first knives in the mid to late 1980s. Memberships: Founding member of New England Custom Knife Association. **Mark:** Name engraved in ricasso area - type of steel on reverse side.

MILLARD, FRED G,
27627 Kopezyk Ln, Richland Center, WI 53581, Phone: 608-647-5376
Specialties: Working/using straight knives of his design or to customer specs. **Patterns:** Bowies, hunters, utility/camp knives, kitchen/steak knives. **Technical:** Grinds ATS-34, O1, D2 and 440C. Makes sheaths. **Prices:** $110 to $300. **Remarks:** Full-time maker; first knife sold in 1993. Doing business as Millard Knives. **Mark:** Mallard duck in flight with serial number.

MILLER, BOB,
7659 Fine Oaks Pl, Oakville, MO 63129, Phone: 314-846-8934
Specialties: Mosaic Damascus; collector using straight knives and folders. **Patterns:** Hunters, Bowies, utility/camp knives, daggers. **Technical:** Forges own Damascus, mosaic-Damascus and 52100. **Prices:** $125 to $500. **Remarks:** Part-time maker; first knife sold in 1983. **Mark:** First and middle initials and last name, or initials.

MILLER, DON,
21049 Uncompahgre Rd., Montrose, CO 81403, Phone: 800-318-8127, masterdon_1@yahoo.com; Web: www.masterdonknives.com, http://uncbb.com (pg. 3)

MILLER, HANFORD J,
Box 97, Cowdrey, CO 80434, Phone: 970-723-4708
Specialties: Working knives in Moran styles, Bowie, period pieces, Cinquedea. **Patterns:** Daggers, Bowies, working knives. **Technical:** All work forged: W2, 1095, 5160 and Damascus. ABS methods; offers fine silver repousse, scabboard mountings and wire inlay, oak presentation cases. **Prices:** $400 to $1000; some to $3000 and up. **Remarks:** Full-time maker; first knife sold in 1968. **Mark:** Initials or name within Bowie logo.

MILLER, JAMES P,
9024 Goeller Rd, RR 2, Box 28, Fairbank, IA 50629, Phone: 319-635-2294, Web: www.damascusknives.biz
Specialties: All tool steel Damascus; working knives and period pieces. **Patterns:** Hunters, Bowies, camp knives and daggers. **Technical:** Forges and grinds 1095, 52100, 440C and his own Damascus. **Prices:** $175 to $500; some to $1500. **Remarks:** Full-time maker; first knife sold in 1970. **Mark:** First and middle initials, last name with knife logo.

MILLER, M A,
11625 Community Center Dr, Unit #1531, Northglenn, CO 80233, Phone: 303-280-3816
Specialties: Using knives for hunting. 3-1/2"-4" Loveless drop-point. Made to customer specs. **Patterns:** Skinners and camp knives. **Technical:** Grinds 440C, D2, O1 and ATS-34 Damascus miniatures. **Prices:** $225 to $350; miniatures $75 to $150. **Remarks:** Part-time maker; first knife sold in 1988. **Mark:** Last name stamped in block letters or first and middle initials, last name, maker, city and state with triangles on either side etched.

MILLER, MICHAEL,
3030 E Calle Cedral, Kingman, AZ 86401, Phone: 928-757-1359, mike@mmilleroriginals.com
Specialties: Hunters, Bowies, and skinners with exotic burl wood, stag, ivory and gemstone handles. **Patterns:** High carbon steel knives. **Technical:** High carbon and nickel alloy Damascus and high carbon and meteorite Damascus. Also mosaic Damascus. **Prices:** $235 to $4500. **Remarks:** Full-time maker since 2002, first knife sold 2000; doing business as M Miller Originals. **Mark:** First initial and last name with 'handmade' underneath.

MILLER, MICHAEL E,
910146 S. 3500 Rd., Chandler, OK 74834, Phone: 918-377-2411, mimiller1@brightok.net
Specialties: Traditional working/using knives of his design. **Patterns:** Bowies, hunters and kitchen knives. **Technical:** Grinds ATS-34, CPM 440V; forges Damascus and cable Damascus and 52100. Prefers scrimshaw, fancy pins, basket weave and embellished sheaths. **Prices:** $80 to $300; some to $500. **Remarks:** Part-time maker; first knife sold in 1984. Doing business as Miller Custom Knives. Member of KGA of Oklahoma and Salt Fork Blacksmith Association. **Mark:** First and middle initials, last name, maker.

MILLER, NATE,
Sportsman's Edge, 1075 Old Steese Hwy N, Fairbanks, AK 99712, Phone: 907-479-4774, sportsmansedge@gci.net Web: www.alaskasportsmansedge.com
Specialties: Fixed blade knives for hunting, fishing, kitchen and collector pieces. **Patterns:** Hunters, skinners, utility, tactical, fishing, camp knives-your pattern or mine. **Technical:** Stock removal maker, ATS-34, 154CM, 440C, D2, 1095, other steels on request. Handle material includes micarta, horn, antler, fossilized ivory and bone, wide selection of woods. **Prices:** $225-$800. **Remarks:** Full time maker since 2002. **Mark:** Nate Miller, Fairbanks, AK.

MILLER, R D,
10526 Estate Lane, Dallas, TX 75238, Phone: 214-348-3496
Specialties: One-of-a-kind collector-grade knives. **Patterns:** Boots, hunters, Bowies, camp and utility knives, fishing and bird knives, miniatures. **Technical:** Grinds a variety of steels to include O1, D2, 440C, 154CM and 1095. **Prices:** $65 to $300; some to $900. **Remarks:** Full-time maker; first knife sold in 1984. **Mark:** R.D. Custom Knives with date or bow and arrow logo.

MILLER, RICK,
516 Kanaul Rd, Rockwood, PA 15557, Phone: 814-926-2059
Specialties: Working/using straight knives of his design and in standard patterns. **Patterns:** Bowies, daggers, hunters and friction folders. **Technical:** Grinds L6. Forges 5160, L6 and Damascus. Patterns for Damascus are random, twist, rose or ladder. **Prices:** $75 to $250; some to $400. **Remarks:** Part-time maker; first knife sold in 1982. **Mark:** Script stamp "R.D.M."

MILLER, RON,
NORTH POLE KNIVES, PO BOX 55301, NORTH POLE, AK 99705, Phone: 907-488-5902, JTMRON@NESCAPE.NET
<**Specialties:** Custom handmade hunting knives built for the extreme conditions of Alaska. Custom fillet blades, tactical fighting knives, custom kitchen knives. Handles are made from mammoth ivory, musk ox, fossilized walrus tusk. Hunters have micarta handles. **Patterns:** Hunters, skinners, fillets, fighters. **Technical:** Stock removal for D2, ATS-34, 109HR, 154CM, and Damascus. **Prices:** $180 and up. **Remarks:** Makes custom sheaths for the above knives. **Mark:** Ron Miller, circle with North Pole Knives with bowie style blade through circle.

MILLER, RONALD T,
12922 127th Ave N, Largo, FL 34644, Phone: 813-595-0378 (after 5 p.m.)
Specialties: Working straight knives in standard patterns. **Patterns:** Combat knives, camp knives, kitchen cutlery, fillet knives, locking folders and butterflies. **Technical:** Grinds D2, 440C and ATS-34; offers brass inlays and scrimshaw. **Prices:** $45 to $325; some to $750. **Remarks:** Part-time maker; first knife sold in 1984. **Mark:** Name, city and state in palm tree logo.

MILLER, SKIP,
13773 Borglum Rd., Keystone, SD 57751, Phone: 605-255-5778, svmlr@mt-rushmore.net
Remarks: Has been making knives since 1994.

MILLER, STEVE,
1376 Pine St., Clearwater, FL 33756, Phone: 727-461-4180, millknives@aol.com
Patterns: Bowies, hunters, skinners, folders. **Technical:** 440-C, ATS-34, Sandvic Stainless, CPM-S30-V, Damascus. Exotic hardwoods, bone, horn, antler, ivory, synthetics. All leather work and sheaths made by me and handstitched. **Remarks:** Have been making custom knives for sale since 1990. Part-time maker, hope to go full time in about five and a half years (after retirement from full-time job). **Mark:** Last name inside a pentagram.

MILLER, TERRY,
P.O. Box 262, Healy, AK 99743, Phone: 907-683-1239, terry@denalidomehome.com
Specialties: Alaskan ulas with wood or horn. **Remarks:** New to knifemaking (4 years).

MILLS, LOUIS G,
9450 Waters Rd, Ann Arbor, MI 48103, Phone: 734-668-1839
Specialties: High-art Japanese-style period pieces. **Patterns:** Traditional tantos, daggers and swords. **Technical:** Makes steel from iron; makes his own Damascus by traditional Japanese techniques. **Prices:** $900 to $2000; some to $8000. **Remarks:** Spare-time maker. **Mark:** Yasutomo in Japanese Kanji.

MILLS, MICHAEL,
151 Blackwell Rd, Colonial Beach, VA 22443-5054, Phone: 804-224-0265
Specialties: Working knives, hunters, skinners, utility and Bowies. **Technical:** Forge 5160 differential heat-treats. **Prices:** $300 and up. **Remarks:** Part-time maker, ABS Journeyman. **Mark:** Last name in script.

MINCHEW, RYAN,
2510 Mary Ellen, Pampa, TX 79065, Phone: 806-669-3983, ryan@minchewknives.com Web: www.minchewknives.com
Specialties: Hunters and folders. **Patterns:** Standard hunter, bird, and trout. **Prices:** $150 to $500. **Mark:** Minchew.

MINK, DAN,
PO Box 861, 196 Sage Circle, Crystal Beach, FL 34681, Phone: 727-786-5408, blademkr@gmail.com
Specialties: Traditional and working knives of his design. **Patterns:** Bowies, fighters, folders and hunters. **Technical:** Grinds ATS-34, 440C and D2. Blades and tanges embellished with fancy filework. Uses natural and rare handle materials. **Prices:** $125 to $450. **Remarks:** Part-time maker; first knife sold in 1985. **Mark:** Name and star encircled by custom made, city, state.

MINNICK, JIM,
144 North 7th St, Middletown, IN 47356, Phone: 765-354-4108
Specialties: Lever-lock folding art knives, liner-locks. **Patterns:** Stilettos, Persian and one-of-a-kind folders. **Technical:** Grinds and carves Damascus, stainless, and high-carbon. **Prices:** $950 to $7000. **Remarks:** Part-time maker; first knife sold in 1976. Husband and wife team. **Mark:** Minnick and JMJ.

MIRABILE, DAVID,
PO BOX 20417, Juneau, AK 99802, Phone: 907-321-1103, dmirabile02@gmail.com; Web: www.mirableknives.com
Specialties: Elegant edged weapons and hard use Alaskan knives. **Patterns:** Fighters, personal carry knives, special studies of the Tlinget dagger. **Technical:** Uses W-2, 1080, 15n20, 1095, 5160, and his own Damascus, and stainless/high carbon San Mai.

MITCHELL, JAMES A,
PO Box 4646, Columbus, GA 31904, Phone: 404-322-8582
Specialties: Fancy working knives. **Patterns:** Hunters, fighters, Bowies and locking folders. **Technical:** Grinds D2, 440C and commercial Damascus. **Prices:** $100 to $400; some to $900. **Remarks:** Part-time maker; first knife sold in 1976. Sells knives in sets. **Mark:** Signature and city.

MITCHELL, MAX DEAN AND BEN,
3803 VFW Rd, Leesville, LA 71440, Phone: 318-239-6416
Specialties: Hatchet and knife sets with folder and belt and holster all match. **Patterns:** Hunters, 200 L6 steel. **Technical:** L6 steel; soft back, hand edge. **Prices:** $300 to $500. **Remarks:** Part-time makers; first knife sold in 1965. Custom orders only; no stock. **Mark:** First names.

MITCHELL, WM DEAN,
PO Box 2, Warren, TX 77664, Phone: 409-547-2213
Specialties: Functional and collectable cutlery. **Patterns:** Personal and collector's designs. **Technical:** Forges own Damascus and carbon steels. **Prices:** Determined by the buyer. **Remarks:** Gentleman knifemaker. ABS Master Smith 1994. **Mark:** Full name with anvil and MS or WDM and MS.

MITSUYUKI, ROSS,
PO Box 29577, Honolulu, HI 96820, Phone: 808-671-3335, Fax: 808-671-3335, rossman@hawaiiantel.net; Web:www.picturetrail.com/homepage/mrbing
Specialties: Working straight knives and folders/engraving titanium & 416 S.S. **Patterns:** Hunting, fighters, utility knives and boot knives. **Technical:** 440C, BG42, ATS-34, S30V, CPM154, and Damascus. **Prices:** $100 and up. **Remarks:** Spare-time maker, first knife sold in 1998. **Mark:** (Honu) Hawaiian sea turtle.

MIVILLE-DESCHENES, ALAIN,
1952 Charles A Parent, Quebec, CANADA G2B 4B2, Phone: 418-845-0950, Fax: 418-845-0950, amd@miville-deschenes.com; Web: www.miville-deschenes.com
Specialties: Working knives of his design or to customer specs and art knives. **Patterns:** Bowies, skinner, hunter, utility, camp knives, fighters, art knives. **Technical:** Grinds ATS-34, CPMS30V, 0-1, D2, and sometime forge carbon steel. **Prices:** $250 to $700; some higher. **Remarks:** Part-time maker; first knife sold in 2001. **Mark:** Logo (small hand) and initials (AMD).

MOEN, JERRY,
4444 Spring Valley Rd, Dallas, TX 75244, Phone: 972-839-1609, jmoen@moencustomknives.com Web: moencustomknives.com
Specialties: Hunting, pocket knives, fighters tactical, and exotic. **Prices:** $750 to $2500.

MOJZIS, JULIUS,
B S Timravy 6, 98511 Halic, SLOVAKIA, mojzisj@stoneline.sk; Web: www.juliusmojzis.com
Specialties: Art Knives. **Prices:** USD $2000. **Mark:** MOJZIS.

MONCUS, MICHAEL STEVEN,
1803 US 19 N, Smithville, GA 31787, Phone: 912-846-2408

MONTANO, GUS A,
11217 Westonhill Dr, San Diego, CA 92126-1447, Phone: 619-273-5357
Specialties: Traditional working/using straight knives of his design. **Patterns:** Boots, Bowies and fighters. **Technical:** Grinds 1095 and 5160; grinds and forges cable. Double or triple hardened and triple drawn; hand-rubbed finish. Prefers natural handle materials. **Prices:** $200 to $400; some to $600. **Remarks:** Spare-time maker; first knife sold in 1997. **Mark:** First initial and last name.

MONTEIRO, VICTOR,
31 Rue D'Opprebais, 1360 Maleves Ste Marie, BELGIUM, Phone: 010 88 0441, victor.monteiro@skynet.be
Specialties: Working and fancy straight knives, folders and integrals of his design. **Patterns:** Fighters, hunters and kitchen knives. **Technical:** Grinds ATS-34, 440C, D2, Damasteel and other commercial Damascus, embellishment, filework and domed pins. **Prices:** $300 to $1000, some higher. **Remarks:** Part-time maker; first knife sold in 1989. **Mark:** Logo with initials connected.

MONTELL, TY,
PO BOX 1312, Thatcher, AZ 85552, Phone: 928-792-4509, Fax: Cell: 575-313-4373, montellfamily@aol.com
Specialties: Automatics, slip-joint folders, hunting and miniatures. **Technical:** Stock removal. Steel of choice is CPM-154, Devin Thomas Damascus. **Prices:** $250 and up. **Remarks:** First knife made in 1980. **Mark:** Tang stamp - Montell.

MOONEY, MIKE,
19432 E Cloud Rd, Queen Creek, AZ 85142, Phone: 480-987-3576, mike@moonblades.com; Web: www.moonblades.com
Specialties: Hand-crafted high-performing straight knives of his or customer's design. **Patterns:** Bowies, fighters, hunting, camp and kitchen users or collectible. **Technical:** Flat-grind, hand-rubbed finish, S30V, CMP-154, Damascus, any steel. **Prices:** $300 to $3000. **Remarks:** Doing business as moonblades.com. Commissions are welcome. **Mark:** M. Mooney followed by crescent moon.

MOORE, DAVY,
Moyriesk, Quin, Co Clare, IRELAND, Phone: 353 (0)65 6825975, davy@mooreireland.com; Web: http://www.mooreireland.com
Specialties: Traditional and Celtic outdoor hunting and utility knives. **Patterns:** Traditional hunters and skinners, Celtic pattern hunting knives, Bushcrafting, fishing, utility/camp knives. **Technical:** Stock removal knives 01, D2, RWL 34, ATS 34, CPM 154, Damasteel (various). **Prices:** 250-1700 Euros. **Remarks:** Full-time maker, first knife sold in 2004. **Mark:** Three stars over rampant lion / MOORE over Ireland.

MOORE, JAMES B,
1707 N Gillis, Ft. Stockton, TX 79735, Phone: 915-336-2113
Specialties: Classic working straight knives and folders of his design. **Patterns:** Hunters, Bowies, daggers, fighters, boots, utility/camp knives, locking folders and slip-joint folders. **Technical:** Grinds 440C, ATS-34, D2, L6, CPM and commercial Damascus. **Prices:** $85 to $700; exceptional knives to $1500. **Remarks:** Full-time maker; first knife sold in 1972. **Mark:** Name, city and state.

MOORE, JON P,
304 South N Rd, Aurora, NE 68818, Phone: 402-849-2616, Web: www.sharpdecisionknives.com
Specialties: Working and fancy straight knives using antler, exotic bone, wood and Micarta. Will use customers antlers on request. **Patterns:** Hunters, skinners, camp Bowies. **Technical:** Hand forged high carbon steel. Makes his own Damascus. **Remarks:** Full-time maker, sold first knife in 2003, member of ABS - apprentice. Does on location knife forging demonstrations. **Mark:** Signature.

MOORE, MARVE,
HC 89 Box 393, Willow, AK 99688, Phone: 907-232-0478, marvemoore@aol.com
Specialties: Fixed blades forged and stock removal. **Patterns:** Hunter, skinners, fighter, short swords. **Technical:** 100 percent of his work is done by hand. **Prices:** $100 to $500. **Remarks:** Also makes his own sheaths. **Mark:** -MM-.

MOORE, MICHAEL ROBERT,
70 Beaulieu St, Lowell, MA 01850, Phone: 978-479-0589, Fax: 978-441-1819

MOORE, TED,
340 E Willow St, Elizabethtown, PA 17022, Phone: 717-367-3939, tedmoore@tedmooreknives.com; Web: www.tedmooreknives.com
Specialties: Damascus folders, cigar cutters, high art. **Patterns:** Slip joints, linerlock, cigar cutters. **Technical:** Grinds Damascus and stainless steels. **Prices:** $250 and up. **Remarks:** Part-time maker; first knife sold 1993. **Mark:** Moore U.S.A.

MORETT, DONALD,
116 Woodcrest Dr, Lancaster, PA 17602-1300, Phone: 717-746-4888

MORGAN, JEFF,
9200 Arnaz Way, Santee, CA 92071, Phone: 619-448-8430
Specialties: Early American style knives. **Patterns:** Hunters, bowies, etc. **Technical:** Carbon steel and carbon steel damascus. **Prices:** $60 to $400

MORGAN, TOM,
14689 Ellett Rd, Beloit, OH 44609, Phone: 330-537-2023
Specialties: Working straight knives and period pieces. **Patterns:** Hunters, boots and presentation tomahawks. **Technical:** Grinds O1, 440C and 154CM. **Prices:** Knives, $65 to $200; tomahawks, $100 to $325. **Remarks:** Full-time maker; first knife sold in 1977. **Mark:** Last name and type of steel used.

MORRIS, C H,
1590 Old Salem Rd, Frisco City, AL 36445, Phone: 334-575-7425
Specialties: LinerLock® folders. **Patterns:** Interframe liner locks. **Technical:** Grinds 440C and ATS-34. **Prices:** Start at $350. **Remarks:** Full-time maker; first knife sold in 1973. Doing business as Custom Knives. **Mark:** First and middle initials, last name.

MORRIS, DARRELL PRICE,
92 Union, St. Plymouth, Devon, ENGLAND PL1 3EZ, Phone: 0752 223546
Specialties: Traditional Japanese knives, Bowies and high-art knives. **Technical:** Nickel Damascus and mokume. **Prices:** $1000 to $4000. **Remarks:** Part-time maker; first knife sold in 1990. **Mark:** Initials and Japanese name—Kuni Shigae.

MORRIS, ERIC,
306 Ewart Ave, Beckley, WV 25801, Phone: 304-255-3951

MORRIS, MICHAEL S.,
609 S. Main St., Yale, MI 48097, Phone: 810-887-7817, mykulmorris@yahoo.com
Specialties: Hunting and Tactical fixed blade knives of his design made from files. **Technical:** All knives hollow ground on 12" wheel. Hand stitches his own sheaths also. **Prices:** From $60 to $350 with most in the $90 to $125 range. **Remarks:** Machinist since 1980, made his first knife in 1984, sold his first knife in 2004. Now full-time maker. **Mark:** Last name with date of manufacture.

MOSES, STEVEN,
1610 W Hemlock Way, Santa Ana, CA 92704

MOSIER, DAVID,
1725 Millburn Ave., Independence, MO 64056, Phone: 816-796-3479, dmknives@aol.com Web: www.dmknives.com
Specialties: Tactical folders and fixed blades. **Patterns:** Fighters and concealment blades. **Technical:** Uses S35VN, CPM 154, S30V, 154CM, ATS-34, 440C, A2, D2, Stainless damascus, and Damasteel. Fixed blades come with Kydex sheaths made by maker. **Prices:** $150 to $1000. **Remarks:** Full-time maker, business name is DM Knives. **Mark:** David Mosier Knives encircling sun.

MOSIER, JOSHUA J,
SPRING CREEK KNIFE WORKS, PO Box 476/608 7th St, Deshler, NE 68340, Phone: 402-365-4386, joshmoiser50@gmail.com; Web:www.sc-kw.com
Specialties: Working straight and folding knives of his designs with customer specs. **Patterns:** Hunter/utility LinerLock® folders. **Technical:** Forges random pattern Damascus, 01, and 5160. **Prices:** $85 and up. **Remarks:** Part-time maker, sold first knife in 1986. **Mark:** SCKW.

MOULTON, DUSTY,
135 Hillview Lane, Loudon, TN 37774, Phone: 865-408-9779, Web: www.moultonknives.com
Specialties: Fancy and working straight knives. **Patterns:** Hunters, fighters, fantasy and miniatures. **Technical:** Grinds ATS-34 and Damascus. **Prices:** $300 to $2000. **Remarks:** Full-time maker; first knife sold in 1991. Now doing engraving on own knives as well as other makers. **Mark:** Last name.

MOYER, RUSS,
1266 RD 425 So, Havre, MT 59501, Phone: 406-395-4423
Specialties: Working knives to customer specs. **Patterns:** Hunters, Bowies and survival knives. **Technical:** Forges W2 & 5160. **Prices:** $150 to $350. **Remarks:** Part-time maker; first knife sold in 1976. **Mark:** Initials in logo.

MULKEY, GARY,
533 Breckenridge Rd, Branson, MO 65616, Phone: 417-335-0123, gary@mulkeyknives.com; Web: www.mulkeyknives.com
Specialties: Sole authorship Damascus and carbon steel. **Patterns:** Fixed blades (hunters, bowies, and fighters). **Technical:** Prefers 1095 or D2 with Damascus, filework, inlets or clay coated blades available on order. **Prices:** $250 and up. **Remarks:** Full-time maker since 1997. **Mark:** MUL above skeleton key.

MULLER, JODY,
3359 S. 225th Rd., Goodson, MO 65663, Phone: 417-752-3260, mullerforge2@hotmail.com; Web: www.mullerforge.com
Specialties: Hand engraving, carving and inlays, fancy folders and oriental styles. **Patterns:** One-of-a-kind fixed blades and folders in all styles. **Technical:** Forges own Damascus and high carbon steel. **Prices:** $300 and up. **Remarks:** Full-time knifemaker, does hand engraving, carving and inlay. All work done by maker. **Mark:** Muller

MUNJAS, BOB,
600 Beebe Rd., Waterford, OH 45786, Phone: 740-336-5538, Web: hairofthebear.com
Specialties: Damascus and carbon steel sheath knives. **Patterns:** Hunters and neck knives. **Technical:** My own Damascus, 5160, 1095, 1984, L6, and W2. Forge and stock removal. Does own heat treating and makes own sheaths. **Prices:** $100 to $500. **Remarks:** Part-time maker. **Mark:** Moon Munjas.

MURSKI, RAY,
12129 Captiva Ct, Reston, VA 22091-1204, Phone: 703-264-1102, rmurski@gmail.com
Specialties: Fancy working/using folders of his design. **Patterns:** Hunters, slip-joint folders and utility/camp knives. **Technical:** Grinds CPM-3V **Prices:** $125 to $500. **Remarks:** Spare-time maker; first knife sold in 1996. **Mark:** Engraved name with serial number under name.

MUTZ, JEFF,
8210 Rancheria Dr. Unit 7, Rancho Cucamonga, CA 91730, Phone: 909-931-9829, jmutzknives@hotmail.com; Web: www.jmutzknives.com
Specialties: Traditional working/using fixed blade and slip-jointed knives of own design and customer specs. **Patterns:** Hunters, skinners, and folders. **Technical:** Forges and grinds all steels Offers scrimshaw. **Prices:** $145 to $500. **Remarks:** Full-time maker, first knife sold in 1998. **Mark:** First initial, last name over "maker."

MYERS, PAUL,
644 Maurice St, Wood River, IL 62095, Phone: 618-258-1707
Specialties: Fancy working straight knives and folders. **Patterns:** Full range of folders, straight hunters and Bowies; tie tacks; knife and fork sets. **Technical:** Grinds D2, 440C, ATS-34 and 154CM. **Prices:** $100 to $350; some to $3000. **Remarks:** Full-time maker; first knife sold in 1974. **Mark:** Initials with setting sun on front; name and number on back.

MYERS, STEVE,
903 Hickory Rd., Virginia, IL 62691-8716, Phone: 217-452-3157, Web: www.myersknives.net
Specialties: Working straight knives and integrals. **Patterns:** Camp knives, hunters, skinners, Bowies, and boot knives. **Technical:** Forges own Damascus and high carbon steels. **Prices:** $250 to $1,000. **Remarks:** Full-time maker, first knife sold in 1985. **Mark:** Last name in logo.

N

NARASADA, MAMORU,
9115-8 Nakaminowa, Minowa-machi, Kamiina-gun, Nagano 399-4601, Phone: 81-265-79-3960, Fax: 81-265-79-3960
Specialties: Utility working straight knife. **Patterns:** Hunting, fishing, and camping knife. **Technical:** Grind and forges / ATS34, VG10, 440C, CRM07. **Prices:** $150 to $500, some higher. **Remarks:** First knife sold in 2003. **Mark:** M.NARASADA with initial logo.

NATEN, GREG,
1804 Shamrock Way, Bakersfield, CA 93304-3921
Specialties: Fancy and working/using folders of his design. **Patterns:** Fighters, hunters and locking folders. **Technical:** Grinds 440C and CPM440V. Heat-treats; prefers desert ironwood, stag and mother-of-pearl. Designs and sews leather sheaths for straight knives. **Prices:** $175 to $600; some to $950. **Remarks:** Spare-time maker; first knife sold in 1992. **Mark:** Last name above battle-ax, handmade.

NAUDE, LOUIS,
15 Auction St, Dalsig, Malmesbury, Western Cape 7560, South Africa, Phone: +27-0-21-981-0079, info@louisnaude.co.za Web: www.louisnaude.co.za
Specialties: Folders, Hunters, Custom.. **Patterns:** See Website. **Technical:** Stock removal, African materials. **Prices:** See website. **Remarks:** Still the tool! **Mark:** Louis Naude Knives with family crest.

NEALY, BUD,
125 Raccoon Way, Stroudsburg, PA 18360, Phone: 570-402-1018, Fax: 570-402-1018, bnealy@ptd.net; Web: www.budnealyknifemaker.com
Specialties: Original design concealment knives with designer multi-concealment sheath system. **Patterns:** Fixed Blades and Folders **Technical:** Grinds CPM 154, XHP, and Damascus. **Prices:** $200 to $2500. **Remarks:** Full-time maker; first knife sold in 1980. **Mark:** Name, city, state or signature.

NEASE, WILLIAM,
2336 Front Rd., LaSalle, Ontario Canada N9J 2C4, wnease@hotmail.com Web: www.unsubtleblades.com
Specialties: Hatchets, choppers, and Japanese-influenced designs. **Technical:** Stock removal. Works A-2, D-2, S-7, O-1, powder stainless alloys, composite laminate blades with steel edges. **Prices:** $125 to $2200. **Remarks:** Part-time maker since 1994. **Mark:** Initials W.M.N. engraved in cursive on exposed tangs or on the spine of blades.

NEDVED, DAN,
206 Park Dr, Kalispell, MT 59901, bushido2222@yahoo.com
Specialties: Slip joint folders, liner locks, straight knives. **Patterns:** Mostly traditional or modern blend with traditional lines. **Technical:** Grinds ATS-34, 440C, 1095 and uses other makers Damascus. **Prices:** $95 and up. Mostly in the $150 to $200 range. **Remarks:** Part-time maker, averages 2 a month. **Mark:** Dan Nedved or Nedved with serial # on opposite side.

NEELY, GREG,
5419 Pine St, Bellaire, TX 77401, Phone: 713-991-2677, gtneely64@comcast.net
Specialties: Traditional patterns and his own patterns for work and/or collecting. **Patterns:** Hunters, Bowies and utility/camp knives. **Technical:** Forges own Damascus, 1084, 5160 and some tool steels. Differentially tempers. **Prices:** $225 to $5000. **Remarks:** Part-time maker; first knife sold in 1987. **Mark:** Last name or interlocked initials, MS.

NEILSON, J,
291 Scouten Rd., Wyalusing, PA 18853, Phone: 570-746-4944, mountainhollow@epix.net; Web: www.mountainhollow.net
Specialties: Working and collectable fixed blade knives. **Patterns:** Hunter/fighters, Bowies, neck knives and daggers. **Technical:** 1084, 1095, 5160, W-2, 52100, maker's own Damascus. **Prices:** $175 to $2500. **Remarks:** ABS Master Smith, full-time maker, first knife sold in 2000, doing business as Neilson's Mountain Hollow. Each knife comes with a sheath. **Mark:** J. Neilson MS.

NELL, CHAD,
75-6201 Hookuku Moho Pl, Kailua-Kona, HI 96740, Phone: 435-229-6442, nellknives@gmail.com; Web: www.nellknives.com
Specialties: Fixed blade working knives. **Patterns:** hunters, fighters, daggers. **Technical:** Grinds CPM-154, ATS-34. **Prices:** Starting at $300. **Remarks:** Full-time maker since Sep 2011. First knife made in May 2010. **Mark:** Nell Knives, Nell Knives Kona, Hi and C. Nell Kona, Hawaii.

NELSON, KEN,
PO BOX 272, Pittsville, WI 54466, Phone: 715-323-0538 or 715-884-6448, ken@ironwolfonline.com Web: www.ironwolfonline.com
Specialties: Working straight knives, period pieces. **Patterns:** Utility, hunters, dirks, daggers, throwers, hawks, axes, swords, pole arms and blade blanks as well. **Technical:** Forges 5160, 52100, W2, 10xx, L6, carbon steels and own Damascus. Does his own heat treating. **Prices:** $50 to $350, some to $3000. **Remarks:** Part-time maker. First knife sold in 1995. Doing business as Iron Wolf Forge. **Mark:** Stylized wolf paw print.

NELSON, TOM,
PO Box 2298, Wilropark 1731, Gauteng, SOUTH AFRICA, Phone: 27 11 7663991, Fax: 27 11 7687161, tom.nelson@telkomsa.net
Specialties: Own Damascus (Hosaic etc.) **Patterns:** One-of-a-kind art knives, swords and axes. **Prices:** $500 to $1000.

NETO JR., NELSON AND DE CARVALHO, HENRIQUE M.,
R. Joao Margarido No 20-V, Guerra, Braganca Paulista, SP-12900-000, BRAZIL, Phone: 011-7843-6889, Fax: 011-7843-6889
Specialties: Straight knives and folders. **Patterns:** Bowies, katanas, jambyias and others. **Technical:** Forges high-carbon steels. **Prices:** $70 to $3000. **Remarks:** Full-time makers; first knife sold in 1990. **Mark:** HandN.

NEUHAEUSLER, ERWIN,
Heiligenangerstrasse 15, 86179 Augsburg, GERMANY, Phone: 0821/81 49 97, ERWIN@AUASBURGKNIVES.DE
Specialties: Using straight knives of his design. **Patterns:** Hunters, boots, Bowies and folders. **Technical:** Grinds ATS-34, RWL-34 and Damascus. **Prices:** $200 to $750. **Remarks:** Spare-time maker; first knife sold in 1991. **Mark:** Etched logo, last name and city.

NEVLING, MARK,
BURR OAK KNIVES, PO Box 9, Hume, IL 61932, Phone: 217-887-2522, burroakknives@aol.com; Web: www.burroakknives.com
Specialties: Straight knives and folders of his own design. **Patterns:** Hunters, fighters, Bowies, folders, and small executive knives. **Technical:** Convex grinds, Forges, uses only high-carbon and Damascus. **Prices:** $200 to $2000. **Remarks:** Full-time maker, first knife sold 1988. Apprentice Damascus smith to George Werth and Doug Ponzio.

NEWBERRY, ALLEN,
PO BOX 301, Lowell, AR 72745, Phone: 479-530-6439, newberry@newberryknives.com Web: www.newberryknives.com
Specialties: Fixed blade knives both forged and stock removal. **Patterns:** Traditional patterns as well as newer designs inspired by historical and international blades. **Technical:** Uses 1095, W2, 5160, 154-CM, other steels by request. **Prices:** $150 to $450+. **Remarks:** Many of the knives feature hamons. **Mark:** Newberry with a capital N for forged pieces and newberry with a lower case n for stock removal pieces.

NEWCOMB, CORBIN,
628 Woodland Ave, Moberly, MO 65270, Phone: 660-263-4639
Specialties: Working straight knives and folders; period pieces. **Patterns:** Hunters, axes, Bowies, folders, buckskinned blades and boots. **Technical:** Hollow-grinds D2, 440C and 154CM; prefers natural handle materials. Makes own Damascus; offers cable Damascus. **Prices:** $100 to $500. **Remarks:** Full-time maker; first knife sold in 1982. Doing business as Corbin Knives. **Mark:** First name and serial number.

NEWHALL, TOM,
3602 E 42nd Stravenue, Tucson, AZ 85713, Phone: 520-721-0562, gggaz@aol.com

NEWTON, LARRY,
1758 Pronghorn Ct, Jacksonville, FL 32225, Phone: 904-537-2066, lnewton1@comcast.net; Web: larrynewtonknives.com
Specialties: Traditional and slender high-grade gentlemen's automatic folders, locking liner type tactical, and working straight knives. **Patterns:** Front release locking folders, interframes, hunters, and skinners. **Technical:** Grinds Damascus, ATS-34, 440C and D2. **Prices:** Folders start at $350, straights start at $150. **Remarks:** Retired teacher. Full-time maker. First knife sold in 1989. Won Best Folder for 2008 - Blade Magazine. **Mark:** Last name.

NEWTON, RON,
223 Ridge Ln, London, AR 72847, Phone: 479-293-3001, rnewton@cei.net Web: ronnewtonknives.com
Specialties: All types of folders and fixed blades. Blackpowder gun knife combos. **Patterns:** Traditional slip joint, multi-blade patterns, antique bowie repros. **Technical:** Forges traditional and mosaid damascus. Performs engraving and gold inlay. **Prices:** $500 and up. **Remarks:** Creates hidden mechanisms in assisted opening folders. **Mark:** NEWTON M.S. in a western invitation font."

NICHOLS, CHAD,
1125 Cr 185, Blue Springs, MS 38828, Phone: 662-538-5966, chadn28@hotmail.com Web: chadnicholsdamascus.com
Specialties: Gents folders and everyday tactical/utility style knives and fixed hunters. **Technical:** Makes own stainless damascus, mosaic damascus, and high carbon damascus. **Prices:** $450 - $1000. **Mark:** Name and Blue Springs.

NICHOLSON, R. KENT,
PO Box 204, Phoenix, MD 21131, Phone: 410-323-6925
Specialties: Large using knives. **Patterns:** Bowies and camp knives in the Moran-style. **Technical:** Forges W2, 9260, 5160; makes Damascus. **Prices:** $150 to $995. **Remarks:** Part-time maker; first knife sold in 1984. **Mark:** Name.

NIELSON, JEFF V,
1060 S Jones Rd, Monroe, UT 84754, Phone: 435-527-4242, jvn1u205@hotmail.com
Specialties: Classic knives of his design and to customer specs. **Patterns:** Fighters, hunters; miniatures. **Technical:** Grinds 440C stainless and Damascus. **Prices:** $100 to $1200. **Remarks:** Part-time maker; first knife sold in 1991. **Mark:** Name, location.

NIEMUTH, TROY,
3143 North Ave, Sheboygan, WI 53083, Phone: 414-452-2927
Specialties: Period pieces and working/using straight knives of his design and to customer specs. **Patterns:** Hunters and utility/camp knives. **Technical:** Grinds 440C, 1095 and A2. **Prices:** $85 to $350; some to $500. **Remarks:** Full-time maker; first knife sold in 1995. **Mark:** Etched last name.

NILSSON, JONNY WALKER,
Tingstigen 11, SE-933 33 Arvidsjaur, SWEDEN, Phone: (46) 960-13048, 0960.1304@telia.com; Web: www.jwnknives.com
Specialties: High-end collectible Nordic hunters, engraved reindeer antler. World class freehand engravings. Matching engraved sheaths in leather, bone and Arctic wood with inlays. Combines traditional techniques and design with his own innovations. Master Bladesmith who specializes in forging mosaic Damascus. Sells unique mosaic Damascus bar stock to folder makers. **Patterns:** Own designs and traditional Sami designs. **Technical:** Mosaic Damascus of UHB 20 C 15N20 with pure nickel, hardness HRC 58-60. **Prices:** $1500 to $6000. **Remarks:** Full-time maker since 1988. Nordic Champion (5 countries) numerous times, 50 first prizes in Scandinavian shows. Yearly award in his name in Nordic Championship. Knives inspired by 10,000 year old indigenous Sami culture. **Mark:** JN on sheath, handle, custom wood box. JWN on blade.

NIRO, FRANK,
1948 Gloaming Dr, Kamloops, B.C. Canada V1S1P8, Phone: 250-372-8332, niro@telus.net
Specialties: Liner locking folding knives in his designs in what might be called standard patterns. **Technical:** Enjoys grinding mosaic Damascus with pure nickel of the make up for blades that are often double ground; as well as meteorite for bolsters which are then etched and heat colored. Uses 416 stainless for spacers with inlays of natural materials, gem stones with also file work. Liners are made from titanium are most often fully file worked and anodized. Only uses natural materials particularly mammoth ivory for scales. **Prices:** $500 to $1500 **Remarks:** Full time maker. Has been selling knives for over thirty years. **Mark:** Last name on the inside of the spacer.

NISHIUCHI, MELVIN S,
6121 Forest Park Dr, Las Vegas, NV 89156, Phone: 702-501-3724, msnknives@yahoo.com
Specialties: Collectable quality using/working knives. **Patterns:** Locking liner folders, fighters, hunters and fancy personal knives. **Technical:** Grinds ATS-34 and Devin Thomas Damascus; prefers semi-precious stone and exotic natural handle materials. **Prices:** $375 to $2000. **Remarks:** Part-time maker; first knife sold in 1985. **Mark:** Circle with a line above it.

NOLEN, STEVE,
2069 Palomino Tr, Keller, TX 76248-3102, Phone: 903-786-2454, nolen_tx@netzero.net; Web: www.nolenknives.com
Specialties: Working knives; display pieces. **Patterns:** Wide variety of straight knives, butterflies and buckles. **Technical:** Grind D2, 440C and 154CM. Offer filework; make exotic handles. **Prices:** $150 to $800; some higher. **Remarks:** Full-time maker; Steve is third generation maker. **Mark:** NK in oval logo.

NORDELL, INGEMAR,
Skarpå 2103, 82041 Fŝrila, SWEDEN, Phone: 0651-23347
Specialties: Classic working and using straight knives. **Patterns:** Hunters, Bowies and fighters. **Technical:** Forges and grinds ATS-34, D2 and Sandvik. **Prices:** $120 to $1500. **Remarks:** Part-time maker; first knife sold in 1985. **Mark:** Initials or name.

NOREN, DOUGLAS E,
14676 Boom Rd, Springlake, MI 49456, Phone: 616-842-4247, gnoren@icsdata.com
Specialties: Hand forged blades, custom built and made to order. Hand file work, carving and casting. Stag and stacked handles. Replicas of Scagel and Joseph Rogers. Hand tooled custom made sheaths. **Technical:** Master smith, 5160, 52100 and 1084 steel. **Prices:** Start at $250. **Remarks:** Sole authorship, works in all mediums, ABS Mastersmith, all knives come with a custom hand-tooled sheath. Also makes anvils. Enjoys the challenge and meeting people.

NORFLEET, ROSS W,
4110 N Courthouse Rd, Providence Forge, VA 23140-3420, Phone: 804-966-2596, rossknife@aol.com
Specialties: Classic, traditional and working/using knives of his design or in standard patterns. **Patterns:** Hunters and folders. **Technical:** Hollow-grinds 440C and ATS-34. **Prices:** $150 to $550. **Remarks:** Part-time maker; first knife sold in 1992. **Mark:** Last name.

NORTON, DON,
95N Wilkison Ave, Port Townsend, WA 98368-2534, Phone: 306-385-1978
Specialties: Fancy and plain straight knives. **Patterns:** Hunters, small Bowies, tantos, boot knives, fillets. **Technical:** Prefers 440C, Micarta, exotic woods and other natural handle materials. Hollow-grinds all knives except fillet knives. **Prices:** $185 to $2800; average is $200. **Remarks:** Full-time maker; first knife sold in 1980. **Mark:** Full name, Hsi Shuai, city, state.

NOWACKI, STEPHEN R.,
167 King Georges Ave, Regents Park, Southampton, Hampshire, England SO154LD, Phone: 023 8032 5405, stephen.nowacki@hotmail.co.uk Web: www.whitetigerknives.com
Specialties: Hand-forged, bowies, daggers, tactical blades, hunters and mountain-man style folders. **Technical:** Flat grinds 0-1, 1084, 5160, and hand forged Damascus. Heat treats and uses natural handle materials. **Prices:** $200 - $1500. **Remarks:** Part-time maker. First knife sold in 2000. Doing business as White Tiger Knives. **Mark:** Stylized W T.

custom knifemakers

NOWLAND, RICK,
3677 E Bonnie Rd, Waltonville, IL 62894, Phone: 618-279-3170, ricknowland@frontiernet.net
Specialties: Slip joint folders in traditional patterns. **Patterns:** Trapper, whittler, sowbelly, toothpick and copperhead. **Technical:** Uses ATS-34, bolsters and liners have integral construction. **Prices:** $225 to $1000. **Remarks:** Part-time maker. **Mark:** Last name.

NUCKELS, STEPHEN J,
1105 Potomac Ave, Hagerstown, MD 21742, Phone: 301-739-1287, sgnucks@myactv.net
Specialties: Traditional using/working/everyday carry knives and small neck knives. **Patterns:** Hunters, bowies, Drop and trailing point knives, frontier styles. **Technical:** Hammer forges carbon steels, stock removal. Modest silver wire inlay and file work. Sheath work. **Prices:** Starting at $500. **Remarks:** Part-time maker forging under Potomac Forge, first knife made in 2008. Member W.F. Moran Jr. Foundation, American Bladesmith Society.

NUNN, GREGORY,
HC64 Box 2107, Castle Valley, UT 84532, Phone: 435-259-8607
Specialties: High-art working and using knives of his design; new edition knife with handle made from anatomized dinosaur bone, first ever made. **Patterns:** Flaked stone knives. **Technical:** Uses gem-quality agates, jaspers and obsidians for blades. **Prices:** $250 to $2300. **Remarks:** Full-time maker; first knife sold in 1989. **Mark:** Name, knife and edition numbers, year made.

O

OATES, LEE,
PO BOX 1391, La Porte, TX 77572, Phone: 281-471-6060, bearoates@att.net
Web: www.bearclawknives.com
Specialties: Friction folders, period correct replicas, traditional, working and primitive knives of my design or to customer specs. **Patterns:** Bowies, teflon-coated fighters, daggers, hunters, fillet and kitchen cutlery. **Technical:** Heat treating services for other makers. Forges carbon, 440C, D2, and makes own Damascus, stock removal on SS and kitchen cutlery, Teflon coatings available on custom hunters/fighters, makes own sheaths. **Prices:** $150 to $2500. **Remarks:** Full-time maker and heat treater since 1996. First knife sold in 1988. **Mark:** Harmony (yin/yang) symbol with two bear tracks inside all forged blades; etched "Commanche Cutlery" on SS kitchen cutlery.

O'BRIEN, MIKE J.,
3807 War Bow, San Antonio, TX 78238, Phone: 210-256-0673, obrien8700@att.net
Specialties: Quality straight knives of his design. **Patterns:** Mostly daggers (safe queens), some hunters. **Technical:** Grinds 440c, ATS-34, and CPM-154. Emphasis on clean workmanship and solid design. Likes hand-rubbed blades and fittings, exotic woods. **Prices:** $300 to $700 and up. **Remarks:** Part-time maker, made first knife in 1988. **Mark:** O'BRIEN in semi-circle.

OCHS, CHARLES F,
124 Emerald Lane, Largo, FL 33771, Phone: 727-536-3827, Fax: 727-536-3827, chuckandbelle@juno.com
Specialties: Working knives; period pieces. **Patterns:** Hunters, fighters, Bowies, buck skinners and folders. **Technical:** Forges 52100, 5160 and his own Damascus. **Prices:** $150 to $1800; some to $2500. **Remarks:** Full-time maker; first knife sold in 1978. **Mark:** OX Forge.

OCHS, ERIC,
PO BOX 1311, Sherwood, OR 97140, Phone: 503-925-9790, Fax: 503-925-9790, eric@ochs.com Web: www.ochssherworx.com
Specialties: Hunting and tactical knives including choppers and folding knives. **Patterns:** Tactical, linear and frame lock folders as well as full-tang knives, tapered tangs available wth handrub, satin or stonewash finishes and synthetic, wood or bone handles. **Technical:** CPM S30V, CPM S35VN, CPM3V, CPM 154CM and Elmax as well as Damasteel and Chad Nichols Damascus. Flat, hollow, and compound grinds. **Prices:** $100 - $950. **Remarks:** Full-time maker; made first knife in 2008 and started selling knives in mid-2009. **Mark:** The words "Ochs Sherworx" separated by an eight point compass insignia.

OGDEN, RANDY W,
10822 Sage Orchard, Houston, TX 77089, Phone: 713-481-3601

ODOM JR., VICTOR L.,
PO Box 572, North, SC 29112, Phone: 803-247-2749, cell 803-608-0829, vlodom3@tds.net Web: www.knifemakercentral.com
Specialties: Forged knives and tomahawks; stock removal knives. **Patterns:** Hunters, Bowies, George Herron patterns, and folders. **Technical:** Use 1095, 5160, 52100 high carbon and alloy steels, ATS-34, and 154 CM. **Prices:** Straight knives $60 and up. Folders $250 and up. **Remarks:** Student of Mr. George Henron. SCAK.ORG. Secretary of the Couth Carolina Association of Knifemakers. **Mark:** Steel stamp "ODOM" and etched "Odom Forge North, SC" plus a serial number.

OGDEN, BILL,
OGDEN KNIVES, PO Box 52, Avis
AVIS, PA 17721, Phone: 570-974-9114
Specialties: One-of-a-kind, liner-lock folders, hunters, skinners, minis. **Technical:** Grinds ATS-34, 440-C, D2, 52100, Damascus, natural and unnatural handle materials, hand-stitched custom sheaths. **Prices:** $50 and up. **Remarks:** Part-time maker since 1992. **Marks:** Last name or "OK" stamp (Ogden Knives).

OGLETREE JR., BEN R,
2815 Israel Rd, Livingston, TX 77351, Phone: 409-327-8315
Specialties: Working/using straight knives of his design. **Patterns:** Hunters, kitchen and utility/camp knives. **Technical:** Grinds ATS-34, W1 and 1075; heat-treats. **Prices:** $200 to $400. **Remarks:** Part-time maker; first knife sold in 1955. **Mark:** Last name, city and state in oval with a tree on either side.

O'HARE, SEAN,
1831 Rte. 776, Grand Manan, NB, CANADA E5G 2H9, Phone: 506-662-8524, sean@ohareknives.com; Web: www.ohareknives.com
Specialties: Fixed blade hunters and folders. **Patterns:** Small to large hunters and daily carry folders. **Technical:** Stock removal, flat ground. **Prices:** $220 USD to $1200 USD. **Remarks:** Strives to balance aesthetics, functionality and durability. **Mark:** 1st line - "OHARE KNIVES", 2nd line - "CANADA."

OLIVE, MICHAEL E,
6388 Angora Mt Rd, Leslie, AR 72645, Phone: 870-363-4668
Specialties: Fixed blades. **Patterns:** Bowies, camp knives, fighters and hunters. **Technical:** Forged blades of 1084, W2, 5160, Damascus of 1084, and1572. **Prices:** $250 and up. **Remarks:** Received J.S. stamp in 2005. **Mark:** Olive.

OLIVER, TODD D,
894 Beaver Hollow, Spencer, IN 47460, Phone: 812-829-1762
Specialties: Damascus hunters and daggers. High-carbon as well. **Patterns:** Ladder, twist random. **Technical:** Sole author of all his blades. **Prices:** $350 and up. **Remarks:** Learned bladesmithing from Jim Batson at the ABS school and Damascus from Billy Merritt in Indiana. **Mark:** T.D. Oliver Spencer IN. Two crossed swords and a battle ax.

OLSON, DARROLD E,
PO Box 1182, McMinnville, OR 97128, Phone: 541-285-1412
Specialties: Straight knives and folders of his design and to customer specs. **Patterns:** Hunters, liner locks and slip joints. **Technical:** Grinds ATS-34, 154CM and 440C. Uses anodized titanium; sheaths wet-molded. **Prices:** $125 to $550 and up. **Remarks:** Part-time maker; first knife sold in 1989. **Mark:** Name, type of steel and year.

OLSON, JOE,
210 W. Simson Ave, Geyser, MT 59447, Phone: 406-735-4404, joekeri@3rivers.net Web: www.olsonhandmade.com
Specialties: Theme based art knives specializing in mosaic Damascus autos, folders, and straight knives, all sole authorship. **Patterns:** Mas. **Technical:** Foix. **Prices:** $300 to $5000 with most in the $3500 range. **Remarks:** Full-time maker for 15 years. **Mark:** Folders marked OLSON relief carved into back bar. Carbon steel straight knives stamped OLSON, forged hunters also stamped JS on reverse side.

OLSON, ROD,
Box 5973, High River, AB, CANADA T1V 1P6, Phone: 403-652-0885, rod.olson@hotmail.com
Patterns: Button lock folders. **Technical:** Grinds RWL 34 blade steel, titanium frames. **Prices:** Mid range. **Remarks:** Full-time maker; first knife sold in 1979. **Mark:** Last name.

OLSZEWSKI, STEPHEN,
1820 Harkney Hill Rd, Coventry, RI 02816, Phone: 401-397-4774, blade5377@yahoo.com; Web: www.olszewskiknives.com
Specialties: Lock back, liner locks, automatics (art knives). **Patterns:** One-of-a-kind art knives specializing in figurals. **Technical:** Damascus steel, titanium file worked liners, fossil ivory and pearl. Double actions. **Prices:** $400 to $20,000. **Remarks:** Will custom build to your specifications. Quality work with guarantee. **Mark:** SCO inside fish symbol. Also "Olszewski."

O'MACHEARLEY, MICHAEL,
129 Lawnview Dr., Wilmington, OH 45177, Phone: 937-728-2818, omachearleycustomknives@yahoo.com
Specialties: Forged and Stock removal; hunters, skinners, bowies, plain to fancy. **Technical:** ATS-34 and 5160, forges own Damascus. **Prices:** $180-$1000 and up. **Remarks:** Full-time maker, first knife made in 1999. **Mark:** Last name and shamrock.

O'MALLEY, DANIEL,
4338 Evanston Ave N, Seattle, WA 98103, Phone: 206-527-0315
Specialties: Custom chef's knives. **Remarks:** Making knives since 1997.

ONION, KENNETH J,
47-501 Hui Kelu St, Kaneohe, HI 96744, Phone: 808-239-1300, shopjunky@aol.com; Web: www.kenonionknives.com
Specialties: Folders featuring speed safe as well as other invention gadgets. **Patterns:** Hybrid, art, fighter, utility. **Technical:** S30V, CPM 154V, Cowry Y, SQ-2 and Damascus. **Prices:** $500 to $20,000. **Remarks:** Full-time maker; designer and inventor. First knife sold in 1991. **Mark:** Name and state.

ORFORD, BEN,
Nethergreen Farm, Ridgeway Cross, Malvern, Worcestershire, England WR13 5JS, Phone: 44 01886 880410, web: www.benorford.com
Specialties: Working knives for woodcraft and the outdoorsman, made to his own designs. **Patterns:** Mostly flat Scandinavian grinds, full and partial tang. Also makes specialist woodcraft tools and hook knives. Custom leather sheaths by Lois, his wife. **Technical:** Grinds and forges 01, EN9, EN43, EN45 plus recycled steels. Heat treats. **Prices:** $25 - $650. **Remarks:** Full-time maker; first knife made in 1997. **Mark:** Celtic knot with name underneath.

ORTEGA, BEN M,
165 Dug Rd, Wyoming, PA 18644, Phone: 717-696-3234
ORTON, RICH,
739 W. Palm Dr., Covina, CA 91722, Phone: 626-332-3441, rorton2@ca.rr.com
Specialties: Straight knives only. **Patterns:** Fighters, hunters, skinners. **Technical:** Grinds ATS-34. Heat treats by Paul Bos.**Prices:** $100 to $1000. **Remarks:** Full-time maker; first knife sold in 1992. Doing business as Orton Knife Works. **Mark:** Last name, city state (maker)
OSBORNE, DONALD H,
5840 N McCall, Clovis, CA 93611, Phone: 559-299-9483, Fax: 559-298-1751, oforge@sbcglobal.net
Specialties: Traditional working using straight knives and folder of his design. **Patterns:** Working straight knives, Bowies, hunters, camp knives and folders. **Technical:** Forges carbon steels and makes Damascus. Grinds ATS-34, 154CM, and 440C. **Prices:** $150 and up. **Remarks:** Part-time maker. **Mark:** Last name logo and J.S.
OSBORNE, WARREN,
#2-412 Alysa Ln, Waxahachie, TX 75167, Phone: 972-935-0899, Fax: 972-937-9004, ossie6@mac.com Web: www.osborneknives.com
Specialties: Investment grade collectible, interframes, one-of-a-kinds; unique locking mechanisms and cutting competition knives. **Patterns:** Folders; bolstered and interframes; conventional lockers, front lockers and back lockers; some slip-joints; some high-art pieces. **Technical:** Grinds CPM M4, BG42, CPM S30V, Damascus - some forged and stock removed cutting competition knives. **Prices:** $1200 to $3500; some to $5000. Interframes $1250 to $3000. **Remarks:** Full-time maker; first knife sold in 1980. **Mark:** Last name in boomerang logo.
OTT, FRED,
1257 Rancho Durango Rd, Durango, CO 81303, Phone: 970-375-9669, fredsknives@durango.net
Patterns: Bowies, hunters tantos and daggers. **Technical:** Forges 1086M, W2 and Damascus. **Prices:** $250 to $1000. **Remarks:** Full-time maker. **Mark:** Last name.
OTT, TED,
154 Elgin Woods Ln., Elgin, TX 78621, Phone: 512-413-2243, tedottknives@aol.com
Specialties: Fixed blades, chef knives, butcher knives, bowies, fillet and hunting knives. Technical: Use mainly CPM powder steel, also ATS-34 and D-2. B>Prices: $250 - $1000, depending on embellishments, including scrimshaw and engraving. **Remarks:** Part-time maker; sold first knife in 1993. Won Blade Show world championship in 2010, along with the Bladesports championship. **Mark:** Ott Knives Elgin Texas.
OUYE, KEITH,
PO Box 25307, Honolulu, HI 96825, Phone: 808-395-7000, keith@keithouyeknives.com; Web: www.keithouyeknives.com
Specialties: Folders with 1/8 blades and titanium handles. **Patterns:** Tactical design with liner lock and flipper. **Technical:** Blades are stainless steel ATS 34, CPM154 and S30V. Titanium liners (.071) and scales 3/16 pivots and stop pin, titanium pocket clip. Heat treat by Paul Bos.**Prices:** $450-$600 with engraved knives starting at $995 and up. **Remarks:** Engraving done by C.J. Cal, Bruce Shaw, Lisa Tomlin and Tom Ferry. Retired, so basically a full time knifemaker. Sold first fixed blade in 2004 and first folder in 2005. **Mark:** Ouye/Hawaii with steel type on back side **Other:** Selected by Blade Magazine (March 2006 issue) as one of five makers to watch in 2006.
OVEREYNDER, T R,
1800 S. Davis Dr, Arlington, TX 76013, Phone: 817-277-4812, Fax: 817-277-4812, trovereynderknives@sbcglobal.net; Web: www.overeynderknives.com
Specialties: Highly finished collector-grade knives. Multi-blades. **Patterns:** Fighters, Bowies, daggers, locking folders, 70 percent collector-grade multi blade slip joints, 25 percent interframe, 5 percent fixed blade **Technical:** Grinds CPM-D2, BG-42, S60V, S30V, CPM154, CPM M4, CTS-XHP, RWL-34 vendor supplied Damascus. Has been making titanium-frame folders since 1977. **Prices:** $750 to $2000, some to $7000. **Remarks:** Full-time maker; first knife sold in 1977. Doing business as TRO Knives. **Mark:** T.R. OVEREYNDER KNIVES, city and state.
OWENS, DONALD,
2274 Lucille Ln, Melbourne, FL 32935, Phone: 321-254-9765
OWENS, JOHN,
14500 CR 270, Nathrop, CO 81236, Phone: 719-207-0067
Specialties: Hunters. **Prices:** $225 to $425 some to $700. **Remarks:** Spare-time maker. **Mark:** Last name.
OWNBY, JOHN C,
708 Morningside Tr., Murphy, TX 75094-4365, Phone: 972-442-7352, john@johnownby.com; Web: www.johnownby.com
Specialties: Hunters, utility/camp knives. **Patterns:** Hunters, locking folders and utility/camp knives. **Technical:** 440C, D2 and ATS-34. All blades are flat ground. Prefers natural materials for handles—exotic woods, horn and antler. **Prices:** $150 to $350; some to $500. **Remarks:** Part-time maker; first knife sold in 1993. Doing business as John C. Ownby Handmade Knives. **Mark:** Name, city, state.

OYSTER, LOWELL R,
543 Grant Rd, Corinth, ME 04427, Phone: 207-884-8663
Specialties: Traditional and original designed multi-blade slip-joint folders. **Patterns:** Hunters, minis, camp and fishing knives. **Technical:** Grinds O1; heat-treats. **Prices:** $55 to $450; some to $750. **Remarks:** Full-time maker; first knife sold in 1981. **Mark:** A scallop shell.

P

PACKARD, BOB,
PO Box 311, Elverta, CA 95626, Phone: 916-991-5218
Specialties: Traditional working/using straight knives of his design and to customer specs. **Patterns:** Hunters, fishing knives, utility/camp knives. **Technical:** Grinds ATS-34, 440C; Forges 52100, 5168 and cable Damascus. **Prices:** $75 to $225. **Mark:** Engraved name and year.
PADILLA, GARY,
PO Box 5706, Bellingham, WA 98227, Phone: 360-756-7573, gkpadilla@yahoo.com
Specialties: Unique knives of all designs and uses. **Patterns:** Hunters, kitchen knives, utility/camp knives and obsidian ceremonial knives. **Technical:** Grinds 440C, ATS-34, O1 and Damascus. **Prices:** Generally $100 to $200. **Remarks:** Part-time maker; first knife sold in 1977. **Mark:** Stylized name.
PAGE, LARRY,
1200 Mackey Scott Rd, Aiken, SC 29801-7620, Phone: 803-648-0001
Specialties: Working knives of his design. **Patterns:** Hunters, boots and fighters. **Technical:** Grinds ATS-34. **Prices:** Start at $85. **Remarks:** Part-time maker; first knife sold in 1983. **Mark:** Name, city and state in oval.
PAGE, REGINALD,
6587 Groveland Hill Rd, Groveland, NY 14462, Phone: 716-243-1643
Specialties: High-art straight knives and one-of-a-kind folders of his design. **Patterns:** Hunters, locking folders and slip-joint folders. **Technical:** Forges O1, 5160 and his own Damascus. Prefers natural handle materials but will work with Micarta. **Remarks:** Spare-time maker; first knife sold in 1985. **Mark:** First initial, last name.
PAINTER, TONY,
87 Fireweed Dr, Whitehorse Yukon, CANADA Y1A 5T8, Phone: 867-633-3323, jimmies@klondiker.com; Web: www.tonypainterdesigns.com
Specialties: One-of-a-kind using knives, some fancy, fixed and folders. **Patterns:** No fixed patterns. **Technical:** Grinds ATS-34, D2, O1, S30V, Damascus satin finish. Prefers to use exotic woods and other natural materials. Micarta and G10 on working knives. **Prices:** Starting at $200. **Remarks:** Full-time knifemaker and carver. First knife sold in 1996. **Mark:** Two stamps used: initials TP in a circle and painter.
PALIKKO, J-T,
B30 bi, Suomenlinna, Helsinki, FINLAND, Phone: 358-400-699687, jt@kp-art.fi; Web: www.art-helsinki.com
Specialties: One of a kind knives and swords. **Patterns:** Own puukko models, hunters, integral & semi-integral knives, swords & other historical waepons and friction folders. **Technical:** Forges 52100 & other carbon steels, Damasteel stainless Damascus & RWL 34, makes own Damascus steel, makes carvings on walrus ivory and antler. **Prices:** Starting at $250. **Remarks:** Full-time maker, first knife sold in 1989. **Mark:** JT
PALM, RIK,
10901 Scripps Ranch Blvd, San Diego, CA 92131, Phone: 858-530-0407, rikpalm@knifesmith.com; Web: www.knifesmith.com
Specialties: Sole authorship of one-of-a-kind unique art pieces, working/using knives and sheaths. **Patterns:** Carved nature themed knives, camp, hunters, friction folders, tomahawks, and small special pocket knives. **Technical:** Makes own Damascus, forges 5160H, 1084, 1095, W2, O1. Does his own heat treating including clay hardening. **Prices:** $80 and up. **Remarks:** American Bladesmith Society Journeyman Smith. First blade sold in 2000. **Mark:** Stamped, hand signed, etched last name signature.
PALMER, TAYLOR,
TAYLOR-MADE SCENIC KNIVES INC., Box 97, Blanding, UT 84511, Phone: 435-678-2523, taylormadewoodeu@citlink.net
Specialties: Bronze carvings inside of blade area. **Prices:** $250 and up. **Mark:** Taylor Palmer Utah.
PANAK, PAUL S,
6103 Leon Rd., Andover, OH 44003, Phone: 330-442-2724, burn@burnknives.com; Web: www.burnknives.com
Specialties: Italian-styled knives. DA OTF's, Italian style stilettos. **Patterns:** Vintage-styled Italians, fighting folders and high art gothic-styles all with various mechanisms. **Technical:** Grinds ATS-34, 154 CM, 440C and Damascus. **Prices:** $800 to $3000. **Remarks:** Full-time maker, first knife sold in 1998. **Mark:** "Burn."
PANCHENKO, SERGE,
5927 El Sol Way, Citrus Heights, CA 95621, Phone: 916-588-8821, serge@sergeknives.com Web: www.sergeknives.com
Specialties: Unique art knives using natural materials, copper and carbon steel for a rustic look. **Patterns:** Art knives, hunting and outdoor knives, Japanese style knives and tactical. **Technical:** Forges and grinds carbon steels. **Prices:** $100 - $600. **Remarks:** Part-time maker, first knife sold in 2008. **Mark:** SERGE

PARDUE, JOE,
PO Box 693, Spurger, TX 77660, Phone: 409-429-7074, Fax: 409-429-5657

PARDUE, MELVIN M,
4461 Jerkins Rd., Repton, AL 36475, Phone: 251-248-2686, mpardue@frontiernet.net; Web: www.pardueknives.com
Specialties: Folders, collectable, combat, utility and tactical. Patterns: Lockback, liner lock, push button; all blade and handle patterns. Technical: Grinds 154CM, 440C, 12C27. Forges mokume and Damascus. Uses titanium. Prices: $400 to $1600. Remarks: Full-time maker, Guild member, ABS member, AFC member. First knife made in 1957; first knife sold professionally in 1974. Mark: Mel Pardue.

PARKER, CLIFF,
6350 Tulip Dr, Zephyrhills, FL 33544, Phone: 813-973-1682, cooldamascus@aol.com Web: cliffparkerknives.com
Specialties: Damascus gent knives. Patterns: Locking liners, some straight knives. Technical: Mostly use 1095, 1084, 15N20, 203E and powdered steel. Prices: $700 to $2100. Remarks: Making own Damascus and specializing in mosaics; first knife sold in 1996. Full-time beginning in 2000. Mark: CP.

PARKER, J E,
11 Domenica Cir, Clarion, PA 16214, Phone: 814-226-4837, jimparkerknives@hotmail.com Web:www.jimparkerknives.com
Specialties: Fancy/embellished, traditional and working straight knives of his design and to customer specs. Engraving and scrimshaw by the best in the business. Patterns: Bowies, hunters and LinerLock® folders. Technical: Grinds 440C, 440V, ATS-34 and nickel Damascus. Prefers mastodon, oosik, amber and malachite handle material. Prices: $75 to $5200. Remarks: Full-time maker; first knife sold in 1991. Doing business as Custom Knife. Mark: J E Parker and Clarion PA stamped or etched in blade.

PARKER, ROBERT NELSON,
1527 E Fourth St, Royal Oak, MI 48067, Phone: 248-545-8211, rnparkerknives@wowway.com; Web:classicknifedesign@wowway.com
Specialties: Traditional working and using straight knives of his design. Patterns: Chutes, subhilts, hunters, and fighters. Technical: Grinds ATS-34; GB-42, S-30V, BG-42, ATS, 34-D-Z, no forging, hollow and flat grinds, full and hidden tangs. Hand-stitched leather sheaths. Prices: $400 to $1400; some to $2000. Remarks: Full-time maker; first knife sold in 1986. I do forge sometimes. Mark: Full name.

PARKS, BLANE C,
15908 Crest Dr, Woodbridge, VA 22191, Phone: 703-221-4680
Specialties: Knives of his design. Patterns: Boots, Bowies, daggers, fighters, hunters, kitchen knives, locking and slip-joint folders, utility/camp knives, letter openers and friction folders. Technical: Grinds ATS-34, 440C, D2 and other carbon steels. Offers filework, silver wire inlay and wooden sheaths. Prices: Start at $250 to $650; some to $1000. Remarks: Part-time maker; first knife sold in 1993. Doing business as B.C. Parks Knives. Mark: First and middle initials, last name.

PARKS, JOHN,
3539 Galilee Church Rd, Jefferson, GA 30549, Phone: 706-367-4916
Specialties: Traditional working and using straight knives of his design. Patterns: Hunters, integral bolsters, and personal knives. Technical: Forges 1095 and 5168. Prices: $275 to $600; some to $800. Remarks: Part-time maker; first knife sold in 1989. Mark: Initials.

PARLER, THOMAS O,
11 Franklin St, Charleston, SC 29401, Phone: 803-723-9433

PARRISH, ROBERT,
271 Allman Hill Rd, Weaverville, NC 28787, Phone: 828-645-2864
Specialties: Heavy-duty working knives of his design or to customer specs. Patterns: Survival and duty knives; hunters and fighters. Technical: Grinds 440C, D2, O1 and commercial Damascus. Prices: $200 to $300; some to $6000. Remarks: Part-time maker; first knife sold in 1970. Mark: Initials connected, sometimes with city and state.

PARRISH III, GORDON A,
940 Lakloey Dr, North Pole, AK 99705, Phone: 907-488-0357, ga-parrish@gci.net
Specialties: Classic and high-art straight knives of his design and to customer specs; working and using knives. Patterns: Bowies and hunters. Technical: Grinds tool steel and ATS-34. Uses mostly Alaskan handle materials. Prices: Starting at $225. Remarks: Spare-time maker; first knife sold in 1980. Mark: Last name, FBKS. ALASKA

PARSONS, LARRY,
1038 W Kyle Way, Mustang, OK 73064, Phone: 405-376-9408, Fax: 405-376-9408, l.j.parsons@sbcglobal.net
Specialties: Variety of sheaths from plain leather, geometric stamped, also inlays of various types. Prices: Starting at $35 and up

PARSONS, PETE,
5905 High Country Dr., Helena, MT 59602, Phone: 406-202-0181, Parsons14@MT.net; Web: www.ParsonsMontanaKnives.com
Specialties: Forged utility blades in straight steel or Damascus (will grind stainless on customer request). Folding knives of my own design. Patterns: Hunters, fighters, Bowies, hikers, camp knives, everyday carry folders, tactical folders, gentleman's folders. Some customer designed pieces. Technical: Forges carbon steel, grinds carbon steel and some stainless. Forges own Damascus. Mark: Left side of blade PARSONS stamp or Parsons Helena, MT etch.

PARTRIDGE, JERRY D.,
P.O. Box 977, DeFuniak Springs, FL 32435, Phone: 850-520-4873, jerry@partridgeknives.com; Web: www.partridgeknives.com
Specialties: Fancy and working straight knives and straight razors of his designs. Patterns: Hunters, skinners, fighters, chef's knives, straight razors, neck knives, and miniatures. Technical: Grinds 440C, ATS-34, carbon Damascus, and stainless Damascus. Prices: $250 and up, depending on materials used. Remarks: Part-time maker, first knife sold in 2007. Mark: Partridge Knives logo on the blade; Partridge or Partridge Knives engraved in script.

PASSMORE, JIMMY D,
316 SE Elm, Hoxie, AR 72433, Phone: 870-886-1922

PATRICK, BOB,
12642 24A Ave, S. Surrey, B.C., CANADA V4A 8H9, Phone: 604-538-6214, Fax: 604-888-2683, bob@knivesonnet.com; Web: www.knivesonnet.com
Specialties: Maker's designs only, No orders. Patterns: Bowies, hunters, daggers, throwing knives. Technical: D2, 5160, Damascus. Prices: Good value. Remarks: Full-time maker; first knife sold in 1987. Doing business as Crescent Knife Works. Mark: Logo with name and province or Crescent Knife Works.

PATRICK, CHUCK,
4650 Pine Log Rd., Brasstown, NC 28902, Phone: 828-837-7627, chuckandpeggypatrick@gmail.com Web: www.chuckandpeggypatrick.com
Specialties: Period pieces. Patterns: Hunters, daggers, tomahawks, pre-Civil War folders. Technical: Forges hardware, his own cable and Damascus, available in fancy pattern and mosaic. Prices: $150 to $1000; some higher. Remarks: Full-time maker. Mark: Hand-engraved name or flying owl.

PATRICK, PEGGY,
4650 Pine Log Rd., Brasstown, NC 28902, Phone: 828-837-7627, chuckandpeggypatrick@gmail.com Web: www.chuckandpeggypatrick.com
Specialties: Authentic period and Indian sheaths, braintan, rawhide, beads and quill work. Technical: Does own braintan, rawhide; uses only natural dyes for quills, old color beads.

PATRICK, WILLARD C,
PO Box 5716, Helena, MT 59604, Phone: 406-458-6552, wilamar@mt.net
Specialties: Working straight knives and one-of-a-kind art knives of his design or to customer specs. Patterns: Hunters, Bowies, fish, patch and kitchen knives. Technical: Grinds ATS-34, 1095, O1, A2 and Damascus. Prices: $100 to $2000. Remarks: Full-time maker; first knife sold in 1989. Doing business as Wil-A-Mar Cutlery. Mark: Shield with last name and a dagger.

PATTAY, RUDY,
8739 N. Zurich Way, Citrus Springs, FL 34434, Phone: 516-318-4538, dolphin51@att.net; Web: www.pattayknives.com
Specialties: Fancy and working straight knives of his design. Patterns: Bowies, hunters, utility/camp knives, drop point, skinners. Technical: Hollow-grinds ATS-34, 440C, O1. Offers commercial Damascus, stainless steel soldered guards; fabricates guard and butt cap on lathe and milling machine. Heat-treats. Prefers synthetic handle materials. Offers hand-sewn sheaths. Prices: $100 to $350; some to $500. Remarks: Full-time maker; first knife sold in 1990. Mark: First initial, last name in sorcerer logo.

PATTERSON, PAT,
Box 246, Barksdale, TX 78828, Phone: 830-234-3586, pat@pattersonknives.com
Specialties: Traditional fixed blades and LinerLock folders. Patterns: Hunters and folders. Technical: Grinds 440C, ATS-34, D2, O1 and Damascus. Prices: $250 to $1000. Remarks: Full-time maker. First knife sold in 1991. Mark: Name and city.

PATTON, DICK AND ROB,
6803 View Ln, Nampa, ID 83687, Phone: 208-468-4123, grpatton@pattonknives.com; Web: www.pattonknives.com
Specialties: Custom Damascus, hand forged, fighting knives, Bowie and tactical. Patterns: Mini Bowie, Merlin Fighter, Mandrita Fighting Bowie. Prices: $100 to $2000.

PATTON, PHILLIP,
PO BOX 113, Yoder, IN 46798, phillip@pattonblades.com Web: www.pattonblades.com
Specialties: Tactical fixed blades, including fighting, camp, and general utility blades. Also makes Bowies and daggers. Known for leaf and recurve blade shapes. Technical: Forges carbon, stainless, and high alloy tool steels. Makes own damascus using 1084/15n20 or O1/L6. Makes own carbon/stainless laminated blades. For handle materials, prefers high end woods and sythetics. Uses 416 ss and bronze for fittings. Prices: $175 - $1000 for knives; $750 and up for swords. Remarks: Full-time maker since 2005. Two-year backlog. ABS member. Mark: "Phillip Patton" with Phillip above Patton.

PAULO, FERNANDES R,
Raposo Tavares No 213, Lencois Paulista, 18680, Sao Paulo, BRAZIL, Phone: 014-263-4281
Specialties: An apprentice of Jose Alberto Paschoarelli, his designs are heavily based on the later designs. Technical: Grinds tool steels and stainless steels. Part-time knifemaker. Prices: Start from $100. Mark: P.R.F.

PAWLOWSKI, JOHN R,
111 Herman Melville Ave, Newport News, VA 23606, Phone: 757-870-4284, Fax: 757-223-5935, www.virginiacustomcutlery.com
> **Specialties:** Traditional working and using straight knives and folders. **Patterns:** Hunters, Bowies, fighters and camp knives. **Technical:** Stock removal, grinds 440C, ATS-34, 154CM and buys Damascus. **Prices:** $150 to $500; some higher. **Remarks:** Part-time maker, first knife sold in 1983, Knifemaker Guild Member. **Mark:** Name with attacking eagle.

PEAGLER, RUSS,
PO Box 1314, Moncks Corner, SC 29461, Phone: 803-761-1008
> **Specialties:** Traditional working straight knives of his design and to customer specs. **Patterns:** Hunters, fighters, boots. **Technical:** Hollow-grinds 440C, ATS-34 and O1; uses Damascus steel. Prefers bone handles. **Prices:** $85 to $300; some to $500. **Remarks:** Spare-time maker; first knife sold in 1983. **Mark:** Initials.

PEARCE, LOGAN,
1013 Dogtown Rd, De Queen, AR 71832, Phone: 580-212-0995, night_everclear@hotmail.com; Web: www.pearceknives.com
> **Specialties:** Edged weapons, art knives, stright working knives. **Patterns:** Bowie, hunters, tomahawks, fantasy, utility, daggers, and slip-joint. **Technical:** Fprges 1080, L6, 5160, 440C, steel cable, and his own Damascus. **Prices:** $35 to $500. **Remarks:** Full-time maker, first knife sold in 1992. Doing business as Pearce Knives **Mark:** Name

PEASE, W D,
657 Cassidy Pike, Ewing, KY 41039, Phone: 606-845-0387, Web: www.wdpeaseknives.com
> **Specialties:** Display-quality working folders. **Patterns:** Fighters, tantos and boots; locking folders and interframes. **Technical:** Grinds ATS-34 and commercial Damascus; has own side-release lock system. **Prices:** $500 to $1000; some to $3000. **Remarks:** Full-time maker; first knife sold in 1970. **Mark:** First and middle initials, last name and state. W. D. Pease Kentucky.

PEELE, BRYAN,
219 Ferry St, PO Box 1363, Thompson Falls, MT 59873, Phone: 406-827-4633, banana_peele@yahoo.com
> **Specialties:** Fancy working and using knives of his design. **Patterns:** Hunters, Bowies and fighters. **Technical:** Grinds 440C, ATS-34, D2, O1 and commercial Damascus. **Prices:** $110 to $300; some to $900. **Remarks:** Part-time maker; first knife sold in 1985. **Mark:** The Elk Rack, full name, city, state.

PELLEGRIN, MIKE,
MP3 Knives, 107 White St., Troy, IL 62294-1126, Phone: 618-667-6777, Web: MP3knives.com
> **Specialties:** Lockback folders with stone inlays, and one-of-a-kind art knives with stainless steel or damascus handles. **Technical:** Stock-removal method of blade making using 440C, Damasteel or high-carbon damascus blades. **Prices:** $800 and up. **Remarks:** Making knives since 2000. **Mark:** MP (combined) 3.

PENDLETON, LLOYD,
24581 Shake Ridge Rd, Volcano, CA 95689, Phone: 209-296-3353, Fax: 209-296-3353
> **Specialties:** Contemporary working knives in standard patterns. **Patterns:** Hunters, fighters and boots. **Technical:** Grinds and ATS-34; mirror finishes. **Prices:** $400 to $900 **Remarks:** Full-time maker; first knife sold in 1973. **Mark:** First initial, last name logo, city and state.

PENDRAY, ALFRED H,
13950 NE 20th St, Williston, FL 32696, Phone: 352-528-6124
> **Specialties:** Working straight knives and folders; period pieces. **Patterns:** Fighters and hunters, axes, camp knives and tomahawks. **Technical:** Forges Wootz steel; makes his own Damascus; makes traditional knives from old files and rasps. **Prices:** $125 to $1000; some to $3500. **Remarks:** Part-time maker; first knife sold in 1954. **Mark:** Last initial in horseshoe logo.

PENFOLD, MICK,
PENFOLD KNIVES, 5 Highview Close, Tremar, Cornwall PL14 5SJ, ENGLAND/UK, Phone: 01579-345783, mickpenfold@btinternet.com
> **Specialties:** Hunters, fighters, Bowies. **Technical:** Grinds 440C, ATS-34, Damasteel, and Damascus. **Prices:** $200 to $1800. **Remarks:** Part-time maker. First knives sold in 1999. **Mark:** Last name.

PENNINGTON, C A,
163 Kainga Rd, Kainga Christchurch 8009, NEW ZEALAND, Phone: 03-3237292, capennington@xtra.co.nz
> **Specialties:** Classic working and collectors knives. Folders a specialty. **Patterns:** Classical styling for hunters and collectors. **Technical:** Forges his own all tool steel Damascus. Grinds D2 when requested. **Prices:** $240 to $2000. **Remarks:** Full-time maker; first knife sold in 1988. Color brochure $3. **Mark:** Name, country.

PEPIOT, STEPHAN,
73 Cornwall Blvd, Winnipeg, Man., CANADA R3J-1E9, Phone: 204-888-1499
> **Specialties:** Working straight knives in standard patterns. **Patterns:** Hunters and camp knives. **Technical:** Grinds 440C and industrial hack-saw blades. **Prices:** $75 to $125. **Remarks:** Spare-time maker; first knife sold in 1982. Not currently taking orders. **Mark:** PEP.

PERRY, CHRIS,
1654 W. Birch, Fresno, CA 93711, Phone: 559-246-7446, chris.perry4@comcast.net
> **Specialties:** Traditional working/using straight knives of his design. **Patterns:** Boots, hunters and utility/camp knives. **Technical:** Grinds ATS-34, Damascus, 416ss fittings, silver and gold fittings, hand-rubbed finishes. **Prices:** Starting at $250. **Remarks:** Part-time maker, first knife sold in 1995. **Mark:** Name above city and state.

PERRY, JIM,
Hope Star PO Box 648, Hope, AR 71801, jenn@comfabinc.com

PERRY, JOHN,
9 South Harrell Rd, Mayflower, AR 72106, Phone: 501-470-3043, jpknives@cyberback.com
> **Specialties:** Investment grade and working folders; Antique Bowies and slip joints. **Patterns:** Front and rear lock folders, liner locks, hunters and Bowies. **Technical:** Grinds CPM440V, D2 and making own Damascus. Offers filework. **Prices:** $375 to $1200; some to $3500. **Remarks:** Part-time maker; first knife sold in 1991. Doing business as Perry Custom Knives. **Mark:** Initials or last name in high relief set in a diamond shape.

PERRY, JOHNNY,
PO Box 35, Inman, SC 29349, Phone: 864-431-6390, perr3838@bellsouth.net
> **Mark:** High Ridge Forge.

PERSSON, CONNY,
PL 588, 820 50 Loos, SWEDEN, Phone: +46 657 10305, Fax: +46 657 413 435, connyknives@swipnet.se; Web: www.connyknives.com
> **Specialties:** Mosaic Damascus. **Patterns:** Mosaic Damascus. **Technical:** Straight knives and folders. **Prices:** $1000 and up. **Mark:** C. Persson.

PETEAN, FRANCISCO AND MAURICIO,
R. Dr. Carlos de Carvalho Rosa 52, Centro, Birigui, SP-16200-000, BRAZIL, Phone: 0186-424786
> **Specialties:** Classic knives to customer specs. **Patterns:** Bowies, boots, fighters, hunters and utility knives. **Technical:** Grinds D6, 440C and high-carbon steels. Prefers natural handle material. **Prices:** $70 to $500. **Remarks:** Full-time maker; first knife sold in 1985. **Mark:** Last name, hand made.

PETERSEN, DAN L,
10610 SW 81st, Auburn, KS 66402, Phone: 785-256-2640, dan@petersenknives.com; Web: www.petersenknives.com
> **Specialties:** Period pieces and forged integral hilts on hunters and fighters. **Patterns:** Texas-style Bowies, boots and hunters in high-carbon and Damascus steel. **Technical:** Precision heat treatments. Bainite blades with mantensite cores. **Prices:** $400 to $5000. **Remarks:** First knife sold in 1978. ABS Master Smith. **Mark:** Stylized initials.

PETERSON, CHRIS,
Box 143, 2175 W Rockyford, Salina, UT 84654, Phone: 435-529-7194
> **Specialties:** Working straight knives of his design. **Patterns:** Large fighters, boots, hunters and some display pieces. **Technical:** Forges O1 and meteor. Makes and sells his own Damascus. Engraves, scrimshaws and inlays. **Prices:** $150 to $600; some to $1500. **Remarks:** Full-time maker; first knife sold in 1986. **Mark:** A drop in a circle with a line through it.

PETERSON, ELDON G,
368 Antelope Trl, Whitefish, MT 59937, Phone: 406-862-2204, draino@digisys.net; Web: http://www.kmg.org/egpeterson
> **Specialties:** Fancy and working folders, any size. **Patterns:** Lockback interframes, integral bolster folders, liner locks, and two-blades. **Technical:** Grinds 440C and ATS-34. Offers gold inlay work, gem stone inlays and engraving. **Prices:** $285 to $5000. **Remarks:** Full-time maker; first knife sold in 1974. **Mark:** Name, city and state.

PETERSON, LLOYD (PETE) C,
64 Halbrook Rd, Clinton, AR 72031, Phone: 501-893-0000, wmblade@cyberback.com
> **Specialties:** Miniatures and mosaic folders. **Prices:** $250 and up. **Remarks:** Lead time is 6-8 months. **Mark:** Pete.

PFANENSTIEL, DAN,
1824 Lafayette Ave, Modesto, CA 95355, Phone: 209-575-5937, dpfan@sbcglobal.net
> **Specialties:** Japanese tanto, swords. One-of-a-kind knives. **Technical:** Forges simple carbon steels, some Damascus. **Prices:** $200 to $1000. **Mark:** Circle with wave inside.

PHILIPPE, D A,
PO Box 306, Cornish, NH 03746, Phone: 603-543-0662
> **Specialties:** Traditional working straight knives. **Patterns:** Hunters, trout and bird, camp knives etc. **Technical:** Grinds ATS-34, 440C, A-2, Damascus, flat and hollow ground. Exotic woods and antler handles. Brass, nickel silver and stainless components. **Prices:** $125 to $800. **Remarks:** Full-time maker, first knife sold in 1984. **Mark:** First initial, last name.

PHILLIPS, ALISTAIR,
Amaroo, ACT, 2914, AUSTRALIA, alistair.phillips@knives.mutantdiscovery.com; Web: http://knives.mutantdiscovery.com
> **Specialties:** Slipjoint folders, forged or stock removal fixed blades. **Patterns:** Single blade slipjoints, smaller neck knives, and hunters. **Technical:** Flat grnds O1, ATS-34, and forged 1055. **Prices:** $80 to $400. **Remarks:** Part-time maker, first knife made in 2005. **Mark:** Stamped signature.

PHILLIPS, DENNIS,
16411 West Bennet Rd, Independence, LA 70443, Phone: 985-878-8275
Specialties: Specializes in fixed blade military combat tacticals.

PHILLIPS, DONAVON,
905 Line Prairie Rd., Morton, MS 39117, Phone: 662-907-0322, bigdknives@gmail.com
Specialties: Flat ground, tapered tang working/using knives. **Patterns:** Hunters, Capers, Fillet, EDC, Field/Camp/Survival, Competition Cutters. Will work with customers on custom designs or changes to own designs. **Technical:** Stock removal maker using CPM-M4, CPM-154, and other air-hardening steels. Will use 5160 or 52100 on larger knives. G-10 or rubber standard, will use natural material if requested including armadillo. Kydex sheath is standard, outsourced leather available.†Heat treat is done by maker. **Prices:** $100 - $1000 **Remarks:** Part-time/hobbyist maker. First knife made in 2004; first sold 2007. **Mark:** Mark is etched, first and last name forming apex of triangle, city and state at the base, D in center.

PHILLIPS, SCOTT C,
671 California Rd, Gouverneur, NY 13642, Phone: 315-287-1280, Web: www.mangusknives.com
Specialties: Sheaths in leather. Fixed blade hunters, boot knives, Bowies, buck skinners (hand forged and stock removal). **Technical:** 440C, 5160, 1095 and 52100. **Prices:** Start at $125. **Remarks:** Part-time maker; first knife sold in 1993. **Mark:** Before "2000" as above after S Mangus.

PICKENS, SELBERT,
2295 Roxalana Rd, Dunbar, WV 25064, Phone: 304-744-4048
Specialties: Using knives. **Patterns:** Standard sporting knives. **Technical:** Stainless steels; stock removal method. **Prices:** Moderate. **Remarks:** Part-time maker. **Mark:** Name.

PICKETT, TERRELL,
66 Pickett Ln, Lumberton, MS 39455, Phone: 601-794-6125, pickettfence66@bellsouth.net
Specialties: Fix blades, camp knives, Bowies, hunters, & skinners. Forge and stock removal and some firework. **Technical:** 5160, 1095, 52100, 440C and ATS-34. **Prices:** Range from $150 to $550. **Mark:** Logo on stock removal T.W. Pickett and on forged knives Terrell Pickett's Forge.

PIENAAR, CONRAD,
19A Milner Rd, Bloemfontein 9300, SOUTH AFRICA, Phone: 027 514364180, Fax: 027 514364180
Specialties: Fancy working and using straight knives and folders of his design, to customer specs and in standard patterns. **Patterns:** Hunters, locking folders, cleavers, kitchen and utility/camp knives. **Technical:** Grinds 12C27, D2 and ATS-34. Uses some Damascus. Embellishments; scrimshaws; inlays gold. Knives come with wooden box and custom-made leather sheath. **Prices:** $300 to $1000. **Remarks:** Part-time maker; first knife sold in 1981. Doing business as C.P. Knifemaker. Makes slip joint folders and liner locking folders. **Mark:** Initials and serial number.

PIERCE, HAROLD L,
106 Lyndon Lane, Louisville, KY 40222, Phone: 502-429-5136
Specialties: Working straight knives, some fancy. **Patterns:** Big fighters and Bowies. **Technical:** Grinds D2, 440C, 154CM; likes sub-hilts. **Prices:** $150 to $450; some to $1200. **Remarks:** Full-time maker; first knife sold in 1982. **Mark:** Last name with knife through the last initial.

PIERCE, RANDALL,
903 Wyndam, Arlington, TX 76017, Phone: 817-468-0138

PIERGALLINI, DANIEL E,
4011 N. Forbes Rd, Plant City, FL 33565, Phone: 813-754-3908, Fax: 813-754-3908, coolnifedad@wildblue.net
Specialties: Traditional and fancy straight knives and folders of his design or to customer's specs. **Patterns:** Hunters, fighters, skinners, working and camp knives. **Technical:** Grinds 440C, O1, D2, ATS-34, some Damascus; forges his own mokume. Uses natural handle material. **Prices:** $450 to $800; some to $1800. **Remarks:** Part-time maker; sold first knife in 1994. **Mark:** Last name, city, state or last name in script.

PIESNER, DEAN,
1786 Sawmill Rd, Conestogo, Ont., CANADA N0B 1N0, Phone: 519-664-3648, dean47@rogers.com
Specialties: Classic and period pieces of his design and to customer specs. **Patterns:** Bowies, skinners, fighters and swords. **Technical:** Forges 5160, 52100, steel Damascus and nickel-steel Damascus. Makes own mokume gane with copper, brass and nickel silver. Silver wire inlays in wood. **Prices:** Start at $150. **Remarks:** Full-time maker; first knife sold in 1990. **Mark:** First initial, last name, JS.

PITMAN, DAVID,
PO Drawer 2566, Williston, ND 58802, Phone: 701-572-3325

PITT, DAVID F,
6812 Digger Pine Ln, Anderson, CA 96007, Phone: 530-357-2393, handcannons@tds.net Web: bearpawcustoms.tds.net
Specialties: Fixed blade, hunters and hatchets. Flat ground mirror finish. **Patterns:** Hatchets with gut hook, small gut hooks, guards, bolsters or guard less. **Technical:** Grinds A2, 440C, 154CM, ATS-34, D2. **Prices:** $100 to $900. **Remarks:** All work done in-house including heat treat. Guild member since 1982. **Mark:** Bear paw with David F. Pitt Maker.

PLUNKETT, RICHARD,
29 Kirk Rd, West Cornwall, CT 06796, Phone: 860-672-3419; Toll free: 888-KNIVES-8
Specialties: Traditional, fancy folders and straight knives of his design. **Patterns:** Slip-joint folders and small straight knives. **Technical:** Grinds O1 and stainless steel. Offers many different file patterns. **Prices:** $150 to $450. **Remarks:** Full-time maker; first knife sold in 1994. **Mark:** Signature and date under handle scales.

PODMAJERSKY, DIETRICH,
9219 15th Ave NE, Seattle, WA 98115, Phone: 206-552-0763, podforge@gmail.com; Web: podforge.com
Specialties: Kitchen, utility and art knives, blending functionality with pleasing lines. **Technical:** Stainless and carbon steel, utilizing stock removal or forging where appropriate. All heat traeting is done in house, including cryogenic as needed. **Prices:** $150 and up.

POLK, CLIFTON,
4625 Webber Creek Rd, Van Buren, AR 72956, Phone: 479-474-3828, cliffpolkknives1@aol.com; Web: www.polkknives.com
Specialties: Fancy working folders. **Patterns:** One blades spring backs in five sizes, LinerLock®, automatics, double blades spring back folder with standard drop & clip blade or bird knife with drop and vent hook or cowboy's knives with drop and hoof pick and straight knives. **Technical:** Uses D2 & ATS-34. Makes all own Damascus using 1084, 1095, O1, 15N20, 5160. Using all kinds of exotic woods. Stag, pearls, ivory, mastodon ivory and other bone and horns. **Prices:** $200 to $3000. **Remarks:** Retired fire fighter, made knives since 1974. **Mark:** Polk.

POLK, RUSTY,
5900 Wildwood Dr, Van Buren, AR 72956, Phone: 870-688-3009, polkknives@yahoo.com; Web: www.facebook.com/polkknives
Specialties: Skinners, hunters, Bowies, fighters and forging working knives fancy Damascus, daggers, boot knives, survival knives, and folders. **Patterns:** Drop point, and forge to shape. **Technical:** ATS-34, 440C, Damascus, D2, 51/60, 1084, 15N20, does all his forging. **Prices:** $200 to $2000. **Mark:** R. Polk.

POLLOCK, WALLACE J,
PO BOX 449, Reserve, NM 87830, Phone: 575-654-4039, wally@pollocknives.com Web: www.pollacknives.com
Specialties: Using knives, skinner, hunter, fighting, camp knives. **Patterns:** Use his own patterns or yours. Traditional hunters, daggers, fighters, camp knives. **Technical:** Grinds ATS-34, D-2, BG-42, makes own Damascus, D-2, 0-1, ATS-34, prefer D-2, handles exotic wood, horn, bone, ivory. **Remarks:** Full-time maker, sold first knife 1973. **Prices:** $250 to $2500. **Mark:** Last name, maker, city/state.

POLZIEN, DON,
1912InlerSuite-L,Lubbock,TX79407,Phone:806-791-0766,blindinglightknives.net
Specialties: Traditional Japanese-style blades; restores antique Japanese swords, scabbards and fittings. **Patterns:** Hunters, fighters, one-of-a-kind art knives. **Technical:** 1045-1050 carbon steels, 440C, D2, ATS-34, standard and cable Damascus. **Prices:** $150 to $2500. **Remarks:** Full-time maker. First knife sold in 1990. **Mark:** Oriental characters inside square border.

PONZIO, DOUG,
10219 W State Rd 81, Beloit, WI 53511, Phone: 608-313-3223, prfgdoug@hughes.net; Web: www.ponziodamascus.com
Specialties: Mosaic Damascus, stainless Damascus. **Mark:** P.F.

POOLE, MARVIN O,
PO Box 552, Commerce, GA 30529, Phone: 803-225-5970
Specialties: Traditional working/using straight knives and folders of his design and in standard patterns. **Patterns:** Bowies, fighters, hunters, locking folders, bird and trout knives. **Technical:** Grinds 440C, D2, ATS-34. **Prices:** $50 to $150; some to $750. **Remarks:** Part-time maker; first knife sold in 1980. **Mark:** First initial, last name, year, serial number.

POSNER, BARRY E,
12501 Chandler Blvd Suite 104, N. Hollywood, CA 91607, Phone: 818-752-8005, Fax: 818-752-8006
Specialties: Working/using straight knives. **Patterns:** Hunters, kitchen and utility/camp knives. **Technical:** Grinds ATS-34; forges 1095 and nickel. **Prices:** $95 to $400. **Remarks:** Part-time maker; first knife sold in 1987. Doing business as Posner Knives. Supplier of finished mosaic handle pin stock. **Mark:** First and middle initials, last name.

POTIER, TIMOTHY F,
PO Box 711, Oberlin, LA 70655, Phone: 337-639-2229, tpotier@hotmail.com
Specialties: Classic working and using straight knives to customer specs; some collectible. **Patterns:** Hunters, Bowies, utility/camp knives and belt axes. **Technical:** Forges carbon steel and his own Damascus; offers filework. **Prices:** $300 to $1800; some to $4000. **Remarks:** Part-time maker; first knife sold in 1981. **Mark:** Last name, MS.

POTTER, BILLY,
6323 Hyland Dr., Dublin, OH 43017, Phone: 614-589-8324, potterknives@yahoo.com; Web: www.potterknives.com
Specialties: Working straight knives; his design or to customers patterns. **Patterns:** Bowie, fighters, utilities, skinners, hunters, folding lock blade, miniatures and tomahawks. **Technical:** Grinds and forges, carbon steel, L6, 0-1, 1095, 5160, 1084 and 52000. Grinds 440C stainless. Forges own

Damascus. Handles: prefers exotic hardwood, curly and birdseye maples. Bone, ivory, antler, pearl and horn. Some scrimshaw. **Prices:** Start at $100 up to $800. **Remarks:** Part-time maker; first knife sold 1996. **Mark:** First and last name (maker).

POWELL, JAMES,
2500 North Robinson Rd, Texarkana, TX 75501

POWELL, ROBERT CLARK,
PO Box 321, 93 Gose Rd., Smarr, GA 31086, Phone: 478-994-5418
Specialties: Composite bar Damascus blades. **Patterns:** Art knives, hunters, combat, tomahawks. **Patterns:** Hand forges all blades. **Prices:** $300 and up. **Remarks:** ABS Journeyman Smith. **Mark:** Powell.

POWERS, WALTER R.,
PO BOX 82, Lolita, TX 77971, Phone: 361-874-4230, carlyn@laward.net Web: waltscustomknives.blademakers.com
Specialties: Skinners and hunters. Technical: Uses mainly CPMD2, CPM154, CPMS35VN and Carpenter CTS XHP, but will occasionally use 3V. Stock removal. **Prices:** $140 - $200. **Remarks:** Part-time maker; first knife made in 2002. **Mark:** WP

PRATER, MIKE,
PRATER AND COMPANY, 81 Sanford Ln., Flintstone, GA 30725, cmprater@aol.com; Web: www.casecustomknives.com
Specialties: Customizing factory knives. **Patterns:** Buck knives, case knives, hen and rooster knives. **Technical:** Manufacture of mica pearl. **Prices:** Varied. **Remarks:** First knife sold in 1980. **Mark:** Mica pearl.

PRESSBURGER, RAMON,
59 Driftway Rd, Howell, NJ 07731, Phone: 732-363-0816
Specialties: BG-42. Only knifemaker in U.S.A. that has complete line of affordable hunting knives made from BG-42. **Patterns:** All types hunting styles. **Technical:** Uses all steels; main steels are D-2 and BG-42. **Prices:** $75 to $500. **Remarks:** Full-time maker; has been making hunting knives for 30 years. Makes knives to your patterning. **Mark:** NA.

PRESTI, MATT,
5280 Middleburg Rd, Union Bridge, MD 21791, Phone: 410-775-1520; Cell: 240-357-3592
Specialties: Hunters and chef's knives, fighters, bowies, and period pieces. **Technical:** Forges 5160, 52100, 1095, 1080, W2, and O1 steels as well as his own Damascus. Does own heat treating and makes sheaths. Prefers natural handle materials, particularly antler and curly maple. **Prices:** $150 and up. **Remarks:** Part-time knifemaker who made his first knife in 2001.

PRICE, TIMMY,
PO Box 906, Blairsville, GA 30514, Phone: 706-745-5111

PRIDGEN JR., LARRY,
POBOX707,Fitzgerald,GA31750,Phone:229-591-0013,pridgencustomknives@gmail.com Web: www.pridgencustomknives.com
Specialties: Bowie and Liner Lock Folders. **Patterns:** Bowie, fighter, skinner, trout, liner lock, and custom orders. **Technical:** I do stock removal and use carbon and stainless Damascus and stainless steel. **Prices:** $250 and up. **Remarks:** Each knife comes with a hand-crafted custom sheath and life-time guarantee. **Mark:** Distinctive logo that looks like a brand with LP and a circle around it.

PRIMOS, TERRY,
932 Francis Dr, Shreveport, LA 71118, Phone: 318-686-6625, tprimos@sport.rr.com or terry@primosknives.com; Web: www.primosknives.com
Specialties: Traditional forged straight knives. **Patterns:** Hunters, Bowies, camp knives, and fighters. **Technical:** Forges primarily 1084 and 5160; also forges Damascus. **Prices:** $250 to $600. **Remarks:** Full-time maker; first knife sold in 1993. **Mark:** Last name.

PRINSLOO, THEUNS,
PO Box 2263, Bethlehem, 9700, SOUTH AFRICA, Phone: 27824663885, theunmesa@telkomsa.net; Web: www.theunsprinsloo.com
Specialties: Fancy folders. **Technical:** Own Damascus and mokume. **Prices:** $450 to $1500.

PRITCHARD, RON,
613 Crawford Ave, Dixon, IL 61021, Phone: 815-284-6005
Specialties: Plain and fancy working knives. **Patterns:** Variety of straight knives, locking folders, interframes and miniatures. **Technical:** Grinds 440C, 154CM and commercial Damascus. **Prices:** $100 to $200; some to $1500. **Remarks:** Part-time maker; first knife sold in 1979. **Mark:** Name and city.

PROVENZANO, JOSEPH D,
39043 Dutch Lane, Ponchatoula, LA 70454, Phone: 225-615-4846
Specialties: Working straight knives and folders in standard patterns. **Patterns:** Hunters, Bowies, folders, camp and fishing knives. **Technical:** Grinds ATS-34, 440C, 154CM, CPM 4400V, CPM420V and Damascus. Hollow-grinds hunters. **Prices:** $110 to $300; some to $1000. **Remarks:** Part-time maker; first knife sold in 1980. **Mark:** Joe-Pro.

PRUYN, PETER,
Brothersville Custom Knives, 1328 NW "B" St., Grants Pass, OR 97526, Phone: 631-793-9052, Fax: 541-479-1889, brothersvilleknife@gmail.com Web: brothersvilleknife.com
Specialties: Fixed blade hunters, fighters, and chef knives. **Technical:** Damascus, hi-carbon and stainless steels. **Prices:** $200 - $600. **Remarks:** Full-time maker, first knife sold in 2009. **Mark:** Anvil with "Brothersville" crested above.

PUGH, JIM,
PO Box 711, Azle, TX 76020, Phone: 817-444-2679, Fax: 817-444-5455
Specialties: Fancy/embellished limited editions by request. **Patterns:** 5- to 7-inch Bowies, wildlife art pieces, hunters, daggers and fighters; some commemoratives. **Technical:** Multi color transplanting in solid 18K gold, fine gems; grinds 440C and ATS-34. Offers engraving, fancy file etching and leather sheaths for wildlife art pieces. Ivory and coco bolo handle material on limited editions. Designs animal head butt caps and paws or bear claw guards; sterling silver heads and guards. **Prices:** $60,000 to $80,000 each in the Big Five 2000 edition. **Remarks:** Full-time maker; first knife sold in 1970. **Mark:** Pugh (Old English).

PULIS, VLADIMIR,
CSA 230-95, SL Republic, 96701 Kremnica, SLOVAKIA, Phone: 00421 903 340076, vpulis@gmail.com; Web: www.vpulis.host.sk
Specialties: Fancy and high-art straight knives of his design. **Patterns:** Daggers and hunters. **Technical:** Forges Damascus steel. All work done by hand. **Prices:** $250 to $3000; some to $10,000. **Remarks:** Full-time maker; first knife sold in 1990. **Mark:** Initials in sixtagon.

PULLIAM, MORRIS C,
560 Jeptha Knob Rd, Shelbyville, KY 40065, Phone: 502-633-2261, mcpulliam@fastballinternet.com
Specialties: Working knives. **Patterns:** Hunters and tomahawks. **Technical:** Forges L6, W2, 1095, Damascus and bar 320 layer Damascus. **Prices:** $165 to $1200. **Remarks:** Full-time maker; first knife sold in 1974. Makes knives for Native American festivals. Doing business as Knob Hill Forge. Member of Piqua Sept Shawnee of Ohio. Indian name Cherokee name Chewla (Fox). As a member of a state tribe, is an American Indian artist and craftsman by federal law. **Mark:** Small and large - Pulliam.

PURSLEY, AARON,
8885 Coal Mine Rd, Big Sandy, MT 59520, Phone: 406-378-3200
Specialties: Fancy working knives. **Patterns:** Locking folders, straight hunters and daggers, personal wedding knives and letter openers. **Technical:** Grinds O1 and 440C; engraves. **Prices:** $900 to $2500. **Remarks:** Full-time maker; first knife sold in 1975. **Mark:** Initials connected with year.

PURVIS, BOB AND ELLEN,
2416 N Loretta Dr, Tucson, AZ 85716, Phone: 520-795-8290, repknives2@cox.net
Specialties: Hunter, skinners, Bowies, using knives, gentlemen folders and collectible knives. **Technical:** Grinds ATS-34, 440C, Damascus, Dama steel, heat-treats and cryogenically quenches. We do gold-plating, salt bluing, scrimshawing, filework and fashion handmade leather sheaths. Materials used for handles include exotic woods, mammoth ivory, mother-of-pearl, G-10 and Micarta. **Prices:** $165 to $800. **Remarks:** Knifemaker since retirement in 1984. Selling them since 1993. **Mark:** Script or print R.E. Purvis ~ Tucson, AZ or last name only.

PUTNAM, DONALD S,
590 Wolcott Hill Rd, Wethersfield, CT 06109, Phone: 860-563-9718, Fax: 860-563-9718, dpknives@cox.net
Specialties: Working knives for the hunter and fisherman. **Patterns:** His design or to customer specs. **Technical:** Uses stock removal method, O1, W2, D2, ATS-34, 154CM, 440C and CPM REX 20; stainless steel Damascus on request. **Prices:** $250 and up. **Remarks:** Full-time maker; first knife sold in 1985. **Mark:** Last name with a knife outline.

Q

QUAKENBUSH, THOMAS C,
2426 Butler Rd, Ft Wayne, IN 46808, Phone: 219-483-0749

QUARTON, BARR,
PO Box 4335, McCall, ID 83638, Phone: 208-634-3641
Specialties: Plain and fancy working knives; period pieces. **Patterns:** Hunters, tantos and swords. **Technical:** Forges and grinds 154CM, ATS-34 and his own Damascus. **Prices:** $180 to $450; some to $4500. **Remarks:** Part-time maker; first knife sold in 1978. Doing business as Barr Custom Knives. **Mark:** First name with bear logo.

QUATTLEBAUM, CRAIG,
5065 Bennetts Pasture Rd., Suffolk, VA 23435-1443, Phone: 757-686-4635, mustang376@gci.net
Specialties: Traditional straight knives and one-of-a-kind knives of his design; period pieces. **Patterns:** Bowies and fighters. **Technical:** Forges 5168, 1095 and own Damascus. **Prices:** $300 to $2000. **Remarks:** Part-time maker; first knife sold in 1988. **Mark:** Stylized initials.

QUESENBERRY, MIKE,
110 Evergreen Cricle, Blairsden, CA 96103, Phone: 775-233-1527, quesenberry@psln.com; Web: www.quesenberryknives.com
Specialties: Hunters, daggers, Bowies, and integrals. **Technical:** Forges 52100, 1095, 1084, 5160. Makes own Damascus. Will use stainless on customer requests. Does own heat-treating and own leather work. **Prices:** Starting at $300. **Remarks:** Parttime maker. ABS member since 2006. Journeyman Bladesmith **Mark:** Last name.

R

RABUCK, JASON,
W3080 Hay Lake Road, Springbrook, WI 54875, Phone: 715-766-8220, sales@rabuckhandmadeknives.com; web: www.rabuckhandmadeknives.com
Patterns: Hunters, skinners, camp knives, fighters, survival/tactical, neck knives, kitchen knives. Include whitetail antler, maple, walnut, as well as stabilized woods and micarta. **Technical:** Flat grinds 1095, 5160, and 0-1 carbon steels. Blades are finished with a hand-rubbed satin blade finish. Hand stitched leather sheaths specifically fit to each knife. Boot clips, swivel sheaths, and leg ties include some of the available sheath options. **Prices:** $140 - $560. **Remarks:** Also knife restoration (handle replacement, etc.) Custom and replacement sheath work available for any knife. **Mark:** "RABUCK" over a horseshoe

RACHLIN, LESLIE S,
1200 W Church St, Elmira, NY 14905, Phone: 607-733-6889, lrachlin@stry.rr.com
Specialties: Classic and working/using straight knives and folders of his design. **Patterns:** Hunters and utility/camp knives. **Technical:** Grinds 440C. **Prices:** $50 to $700. **Remarks:** Spare-time maker; first knife sold in 1989. Doing business as Tinkermade Knives. **Mark:** LSR

RADER, MICHAEL,
P.O. Box 393, Wilkeson, WA 98396, Phone: 253-255-7064, michael@raderblade.com; Web: www.raderblade.com
Specialties: Swords, kitchen knives, integrals. **Patterns:** Non traditional designs. Inspired by various cultures. **Technical:** Damascus is made with 1084 and 15N-20, forged blades in 52100, W2 and 1084. **Prices:** $350 - $5,000 **Remarks:** ABS Journeyman Smith **Mark:** ABS Mastersmith Mark "Rader" on one side, "M.S." on other

RADOS, JERRY F,
134 Willie Nell Rd., Columbia, KY 42728, Phone: 606-303-3334, jerry@radosknives.com Web: www.radosknives.com
Specialties: Deluxe period pieces. **Patterns:** Hunters, fighters, locking folders, daggers and camp knives. **Technical:** Forges and grinds his own Damascus which he sells commercially; makes pattern-welded Turkish Damascus. **Prices:** Start at $900. **Remarks:** Full-time maker; first knife sold in 1981. **Mark:** Last name.

RAFN, DAN C.,
Smedebakken 24, 8370 Hadsten, Denmark, contact@dcrknives.com Web: www.dcrknives.com
Specialties: One of a kind collector art knives of own design. **Patterns:** Mostly fantasy style fighters and daggers. But also swords, hunters, and folders. **Technical:** Grinds RWL-34, sleipner steel, damasteel, and hand forges Damascus. **Prices:** Start at $500. **Remarks:** Part-time maker since 2003. **Mark:** Rafn. or DCR. or logo.

RAGSDALE, JAMES D,
160 Clear Creek Valley, Ellijay, GA 30536, Phone: 706-636-3180, jimmarrags@etcmail.com
Specialties: Fancy and embellished working knives of his design or to customer specs. **Patterns:** Hunters, folders and fighters. **Technical:** Grinds 440C, ATS-34 and A2. Uses some Damascus **Prices:** $150 and up. **Remarks:** Full-time maker; first knife sold in 1984. **Mark:** Fish symbol with name above, town below.

RAINVILLE, RICHARD,
126 Cockle Hill Rd, Salem, CT 06420, Phone: 860-859-2776, w1jo@snet.net
Specialties: Traditional working straight knives. **Patterns:** Outdoor knives, including fishing knives. **Technical:** L6, 400C, ATS-34. **Prices:** $100 to $800. **Remarks:** Full-time maker; first knife sold in 1982. **Mark:** Name, city, state in oval logo.

RALEY, R. WAYNE,
825 Poplar Acres Rd, Collierville, TN 38017, Phone: 901-853-2026

RALPH, DARREL,
BRIAR KNIVES, 4185 S St Rt 605, Galena, OH 43021, Phone: 740-965-9970, dralph@earthlink.net; Web: www.darrelralph.com
Specialties: Fancy, high-art, high-tech, collectible straight knives and folders of his design and to customer specs; unique mechanisms, some disassemble. **Patterns:** Daggers, fighters and swords. **Technical:** Forges his own Damascus, nickel and high-carbon. Uses mokume and Damascus; mosaics and special patterns. Engraves and heat-treats. Prefers pearl, ivory and abalone handle material; uses stones and jewels. **Prices:** $250 to six figures. **Remarks:** Full-time maker; first knife sold in 1987. Doing business as Briar Knives. **Mark:** DDR.

RAMONDETTI, SERGIO,
VIA MARCONI N 24, 12013 CHIUSA DI PESIO (CN), ITALY, Phone: 0171 734490, Fax: 0171 734490, info@ramon-knives.com Web: www.ramon-knives.com
Specialties: Folders and straight knives of his design. **Patterns:** Utility, hunters and skinners. **Technical:** Grinds RWL-34 and Damascus. **Prices:** $500 to $2000. **Remarks:** Part-time maker; first knife sold in 1999. **Mark:** Logo (S.Ramon) with last name.

RAMSEY, RICHARD A,
8525 Trout Farm Rd, Neosho, MO 64850, Phone: 417-451-1493, rams@direcway.com; Web: www.ramseyknives.com
Specialties: Drop point hunters. **Patterns:** Various Damascus. **Prices:** $125 to $1500. **Mark:** RR double R also last name-RAMSEY.

RANDALL, PATRICK,
160 Mesa Ave., Newbury Park, CA 91320, Phone: 805-754-8093, pat@patrickknives.com; Web: www.patrickknives.com
Specialties: EDC slipjoint folders, drop point hunters, and dive knives of own design. **Technical:** Materials are mostly O1, A2, and ATS-34. Wood, stag, jigged bone, and micarta handles. **Prices:** $125 to $225. **Remarks:** Part-time maker, 4 years of experience, makes about 50 knives per year.

RANDALL JR., JAMES W,
11606 Keith Hall Rd, Keithville, LA 71047, Phone: 318-925-6480, Fax: 318-925-1709, jw@jwrandall.com; Web: www.jwrandall.com
Specialties: Collectible and functional knives. **Patterns:** Bowies, hunters, daggers, swords, folders and combat knives. **Technical:** Forges 5160, 1084, O1 and his Damascus. **Prices:** $400 to $8000. **Remarks:** Part-time. First knife sold in 1998. **Mark:** JW Randall, MS.

RANDALL MADE KNIVES,
4857 South Orange Blossom Trail, Orlando, FL 32839, Phone: 407-855-8075, Fax: 407-855-9054, Web: http://www.randallknives.com
Specialties: Working straight knives. **Patterns:** Hunters, fighters and Bowies. **Technical:** Forges and grinds O1 and 440B. **Prices:** $170 to $550; some to $450. **Remarks:** Part-time maker; first knife sold in 1937. **Mark:** Randall made, city and state in scimitar logo.

RANDOW, RALPH,
4214 Blalock Rd, Pineville, LA 71360, Phone: 318-640-3369

RANKL, CHRISTIAN,
Possenhofenerstr 33, 81476 Munchen, GERMANY, Phone: 0049 01 71 3 66 26 79, Fax: 0049 8975967265, Web: http://www.german-knife.com/german-knifemakers-guild.html
Specialties: Tail-lock knives. **Patterns:** Fighters, hunters and locking folders. **Technical:** Grinds ATS-34, D2, CPM1440V, RWL 34 also stainless Damascus. **Prices:** $450 to $950; some to $2000. **Remarks:** Part-time maker; first knife sold in 1989. **Mark:** Electrochemical etching on blade.

RAPP, STEVEN J,
8033 US Hwy 25-70, Marshall, NC 28753, Phone: 828-649-1092
Specialties: Gold quartz; mosaic handles. **Patterns:** Daggers, Bowies, fighters and San Francisco knives. **Technical:** Hollow- and flat-grinds 440C and Damascus. **Prices:** Start at $500. **Remarks:** Full-time maker; first knife sold in 1981. **Mark:** Name and state.

RAPPAZZO, RICHARD,
142 Dunsbach Ferry Rd, Cohoes, NY 12047, Phone: 518-783-6843
Specialties: Damascus locking folders and straight knives. **Patterns:** Folders, dirks, fighters and tantos in original and traditional designs. **Technical:** Hand-forges all blades; specializes in Damascus; uses only natural handle materials. **Prices:** $400 to $1500. **Remarks:** Part-time maker; first knife sold in 1985. **Mark:** Name, date, serial number.

RARDON, A D,
1589 SE Price Dr, Polo, MO 64671, Phone: 660-354-2330
Specialties: Folders, miniatures. **Patterns:** Hunters, buck skinners, Bowies, miniatures and daggers. **Technical:** Grinds O1, D2, 440C and ATS-34. **Prices:** $150 to $2000; some higher. **Remarks:** Full-time maker; first knife sold in 1954. **Mark:** Fox logo.

RARDON, ARCHIE F,
1589 SE Price Dr, Polo, MO 64671, Phone: 660-354-2330
Specialties: Working knives. **Patterns:** Hunters, Bowies and miniatures. **Technical:** Grinds O1, D2, 440C, ATS-34, cable and Damascus. **Prices:** $50 to $500. **Remarks:** Part-time maker. **Mark:** Boar hog.

RAY, ALAN W,
1287 FM 1280 E, Lovelady, TX 75851, awray@rayzblades.com; Web: www.rayzblades.com
Specialties: Working straight knives of his design. **Patterns:** Hunters. **Technical:** Forges 01, L6 and 5160 for straight knives. **Prices:** $200 to $1000. **Remarks:** Full-time maker; first knife sold in 1979. **Mark:** Stylized initials.

REBELLO, INDIAN GEORGE,
358 Elm St, New Bedford, MA 02740-3837, Phone: 508-951-2719, indgeo@juno.com; Web: www.indiangeorgesknives.com
Specialties: One-of-a-kind fighters and Bowies. **Patterns:** To customer's specs, hunters and utilities. **Technical:** Forges his own Damascus, 5160, 52100, 1084, 1095, cable and O1. Grinds S30V, ATS-34, 154CM, 440C, D2 and A2. **Prices:** Starting at $250. **Remarks:** Full-time maker, first knife sold in 1991. Doing business as Indian George's Knives. Founding father and President of the Southern New England Knife-Makers Guild. Member of the N.C.C.A. and A.B.S. **Mark:** Indian George's Knives.

RED, VERNON,
2020 Benton Cove, Conway, AR 72034, Phone: 501-450-7284, knivesvr@conwaycorp.net
Specialties: Custom design straight knives or folders of own design or customer's. **Patterns:** Hunters, fighters, Bowies, folders. **Technical:** Hollow grind, flat grind, stock removal and forged blades. Uses 440C, D-2, ATS-34, 1084, 1095, and Damascus. **Prices:** $150 and up. **Remarks:** Made first knife in 1982, first folder in 1992. Member of (AKA) Arkansas Knives Association. Doing business as Custom Made Knives by Vernon Red. **Mark:** Last name.

REDD, BILL,
2647 West 133rd Circle, Broomfield, Colorado 80020, Phone: 303-469-9803, knifeinfo@reddknives.com and unlimited_design@msn.com; Web: www.reddknives.com
Prices: Contact maker. **Remarks:** Full-time custom maker, member of PKA. **Mark:** Redd Knives, Bill Redd.

REDDIEX, BILL,
27 Galway Ave, Palmerston North, NEW ZEALAND, Phone: 06-357-0383, Fax: 06-358-2910
Specialties: Collector-grade working straight knives. **Patterns:** Traditional-style Bowies and drop-point hunters. **Technical:** Grinds 440C, D2 and O1; offers variety of grinds and finishes. **Prices:** $130 to $750. **Remarks:** Full-time maker; first knife sold in 1980. **Mark:** Last name around kiwi bird logo.

REED, DAVE,
Box 132, Brimfield, MA 01010, Phone: 413-245-3661
Specialties: Traditional styles. Makes knives from chains, rasps, gears, etc. **Patterns:** Bush swords, hunters, working minis, camp and utility knives. **Technical:** Forges 1075 and his own Damascus. **Prices:** Start at $50. **Remarks:** Part-time maker; first knife sold in 1970. **Mark:** Initials.

REED, JOHN M,
3937 Sunset Cove Dr., Port Orange, FL 32129, Phone: 386-310-4569
Specialties: Hunter, utility, some survival knives. **Patterns:** Trailing Point, and drop point sheath knives. **Technical:** ATS-34, Rockwell 60 exotic wood or natural material handles. **Prices:** $135 to $450. Depending on handle material. **Remarks:** Likes the stock removal method. "Old Fashioned trainling point blades." Handmade and sewn leather sheaths. **Mark:** "Reed" acid etched on left side of blade.

REEVE, CHRIS,
2949 Victory View Way, Boise, ID 83709-2946, Phone: 208-375-0367, Fax: 208-375-0368, crkinfo@chrisreeve.com; Web: www.chrisreeve.com
Specialties: Originator and designer of the One Piece range of fixed blade utility knives and of the Sebenza Integral Lock folding knives made by Chris Reeve Knives. Currently makes only one or two pieces per year himself. **Patterns:** Art folders and fixed blades; one-of-a-kind. **Technical:** Grinds specialty stainless steels, Damascus and other materials to his own design. **Prices:** $1000 and upwards. **Remarks:** Full-time in knife business; first knife sold in 1982. **Mark:** Signature and date.

REEVES, J.R.,
5181 South State Line, Texarkana, Arkansas 71854, Phone: 870-773-5777, jos123@netscape.com
Specialties: Working straight knives of my design or customer design if a good flow. **Patterns:** Hunters, fighters, bowies, camp, bird, and trout knives. **Technical:** Forges and grinds 5160, 1084, 15n20, L6, 52100 and some damascus. Also some stock removal 440C, 01, D2, and 154 CM steels. I offer flat or hollow grinds. Natural handle material to include Sambar stag, desert Ironwood, sheep horn, other stabilized exotic woods and ivory. Custom filework offered. **Prices:** $200 - $1500. **Remarks:** Full-time maker, first knife sold in 1985. **Mark:** JR Reeves.

REGGIO JR., SIDNEY J,
PO Box 851, Sun, LA 70463, Phone: 504-886-5886
Specialties: Miniature classic and fancy straight knives of his design or in standard patterns. **Patterns:** Fighters, hunters and utility/camp knives. **Technical:** Grinds 440C, ATS-34 and commercial Damascus. Engraves; scrimshaws; offers filework. Hollow grinds most blades. Prefers natural handle material. Offers handmade sheaths. **Prices:** $85 to $250; some to $500. **Remarks:** Part-time maker; first knife sold in 1988. Doing business as Sterling Workshop. **Mark:** Initials.

REID, JIM,
6425 Cranbrook St. NE, Albuquerque, NM 87111, jhrabq7@Q.com
Specialties: Fixed-blade knives. **Patterns:** Hunting, neck, and cowboy bowies. **Technical:** A2, D2, and damascus, stock removal. **Prices:** $125 to $300. **Mark:** Jim Reid over New Mexico zia sign.

RENNER, TERRY,
TR Blades, Inc., 707 13th Ave. Cir. W, Palmetto, FL 34221, Phone: 941-729-3226; 941-545-6320, terrylmusic@gmail.com Web: www.trblades.com
Specialties: High art folders and straight-blades, specialty locking mechanisms. Designer of the Neckolas knife by CRKT. Deep-relief carving. **Technical:** Prefer CPM154, S30V, 1095 carbon, damascus by Rob Thomas, Delbert Ealey, Bertie Reitveld, Todd Fischer, Joel Davis. Does own heat treating. **Remarks:** Full-time maker as of 2005. Formerly in bicylce manufacturing business, with patents for tooling and fixtures. President of the Florida Knifemaker's Association since 2009. **Mark:** TR* stylized

REPKE, MIKE,
4191 N. Euclid Ave., Bay City, MI 48706, Phone: 517-684-3111
Specialties: Traditional working and using straight knives of his design or to customer specs; classic knives; display knives. **Patterns:** Hunters, Bowies, skinners, fighters boots, axes and swords. **Technical:** Grind 440C. Offer variety of handle materials. **Prices:** $99 to $1500. **Remarks:** Full-time makers. Doing business as Black Forest Blades. **Mark:** Knife logo.

REVERDY, NICOLE AND PIERRE,
5 Rue de L'egalite', 26100 Romans, FRANCE, Phone: 334 75 05 10 15, Web: http://www.reverdy.com
Specialties: Art knives; legend pieces. Pierre and Nicole, his wife, are creating knives of art with combination of enamel on pure silver (Nicole) and poetic Damascus (Pierre) such as the "La dague a la licorne." **Patterns:** Daggers, folding knives Damascus and enamel, Bowies, hunters and other large patterns. **Technical:** Forges his Damascus and "poetic Damascus"; where animals such as unicorns, stags, dragons or star crystals appear, works with his own EDM machine to create any kind of pattern inside the steel with his own touch. **Prices:** $2000 and up. **Remarks:** Full-time maker since 1989; first knife sold in 1986. Nicole (wife) collaborates with enamels. **Mark:** Reverdy.

REVISHVILI, ZAZA,
2102 Linden Ave, Madison, WI 53704, Phone: 608-243-7927
Specialties: Fancy/embellished and high-art straight knives and folders of his design. **Patterns:** Daggers, swords and locking folders. **Technical:** Uses Damascus; silver filigree, silver inlay in wood; enameling. **Prices:** $1000 to $9000; some to $15,000. **Remarks:** Full-time maker; first knife sold in 1987. **Mark:** Initials, city.

REXFORD, TODD,
518 Park Dr., Woodland Park, CO 80863, Phone: 719-650-6799, todd@rexfordknives.com; Web: www.rexfordknives.com
Specialties: Dress tactical and tactical folders and fixed blades. **Technical:** I work in stainless steels, stainless damascus, titanium, Stellite and other high performance alloys. All machining and part engineering is done in house.

REXROAT, KIRK,
527 Sweetwater Circle Box 224, Wright, WY 82732, Phone: 307-464-0166, rexknives@vcn.com; Web: www.rexroatknives.com
Specialties: Using and collectible straight knives and folders of his design or to customer specs. **Patterns:** Bowies, hunters, folders. **Technical:** Forges Damascus patterns, mosaic and 52100. **Prices:** $400 and up. **Remarks:** Part-time maker, Master Smith in the ABS; first knife sold in 1984. Doing business as Rexroat Knives. **Mark:** Last name.

REYNOLDS, DAVE,
Rt 2 Box 36, Harrisville, WV 26362, Phone: 304-643-2889, wvreynolds@zoomintevnet.net
Specialties: Working straight knives of his design. **Patterns:** Bowies, kitchen and utility knives. **Technical:** Grinds and forges L6, 1095 and 440C. Heat-treats. **Prices:** $50 to $85; some to $175. **Remarks:** Full-time maker; first knife sold in 1980. Doing business as Terra-Gladius Knives. **Mark:** Mark on special orders only; serial number on all knives.

REYNOLDS, JOHN C,
#2 Andover HC77, Gillette, WY 82716, Phone: 307-682-6076
Specialties: Working knives, some fancy. **Patterns:** Hunters, Bowies, tomahawks and buck skinners; some folders. **Technical:** Grinds D2, ATS-34, 440C and forges own Damascus and knives. Scrimshaws. **Prices:** $200 to $3000. **Remarks:** Spare-time maker; first knife sold in 1969. **Mark:** On ground blades JC Reynolds Gillette WY, on forged blades, initials make the mark-JCR.

RHEA, LIN,
413 Grant 291020, Prattsville, AR 72129, Phone: 870-699-5095, lwrhea2@windstream.net; Web: www.rheaknives.com
Specialties: Traditional and early American styled Bowies in high carbon steel or Damascus. **Patterns:** Bowies, hunters and fighters. **Technical:** Filework wire inlay. Sole authorship of construction, Damascus and embellishment. **Prices:** $280 to $1500. **Remarks:** Serious part-time maker and rated as a Master Smith in the ABS.

RHO, NESTOR LORENZO,
Primera Junta 589, (6000) Junin, Buenos Aires, ARGENTINA, Phone: (02362) 15670686
Specialties: Classic and fancy straight knives of his design. **Patterns:** Bowies, fighters and hunters. **Technical:** Grinds 420C, 440C, 1084, 51-60, 52100, L6, and W1. Offers semi-precious stones on handles, acid etching on blades and blade engraving. **Prices:** $90 to $500, some to $1500. **Remarks:** Full-time maker; first knife sold in 1975. **Mark:** Name.

RIBONI, CLAUDIO,
Via L Da Vinci, Truccazzano (MI), ITALY, Phone: 02 95309010, Web: www.riboni-knives.com

RICARDO ROMANO, BERNARDES,
Ruai Coronel Rennò 1261, Itajuba MG, BRAZIL 37500, Phone: 0055-2135-622-5896
Specialties: Hunters, fighters, Bowies. **Technical:** Grinds blades of stainless and tools steels. **Patterns:** Hunters. **Prices:** $100 to $700. **Mark:** Romano.

RICHARD, RAYMOND,
31047 SE Jackson Rd., Gresham, OR 97080, Phone: 503-663-1219, rayskee13@hotmail.com; Web: www.hawknknives.com
Specialties: Hand-forged knives, tomahawks, axes, and spearheads, all one-of-a-kind. **Prices:** $200 and up, some to $3000. **Remarks:** Full-time maker since 1994. **Mark:** Name on spine of blades.

RICHARDS, CHUCK,
7243 Maple Tree Lane SE, Salem, OR 97317, Phone: 503-569-5549, chuck@woodchuckforge.com; Web: www.woodchuckforge.com
Specialties: Fixed blade Damascus. One-of-a-kind. **Patterns:** Hunters, fighters. **Prices:** $200 to $1200+ **Remarks:** Likes to work with customers on a truly custom knife. **Mark:** A.C. Richards J.S. or ACR J.S.

RICHARDS, RALPH (BUD),
6413 Beech St, Bauxite, AR 72011, Phone: 501-602-5367, DoubleR042@aol.com; Web: SwampPoodleCreations.com
Specialties: Forges 55160, 1084, and 15N20 for Damascus. S30V, 440C, and others. Wood, mammoth, giraffe and mother of pearl handles.

RICHARDSON JR., PERCY,
1117 Kettler St., Navasota, TX 77868, Phone: 936-288-1690, 936-825-2899, Percy@Richardsonhandmadeknives.com; Web: www.Richardsonhandmadeknives.com
Specialties: Working straight knives and folders. **Patterns:** Hunters, skinners, bowies, fighters and folders. **Technical:** Grinds 154CM, ATS-34, and D2. **Prices:** $175 - $750 some bowies to $1200. **Remarks:** Part time maker, first knife sold in 1990. Doing business as Richardsons Handmade Knives. **Mark:** Texas star with last name across it.

RICHERSON, RON,
P.O. Box 51, Greenburg, KY 42743, Phone: 270-405-0491, Fax: 270-932-5601, RRicherson1@windstream.net
Specialties: Collectible and functional fixed blades, locking liners, and autos of his design. **Technical:** Grinds ATS-34, S30V, S60V, CPM-154, D2, 440, high carbon steel, and his and others' Damascus. Prefers natural materials for handles and does both stock removal and forged work, some with embellishments. **Prices:** $250 to $850, some higher. **Remarks:** Full-time maker. Member American Bladesmith Society. Made first knife in September 2006, sold first knife in December 2006. **Mark:** Name in oval with city and state. Also name in center of oval Green River Custom Knives.

RICKE, DAVE,
1209 Adams St, West Bend, WI 53090, Phone: 262-334-5739, R.L5710@sbcglobal.net
Specialties: Working knives; period pieces. **Patterns:** Hunters, boots, Bowies; locking folders and slip joints. **Technical:** Grinds ATS-34, A2, 440C and 154CM. **Prices:** $145 and up. **Remarks:** Full-time maker; first knife sold in 1976. Knifemakers Guild voting member. **Mark:** Last name.

RICKS, KURT J.,
Darkhammer Forge, 29 N. Center, Trenton, UT 84338, Phone: 435-563-3471, kopsh@hotmail.com; http://darkhammerworks.tripod.com
Specialties: Fixed blade working knives of all designs and to customer specs. **Patterns:** Fighters, daggers, hunters, swords, axes, and spears. **Technical:** Uses a coal fired forge. Forges high carbon, tool and spring steels. Does own heat treat on forge. Prefers natural handle materials. Leather sheaths available. **Prices:** Start at $50 plus shipping. **Remarks:** A knife should be functional first and pretty second. Part-time maker; first knife sold in 1994. **Mark:** Initials.

RIDER, DAVID M,
PO Box 5946, Eugene, OR 97405-0911, Phone: 541-343-8747

RIDLEY, ROB,
RR1, Sundre, AB CANADA T0M 1X0, Phone: 405-556-1113, rob@rangeroriginal.com; www.rangeroriginal.com, www.knifemaker.ca
Specialties: The knives I make are mainly fixed blades, though I'm exploring the complex world of folders. **Technical:** I favour high-end stainless alloys and exotic handle materials because a knife should provide both cutting ability and bragging rights. **Remarks:** I made my first knife in 1998 and still use that blade today. I've gone from full time, to part time, to hobby maker, but I still treasure time in the shop or spent with other enthusiasts. Operates Canadian Knifemakers Supply

RIEPE, RICHARD A,
17604 E 296 St, Harrisonville, MO 64701

RIETVELD, BERTIE,
PO Box 53, Magaliesburg 1791, SOUTH AFRICA, Phone: 2783 232 8766, bertie@rietveldknives.com; Web: www.rietveldknives.com
Specialties: Art daggers, Bolster lock folders, Persian designs, embraces elegant designs. **Patterns:** Mostly one-of-a-kind. **Technical:** Sole authorship, work only in own Damascus, gold inlay, blued stainless fittings. **Prices:** $500 - $8,000 **Remarks:** First knife made in 1979. Annual shows attended: ECCKS, Blade Show, Milan Show, South African Guild Show. **Marks:** Logo is elephant in half circle with name, enclosed in Stanhope lens

RIGNEY JR., WILLIE,
191 Colson Dr, Bronston, KY 42518, Phone: 606-679-4227
Specialties: High-tech period pieces and fancy working knives. **Patterns:** Fighters, boots, daggers and push knives. **Technical:** Grinds 440C and 154CM; buys Damascus. Most knives are embellished. **Prices:** $150 to $1500; some to $10,000. **Remarks:** Full-time maker; first knife sold in 1978. **Mark:** First initial, last name.

RINKES, SIEGFRIED,
Am Sportpl 2, D 91459, Markterlbach, GERMANY

RIZZI, RUSSELL J,
37 March Rd, Ashfield, MA 01330, Phone: 413-625-2842
Specialties: Fancy working and using straight knives and folders of his design or to customer specs. **Patterns:** Hunters, locking folders and fighters. **Technical:** Grinds 440C, D2 and commercial Damascus. **Prices:** $150 to $750; some to $2500. **Remarks:** Part-time maker; first knife sold in 1990. **Mark:** Last name, Ashfield, MA.

ROBBINS, BILL,
192 S. Fairview St, Globe, AZ 85501, Phone: 928-402-0052, billrknifemaker@aol.com
Specialties: Plain and fancy working straight knives. Makes to his designs and most anything you can draw. **Patterns:** Hunting knives, utility knives, and Bowies. **Technical:** Grinds ATS-34, 440C, tool steel, high carbon, buys Damascus. **Prices:** $70 to $450. **Remarks:** Part-time maker, first knife sold in 2001. **Mark:** Last name or desert scene with name.

ROBBINS, HOWARD P,
1310 E. 310th Rd., Flemington, MO 65650, Phone: 417-282-5055, ARobb1407@aol.com
Specialties: High-tech working knives with clean designs, some fancy. **Patterns:** Folders, hunters and camp knives. **Technical:** Grinds 440C. Heat-treats; likes mirror finishes. Offers leatherwork. **Prices:** $100 to $500; some to $1000. **Remarks:** Full-time maker; first knife sold in 1982. **Mark:** Name, city and state.

ROBERTS, CHUCK,
PO Box 7174, Golden, CO 80403, Phone: 303-642-2388, chuck@crobertsart.com; Web: www.crobertsart.com
Specialties: Price daggers, large Bowies, hand-rubbed satin finish. **Patterns:** Bowies and California knives. **Technical:** Grinds 440C, 5160 and ATS-34. Handles made of stag, ivory or mother-of-pearl. **Prices:** $1250. **Remarks:** Full-time maker. Company name is C. Roberts - Art that emulates the past. **Mark:** Last initial or last name.

ROBERTS, GEORGE A,
PO Box 31228, 211 Main St., Whitehorse, YT, CANADA Y1A 5P7, Phone: 867-667-7099, Fax: 867-667-7099, gr1898@northwestel.net; Web: www.yuk-biz.com/bandit blades
Specialties: Mastadon ivory, fossil walrus ivory handled knives, scrimshawed or carved. **Patterns:** Side lockers, fancy bird and trout knives, hunters, fillet blades. **Technical:** Grinds stainless Damascus, all surgical steels. **Prices:** Up to $3500 U.S. **Remarks:** Full-time maker; first knives sold in 1986. Doing business as Bandit Blades. Most recent works have gold nuggets in fossilized Mastodon ivory. Something new using mosaic pins in mokume bolster and in mosaic Damascus, it creates a new look. **Mark:** Bandit Yukon with pick and shovel crossed.

ROBERTS, JACK,
10811 Sagebluff Dr, Houston, TX 77089, Phone: 281-481-1784, jroberts59@houston.rr.com
Specialties: Hunting knives and folders, offers scrimshaw by wife Barbara. **Patterns:** Drop point hunters and LinerLock® folders. **Technical:** Grinds 440-C, offers file work, texturing, natural handle materials and Micarta. **Prices:** $200 to $800 some higher. **Remarks:** Part-time maker, sold first knife in 1965. **Mark:** Name, city, state.

ROBERTS, MICHAEL,
601 Oakwood Dr, Clinton, MS 39056, Phone: 601-540-6222, Fax: 601-213-4891
Specialties: Working and using knives in standard patterns and to customer specs. **Patterns:** Hunters, Bowies, tomahawks and fighters. **Technical:** Forges 5160, O1, 1095 and his own Damascus. Uses only natural handle materials. **Prices:** $145 to $500; some to $1100. **Remarks:** Part-time maker; first knife sold in 1988. **Mark:** Last name or first and last name in Celtic script.

ROBERTS, T. C. (TERRY),
1795 Berry Lane, Fayetteville, AR 72701, Phone: 479-442-4493, carolcroberts@cox.net
Specialties: Working straight knives and folders of the maker's original design. **Patterns:** Bowies, daggers, fighters, locking folders, slip joints to include multiblades and whittlers. **Technical:** Grinds all types of carbon and stainless steels and commercially available Damascus. Works in stone and casts in bronze and silver. Some inlays and engraving. **Prices:** $250 - $3500. **Remarks:** Full-time maker; sold first knife in 1983. **Mark:** Stamp is oval with initials inside.

ROBERTSON, LEO D,
3728 Pleasant Lake Dr, Indianapolis, IN 46227, Phone: 317-882-9899, ldr52@juno.com
Specialties: Hunting and folders. **Patterns:** Hunting, fillet, Bowie, utility, folders and tantos. **Technical:** Uses ATS-34, 154CM, 440C, 1095, D2 and Damascus steels. **Prices:** Fixed knives $75 to $350, folders $350 to $600. **Remarks:** Handles made with stag, wildwoods, laminates, mother-of-pearl. Made first knife in 1990. Member of American Bladesmith Society. **Mark:** Logo with full name in oval around logo.

ROBINSON, CALVIN,
5501 Twin Creek Circle, Pace, FL 32571, Phone: 850 572 1504, calvinshandmadeknives@yahoo.com; Web: www.CalvinRobinsonKnives.com
Specialties: Working knives of my own design. **Patterns:** Hunters, fishing, folding and kitchen and purse knives. **Technical:** Now using 13-C-26 stainless. **Prices:** $180 to $2500. **Remarks:** Full-time maker. Probationary member and voting member of the Knifemaker's Guild. **Mark:** Calvin Robinson Pace, Florida.

ROBINSON, CHARLES (DICKIE),
PO Box 221, Vega, TX 79092, Phone: 806-676-6428, dickie@amaonline.com; Web: www.robinsonknives.com
Specialties: Classic and working/using knives. Does his own engraving. **Patterns:** Bowies, daggers, fighters, hunters and camp knives. **Technical:** Forges O1, 5160, 52100 and his own Damascus. **Prices:** $350 to $850; some to $5000. **Remarks:** Part-time maker; first knife sold in 1988. Doing business as Robinson Knives. ABS Master Smith. **Mark:** Robinson MS.

ROBINSON, CHUCK,
SEA ROBIN FORGE, 1423 Third Ave., Picayune, MS 39466, Phone: 601-798-0060, robi5515@bellsouth.net
Specialties: Deluxe period pieces and working / using knives of his design and to customer specs. **Patterns:** Bowies, fighters, hunters, utility knives and original designs. **Technical:** Forges own Damascus, 52100, O1, L6 and 1070 thru 1095. **Prices:** Start at $225. **Remarks:** First knife 1958. **Mark:** Fish logo, anchor and initials C.R.

ROBINSON III, REX R,
10531 Poe St, Leesburg, FL 34788, Phone: 352-787-4587
Specialties: One-of-a-kind high-art automatics of his design. **Patterns:** Automatics, liner locks and lock back folders. **Technical:** Uses tool steel and stainless Damascus and mokume; flat grinds. Hand carves folders. **Prices:** $1800 to $7500. **Remarks:** First knife sold in 1988. **Mark:** First name inside oval.

ROCHFORD, MICHAEL R,
PO Box 577, Dresser, WI 54009, Phone: 715-755-3520, mrrochford@centurytel.net
Specialties: Working straight knives and folders. Classic Bowies and Moran traditional. **Patterns:** Bowies, fighters, hunters: slip-joint, locking and liner locking folders. **Technical:** Grinds ATS-34, 440C, 154CM and D-2; forges W2, 5160, and his own Damascus. Offers metal and metal and leather sheaths. Filework and wire inlay. **Prices:** $150 to $1000; some to $2000. **Remarks:** Part-time maker; first knife sold in 1984. **Mark:** Name.

RODEBAUGH, JAMES L,
4875 County Rd, Carpenter, WY 82054

RODEWALD, GARY,
447 Grouse Ct, Hamilton, MT 59840, Phone: 406-363-2192
Specialties: Bowies of his design as inspired from historical pieces. **Patterns:** Hunters, Bowies and camp/combat. Forges 5160 1084 and his own Damascus of 1084, 15N20, field grade hunters AT-34-440C, 440V, and BG42. **Prices:** $200 to $1500. **Remarks:** Sole author on knives, sheaths done by saddle maker. **Mark:** Rodewald.

RODKEY, DAN,
18336 Ozark Dr, Hudson, FL 34667, Phone: 727-863-8264
Specialties: Traditional straight knives of his design and in standard patterns. **Patterns:** Boots, fighters and hunters. **Technical:** Grinds 440C, D2 and ATS-34. **Prices:** Start at $200. **Remarks:** Full-time maker; first knife sold in 1985. Doing business as Rodkey Knives. **Mark:** Etched logo on blade.

ROE JR., FRED D,
4005 Granada Dr, Huntsville, AL 35802, Phone: 205-881-6847
Specialties: Highly finished working knives of his design; period pieces. **Patterns:** Hunters, fighters and survival knives; locking folders; specialty designs like diver's knives. **Technical:** Grinds 154CM, ATS-34 and Damascus. Field-tests all blades. **Prices:** $125 to $250; some to $2000. **Remarks:** Part-time maker; first knife sold in 1980. **Mark:** Last name.

ROEDER, DAVID,
812 W. 45 Pl., Kennewick, WA 99337, d.roeder1980@yahoo.com
Specialties: Fixed blade field and exposition grade knives. **Patterns:** Favorite styles are Bowie and hunter. **Technical:** Forges primarily 5160 and 52100. Makes own Damascus. **Prices:** Start at $150. **Remarks:** Made first knife in September, 1996. **Mark:** Maker's mark is a D and R with the R resting at a 45-degree angle to the lower right of the D.

ROGERS, RAY,
PO Box 126, Wauconda, WA 98859, Phone: 509-486-8069, knives@rayrogers.com; Web: www.rayrogers.com
Specialties: LinerLock® folders. Asian and European professional chef's knives. **Patterns:** Rayzor folders, chef's knives and cleavers of his own and traditional designs, drop point hunters and fillet knives. **Technical:** Stock removal S30V, 440, 1095, O1 Damascus and other steels. Does all own heat treating, clay tempering, some forging G-10, Micarta, carbon fiber on folders, stabilized burl woods on fixed blades. **Prices:** $200 to $450. **Remarks:** Knives are made one-at-a-time to the customer's order. Happy to consider customizing knife designs to suit your preferences and sometimes create entirely new knives when necessary. As a full-time knifemaker is willing to spend as much time as it takes (usually through email) discussing the options and refining details of a knife's design to insure that you get the knife you really want.

ROGERS, RICHARD,
PO Box 769, Magdalena, NM 87825, Phone: 575-838-7237, r.s.rogers@hotmail.com
Specialties: Sheffield-style folders and multi-blade folders. **Patterns:** Folders: various traditional patterns. One-of-a-kind fixed blades: Bowies, daggers, hunters, utility knives. **Technical:** Mainly uses ATS-34 and prefer natural handle materials. **Prices:** $400 and up. **Mark:** Last name.

ROGHMANS, MARK,
607 Virginia Ave, LaGrange, GA 30240, Phone: 706-885-1273
Specialties: Classic and traditional knives of his design. **Patterns:** Bowies, daggers and fighters. **Technical:** Grinds ATS-34, D2 and 440C. **Prices:** $250 to $500. **Remarks:** Part-time maker; first knife sold in 1984. Doing business as LaGrange Knife. **Mark:** Last name and/or LaGrange Knife.

ROHN, FRED,
7675 W Happy Hill Rd, Coeur d'Alene, ID 83814, Phone: 208-667-0774
Specialties: Hunters, boot knives, custom patterns. **Patterns:** Drop points, double edge, etc. **Technical:** Grinds 440 or 154CM. **Prices:** $85 and up. **Remarks:** Part-time maker. **Mark:** Logo on blade; serial numbered.

ROLLERT, STEVE,
PO Box 65, Keenesburg, CO 80643-0065, Phone: 303-732-4858, steve@doveknives.com; Web: www.doveknives.com
Specialties: Highly finished working knives. **Patterns:** Variety of straight knives; locking folders and slip-joints. **Technical:** Forges and grinds W2, 1095, ATS-34 and his pattern-welded, cable Damascus and nickel Damascus. **Prices:** $300 to $1000; some to $3000. **Remarks:** Full-time maker; first knife sold in 1980. Doing business as Dove Knives. **Mark:** Last name in script.

ROMEIS, GORDON,
1521 Coconut Dr., Fort Myers, FL 33901, Phone: 239-940-5060, gordonromeis@gmail.com Web: Romeisknives.com
Specialties: Smaller using knives. **Patterns:** I have a number of standard designs that include both full tapered tangs and narrow tang knives. Custom designs are welcome. Many different types. No folders. **Technical:** Standard steel is 440C. Also uses Alabama Damascus steel. **Prices:** Start at $165. **Remarks:** I am a part-time maker however I do try to keep waiting times to a minimum. **Mark:** Either my name, city, and state or simply ROMEIS depending on the knife.

RONZIO, N. JACK,
PO Box 248, Fruita, CO 81521, Phone: 970-858-0921

ROOT, GARY,
644 East 14th St, Erie, PA 16503, Phone: 814-459-0196
Specialties: Damascus Bowies with hand carved eagles, hawks and snakes for handles. Few folders made. **Patterns:** Daggers, hunter/field knives. **Technical:** Using handforged Damascus from Ray Bybar Jr (M.S.) and Robert Eggerling. Grinds D2, 440C, 1095 and 5160. Some 5160 is hand forged. **Prices:** $80 to $300 some to $1000. **Remarks:** Full time maker, first knife sold in 1976. **Mark:** Name over Erie, PA.

ROSE, BOB,
PO BOX 126, Wagontown, PA 19376, Phone: 484-883-3925, medit8@meditationsociety.com Web: www.bobroseknives.com
Patterns: Bowies, fighters, drop point hunters, daggers, bird and trout, camp, and other fixed blade styles. **Technical:** Mostly using 1095 and damascus steel, desert ironwood and other top-of-the-line exotic woods as well as mammoth tooth. **Prices:** $49 - $300. **Remarks:** Been making and selling knives since 2004. "Knife Making is a meditation technique for me."

ROSE, DEREK W,
14 Willow Wood Rd, Gallipolis, OH 45631, Phone: 740-446-4627

ROSE II, DOUN T,
Ltc US Special Operations Command (ret), 1795/96 W Sharon Rd SW, Fife Lake, MI 49633, Phone: 231-645-1369, Web: www.rosecutlery.com
Specialties: Straight working, collector and presentation knives to a high level of fit and finish. Design in collaboration with customer. **Patterns:** Field knives, Scagel, Bowies, period pieces, axes and tomahawks, fishing and hunting spears and fine. **Technical:** Forged and billet ground, high carbon and stainless steel appropriate to end use. Sourced from: Crucible, Frye, Admiral and Starret. Some period pieces from recovered stock. Makes own damascus and mokume gane. **Remarks:** Full-time maker, ABS since 2000, William Scagel Memorial Scholarship 2002, Bill Moran School of Blade Smithing 2003, Apprentice under Master Blacksmith Dan Nickels at Black Rock Forge current. **Mark:** Last name ROSE in block letters with five petal "wild rose" in place of O. Doing business as Rose Cutlery.

ROSENBAUGH, RON,
2806 Stonegate Dr, Crystal Lake, IL 60012, Phone: 815-477-0027, ron@rosenbaughknives.com; Web: www.rosenbaughknives.com
Specialties: Fancy and plain working knives using own designs, collaborations, and traditional patterns. **Patterns:** Bird, trout, boots, hunters, fighters, some Bowies. **Technical:** Grinds high alloy stainless, tool steels, and Damascus; forges 1084, 5160, 52100, carbon and spring steels. **Prices:** $150 to $1000. **Remarks:** Part-time maker, first knife sold in 1004. **Mark:** Last name, logo, city.

ROSENFELD, BOB,
955 Freeman Johnson Rd, Hoschton, GA 30548, Phone: 770-867-2647, www.1bladesmith@msn.com
Specialties: Fancy and embellished working/using straight knives of his design and in standard patterns. **Patterns:** Daggers, hunters and utility/camp knives. **Technical:** Forges 52100, A203E, 1095 and L6 Damascus. Offers engraving. **Prices:** $125 to $650; some to $1000. **Remarks:** Full-time maker; first knife sold in 1984. Also makes folders; ABS Journeyman. **Mark:** Last name or full name, Knifemaker.

ROSS, D L,
27 Kinsman St, Dunedin, NEW ZEALAND, Phone: 64 3 464 0239, Fax: 64 3 464 0239
Specialties: Working straight knives of his design. **Patterns:** Hunters, various others. **Technical:** Grinds 440C. **Prices:** $100 to $450; some to $700 NZ (not U.S. $). **Remarks:** Part-time maker; first knife sold in 1988. **Mark:** Dave Ross, Maker, city and country.

ROSS, STEPHEN,
534 Remington Dr, Evanston, WY 82930, Phone: 307-789-7104
Specialties: One-of-a-kind collector-grade classic and contemporary straight knives and folders of his design and to customer specs; some fantasy pieces. **Patterns:** Combat and survival knives, hunters, boots and folders. **Technical:** Grinds stainless and tool steels. Engraves, scrimshaws. Makes leather sheaths. **Prices:** $160 to $3000. **Remarks:** Part-time-time maker; first knife sold in 1971. **Mark:** Last name in modified Roman; sometimes in script.

ROSS, TIM,
3239 Oliver Rd, Thunder Bay, Ont., CANADA P7G 1S9, Phone: 807-935-2667, Fax: 807-935-3179
Specialties: Fixed blades, natural handle material. **Patterns:** Hunting, fishing, Bowies, fighters. **Technical:** 440C, D2, 52100, Cable, 5160, 1084, 66, W2. **Prices:** $150 to $750 some higher. **Remarks:** Forges and stock removal. **Mark:** Ross Custom Knives.

ROSSDEUTSCHER, ROBERT N,
133 S Vail Ave, Arlington Heights, IL 60005, Phone: 847-577-0404, Web: www.rnrknives.com
Specialties: Frontier-style and historically inspired knives. **Patterns:** Trade knives, Bowies, camp knives and hunting knives, tomahawks and lances. **Technical:** Most knives are hand forged, a few are stock removal. **Prices:** $135 to $1500. **Remarks:** Journeyman Smith of the American Bladesmith Society. **Mark:** Back-to-back "R's", one upside down and backwards, one right side up and forward in an oval. Sometimes with name, town and state; depending on knife style.

ROTELLA, RICHARD A,
643 75th St, Niagara Falls, NY 14304
Specialties: Working knives of his design. **Patterns:** Various fishing, hunting and utility knives; folders. **Technical:** Grinds ATS-34. Prefers hand-rubbed finishes. **Prices:** $65 to $450; some to $900. **Remarks:** Spare-time maker; first knife sold in 1977. Not taking orders at this time; only sells locally. **Mark:** Name and city in stylized waterfall logo.

ROULIN, CHARLES,
113 B Rt. de Soral, 1233 Geneva, SWITZERLAND, Phone: 022-757-4479, Fax: 079-218-9754, charles.roulin@bluewin.ch; Web: www.coutelier-roulin.com
Specialties: Fancy high-art straight knives and folders of his design. **Patterns:** Bowies, locking folders, slip-joint folders and miniatures. **Technical:** Grinds 440C, ATS-34 and D2. Engraves; carves nature scenes and detailed animals in steel, ivory, on handles and blades. **Prices:** $500 to $3000; some to Euro: 14,600. **Remarks:** Full-time maker; first knife sold in 1988. **Mark:** Symbol of fish with name or name engraved.

ROUSH, SCOTT,
Big Rock Forge, 31920 Maki Rd, Washburn, WI 54891, Phone: 715-373-2334, scott@bigrockforge.com; Web: bigrockforge.com
Specialties: Forged blades representing a diversity of styles from trasditional hunters, fighters, camp knives, and EDC's to artistic pieces of cultural and historical inspiration with an emphasis on unique materials. **Technical:** Forges Aldo 1084, W2, low MN 1075, stainless/high carbon san mai, wrought iron/high carbon san mai, damascus. **Prices:** $85 to $1000 **Remarks:** Full-time maker; first knife sold in 2010. **Mark:** Stamped initials (SAR) set in a diamond.

ROWE, FRED,
BETHEL RIDGE FORGE, 3199 Roberts Rd, Amesville, OH 45711, Phone: 866-325-2164, fred.rowe@bethelridgeforge.com; Web: www.bethelridgeforge.com
Specialties: Damascus and carbon steel sheath knives. **Patterns:** Bowies, hunters, fillet small kokris. **Technical:** His own Damascus, 52100, O1, L6, 1095 carbon steels, mosaics. **Prices:** $200 to $2000. **Remarks:** All blades are clay hardened. **Mark:** Bethel Ridge Forge.

ROYER, KYLE,
1962 State Route W, Mountain View, MO 65548, Phone: 417-934-6394, Fax: 417-247-5572, royerknifeworks@live.com Web: www.royerknifeworks.com
Specialties: I currently specialize in fixed blades. **Technical:** I forge many different patterns of damascus using mostly 1080 and 15n20. **Remarks:** I am a full-time maker and nineteen years old (12-05-90). I received my ABS Journeyman Smith Stamp at the 2009 Blade Show in Atlanta.

ROZAS, CLARK D,
1436 W "G" St, Wilmington, CA 90744, Phone: 310-518-0488
Specialties: Hand forged blades. **Patterns:** Pig stickers, toad stabbers, whackers, choppers. **Technical:** Damascus, 52100, 1095, 1084, 5160. **Prices:** $200 to $600. **Remarks:** A.B.S. member; part-time maker since 1995. **Mark:** Name over dagger.

RUA, GARY,
396 Snell Street, Fall River, MA 02721, Phone: 508-677-2664
Specialties: Working straight knives of his design. 1800 to 1900 century standard patterns. **Patterns:** Bowies, hunters, fighters, and patch knives. **Technical:** Forges and grinds. Damascus, 5160, 1095, old files. Uses only natural handle material. **Prices:** $350 - $2000. **Remarks:** Part-time maker. (Harvest Moon Forge) **Mark:** Last name.

RUANA KNIFE WORKS,
Box 520, Bonner, MT 59823, Phone: 406-258-5368, Fax: 406-258-2895, info@ruanaknives.com; Web: www.ruanaknives.com
Specialties: Working knives and period pieces. **Patterns:** Variety of straight knives. **Technical:** Forges 5160 chrome alloy for Bowies and 1095. **Prices:** $200 and up. **Remarks:** Full-time maker; first knife sold in 1938. Brand new non catalog knives available on ebay under seller name ruanaknives. For free catalog email regular mailing address to info@ruanaknives.com **Mark:** Name.

RUCKER, THOMAS,
194 Woodhaven Ct., Nacogdoches, TX 75965, Phone: 832-216-8122, admin@knivesbythomas.com Web: www.knivesbythomas.com
Specialties: Personal design and custom design. Hunting, tactical, folding knives, and cutlery. **Technical:** Design and grind ATS34, D2, O1, Damascus, and VG10. **Prices:** $150 - $5,000. **Remarks:** Full-time maker and custom scrimshaw and engraving done by wife, Debi Rucker. First knife done in 1969; first design sold in 1975 **Mark:** Etched logo and signature.

RUPERT, BOB,
301 Harshaville Rd, Clinton, PA 15026, Phone: 724-573-4569, rbrupert@aol.com
Specialties: Wrought period pieces with natural elements. **Patterns:** Elegant straight blades, friction folders. **Technical:** Forges colonial 7; 1095; 5160; diffuse mokume-gane and Damascus. **Prices:** $150 to $1500; some higher. **Remarks:** Part-time maker; first knife sold in 1980. Evening hours studio since 1980. Likes simplicity that disassembles. **Mark:** R etched in Old English.

RUPLE, WILLIAM H,
201 Brian Dr., Pleasanton, TX 78064, Phone: 830-569-0007, bknives@devtex.net
Specialties: Multi-blade folders, slip joints, some lock backs. **Patterns:** Like to reproduce old patterns. Offers filework and engraving. **Technical:** Grinds CPM-154 and other carbon and stainless steel and commercial Damascus. **Prices:** $950 to $2500. **Remarks:** Full-time maker; first knife sold in 1988. **Mark:** Ruple.

RUSS, RON,
5351 NE 160th Ave, Williston, FL 32696, Phone: 352-528-2603, RussRs@aol.com
Specialties: Damascus and mokume. **Patterns:** Ladder, rain drop and butterfly. **Technical:** Most knives, including Damascus, are forged from 52100-E. **Prices:** $65 to $2500. **Remarks:** Mark: Russ.

RUSSELL, MICK,
4 Rossini Rd, Pari Park, Port Elizabeth 6070, SOUTH AFRICA
Specialties: Art knives. **Patterns:** Working and collectible bird, trout and hunting knives, defense knives and folders. **Technical:** Grinds D2, 440C, ATS-34 and Damascus. Offers mirror or satin finishes. **Prices:** Start at $100. **Remarks:** Full-time maker; first knife sold in 1986. **Mark:** Stylized rhino incorporating initials.

RUSSELL, TOM,
6500 New Liberty Rd, Jacksonville, AL 36265, Phone: 205-492-7866
Specialties: Straight working knives of his design or to customer specs. **Patterns:** Hunters, folders, fighters, skinners, Bowies and utility knives. **Technical:** Grinds D2, 440C and ATS-34; offers filework. **Prices:** $75 to $225. **Remarks:** Part-time maker; first knife sold in 1987. Full-time tool and die maker. **Mark:** Last name with tulip stamp.

RUTH, MICHAEL G,
3101 New Boston Rd, Texarkana, TX 75501, Phone: 903-832-7166/cell:903-277-3663, Fax: 903-832-4710, mike@ruthknives.com; Web: www.ruthknives.com
Specialties: Hunters, bowies & fighters. Damascus & carbon steel. **Prices:** $375 & up. **Mark:** Last name.

RUTH, JR., Michael,
, Texarkana, TX 75503, Phone: 903-293-2663, michael@ruthlesscustomknives.com; Web: www.ruthlesscustomknives.com
Specialties: Custom hand-forged blades, utilizing high carbon and Damascus steels. **Patterns:** Bowies, hunters and fighters ranging from field to presentation-grade pieces. **Technical:** Steels include 5160, 1084, 15n20, W-2, 1095, and O-1. Handle materials include a variety of premium hardwoods, stag, assorted ivories and micarta. **Mark:** 8-pointed star with capital "R" in center.

RUUSUVUORI, ANNSSI,
Verkkotie 38, 21500 Piikkio, FINLAND, Phone: 358-50-520 8057, anssi.ruusuvuori@akukon.fi
Specialties: Traditional and modern puukko knives and hunters. Sole author except for Damascus steel.**Technical:** Forges mostly 1080 steel.**Prices:** $200 to $500; some to $1200. **Remarks:** Part-time maker.**Mark:** A inside a circle (stamped)

RYBAR JR., RAYMOND B,
2328 South Sunset Dr., Came Verde, AZ 86322, Phone: 928-567-6372, ray@rybarknives.com; Web: www.rybarknives.com
Specialties: Straight knives or folders with customers name, logo, etc. in mosaic pattern. **Patterns:** Common patterns plus mosaics of all types. **Technical:** Forges own Damascus. Primary forging of self smelted steel - smelting classes. **Prices:** $200 to $2000; Bible blades to $10,000. **Remarks:** Master Smith (A.B.S.) Primary focus toward Biblicaly themed blades **Mark:** Rybar or stone church forge or Rev. 1:3 or R.B.R. between diamonds.

RYBERG, GOTE,
Faltgatan 2, S-562 00 Norrahammar, SWEDEN, Phone: 4636-61678

RYDBOM, JEFF,
PO Box 548, Annandale, MN 55302, Phone: 320-274-9639, jry1890@hotmail.com
Specialties: Ring knives. **Patterns:** Hunters, fighters, Bowie and camp knives. **Technical:** Straight grinds O1, A2, 1566 and 5150 steels. **Prices:** $150 to $1000. **Remarks:** No pinning of guards or pommels. All silver brazed. **Mark:** Capital "C" with J R inside.

RYUICHI, KUKI,
504-7 Tokorozawa-Shinmachi, Tokorozawa-city, Saitama, JAPAN, Phone: 042-943-3451

RZEWNICKI, GERALD,
8833 S Massbach Rd, Elizabeth, IL 61028-9714, Phone: 815-598-3239

S

SAINDON, R BILL,
233 Rand Pond Rd, Goshen, NH 03752, Phone: 603-863-1874, dayskiev71@aol.com
Specialties: Collector-quality folders of his design or to customer specs. **Patterns:** Latch release, LinerLock® and lockback folders. **Technical:** Offers limited amount of own Damascus; also uses Damas makers steel. Prefers natural handle material, gold and gems. **Prices:** $500 to $4000. **Remarks:** Full-time maker; first knife sold in 1981. Doing business as Daynia Forge. **Mark:** Sun logo or engraved surname.

SAKAKIBARA, MASAKI,
20-8 Sakuragaoka, 2-Chome Setagaya-ku, Tokyo 156-0054, JAPAN, Phone: 81-3-3420-0375

SAKMAR, MIKE,
903 S. Latson Rd. #257, Howell, MI 48843, Phone: 517-546-6388, Fax: 517-546-6399, sakmarent@yahoo.com; Web: www.sakmarenterprises.com
Specialties: Mokume in various patterns and alloy combinations. **Patterns:** Bowies, fighters, hunters and integrals. **Technical:** Grinds ATS-34, Damascus and high-carbon tool steels. Uses mostly natural handle materials—elephant ivory, walrus ivory, stag, wildwood, oosic, etc. Makes mokume for resale. **Prices:** $250 to $2500; some to $4000. **Remarks:** Part-time maker; first knife sold in 1990. Supplier of mokume. **Mark:** Last name.

SALLEY, JOHN D,
3965 Frederick-Ginghamsburg Rd., Tipp City, OH 45371, Phone: 937-698-4588, Fax: 937-698-4131
Specialties: Fancy working knives and art pieces. **Patterns:** Hunters, fighters, daggers and some swords. **Technical:** Grinds ATS-34, 12C27 and W2; buys Damascus. **Prices:** $85 to $1000; some to $6000. **Remarks:** Part-time maker; first knife sold in 1979. **Mark:** First initial, last name.

SAMPSON, LYNN,
381 Deakins Rd, Jonesborough, TN 37659, Phone: 423-348-8373
Specialties: Highly finished working knives, mostly folders. **Patterns:** Locking folders, slip-joints, interframes and two-blades. **Technical:** Grinds D2, 440C and ATS-34; offers extensive filework. **Prices:** Start at $300. **Remarks:** Full-time maker; first knife sold in 1982. **Mark:** Name and city in logo.

SANDBERG, RONALD B,
24784 Shadowwood Ln, Brownstown, MI 48134-9560, Phone: 734-671-6866, msc2009@comcast.net
Specialties: Good looking and functional hunting knives, filework, mixing of handle materials. **Patterns:** Hunters, skinners and Bowies. **Prices:** $120 and up. **Remarks:** Full lifetime workmanship guarantee. **Mark:** R.B. SANDBERG

SANDERS, BILL,
335 Bauer Ave, PO Box 957, Mancos, CO 81328, Phone: 970-533-7223, Fax: 970-533-7390, billsand@frontier.net; Web: www.billsandershandmadeknives.com
Specialties: Survival knives, working straight knives, some fancy and some fantasy, of his design. **Patterns:** Hunters, boots, utility knives, using belt knives. **Technical:** Grinds 440C, ATS-34 and commercial Damascus. Provides wide variety of handle materials. **Prices:** $170 to $800. **Remarks:** Full-time maker. Formerly of Timberline Knives. **Mark:** Name, city and state.

SANDERS, MICHAEL M,
PO Box 1106, Ponchatoula, LA 70454, Phone: 225-294-3601, sanders@bellsouth.net
Specialties: Working straight knives and folders, some deluxe. **Patterns:** Hunters, fighters, Bowies, daggers, large folders and deluxe Damascus miniatures. **Technical:** Grinds O1, D2, 440C, ATS-34 and Damascus. **Prices:** $75 to $650; some higher. **Remarks:** Full-time maker; first knife sold in 1967. **Mark:** Name and state.

SANDOW, BRENT EDWARD,
50 O'Halloran Road, Howick, Manukau 2014, Auckland, New Zealand, Phone: 64 9 537 4166, Fax: 64 9 533 6655, knifebug@vodafone.co.nz
Specialties: Tactical fixed blades, hunting, camp, Bowie. **Technical:** All blades made by stock removal method. **Prices:** From US $200 upward.

SANDOW, NORMAN E,
63 B Moore St, Howick, Auckland, NEW ZEALAND, Phone: 095328912, sanknife@xtra.co.nz
Specialties: Quality LinerLock® folders. Working and fancy straight knives. Some one-of-a-kind. Embellishments available. **Patterns:** Most patterns, hunters, boot, bird and trout, etc., and to customer's specs. **Technical:** Predominate knife steel ATS-34. Also in use 12C27, D2 and Damascus. High class handle material used on both folders and straight knives. All blades made via the stock removal method. **Prices:** $350 to $4000. **Remarks:** Full-time maker. **Mark:** Norman E Sandow in semi-circular design.

SANDS, SCOTT,
2 Lindis Ln, New Brighton, Christchurch 9, NEW ZEALAND
Specialties: Classic working and fantasy swords. **Patterns:** Fantasy, medieval, celtic, viking, katana, some daggers. **Technical:** Forges own Damascus; 1080

and L6; 5160 and L6; O1 and L6. All hand-polished, does own heat-treating, forges non-Damascus on request. **Prices:** $1500 to $15,000+. **Remarks:** Full-time maker; first blade sold in 1996. **Mark:** Stylized Moon.

SANFORD, DICK,
9 Satsop Court, Montesano, WA 98563, Phone: 360-249-5776, richardsanfo364@centurytel.net
Specialties: Ten years experience hand forging knives

SANTIAGO, ABUD,
Av Gaona 3676 PB A, Buenos Aires 1416, ARGENTINA, Phone: 5411 4612 8396, info@phi-sabud.com; Web: www.phi-sabud.com/blades.html

SANTINI, TOM,
101 Clayside Dr, Pikeville, NC 27863, Phone: 919-288-2071, tomsantiniknives@hotmail.com; Web: www.tomsantiniknives.com
Specialties: working/using straight knives, tactical, and some slipjoints **Technical:** Grinds ATS-34, S-90-V, D2, and damascus. I handstitch my leather sheaths. **Prices:** $150 - $500. **Remarks:** Full-time maker, first knife sold in 2004. **Mark:** Full name.

SARGANIS, PAUL,
2215 Upper Applegate Rd, Jacksonville, OR 97530, Phone: 541-899-2831, paulsarganis@hotmail.com; Web: www.sarganis.50megs.com
Specialties: Hunters, folders, Bowies. **Technical:** Forges 5160, 1084. Grinds ATS-34 and 440C. **Prices:** $120 to $500. **Remarks:** Spare-time maker, first knife sold in 1987. **Mark:** Last name.

SASS, GARY N,
2048 Buckeye Dr, Sharpsville, PA 16150, Phone: 724-866-6165, gnsass@yahoo.com
Specialties: Working straight knives of his design or to customer specifications. **Patterns:** Hunters, fighters, utility knives, push daggers. **Technical:** Grinds 440C, ATS-34 and Damascus. Uses exotic wood, buffalo horn, warthog tusk and semi-precious stones. **Prices:** $50 to $250, some higher. **Remarks:** Part-time maker. First knife sold in 2003. **Mark:** Initials G.S. formed into a diamond shape or last name.

SAVIANO, JAMES,
124 Wallis St., Douglas, MA 01516, Phone: 508-476-7644, jimsaviano@gmail.com
Specialties: Straight knives. **Patterns:** Hunters, bowies, fighters, daggers, short swords. **Technical:** Hand-forged high-carbon and my own damascus steel. **Prices:** Starting at $300. **Remarks:** ABS mastersmith, maker since 2000, sole authorship. **Mark:** Last name or stylized JPS initials.

SAWBY, SCOTT,
480 Snowberry Ln, Sandpoint, ID 83864, Phone: 208-263-4253, scotmar@dishmail.net; Web: www.sawbycustomknives.com
Patterns: Locking folders, patent locking systems and interframes. **Technical:** Grinds D2, 440C, CPM154, ATS-34, S30V, and Damascus. **Prices:** $700 to $3000. **Remarks:** Full-time maker; first knife sold in 1974. Engraving by wife Marian. **Mark:** Last name, city and state.

SCARROW, WIL,
c/o LandW Mail Service, PO Box 1036, Gold Hill, OR 97525, Phone: 541-855-1236, willsknife@earthlink.net
Specialties: Carving knives, also working straight knives in standard patterns or to customer specs. **Patterns:** Carving, fishing, hunting, skinning, utility, swords and Bowies. **Technical:** Forges and grinds: A2, L6, W1, D2, 5160, 1095, 440C, AEB-L, ATS-34 and others on request. Offers some filework. **Prices:** $105 to $850; some higher. Prices include sheath (carver's $40 and up). **Remarks:** Spare-time maker; first knife sold in 1983. Two to eight month construction time on custom orders. Doing business as Scarrow's Custom Stuff and Gold Hill Knife works (in Oregon). Carving knives available at Raven Dog Enterprises. Contact at Ravedog@aol.com. **Mark:** SC with arrow and year made.

SCHALLER, ANTHONY BRETT,
5609 Flint Ct. NW, Albuquerque, NM 87120, Phone: 505-899-0155, brett@schallerknives.com; Web: www.schallerknives.com
Specialties: Straight knives and locking-liner folders of his design and in standard patterns. **Patterns:** Boots, fighters, utility knives and folders. **Technical:** Grinds CPM154, S30V, and stainless Damascus. Offers filework, hand-rubbed finishes and full and narrow tangs. Prefers exotic woods or Micarta for handle materials, G-10 and carbon fiber to handle materials. **Prices:** $100 to $350; some to $500. **Remarks:** Part-time maker; first knife sold in 1990. **Mark:** A.B. Schaller - Albuquerque NM - handmade.

SCHEID, MAGGIE,
124 Van Stallen St, Rochester, NY 14621-3557
Specialties: Simple working straight knives. **Patterns:** Kitchen and utility knives; some miniatures. **Technical:** Forges 5160 high-carbon steel. **Prices:** $100 to $200. **Remarks:** Part-time maker; first knife sold in 1986. **Mark:** Full name.

SCHEMPP, ED,
PO Box 1181, Ephrata, WA 98823, Phone: 509-754-2963, Fax: 509-754-3212
Specialties: Mosaic Damascus and unique folder designs. **Patterns:** Primarily folders. **Technical:** Grinds CPM440V; forges many patterns of mosaic using powdered steel. **Prices:** $100 to $400; some to $2000. **Remarks:** Part-time maker; first knife sold in 1991. Doing business as Ed Schempp Knives. **Mark:** Ed Schempp Knives over five heads of wheat, city and state.

SCHEMPP, MARTIN,
PO Box 1181, 5430 Baird Springs Rd NW, Ephrata, WA 98823, Phone: 509-754-2963, Fax: 509-754-3212
Specialties: Fantasy and traditional straight knives of his design, to customer specs and in standard patterns; Paleolithic-styles. **Patterns:** Fighters and Paleolithic designs. **Technical:** Uses opal, Mexican rainbow and obsidian. Offers scrimshaw. **Prices:** $15 to $100; some to $250. **Remarks:** Spare-time maker; first knife sold in 1995. **Mark:** Initials and date.

SCHEPERS, GEORGE B,
PO Box 395, Shelton, NE 68876-0395
Specialties: Fancy period pieces of his design. **Patterns:** Bowies, swords, tomahawks; locking folders and miniatures. **Technical:** Grinds W1, W2 and his own Damascus; etches. **Prices:** $125 to $600; some higher. **Remarks:** Full-time maker; first knife sold in 1981. **Mark:** Schep.

SCHEURER, ALFREDO E FAES,
Av Rincon de los Arcos 104, Col Bosque Res del Sur, C.P. 16010, MEXICO, Phone: 5676 47 63
Specialties: Fancy and fantasy knives of his design. **Patterns:** Daggers. **Technical:** Grinds stainless steel; casts and grinds silver. Sets stones in silver. **Prices:** $2000 to $3000. **Remarks:** Spare-time maker; first knife sold in 1989. **Mark:** Symbol.

SCHIPPNICK, JIM,
PO Box 326, Sanborn, NY 14132, Phone: 716-731-3715, ragnar@ragweedforge.com; Web: www.ragweedforge.com
Specialties: Nordic, early American, rustic. **Mark:** Runic R. **Remarks:** Also imports Nordic knives from Norway, Sweden and Finland.

SCHLUETER, DAVID,
2136 Cedar Gate Rd., Madison Heights, VA 24572, Phone: 434-384-8642, drschlueter@hotmail.com
Specialties: Japanese-style swords. **Patterns:** Larger blades. O-tanto to Tachi, with focus on less common shapes. **Technical:** Forges and grinds carbon steels, heat-treats and polishes own blades, makes all fittings, does own mounting and finishing. **Prices:** Start at $3000. **Remarks:** Sells fully mounted pieces only, doing business as Odd Frog Forge. **Mark:** Full name and date.

SCHMITZ, RAYMOND E,
PO Box 1787, Valley Center, CA 92082, Phone: 760-749-4318

SCHNEIDER, CRAIG M,
5380 N Amity Rd, Claremont, IL 62421, Phone: 217-377-5715, raephtownslam@att.blackberry.net
Specialties: Straight knives of his own design. **Patterns:** Bowies, hunters, tactical, bird & trout. **Technical:** Forged high-carbon steel and Damascus. Flat grind and differential heat treatment use a wide selection of handle, guard and bolster material, also offers leather sheaths. **Prices:** $150 to $3000. **Remarks:** Part-time maker; first knife sold in 1985. **Mark:** Stylized initials.

SCHNEIDER, HERMAN,
14084 Apple Valley Rd, Apple Valley, CA 92307, Phone: 760-946-9096
Specialties: Presentation pieces, Fighters, Hunters. **Prices:** Starting at $900. **Mark:** H.J. Schneider-Maker or maker's last name.

SCHOEMAN, CORRIE,
Box 28596, Danhof 9310, SOUTH AFRICA, Phone: 027 51 4363528 Cell: 027 82-3750789, corries@intekom.co.za
Specialties: High-tech folders of his design or to customer's specs. **Patterns:** Linerlock folders and automatics. **Technical:** ATS-34, Damascus or stainless Damascus with titanium frames; prefers exotic materials for handles. **Prices:** $650 to $2000. **Remarks:** Full-time maker; first knife sold in 1984. All folders come with filed liners and back and jeweled inserts. **Mark:** Logo in knife shape engraved on inside of back bar.

SCHOENFELD, MATTHEW A,
RR #1, Galiano Island, B.C., CANADA V0N 1P0, Phone: 250-539-2806
Specialties: Working knives of his design. **Patterns:** Kitchen cutlery, camp knives, hunters. **Technical:** Grinds 440C. **Prices:** $85 to $500. **Remarks:** Part-time maker; first knife sold in 1978. **Mark:** Signature, Galiano Is. B.C., and date.

SCHOENINGH, MIKE,
49850 Miller Rd, North Powder, OR 97867, Phone: 541-856-3239

SCHOLL, TIM,
1389 Langdon Rd, Angier, NC 27501, Phone: 910-897-2051, tschollknives@live.com
Specialties: Fancy and working/using straight knives and folders of his design and to customer specs. **Patterns:** Bowies, hunters, tomahawks, daggers & fantasy knives. **Technical:** Forges high carbon and tool steel makes Damascus, grinds ATS-34 and D2 on request. **Prices:** $150 to $6000. **Remarks:** Part-time maker; first knife sold in 1990. Doing business as Tim Scholl Custom Knives. President North Carolina Custom Knifemakers Guild. Journeyman Smith American Bladesmith Society member Professional Knifemakers Association. **Mark:** S pierced by arrow.

SCHRADER, ROBERT,
55532 Gross De, Bend, OR 97707, Phone: 541-598-7301
Specialties: Hunting, utility, Bowie. **Patterns:** Fixed blade. **Prices:** $150 to $600.

SCHRAP, ROBERT G,
CUSTOM LEATHER KNIFE SHEATH CO., 7024 W Wells St, Wauwatosa, WI 53213-3717, Phone: 414-771-6472, Fax: 414-479-9765, knifesheaths@aol.com; Web: www.customsheaths.com
Specialties: Leatherwork. **Prices:** $35 to $100. **Mark:** Schrap in oval.

SCHROEN, KARL,
4042 Bones Rd, Sebastopol, CA 95472, Phone: 707-823-4057, Fax: 707-823-2914, Web: http://users.ap.net/~schroen
Specialties: Using knives made to fit. **Patterns:** Sgian dubhs, carving sets, wood-carving knives, fishing knives, kitchen knives and new cleaver design. **Technical:** Forges A2, ATS-34, D2 and L6 cruwear S30V S90V. **Prices:** $150 to $6000. **Remarks:** Full-time maker; first knife sold in 1968. Author of *The Hand Forged Knife.* **Mark:** Last name.

SCHUCHMANN, RICK,
3975 Hamblen Dr, Cincinnati, OH 45255, Phone: 513-553-4316
Specialties: Replicas of antique and out-of-production Scagels and Randalls, primarily miniatures. **Patterns:** All sheath knives, mostly miniatures, hunting and fighting knives, some daggers and hatchets. **Technical:** Stock removal, 440C and O1 steel. Most knives are flat ground, some convex. **Prices:** $175 to $600 and custom to $4000. **Remarks:** Part-time maker, sold first knife in 1997. Knives on display in the Randall Museum. Sheaths are made exclusively at Sullivan's Holster Shop, Tampa, FL. **Mark:** SCAR.

SCHWARZER, LORA SUE,
119 Shoreside Trail, Crescent City, FL 32112, Phone: 386-698-2840, steveschwarzer@GBSO.net
Specialties: Scagel style knives. **Patterns:** Hunters and miniatures **Technical:** Forges 1084 and Damascus. **Prices:** Start at $400. **Remarks:** Part-time maker; first knife sold in 1997. Journeyman Bladesmith, American Bladesmith Society. Now working with Steve Schwarzer on some projects. **Mark:** Full name - JS on reverse side.

SCHWARZER, STEPHEN,
119 Shoreside Trail, Crescent City, FL 32112, Phone: 386-698-2840, Fax: 386-698-2840, steveschwarzer@gbso.net; Web: www.steveschwarzer.com
Specialties: Mosaic Damascus and picture mosaic in folding knives. All Japanese blades are finished working with Wally Hostetter considered the top Japanese lacquer specialist in the U.S.A. Also produces a line of carbon steel skinning knives at $300. **Patterns:** Folders, axes and buckskinner knives. **Technical:** Specializes in picture mosaic Damascus and powder metal mosaic work. Sole authorship; all work including carving done in-house. Most knives have file work and carving. Hand carved steel and precious metal guards. **Prices:** $1500 to $5000, some higher; carbon steel and primitive knives much less. **Remarks:** Full-time maker; first knife sold in 1976, considered by many to be one of the top mosaic Damascus specialists in the world. Mosaic Master level work. I am now working with Lora Schwarzer on some projects. **Mark:** Schwarzer + anvil.

SCIMIO, BILL,
4554 Creek Side Ln., Spruce Creek, PA 16683, Phone: 814-632-3751, sprucecreekforge@gmail.com Web: www.sprucecreekforge.com
Specialties: Hand-forged primitive-style knives with curly maple, antler, bone and osage handles.

SCORDIA, PAOLO,
Via Terralba 144, 00050 Torrimpietra, Roma, ITALY, Phone: 06-61697231, paolo.scordia@uni.net; Web: www.scordia-knives.com
Specialties: Working, fantasy knives, Italian traditional folders and fixed blades of own design. **Patterns:** Any. **Technical:** Forge mosaic Damascus, forge blades, welds own mokume and grinds ATS-34, etc. use hardwoods and Micarta for handles, brass and nickel-silver for fittings. Makes sheaths. **Prices:** $200 to $2000, some to $4000. **Remarks:** Part-time maker; first knife sold in 1988. **Mark:** Sun and moon logo and ititials.

SCOTT, AL,
2245 Harper Valley Rd, Harper, TX 78631, Phone: 830-928-1742, deadlybeautybladeart@ctesc.net
Specialties: High-art straight knives of his design. **Patterns:** Daggers, swords, early European, Middle East and Japanese knives. **Technical:** Uses ATS-34, 440C and Damascus. Hand engraves; does file work; cuts filigree in the blade; offers ivory carving and precious metal inlay. **Remarks:** Full-time maker; first knife sold in 1994. Doing business as Al Scott Maker of Fine Blade Art. **Mark:** Name engraved in Old English, sometime inlaid in 24K gold.

SCROGGS, JAMES A,
108 Murray Hill Dr, Warrensburg, MO 64093, Phone: 660-747-2568, jscroggsknives@embarqmail.com
Specialties: Straight knives, prefers light weight. **Patterns:** Hunters, hideouts, and fighters. **Technical:** Grinds CPM154 stainless plus experiments in steels. Uses high and low temperature of salt pots for heat treat. Prefers handles of walnut in English, bastonge, American black. Also uses myrtle, maple, Osage orange. **Prices:** $200 to $1000. **Remarks:** 1st knife sold in 1985. Full-time maker, no orders taken. **Mark:** SCROGGS in block or script.

SCULLEY, PETER E,
340 Sunset Dr, Rising Fawn, GA 30738, Phone: 706-398-0169

SEARS, MICK,
8146 Featherun Rd, Kershaw, SC 29067, Phone: 803-475-4937
Specialties: Scots and confederate reproductions; Bowies and fighters. **Patterns:** Bowies, fighters. **Technical:** Grinds 440C and 1095. **Prices:** $50 to $150; some to $300. **Remarks:** Full-time maker; first knife sold in 1975. Doing business as Mick's Custom Knives. **Mark:** First name.

SEATON, DAVID D,
1028 South Bishop Avenue, #237 Rolla MO 665401 Phone: 573-465-3193, aokcustomknives@gmail.com
Specialties: Gentleman's and Lady's folders. **Patterns:** Liner lock folders of

own design and to customer specs, lock backs, slip joints, some straight knives, tactical folders, skinners, fighters, and utility knives. **Technical:** Grinds ATS-34, O1, 1095, 154CM, CPM154, commercial Damascus. Blades are mostly flat ground, some hollow ground. Does own heat treating, tempering, and Nitre Bluing. Prefers natural handle materials such as ivory, mother of pearl, bone, and exotic woods, some use of G10 and micarta on hard use knives. Use gem stones, gold, silver on upscale knives, offers some carving, filework, and engrving. **Prices:** $150 to $600 avg; some to $1500 and up depending on materials and embellishments. **Remarks:** First knife sold in 2002, part-time maker, doing business at AOK Custom Knives. **Mark:** full or last name engraved on blade.

SEIB, STEVE,
7914 Old State Road, Evansville, IN 47710, Phone: 812-867-2231, sseib@insightbb.com
   Specialties: Working straight knives. **Pattern:** Skinners, hunters, bowies and camp knives. **Technical:** Forges high-carbon and makes own damascus. **Remarks:** Part-time maker. ABS member. **Mark:** Last name.

SELF, ERNIE,
950 O'Neill Ranch Rd, Dripping Springs, TX 78620-9760, Phone: 512-940-7134, ernieself@hillcountrytx.net
   Specialties: Traditional and working straight knives and folders of his design and in standard patterns. **Patterns:** Hunters, locking folders and slip-joints. **Technical:** Grinds 440C, D2, 440V, ATS-34 and Damascus. Offers fancy filework. **Prices:** $250 to $1000; some to $2500. **Remarks:** Full-time maker; first knife sold in 1982. Also customizes Buck 110's and 112's folding hunters. **Mark:** In oval shape - Ernie Self Maker Dripping Springs TX.

SELLEVOLD, HARALD,
S Kleivesmau:2, PO Box 4134, N5835 Bergen, NORWAY, Phone: 47 55-310682, haraldsellevold@c2i.net; Web:knivmakeren.com
   Specialties: Norwegian-styles; collaborates with other Norse craftsmen. **Patterns:** Distinctive ferrules and other mild modifications of traditional patterns; Bowies and friction folders. **Technical:** Buys Damascus blades; blacksmiths his own blades. Semi-gemstones used in handles; gemstone inlay. **Prices:** $350 to $2000. **Remarks:** Full-time maker; first knife sold in 1980. **Mark:** Name and country in logo.

SELZAM, FRANK,
Martin Reinhard Str 23 97631, Bad Koenigshofen, GERMANY, Phone: 09761-5980, frankselzam.de
   Specialties: Hunters, working knives to customers specs, hand tooled and stitched leather sheaths large stock of wood and German stag horn. **Patterns:** Mostly own design. **Technical:** Forged blades, own Damascus, also stock removal stainless. **Prices:** $250 to $1500. **Remark:** First knife sold in 1978. **Mark:** Last name stamped.

SENTZ, MARK C,
4084 Baptist Rd, Taneytown, MD 21787, Phone: 410-756-2018
   Specialties: Fancy straight working knives of his design. **Patterns:** Hunters, fighters, folders and utility/camp knives. **Technical:** Forges 1085, 1095, 5160, 5155 and his Damascus. Most knives come with wood-lined leather sheath or wooden presentation sheath. **Prices:** Start at $275. **Remarks:** Full-time maker; first knife sold in 1989. Doing business as M. Charles Sentz Gunsmithing, Inc. **Mark:** Last name.

SERAFEN, STEVEN E,
24 Genesee St, New Berlin, NY 13411, Phone: 607-847-6903
   Specialties: Traditional working/using straight knives of his design and to customer specs. **Patterns:** Bowies, fighters, hunters. **Technical:** Grinds ATS-34, 440C, high-carbon steel. **Prices:** $175 to $600; some to $1200. **Remarks:** Part-time maker; first knife sold in 1990. **Mark:** First and middle initial, last name in script.

SERVEN, JIM,
PO Box 1, Fostoria, MI 48435, Phone: 517-795-2255
   Specialties: Highly finished unique folders. **Patterns:** Fancy working folders, axes, miniatures and razors; some straight knives. **Technical:** Grinds 440C; forges his own Damascus. **Prices:** $150 to $800; some to $1500. **Remarks:** Full-time maker; first knife sold in 1971. **Mark:** Name in map logo.

SEVEY CUSTOM KNIFE,
94595 Chandler Rd, Gold Beach, OR 97444, Phone: 541-247-2649, sevey@charter.net; Web: www.seveyknives.com
   Specialties: Fixed blade hunters. **Patterns:** Drop point, trailing paint, clip paint, full tang, hidden tang. **Technical:** D-2, and ATS-34 blades, stock removal. Heat treatment by Paul Bos. **Prices:** $225 and up depending on overall length and grip material. **Mark:** Sevey Custom Knife.

SFREDDO, RODRIGO MENEZES,
Rua 15 De Setembro 66, Centro Nova Petropolis RS, cep g5 150-000, BRAZIL 95150-000, Phone: 011-55-54-303-303-90, www.brazilianbladesmiths.com.br; www.sbccutelaria.org.br
   Specialties: Integrals, Bowies, hunters, dirks & swords. **Patterns:** Forges his own Damascus and 52100 steel. **Technical:** Specialized in integral knives and Damascus. **Prices:** From $350 and up. Most around $750 to $1000. **Remarks:** Considered by many to be the Brazil's best bladesmith. ABS SBC Member. **Mark:** S. Sfreddo on the left side of the blade.

SHADLEY, EUGENE W,
209 NW 17th Street, Grand Rapids, MN 55744, Phone: 218-999-7197 or 218-244-8628, Fax: call first, ShadleyKnives@hotmail.com
   Specialties: Gold frames are available on some models. **Patterns:** Whittlers, stockman, sowbelly, congress, trapper, etc. **Technical:** Grinds ATS-34, 416 frames. **Prices:** Starts at $600, some models up to $10000. **Remarks:** Full-time maker; first knife sold in 1985. Doing business as Shadley Knives. **Mark:** Last name.

SHADMOT, BOAZ,
MOSHAV PARAN D N, Arava, ISRAEL 86835, srb@arava.co.il

SHARRIGAN, MUDD,
111 Bradford Rd, Wiscasset, ME 04578-4457, Phone: 207-882-9820, Fax: 207-882-9835
   Specialties: Custom designs; repair straight knives, custom leather sheaths. **Patterns:** Daggers, fighters, hunters, crooked knives and seamen working knives; traditional Scandinavian-styles. **Technical:** Forges 1095, 5160, and W2. **Prices:** $50 to $325; some to $1200. **Remarks:** Full-time maker; first knife sold in 1982. **Mark:** Swallow tail carving. Mudd engraved.

SHEEHY, THOMAS J,
4131 NE 24th Ave, Portland, OR 97211-6411, Phone: 503-493-2843
   Specialties: Hunting knives and ulus. **Patterns:** Own or customer designs. **Technical:** 1095/O1 and ATS-34 steel. **Prices:** $35 to $200. **Remarks:** Do own heat treating; forged or ground blades. **Mark:** Name.

SHEELY, "BUTCH" FOREST,
15784 Custar rd, Grand Rapids, OH 43522, Phone: 419-308-3471, sheelyblades@gmail.com
   Specialties: Traditional bowies and pipe tomahawks. **Patterns:** Bowies, hunters, integrals, dirks, axes and hawks. **Technical:** Forges 5160, 52100, 1084, 1095, and Damascus. **Prices:** $150 to $1500; **Remarks:** Full-time bladesmith part-time blacksmith; first knife sold in 1982. ABS Journeysmith, sole author of all knives and hawks including hand sewn leather sheaths, doing business as Beaver Creek Forge. **Mark:** First and last name above Bladesmith.

SHEETS, STEVEN WILLIAM,
6 Stonehouse Rd, Mendham, NJ 07945, Phone: 201-543-5882

SHIFFER, STEVE,
PO Box 582, Leakesville, MS 39451, Phone: 601-394-4425, aiifish2@yahoo.com; Web: wwwchoctawplantationforge.com
   Specialties: Bowies, fighters, hard use knives. **Patterns:** Fighters, hunters, combat/utility knives. Walker pattern LinerLock® folders. Allen pattern scale and bolster release autos. **Technical:** Most work forged, stainless stock removal. Makes own Damascus. O1 and 5160 most used also 1084, 440c, 154cm, s30v. **Prices:** $125 to $1000. **Remarks:** First knife sold in 2000, all heat treatment done by maker. Doing business as Choctaw Plantation Forge. **Mark:** Hot mark sunrise over creek.

SHINOSKY, ANDY,
3117 Meanderwood Dr, Canfield, OH 44406, Phone: 330-702-0299, andrew@shinosky.com; Web: www.shinosky.com
   Specialties: Collectable folders and interframes. **Patterns:** Drop point, spear point, trailing point, daggers. **Technical:** Grinds ATS-34 and Damascus. Prefers natural handle materials. Most knives are engraved by Andy himself. **Prices:** Start at $800. **Remarks:** Part-time maker/engraver. First knife sold in 1992. **Mark:** Name.

SHIPLEY, STEVEN A,
800 Campbell Rd Ste 137, Richardson, TX 75081, Phone: 972-644-7981, Fax: 972-644-7985, steve@shipleysphotography.com
   Specialties: Hunters, skinners and traditional straight knives. **Technical:** Hand grinds ATS-34, 440C and Damascus steels. Each knife is custom sheathed by his son, Dan. **Prices:** $175 to $2000. **Remarks:** Part-time maker; like smooth lines and unusual handle materials. **Mark:** S A Shipley.

SHOEMAKER, CARROLL,
380 Yellowtown Rd, Northup, OH 45658, Phone: 740-446-6695
   Specialties: Working/using straight knives of his design. **Patterns:** Hunters, utility/camp and early American backwoodsmen knives. **Technical:** Grinds ATS-34; forges old files, O1 and 1095. Uses some Damascus; offers scrimshaw and engraving. **Prices:** $100 to $175; some to $350. **Remarks:** Spare-time maker; first knife sold in 1977. **Mark:** Name and city or connected initials.

SHOEMAKER, SCOTT,
316 S Main St, Miamisburg, OH 45342, Phone: 513-859-1935
   Specialties: Twisted, wire-wrapped handles on swords, fighters and fantasy blades; new line of seven models with quick-draw, multi-carry Kydex sheaths. **Patterns:** Bowies, boots and one-of-a-kinds in his design or to customer specs. **Technical:** Grinds A6 and ATS-34; buys Damascus. Hand satin finish is standard. **Prices:** $100 to $1500; swords to $8000. **Remarks:** Part-time maker; first knife sold in 1984. **Mark:** Angel wings with last initial, or last name.

SHOGER, MARK O,
14780 SW Osprey Dr Suite 345, Beaverton, OR 97007, Phone: 503-579-2495, mosdds@msn.com
   Specialties: Working and using straight knives and folders of his design; fancy and embellished knives. **Patterns:** Hunters, Bowies, daggers and folders. **Technical:** Forges O1, W2, 1084, 5160, 52100 and 1084/15n20 pattern weld. **Remarks:** Spare-time maker. **Mark:** Last name or stamped last initial over anvil.

SHROPSHIRE, SHAWN,
PO Box 453, Piedmont, OK 73078, Phone: 405-833-5239, shawn@ sdsknifeworks.com; Web: www.sdsknifeworks.com
 Specialties: Working straight knives and frontier style period pieces. **Patterns:** Bowies, hunters, skinners, fighters, patch/neck knives. **Technical:** Grinds D2, 154CM and some Damascus, forges 1084, 5160. **Prices:** Starting at $125. **Remarks:** Part-time maker; first knife sold in 1997. Doing business at SDS Knifeworks. **Mark:** Etched "SDS Knifeworks - Oklahoma" in an oval or "SDS" tang stamp.

SHULL, JAMES,
5146 N US 231 W, Rensselaer, IN 47978, Phone: 219-866-0436, nbjs@netnitco.net Web: www.shullhandforgedknives.com
 Specialties: Working knives of hunting, fillet, Bowie patterns. **Technical:** Forges or uses 1095, 5160, 52100 & O1. **Prices:** $100 to $300. **Remarks:** DBA Shull Handforged Knives. **Mark:** Last name in arc.

SIBERT, SHANE,
PO BOX 241, Gladstone, OR 97027, Phone: 503-650-2082, shane.sibert@ comcast.net Web: www.sibertknives.com
 Specialties: Innovative light weight hiking and backpacking knives for outdoorsman and adventurers, progressive fixed blade combat and fighting knives. One-of-a-kind knives of various configurations. Titanium frame lock folders. **Patterns:** Modern configurations of utility/camp knives, bowies, modified spear points, daggers, tantos, recurves, clip points and spine serrations. **Technical:** Stock removal. Specializes in CPM S30V, CPM S35VN, CPM D2, CPM 3V, stainless damascus. Micarta, G-10, stabilized wood and titanium. **Prices:** $200 - $1000, some pieces $1500 and up. **Remarks:** Full-time maker, first knife sold in 1994. **Mark:** Stamped "SIBERT" and occasionally uses electro-etch with oval around last name.

SIBRIAN, AARON,
4308 Dean Dr, Ventura, CA 93003, Phone: 805-642-6950
 Specialties: Tough working knives of his design and in standard patterns. **Patterns:** Makes a "Viper utility"—a kukri derivative and a variety of straight using knives. **Technical:** Grinds 440C and ATS-34. Offers traditional Japanese blades; soft backs, hard edges, temper lines. **Prices:** $60 to $100; some to $250. **Remarks:** Spare-time maker; first knife sold in 1989. **Mark:** Initials in diagonal line.

SIMMONS, H R,
1100 Bay City Rd, Aurora, NC 27806, Phone: 252-322-5969
 Specialties: Working/using straight knives of his design. **Patterns:** Fighters, hunters and utility/camp knives. **Technical:** Forges and grinds Damascus and L6; grinds ATS-34. **Prices:** $150 to $250; some to $400. **Remarks:** Part-time maker; first knife sold in 1987. Doing business as HRS Custom Knives, Royal Forge and Trading Company. **Mark:** Initials.

SIMONELLA, GIANLUIGI,
Via Battiferri 33, 33085 Maniago, ITALY, Phone: 01139-427-730350
 Specialties: Traditional and classic folding and working/using knives of his design and to customer specs. **Patterns:** Bowies, fighters, hunters, utility/camp knives. **Technical:** Forges ATS-34, D2, 440C. **Prices:** $250 to $400; some to $1000. **Remarks:** Full-time maker; first knife sold in 1988. **Mark:** Wilson.

SIMS, BOB,
PO Box 772, Meridian, TX 76665, Phone: 254-435-6240
 Specialties: Traditional working straight knives and folders in standard patterns. **Patterns:** Locking folders, slip-joint folders and hunters. **Technical:** Grinds D2, ATS-34 and O1. Offers filework on some knives. **Prices:** $150 to $275; some to $600. **Remarks:** Full-time maker; first knife sold in 1975. **Mark:** The division sign.

SINCLAIR, J E,
520 Francis Rd, Pittsburgh, PA 15239, Phone: 412-793-5778
 Specialties: Fancy hunters and fighters, liner locking folders. **Patterns:** Fighters, hunters and folders. **Technical:** Flat-grinds and hollow grind, prefers hand rubbed satin finish. Uses natural handle materials. **Prices:** $185 to $800. **Remarks:** Part-time maker; first knife sold in 1995. **Mark:** First and middle initials, last name and maker.

SINYARD, CLESTON S,
27522 Burkhardt Dr, Elberta, AL 36530, Phone: 334-987-1361, nimoforge1@ gulftel.com; Web: www.knifemakersguild
 Specialties: Working straight knives and folders of his design. **Patterns:** Hunters, buckskinners, Bowies, daggers, fighters and all-Damascus folders. **Technical:** Makes Damascus from 440C, stainless steel, D2 and regular high-carbon steel; forges "forefinger pad" into hunters and skinners. **Prices:** In Damascus $450 to $1500; some $2500. **Remarks:** Full-time maker; first knife sold in 1980. Doing business as Nimo Forge. **Mark:** Last name, U.S.A. in anvil.

SISKA, JIM,
48 South Maple St, Westfield, MA 01085, Phone: 413-642-3059, siskaknives@ comcast.net
 Specialties: Traditional working straight knives, no folders. **Patterns:** Hunters, fighters, Bowies and one-of-a-kinds; folders. **Technical:** Grinds D2, A2, 54CM and ATS-34; buys Damascus. Likes exotic woods. **Prices:** $300 and up. **Remarks:** Part-time. **Mark:** Siska in Old English.

SJOSTRAND, KEVIN,
1541 S Cain St, Visalia, CA 93292, Phone: 559-625-5254
 Specialties: Traditional and working/using straight knives and folders of his design or to customer specs. **Patterns:** Fixed blade hunters, Bowies, utility/camp knives. **Technical:** Grinds ATS-34, 440C and 1095. Prefers high polished blades and full tang. Natural and stabilized hardwoods, Micarta and stag handle material. **Prices:** $150 to $400. **Remarks:** Part-time maker; first knife sold in 1992. Doing business as Black Oak Blades. **Mark:** SJOSTRAND

SKIFF, STEVEN,
SKIFF MADE BLADES, PO Box 537, Broadalbin, NY 12025, Phone: 518-883-4875, skiffmadeblades @hotmail.com; Web: www.skiffmadeblades.com
 Specialties: Custom using/collector grade straight blades and LinerLock® folders of maker's design or customer specifications. **Patterns:** Hunters, utility/camp knives, tactical/fancy art folders. **Prices:** Straight blades $225 and up. Folders $450 and up. **Technical:** Stock removal hollow ground ATS-34, 154 CM, S30V, and tool steel. Damascus-Devon Thomas, Robert Eggerling, Mike Norris and Delbert Ealy. Nickel silver and stainless in-house heat treating. Handle materials: man made and natural woods (stablilized). Horn shells sheaths for straight blades, sews own leather and uses sheaths by "Tree-Stump Leather." **Remarks:** First knife sold 1997. Started making folders in 2000. **Mark:** SKIFF on blade of straight blades and in inside of backspacer on folders.

SLEE, FRED,
9 John St, Morganville, NJ 07751, Phone: 732-591-9047
 Specialties: Working straight knives, some fancy, to customer specs. **Patterns:** Hunters, fighters, fancy daggers and folders. **Technical:** Grinds D2, 440C and ATS-34. **Prices:** $285 to $1100. **Remarks:** Part-time maker; first knife sold in 1980. **Mark:** Letter "S" in Old English.

SLOAN, DAVID,
PO BOX 83, Diller, NE 68342, Phone: 402-793-5755, sigp22045@hotmail.com
 Specialties: Hunters, choppers and fighters. **Technical:** Forged blades of W2, 1084 and Damascus. **Prices:** Start at $225. **Remarks:** Part-time maker, made first knife in 2002, received JS stamp 2010. **Mark:** Sloan JS.

SLOAN, SHANE,
4226 FM 61, Newcastle, TX 76372, Phone: 940-846-3290
 Specialties: Collector-grade straight knives and folders. **Patterns:** Uses stainless Damascus, ATS-34 and 12C27. Bowies, lockers, slip-joints, fancy folders, fighters and period pieces. **Technical:** Grinds D2 and ATS-34. Uses hand-rubbed satin finish. Prefers rare natural handle materials. **Prices:** $250 to $6500. **Remarks:** Full-time maker; first knife sold in 1985. **Mark:** Name and city.

SLOBODIAN, SCOTT,
PO Box 1498, San Andreas, CA 95249, Phone: 209-286-1980, Fax: 209-286-1982, info@slobodianswords.com; Web: www.slobodianswords.com
 Specialties: Japanese-style knives and swords, period pieces, fantasy pieces and miniatures. **Patterns:** Small kweikens, tantos, wakazashis, katanas, traditional samurai swords. **Technical:** Flat-grinds 1050, commercial Damascus. **Prices:** Prices start at $1500. **Remarks:** Full-time maker; first knife sold in 1987. **Mark:** Blade signed in Japanese characters and various scripts.

SMALE, CHARLES J,
509 Grove Ave, Waukegan, IL 60085, Phone: 847-244-8013

SMALL, ED,
Rt 1 Box 178-A, Keyser, WV 26726, Phone: 304-298-4254, coldanvil@gmail.com
 Specialties: Working knives of his design; period pieces. **Patterns:** Hunters, daggers, buckskinners and camp knives; likes one-of-a-kinds, very primative bowies. **Technical:** Forges and grinds W2, L6 and his own Damascus. **Prices:** $150 to $1500. **Remarks:** Full-time maker; first knife sold in 1978. **Mark:** Script initials connected.

SMART, STEVE,
907 Park Row Cir, McKinney, TX 75070-3847, Phone: 214-837-4216, Fax: 214-837-4111
 Specialties: Working/using straight knives and folders of his design, to customer specs and in standard patterns. **Patterns:** Bowies, hunters, kitchen knives, locking folders, utility/camp, fishing and bird knives. **Technical:** Grinds ATS-34, D2, 440C and O1. Prefers mirror polish or satin finish; hollow-grinds all blades. All knives come with sheath. Offers some filework. **Prices:** $95 to $225; some to $500. **Remarks:** Spare-time maker; first knife sold in 1983. **Mark:** Name, Custom, city and state in oval.

SMIT, GLENN,
627 Cindy Ct, Aberdeen, MD 21001, Phone: 410-272-2959, wolfsknives@ comcast.net
 Specialties: Working and using straight and folding knives of his design or to customer specs. Customizes and repairs all types of cutlery. Exclusive maker of Dave Murphy Style knives. **Patterns:** Hunters, Bowies, daggers, fighters, utility/camp, folders, kitchen knives and miniatures, Murphy combat, C.H.A.I.K., Little 88 and Tiny 90-styles. **Technical:** Grinds 440C, ATS-34, O1, A2 also grinds 6AL4V titanium allox for blades. Reforges commercial Damascus and makes own Damascus, cast aluminum handles. **Prices:** Miniatures start at $30; full-size knives start at $50. **Remarks:** Spare-time maker; first knife sold in 1986. Doing business as Wolf's Knives. **Mark:** G.P. SMIT, with year on reverse side, Wolf's Knives-Murphy's way with date.

SMITH, J D,
69 Highland, Roxbury, MA 02119, Phone: 617-989-0723, jdsmith02119@yahoo.com

Specialties: Fighters, Bowies, Persian, locking folders and swords. **Patterns:** Bowies, fighters and locking folders. **Technical:** Forges and grinds D2, his Damascus, O1, 52100 etc. and wootz-pattern hammer steel. **Prices:** $500 to $2000; some to $5000. **Remarks:** Full-time maker; first knife sold in 1987. Doing business as Hammersmith. **Mark:** Last initial alone or in cartouche.

SMITH, J.B.,
21 Copeland Rd., Perkinston, MS 39573, Phone: 228-380-1851

Specialties: Traditional working knives for the hunter and fisherman. **Patterns:** Hunters, Bowies, and fishing knives; copies of 1800 period knives. **Technical:** Grinds ATS-34, 440C. **Prices:** $100 to $800. **Remarks:** Full-time maker, first knife sold in 1972. **Mark:** J.B. Smith MAKER PERKINSTON, MS.

SMITH, JERRY,
JW Smith & Sons Custom Knives, 111 S Penn Ave, Oberlin, KS 67749, Phone: 785-475-2695, jerry@jwsmithandsons.com Web: www.jwsmithandsons.com

Specialties: Fixed blade and folding knives. **Technical:** Steels used D2, A2, O1, 154 CM, 154 CPM. Stock removal, heat treat in house, all leather work in house. **Prices:** $240. **Remarks:** Full-time knifemaker. First knife made in 2004. Slogan: "Cut Like You Mean It"

SMITH, JOHN M,
3450 E Beguelin Rd, Centralia, IL 62801, Phone: 618-249-6444, jknife@frontiernet.net

Specialties: Folders. **Patterns:** Folders. **Prices:** $250 to $2500. **Remarks:** First knife sold in 1980. Not taking orders at this time on fixed blade knives. Part-time maker. **Mark:** Etched signature or logo.

SMITH, JOHN W,
1322 Cow Branch Rd, West Liberty, KY 41472, Phone: 606-743-3599, jwsknive@mrtc.com; Web: www.jwsmithknives.com

Specialties: Fancy and working locking folders of his design or to customer specs. **Patterns:** Interframes, traditional and daggers. **Technical:** Grinds 530V and his own Damascus. Offers gold inlay, engraving with gold inlay, hand-fitted mosaic pearl inlay and filework. Prefers hand-rubbed finish. Pearl and ivory available. **Prices:** Utility pieces $375 to $650. Art knives $1200 to $10,000. **Remarks:** Full-time maker. **Mark:** Initials engraved inside diamond.

SMITH, JOSH,
Box 753, Frenchtown, MT 59834, Phone: 406-626-5775, joshsmithknives@gmail.com; Web: www.joshsmithknives.com

Specialties: Mosaic, Damascus, LinerLock folders, automatics, Bowies, fighters, etc. **Patterns:** All kinds. **Technical:** Advanced Mosaic and Damascus. **Prices:** $450 and up. **Remarks:** A.B.S. Master Smith. **Mark:** Josh Smith with last two digits of the current year.

SMITH, LACY,
PO BOX 188, Jacksonville, AL 36265, Phone: 256-310-4619, sales@smith-knives.com; Web: www.smith-knives.com

SMITH, LENARD C,
PO Box D68, Valley Cottage, NY 10989, Phone: 914-268-7359

SMITH, MICHAEL J,
1418 Saddle Gold Ct, Brandon, FL 33511, Phone: 813-431-3790, smithknife@hotmail.com; Web: www.smithknife.com

Specialties: Fancy high art folders of his design. **Patterns:** Locking locks and automatics. **Technical:** Uses ATS-34, non-stainless and stainless Damascus; hand carves folders, prefers ivory and pearl. Hand-rubbed satin finish. Liners are 6AL4V titanium. **Prices:** $500 to $3000. **Remarks:** Full-time maker; first knife sold in 1989. **Mark:** Name, city, state.

SMITH, NEWMAN L.,
865 Glades Rd Shop #3, Gatlinburg, TN 37738, Phone: 423-436-3322, thesmithshop@aol.com; Web: www.thesmithsshop.com

Specialties: Collector-grade and working knives. **Patterns:** Hunters, slip-joint and lock-back folders, some miniatures. **Technical:** Grinds O1 and ATS-34; makes fancy sheaths. **Prices:** $165 to $750; some to $1000. **Remarks:** Full-time maker; first knife sold in 1984. Partners part-time to handle Damascus blades by Jeff Hurst; marks these with SH connected. **Mark:** First and middle initials, last name.

SMITH, RALPH L,
525 Groce Meadow Rd, Taylors, SC 29687, Phone: 864-444-0819, ralph_smith1@charter.net; Web: www.smithhandcraftedknives.com

Specialties: Working knives: straight and folding knives. Hunters, skinners, fighters, bird, boot, Bowie and kitchen knives. **Technical:** Concave Grind D2, ATS 34, 440C, steel hand finish or polished. **Prices:** $125 to $350 for standard models. **Remarks:** First knife sold in 1976. KMG member since 1981. SCAK founding member and past president. **Mark:** SMITH handcrafted knives in SC state outline.

SMITH, RAYMOND L,
217 Red Chalk Rd, Erin, NY 14838, Phone: 607-795-5257, Bladesmith@wildblue.net; Web: www.theanvilsedge.com

Specialties: Working/using straight knives and folders to customer specs and in standard patterns; period pieces. **Patterns:** Bowies, hunters, skip-joints. **Technical:** Forges 5160, 52100, 1018, 15N20, 1084, ATS 34. Damascus and wire cable Damascus. Filework. **Prices:** $125 to $1500; estimates for custom orders. **Remarks:** Full-time maker; first knife sold in 1991. ABS Master Smith. Doing business as The Anvils Edge. **Mark:** Ellipse with RL Smith, Erin NY MS in center.

SMITH, RICHARD J.,
PO BOX 116, Milford, PA 18337, Phone: 908-627-5934, rs@smithknives.com Web: www.smithknives.com

Specialties: Straight working and collector knives with a high level of fit and finish in traditional and collector knives with a high level of fit and finish in traditional and own designs. **Technical:** Grinds CPM 154 CM, ATS-34, 154CM, O1 tool steel and others. **Prices:** $180 to $600. **Remarks:** Part-time maker, first knife sold in 2005. **Mark:** RJ Smith with U.S.A. beneath name.

SMITH, RICK,
BEAR BONE KNIVES, 1843 W Evans Creek Rd., Rogue River, OR 97537, Phone: 541-582-4144, BearBoneSmith@msn.com; Web: www.bearbone.com

Specialties: Classic, historical style Bowie knives, hunting knives and various contemporary knife styles. **Technical:** Blades are either forged or made by stock removal method depending on steel used. Also forge weld wire Damascus. Does own heat treating and tempering using digital even heat kiln. Stainless blades are sent out for cryogenic "freeze treat." Preferred steels are O1, tool, 5160, 1095, 1084, ATS-34, 154CM, 440C and various high carbon Damascus. **Prices:** $350 to $1500. Custom leather sheaths available for knives. **Remarks:** Full-time maker since 1997. Serial numbers no longer put on knives. Official business name is "Bear Bone Knives." **Mark:** Early maker's mark was "Bear Bone" over capital letters "RS" with downward arrow between letters and "Hand Made" underneath letters. Mark on small knives is 3/8 circle containing "RS" with downward arrow between letters. Current mark since 2003 is "R Bear Bone Smith" arching over image of coffin Bowie knife with two shooting stars and "Rogue River, Oregon" underneath.

SMITH, SHAWN,
2644 Gibson Ave, Clouis, CA 93611, Phone: 559-323-6234, kslc@sbcglobal.net

Specialties: Working and fancy straight knives. **Patterns:** Hunting, trout, fighters, skinners. **Technical:** Hollow grinds ATS-34, 154CM, A-2. **Prices:** $150.00 and up. **Remarks:** Part time maker. **Mark:** Shawn Smith handmade.

SMITH JR., JAMES B "RED",
Rt 2 Box 1525, Morven, GA 31638, Phone: 912-775-2844

Specialties: Rotating rear-lock folders. **Technical:** Grinds ATS-34, D2 and Vascomax 350. **Prices:** Start at $350. **Remarks:** Full-time maker; first knife sold in 1985. **Mark:** GA RED in cowboy hat.

SMOCK, TIMOTHY E,
1105 N Sherwood Dr, Marion, IN 46952, Phone: 765-664-0123

SNODY, MIKE,
135 Triple Creek Rd, Fredericksburg, TX 78624, Phone: 361-443-0161, info@snodyknives.com; Web: www.snodyknives.com

Specialties: High performance straight knives in traditional and Japanese-styles. **Patterns:** Skinners, hunters, tactical, Kwaiken and tantos. **Technical:** Grinds BG42, ATS-34, 440C and A2. Offers full or tapered tangs, upgraded handle materials such as fossil ivory, coral and exotic woods. Traditional diamond wrap over stingray on Japanese-style knives. Sheaths available in leather or Kydex. **Prices:** $100 to $1000. **Remarks:** Part-time maker; first knife sold in 1999. **Mark:** Name over knife maker.

SNOW, BILL,
4824 18th Ave, Columbus, GA 31904, Phone: 706-576-4390, tipikw@knology.net

Specialties: Traditional working/using straight knives and folders of his design and to customer specs. Offers engraving and scrimshaw. **Patterns:** Bowies, fighters, hunters and folders. **Technical:** Grinds ATS-34, 440V, 440C, 420V, CPM350, BG42, A2, D2, 5160, 52100 and O1; forges if needed. Cryogenically quenches all steels; inlaid handles; some integrals; leather or Kydex sheaths. **Prices:** $125 to $700; some to $3500. **Remarks:** Now also have 530V, 10V and 3V steels in use. Full-time maker; first knife sold in 1958. Doing business as Tipi Knife works. **Mark:** Old English scroll "S" inside a tipi.

SNYDER, MICHAEL TOM,
PO Box 522, Zionsville, IN 46077-0522, Phone: 317-873-6807, wildcatcreek@indy.pr.com

SOAPER, MAX H.,
2375 Zion Rd, Henderson, KY 42420, Phone: 270-827-8143

Specialties: Primitive Longhunter knives, scalpers, camp knives, cowboy Bowies, neck knives, working knives, period pieces from the 18th century. **Technical:** Forges 5160, 1084, 1095; all blades differentially heat treated. **Prices:** $80 to $800. **Remarks:** Part-time maker since 1989. **Mark:** Initials in script.

SOLOMON, MARVIN,
23750 Cold Springs Rd, Paron, AR 72122, Phone: 501-821-3170, mardot@swbell.net; Web: www.coldspringsforge.com

Specialties: Traditional working and using straight knives of his design and to customer specs, also lock back 7 LinerLock® folders. **Patterns:** Single blade folders. **Technical:** Forges 5160, 1095, O1 and random Damascus. **Prices:** $125 to $1000. **Remarks:** Part-time maker; first knife sold in 1990. Doing business as Cold Springs Forge. **Mark:** Last name.

SONNTAG, DOUGLAS W,
902 N 39th St, Nixa, MO 65714, Phone: 417-693-1640, Fax: 417-582-1392, dougsonntag@gmail.com

Specialties: Working knives; art knives. **Patterns:** Hunters, boots, straight working knives; Bowies, some folders, camp/axe sets. **Technical:** Grinds D2, ATS-34, forges own Damascus; does own heat treating. **Prices:** $225 and up. **Remarks:** Full-time maker; first knife sold in 1986. **Mark:** Etched name in arch.

SONNTAG, JACOB D,
14148 Trisha Drive St, Robert, MO 65584, Phone: 337-378-7090, Jake0372@live.com
Specialties: Working knives, some art knives. **Patterns:** Hunters, bowies, and tomahawks. **Technical:** Grinds D2, ATS34 and Damascus. Forges some Damascus and tomahawks; does own heat treating. **Prices:** $200 and up. **Remarks:** Part-time maker; first knife sold in 2010. **Mark:** Etched name or stamped

SONNTAG, KRISTOPHER D,
902 N 39th St, Nixa, MO 65714, Phone: 417-838-8327, kriss@buildit.us
Specialties: Working fixed blades, hunters, skinners, using knives. **Patterns:** Hunters, bowies, skinners. **Technical:** Grinds D2, ATS 34, Damascus. Makes some Damascus; does own heat treating. **Prices:** $200 and up. **Remarks:** Part-time maker; first knife sold in 2010. **Mark:** Etched name or stamped

SONTHEIMER, G DOUGLAS,
12604 Bridgeton Dr, Potomac, MD 20854, Phone: 301-948-5227
Specialties: Fixed blade knives. **Patterns:** Whitetail deer, backpackers, camp, claws, fillet, fighters. **Technical:** Hollow Grinds. **Price:** $500 and up. **Remarks:** Spare-time maker; first knife sold in 1976. **Mark:** LORD.

SOPPERA, ARTHUR,
"Pilatusblick", Oberer Schmidberg, CH-9631 Ulisbach, SWITZERLAND, Phone: 71-988 23 27, Fax: 71-988 47 57, doublelock@hotmail.com; Web: www.sopperaknifeart.ch
Specialties: High-art, high-tech knives of his design. **Patterns:** Locking folders, and fixed blade knives. **Technical:** Grinds ATS-34 and commercial Damascus. Folders have button lock of his own design; some are fancy folders in jeweler's fashion. Also makes jewelry with integrated small knives. **Prices:** $300 to $1500, some $2500 and higher. **Remarks:** Full-time maker; first knife sold in 1986. **Mark:** Stylized initials, name, country.

SORNBERGER, JIM,
25126 Overland Dr, Volcano, CA 95689, Phone: 209-295-7819
Specialties: Classic San Francisco-style knives. Collectible straight knives. **Patterns:** Forges 1095-1084/15W2. Makes own Damascus and powder metal. Fighters, daggers, Bowies; miniatures; hunters, custom canes, liner locks folders. **Technical:** Grinds 440C, 154CM and ATS-34; engraves, carves and embellishes. **Prices:** $500 to $20,000 in gold with gold quartz inlays. **Remarks:** Full-time maker; first knife sold in 1970. **Mark:** First initial, last name, city and state.

SOWELL, BILL,
100 Loraine Forest Ct, Macon, GA 31210, Phone: 478- 994-9863, billsowell@reynoldscable.net
Specialties: Antique reproduction Bowies, forging Bowies, hunters, fighters, and most others. Also folders. **Technical:** Makes own Damascus, using 1084/15N20, also making own designs in powder metals, forges 5160-1095-1084, and other carbon steels, grinds ATS-34. **Prices:** Starting at $150 and up. **Remarks:** Part-time maker. Sold first knife in 1998. Does own leather work. ABS Master Smith. **Mark:** Iron Horse Forge - Sowell - MS.

SPARKS, BERNARD,
PO Box 73, Dingle, ID 83233, Phone: 208-847-1883, dogknifeii@juno.com; Web: www.sparksknives.com
Specialties: Maker engraved, working and art knives. Straight knives and folders of his own design. **Patterns:** Locking inner-frame folders, hunters, fighters, one-of-a-kind art knives. **Technical:** Grinds 530V steel, 440-C, 154CM, ATS-34, D-2 and forges by special order; triple temper, cryogenic soak. Mirror or hand finish. New Liquid metal steel. **Prices:** $300 to $2000. **Remarks:** Full-time maker, first knife sold in 1967. **Mark:** Last name over state with a knife logo on each end of name. Prior 1980, stamp of last name.

SPICKLER, GREGORY NOBLE,
5614 Mose Cir, Sharpsburg, MD 21782, Phone: 301-432-2746

SPINALE, RICHARD,
4021 Canterbury Ct, Lorain, OH 44053, Phone: 440-282-1565
Specialties: High-art working knives of his design. **Patterns:** Hunters, fighters, daggers and locking folders. **Technical:** Grinds 440C, ATS-34 and 07; engraves. Offers gold bolsters and other deluxe treatments. **Prices:** $300 to $1000; some to $3000. **Remarks:** Spare-time maker; first knife sold in 1976. **Mark:** Name, address, year and model number.

SPIVEY, JEFFERSON,
9244 W Wilshire, Yukon, OK 73099, Phone: 405-371-9304, jspivey5@cox.net
Specialties: The Saber tooth: a combination hatchet, saw and knife. **Patterns:** Built for the wilderness, all are one-of-a-kind. **Technical:** Grinds chromemoly steel. The saw tooth spine curves with a double row of biangular teeth. **Prices:** Start at $275. **Remarks:** First knife sold in 1977. As of September 2006 Spivey knives has resumed production of the Sabertooth knife (one word trademark). **Mark:** Name and serial number.

SPRAGG, WAYNE E,
252 Oregon Ave, Lovell, WY 82431, Phone: 307-548-7212
Specialties: Working straight knives, some fancy. **Patterns:** Folders. **Technical:** Forges carbon steel and makes Damascus. **Prices:** $200 and up. **Remarks:** All stainless heat-treated by Paul Bos. Carbon steel in shop heat treat. **Mark:** Last name front side w/s initials on reverse side.

SPROKHOLT, ROB,
GATHERWOOD, Burgerweg 5, Netherlands, Netherlands 1754 KB Burgerbrug, Phone: 0031 6 51230225, Fax: 0031 84 2238446, info@gatherwood.nl; Web: www.gatherwood.nl
Specialties: One-of-a-kind knives. Top materials collector grade, made to use. **Patterns:** Outdoor knives (hunting, sailing, hiking), Bowies, man's surviving companions MSC, big tantos, folding knives. **Technical:** Handles mostly stabilized or oiled wood, ivory, Micarta, carbon fibre, G10. Stiff knives are full tang. Characteristic one row of massive silver pins or tubes. Folding knives have a LinerLock® with titanium or Damascus powdersteel liner thumb can have any stone you like. Stock removal grinder: flat or convex. Steel 440-C, RWL-34, ATS-34, PM damascener steel. **Prices:** Start at 320 euro. **Remarks:** Writer of the first Dutch knifemaking book, supply shop for knife enthusiastic. First knife sold in 2000. **Mark:** Gatherwood in an eclipse etched blade or stamped in an intarsia of silver in the spine.

ST. AMOUR, MURRAY,
RR 3, 222 Dicks Rd, Pembroke ON, CANADA K8A 6W4, Phone: 613-735-1061, knives@webhart.net; Web: www.stamourknives.com
Patterns: Working fixed blades. **Patterns:** Hunters, fish, fighters, Bowies and utility knives. **Technical:** Grinds ATS-34, 154CM, CPM-S-30-Y-60-Y-904 and Damascus. **Prices:** $75 and up. **Remarks:** Full-time maker; sold first knife in 1992. **Mark:** Last name over Canada.

ST. CLAIR, THOMAS K,
12608 Fingerboard Rd, Monrovia, MD 21770, Phone: 301-482-0264

ST. CYR, H RED,
1218 N Cary Ave, Wilmington, CA 90744, Phone: 310-518-9525

STAFFORD, RICHARD,
104 Marcia Ct, Warner Robins, GA 31088, Phone: 912-923-6372, Fax: Cell: 478-508-5821, rnrstafford@cox.net
Specialties: High-tech straight knives and some folders. **Patterns:** Hunters in several patterns, fighters, boots, camp knives, combat knives and period pieces. **Technical:** Grinds ATS-34 and 440C. Machine satin finish offered. **Prices:** Starting at $150. **Remarks:** Part-time maker; first knife sold in 1983. **Mark:** R. W. STAFFORD GEORGIA.

STAINTHORP, GUY,
4 Fisher St, Brindley Ford, Stoke-on-Trent ST8 7QJ ENGLAND, Phone: 07946 469 888, guystainthorp@hotmail.com Web: http://stainthorpknives.co.uk/index.html
Specialties: Tactical and outdoors knives to his own design. **Patterns:** Hunting, survival and occasionally folding knives. **Technical:** Grinds RWL-34, O1, S30V, Damasteel. Micarta, G10 and stabilised wood/bone for handles. **Prices:** $200 - $1000. **Remarks:** Full-time knifemaker. **Mark:** Squared stylised GS over "Stainthorp".

STALCUP, EDDIE,
PO Box 2200, Gallup, NM 87305, Phone: 505-863-3107, sharon.stalcup@gmail.com
Specialties: Working and fancy hunters, bird and trout. Special custom orders. **Patterns:** Drop point hunters, locking liner and multi blade folders. **Technical:** ATS-34, 154 CM, 440C, CPM 154 and S30V. **Prices:** $150 to $1500. **Remarks:** Scrimshaw, exotic handle material, wet formed sheaths. Membership Arizona Knife Collectors Association. Southern California blades collectors & professional knife makers assoc. **Mark:** E.F. Stalcup, Gallup, NM.

STANCER, CHUCK,
62 Hidden Ranch Rd NW, Calgary, AB, CANADA T3A 5S5, Phone: 403-295-7370, stancerc@telusplanet.net
Specialties: Traditional and working straight knives. **Patterns:** Bowies, hunters and utility knives. **Technical:** Forges and grinds most steels. **Prices:** $175 and up. **Remarks:** Part-time maker. **Mark:** Last name.

STANFORD, PERRY,
405N Walnut #9, Broken Arrow, OK 74012, Phone: 918-251-7983 or 866-305-5690, stanfordoutdoors@valornet; Web: www.stanfordoutdoors.homestead.com
Specialties: Drop point, hunting and skinning knives, handmade sheaths. **Patterns:** Stright, hunting, and skinners. **Technical:** Grinds 440C, ATS-34 and Damascus. **Prices:** $65 to $275. **Remarks:** Part-time maker, first knife sold in 2007. Knifemaker supplier, manufacturer of paper sharpening systems. Doing business as Stanford Outdoors. **Mark:** Company name and nickname.

STANLEY, JOHN,
604 Elm St, Crossett, AR 71635, Phone: 970-304-3005
Specialties: Hand forged fixed blades with engraving and carving. **Patterns:** Scottish dirks, skeans and fantasy blades. **Technical:** Forge high-carbon steel, own Damascus. Prices $70 to $500. **Remarks:** All work is sole authorship. Offers engraving and carving services on other knives and handles. **Mark:** Varies.

STAPEL, CHUCK,
Box 1617, Glendale, CA 91209, Phone: 213-66-KNIFE, Fax: 213-669-1577, www.stapelknives.com
Specialties: Working knives of his design. **Patterns:** Variety of straight knives, tantos, hunters, folders and utility knives. **Technical:** Grinds D2, 440C and AEB-L. **Prices:** $185 to $12,000. **Remarks:** Full-time maker; first knife sold in 1974. **Mark:** Last name or last name, U.S.A.

STAPLETON, WILLIAM E,
BUFFALO 'B' FORGE, 5425 Country Ln, Merritt Island, FL 32953
Specialties: Classic and traditional knives of his design and customer spec. **Patterns:** Hunters and using knives. **Technical:** Forges, O1 and L6 Damascus, cable Damascus and 5160; stock removal on request. **Prices:** $150 to $1000. **Remarks:** Part-time maker, first knife sold 1990. Doing business as Buffalo "B" Forge. **Mark:** Anvil with S initial in center of anvil.

STATES, JOSHUA C,
43905 N 16th St, New River, AZ 85087, Phone: 623-826-3809
Specialties: Design and fabrication of forged working and art knives from O1 and my own Damascuz. Stock removal from 440C and CM154 upon request. Folders from 440C, CM154 and Damascus. Flat and Hollow grinds. Knives made to customer specs and/or design. **Patterns:** Bowies, hunters, daggers, chef knives, and exotic shapes. **Technical:** Damascus is 1095, 1084, O1, or 15N20. Carved or file-worked fittings from various metals including my own mokume gane and Damascus. **Prices:** $150 to $1500. **Remarks:** Part-time maker with waiting list. First knife sold in 2006. **Mark:** Initials JCS inside small oval, or Dos Gatos Forge. Unmarked knives come with certificate of authorship.

STECK, VAN R,
260 W Dogwood Ave, Orange City, FL 32763, Phone: 407-416-1723, van@thudknives.com
Specialties: Specializing in double-edged grinds. Free-hand grinds: folders, spears, bowies, swords and miniatures. **Patterns:** Tomahawks with a crane for the spike, tactical merged with nature. **Technical:** Hamon lines, folder lock of own design, the arm-lock! **Prices:** $50 - $1500. **Remarks:** Builds knives designed by Laci Szabo or builds to customer design. Studied with Reese Weiland on folders and automatics. **Mark:** GEISHA holding a sword with initials and THUD KNIVES in a circle.

STEGALL, KEITH,
701 Outlet View Dr, Wasilla, AK 99654, Phone: 907-376-0703, kas5200@yahoo.com
Specialties: Traditional working straight knives. **Patterns:** Most patterns. **Technical:** Grinds 440C and 154CM. **Prices:** $100 to $300. **Remarks:** Spare-time maker; first knife sold in 1987. **Mark:** Name and state with anchor.

STEGNER, WILBUR G,
9242 173rd Ave SW, Rochester, WA 98579, Phone: 360-273-0937, wilbur@wgsk.net; Web: www.wgsk.net
Specialties: Working/using straight knives and folders of his design. **Patterns:** Hunters and locking folders. **Technical:** Makes his own Damascus steel. **Prices:** $100 to $1000; some to $5000. **Remarks:** Full-time maker; first knife sold in 1979. Google search key words-"STEGNER KNIVES." Best folder awards NWKC 2009, 2010 and 2011. **Mark:** First and middle initials, last name in bar over shield logo.

STEIER, DAVID,
7722 Zenith Way, Louisville, KY 40219, Web: www.steierknives.com
Specialties: Folding LinerLocks, Bowies, slip joints, lockbacks, and straight hunters. **Technical:** Stock removal blades of 440C, ATS-34, and Damascus from outside sources like Robert Eggerling and Mike Norris. **Prices:** $150 for straight hunters to $1400 for fully decked-out folders. **Remarks:** First knife sold in 1979. **Mark:** Last name STEIER.

STEIGER, MONTE L,
Box 186, Genesee, ID 83832, Phone: 208-285-1769, montesharon@genesee-id.com
Specialties: Traditional working/using straight knives of all designs. **Patterns:** Hunters, utility/camp knives, fillet and chefs. Carving sets and steak knives. **Technical:** Grinds 1095, O1, 440C, ATS-34. Handles of stacked leather, natural wood, Micarta or pakkawood. Each knife comes with right- or left-handed sheath. **Prices:** $110 to $600. **Remarks:** Spare-time maker; first knife sold in 1988. Retired librarian **Mark:** First initial, last name, city and state.

STEIGERWALT, KEN,
507 Savagehill Rd, Orangeville, PA 17859, Phone: 570-683-5156, Web: www.steigerwaltknives.com
Specialties: Carving on bolsters and handle material. **Patterns:** Folders, button locks and rear locks. **Technical:** Grinds ATS-34, 440C and commercial Damascus. Experiments with unique filework. **Prices:** $500 to $5000. **Remarks:** Full-time maker; first knife sold in 1981. **Mark:** Kasteigerwalt

STEINAU, JURGEN,
Julius-Hart Strasse 44, Berlin 0-1162, GERMANY, Phone: 372-6452512, Fax: 372-645-2512
Specialties: Fantasy and high-art straight knives of his design. **Patterns:** Boots, daggers and switch-blade folders. **Technical:** Grinds 440B, 2379 and X90 Cr.Mo.V. 78. **Prices:** $1500 to $2500; some to $3500. **Remarks:** Full-time maker; first knife sold in 1984. **Mark:** Symbol, plus year, month day and serial number.

STEINBERG, AL,
5244 Duenas, Laguna Woods, CA 92653, Phone: 949-951-2889, lagknife@fea.net
Specialties: Fancy working straight knives to customer specs. **Patterns:** Hunters, Bowies, fishing, camp knives, push knives and high end kitchen knives. **Technical:** Grinds O1, 440C and 154CM. **Prices:** $60 to $2500. **Remarks:** Full-time maker; first knife sold in 1972. **Mark:** Signature, city and state.

STEINBRECHER, MARK W,
1122 92nd Place, Pleasant Prairie, WI 53158-4939
Specialties: Working and fancy folders. **Patterns:** Daggers, pocket knives, fighters and gents of his own design or to customer specs. **Technical:** Hollow grinds ATS-34, O1 other makers Damascus. Uses natural handle materials: stag, ivories, mother-of-pearl. File work and some inlays. **Prices:** $500 to $1200, some to $2500. **Remarks:** Part-time maker, first folder sold in 1989. **Mark:** Name etched or handwritten on ATS-34; stamped on Damascus.

STEINGASS, T.K.,
194 Mesquite Lane, Hedgesville, WV 25427, Phone: 304-268-1161, tksteingass@frontier.com; Web: http://steingassknives.com
Specialties: Loveless style hunters and fighters and sole authorship knives: Man Knife, Silent Hunter, and Silent Fighter. Harpoon Grind Camp Knife and Harpoon Grind Man Hunter. **Technical:** Stock removal, use CPM 154, S3V and occasionally 1095 or O1 for camp choppers. **Prices:** $200 to $500. **Remarks:** Part-time maker; first knife made in 2010. **Mark:** STEINGASS.

STEKETEE, CRAIG A,
871 NE US Hwy 60, Billings, MO 65610, Phone: 417-744-2770, stekknives04@yahoo.com
Specialties: Classic and working straight knives and swords of his design. **Patterns:** Bowies, hunters, and Japanese-style swords. **Technical:** Forges his own Damascus; bronze, silver and Damascus fittings, offers filework. Prefers exotic and natural handle materials. **Prices:** $200 to $4000. **Remarks:** Full-time maker. **Mark:** STEK.

STEPHAN, DANIEL,
2201 S Miller Rd, Valrico, FL 33594, Phone: 727-580-8617, knifemaker@verizon.net
Specialties: Art knives, one-of-a-kind.

STERLING, MURRAY,
693 Round Peak Church Rd, Mount Airy, NC 27030, Phone: 336-352-5110, Fax: Fax: 336-352-5105, sterck@surry.net; Web: www.sterlingcustomknives.com
Specialties: Single and dual blade folders. Interframes and integral dovetail frames. **Technical:** Grinds ATS-34 or Damascus by Mike Norris and/or Devin Thomas. **Prices:** $300 and up. **Remarks:** Full-time maker; first knife sold in 1991. **Mark:** Last name stamped.

STERLING, THOMAS J,
ART KNIVES BY, 120 N Pheasant Run, Coupeville, WA 98239, Phone: 360-678-9269, Fax: 360-678-9269, netsuke@comcast.net; Web: www.bladegallery.com Or www.sterlingsculptures.com
Specialties: Since 2003 Tom Sterling and Dr. J.P. Higgins have created a unique collaboration of one-of-a-kind, ultra-quality art knives with percussion or pressured flaked stone blades and creatively sculpted handles. Their knives are often highly influenced by the traditions of Japanese netsuke and unique fusions of cultures, reflecting stylistically integrated choices of exotic hardwoods, fossil ivories and semi-precious materials, contrasting inlays and polychromed and pyrographed details. **Prices:** $300 to $900. **Remarks:** Limited output ensures highest quality artwork and exceptional levels of craftsmanship. **Mark:** Signatures Sterling and Higgins.

STETTER, J. C.,
115 E College Blvd PMB 180, Roswell, NM 88201, Phone: 505-627-0978
Specialties: Fixed and folding. **Patterns:** Traditional and yours. **Technical:** Forged and ground of varied materials including his own pattern welded steel. **Prices:** Start at $250. **Remarks:** Full-time maker, first knife sold 1989. **Mark:** Currently "J.C. Stetter."

STEWART, EDWARD L,
4297 Audrain Rd 335, Mexico, MO 65265, Phone: 573-581-3883
Specialties: Fixed blades, working knives some art. **Patterns:** Hunters, Bowies, utility/camp knives. **Technical:** Forging 1095-W-2-I-6-52100 makes own Damascus. **Prices:** $85 to $500. **Remarks:** Part-time maker first knife sold in 1993. **Mark:** First and last initials-last name.

STEYN, PETER,
PO Box 76, Welkom 9460, Freestate, SOUTH AFRICA, Phone: 27573522015, Fax: 27573523566, Web: www.petersteynknives.com email: info@petersteynknives.com
Specialties: Fixed blade working knives of own design, tendency toward tactical creative & artistic styles all with hand stitched leather sheaths. **Patterns:** Hunters, skinners, fighters & wedge ground daggers. **Technical:** Grinds 12C27, D2, N690. Blades are bead-blasted in plain or camo patterns & own leanings crator finish. Prefers synthetic handle materials also uses cocobolo & ironwood. **Prices:** $200-$600. **Remarks:** Full time maker, first knife sold 2005, member of South African Guild. **Mark:** Letter 'S' in shape of pyramid with full name above & 'Handcrafted' below.

STICE, DOUGLAS W,
4113 W 18th St N, Wichita, KS 67212, Phone: 316-295-6855, doug@sticecraft.com; Web: www.sticecraft.com
Specialties: Working fixed blade knives of own design. **Patterns:** Tacticals, hunters, skinners, utility, and camp knives. **Technical:** Grinds CPM154CM, 154CM, CPM3V, Damascus; uses 18" contact grinds where wheel for hollow grinds, also flat. **Prices:** $100 to $750. **Remarks:** Full-time maker; first professional knife made in 2009. All knives have serial numbers and include certificate of authenticity. **Mark:** Stylized "Stice" stamp.

custom knifemakers

STIDHAM, DANIEL,
3106 Mill Cr. Rd., Gallipolis, Ohio 45631, Phone: 740-446-1673, danstidham@yahoo.com
Specialties: Fixed blades, folders, Bowies and hunters. **Technical:** 440C, Alabama Damascus, 1095 with filework. **Prices:** Start at $150. **Remarks:** Has made fixed blades since 1961, folders since 1986. Also sells various knife brands. **Mark:** Stidham Knives Gallipolis, Ohio 45631.

STIMPS, JASON M,
374 S Shaffer St, Orange, CA 92866, Phone: 714-744-5866

STIPES, DWIGHT,
2651 SW Buena Vista Dr, Palm City, FL 34990, Phone: 772-597-0550, dwightstipes@adelphia.net
Specialties: Traditional and working straight knives in standard patterns. **Patterns:** Boots, Bowies, daggers, hunters and fighters. **Technical:** Grinds 440C, D2 and D3 tool steel. Handles of natural materials, animal, bone or horn. **Prices:** $75 to $150. **Remarks:** Full-time maker; first knife sold in 1972. **Mark:** Stipes.

STOCKWELL, WALTER,
368 San Carlos Ave, Redwood City, CA 94061, Phone: 650-363-6069, walter@stockwellknives.com; Web: www.stockwellknives.com
Specialties: Scottish dirks, sgian dubhs. **Patterns:** All knives one-of-a-kind. **Technical:** Grinds ATS-34, forges 5160, 52100, L6. **Prices:** $125 to $500. **Remarks:** Part-time maker since 1992; graduate of ABS bladesmithing school. **Mark:** Shooting star over "STOCKWELL." Pre-2000, "WKS."

STODDART, JEFF,
77 Sheehan Ave, Cincinnati, OH 45216, Phone: 513-821-2880
Specialties: Sportsmen's working knives and multi-blade folders. **Patterns:** Hunters, camp and fish knives; multi-blade reproductions of old standards. **Technical:** Grinds A2, 440C and ATS-34; makes sheaths to match handle materials. **Prices:** $80 to $300; some to $850. **Remarks:** Part-time maker. **Mark:** Name, Cincinnati, state.

STOKES, ED,
22614 Cardinal Dr, Hockley, TX 77447, Phone: 713-351-1319
Specialties: Working straight knives and folders of all designs. **Patterns:** Boots, Bowies, daggers, fighters, hunters and miniatures. **Technical:** Grinds ATS-34, 440C and D2. Offers decorative butt caps, tapered spacers on handles and finger grooves, nickel-silver inlays, handmade sheaths. **Prices:** $185 to $290; some to $350. **Remarks:** Full-time maker; first knife sold in 1973. **Mark:** First and last name, Custom Knives with Apache logo.

STONE, JERRY,
PO Box 1027, Lytle, TX 78052, Phone: 830-709-3042
Specialties: Traditional working and using folders of his design and to customer specs; fancy knives. **Patterns:** Fighters, hunters, locking folders and slip joints. Also make automatics. **Technical:** Grinds 440C and ATS-34. Offers filework. **Prices:** $175 to $1000. **Remarks:** Full-time maker; first knife sold in 1973. **Mark:** Name over Texas star/town and state underneath.

STORCH, ED,
RR 4 Mannville, Alberta T0B 2W0, CANADA, Phone: 780-763-2214, storchkn@agt.net; Web: www.storchknives.com
Specialties: Working knives, fancy fighting knives, kitchen cutlery and art knives. Knifemaking classes. **Patterns:** Working patterns, Bowies and folders. **Technical:** Forges his own Damascus. Grinds ATS-34. Builds friction folders. Salt heat treating. **Prices:** $45 to $750 (U.S). **Remarks:** Part-time maker; first knife sold in 1984. Hosts annual Northwest Canadian Knifemakers Symposium; 60 to 80 knifemakers and families. **Mark:** Last name.

STORMER, BOB,
34354 Hwy E, Dixon, MO 65459, Phone: 636-734-2693, bs34354@gmail.com
Specialties: Straight knives, using collector grade. **Patterns:** Bowies, skinners, hunters, camp knives. **Technical:** Forges 5160, 1095. **Prices:** $200 to $500. **Remarks:** Part-time maker, ABS Journeyman Smith 2001. **Mark:** Setting sun/fall trees/initials.

STOUT, CHARLES,
RT3 178 Stout Rd, Gillham, AR 71841, Phone: 870-386-5521

STOUT, JOHNNY,
1205 Forest Trail, New Braunfels, TX 78132, Phone: 830-606-4067, johnny@stoutknives.com; Web: www.stoutknives.com
Specialties: Folders, some fixed blades. Working knives, some fancy. **Patterns:** Hunters, tactical, Bowies, automatics, liner locks and slip-joints. **Technical:** Grinds stainless and carbon steels; forges own Damascus. **Prices:** $450 to $895; some to $3500. **Remarks:** Full-time maker; first knife sold in 1983. Hosts semi-annual Guadalupe Forge Hammer-in and Knifemakers Rendezvous. **Mark:** Name and city in logo with serial number.

STRAIGHT, KENNETH J,
11311 103 Lane N, Largo, FL 33773, Phone: 813-397-9817

STRANDE, POUL,
Soster Svenstrup Byvej 16, Dastrup 4130 Viby Sj., DENMARK, Phone: 46 19 43 05, Fax: 46 19 53 19, Web: www.poulstrande.com
Specialties: Classic fantasy working knives; Damasceret blade, Nikkel Damasceret blade, Lamineret: Lamineret blade with Nikkel. **Patterns:** Bowies, daggers, fighters, hunters and swords. **Technical:** Uses carbon steel and 15C20 steel. **Prices:** NA. **Remarks:** Full-time maker; first knife sold in 1985. **Mark:** First and last initials.

STRAUB, SALEM F.,
324 Cobey Creek Rd., Tonasket, WA 98855, Phone: 509-486-2627, vorpalforge@hotmail.com Web: www.prometheanknives.com
Specialties: Elegant working knives, fixed blade hunters, utility, skinning knives; liner locks. Makes own horsehide sheaths. **Patterns:** A wide range of syles, everything from the gentleman's pocket to the working kitchen, integrals, Bowies, folders, check out my website to see some of my work for ideas. **Technical:** Forges several carbon steels, 52100, W1, etc. Grinds stainless and makes/uses own damascus, cable, san mai, stadard patterns. Likes clay quenching, hamons, hand rubbed finishes. Flat, hollow, or convex grinds. Prefers synthetic handle materials. Hidden and full tapered tangs. **Prices:** $150 - $600, some higher. **Remarks:** Full-time maker. Doing what it takes to make your knife ordering and buying experience positive and enjoyable; striving to exceed expectations. All knives backed by lifetime guarantee. **Mark:** "Straub" stamp or "Promethean Knives" etched. Some older pieces stamped "Vorpal" though no longer using this mark. **Other:** Feel free to call or e-mail anytime. I love to talk knives.

STRICKLAND, DALE,
1440 E Thompson View, Monroe, UT 84754, Phone: 435-896-8362
Specialties: Traditional and working straight knives and folders of his design and to customer specs. **Patterns:** Hunters, folders, miniatures and utility knives. **Technical:** Grinds Damascus and 440C. **Prices:** $120 to $350; some to $500. **Remarks:** Part-time maker; first knife sold in 1991. **Mark:** Oval stamp of name, Maker.

STRIDER, MICK,
STRIDER KNIVES, 120 N Pacific Unit L-7, San Marcos, CA 92069, Phone: 760-471-8275, Fax: 503-218-7069, striderguys@striderknives.com; Web: www.striderknives.com

STRONG, SCOTT,
1599 Beaver Valley Rd, Beavercreek, OH 45434, Phone: 937-426-9290
Specialties: Working knives, some deluxe. **Patterns:** Hunters, fighters, survival and military-style knives, art knives. **Technical:** Forges and grinds O1, A2, D2, 440C and ATS-34. Uses no solder; most knives disassemble. **Prices:** $75 to $450; some to $1500. **Remarks:** Spare-time maker; first knife sold in 1983. **Mark:** Strong Knives.

STROYAN, ERIC,
Box 218, Dalton, PA 18414, Phone: 717-563-2603
Specialties: Classic and working/using straight knives and folders of his design. **Patterns:** Hunters, locking folders, slip-joints. **Technical:** Forges Damascus; grinds ATS-34, D2. **Prices:** $200 to $600; some to $2000. **Remarks:** Part-time maker; first knife sold in 1968. **Mark:** Signature or initials stamp.

STUART, MASON,
24 Beech Street, Mansfield, MA 02048, Phone: 508-339-8236, smasonknives@verizon.net Web: smasonknives.com
Specialties: Straight knives of his design, standard patterns. **Patterns:** Bowies, hunters, fighters and neck knives. **Technical:** Forges and grinds. Damascus, 5160, 1095, 1084, old files. Uses only natural handle material. **Prices:** $350 - 2,000. **Remarks:** Part-time maker. **Mark:** First initial and last name.

STUART, STEVE,
Box 168, Gores Landing, Ont., CANADA K0K 2E0, Phone: 905-440-6910, stevestuart@xplornet.com
Specialties: Straight knives. **Patterns:** Tantos, fighters, skinners, file and rasp knives. **Technical:** Uses 440C, CPM154, CPMS30V, Micarta and natural handle materials. **Prices:** $60 to $400. **Remarks:** Part-time maker. **Mark:** SS.

STYREFORS, MATTIAS,
Unbyn 23, SE-96193 Boden, SWEDEN, infor@styrefors.com
Specialties: Damascus and mosaic Damascus. Fixed blade Nordic hunters, folders and swords. **Technical:** Forges, shapes and grinds Damascus and mosaic Damascus from mostly UHB 15N20 and 20C with contrasts in nickel and 15N20. Hardness HR 58. **Prices:** $800 to $3000. **Remarks:** Full-time maker since 1999. International reputation for high end Damascus blades. Uses stabilized Arctic birch and willow burl, horn, fossils, exotic materials, and scrimshaw by Viveca Sahlin for knife handles. Hand tools and hand stitches leather sheaths in cow raw hide. Works in well equipped former military forgery in northern Sweden. **Mark:** MS.

SUEDMEIER, HARLAN,
762 N 60th Rd, Nebraska City, NE 68410, Phone: 402-873-4372
Patterns: Straight knives. **Technical:** Forging hi carbon Damascus. **Prices:** Starting at $175. **Mark:** First initials & last name.

SUGIHARA, KEIDOH,
4-16-1 Kamori-Cho, Kishiwada City, Osaka, F596-0042, JAPAN, Fax: 0724-44-2677
Specialties: High-tech working straight knives and folders of his design. **Patterns:** Bowies, hunters, fighters, fishing, boots, some pocket knives and liner-lock folders. **Technical:** Grinds ATS-34, COS-25, buys Damascus and high-carbon steels. **Prices:** $60 to $4000. **Remarks:** Full-time maker, first knife sold in 1980. **Mark:** Initial logo with fish design.

SUGIYAMA, EDDY K,
2361 Nagayu, Naoirimachi Naoirigun, Ohita, JAPAN, Phone: 0974-75-2050
Specialties: One-of-a-kind, exotic-style knives. **Patterns:** Working, utility and miniatures. **Technical:** CT rind, ATS-34 and D2. **Prices:** $400 to $1200. **Remarks:** Full-time maker. **Mark:** Name or cedar mark.

SUMMERS, ARTHUR L,
1310 Hess Rd, Concord, NC 28025, Phone: 704-787-9275 Cell: 704-305-0735, arthursummers88@hotmail.com
Specialties: Drop points, clip points, straight blades. Patterns: Hunters, Bowies and personal knives. Technical: Grinds 440C, ATS-34, D2 and Damascus. Prices: $250 to $1000. Remarks: Full-time maker; first knife sold in 1988. Mark: Serial number is the date.

SUMMERS, DAN,
2675 NY Rt. 11, Whitney Pt., NY 13862, Phone: 607-692-2391, dansumm11@msn.com
Specialties: Period knives and tomahawks. Technical: All hand forging. Prices: Most $100 to $400.

SUMMERS, DENNIS K,
827 E. Cecil St, Springfield, OH 45503, Phone: 513-324-0624
Specialties: Working/using knives. Patterns: Fighters and personal knives. Technical: Grinds 440C, A2 and D2. Makes drop and clip point. Prices: $75 to $200. Remarks: Part-time maker; first knife sold in 1995. Mark: First and middle initials, last name, serial number.

SUNDERLAND, RICHARD,
Av Infraganti 23, Col Lazaro Cardenas, Puerto Escondido Oaxaca, MEXICO 71980, Phone: 011 52 94 582 1451, sunamerica@prodigy.net.mx7
Specialties: Personal and hunting knives with carved handles in oosic and ivory. Patterns: Hunters, Bowies, daggers, camp and personal knives. Technical: Grinds 440C, ATS-34 and O1. Handle materials of rosewoods, fossil mammoth ivory and oosic. Prices: $150 to $1000. Remarks: Part-time maker; first knife sold in 1983. Doing business as Sun Knife Co. Mark: SUN.

SUTTON, S RUSSELL,
4900 Cypress Shores Dr, New Bern, NC 28562, Phone: 252-637-3963, srsutton@suddenlink.net; Web: www.suttoncustomknives.com
Specialties: Straight knives and folders to customer specs and in standard patterns. Patterns: Boots, hunters, interframes, slip joints and locking liners. Technical: Grinds ATS-34, 440C and stainless Damascus. Prices: $220 to $2000. Remarks: Full-time maker; first knife sold in 1992. Provides relief engraving on bolsters and guards. Mark: Etched last name.

SWEAZA, DENNIS,
4052 Hwy 321 E, Austin, AR 72007, Phone: 501-941-1886, knives4den@aol.com

SWEENEY, COLTIN D,
1216 S 3 St W, Missoula, MT 59801, Phone: 406-721-6782

SWYHART, ART,
509 Main St, PO Box 267, Klickitat, WA 98628, Phone: 509-369-3451, swyhart@gorge.net; Web: www.knifeoutlet.com/swyhart.htm
Specialties: Traditional working and using knives of his design. Patterns: Bowies, hunters and utility/camp knives. Technical: Forges 52100, 5160 and Damascus 1084 mixed with either 15N20 or O186. Blades differentially heat-treated with visible temper line. Prices: $75 to $250; some to $350. Remarks: Part-time maker; first knife sold in 1983. Mark: First name, last initial in script.

SYLVESTER, DAVID,
465 Sweede Rd., Compton, Quebec CANADA, Phone: 819-837-0304, david@swedevilleforge.com Web: swedevilleforge.com
Patterns: I hand forge all my knives and I like to make hunters and integrals and some Bowies and fighters. I work with W2, 1084, 1095, and my damascus. Prices: $200 - $1500. Remarks: Part-time maker. ABS Journeyman Smith. Mark: D.Sylvester

SYMONDS, ALBERTO E,
Rambla M Gandhi 485, Apt 901, Montevideo 11300, URUGUAY, Phone: 011 598 27103201, Fax: 011 598 2 7103201, albertosymonds@hotmail.com
Specialties: All kinds including puukos, nice sheaths, leather and wood. Prices: $300 to $2200. Mark: AESH and current year.

SYSLO, CHUCK,
3418 South 116 Ave, Omaha, NE 68144, Phone: 402-333-0647, ciscoknives@cox.net
Specialties: Hunters, working knives, daggers & misc. Patterns: Hunters, daggers and survival knives; locking folders. Technical: Flat-grinds D2, 440C and 154CM; hand polishes only. Prices: $250 to $1000; some to $3000. Remarks: Part-time maker; first knife sold in 1978. Uses many natural materials. Mark: CISCO in logo.

SZILASKI, JOSEPH,
52 Woods Dr, Pine Plains, NY 12567, Phone: 518-398-0309, Web: www.szilaski.com
Specialties: Straight knives, folders and tomahawks of his design, to customer specs and in standard patterns. Many pieces are one-of-a-kind. Patterns: Bowies, daggers, fighters, hunters, art knives and early American-styles. Technical: Forges A2, D2, O1 and Damascus. Prices: $450 to $4000; some to $10,000. Remarks: Full-time maker; first knife sold in 1990. ABS Master Smith and voting member KMG. Mark: Snake logo.

T

TABOR, TIM,
18925 Crooked Lane, Lutz, FL 33548, Phone: 813-948-6141, taborknives.com
Specialties: Fancy folders, Damascus Bowies and hunters. Patterns: My own design folders & customer requests. Technical: ATS-34, hand forged Damascus, 1084, 15N20 mosaic Damascus, 1095, 5160 high carbon blades, flat grind, file work & jewel embellishments. Prices: $175 to $1500. Remarks: Part-time maker, sold first knife in 2003. Mark: Last name

TAKACH, ANDREW,
1390 Fallen Timber Rd., Elizabeth, PA 15037, Phone: 724-691-2271, a-takach@takachforge.com; Web: www.takachforge.com
Specialties: One-of-a-kind fixed blade working knives (own design or customer's). Mostly all fileworked. Patterns: Hunters, skinners, caping, fighters, and designs of own style. Technical: Forges mostly 5160, 1090, 01, an down pattern welded Damascus, nickle Damascus, and cable and various chain Damascus. Also do some San Mai. Prices: $100 to $350, some over $550. Remarks: Doing business as Takach Forge. First knife sold in 2004. Mark: Takach (stamped).

TAKAHASHI, MASAO,
39-3 Sekine-machi, Maebashi-shi, Gunma 371 0047, JAPAN, Phone: 81 27 234 2223, Fax: 81 27 234 2223
Specialties: Working straight knives. Patterns: Daggers, fighters, hunters, fishing knives, boots. Technical: Grinds ATS-34 and Damascus. Prices: $350 to $1000 and up. Remarks: Full-time maker; first knife sold in 1982. Mark: M. Takahashi.

TALLY, GRANT,
26961 James Ave, Flat Rock, MI 48134, Phone: 313-414-1618
Specialties: Straight knives and folders of his design. Patterns: Bowies, daggers, fighters. Technical: Grinds ATS-34, 440C and D2. Offers filework. Prices: $250 to $1000. Remarks: Part-time maker; first knife sold in 1985. Doing business as Tally Knives. Mark: Tally (last name).

TAMBOLI, MICHAEL,
12447 N 49 Ave, Glendale, AZ 85304, Phone: 602-978-4308, mnbtamboli@gmail.com
Specialties: Miniatures, some full size. Patterns: Miniature hunting knives to fantasy art knives. Technical: Grinds ATS-34 & Damascus. Prices: $75 to $500; some to $2000. Remarks: Full time maker; first knife sold in 1978. Mark: Initials, last name, last name city and state, MT Custom Knives or Mike Tamboli in Japanese script.

TASMAN, KERLEY,
9 Avignon Retreat, Pt Kennedy 6172, Western Australia, AUSTRALIA, Phone: 61 8 9593 0554, Fax: 61 8 9593 0554, taskerley@optusnet.com.au
Specialties: Knife/harness/sheath systems for elite military personnel and body guards. Patterns: Utility/tactical knives, hunters small game and presentation grade knives. Technical: ATS-34 and 440C, Damascus, flat and hollow grids. Prices: $200 to $1800 U.S. Remarks: Will take presentation grade commissions. Multi award winning maker and custom jeweler. Mark: Maker's initials.

TAYLOR, BILLY,
10 Temple Rd, Petal, MS 39465, Phone: 601-544-0041
Specialties: Straight knives of his design. Patterns: Bowies, skinners, hunters and utility knives. Technical: Flat-grinds 440C, ATS-34 and 154CM. Prices: $60 to $300. Remarks: Part-time maker; first knife sold in 1991. Mark: Full name, city and state.

TAYLOR, C GRAY,
560 Poteat Ln, Fall Branch, TN 37656, Phone: 423-348-8304, graysknives@aol.com or graysknives@hotmail.com; Web: www.cgraytaylor.com
Specialties: Traditonal multi-blade lobster folders, also art display Bowies and daggers. Patterns: Orange Blossom, sleeveboard and gunstocks. Technical: Grinds. Prices: Upscale. Remarks: Full-time maker; first knife sold in 1975. Mark: Name, city and state.

TAYLOR, DAVID,
113 Stewart Hill Dr, Rogersville, TN 37857, Phone: 423-921-0733, dtaylor0730@charter.net; Web: www.dtguitars.com
Patterns: Multi-blade folders, traditional patterns. Technical: Grinds ATS-34. Prices: $400 and up. Remarks: First sold knife in 1981 at age 14. Became a member of Knifemakers Guild at age 14. Made first folder in 1983. Full-time pastor of Baptist Church and part-time knifemaker.

TAYLOR, SHANE,
42 Broken Bow Ln, Miles City, MT 59301, Phone: 406-234-7175, shane@taylorknives.com; Web: www.taylorknives.com
Specialties: One-of-a-kind fancy Damascus straight knives and folders. Patterns: Bowies, folders and fighters. Technical: Forges own mosaic and pattern welded Damascus. Prices: $450 and up. Remarks: ABS Master Smith, full-time maker; first knife sold in 1982. Mark: First name.

TEDFORD, STEVEN,
7486 Bamsey Rd., PO Box 445 RR#2, Bewdley, Ontario, Canada K0L 1E0, Phone: 905-342-3696, firebornswords@yahoo.com; Web: www.facebook.com/profile.php?id=544811568&ref=ts
Specialties: Functional outdoorsman knives such as hunters, skinners, Bowies and fillets. One of a kind custom knives and collector's knives. Technical: >Combination forging and stock removal. Full-tang ATS-34 stainless blades.

TENDICK, BEN,
798 Nadine Ave, Eugene, OR 97404, Phone: 541-912-1280, bentendick@gmail.com
Specialties: Hunter/utility, tactical, bushcraft, and kitchen. Technical: Preferred steel - L6, 5160, and 15N20. Stock Removal. Prices: $75 to $500. Remarks: Part-time; has been making knives since early 90's but started seriously making knives in 2010. In business at BRT Bladeworks, no website yet but can be found on Facebook. Mark: Initials (BRT) with B backwards and T between the B and R.

TERRILL, STEPHEN,
16357 Goat Ranch Rd, Springville, CA 93265, Phone: 559-539-3116, slterrill@yahoo.com
Specialties: Deluxe working straight knives and folders. **Patterns:** Fighters, tantos, boots, locking folders and axes; traditional oriental patterns. **Technical:** Forges 1095, 5160, Damascus, stock removal ATS-34. **Prices:** $300+. **Remarks:** Full-time maker; first knife sold in 1972. **Mark:** Name, city, state in logo.

TERZUOLA, ROBERT,
10121 Eagle Rock NE, Albuquerque, NM 87122, Phone: 505-856-7077, terzuola@earthlink.net
Specialties: Working folders of his design; period pieces. **Patterns:** High-tech utility, defense and gentleman's folders. **Technical:** Grinds CPM154, Damascus, and CPM S30V. Offers titanium, carbon fiber and G10 composite for side-lock folders and tactical folders. **Prices:** $550 to $2000. **Remarks:** Full-time maker; first knife sold in 1980. **Mark:** Mayan dragon head, name.

THAYER, DANNY O,
8908S 100W, Romney, IN 47981, Phone: 765-538-3105, dot61h@juno.com
Specialties: Hunters, fighters, Bowies. **Prices:** $250 and up.

THEIS, TERRY,
21452 FM 2093, Harper, TX 78631, Phone: 830-864-4438
Specialties: All European and American engraving styles. **Prices:** $200 to $2000. **Remarks:** Engraver only.

THEVENOT, JEAN-PAUL,
16 Rue De La Prefecture, Dijon, FRANCE 21000
Specialties: Traditional European knives and daggers. **Patterns:** Hunters, utility-camp knives, daggers, historical or modern style. **Technical:** Forges own Damascus, 5160, 1084. **Remarks:** Part-time maker. ABS Master Smith. **Mark:** Interlocked initials in square.

THIE, BRIAN,
13250 150th St, Burlington, IA 52601, Phone: 319-850-2188, thieknives@gmail.com; Web: www.mepotelco.net/web/tknives
Specialties: Working using knives from basic to fancy. **Patterns:** Hunters, fighters, camp and folders. **Technical:** Forges blades and own Damascus. **Prices:** $250 and up. **Remarks:** ABS Journeyman Smith, part-time maker. Sole author of blades including forging, heat treat, engraving and sheath making. **Mark:** Last name hand engraved into the blade, JS stamped into blade.

THILL, JIM,
10242 Bear Run, Missoula, MT 59803, Phone: 406-251-5475
Specialties: Traditional and working/using knives of his design. **Patterns:** Fighters, hunters and utility/camp knives. **Technical:** Grinds D2 and ATS-34; forges 10-95-85, 52100, 5160, 10 series, reg. Damascus-mosaic. Offers hand cut sheaths with rawhide lace. **Prices:** $145 to $350; some to $1250. **Remarks:** Full-time maker; first knife sold in 1962. **Mark:** Running bear in triangle.

THOMAS, DAVID E,
8502 Hwy 91, Lillian, AL 36549, Phone: 251-961-7574, redbluff@gulftel.com
Specialties: Bowies and hunters. **Technical:** Hand forged blades in 5160, 1095 and own Damascus. **Prices:** $400 and up. **Mark:** Stylized DT, maker's last name, serial number.

THOMAS, DEVIN,
PO Box 568, Panaca, NV 89042, Phone: 775-728-4363, hoss@devinthomas.com; Web: www.devinthomas.com
Specialties: Traditional straight knives and folders in standard patterns. **Patterns:** Bowies, fighters, hunters. **Technical:** Forges stainless Damascus, nickel and 1095. Uses, makes and sells mokume with brass, copper and nickel-silver. **Prices:** $300 to $1200. **Remarks:** Full-time maker; first knife sold in 1979. **Mark:** First and last name, city and state with anvil, or first name only.

THOMAS, KIM,
PO Box 531, Seville, OH 44273, Phone: 330-769-9906
Specialties: Fancy and traditional straight knives of his design and to customer specs; period pieces. **Patterns:** Boots, daggers, fighters, swords. **Technical:** Forges own Damascus from 5160, 1010 and nickel. **Prices:** $135 to $1500; some to $3000. **Remarks:** Part-time maker; first knife sold in 1986. Doing business as Thomas Iron Works. **Mark:** KT.

THOMAS, ROCKY,
1716 Waterside Blvd, Moncks Corner, SC 29461, Phone: 843-761-7761
Specialties: Traditional working knives in standard patterns. **Patterns:** Hunters and utility/camp knives. **Technical:** ATS-34 and commercial Damascus. **Prices:** $130 to $350. **Remarks:** Spare-time maker; first knife sold in 1986. **Mark:** First name in script and/or block.

THOMPSON, KENNETH,
4887 Glenwhite Dr, Duluth, GA 30136, Phone: 770-446-6730
Specialties: Traditional working and using knives of his design. **Patterns:** Hunters, Bowies and utility/camp knives. **Technical:** Forges 5168, O1, 1095 and 52100. **Prices:** $75 to $1500; some to $2500. **Remarks:** Part-time maker; first knife sold in 1990. **Mark:** P/W; or name, P/W, city and state.

THOMPSON, LEON,
45723 SW Saddleback Dr, Gaston, OR 97119, Phone: 503-357-2573
Specialties: Working knives. **Patterns:** Locking folders, slip-joints and liner locks. **Technical:** Grinds ATS-34, D2 and 440C. **Prices:** $450 to $1000. **Remarks:** Full-time maker; first knife sold in 1976. **Mark:** First and middle initials, last name, city and state.

THOMPSON, LLOYD,
PO Box 1664, Pagosa Springs, CO 81147, Phone: 970-264-5837
Specialties: Working and collectible straight knives and folders of his design. **Patterns:** Straight blades, lock back folders and slip joint folders. **Technical:** Hollow-grinds ATS-34, D2 and O1. Uses sambar stag and exotic woods. **Prices:** $150 to upscale. **Remarks:** Full-time maker; first knife sold in 1985. Doing business as Trapper Creek Knife Co. **Remarks:** Offers three-day knife-making classes. **Mark:** Name.

THOMPSON, TOMMY,
4015 NE Hassalo, Portland, OR 97232-2607, Phone: 503-235-5762
Specialties: Fancy and working knives; mostly liner-lock folders. **Patterns:** Fighters, hunters and liner locks. **Technical:** Grinds D2, ATS-34, CPM440V and T15. Handles are either hardwood inlaid with wood banding and stone or shell, or made of agate, jasper, petrified woods, etc. **Prices:** $75 to $500; some to $1000. **Remarks:** Part-time maker; first knife sold in 1987. Doing business as Stone Birds. Knife making temporarily stopped due to family obligations. **Mark:** First and last name, city and state.

THOMSEN, LOYD W,
30173 Black Banks Rd, Oelrichs, SD 57763, Phone: 605-535-6162, loydt@yahoo.com; Web: horseheadcreekknives.com
Specialties: High-art and traditional working/using straight knives and presentation pieces of his design and to customer specs; period pieces. Hand carved animals in crown of stag on handles and carved display stands. **Patterns:** Bowies, hunters, daggers and utility/camp knives. **Technical:** Forges and grinds 1095HC, 1084, L6, 15N20, 440C stainless steel, nickel 200; special restoration process on period pieces. Makes sheaths. Uses natural materials for handles. **Prices:** $350 to $1000. **Remarks:** Full-time maker; first knife sold in 1995. Doing business as Horsehead Creek Knives. **Mark:** Initials and last name over a horse's head.

THORBURN, ANDRE E.,
P.O. Box 1748, Bela Bela, Warmbaths 0480, SOUTH AFRICA, Phone: 27-82-650-1441, andrethorburn@gmail.com; Web: www.thorburnknives.com
Specialties: Working and fancy folders of own design to customer specs. **Technical:** Uses RWL34, 12C27, 19C27, D2, Danzer36, CPM steels and Carbon and stainless Damascus. **Prices:** Starting at $350. **Remarks:** Full-time maker since 1996, first knife sold in 1990. Member of American Knifemakers Guild and South African, Italian, and German guilds; chairman of Knifemakers Guild of South Africa. **Mark:** Initials and name in a double circle.

THOUROT, MICHAEL W,
T-814 Co Rd 11, Napoleon, OH 43545, Phone: 419-533-6832, Fax: 419-533-3516, mike2row@henry-net.com; Web: wwwsafariknives.com
Specialties: Working straight knives to customer specs. Designed two-handled skinning ax and limited edition engraved knife and art print set. **Patterns:** Fishing and fillet knives, Bowies, tantos and hunters. **Technical:** Grinds O1, D2, 440C and Damascus. **Prices:** $200 to $5000. **Remarks:** Part-time maker; first knife sold in 1968. **Mark:** Initials.

THUESEN, ED,
21211 Knolle Rd, Damon, TX 77430, Phone: 979-553-1211, Fax: 979-553-1211
Specialties: Working straight knives. **Patterns:** Hunters, fighters and survival knives. **Technical:** Grinds D2, 440C, ATS-34 and Vascowear. **Prices:** $150 to $275; some to $600. **Remarks:** Part-time maker; first knife sold in 1979. Runs knifemaker supply business. **Mark:** Last name in script.

TIENSVOLD, ALAN L,
PO Box 355, Rushville, NE 69360, Phone: 308-327-2046
Specialties: Working knives, tomahawks and period pieces, high end Damascus knives. **Patterns:** Random, ladder, twist and many more. **Technical:** Hand forged blades, forges own Damascus. **Prices:** Working knives start at $300. **Remarks:** Received Journeyman rating with the ABS in 2002. Does own engraving and fine work. **Mark:** Tiensvold hand made U.S.A. on left side, JS on right.

TIENSVOLD, JASON,
PO Box 795, Rushville, NE 69360, Phone: 308-360-0613, tiensvoldknives@gpcom.net
Specialties: Working and using straight knives of his design; period pieces. Gentlemen folders, art folders. Single action automatics. **Patterns:** Hunters, skinners, Bowies, fighters, daggers, liner locks. **Technical:** Forges own Damascus using 15N20 and 1084, 1095, nickel, custom file work. **Prices:** $200 to $4000. **Remarks:** Full-time maker, first knife sold in 1994; doing business under Tiensvold Custom Knives. **Mark:** A. Tiensvold on left side, JS on right.

TIGHE, BRIAN,
12-111 Fourth Ave, Suite 376 Ridley Square, St. Catharines, Ont., CANADA L0S 1M0, Phone: 905-892-2734, Web: www.tigheknives.com
Specialties: Folding knives, bearing pivots. High tech tactical folders. **Patterns:** Boots, daggers and locking. **Technical:** BG-42, RWL-34, Damasteel, 154CM, S30V, CPM 440V and CPM 420V. Prefers natural handle material inlay; hand finishes. **Prices:** $450 to $4000. **Remarks:** Full-time maker; first knife sold in 1989. **Mark:** Etched signature.

TILL, CALVIN E AND RUTH,
211 Chaping, Chadron, NE 69337
Specialties: Straight knives, hunters, Bowies; no folders **Patterns:** Training point, drop point hunters, Bowies. **Technical:** ATS-34 sub zero quench RC59, 61. **Prices:** $700 to $1200. **Remarks:** Sells only the absolute best knives they can make. Manufactures every part in their knives. **Mark:** RC Till. The R is for Ruth.

TILTON, JOHN,
24041 Hwy 383, Iowa, LA 70647, Phone: 337-582-6785, john@jetknives.com
Specialties: Bowies, camp knives, skinners and folders. **Technical:** All forged blades. Makes own Damascus. **Prices:** $150 and up. **Remarks:** ABS Journeyman Smith. **Mark:** Initials J.E.T.

TINDERA, GEORGE,
BURNING RIVER FORGE, 751 Hadcock Rd, Brunswick, OH 44212-2648, Phone: 330-220-6212
Specialties: Straight knives; his designs. **Patterns:** Personal knives; classic Bowies and fighters. **Technical:** Hand-forged high-carbon; his own cable and pattern welded Damascus. **Prices:** $125 to $600. **Remarks:** Spare-time maker; sold first knife in 1995. Natural handle materials.

TINGLE, DENNIS P,
19390 E Clinton Rd, Jackson, CA 95642, Phone: 209-223-4586, dtknives@earthlink.net
Specialties: Swords, fixed blades: small to medium, tomahawks. **Technical:** All blades forged. **Remarks:** ABS, JS. **Mark:** D. Tingle over JS.

TIPPETTS, COLTEN,
4068 W Miners Farm Dr, Hidden Springs, ID 83714, Phone: 208-229-7772, coltentippetts@gmail.com
Specialties: Fancy and working straight knives and fancy locking folders of his own design or to customer specifications. **Patterns:** Hunters and skinners, fighters and utility. **Technical:** Grinds BG-42, high-carbon 1095 and Damascus. **Prices:** $200 to $1000. **Remarks:** Part-time maker; first knife sold in 1996. **Mark:** Fused initials.

TODD, RICHARD C,
375th LN 46001, Chambersburg, IL 62323, Phone: 217-327-4380, ktodd45@yahoo.com
Specialties: Multi blade folders and silver sheaths. **Patterns:** Jewel setting and hand engraving. **Mark:** RT with letter R crossing the T or R Todd.

TOICH, NEVIO,
Via Pisacane 9, Rettorgole di Caldogna, Vincenza, ITALY 36030, Phone: 0444-985065, Fax: 0444-301254
Specialties: Working/using straight knives of his design or to customer specs. **Patterns:** Bowies, hunters, skinners and utility/camp knives. **Technical:** Grinds 440C, D2 and ATS-34. Hollow-grinds all blades and uses mirror polish. Offers hand-sewn sheaths. Uses wood and horn. **Prices:** $120 to $300; some to $450. **Remarks:** Spare-time maker; first knife sold in 1989. Doing business as Custom Toich. **Mark:** Initials and model number punched.

TOKAR, DANIEL,
Box 1776, Shepherdstown, WV 25443
Specialties: Working knives; period pieces. **Patterns:** Hunters, camp knives, buckskinners, axes, swords and battle gear. **Technical:** Forges L6, 1095 and his Damascus; makes mokume, Japanese alloys and bronze daggers; restores old edged weapons. **Prices:** $25 to $800; some to $3000. **Remarks:** Part-time maker; first knife sold in 1979. Doing business as The Willow Forge. **Mark:** Arrow over rune and date.

TOLLEFSON, BARRY A,
104 Sutter Pl, PO Box 4198, Tubac, AZ 85646, Phone: 520-398-9327
Specialties: Working straight knives, some fancy. **Patterns:** Hunters, skinners, fighters and camp knives. **Technical:** Grinds 440C, ATS-34 and D2. Likes mirror-finishes; offers some fancy filework. Handles made from elk, deer and exotic hardwoods. **Prices:** $75 to $300; some higher. **Remarks:** Part-time maker; first knife sold in 1990. **Mark:** Stylized initials.

TOMBERLIN, BRION R,
ANVIL TOP CUSTOM KNIVES, 825 W Timberdell, Norman, OK 73072, Phone: 405-202-6832, anviltopp@aol.com
Specialties: Hand forged blades, working pieces, standard classic patterns, some swords, and customer designs. **Patterns:** Bowies, hunters, fighters, Persian and eastern-styles. Likes Japanese blades. **Technical:** Forge 1050, 1075, 1084, 1095, 5160, some forged stainless, also do some stock removal in stainless. Also makes own damascus. **Prices:** Start at $275 up to $2000 or higher for swords and custom pieces. **Remarks:** Part-time maker, Mastersmith America Bladesmith Society. Prefers natural handle materials, hand rubbed finishes. Likes temperlines. **Mark:** BRION with MS.

TOMES, P J,
594 High Peak Ln, Shipman, VA 22971, Phone: 434-263-8662, tomgsknives@juno.com; Web: www.tomesknives.com
Specialties: Scagel reproductions. **Patterns:** Front-lock folders. **Technical:** Forges 52100. **Prices:** $150 to $750. **Mark:** Last name, USA, MS, stamped in forged blades.

TOMEY, KATHLEEN,
146 Buford Pl, Macon, GA 31204, Phone: 478-746-8454, ktomey@tomeycustomknives.com; Web: www.tomeycustomknives.com
Specialties: Working hunters, skinners, daily users in fixed blades, plain and embellished. Tactical neck and belt carry. Japanese influenced. Bowies. **Technical:** Grinds O1, ATS-34, flat or hollow grind, filework, satin and mirror polish finishes. High quality leather sheaths with tooling. Kydex with tactical. **Prices:** $150 to $500. **Remarks:** Almost full-time maker. **Mark:** Last name in diamond.

TOMPKINS, DAN,
PO Box 398, Peotone, IL 60468, Phone: 708-258-3620
Specialties: Working knives, some deluxe, some folders. **Patterns:** Hunters,

boots, daggers and push knives. **Technical:** Grinds D2, 440C, ATS-34 and 154CM. **Prices:** $85 to $150; some to $400. **Remarks:** Part-time maker; first knife sold in 1975. **Mark:** Last name, city, state.

TONER, ROGER,
531 Lightfoot Pl, Pickering, Ont., CANADA L1V 5Z8, Phone: 905-420-5555
Specialties: Exotic sword canes. **Patterns:** Bowies, daggers and fighters. **Technical:** Grinds 440C, D2 and Damascus. Scrimshaws and engraves. Silver cast pommels and guards in animal shapes; twisted silver wire inlays. Uses semi-precious stones. **Prices:** $200 to $2000; some to $3000. **Remarks:** Part-time maker; first knife sold in 1982. **Mark:** Last name.

TORRES, HENRY,
2329 Moody Ave., Clovis, CA 93619, Phone: 559-297-9154, Web: www.htknives.com
Specialties: Forged high-performance hunters and working knives, Bowies, and fighters. **Technical:** 52100 and 5160 and makes own Damascus. **Prices:** $350 to $3000. **Remarks:** Started forging in 2004. Has mastersmith with American Bladesmith Association.

TOSHIFUMI, KURAMOTO,
3435 Higashioda, Asakura-gun, Fukuoka, JAPAN, Phone: 0946-42-4470

TOWELL, DWIGHT L,
2375 Towell Rd, Midvale, ID 83645, Phone: 208-355-2419
Specialties: Solid, elegant working knives; art knives, high quality hand engraving and gold inlay. **Patterns:** Hunters, Bowies, daggers and folders. **Technical:** Grinds 154CM, ATS-34, 440C and other maker's Damascus. **Prices:** Upscale. **Remarks:** Full-time maker. First knife sold in 1970. Member of AKI. **Mark:** Towell, sometimes hand engraved.

TOWNSEND, ALLEN MARK,
6 Pine Trail, Texarkana, AR 71854, Phone: 870-772-8945

TOWNSLEY, RUSSELL,
PO BOX 185, Concord, AR 72523, Phone: 870-307-8069, circleTRMtownsley@yahoo.com
Specialties: Using knives of his own design. **Patterns:** Hunters, skinners, folders. **Technical:** Hollow grinds D2 and O1. Handle material - antler, tusk, bone, exotic woods. **Prices:** Prices start at $125. **Remarks:** Arkansas knifemakers association. Sold first knife in 2009. Doing business as Circle-T knives.**Mark:** Encircled T.

TRACE RINALDI CUSTOM BLADES,
1470 Underpass Rd, Plummer, ID 83851, Trace@thrblades.com; Web: www.thrblades.com
Technical: Grinds S30V, 3V, A2 and talonite fixed blades. **Prices:** $300-$1000. **Remarks:** Tactical and utility for the most part. **Mark:** Diamond with THR inside.

TRACY, BUD,
495 Flanders Rd, Reno, NV 8951-4784

TREML, GLENN,
RR #14 Site 12-10, Thunder Bay, Ont., CANADA P7B 5E5, Phone: 807-767-1977
Specialties: Working straight knives of his design and to customer specs. **Patterns:** Hunters, kitchen knives and double-edged survival knives. **Technical:** Grinds 440C, ATS-34 and O1; stock removal method. Uses various woods and Micarta for handle material. **Prices:** $150 and up. **Mark:** Stamped last name.

TRINDLE, BARRY,
1660 Ironwood Trail, Earlham, IA 50072-8611, Phone: 515-462-1237
Specialties: Engraved folders. **Patterns:** Mostly small folders, classical-styles and pocket knives. **Technical:** 440 only. Engraves. Handles of wood or mineral material. **Prices:** Start at $1000. **Mark:** Name on tang.

TRISLER, KENNETH W,
6256 Federal 80, Rayville, LA 71269, Phone: 318-728-5541

TRITZ, JEAN JOSE,
Schopstrasse 23, 20255 Hamburg, GERMANY, Phone: 040-49 78 21
Specialties: Scandinavian knives, Japanese kitchen knives, friction folders, swords. **Patterns:** Puukkos, Tollekniven, Hocho, friction folders, swords. **Technical:** Forges tool steels, carbon steels, 52100 Damascus, mokume, San Maj. **Prices:** $200 to $2000; some higher. **Remarks:** Full-time maker; first knife sold in 1989. Does own leatherwork, prefers natural materials. Sole authorship. Speaks French, German, English, Norwegian. **Mark:** Initials in monogram.

TROUT, GEORGE H.,
727 Champlin Rd, Wilmington, OH 45177, Phone: 937-382-2331, gandjtrout@msn.com
Specialties: Working knives, some fancy. **Patterns:** Hunters, drop points, Bowies and fighters. **Technical:** Stock removal: ATS-34, 440C Forged: 5160, W2, 1095, O1 Full integrals: 440C, A2, O1. **Prices:** $150 and up. **Remarks:** Makes own sheaths and mosaic pins. Fileworks most knives. First knife 1985. **Mark:** Etched name and state on stock removal. Forged: stamped name and forged.

TRUJILLO, ALBERT M B,
2035 Wasmer Cir, Bosque Farms, NM 87068, Phone: 505-869-0428, trujilloscutups@comcast.net
Specialties: Working/using straight knives of his design or to customer specs. **Patterns:** Hunters, skinners, fighters, working/using knives. File work offered. **Technical:** Grinds ATS-34, D2, 440C, S30V. Tapers tangs, all blades cryogenically treated. **Prices:** $75 to $500. **Remarks:** Part-time maker; first knife sold in 1997. **Mark:** First and last name under logo.

TRUJILLO, MIRANDA,
6366 Commerce Blvd, Rohnert Park, CA 94928
  Specialties: Working/using straight knives of her design. **Patterns:** Hunters and utility/camp knives. **Technical:** Grinds ATS-34 and 440C. Sheaths are water resistant. **Prices:** $145 - $400; some to $600. **Remarks:** Spare-time maker; first knife sold in 1989. Doing business as Alaska Knife and Service Co. **Mark:** NA.

TRUNCALI, PETE,
2914 Anatole Court, Garland, TX 75043, Phone: 214-763-7127, truncaliknives@yahoo.com Web:www.truncaliknives.com
  Specialties: Lockback folders, locking liner folders, automatics and fixed blades. Does business as Truncali Custom Knives.

TSCHAGER, REINHARD,
Piazza Parrocchia 7, I-39100 Bolzano, ITALY, Phone: 0471-970642, Fax: 0471-970642, reinhardtschager@virgilio.it
  Specialties: Classic, high-art, collector-grade straight knives of his design. **Patterns:** Jewel knife, daggers, and hunters. **Technical:** Grinds ATS-34, D2 and Damascus. Oval pins. Gold inlay. Offers engraving. **Prices:** $900 to $2000; some to $3000. **Remarks:** Spare-time maker; first knife sold in 1979. **Mark:** Gold inlay stamped with initials.

TUOMINEN, PEKKA,
Pohjois-Keiteleentie20, 72930 Tossavanlahti, FINLAND, Phone: 358405167853, puukkopekka@luukku.com; Web: www.puukkopekka.com
  Specialties: Puukko knives. **Patterns:** Puukkos, hunters, leukus, and folders. **Technical:** Forges silversteel, 1085, 52100, and makes own Damascus 15N20 and 1095. Grinds RWL-34 and ATS-34. **Prices:** Starting at $170. **Remarks:** Part-time maker. **Mark:** Name.

TURCOTTE, LARRY,
1707 Evergreen, Pampa, TX 79065, Phone: 806-665-9369, 806-669-0435
  Specialties: Fancy and working/using knives of his design and to customer specs. **Patterns:** Hunters, kitchen knives, utility/camp knives. **Technical:** Grinds 440C, D2, ATS-34. Engraves, scrimshaws, silver inlays. **Prices:** $150 to $350; some to $1000. **Remarks:** Part-time maker; first knife sold in 1977. Doing business as Knives by Turcotte. **Mark:** Last name.

TURECEK, JIM,
12 Elliott Rd, Ansonia, CT 06401, Phone: 203-734-8406
  Specialties: Exotic folders, art knives and some miniatures. **Patterns:** Trout and bird knives with split bamboo handles and one-of-a-kind folders. **Technical:** Grinds and forges stainless and carbon Damascus. **Prices:** $750 to $1500; some to $3000. **Remarks:** Full-time maker; first knife sold in 1983. **Mark:** Last initial in script, or last name.

TURNBULL, RALPH A,
14464 Linden Dr, Spring Hill, FL 34609, Phone: 352-688-7089, tbull2000@bellsouth.net; Web: www.turnbullknives.com
  Specialties: Fancy folders. **Patterns:** Primarily gents pocket knives. **Technical:** Wire EDM work on bolsters. **Prices:** $300 and up. **Remarks:** Full-time maker; first knife sold in 1973. **Mark:** Signature or initials.

TURNER, KEVIN,
17 Hunt Ave, Montrose, NY 10548, Phone: 914-739-0535
  Specialties: Working straight knives of his design and to customer specs; period pieces. **Patterns:** Daggers, fighters and utility knives. **Technical:** Forges 5160 and 52100. **Prices:** $90 to $500. **Remarks:** Part-time maker; first knife sold in 1991. **Mark:** Acid-etched signed last name and year.

TURNER, MIKE,
PO BOX 194, Williams, OR 97544, Phone: 541-846-0204, mike@turnerknives.com Web: www.turnerknives.com
  Specialties: Forged and stock removed full tang, hidden and thru tang knives. **Patterns:** Hunters, fighters, Bowies, boot knives, skinners and kitchen knives. **Technical:** I make my own damascus. **Prices:** $200 - $1,000. **Remarks:** Part-time maker, sold my first knife in 2008, doing business as Mike Turner Custom Knives. **Mark:** Name, City, & State.

TYRE, MICHAEL A,
1219 Easy St, Wickenburg, AZ 85390, Phone: 928-684-9601/602-377-8432, michaeltyre@msn.com
  Specialties: Quality folding knives upscale gents folders one-of-a-kind collectable models. **Patterns:** Working fixed blades for hunting, kitchen and fancy Bowies. **Technical:** Grinds prefer hand rubbed satin finishes and use natural handle materials. **Prices:** $250 to $1300.

TYSER, ROSS,
1015 Hardee Court, Spartanburg, SC 29303, Phone: 864-585-7616
  Specialties: Traditional working and using straight knives and folders of his design and in standard patterns. **Patterns:** Bowies, hunters and slip-joint folders. **Technical:** Grinds 440C and commercial Damascus. Mosaic pins; stone inlay. Does filework and scrimshaw. Offers engraving and cut-work and some inlay on sheaths. **Prices:** $45 to $125; some to $400. **Remarks:** Part-time maker; first knife sold in 1995. Doing business as RT Custom Knives. **Mark:** Stylized initials.

U

UCHIDA, CHIMATA,
977-2 Oaza Naga Shisui Ki, Kumamoto, JAPAN 861-1204

V

VAGNINO, MICHAEL,
PO Box 67, Visalia, CA 93279, Phone: 559-636-0501, mvknives@lightspeed.net; Web: www.mvknives.com
  Specialties: Folders and straight knives, working and fancy. **Patterns:** Folders--locking liners, slip joints, lock backs, double and single action autos. Straight knives--hunters, Bowies, camp and kitchen. **Technical:** Forges 52100, W2, 15N20 and 1084. Grinds stainless. Makes own damascus and does engraving. **Prices:** $275 to $4000 and above. **Remarks:** Full-time maker, ABS Mastersmith. **Mark:** Logo, last name.

VAIL, DAVE,
554 Sloop Point Rd, Hampstead, NC 28443, Phone: 910-270-4456
  Specialties: Working/using straight knives of his own design or to the customer's specs. **Patterns:** Hunters/skinners, camp/utility, fillet, Bowies. **Technical:** Grinds ATS-34, 440c, 154 CM and 1095 carbon steel. **Prices:** $90 to $450. **Remarks:** Part-time maker. Member of NC Custom Knifemakers Guild. **Mark:** Etched oval with "Dave Vail Hampstead NC" inside.

VALLOTTON, BUTCH AND AREY,
621 Fawn Ridge Dr, Oakland, OR 97462, Phone: 541-459-2216, Fax: 541-459-7473
  Specialties: Quick opening knives w/complicated mechanisms. **Patterns:** Tactical, fancy, working, and some art knives. **Technical:** Grinds all steels, uses others' Damascus. Uses Spectrum Metal. **Prices:** From $350 to $4500. **Remarks:** Full-time maker since 1984; first knife sold in 1981. Co/designer, Applegate Fairbarn folding w/Bill Harsey. **Mark:** Name w/viper head in the "V."

VALLOTTON, RAINY D,
1295 Wolf Valley Dr, Umpqua, OR 97486, Phone: 541-459-0465
  Specialties: Folders, one-handed openers and art pieces. **Patterns:** All patterns. **Technical:** Stock removal all steels; uses titanium liners and bolsters; uses all finishes. **Prices:** $350 to $3500. **Remarks:** Full-time maker. **Mark:** Name.

VALLOTTON, SHAWN,
621 Fawn Ridge Dr, Oakland, OR 97462, Phone: 503-459-2216
  Specialties: Left-hand knives. **Patterns:** All styles. **Technical:** Grinds 440C, ATS-34 and Damascus. Uses titanium. Prefers bead-blasted or anodized finishes. **Prices:** $250 to $1400. **Remarks:** Full-time maker. **Mark:** Name and specialty.

VALLOTTON, THOMAS,
621 Fawn Ridge Dr, Oakland, OR 97462, Phone: 541-459-2216
  Specialties: Custom autos. **Patterns:** Tactical, fancy. **Technical:** File work, uses Damascus, uses Spectrum Metal. **Prices:** From $350 to $700. **Remarks:** Full-time maker. Maker of ProtŽgé 3 canoe. **Mark:** T and a V mingled.

VALOIS, A. DANIEL,
3552 W Lizard Ck Rd, Lehighton, PA 18235, Phone: 717-386-3636
  Specialties: Big working knives; various sized lock-back folders with new safety releases. **Patterns:** Fighters in survival packs, sturdy working knives, belt buckle knives, military-style knives, swords. **Technical:** Forges and grinds A2, O1 and 440C; likes full tangs. **Prices:** $65 to $240; some to $600. **Remarks:** Full-time maker; first knife sold in 1969. **Mark:** Anvil logo with last name inside.

VAN CLEVE, STEVE,
Box 372, Sutton, AK 99674, Phone: 907-745-3038

VAN DE MANAKKER, THIJS,
Koolweg 34, 5759 px Helenaveen, HOLLAND, Phone: 0493539369, www.ehijsvandemanakker.com
  Specialties: Classic high-art knives. **Patterns:** Swords, utility/camp knives and period pieces. **Technical:** Forges soft iron, carbon steel and Bloomery Iron. Makes own Damascus, Bloomery Iron and patterns. **Prices:** $20 to $2000; some higher. **Remarks:** Full-time maker; first knife sold in 1969. **Mark:** Stylized "V."

VAN DEN ELSEN, GERT,
Purcelldreef 83, 5012 AJ Tilburg, NETHERLANDS, Phone: 013-4563200, gvdelsen@home.nl
  Specialties: Fancy, working/using, miniatures and integral straight knives of the maker's design or to customer specs. **Patterns:** Bowies, fighters, hunters and Japanese-style blades. **Technical:** Grinds ATS-34 and 440C; forges Damascus. Offers filework, differentially tempered blades and some mokume-gane fittings. **Prices:** $350 to $1000; some to $4000. **Remarks:** Part-time maker; first knife sold in 1982. Doing business as G-E Knives. **Mark:** Initials GE in lozenge shape.

VAN DER WESTHUIZEN, PETER,
PO Box 1698, Mossel Bay 6500, SOUTH AFRICA, Phone: 27 446952388, pietvdw@telkomsa.net
  Specialties: Working knives, folders, daggers and art knives. **Patterns:** Hunters, skinners, bird, trout and sidelock folders. **Technical:** Sandvik, 12627. Damascus indigenous wood and ivory. **Prices:** From $450 to $5500. **Remarks:** First knife sold in 1987. Full-time since 1996. **Mark:** Initial & surname. Handmade RSA.

VAN DIJK, RICHARD,
76 Stepney Ave Rd 2, Harwood Dunedin, NEW ZEALAND, Phone: 0064-3-4780401, Web: www.hoihoknives.com
Specialties: Damascus, Fantasy knives, sgiandubhs, dirks, swords, and hunting knives. **Patterns:** Mostly one-offs, anything from bird and trout to swords, no folders. **Technical:** Forges mainly own Damascus, some 5160, O1, 1095, L6. Prefers natural handle materials, over 35 years experience as goldsmith, handle fittings are often made from sterling silver and sometimes gold, manufactured to cap the handle, use gemstones if required. Makes own sheaths. **Prices:** $300 and up. **Remarks:** Full-time maker, first knife sold in 1980. Doing business as HOIHO KNIVES. **Mark:** Stylized initials RvD in triangle.

VAN EIZENGA, JERRY W,
14281 Cleveland, Nunica, MI 49448, Phone: 616-638-2275
Specialties: Hand forged blades, Scagel patterns and other styles. **Patterns:** Camp, hunting, bird, trout, folders, axes, miniatures. **Technical:** 5160, 52100, 1084. **Prices:** Start at $250. **Remarks:** Part-time maker, sole author of knife and sheath. First knife made 1970s. ABS member who believes in the beauty of simplicity. **Mark:** J.S. stamp.

VAN ELDIK, FRANS,
Ho Flaan 3, 3632BT Loenen, NETHERLANDS, Phone: 0031 294 233 095, Fax: 0031 294 233 095
Specialties: Fancy collector-grade straight knives and folders of his design. **Patterns:** Hunters, fighters, boots and folders. **Technical:** Forges and grinds D2, 154CM, ATS-34 and stainless Damascus. **Prices:** Start at $450. **Remarks:** Spare-time maker; first knife sold in 1979. Knifemaker 30 years, 25 year member of Knifemakers Guild. **Mark:** Lion with name and Amsterdam.

VAN HEERDEN, ANDRE,
P.O. Box 905-417, Garsfontein, Pretoria, SOUTH AFRICA 0042, Phone: 27 82 566 6030, andrevh@iafrica.com; Web: www.andrevanheerden.com
Specialties: Fancy and working folders of his design to customer specs. **Technical:** Grinds RWL34, 19C27, D2, carbon and stainless Damascus. **Prices:** Starting at $350. **Remarks:** Part-time maker, first knife sold in 2003. **Mark:** Initials and name in a double circle.

VAN REENEN, IAN,
6003 Harvard St, Amarillo, TX 79109, Phone: 806-236-8333, ianvanreenen@suddenlink.net Web: www.ianvanreenenknives.com
Specialties: Slipjoints, single and double blades. **Patterns:** Trappers, peanuts, saddle horn trappers. **Technical:** ATS-34 and CPM 154. **Prices:** $400 to $700. **Remarks:** Specializing in slipjoints. **Mark:** VAN REENEN

VAN RYSWYK, AAD,
AVR KNIVES, Werf Van Pronk 8, 3134 HE Vlaardingen, NETHERLANDS, Phone: +31 10 4742952, info@avrknives.com; Web: www.avrknives.com
Specialties: High-art interframe knives of his design. **Patterns:** Hunters and locking folders. **Technical:** Uses semi-precious stones, mammoth ivory, iron wood, etc. **Prices:** $550 to $3800. **Remarks:** Full-time maker; first knife sold in 1993.

VANDERFORD, CARL G,
2290 Knob Creek Rd, Columbia, TN 38401, Phone: 931-381-1488
Specialties: Traditional working straight knives and folders of his design. **Patterns:** Hunters, Bowies and locking folders. **Technical:** Forges and grinds 440C, O1 and wire Damascus. **Prices:** $60 to $125. **Remarks:** Part-time maker; first knife sold in 1987. **Mark:** Last name.

VANDERKOLFF, STEPHEN,
5 Jonathan Crescent, Mildmay Ontario, CANADA N0g 2JO, Phone: 519-367-3401, steve@vanderkolffknives.com; Web: www.vanderkolffknives.com
Specialties: Fixed blades from gent's pocketknives and drop hunters to full sized Bowies and art knives. **Technical:** Primary blade steel 440C, Damasteel or custom made Damascus. All heat treat done by maker and all blades hardness tested. Handle material: stag, stabilized woods or MOP. **Prices:** $150 to $1200. **Remarks:** Started making knives in 1998 and sold first knife in 2000. Winner of the best of show art knife 2005 Wolverine Knife Show.

VANDEVENTER, TERRY L,
3274 Davis Rd, Terry, MS 39170-8719, Phone: 601-371-7414, tvandeventer@comcast.net
Specialties: Bowies, hunters, camp knives, friction folders. **Technical:** 1084, 1095, 15N20 and L6 steels. Damascus and mokume. Natural handle materials. **Prices:** $600 to $3000. **Remarks:** Sole author; makes everything here. First ABS MS from the state of Mississippi. **Mark:** T.L. Vandeventer (silhouette of snake underneath). MS on ricasso.

VANHOY, ED AND TANYA,
24255 N Fork River Rd, Abingdon, VA 24210, Phone: 276-944-4885, vanhoyknives@centurylink.net
Specialties: Traditional and working/using straight knives and folders and innovative locking mechanisms. **Patterns:** Fighters, straight knives, folders, hunters, art knives and Bowies. **Technical:** Grinds ATS-34 and carbon/stainless steel Damascus; forges carbon and stainless Damascus. Offers filework and engraving with hammer and chisel. **Prices:** $250 to $3000. **Remarks:** Full-time maker; first knife sold in 1977. Wife also engraves. Doing business as Van Hoy Custom Knives. **Mark:** Acid etched last name.

VARDAMAN, ROBERT,
2406 Mimosa Lane, Hattiesburg, MS 39402, Phone: 601-268-3889, rv7x@comcast.net
Specialties: Working straight knives of his design or to customer specs.

Patterns: Bowies, hunters, skinners, utility and camp knives. **Technical:** Forges 52100, 5160, 1084 and 1095. Filework. **Prices:** $100 to $500. **Remarks:** Part-time maker. First knife sold in 2004. **Mark:** Last name, last name with Mississippi state logo.

VASQUEZ, JOHNNY DAVID,
1552 7th St, Wyandotte, MI 48192, Phone: 734-281-2455

VAUGHAN, IAN,
351 Doe Run Rd, Manheim, PA 17545-9368, Phone: 717-665-6949

VEIT, MICHAEL,
3289 E Fifth Rd, LaSalle, IL 61301, Phone: 815-223-3538, whitebear@starband.net
Specialties: Damascus folders. **Technical:** Engraver, sole author. **Prices:** $2500 to $6500. **Remarks:** Part-time maker; first knife sold in 1985. **Mark:** Name in script.

VELARDE, RICARDO,
7240 N Greenfield Dr, Park City, UT 84098, Phone: 435-901-1773, velardeknives@mac.com Web: www.velardeknives.com
Specialties: Investment grade integrals and interframs. **Patterns:** Boots, fighters and hunters; hollow grind. **Technical:** BG on Integrals. **Prices:** $1450 to $5200. **Remarks:** First knife sold in 1992. **Mark:** First initial and last name.

VELICK, SAMMY,
3457 Maplewood Ave, Los Angeles, CA 90066, Phone: 310-663-6170, metaltamer@gmail.com
Specialties: Working knives and art pieces. **Patterns:** Hunter, utility and fantasy. **Technical:** Stock removal and forges. **Prices:** $100 and up. **Mark:** Last name.

VENSILD, HENRIK,
Gl Estrup, Randersvei 4, DK-8963 Auning, DENMARK, Phone: +45 86 48 44 48
Specialties: Classic and traditional working and using knives of his design; Scandinavian influence. **Patterns:** Hunters and using knives. **Technical:** Forges Damascus. Hand makes handles, sheaths and blades. **Prices:** $350 to $1000. **Remarks:** Part-time maker; first knife sold in 1967. **Mark:** Initials.

VESTAL, CHARLES,
26662 Shortsville Rd., Abingdon, VA 24210, Phone: 276-492-3262, charles@vestalknives.com; Web: www.vestalknives.com
Specialties: Hunters and double ground fighters in traditional designs and own designs. **Technical:** Grinds CPM-154, ATS-134, 154-CM and other steels. **Prices:** $300 to $1000, some higher. **Remarks:** First knife sold in 1995.

VIALLON, HENRI,
Les Belins, 63300 Thiers, FRANCE, Phone: 04-73-80-24-03, Fax: 04 73-51-02-02
Specialties: Folders and complex Damascus **Patterns:** His draws. **Technical:** Forge. **Prices:** $1000 to $5000. **Mark:** H. Viallon.

VICKERS, DAVID,
11620 Kingford Dr., Montgomery, TX 77316, Phone: 936-537-4900, jdvickers@gmail.com
Specialties: Working/using blade knives especially for hunters. His design or to customer specs. **Patterns:** Hunters, skinners, camp/utility. **Technical:** Grinds ATS-34, 440C, and D-2. Uses stag, various woods, and micarta for handle material. Hand-stitched sheaths. **Remark:** Full-time maker. **Prices:** $125 - $350. **Mark:** VICKERS

VIELE, H J,
88 Lexington Ave, Westwood, NJ 07675, Phone: 201-666-2906, h.viele@verizon.net
Specialties: Folding knives of distinctive shapes. **Patterns:** High-tech folders and one-of-a-kind. **Technical:** Grinds ATS-34 and S30V. **Prices:** Start at $575. **Remarks:** Full-time maker; first knife sold in 1973. **Mark:** Japanese design for the god of war.

VILAR, RICARDO AUGUSTO FERREIRA,
Rua Alemada Dos Jasmins NO 243, Parque Petropolis, Mairipora Sao Paulo, BRAZIL 07600-000, Phone: 011-55-11-44-85-43-46, ricardovilar@ig.com.br.
Specialties: Traditional Brazilian-style working knives of the Sao Paulo state. **Patterns:** Fighters, hunters, utility, and camp knives, welcome customer design. Specialize in the "true" Brazilian camp knife "Soracabana." **Technical:** Forges only with sledge hammer to 100 percent shape in 5160 and 52100 and his own Damascus steels. Makes own sheaths in the "true" traditional "Paulista"-style of the state of Sao Paulo. **Remark:** Full-time maker. **Prices:** $250 to $600. Uses only natural handle materials. **Mark:** Special designed signature styled name R. Vilar.

VILLA, LUIZ,
R. Com. Miguel Calfat, 398 Itaim Bibi, Sao Paulo, SP-04537-081, BRAZIL, Phone: 011-8290649
Specialties: One-of-a-kind straight knives and jewel knives of all designs. **Patterns:** Bowies, hunters, utility/camp knives and jewel knives. **Technical:** Grinds D6, Damascus and 440C; forges 5160. Prefers natural handle material. **Prices:** $70 to $200. **Remarks:** Part-time maker; first knife sold in 1990. **Mark:** Last name and serial number.

VILLAR, RICARDO,
Al. dos Jasmins 243 Mairipora, S.P. 07600-000, BRAZIL, Phone: 011-4851649
Specialties: Straight working knives to customer specs. **Patterns:** Bowies, fighters and utility/camp knives. **Technical:** Grinds D6, ATS-34 and 440C stainless. **Prices:** $80 to $200. **Remarks:** Part-time maker; first knife sold in 1993. **Mark:** Percor over sword and circle.

VILPPOLA, MARKKU,
Arkeologinen Kokeiluverstas, Kuralan Kylamaki, Jaanintie 45 20540 Turku, Finland, Phone: +358 (0)50 566 1563, markku@mvforge.fi Web: www.mvforge.fi
Specialties: All kinds of swords and knives. **Technical:** Forges silver steel, CO, 8%, nickel, 1095, A203E, etc. Mokume (sterling silver/brass/copper). Bronze casting (sand casting, lost-wax casting). **Prices:** Starting at $200.

VINING, BILL,
9 Penny Lane, Methuen, MA 01844, Phone: 978-688-4729, billv@medawebs.com; Web: www.medawebs.com/knives
Specialties: Liner locking folders. Slip joints & lockbacks. **Patterns:** Likes to make patterns of his own design. **Technical:** S30V, 440C, ATS-34. Damascus from various makers. **Prices:** $450 and up. **Remarks:** Part-time maker. **Mark:** VINING or B. Vining.

VISTE, JAMES,
EDGE WISE FORGE, 13401 Mt Elliot, Detroit, MI 48212, Phone: 313-664-7455, grumblejunky@hotmail.com
Mark: EWF touch mark.

VISTNES, TOR,
N-6930 Svelgen, NORWAY, Phone: 047-57795572
Specialties: Traditional and working knives of his design. **Patterns:** Hunters and utility knives. **Technical:** Grinds Uddeholm Elmax. Handles made of rear burls of different Nordic stabilized woods. **Prices:** $300 to $1100. **Remarks:** Part-time maker; first knife sold in 1988. **Mark:** Etched name and deer head.

VITALE, MACE,
925 Rt 80, Guilford, CT 06437, Phone: 203-457-5591, Web: www.laurelrockforge.com
Specialties: Hand forged blades. **Patterns:** Hunters, utility, chef, Bowies and fighters. **Technical:** W2, 1095, 1084, L6. Hand forged and finished. **Prices:** $100 to $1000. **Remarks:** American Bladesmith Society, Journeyman Smith. Full-time maker; first knife sold 2001. **Mark:** MACE.

VOGT, DONALD J,
9007 Hogans Bend, Tampa, FL 33647, Phone: 813-973-3245, vogtknives@verizon.net
Specialties: Art knives, folders, automatics. **Technical:** Uses Damascus steels for blade and bolsters, filework, hand carving on blade bolsters and handles. Other materials used: jewels, gold, mother-of-pearl, gold-lip pearl, black-lip pearl, ivory. **Prices:** $4,000 to $10,000. **Remarks:** Part-time maker; first knife sold in 1997. **Mark:** Last name.

VOGT, PATRIK,
Kungsvagen 83, S-30270 Halmstad, SWEDEN, Phone: 46-35-30977
Specialties: Working straight knives. **Patterns:** Bowies, hunters and fighters. **Technical:** Forges carbon steel and own Damascus. **Prices:** From $100. **Remarks:** Not currently making knives. **Mark:** Initials or last name.

VOORHIES, LES,
14511 Lk Mazaska Tr, Faribault, MN 55021, Phone: 507-332-0736, lesvor@msn.com; Web: www.lesvoorhiesknives.com
Specialties: Steels. **Patterns:** Liner locks & autos. **Technical:** ATS-34 Damascus. **Prices:** $250 to $1200. **Mark:** L. Voorhies.

VOSS, BEN,
2212 Knox Rd. 1600 Rd. E, Victoria, IL 61485-9644, Phone: 309-879-2940
Specialties: Fancy working knives of his design. **Patterns:** Bowies, fighters, hunters, boots and folders. **Technical:** Grinds 440C, ATS-34 and D2. **Prices:** $35 to $1200. **Remarks:** Part-time maker; first knife sold in 1986. **Mark:** Name, city and state.

VOTAW, DAVID P,
305 S State St, Pioneer, OH 43554, Phone: 419-737-2774
Specialties: Working knives; period pieces. **Patterns:** Hunters, Bowies, camp knives, buckskinners and tomahawks. **Technical:** Grinds O1 and D2. **Prices:** $100 to $200; some to $500. **Remarks:** Part-time maker; took over for the late W.K. Kneubuhler. Doing business as W-K Knives. **Mark:** WK with V inside anvil.

W

WACHOLZ, DOC,
95 Anne Rd, Marble, NC 28905, Phone: 828-557-1543, killdrums@aol.com; web: rackforge.com
Specialties: Forged tactical knives and tomahawks. **Technical:** Use 52100 and 1084 high carbon steel; make own Damascus; design and dew own sheaths. Grind up and down fashion on a 3" wheel. **Prices:** $300 to $800. **Remarks:** Part-time maker; started forging in 1999, with ABS master Charles Ochs.. **Mark:** Early knives stamped RACK, newer knives since 2005 stamped WACHOLZ.

WADA, YASUTAKA,
2-6-22 Fujinokidai, Nara City, Nara prefect 631-0044, JAPAN, Phone: 0742 46-0689
Specialties: Fancy and embellished one-of-a-kind straight knives of his design. **Patterns:** Bowies, daggers and hunters. **Technical:** Grinds ATS-34. All knives hand-filed and flat grinds. **Prices:** $400 to $2500; some higher. **Remarks:** Part-time maker; first knife sold in 1990. **Mark:** Owl eyes with initial and last name underneath or last name.

WAGAMAN, JOHN K,
107 E Railroad St, Selma, NC 27576, Phone: 919-965-9659, Fax: 919-965-9901
Specialties: Fancy working knives. **Patterns:** Bowies, miniatures, hunters, fighters and boots. **Technical:** Grinds D2, 440C, 154CM and commercial

Damascus; inlays mother-of-pearl. **Prices:** $110 to $2000. **Remarks:** Part-time maker; first knife sold in 1975. **Mark:** Last name.

WAITES, RICHARD L,
PO Box 188, Broomfield, CO 80038, Phone: 303-465-9970, Fax: 303-465-9971, dickknives@aol.com
Specialties: Working fixed blade knives of all kinds including "paddle blade" skinners. Hand crafted sheaths, some upscale and unusual. **Technical:** Grinds 440C, ATS 34, D2. **Prices:** $100 to $500. **Remarks:** Part-time maker. First knife sold in 1998. Doing business as R.L. Waites Knives. **Mark:** Oval etch with first and middle initial and last name on top and city and state on bottom. Memberships; Professional Knifemakers Association and Rocky Mountain Blade Collectors Club.

WALKER, BILL,
431 Walker Rd, Stevensville, MD 21666, Phone: 410-643-5041

WALKER, DON,
2850 Halls Chapel Rd, Burnsville, NC 28714, Phone: 828-675-9716, dlwalkernc@gmail.com

WALKER, JIM,
22 Walker Ln, Morrilton, AR 72110, Phone: 501-354-3175, jwalker46@att.net
Specialties: Period pieces and working/using knives of his design and to customer specs. **Patterns:** Bowies, fighters, hunters, camp knives. **Technical:** Forges 5160, O1, L6, 52100, 1084, 1095. **Prices:** Start at $450. **Remarks:** Full-time maker; first knife sold in 1993. **Mark:** Three arrows with last name/MS.

WALKER, MICHAEL L,
925-A Paseo del, Pueblo Sur Taos, NM 87571, Phone: 505-751-3409, Fax: 505-751-3417, metalwerkr@msn.com
Specialties: Innovative knife designs and locking systems; titanium and SS furniture and art. **Patterns:** Folders from utility grade to museum quality art; others upon request. **Technical:** State-of-the-art materials: titanium, stainless Damascus, gold, etc. **Prices:** $3500 and above. **Remarks:** Designer/MetalCrafts; full-time professional knifemaker since 1980; four U.S. patents; invented LinerLock® and was awarded registered U.S. trademark no. 1,585,333. **Mark:** Early mark MW, Walker's Lockers by M.L. Walker; current M.L. Walker or Michael Walker.

WALLINGFORD JR., CHARLES W,
9024 Old Union Rd, Union, KY 41091, Phone: 859-384-4141, Web: www.cwknives.com
Specialties: 18th and 19th century styles, patch knives, rifleman knives. **Technical:** 1084 and 5160 forged blades. **Prices:** $125 to $300. **Mark:** CW.

WALTERS, A F,
PO Box 523, 275 Crawley Rd., TyTy, GA 31795, Phone: 229-528-6207
Specialties: Working knives, some to customer specs. **Patterns:** Locking folders, straight hunters, fishing and survival knives. **Technical:** Grinds D2, 154CM and 13C26. **Prices:** Start at $200. **Remarks:** Part-time maker. Label: "The jewel knife." **Mark:** "J" in diamond and knife logo.

WARD, CHUCK,
PO Box 2272, 1010 E North St, Benton, AR 72018-2272, Phone: 501-778-4329, chuckbop@aol.com
Specialties: Traditional working and using straight knives and folders of his design. **Technical:** Grinds 440C, D2, A2, ATS-34 and O1; uses natural and composite handle materials. **Prices:** $90 to $400, some higher. **Remarks:** Part-time maker; first knife sold in 1990. **Mark:** First initial, last name.

WARD, J J,
7501 S R 220, Waverly, OH 45690, Phone: 614-947-5328
Specialties: Traditional and working/using straight knives and folders of his design. **Patterns:** Hunters and locking folders. **Technical:** Grinds ATS-34, 440C and Damascus. Offers handmade sheaths. **Prices:** $125 to $250; some to $500. **Remarks:** Spare-time maker; first knife sold in 1980. **Mark:** Etched name.

WARD, KEN,
1125 Lee Roze Ln, Grants Pass, OR 97527, Phone: 541-956-8864
Specialties: Working knives, some to customer specs. **Patterns:** Straight, axes, Bowies, buckskinners and miniatures. **Technical:** Grinds ATS-34, Damascus. **Prices:** $100 to $700. **Remarks:** Part-time maker; first knife sold in 1977. **Mark:** Name.

WARD, RON,
PO BOX 21, Rose Hill, VA 24281, Phone: 276-445-4757
Specialties: Classic working and using straight knives, fantasy knives. **Patterns:** Bowies, hunter, fighters, and utility/camp knives. **Technical:** Grinds 440C, 154CM, ATS-34, uses composite and natural handle materials. **Prices:** $50 to $750. **Remarks:** Part-time maker; first knife sold in 1992. Doing business as Ron Ward Blades. **Mark:** Ron Ward Blades, Loveland OH.

WARD, W C,
817 Glenn St, Clinton, TN 37716, Phone: 615-457-3568
Specialties: Working straight knives; period pieces. **Patterns:** Hunters, Bowies, swords and kitchen cutlery. **Technical:** Grinds O1. **Prices:** $85 to $150; some to $500. **Remarks:** Part-time maker; first knife sold in 1969. He styled the Tennessee Knife Maker. **Mark:** TKM.

WARDELL, MICK,
20 Clovelly Rd, Bideford, N Devon EX39 3BU, ENGLAND, wardellknives@hotmail.co.uk Web: www.wardellscustomknives.com
Specialties: Spring back folders and a few fixed blades. **Patterns:** Locking and slip-joint folders, Bowies. **Technical:** Grinds stainless Damascus and

RWL34. Heat-treats. **Prices:** $300 to $2500. **Remarks:** Full-time maker; first knife sold in 1986. Takes limited Comissions. **Mark:** Wardell.

WARDEN, ROY A,
275 Tanglewood Rd, Union, MO 63084, Phone: 314-583-8813, rwarden@yhti.net
Specialties: Complex mosaic designs of "EDM wired figures" and "stack up" patterns and "lazer cut" and "torch cut" and "sawed" patterns combined. **Patterns:** Mostly "all mosaic" folders, automatics, fixed blades. **Technical:** Mosaic Damascus with all tool steel edges. **Prices:** $100 to $1000. **Remarks:** Part-time maker; first knife sold in 1987. **Mark:** WARDEN stamped or initials connected.

WARE, TOMMY,
158 Idlewilde, Onalaska, TX 77360, Phone: 936-646-4649
Specialties: Traditional working and using straight knives, folders and automatics of his design and to customer specs. **Patterns:** Hunters, automatics and locking folders. **Technical:** Grinds ATS-34, 440C and D2. Offers engraving and scrimshaw. **Prices:** $425 to $650; some to $1500. **Remarks:** Full-time maker; first knife sold in 1990. Doing business as Wano Knives. **Mark:** Last name inside oval, business name above, city and state below, year on side.

WARREN, AL,
1423 Sante Fe Circle, Roseville, CA 95678, Phone: 916-784-3217/Cell phone 916-257-5904, Fax: 215-318-2945, al@warrenknives.com; Web: www.warrenknives.com
Specialties: Working straight knives and folders, some fancy. **Patterns:** Hunters, Bowies, fillets, lockback, folders & multi blade. **Technical:** Grinds ATS-34 and S30V.440V. **Prices:** $135 to $3200. **Remarks:** Part-time maker; first knife sold in 1978. **Mark:** First and middle initials, last name.

WARREN, DANIEL,
571 Lovejoy Rd, Canton, NC 28716, Phone: 828-648-7351
Specialties: Using knives. **Patterns:** Drop point hunters. **Prices:** $200 to $500. **Mark:** Warren-Bethel NC.

WASHBURN, ARTHUR D,
ADW CUSTOM KNIVES, 211 Hinman St / PO Box 625, Pioche, NV 89043, Phone: 775-962-5463, knifeman@lcturbonet.com; Web: www.adwcustomknives.com
Specialties: Locking liner folders. **Patterns:** Slip joint folders (single and multiplied), lock-back folders, some fixed blades. Do own heat-treating; Rockwell test each blade. **Technical:** Carbon and stainless Damascus, some 1084, 1095, AEBL, 12C27, S30V. **Prices:** $200 to $1000 and up. **Remarks:** Sold first knife in 1997. Part-time maker. **Mark:** ADW enclosed in an oval or ADW.

WASHBURN JR., ROBERT LEE,
441 Sunland Dr., Apt 24, St George, UT 84790, Phone: 435-619-4432, Fax: 435-574-8554, rlwashburn@excite.com
Hand-forged period, Bowies, tactical, boot and hunters.
Patterns: Bowies, tantos, loot hunters, tactical and folders. **Prices:** $100 to $2500. **Remarks:** All hand forged. 52100 being his favorite steel. **Mark:** Washburn Knives W.

WATANABE, MELVIN,
1297 Kika St., Kailua, HI 96734, Phone: 808-261-2842, meltod808@yahoo.com
Specialties: Fancy folding knives. Some hunters. **Patterns:** Liner-locks and hunters. **Technical:** Grinds ATS-34, stainless Damascus. **Prices:** $350 and up. **Remarks:** Part-time maker, first knife sold in 1985. **Mark:** Name and state.

WATANABE, WAYNE,
PO Box 3563, Montebello, CA 90640, wwknives@gmail.com; Web: www.geocities.com/ww-knives
Specialties: Straight knives in Japanese-styles. One-of-a-kind designs; welcomes customer designs. **Patterns:** Tantos to katanas, Bowies. **Technical:** Flat grinds A2, O1 and ATS-34. Offers hand-rubbed finishes and wrapped handles. **Prices:** Start at $200. **Remarks:** Part-time maker. **Mark:** Name in characters with flower.

WATERS, GLENN,
11 Doncaster Place, Hyland Park, AUSTRALIA NSW 2448, Phone: 172-33-8881, watersglenn@hotmail.com; Web: www.glennwaters.com
Specialties: One-of-a-kind collector-grade highly embellished art knives. Folders, fixed blades, and automatics. **Patterns:** Locking liner folders, automatics and fixed art knives. **Technical:** Grinds blades from Damasteel, and selected Damascus makers, mostly stainless. Does own engraving, gold inlaying and stone setting, filework, and carving. Gold and Japanese precious metal fabrication. Prefers exotic material, high karat gold, silver, Shyaku Dou, Shibu Ichi Gin, precious gemstones. **Prices:** Upscale. **Remarks:** Designs and makes some-of-a-kind highly embellished art knives often with fully engraved handles and blades. A jeweler by trade for 20 years before starting to make knives. Full-time since 1999, first knife sold in 1994. **Mark:** Glenn Waters maker Japan, G. Waters or Glen in Japanese writing.

WATSON, BERT,
PO Box 26, Westminster, CO 80036-0026, Phone: 303-587-3064, watsonbd21960@q.com
Specialties: Working/using straight knives of his design and to customer specs. **Patterns:** Hunters, utility/camp knives. **Technical:** Grinds O1, ATS-34, 440C, D2, A2 and others. **Prices:** $150 to $800. **Remarks:** Full-time maker. **Mark:** GTK and/or Bert.

WATSON, BILLY,
440 Forge Rd, Deatsville, AL 36022, Phone: 334-365-1482, billy@watsonknives.com; Web: www.watsonknives.com
Specialties: Working and using straight knives and folders of his design; period pieces. **Patterns:** Hunters, Bowies and utility/camp knives. **Technical:** Forges and grinds his own Damascus, 1095, 5160 and 52100. **Prices:** $40 to $1500. **Remarks:** Full-time maker; first knife sold in 1970. Doing business as Billy's Blacksmith Shop. **Mark:** Last name.

WATSON, DANIEL,
350 Jennifer Ln, Driftwood, TX 78619, Phone: 512-847-9679, info@angelsword.com; Web: http://www.angelsword.com
Specialties: One-of-a-kind knives and swords. **Patterns:** Hunters, daggers, swords. **Technical:** Hand-purify and carbonize his own high-carbon steel, pattern-welded Damascus, cable and carbon-induced crystalline Damascus. Teehno-Wootz™ Damascus steel, heat treats including cryogenic processing. European and Japanese tempering. **Prices:** $125 to $25,000. **Remarks:** Full-time maker; first knife sold in 1979. **Mark:** "Angel Sword" on forged pieces; "Bright Knight" for stock removal. Avatar on Techno-Wootz™ Damascus. Bumon on traditional Japanese blades.

WATSON, PETER,
66 Kielblock St, La Hoff 2570, SOUTH AFRICA, Phone: 018-84942
Specialties: Traditional working and using straight knives and folders of his design. **Patterns:** Hunters, locking folders and utility/camp knives. **Technical:** Sandvik and 440C. **Prices:** $120 to $250; some to $1500. **Remarks:** Part-time maker; first knife sold in 1989. **Mark:** Buffalo head with name.

WATSON, TOM,
1103 Brenau Terrace, Panama City, FL 32405, Phone: 850-785-9209, tom@tomwatsonknives.com; Web: www.tomwatsonknives.com
Specialties: Utility/tactical linerlocks. **Patterns:** Tactical and utility. **Technical:** Flat grinds satin finished D2 and Damascus. **Prices:** Starting at $375. **Remarks:** Full time maker. In business since 1978. **Mark:** Name and city.

WATTELET, MICHAEL A,
PO Box 649, 125 Front, Minocqua, WI 54548, Phone: 715-356-3069, redtroll@frontier.com
Specialties: Working and using straight knives of his design and to customer specs; fantasy knives. **Patterns:** Daggers, fighters and swords. **Technical:** Grinds 440C and L6; forges and grinds O1. Silversmith. **Prices:** $75 to $1000; some to $5000. **Remarks:** Full-time maker; first knife sold in 1966. Doing business as M and N Arts Ltd. **Mark:** First initial, last name.

WATTS, JOHNATHAN,
9560 S Hwy 36, Gatesville, TX 76528, Phone: 254-487-2866
Specialties: Traditional folders. **Patterns:** One and two blade folders in various blade shapes. **Technical:** Grinds ATS-34 and Damascus on request. **Prices:** $120 to $400. **Remarks:** Part-time maker; first knife sold in 1997. **Mark:** J Watts.

WATTS, WALLY,
9560 S Hwy 36, Gatesville, TX 76528, Phone: 254-223-9669
Specialties: Unique traditional folders of his design. **Patterns:** One- to five-blade folders and single-blade gents in various blade shapes. **Technical:** Grinds ATS-34; Damascus on request. **Prices:** $150 to $400. **Remarks:** Full-time maker; first knife sold in 1986. **Mark:** Last name.

WEBSTER, BILL,
58144 West Clear Lake Rd, Three Rivers, MI 49093, Phone: 269-244-2873, wswebster_5@msn.com Web: www.websterknifeworks.com
Specialties: Working and using straight knives, especially for hunters. His patterns are custom designed. **Patterns:** Hunters, skinners, camp knives, Bowies and daggers. **Technical:** Hand-filed blades made of D2 steel only, unless other steel is requested. Preferred handle material is stabilized and exotic wood and stag. Sheaths are made by Green River Leather in Kentucky. Hand-sewn sheaths by Bill Dehn in Three Rivers, MI. **Prices:** $75 to $500. **Remarks:** Part-time maker, first knife sold in 1978. **Mark:** Originally WEB stamped on blade, at present, Webster Knifeworks Three Rivers, MI laser etched on blade.

WEEKS, RYAN,
PO Box 1101, Bountiful, UT 84001, Phone: 801-755-6789, ryan@ryanwknives.com; Web: www.ryanwknives.com
Specialties: Military and Law Enforcement applications as well as hunting and utility designs. **Patterns:** Fighters, bowies, hunters, and custom designs, I use man made as well as natural wood and exotic handle materials. **Technical:** Make via forge and stock removal methods, preferred steel includes high carbon, CPM154 CM and ATS34, Damascus and San Mai. **Prices:** $160 to $750. **Remarks:** Part-time maker; Business name is "Ryan W. Knives." First knife sold in 2009. **Mark:** Encircled "Ryan" beneath the crossed "W" UTAH, USA.

WEEVER, JOHN,
2400 N FM 199, Cleburne, TX 76033, Phone: 254-898-9595, john.weever@gmail.com; Web: WeeverKnives.com
Specialties: Traditional hunters (fixed blade, slip joint, and lockback) and tactical. **Patterns:** See website. **Technical:** Types of steel: S30V, Damascus or customer choice. Handles in mammoth ivory, oosic, horn, sambar, stag, etc. Sheaths in exotic leathers. **Prices:** $400 to $1200. **Remarks:** Stock removal maker full-time; began making knives in 1985. Member of knifemakers guild. **Mark:** Tang stamp: head of charging elephant with ears extended and WEEVER curved over the top.

WEHNER, RUDY,
297 William Warren Rd, Collins, MS 39428, Phone: 601-765-4997
Specialties: Reproduction antique Bowies and contemporary Bowies in full and miniature. **Patterns:** Skinners, camp knives, fighters, axes and Bowies. **Technical:** Grinds 440C, ATS-34, 154CM and Damascus. **Prices:** $100 to $500; some to $850. **Remarks:** Full-time maker; first knife sold in 1975. **Mark:** Last name on Bowies and antiques; full name, city and state on skinners.

WEILAND JR., J REESE,
PO Box 2337, Riverview, FL 33568, Phone: 813-671-0661, RWPHIL413@ earthlink.net; Web: www.rwcustomknive.som
Specialties: Hawk bills; tactical to fancy folders. **Patterns:** Hunters, tantos, Bowies, fantasy knives, spears and some swords. **Technical:** Grinds ATS-34, 154CM, 440C, D2, O1, A2, Damascus. Titanium hardware on locking liners and button locks. **Prices:** $150 to $4000. **Remarks:** Full-time maker, first knife sold in 1978. Knifemakers Guild member since 1988.

WEINAND, GEROME M,
14440 Harpers Bridge Rd, Missoula, MT 59808, Phone: 406-543-0845
Specialties: Working straight knives. **Patterns:** Bowies, fishing and camp knives, large special hunters. **Technical:** Grinds O1, 440C, ATS-34, 1084, L6, also stainless Damascus, Aebl and 304; makes all-tool steel Damascus; Dendritic D2 from powdered steel. Heat-treats. **Prices:** $30 to $100; some to $500. **Remarks:** Full-time maker; first knife sold in 1982. **Mark:** Last name.

WEINSTOCK, ROBERT,
PO Box 170028, San Francisco, CA 94117-0028, Phone: 415-731-5968, robertweinstock@att.net
Specialties: Folders, slip joins, lockbacks, autos. **Patterns:** Daggers, folders. **Technical:** Grinds A2, O1 and 440C. Chased and hand-carved blades and handles. Also using various Damascus steels from other makers. **Prices:** $3000 to 7000. **Remarks:** Full-time maker; first knife sold in 1994. **Mark:** Last name carved in steel.

WEISS, CHARLES L,
PO BOX 1037, Waddell, AZ 85355, Phone: 623-935-0924, weissknife@live.com
Specialties: High-art straight knives and folders; deluxe period pieces. **Patterns:** Daggers, fighters, boots, push knives and miniatures. **Technical:** Grinds 440C, 154CM and ATS-34. **Prices:** $300 to $1200; some to $2000. **Remarks:** Full-time maker; first knife sold in 1975. **Mark:** Name and city.

WELLING, RONALD L,
15446 Lake Ave, Grand Haven, MI 49417, Phone: 616-846-2274
Specialties: Scagel knives of his design or to customer specs. **Patterns:** Hunters, camp knives, miniatures, bird, trout, folders, double edged, hatchets, skinners and some art pieces. **Technical:** Forges Damascus 1084 and 1095. Antler, ivory and horn. **Prices:** $250 to $3000. **Remarks:** Full-time maker. ABS Journeyman maker. **Mark:** First initials and or name and last name. City and state. Various scagel kris (1or 2).

WELLING, WILLIAM,
Up-armored Knives, 5437 Pinecliff Dr., West Valley, NY 14171, Phone: 716-942-6031, uparmored@frontier.net; Web: www.up-armored.com
Specialties: Innovative tactical fixed blades each uniquely coated in a variety of Up-armored designed patterns and color schemes.Convexed edged bushcraft knives for the weekend camper, backpacker, or survivalist. Knives developed specifically for tactical operators. Leather lined kydex sheaths. **Patterns:** Modern samples of time tested designs as well as contemporary developed cutting tools. **Technical:** Stock removal specializing in tested 1095CV and 5160 steels. **Prices:** $200 to $500. **Remarks:** Part-time maker; first knife sold in 2010. **Mark:** Skull rounded up by Up-Armored USA.

WERTH, GEORGE W,
5223 Woodstock Rd, Poplar Grove, IL 61065, Phone: 815-544-4408
Specialties: Period pieces, some fancy. **Patterns:** Straight fighters, daggers and Bowies. **Technical:** Forges and grinds O1, 1095 and his Damascus, including mosaic patterns. **Prices:** $200 to $650; some higher. **Remarks:** Full-time maker. Doing business as Fox Valley Forge. **Mark:** Name in logo or initials connected.

WESCOTT, CODY,
5330 White Wing Rd, Las Cruces, NM 88012, Phone: 575-382-5008
Specialties: Fancy and presentation grade working knives. **Patterns:** Hunters, locking folders and Bowies. **Technical:** Hollow-grinds D2 and ATS-34; all knives file worked. Offers some engraving. Makes sheaths. **Prices:** $110 to $500; some to $1200. **Remarks:** Full-time maker; first knife sold in 1982. **Mark:** First initial, last name.

WEST, CHARLES A,
1315 S Pine St, Centralia, IL 62801, Phone: 618-532-2777
Specialties: Classic, fancy, high tech, period pieces, traditional and working/using straight knives and folders. **Patterns:** Bowies, fighters and locking folders. **Technical:** Grinds ATS-34, O1 and Damascus. Prefers hot blued finishes. **Prices:** $100 to $1000; some to $2000. **Remarks:** Full-time maker; first knife sold in 1963. Doing business as West Custom Knives. **Mark:** Name or name, city and state.

WESTBERG, LARRY,
305 S Western Hills Dr, Algona, IA 50511, Phone: 515-295-9276
Specialties: Traditional and working straight knives of his design and in standard patterns. **Patterns:** Bowies, hunters, fillets and folders. **Technical:** Grinds 440C, D2 and 1095. Heat-treats. Uses natural handle materials. **Prices:**

$85 to $600; some to $1000. **Remarks:** Part-time maker; first knife sold in 1987. **Mark:** Last name-town and state.

WHEELER, GARY,
351 Old Hwy 48, Clarksville, TN 37040, Phone: 931-552-3092, LR22SHTR@ charter.net
Specialties: Working to high end fixed blades. **Patterns:** Bowies, Hunters, combat knives, daggers and a few knives. **Technical:** Forges 5160, 1095, 52100 and his own Damascus. **Prices:** $125 to $2000. **Remarks:** Full-time maker since 2001, first knife sold in 1985 collaborates/works at B&W Blade Works. ABS Journeyman Smith 2008. **Mark:** Stamped last name.

WHEELER, ROBERT,
289 S Jefferson, Bradley, IL 60915, Phone: 815-932-5854, b2btaz@brmemc.net

WHETSELL, ALEX,
PO Box 215, Haralson, GA 30229, Phone: 770-463-4881, www.KnifeKits.com
Specialties: Knifekits.com, a source for fold locking liner type and straight knife kits. These kits are industry standard for folding knife kits. **Technical:** Many selections of colored G10 carbon fiber and wood handle material for kits, as well as bulk sizes for the custom knifemaker, heat treated folding knife pivots, screws, bushings, etc.

WHIPPLE, WESLEY A,
1002 Shoshoni St, Thermopolis, WY 82443, Phone: 307-921-2445, wildernessknife@yahoo.com
Specialties: Working straight knives, some fancy. **Patterns:** Hunters, Bowies, camp knives, fighters. **Technical:** Forges high-carbon steels, Damascus, offers relief carving and silver wire inlay and checkering. **Prices:** $300 to $1400; some higher. **Remarks:** Full-time maker; first knife sold in 1989. A.K.A. Wilderness Knife and Forge. **Mark:** Last name/JS.

WHITE, BRYCE,
1415 W Col Glenn Rd, Little Rock, AR 72210, Phone: 501-821-2956
Specialties: Hunters, fighters, makes Damascus, file work, handmade only. **Technical:** L6, 1075, 1095, O1 steels used most. **Patterns:** Will do any pattern or use his own. **Prices:** $200 to $300. Sold first knife in 1995. **Mark:** White.

WHITE, DALE,
525 CR 212, Sweetwater, TX 79556, Phone: 325-798-4178, dalew@taylortel.net
Specialties: Working and using knives. **Patterns:** Hunters, skinners, utilities and Bowies. **Technical:** Grinds 440C, offers file work, fancy pins and scrimshaw by Sherry Sellers. **Prices:** From $45 to $300. **Remarks:** Sold first knife in 1975. **Mark:** Full name, city and state.

WHITE, GARRETT,
871 Sarijon Rd, Hartwell, GA 30643, Phone: 706-376-5944
Specialties: Gentlemen folders, fancy straight knives. **Patterns:** Locking liners and hunting fixed blades. **Technical:** Grinds 440C, S30V, and stainless Damascus. **Prices:** $150 to $1000. **Remarks:** Part-time maker. **Mark:** Name.

WHITE, JOHN PAUL,
231 S Bayshore, Valparaiso, FL 32580, Phone: 850-729-9174, johnwhiteknives@ gmail.com
Specialties: Forged hunters, fighters, traditional Bowies and personal carry knives with handles of natural materials and fittings with detailed file work. **Technical:** Forges carbon steel and own Damascus. **Prices:** $500 to $3500**Remarks:** Master Smith, American Bladesmith Society. **Mark:** First initial, last name.

WHITE, LOU,
7385 Red Bud Rd NE, Ranger, GA 30734, Phone: 706-334-2273

WHITE, RICHARD T,
359 Carver St, Grosse Pointe Farms, MI 48236, Phone: 313-881-4690

WHITE, ROBERT J,
RR 1 641 Knox Rd 900 N, Gilson, IL 61436, Phone: 309-289-4487
Specialties: Working knives, some deluxe. **Patterns:** Bird and trout knives, hunters, survival knives and locking folders. **Technical:** Grinds A2, D2 and 440C; commercial Damascus. Heat-treats. **Prices:** $125 to $250; some to $600. **Remarks:** Full-time maker; first knife sold in 1976. **Mark:** Last name in script.

WHITE JR., ROBERT J BUTCH,
RR 1, Gilson, IL 61436, Phone: 309-289-4487
Specialties: Folders of all sizes. **Patterns:** Hunters, fighters, boots and folders. **Technical:** Forges Damascus; grinds tool and stainless steel. **Prices:** $500 to $1800. **Remarks:** Spare-time maker; first knife sold in 1980. **Mark:** Last name in block letters.

WHITENECT, JODY,
Elderbank, Halifax County, Nova Scotia, CANADA B0N 1K0, Phone: 902-384-2511
Specialties: Fancy and embellished working/using straight knives of his design and to customer specs. **Patterns:** Bowies, fighters and hunters. **Technical:** Forges 1095 and O1; forges and grinds ATS-34. Various filework on blades and bolsters. **Prices:** $200 to $400; some to $800. **Remarks:** Part-time maker; first knife sold in 1996. **Mark:** Longhorn stamp or engraved.

WHITESELL, J. DALE,
P.O. Box 455, Stover, MO 65078, Phone: 573-569-0753, dalesknives@yahoo. com; Web: whitesell-knives.webs.com
Specialties: Fixed blade working knives, and some collector pieces. **Patterns:** Hunting and skinner knives, camp knives, and kitchen knives. **Technical:** Blades ground from O1, 1095, and 440C in hollow, flat and saber grinds. Wood, bone, deer antler, and G10 are basic handle materials. **Prices:** $100 to $450. **Remarks:** Part-time maker, first knife sold in 2003. Doing business as Dale's

Knives. All knives have serial number to indicate steel (since June 2010).**Mark:** Whitesell on the left side of the blade.

WHITLEY, L WAYNE,
1675 Carrow Rd, Chocowinity, NC 27817-9495, Phone: 252-946-5648

WHITLEY, WELDON G,
4308 N Robin Ave, Odessa, TX 79764, Phone: 432-530-0448, Fax: 432-530-0048, wgwhitley@juno.com
Specialties: Working knives of his design or to customer specs. **Patterns:** Hunters, folders and various double-edged knives. **Technical:** Grinds 440C, 154CM and ATS-34. **Prices:** $150 to $1250. **Mark:** Name, address, road-runner logo.

WHITTAKER, ROBERT E,
PO Box 204, Mill Creek, PA 17060
Specialties: Using straight knives. Has a line of knives for buckskinners. **Patterns:** Hunters, skinners and Bowies. **Technical:** Grinds O1, A2 and D2. Offers filework. **Prices:** $35 to $100. **Remarks:** Part-time maker; first knife sold in 1980. **Mark:** Last initial or full initials.

WHITTAKER, WAYNE,
2900 Woodland Ct, Metamore, MI 48455, Phone: 810-797-5315, lindorwayne@yahoo.com
Specialties: Liner locks and autos.**Patterns:** Folders. **Technical:** Damascus, mammoth, ivory, and tooth. **Prices:** $500 to $1500. **Remarks:** Full-time maker. **Mark:** Inside of backbar.

WICK, JONATHAN P.,
300 Cole Ave., Bisbee, AZ 85603, Phone: 520-227-5228, vikingwick@aol.com Web: jpwickbladeworks.com
Specialties: Fixed blades, Bowies, hunters, neck knives, copper clad sheaths, collectibles, most handle styles and materials. **Technical:** Forged blades and own Damascus, along with shibuichi, mokume, lost wax casting. **Prices:** $250 - $1800 and up. **Remarks:** Full-time maker, ABS member, sold first knife in 2008. **Mark:** J P Wick, also on small blades a JP over a W.

WICKER, DONNIE R,
2544 E 40th Ct, Panama City, FL 32405, Phone: 904-785-9158
Specialties: Traditional working and using straight knives of his design or to customer specs. **Patterns:** Hunters, fighters and slip-joint folders. **Technical:** Grinds 440C, ATS-34, D2 and 154CM. Heat-treats and does hardness testing. **Prices:** $90 to $200; some to $400. **Remarks:** Part-time maker; first knife sold in 1975. **Mark:** First and middle initials, last name.

WIGGINS, BILL,
105 Kaolin Lane, Canton, NC 28716, Phone: 828-226-2551, wncbill@bellsouth.net Web: www.wigginsknives.com
Specialties: Forged working knives. **Patterns:** Hunters, Bowies, camp knives and utility knives of own design or will work with customer on design. **Technical:** Forges 1084 and 52100 as well as making own Damascus. **Prices:** $250 - $1500. **Remarks:** Part-time maker. First knife sold in 1989. ABS board member. **Mark:** Wiggins

WIGGINS, HORACE,
203 Herndon Box 152, Mansfield, LA 71502, Phone: 318-872-4471
Specialties: Fancy working knives. **Patterns:** Straight and folding hunters. **Technical:** Grinds O1, D2 and 440C. **Prices:** $90 to $275. **Remarks:** Part-time maker; first knife sold in 1970. **Mark:** Name, city and state in diamond logo.

WILCHER, WENDELL L,
RR 6 Box 6573, Palestine, TX 75801, Phone: 903-549-2530
Specialties: Fantasy, miniatures and working/using straight knives and folders of his design and to customer specs. **Patterns:** Fighters, hunters, locking folders. **Technical:** Hand works (hand file and hand sand knives), not grind. **Prices:** $75 to $250; some to $600. **Remarks:** Part-time maker; first knife sold in 1987. **Mark:** Initials, year, serial number.

WILKINS, MITCHELL,
15523 Rabon Chapel Rd, Montgomery, TX 77316, Phone: 936-588-2696, mwilkins@consolidated.net

WILLEY, WG,
14210 Sugar Hill Rd, Greenwood, DE 19950, Phone: 302-349-4070, Web: www.willeyknives.com
Specialties: Fancy working straight knives. **Patterns:** Small game knives, Bowies and throwing knives. **Technical:** Grinds 440C and 154CM. **Prices:** $350 to $600; some to $1500. **Remarks:** Part-time maker; first knife sold in 1975. Owns retail store. **Mark:** Last name inside map logo.

WILLIAMS, JASON L,
PO Box 67, Wyoming, RI 02898, Phone: 401-539-8353, Fax: 401-539-0252
Specialties: Fancy and high tech folders of his design, co-inventor of the Axis Lock. **Patterns:** Fighters, locking folders, automatics and fancy pocket knives. **Technical:** Forges Damascus and other steels by request. Uses exotic handle materials and precious metals. Offers inlaid spines and gemstone thumb knobs. **Prices:** $1000 and up. **Remarks:** Full-time maker; first knife sold in 1989. **Mark:** First and last initials on pivot.

WILLIAMS, MICHAEL,
Rt. 3 Box 276, Broken Bow, OK 74728, Phone: 580-420-3051, hforge@pine-net.com
Specialties: Functional, personalized, edged weaponry. Working and collectible art. **Patterns:** Bowies, hunters, camp knives, daggers, others. **Technical:** Forges high carbon steel and own forged Damascus. **Prices:** $500 - $12000. **Remarks:** Full-time ABS Master Smith. **Mark:** Williams MS.

WILLIAMS JR., RICHARD,
1440 Nancy Circle, Morristown, TN 37814, Phone: 615-581-0059
Specialties: Working and using straight knives of his design or to customer specs. **Patterns:** Hunters, dirks and utility/camp knives. **Technical:** Forges 5160 and uses file steel. Hand-finish is standard; offers filework. **Prices:** $80 to $180; some to $250. **Remarks:** Spare-time maker; first knife sold in 1985. **Mark:** Last initial or full initials.

WILLIAMSON, TONY,
Rt 3 Box 503, Siler City, NC 27344, Phone: 919-663-3551
Specialties: Flint knapping: knives made of obsidian flakes and flint with wood, antler or bone for handles. **Patterns:** Skinners, daggers and flake knives. **Technical:** Blades have width/thickness ratio of at least 4 to 1. Hafts with methods available to prehistoric man. **Prices:** $58 to $160. **Remarks:** Student of Errett Callahan. **Mark:** Initials and number code to identify year and number of knives made.

WILLIS, BILL,
RT 7 Box 7549, Ava, MO 65608, Phone: 417-683-4326
Specialties: Forged blades, Damascus and carbon steel. **Patterns:** Cable, random or ladder lamented. **Technical:** Professionally heat treated blades. **Prices:** $75 to $600. **Remarks:** Lifetime guarantee on all blades against breakage. All work done by maker; including leather work. **Mark:** WF.

WILLUMSEN, MIKKEL,
Nyrnberggade 23, 2300 Copenhagen S, Denmark, Phone: 4531176333, mw@willumsen-cph.com Web: www.wix.com/willumsen/urbantactical
Specialties: Folding knives, fixed blades, and balisongs. Also kitchen knives. **Patterns:** Primarily influenced by design that is function and quality based. Tactical style knives inspired by classical designs mixed with modern tactics. **Technical:** Uses CPM 154, RW 134, S30V, and carbon fiber titanium G10 for handles.**Prices:** Starting at $600.

WILSON, CURTIS M,
PO Box 383, Burleson, TX 76097, Phone: 817-295-3732, cwknifeman2026@att.net; Web: www.cwilsonknives.com
Specialties: Traditional working/using knives, fixed blade, folders, slip joint, LinerLock® and lock back knives. Art knives, presentation grade Bowies, folder repair, heat treating services. Sub-zero quench. **Patterns:** Hunters, camp knives, military combat, single and multi-blade folders. Dr's knives large or small or custom design knives. **Technical:** Grinds ATS-34, 440C 52100, D2, S30V, CPM 154, mokume gane, engraves, scrimshaw, sheaths leather of kykex heat treating and file work. **Prices:** $150-750. **Remarks:** Part-time maker since 1984. Sold first knife in 1993. **Mark:** Curtis Wilson in ribbon or Curtis Wilson with hand made in a half moon.

WILSON, JAMES G,
PO Box 4024, Estes Park, CO 80517, Phone: 303-586-3944
Specialties: Bronze Age knives; Medieval and Scottish-styles; tomahawks. **Patterns:** Bronze knives, daggers, swords, spears and battle axes; 12-inch steel Misericorde daggers, sgian dubhs, "his and her" skinners, bird and fish knives, capers, boots and daggers. **Technical:** Casts bronze; grinds D2, 440C and ATS-34. **Prices:** $49 to $400; some to $1300. **Remarks:** Part-time maker; first knife sold in 1975. **Mark:** WilsonHawk.

WILSON, MIKE,
1416 McDonald Rd, Hayesville, NC 28904, Phone: 828-389-8145
Specialties: Fancy working and using straight knives of his design or to customer specs, folders. **Patterns:** Hunters, Bowies, utility knives, gut hooks, skinners, fighters and miniatures. **Technical:** Hollow grinds 440C, L6, O1 and D2. Mirror finishes are standard. Offers filework. **Prices:** $50 to $600. **Remarks:** Full-time maker; first knife sold in 1985. **Mark:** Last name.

WILSON, PHILIP C,
SEAMOUNT KNIFEWORKS, PO Box 846, Mountain Ranch, CA 95246, Phone: 209-754-1990, seamount@bigplanet.com; Web: www.seamountknifeworks.com
Specialties: Working knives; emphasis on salt water fillet knives and utility hunters of his design. **Patterns:** Fishing knives, hunters, utility knives. **Technical:** Grinds CPM10V, S-90V, CPMS110V, K390, K294, CPM154, M-390, ELMAX. Heat-treats and Rockwell tests all blades. **Prices:** Start at $400. **Remarks:** First knife sold in 1985. Doing business as Sea-Mount Knife Works. **Mark:** Signature.

WILSON, RON,
2639 Greenwood Ave, Morro Bay, CA 93442, Phone: 805-772-3381
Specialties: Classic and fantasy straight knives of his design. **Patterns:** Daggers, fighters, swords and axes, mostly all miniatures. **Technical:** Forges and grinds Damascus and various tool steels; grinds meteorite. Uses gold, precious stones and exotic wood. **Prices:** Vary. **Remarks:** Part-time maker; first knives sold in 1995. **Mark:** Stamped first and last initials.

WILSON, RW,
PO Box 2012, Weirton, WV 26062, Phone: 304-723-2771, rwknives@comcast.net
Specialties: Working straight knives; period pieces. **Patterns:** Bowies, tomahawks and patch knives. **Technical:** Grinds 440C; scrimshaws. **Prices:** $85 to $175; some to $1000. **Remarks:** Part-time maker; first knife sold in 1966. Knifemaker supplier. Offers free knife-making lessons. **Mark:** Name in tomahawk.

WILSON, STAN,
8931 Pritcher Rd, Lithia, FL 33547, Phone: 727-461-1992, swilson@stanwilsonknives.com; Web: www.stanwilsonknives.com
Specialties: Fancy folders and automatics of his own design. **Patterns:** Locking liner folders, single and dual action autos, daggers. **Technical:** Stock removal, uses Damascus, stainless and high carbon steels, prefers ivory and pearl,

custom knifemakers

WILSON—YASHINSKI

Damascus with blued finishes and filework. **Prices:** $400 and up. **Remarks:** Member of Knifemakers Guild and Florida Knifemakers Association. Full-time maker will do custom orders. **Mark:** Name in script.

WILSON, VIC,
9130 Willow Branch Dr, Olive Branch, MS 38654, Phone: 901-233-7126, vdubjr55@earthlink.net
Specialties: Classic working and using knives and folders. **Patterns:** Hunters, boning, utility, camp, my patterns or customers. **Technical:** Grinds O1 and D2. Also does own heat treating. Offer file work and decorative liners on folders. Fabricate custome leather sheaths for all knives. **Prices:** $150 to $400. **Remarks:** Part-time maker, first knife sold in 1989. **Mark:** Etched V over W with oval circle around it, name, Memphis, MS.

WINGO, GARY,
240 Ogeechee, Ramona, OK 74061, Phone: 918-536-1067, wingg_2000@yahoo.com; Web: www.geocities.com/wingg_2000/gary.html
Specialties: Folder specialist. Steel 44OC, D2, others on request. Handle bone-stag, others on request. **Patterns:** Trapper three-blade stockman, four-blade congress, single- and two-blade barlows. **Prices:** 150 to $400. **Mark:** First knife sold 1994. Steer head with Wingo Knives or Straight line Wingo Knives.

WINGO, PERRY,
22 55th St, Gulfport, MS 39507, Phone: 228-863-3193
Specialties: Traditional working straight knives. **Patterns:** Hunters, skinners, Bowies and fishing knives. **Technical:** Grinds 440C. **Prices:** $75 to $1000. **Remarks:** Full-time maker; first knife sold in 1988. **Mark:** Last name.

WINKLER, DANIEL,
PO Box 2166, Blowing Rock, NC 28605, Phone: 828-295-9156, danielwinkler@bellsouth.net; Web: www.winklerknives.com
Specialties: Forged cutlery styled in the tradition of an era past as well as producing a custom-made stock removal line. **Patterns:** Fixed blades, friction folders, lock back folders, and axes/tomahawks. **Technical:** Forges, grinds, and heat treats carbon steels, specialty steels, and his own Damascus steel. **Prices:** $350 to $4000+. **Remarks:** Full-time maker since 1988. Exclusively offers leatherwork by Karen Shook. ABS Master Smith; Knifemakers Guild voting member. **Mark:** Hand forged: Dwinkler; Stock removal: Winkler Knives

WINN, MARVIN,
Maxcutter Custom Knives, 8711 Oakwood Ln., Frisco, TX 75035, Phone: 214-471-7012, maxcutter03@yahoo.com Web: www.maxcutterknives.com
Patterns: Hunting knives, some tactical and some miniatures. **Technical:** 1095, 5160, 154 CM, 12C27, CPMS30V and CPM154CM, Damascus or customer specs. Stock removal. **Prices:** $75 - $850. **Remarks:** Part-time maker. First knife made in 2002. **Mark:** Name, city, state.

WINN, TRAVIS A.,
558 E 3065 S, Salt Lake City, UT 84106, Phone: 801-467-5957
Specialties: Fancy working knives and knives to customer specs. **Patterns:** Hunters, fighters, boots, Bowies and fancy daggers, some miniatures, tantos and fantasy knives. **Technical:** Grinds D2 and 440C. Embellishes. **Prices:** $125 to $500; some higher. **Remarks:** Part-time maker; first knife sold in 1976. **Mark:** TRAV stylized.

WINSTON, DAVID,
1671 Red Holly St, Starkville, MS 39759, Phone: 601-323-1028
Specialties: Fancy and traditional knives of his design and to customer specs. **Patterns:** Bowies, daggers, hunters, boot knives and folders. **Technical:** Grinds 440C, ATS-34 and D2. Offers filework; heat-treats. **Prices:** $40 to $750; some higher. **Remarks:** Part-time maker; first knife sold in 1984. Offers lifetime sharpening for original owner. **Mark:** Last name.

WIRTZ, ACHIM,
Mittelstrasse 58, Wuerselen, D-52146, GERMANY, Phone: 0049-2405-462-486, wootz@web.de
Specialties: Medieval, Scandinavian and Middle East-style knives. **Technical:** Forged blades only, Damascus steel, Wootz, Mokume. **Prices:** Start at $200. **Remarks:** Part-time maker. First knife sold in 1997. **Mark:** Stylized initials.

WISE, DONALD,
304 Bexhill Rd, St Leonardo-On-Sea, East Sussex, TN3 8AL, ENGLAND
Specialties: Fancy and embellished working straight knives to customer specs. **Patterns:** Hunters, Bowies and daggers. **Technical:** Grinds Sandvik 12C27, D2 D3 and O1. Scrimshaws. **Prices:** $110 to $300; some to $500. **Remarks:** Full-time maker; first knife sold in 1983. **Mark:** KNIFECRAFT.

WOLF, BILL,
4618 N 79th Ave, Phoenix, AZ 85033, Phone: 623-910-3147, bwcustomknives143@gmail.com Web: billwolfcustomknives.com
Specialties: Investment grade knives. **Patterns:** Own designs or customer's. **Technical:** Grinds stainless and all steels. **Prices:** $400 to ? **Remarks:** First knife made in 1988. **Mark:** WOLF

WOLF JR., WILLIAM LYNN,
4006 Frank Rd, Lagrange, TX 78945, Phone: 409-247-4626

WOOD, ALAN,
Greenfield Villa, Greenhead, Brampton CA8 7HH, ENGLAND, a.wood@knivesfreeserve.co.uk; Web: www.alanwoodknives.co.uk
Specialties: High-tech working straight knives of his design. **Patterns:** Hunters, utility/camp and bushcraft knives. **Technical:** Grinds 12027, RWL-34, stainless Damascus and O1. Blades are cryogenic treated. **Prices:** $200 to $800; some to $750. **Remarks:** Full-time maker; first knife sold in 1979. Not currently taking orders. **Mark:** Full name with stag tree logo.

WOOD, OWEN DALE,
6492 Garrison St, Arvada, CO 80004-3157, Phone: 303-456-2748, wood.owen@gmail.com; Web: www.owenwoodcustomknives.com
Specialties: Folding knives and daggers. **Patterns:** Own Damascus, specialties in 456 composite blades. **Technical:** Materials: Damascus stainless steel, exotic metals, gold, rare handle materials. **Prices:** $1000 to $9000. **Remarks:** Folding knives in art deco and art noveau themes. Full-time maker from 1981. **Mark:** OWEN WOOD.

WOOD, WEBSTER,
22041 Shelton Trail, Atlanta, MI 49709, Phone: 989-785-2996, mainganikan@src-milp.com
Specialties: Works mainly in stainless; art knives, Bowies, hunters and folders. **Remarks:** Full-time maker; first knife sold in 1980. Retired guild member. All engraving done by maker. **Mark:** Initials inside shield and name.

WORLEY, JOEL A.,
PO BOX 64, Maplewood, OH 45340, Phone: 937-638-9518, j.a.worleyknives@woh.rr.com
Specialties: Bowies, hunters, fighters, utility/camp knives also period style friction folders. **Patterns:** Classic styles, recurves, his design or customer specified. **Technical:** Most knives are fileworked and include a custom made leather sheath. Forges 5160, W2, Cru forge V, files own Damascus of 1080 and 15N20. **Prices:** $250 and up. **Remarks:** Part-time maker. ABS member. First knife sold in 2005. **Mark:** First name, middle initial and last name over a shark incorporating initials.

WRIGHT, KEVIN,
671 Leland Valley Rd W, Quilcene, WA 98376-9517, Phone: 360-765-3589, kevinw@ptpc.com
Specialties: Fancy working or collector knives to customer specs. **Patterns:** Hunters, boots, buckskinners, miniatures. **Technical:** Forges and grinds L6, 1095, 440C and his own Damascus. **Prices:** $75 to $500; some to $2000. **Remarks:** Part-time maker; first knife sold in 1978. **Mark:** Last initial in anvil.

WRIGHT, L T,
1523 Pershing Ave, Steubenville, OH 43952, Phone: 740-282-4947, knifemkr@sbcglobal.net; Web: www.ltwrightknives.com
Specialties: Hunting and tactical knives. **Patterns:** Drop point hunters, bird, trout and tactical. **Technical:** Grinds D2, 440C and O1. **Remarks:** Full-time maker.

WRIGHT, RICHARD S,
PO Box 201, 111 Hilltop Dr, Carolina, RI 02812, Phone: 401-364-3579, rswswitchblades@hotmail.com; Web: www.richardswright.com
Specialties: Bolster release switchblades, tactical automatics. **Patterns:** Folding fighters, gents pocket knives, one-of-a-kind high-grade automatics. **Technical:** Reforges and grinds various makers Damascus. Uses a variety of tool steels. Uses natural handle material such as ivory and pearl, extensive file-work on most knives. **Prices:** $850 and up. **Remarks:** Full-time knifemaker with background as a gunsmith. Made first folder in 1991. **Mark:** RSW on blade, all folders are serial numbered.

WRIGHT, ROBERT A,
21 Wiley Bottom Rd, savannah, GA 31411, Phone: 912-598-8239; Cell: 912-656-9085, Fax: 912-598-8239, robwright57@yahoo.com; Web: www.RobWrightKnives.com
Specialties: Fixed blade fighters, hunting and skinning, fillets, small backpacker knives. **Patterns:** Customer and maker designs; sculpted handles of high quality materials. **Technical:** All types of steel (CPMS30V, D2< 440C, Damascus, etc.). **Prices:** $200 and up depending on design and materials. **Remarks:** Full-time maker, member of the Georgia knifemakers guild. Proven high quality steel and handle materials; exotic wood and other materials. **Mark:** Etched maple leaf with makers name.

WRIGHT, TIMOTHY,
PO Box 3746, Sedona, AZ 86340, Phone: 928-282-4180
Specialties: High-tech folders and working knives. **Patterns:** Interframe locking folders, non-inlaid folders, straight hunters and kitchen knives. **Technical:** Grinds BG-42, AEB-L, K190 and Cowry X; works with new steels. All folders can disassemble and are furnished with tools. **Prices:** $150 to $1800; some to $3000. **Remarks:** Full-time maker; first knife sold in 1975. **Mark:** Last name and type of steel used.

WUERTZ, TRAVIS,
2487 E Hwy 287, Casa Grande, AZ 85222, Phone: 520-723-4432

WULF, DERRICK,
25 Sleepy Hollow Rd, Essex, VT 05452, Phone: 802-777-8766, dickwulf@yahoo.com Web: www.dicksworkshop.com
Specialties: Makes predominantly forged fixed blade knives using carbon steels and his own Damascus. **Mark:** "WULF".

WYATT, WILLIAM R,
Box 237, Rainelle, WV 25962, Phone: 304-438-5494
Specialties: Classic and working knives of all designs. **Patterns:** Hunters and utility knives. **Technical:** Forges and grinds saw blades, files and rasps. Prefers stag handles. **Prices:** $45 to $95; some to $350. **Remarks:** Part-time maker; first knife sold in 1990. **Mark:** Last name in star with knife logo.

Y

YASHINSKI, JOHN L,
207 N Platt, PO Box 1284, Red Lodge, MT 59068, Phone: 406-446-3916
Specialties: Native American beaded sheaths, painted rawhide sheaths and tack sheaths. **Prices:** Vary.

YEATES, JOE A,
730 Saddlewood Circle, Spring, TX 77381, Phone: 281-367-2765, joeyeates291@cs.com; Web: www.yeatesBowies.com
Specialties: Bowies and period pieces. **Patterns:** Bowies, toothpicks and combat knives. **Technical:** Grinds 440C, D2 and ATS-34. **Prices:** $600 to $2500. **Remarks:** Full-time maker; first knife sold in 1975. **Mark:** Last initial within outline of Texas; or last initial.

YESKOO, RICHARD C,
76 Beekman Rd, Summit, NJ 07901

YORK, DAVID C,
PO Box 3166, Chino Valley, AZ 86323, Phone: 928-636-1709, dmatj@msn.com
Specialties: Working straight knives and folders. **Patterns:** Prefers small hunters and skinners; locking folders. **Technical:** Grinds D2. **Prices:** $75 to $300; some to $600. **Remarks:** Part-time maker; first knife sold in 1975. **Mark:** Last name.

YOSHIHARA, YOSHINDO,
8-17-11 Takasago Katsushi, Tokyo, JAPAN

YOSHIKAZU, KAMADA,
, 540-3 Kaisaki Niuta-cho, Tokushima, JAPAN, Phone: 0886-44-2319

YOSHIO, MAEDA,
, 3-12-11 Chuo-cho tamashima Kurashiki-city, Okayama, JAPAN, Phone: 086-525-2375

YOUNG, BUD,
Box 336, Port Hardy, BC, CANADA V0N 2P0, Phone: 250-949-6478
Specialties: Fixed blade, working knives, some fancy. **Patterns:** Drop-points to skinners. **Technical:** Hollow or flat grind, 5160, 440C, mostly ATS-34, satin finish. Using supplied damascus at times. **Prices:** $150 to $2000 CDN. **Remarks:** Spare-time maker; making knives since 1962; first knife sold in 1985. Not taking orders at this time, sell as produced. **Mark:** Name.

YOUNG, CLIFF,
Fuente De La Cibeles No 5, Atascadero, San Miguel De Allende, GTO., MEXICO, Phone: 37700, Fax: 011-52-415-2-57-11
Specialties: Working knives. **Patterns:** Hunters, fighters and fishing knives. **Technical:** Grinds all; offers D2, 440C and 154CM. **Prices:** Start at $250. **Remarks:** Part-time maker; first knife sold in 1980. **Mark:** Name.

YOUNG, ERROL,
4826 Storey Land, Alton, IL 62002, Phone: 618-466-4707
Specialties: Traditional working straight knives and folders. **Patterns:** Wide range, including tantos, Bowies, miniatures and multi-blade folders. **Technical:** Grinds D2, 440C and ATS-34. **Prices:** $75 to $650; some to $800. **Remarks:** Part-time maker; first knife sold in 1987. **Mark:** Last name with arrow.

YOUNG, GEORGE,
713 Pinoak Dr, Kokomo, IN 46901, Phone: 765-457-8893
Specialties: Fancy/embellished and traditional straight knives and folders of his design and to customer specs. **Patterns:** Hunters, fillet/camp knives and locking folders. **Technical:** Grinds 440C, CPM440V, and stellite 6K. Fancy ivory, black pearl and stag for handles. Filework: all stellite construction (6K and 25 alloys). Offers engraving. **Prices:** $350 to $750; some $1500 to $3000. **Remarks:** Full-time maker; first knife sold in 1954. Doing business as Young's Knives. **Mark:** Last name integral inside Bowie.

YOUNG, RAYMOND L,
CUTLER/BLADESMITH, 2922 Hwy 188E, Mt. Ida, AR 71957, Phone: 870-867-3947
Specialties: Cutler-Bladesmith, sharpening service. **Patterns:** Hunter, skinners, fighters, no guard, no ricasso, chef tools. **Technical:** Edge tempered 1095, 516C, mosaic handles, water buffalo and exotic woods. **Prices:** $100 and up. **Remarks:** Federal contractor since 1995. Surgical steel sharpening. **Mark:** R.

YURCO, MIKEY,
PO Box 712, Canfield, OH 44406, Phone: 330-533-4928, shorinki@aol.com
Specialties: Working straight knives. **Patterns:** Hunters, utility knives, Bowies and fighters, push knives, claws and other hideouts. **Technical:** Grinds 440C, ATS-34 and 154CM; likes mirror and satin finishes. **Prices:** $20 to $500. **Remarks:** Part-time maker; first knife sold in 1983. **Mark:** Name, steel, serial number.

Z

ZACCAGNINO JR., DON,
2256 Bacom Point Rd, Pahokee, FL 33476-2622, Phone: 561-985-0303, zackknife@gmail.com Web: www.zackknives.com
Specialties: Working knives and some period pieces of their designs. **Patterns:** Heavy-duty hunters, axes and Bowies; a line of light-weight hunters, fillets and personal knives. **Technical:** Grinds 440C and 17-4 PH; highly finished in complex handle and blade treatments. **Prices:** $165 to $500; some to $2500. **Remarks:** Part-time maker; first knife sold in 1969 by Don Zaccagnino Sr. **Mark:** ZACK, city and state inside oval.

ZAHM, KURT,
488 Rio Casa, Indialantic, FL 32903, Phone: 407-777-4860
Specialties: Working straight knives of his design or to customer specs. **Patterns:** Daggers, fancy fighters, Bowies, hunters and utility knives. **Technical:** Grinds D2, 440C; likes filework. **Prices:** $75 to $1000. **Remarks:** Part-time maker; first knife sold in 1985. **Mark:** Last name.

ZAKABI, CARL S,
PO Box 893161, Mililani Town, HI 96789-0161, Phone: 808-626-2181
Specialties: User-grade straight knives of his design, cord wrapped and bare steel handles exclusively. **Patterns:** Fighters, hunters and utility/camp knives. **Technical:** Grinds 440C and ATS-34. **Prices:** $90 to $400. **Remarks:** Spare-time maker; first knife sold in 1988. Doing business as Zakabi's Knifeworks LLC. **Mark:** Last name and state inside a Hawaiian sharktooth dagger.

ZAKHAROV, GLADISTON,
Bairro Rio Comprido, Rio Comprido Jacarei, Jacaret SP, BRAZIL 12302-070, Phone: 55 12 3958 4021, Fax: 55 12 3958 4103, arkhip@terra.com.br; Web: www.arkhip.com.br
Specialties: Using straight knives of his design. **Patterns:** Hunters, kitchen, utility/camp and barbecue knives. **Technical:** Grinds his own "secret steel." **Prices:** $30 to $200. **Remarks:** Full-time maker. **Mark:** Arkhip Special Knives.

ZBORIL, TERRY,
5320 CR 130, Caldwell, TX 77836, Phone: 979-535-4157, tzboril@tconline.net
Specialties: ABS Journeyman Smith.

ZEMBKO III, JOHN,
140 Wilks Pond Rd, Berlin, CT 06037, Phone: 860-828-3503, johnzembko@hotmail.com
Specialties: Working knives of his design or to customer specs. **Patterns:** Likes to use stabilized high-figured woods. **Technical:** Grinds ATS-34, A2, D2; forges O1, 1095; grinds Damasteel. **Prices:** $50 to $400; some higher. **Remarks:** First knife sold in 1987. **Mark:** Name.

ZEMITIS, JOE,
14 Currawong Rd, Cardiff Hts, 2285 Newcastle, AUSTRALIA, Phone: 0249549907, jjvzem@bigpond.com
Specialties: Traditional working straight knives. **Patterns:** Hunters, Bowies, tantos, fighters and camp knives. **Technical:** Grinds O1, D2, W2 and 440C; makes his own Damascus. Embellishes; offers engraving. **Prices:** $150 to $3000. **Remarks:** Full-time maker; first knife sold in 1983. **Mark:** First initial, last name and country, or last name.

ZERMENO, WILLIAM D.,
9131 Glenshadow Dr, Houston, TX 77088, Phone: 281-726-2459, will@wdzknives.com Web: www.wdzknives.com
Specialties: Tactical/utility folders and fixed blades. **Patterns:** Frame lock and liner lock folders the majority of which incorporate flippers and utility fixed blades. **Technical:** Grinds CPM 154, S30V, 3V and stainless Damascus. **Prices:** $250 - $600. **Remarks:** Part-time maker, first knife sold in 2008. Doing business as www.wdzknives.com. **Mark:** WDZ over logo.

ZIMA, MICHAEL F,
732 State St, Ft. Morgan, CO 80701, Phone: 970-867-6078, Web: http://www.zimaknives.com
Specialties: Working and collector quality straight knives and folders. **Patterns:** Hunters, lock backs, LinerLock®, slip joint and automatic folders. **Technical:** Grinds Damascus, 440C, ATS-34 and 154CM. **Prices:** $200 and up. **Remarks:** Full-time maker; first knife sold in 1982. **Mark:** Last name.

ZINKER, BRAD,
BZ KNIVES, 1591 NW 17 St, Homestead, FL 33030, Phone: 305-216-0404, bzknives@aol.com
Specialties: Fillets, folders and hunters. **Technical:** Uses ATS-34 and stainless Damascus. **Prices:** $200 to $600. **Remarks:** Voting member of Knifemakers Guild and Florida Knifemakers Association. **Mark:** Offset connected initials BZ.

ZIRBES, RICHARD,
Neustrasse 15, D-54526 Niederkail, GERMANY, Phone: 0049 6575 1371, r.zirbes@freenet.de Web: www.zirbes-knives.com www.zirbes-messer.de
Specialties: Fancy embellished knives with engraving and self-made scrimshaw (scrimshaw made by maker). High-tech working knives and high-tech hunters, boots, fighters and folders. All knives made by hand. **Patterns:** Boots, fighters, folders, hunters. **Technical:** Uses only the best steels for blade material like CPM-T 440V, CPM-T 420V, ATS-34, D2, C440, stainless Damascus or steel according to customer's desire. **Prices:** Working knives and hunters: $200 to $600. Fancy embellished knives with engraving and/or scrimshaw: $800 to $3000. **Remarks:** Part-time maker; first knife sold in 1991. Member of the German Knifemaker Guild. **Mark:** Zirbes or R. Zirbes.

ZOWADA, TIM,
4509 E Bear River Rd, Boyne Falls, MI 49713, Phone: 231-881-5056, tim@tzknives.com Web: www.tzknives.com
Specialties: Working knives and straight razors. **Technical:** Forges O1, L6, his own Damascus and smelted steel "Michi-Gane". **Prices:** $200 to $2500; some to $5000. **Remarks:** Full-time maker; first knife sold in 1980. **Mark:** Gothic, lower case "TZ"

ZSCHERNY, MICHAEL,
1840 Rock Island Dr, Ely, IA 52227, Phone: 319-848-3629, zschernyknives@aol.com
Specialties: Quality folding knives. **Patterns:** Liner-lock and lock-back folders in titanium, working straight knives. **Technical:** Grinds ATS-34 and commercial Damascus, prefers natural materials such as pearls and ivory. **Prices:** Starting at $500. **Remarks:** Full-time maker, first knife sold in 1978. **Mark:** Last name, city and state; folders, last name with stars inside folding knife.

AK

Barlow, Jana Poirier	Anchorage
Brennan, Judson	Delta Junction
Breuer, Lonnie	Wasilla
Broome, Thomas A	Kenai
Cawthorne, Christopher A	Wrangell
Chamberlin, John A	Anchorage
Dempsey, Gordon S	N. Kenai
Desrosiers, Adam	Petersburg
Desrosiers, Haley	Petersburg
Dufour, Arthur J	Anchorage
England, Virgil	Anchorage
Flint, Robert	Anchorage
Gouker, Gary B	Sitka
Grebe, Gordon S	Anchor Point
Harvey, Mel	Nenana
Hibben, Westley G	Anchorage
Hook, Bob	North Pole
Kelsey, Nate	Anchorage
Knapp, Mark	Fairbanks
Lance, Bill	Eagle River
Malaby, Raymond J	Juneau
Mcfarlin, Eric E	Kodiak
Miller, Nate	Fairbanks
Miller, Ron	North Pole
Miller, Terry	Healy
Mirabile, David	Juneau
Moore, Marve	Willow
Parrish Iii, Gordon A	North Pole
Stegall, Keith	Wasilla
Van Cleve, Steve	Sutton

AL

Batson, James	Madison
Baxter, Dale	Trinity
Bell, Tony	Woodland
Bowles, Chris	Reform
Brothers, Dennis L.	Oneonta
Coffman, Danny	Jacksonville
Conn Jr., C T	Attalla
Daniels, Alex	Town Creek
Dark, Robert	Oxford
Di Marzo, Richard	Birmingham
Durham, Kenneth	Cherokee
Elrod, Roger R	Enterprise
Gilbreath, Randall	Dora
Golden, Randy	Montgomery
Grizzard, Jim	Oxford
Hammond, Jim	Arab
Howard, Durvyn M	Hokes Bluff
Howell, Len	Opelika
Howell, Ted	Wetumpka
Huckabee, Dale	Maylene
Hulsey, Hoyt	Attalla
Mccullough, Jerry	Georgiana
Mcnees, Jonathan	Northport
Militano, Tom	Jacksonville
Morris, C H	Frisco City
Pardue, Melvin M	Repton
Roe Jr., Fred D	Huntsville
Russell, Tom	Jacksonville
Sinyard, Cleston S	Elberta
Smith, Lacy	Jacksonville
Thomas, David E	Lillian
Watson, Billy	Deatsville

AR

Anders, David	Center Ridge
Ardwin, Corey	North Little Rock
Barnes Jr., Cecil C.	Center Ridge
Brown, Jim	Little Rock
Browning, Steven W	Benton
Bullard, Benoni	Bradford
Bullard, Tom	Flippin
Cabe, Jerry (Buddy)	Hattieville

Cook, James R	Nashville
Copeland, Thom	Nashville
Cox, Larry	Murfreesboro
Crawford, Pat And Wes	West Memphis
Crotts, Dan	Elm Springs
Crowell, James L	Mtn. View
Dozier, Bob	Springdale
Duvall, Fred	Benton
Echols, Rodger	Nashville
Edge, Tommy	Cash
Ferguson, Lee	Hindsville
Ferguson, Linda	Hindsville
Fisk, Jerry	Nashville
Fitch, John S	Clinton
Flournoy, Joe	El Dorado
Foster, Ronnie E	Morrilton
Foster, Timothy L	El Dorado
Frizzell, Ted	West Fork
Gadberry, Emmet	Hattieville
Greenaway, Don	Fayetteville
Herring, Morris	Dyer
Hutchinson, Alan	Conway
Lawrence, Alton	De Queen
Lemoine, David C	Mountain Home
Livesay, Newt	Siloam Springs
Lunn, Gail	Mountain Home
Lunn, Larry A	Mountain Home
Lynch, Tad	Beebe
Maringer, Tom	Springdale
Martin, Bruce E	Prescott
Martin, Hal W	Morrilton
Massey, Roger	Texarkana
Newberry, Allen	Lowell
Newton, Ron	London
Olive, Michael E	Leslie
Passmore, Jimmy D	Hoxie
Pearce, Logan	De Queen
Perry, Jim	Hope
Perry, John	Mayflower
Peterson, Lloyd (Pete) C	Clinton
Polk, Clifton	Van Buren
Polk, Rusty	Van Buren
Red, Vernon	Conway
Reeves, J.R.	Texarkana
Rhea, Lin	Prattsville
Richards, Ralph (Bud)	Bauxite
Roberts, T. C. (Terry)	Fayetteville
Solomon, Marvin	Paron
Stanley, John	Crossett
Stout, Charles	Gillham
Sweaza, Dennis	Austin
Townsend, Allen Mark	Texarkana
Townsley, Russell	Concord
Walker, Jim	Morrilton
Ward, Chuck	Benton
White, Bryce	Little Rock
Young, Raymond L	Mt. Ida

AZ

Ammons, David C	Tucson
Bennett, Glen C	Tucson
Birdwell, Ira Lee	Congress
Boye, David	Dolan Springs
Bryan, Tom	Gilbert
Cheatham, Bill	Laveen
Choate, Milton	Somerton
Clark, R W	Surprise
Dawson, Barry	Prescott Valley
Dawson, Lynn	Prescott Valley
Deubel, Chester J.	Tucson
Dodd, Robert F	Camp Verde
Fuegen, Larry	Prescott
Goo, Tai	Tucson
Hancock, Tim	Scottsdale
Hoel, Steve	Pine
Holder, D'Alton	Wickenburg

Karp, Bob	Phoenix
Kiley, Mike And Jandy	Chino Valley
Kopp, Todd M	Apache Jct.
Lampson, Frank G	Rimrock
Lee, Randy	St. Johns
Mcfall, Ken	Lakeside
Mcfarlin, J W	Lake Havasu City
Miller, Michael	Kingman
Montell, Ty	Thatcher
Mooney, Mike	Queen Creek
Newhall, Tom	Tucson
Purvis, Bob And Ellen	Tucson
Robbins, Bill	Globe
Rybar Jr., Raymond B	Came Verde
States, Joshua C	New River
Tamboli, Michael	Glendale
Tollefson, Barry A	Tubac
Tyre, Michael A	Wickenburg
Weiss, Charles L	Waddell
Wick, Jonathan P.	Bisbee
Wolf, Bill	Phoenix
Wright, Timothy	Sedona
Wuertz, Travis	Casa Grande
York, David C	Chino Valley

CA

Abegg, Arnie	Huntington Beach
Adkins, Richard L	Mission Viejo
Athey, Steve	Riverside
Barnes, Gregory	Altadena
Barron, Brian	San Mateo
Benson, Don	Escalon
Berger, Max A.	Carmichael
Biggers, Gary	Ventura
Bost, Roger E	Palos Verdes
Boyd, Francis	Berkeley
Breshears, Clint	Manhattan Beach
Brooks, Buzz	Los Angles
Brous, Jason	Goleta
Browne, Rick	Upland
Bruce, Richard L.	Yankee Hill
Bruce, Richard L.	Yankee Hill
Butler, Bart	Ramona
Cabrera, Sergio B	Wilmington
Cantrell, Kitty D	Ramona
Caston, Darriel	Folsom
Caswell, Joe	Newbury
Clinco, Marcus	Venice
Coffey, Bill	Clovis
Coleman, John A	Citrus Heights
Connolly, James	Oroville
Cucchiara, Matt	Fresno
Davis, Charlie	Santee
De Maria Jr., Angelo	Carmel Valley
Dion, Greg	Oxnard
Dixon Jr., Ira E	Ventura
Dobratz, Eric	Laguna Hills
Doolittle, Mike	Novato
Driscoll, Mark	La Mesa
Dwyer, Duane	San Marcos
Ellis, Dave/Abs Mastersmith	Vista
Ellis, William Dean	Sanger
Emerson, Ernest R	Torrance
English, Jim	Jamul
English, Jim	Jamul
Ernest, Phil (Pj)	Whittier
Essegian, Richard	Fresno
Felix, Alexander	Torrance
Ferguson, Jim	Temecula
Forrest, Brian	Descanso
Fraley, D B	Dixon
Fred, Reed Wyle	Sacramento
Freer, Ralph	Seal Beach
Fulton, Mickey	Willows
Girtner, Joe	Brea
Gofourth, Jim	Santa Paula

Guarnera, Anthony R — Quartzhill
Hall, Jeff — Paso Robles
Hardy, Scott — Placerville
Harris, Jay — Redwood City
Harris, John — Riverside
Helton, Roy — San Diego
Herndon, Wm R "Bill" — Acton
Hink Iii, Les — Stockton
Hoy, Ken — North Fork
Humenick, Roy — Rescue
Iames, Gary — Tahoe
Jacks, Jim — Covina
Jackson, David — Lemoore
Jensen, John Lewis — Pasadena
Johnson, Randy — Turlock
Kazsuk, David — Perris
Kelly, Dave — Los Angeles
Keyes, Dan — Chino
Kilpatrick, Christian A — Citrus Hieghts
Koster, Steven C — Huntington Beach
Larson, Richard — Turlock
Leland, Steve — Fairfax
Lin, Marcus — Los Angeles
Lockett, Sterling — Burbank
Luchini, Bob — Palo Alto
Mackie, John — Whittier
Massey, Ron — Joshua Tree
Mata, Leonard — San Diego
Maxwell, Don — Clovis
Mcabee, William — Colfax
Mcclure, Michael — Menlo Park
Mcgrath, Patrick T — Westchester
Melin, Gordon C — La Mirada
Meloy, Sean — Lemon Grove
Montano, Gus A — San Diego
Morgan, Jeff — Santee
Moses, Steven — Santa Ana
Mutz, Jeff — Rancho Cucamonga
Naten, Greg — Bakersfield
Orton, Rich — Covina
Osborne, Donald H — Clovis
Packard, Bob — Elverta
Palm, Rik — San Diego
Panchenko, Serge — Citrus Heights
Pendleton, Lloyd — Volcano
Perry, Chris — Fresno
Pfanenstiel, Dan — Modesto
Pitt, David F — Anderson
Posner, Barry E — N. Hollywood
Quesenberry, Mike — Blairsden
Randall, Patrick — Newbury Park
Rozas, Clark D — Wilmington
Schmitz, Raymond E — Valley Center
Schneider, Herman — Apple Valley
Schroen, Karl — Sebastopol
Sibrian, Aaron — Ventura
Sjostrand, Kevin — Visalia
Slobodian, Scott — San Andreas
Smith, Shawn — Clouis
Sornberger, Jim — Volcano
St. Cyr, H Red — Wilmington
Stapel, Chuck — Glendale
Steinberg, Al — Laguna Woods
Stimps, Jason M — Orange
Stockwell, Walter — Redwood City
Strider, Mick — San Marcos
Terrill, Stephen — Springville
Tingle, Dennis P — Jackson
Torres, Henry — Clovis
Trujillo, Miranda — Rohnert Park
Vagnino, Michael — Visalia
Velick, Sammy — Los Angeles
Warren, Al — Roseville
Watanabe, Wayne — Montebello
Weinstock, Robert — San Francisco
Wilson, Philip C — Mountain Ranch
Wilson, Ron — Morro Bay

CO

Anderson, Mark Alan — Denver
Anderson, Mel — Hotchkiss
Booco, Gordon — Hayden
Brock, Kenneth L — Allenspark
Burrows, Chuck — Durango
Dannemann, Randy — Hotchkiss
Davis, Don — Loveland
Dennehy, John D — Loveland
Dill, Robert — Loveland
Fairly, Daniel — Bayfield
Fredeen, Graham — Colorado Springs
Fronefield, Daniel — Peyton
Hackney, Dana A. — Monument
High, Tom — Alamosa
Hockensmith, Dan — Berthoud
Hughes, Ed — Grand Junction
Irie, Michael L — Colorado Springs
Kitsmiller, Jerry — Montrose
Leck, Dal — Hayden
Miller, Don — Montrose
Miller, Hanford J — Cowdrey
Miller, M A — Northglenn
Ott, Fred — Durango
Owens, John — Nathrop
Rexford, Todd — Woodland Park
Roberts, Chuck — Golden
Rollert, Steve — Keenesburg
Ronzio, N. Jack — Fruita
Sanders, Bill — Mancos
Thompson, Lloyd — Pagosa Springs
Waites, Richard L — Broomfield
Watson, Bert — Westminster
Wilson, James G — Estes Park
Wood, Owen Dale — Arvada
Zima, Michael F — Ft. Morgan
Redd, Bill — Broomfield

CT

Buebendorf, Robert E — Monroe
Chapo, William G — Wilton
Cross, Kevin — Higganum
Framski, Walter P — Prospect
Jean, Gerry — Manchester
Loukides, David E — Cheshire
Meyer, Christopher J — Tolland
Plunkett, Richard — West Cornwall
Putnam, Donald S — Wethersfield
Rainville, Richard — Salem
Turecek, Jim — Ansonia
Vitale, Mace — Guilford
Zembko Iii, John — Berlin

DE

Willey, Wg — Greenwood

FL

Adams, Les — Hialeah
Alexander,, Oleg, And Cossack Blades — Wellington
Anders, Jerome — Miramar
Angell, Jon — Hawthorne
Atkinson, Dick — Wausau
Bacon, David R. — Bradenton
Barry Iii, James J. — West Palm Beach
Beers, Ray — Lake Wales
Benjamin Jr., George — Kissimmee
Blackwood, Neil — Lakeland
Bosworth, Dean — Key Largo
Bradley, John — Pomona Park
Bray Jr., W Lowell — New Port Richey
Brown, Harold E — Arcadia
Burris, Patrick R — Jacksonville
Butler, John — Havana

Chase, Alex — DeLand
Cole, Dave — Satellite Beach
D'Andrea, John — Citrus Springs
Davis Jr., Jim — Zephyrhills
Dietzel, Bill — Middleburg
Dintruff, Chuck — Seffner
Doggett, Bob — Brandon
Dotson, Tracy — Baker
Ellerbe, W B — Geneva
Ellis, Willy B — Palm Harbor
Enos Iii, Thomas M — Orlando
Ferrara, Thomas — Naples
Fowler, Charles R — Ft McCoy
Gamble, Roger — Newberry
Gibson Sr., James Hoot — Bunnell
Goers, Bruce — Lakeland
Granger, Paul J — Largo
Greene, Steve — Intercession City
Griffin Jr., Howard A — Davie
Grospitch, Ernie — Orlando
Harris, Ralph Dewey — Brandon
Heaney, John D — Haines City
Heitler, Henry — Tampa
Hodge Iii, John — Palatka
Hostetler, Larry — Fort Pierce
Humphreys, Joel — Lake Placid
Hunter, Richard D — Alachua
Hytovick, Joe "Hy" — Dunnellon
Jernigan, Steve — Milton
Johanning Custom Knives, Tom — Sarasota
Johnson, John R — Plant City
King, Bill — Tampa
Krapp, Denny — Apopka
Levengood, Bill — Tampa
Lewis, Mike — DeBary
Long, Glenn A — Dunnellon
Lovestrand, Schuyler — Vero Beach
Lozier, Don — Ocklawaha
Lyle Iii, Ernest L — Chiefland
Mandt, Joe — St. Petersburg
Mcdonald, Robert J — Loxahatchee
Mcgowan, Frank E — Sebring
Miller, Ronald T — Largo
Miller, Steve — Clearwater
Mink, Dan — Crystal Beach
Newton, Larry — Jacksonville
Ochs, Charles F — Largo
Owens, Donald — Melbourne
Parker, Cliff — Zephyrhills
Partridge, Jerry D. — DeFuniak Springs
Pattay, Rudy — Citrus Springs
Pendray, Alfred H — Williston
Piergallini, Daniel E — Plant City
Randall Made Knives, — Orlando
Reed, John M — Port Orange
Renner, Terry — Palmetto
Robinson, Calvin — Pace
Robinson Iii, Rex R — Leesburg
Rodkey, Dan — Hudson
Romeis, Gordon — Fort Myers
Russ, Ron — Williston
Schwarzer, Lora Sue — Crescent City
Schwarzer, Stephen — Crescent City
Smith, Michael J — Brandon
Stapleton, William E — Merritt Island
Steck, Van R — Orange City
Stephan, Daniel — Valrico
Stipes, Dwight — Palm City
Straight, Kenneth J — Largo
Tabor, Tim — Lutz
Turnbull, Ralph A — Spring Hill
Vogt, Donald J — Tampa
Watson, Tom — Panama City
Weiland Jr., J Reese — Riverview
White, John Paul — Valparaiso
Wicker, Donnie R — Panama City
Wilson, Stan — Lithia

Zaccagnino Jr., Don	Pahokee
Zahm, Kurt	Indialantic
Zinker, Brad	Homestead

GA

Arrowood, Dale	Sharpsburg
Ashworth, Boyd	Powder Springs
Barker, John	Cumming
Barker, Robert G.	Bishop
Bentley, C L	Albany
Bish, Hal	Jonesboro
Bradley, Dennis	Blairsville
Buckner, Jimmie H	Putney
Chamblin, Joel	Concord
Cole, Welborn I	Athens
Crockford, Jack	Chamblee
Daniel, Travis E	Thomaston
Davis, Steve	Powder Springs
Dunn, Charles K	Shiloh
Frost, Dewayne	Barnesville
Gaines, Buddy	Commerce
Glover, Warren D	Cleveland
Greene, David	Covington
Hammond, Hank	Leesburg
Hardy, Douglas E	Franklin
Hawkins, Rade	Fayetteville
Hensley, Wayne	Conyers
Hinson And Son, R	Columbus
Hoffman, Kevin L	Savannah
Hossom, Jerry	Duluth
Jones, Franklin (Frank) W	Columbus
Kimsey, Kevin	Cartersville
King, Fred	Cartersville
Knott, Steve	Guyton
Landers, John	Newnan
Lonewolf, J Aguirre	Demorest
Mathews, Charlie And Harry	Statesboro
Mcgill, John	Blairsville
Mclendon, Hubert W	Waco
Mitchell, James A	Columbus
Moncus, Michael Steven	Smithville
Parks, John	Jefferson
Poole, Marvin O	Commerce
Powell, Robert Clark	Smarr
Prater, Mike	Flintstone
Price, Timmy	Blairsville
Pridgen Jr., Larry	Fitzgerald
Ragsdale, James D	Ellijay
Roghmans, Mark	LaGrange
Rosenfeld, Bob	Hoschton
Sculley, Peter E	Rising Fawn
Smith Jr., James B "Red"	Morven
Snow, Bill	Columbus
Sowell, Bill	Macon
Stafford, Richard	Warner Robins
Thompson, Kenneth	Duluth
Tomey, Kathleen	Macon
Walters, A F	TyTy
Whetsell, Alex	Haralson
White, Garrett	Hartwell
White, Lou	Ranger
Wright, Robert A	savannah

HI

Evans, Vincent K And Grace	Keaau
Fujisaka, Stanley	Kaneohe
Gibo, George	Hilo
Lui, Ronald M	Honolulu
Mann, Tim	Honokaa
Matsuoka, Scot	Mililani
Mayo Jr., Tom	Waialua
Mitsuyuki, Ross	Honolulu
Nell, Chad	Kailua-Kona
Onion, Kenneth J	Kaneohe
Ouye, Keith	Honolulu

Watanabe, Melvin	Kailua
Zakabi, Carl S	Mililani Town

IA

Brooker, Dennis	Chariton
Brower, Max	Boone
Clark, Howard F	Runnells
Cockerham, Lloyd	Denham Springs
Helscher, John W	Washington
Lainson, Tony	Council Bluffs
Lewis, Bill	Riverside
Mckiernan, Stan	Lamoni
Miller, James P	Fairbank
Thie, Brian	Burlington
Trindle, Barry	Earlham
Westberg, Larry	Algona
Zscherny, Michael	Ely

ID

Alderman, Robert	Sagle
Alverson, Tim (R.V.)	Moscow
Bloodworth Custom Knives,	Meridian
Burke, Bill	Boise
Eddy, Hugh E	Caldwell
Hawk, Grant And Gavin	Idaho City
Hogan, Thomas R	Boise
Horton, Scot	Buhl
Howe, Tori	Athol
Mann, Michael L	Spirit Lake
Metz, Greg T	Cascade
Patton, Dick And Rob	Nampa
Quarton, Barr	McCall
Reeve, Chris	Boise
Rohn, Fred	Coeur d'Alene
Sawby, Scott	Sandpoint
Sparks, Bernard	Dingle
Steiger, Monte L	Genesee
Tippetts, Colten	Hidden Springs
Towell, Dwight L	Midvale
Trace Rinaldi Custom Blades,	Plummer

IL

Andersen, Karl B.	Watseka
Bloomer, Alan T	Maquon
Camerer, Craig	Chesterfield
Cook, Louise	Ozark
Cook, Mike	Ozark
Detmer, Phillip	Breese
Dicristofano, Anthony P	Northlake
Eaker, Allen L	Paris
Fiorini, Bill	Grayville
Hawes, Chuck	Weldon
Heath, William	Bondville
Hill, Rick	Maryville
Knuth, Joseph E	Rockford
Kovar, Eugene	Evergreen Park
Leone, Nick	Pontoon Beach
Markley, Ken	Sparta
Meers, Andrew	Carbondale
Meier, Daryl	Carbondale
Myers, Paul	Wood River
Myers, Steve	Virginia
Nevling, Mark	Hume
Nowland, Rick	Waltonville
Pellegrin, Mike	Troy
Pritchard, Ron	Dixon
Rosenbaugh, Ron	Crystal Lake
Rossdeutscher, Robert N	Arlington Heights
Rzewnicki, Gerald	Elizabeth
Schneider, Craig M	Claremont
Smale, Charles J	Waukegan
Smith, John M	Centralia
Todd, Richard C	Chambersburg

Tompkins, Dan	Peotone
Veit, Michael	LaSalle
Voss, Ben	Victoria
Werth, George W	Poplar Grove
West, Charles A	Centralia
Wheeler, Robert	Bradley
White, Robert J	Gilson
White Jr., Robert J Butch	Gilson
Young, Errol	Alton

IN

Adkins, Larry	Indianapolis
Ball, Ken	Mooresville
Barkes, Terry	Edinburgh
Barrett, Rick L. (Toshi Hisa)	Goshen
Bose, Reese	Shelburn
Bose, Tony	Shelburn
Chaffee, Jeff L	Morris
Claiborne, Jeff	Franklin
Cramer, Brent	Wheatland
Crowl, Peter	Waterloo
Damlovac, Sava	Indianapolis
Darby, Jed	Greensburg
Fitzgerald, Dennis M	Fort Wayne
Fraps, John R	Indianapolis
Good, D.R.	Tipton
Harding, Chad	Solsberry
Hunt, Maurice	Brownsburg
Imel, Billy Mace	New Castle
Johnson, C E Gene	Chesterton
Kain, Charles	Indianapolis
Keeslar, Steven C	Hamilton
Keeton, William L	Laconia
Kinker, Mike	Greensburg
Mayville, Oscar L	Marengo
Minnick, Jim	Middletown
Oliver, Todd D	Spencer
Patton, Phillip	Yoder
Quakenbush, Thomas C	Ft Wayne
Robertson, Leo D	Indianapolis
Seib, Steve	Evansville
Shull, James	Rensselaer
Smock, Timothy E	Marion
Snyder, Michael Tom	Zionsville
Thayer, Danny O	Romney
Young, George	Kokomo

KS

Bradburn, Gary	Wichita
Burrows, Stephen R	Humboldt
Chard, Gordon R	Iola
Craig, Roger L	Topeka
Culver, Steve	Meriden
Darpinian, Dave	Olathe
Davison, Todd A.	Lyons
Dawkins, Dudley L	Topeka
Dick, Dan	Hutchinson
Evans, Phil	Columbus
Hegwald, J L	Humboldt
Herman, Tim	Olathe
Keranen, Paul	Tacumseh
King, Jason M	Eskridge
King Jr., Harvey G	Alta Vista
Kraft, Steve	Abilene
Lamb, Curtis J	Ottawa
Magee, Jim	Salina
Petersen, Dan L	Auburn
Smith, Jerry	Oberlin
Stice, Douglas W	Wichita

KY

Addison, Kyle A	Hazel
Baskett, Barbara	Eastview
Baskett, Lee Gene	Eastview

Bodner, Gerald "Jerry" — Louisville
Bybee, Barry J — Cadiz
Carson, Harold J "Kit" — Vine Grove
Carter, Mike — Louisville
Coil, Jimmie J — Owensboro
Downing, Larry — Bremen
Dunn, Steve — Smiths Grove
Edwards, Mitch — Glasgow
Finch, Ricky D — West Liberty
Fister, Jim — Simpsonville
France, Dan — Cawood
Frederick, Aaron — West Liberty
Greco, John — Greensburg
Hibben, Daryl — LaGrange
Hibben, Gil — LaGrange
Hibben, Joleen — LaGrange
Hoke, Thomas M — LaGrange
Holbrook, H L — Sandy Hook
Howser, John C — Frankfort
Keeslar, Joseph F — Almo
Lott, Sherry — Greensburg
Pease, W D — Ewing
Pierce, Harold L — Louisville
Pulliam, Morris C — Shelbyville
Rados, Jerry F — Columbia
Richerson, Ron — Greenburg
Rigney Jr., Willie — Bronston
Smith, John W — West Liberty
Soaper, Max H. — Henderson
Steier, David — Louisville
Wallingford Jr., Charles W — Union

LA

Barker, Reggie — Springhill
Blaum, Roy — Covington
Caldwell, Bill — West Monroe
Calvert Jr., Robert W (Bob) — Rayville
Capdepon, Randy — Carencro
Capdepon, Robert — Carencro
Chauvin, John — Scott
Dake, C M — New Orleans
Dake, Mary H — New Orleans
Durio, Fred — Opelousas
Faucheaux, Howard J — Loreauville
Fontenot, Gerald J — Mamou
Gorenflo, James T (Jt) — Baton Rouge
Graves, Dan — Shreveport
Johnson, Gordon A. — Choudrant
Ki, Shiva — Baton Rouge
Laurent, Kermit — LaPlace
Leonard, Randy Joe — Sarepta
Mitchell, Max Dean And Ben — Leesville
Phillips, Dennis — Independence
Potier, Timothy F — Oberlin
Primos, Terry — Shreveport
Provenzano, Joseph D — Ponchatoula
Randall Jr., James W — Keithville
Randow, Ralph — Pineville
Reggio Jr., Sidney J — Sun
Sanders, Michael M — Ponchatoula
Tilton, John — Iowa
Trisler, Kenneth W — Rayville
Wiggins, Horace — Mansfield

MA

Banaitis, Romas — Medway
Cooper, Paul — Woburn
Dailey, G E — Seekonk
Dugdale, Daniel J. — Walpole
Entin, Robert — Boston
Gaudette, Linden L — Wilbraham
Gedraitis, Charles J — Holden
Grossman, Stewart — Clinton
Hinman, Theodore — Greenfield
Jarvis, Paul M — Cambridge

Khalsa, Jot Singh — Millis
Kubasek, John A — Easthampton
Lapen, Charles — W. Brookfield
Little, Larry — Spencer
Martin, Randall J — Bridgewater
Mcluin, Tom — Dracut
Moore, Michael Robert — Lowell
Rebello, Indian George — New Bedford
Reed, Dave — Brimfield
Rizzi, Russell J — Ashfield
Rua, Gary — Fall River
Saviano, James — Douglas
Siska, Jim — Westfield
Smith, J D — Roxbury
Stuart, Mason — Mansfield
Vining, Bill — Methuen

MD

Bagley, R. Keith — White Plains
Barnes, Aubrey G. — Hagerstown
Barnes, Gary L. — New Windsor
Cohen, N J (Norm) — Baltimore
Dement, Larry — Prince Fredrick
Fuller, Jack A — New Market
Gossman, Scott — Whiteford
Hart, Bill — Pasadena
Hendrickson, E Jay — Frederick
Hendrickson, Shawn — Knoxville
House, Nathan — Lonaconing
Kreh, Lefty — "Cockeysville"
Mccarley, John — Taneytown
Mcgowan, Frank E — Sykesvile
Merchant, Ted — White Hall
Nicholson, R. Kent — Phoenix
Nuckels, Stephen J — Hagerstown
Presti, Matt — Union Bridge
Sentz, Mark C — Taneytown
Smit, Glenn — Aberdeen
Sontheimer, G Douglas — Potomac
Spickler, Gregory Noble — Sharpsburg
St. Clair, Thomas K — Monrovia
Walker, Bill — Stevensville

ME

Bohrmann, Bruce — Yarmouth
Ceprano, Peter J. — Auburn
Coombs Jr., Lamont — Bucksport
Fogg, Don — Auburn
Gray, Daniel — Brownville
Hillman, Charles — Friendship
Leavitt Jr., Earl F — E. Boothbay
Oyster, Lowell R — Corinth
Sharrigan, Mudd — Wiscasset

MI

Ackerson, Robin E — Buchanan
Alcorn, Douglas A. — Chesaning
Andrews, Eric — Grand Ledge
Arms, Eric — Tustin
Behnke, William — Kingsley
Booth, Philip W — Ithaca
Buckbee, Donald M — Grayling
Carr, Tim — Muskegon
Carroll, Chad — Grant
Casey, Kevin — Hickory Corners
Cashen, Kevin R — Hubbardston
Cook, Mike A — Portland
Cousino, George — Onsted
Cowles, Don — Royal Oak
Dilluvio, Frank J — Prudenville
Ealy, Delbert — Indian River
Erickson, Walter E. — Atlanta
Gordon, Larry B — Farmington Hills

Gottage, Dante — Clinton Twp.
Gottage, Judy — Clinton Twp.
Harm, Paul W — Attica
Harrison, Brian — Cedarville
Hartman, Arlan (Lanny) — Baldwin
Hoffman, Jay — Munising
Hughes, Daryle — Nunica
Krause, Roy W — St. Clair Shores
Lankton, Scott — Ann Arbor
Lark, David — Kingsley
Leach, Mike J — Swartz Creek
Lucie, James R — Fruitport
Mankel, Kenneth — Cannonsburg
Marsh, Jeremy — Ada
Mills, Louis G — Ann Arbor
Morris, Michael S. — Yale
Noren, Douglas E — Springlake
Parker, Robert Nelson — Royal Oak
Repke, Mike — Bay City
Rose Ii, Doun T — Fife Lake
Sakmar, Mike — Howell
Sandberg, Ronald B — Brownstown
Serven, Jim — Fostoria
Tally, Grant — Flat Rock
Van Eizenga, Jerry W — Nunica
Vasquez, Johnny David — Wyandotte
Viste, James — Detroit
Webster, Bill — Three Rivers
Welling, Ronald L — Grand Haven
White, Richard T — Grosse Pointe Farms
Whittaker, Wayne — Metamore
Wood, Webster — Atlanta
Zowada, Tim — Boyne Falls

MN

Davis, Joel — Albert Lea
Gingrich, Justin — Blue Earth
Hagen, Doc — Pelican Rapids
Hansen, Robert W — Cambridge
Hebeisen, Jeff — Hopkins
Johnson, Jerry L — Worthington
Johnson, R B — Clearwater
Knipschield, Terry — Rochester
Leblanc, Gary E — Royalton
Maines, Jay — Wyoming
Metsala, Anthony — Princeton
Mickley, Tracy — North Mankato
Rydbom, Jeff — Annandale
Shadley, Eugene W — Grand Rapids
Voorhies, Les — Faribault

MO

Allred, Elvan — St. Charles
Andrews, Russ — Sugar Creek
Betancourt, Antonio L. — St. Louis
Braschler, Craig W. — Doniphan
Buxton, Bill — Kaiser
Chinnock, Daniel T. — Union
Cover, Jeff — Potosi
Cover, Raymond A — Festus
Cover, Raymond A — Mineral Point
Cox, Colin J — Raymore
Davis, W C — El Dorado Springs
Dippold, Al — Perryville
Duncan, Ron — Cairo
Ehrenberger, Daniel Robert — Mexico
Engle, William — Boonville
Hanson Iii, Don L. — Success
Harris, Jeffery A — Chesterfield
Harrison, Jim (Seamus) — St. Louis
Jim, Krause — Farmington
Jones, John A — Holden
Kinnikin, Todd — Pacific
Knickmeyer, Hank — Cedar Hill
Knickmeyer, Kurt — Cedar Hill

Martin, Tony	Arcadia
Mason, Bill	Excelsior Springs
Mccrackin, Kevin	House Spings
Mccrackin And Son, V J	House Spings
Miller, Bob	Oakville
Mosier, David	Independence
Mulkey, Gary	Branson
Muller, Jody	Goodson
Newcomb, Corbin	Moberly
Ramsey, Richard A	Neosho
Rardon, A D	Polo
Rardon, Archie F	Polo
Riepe, Richard A	Harrisonville
Robbins, Howard P	Flemington
Royer, Kyle	Mountain View
Scroggs, James A	Warrensburg
Seaton, David D	Rolla
Sonntag, Douglas W	Nixa
Sonntag, Jacob D	Robert
Sonntag, Kristopher D	Nixa
Steketee, Craig A	Billings
Stewart, Edward L	Mexico
Stormer, Bob	Dixon
Warden, Roy A	Union
Whitesell, J. Dale	Stover
Willis, Bill	Ava

MS

Black, Scott	Picayune
Boleware, David	Carson
Cohea, John M	Nettleton
Davis, Jesse W	Sarah
Evans, Bruce A	Booneville
Flynt, Robert G	Gulfport
Jones, Jack P.	Ripley
Lamey, Robert M	Biloxi
Lebatard, Paul M	Vancleave
May, Charles	Aberdeen
Mayo Jr., Homer	Biloxi
Nichols, Chad	Blue Springs
Phillips, Donavon	Morton
Pickett, Terrell	Lumberton
Roberts, Michael	Clinton
Robinson, Chuck	Picayune
Shiffer, Steve	Leakesville
Smith, J.B.	Perkinston
Taylor, Billy	Petal
Vandeventer, Terry L	Terry
Vardaman, Robert	Hattiesburg
Wehner, Rudy	Collins
Wilson, Vic	Olive Branch
Wingo, Perry	Gulfport
Winston, David	Starkville

MT

Barnes, Jack	Whitefish
Barnes, Wendell	Clinton
Barth, J.D.	Alberton
Beam, John R.	Kalispell
Beaty, Robert B.	Missoula
Bell, Don	Lincoln
Bizzell, Robert	Butte
Boxer, Bo	Whitefish
Brooks, Steve R	Walkerville
Caffrey, Edward J	Great Falls
Campbell, Doug	McLeod
Carlisle, Jeff	Simms
Christensen, Jon P	Stevensville
Colter, Wade	Colstrip
Conklin, George L	Ft. Benton
Crowder, Robert	Thompson Falls
Curtiss, Steve L	Eureka
Dunkerley, Rick	Lincoln
Eaton, Rick	Broadview

Ellefson, Joel	Manhattan
Fassio, Melvin G	Lolo
Forthofer, Pete	Whitefish
Fritz, Erik L	Forsyth
Gallagher, Barry	Lewistown
Harkins, J A	Conner
Hill, Howard E	Polson
Hintz, Gerald M	Helena
Hulett, Steve	West Yellowstone
Kajin, Al	Forsyth
Kauffman, Dave	Montana City
Kelly, Steven	Bigfork
Luman, James R	Anaconda
Mcguane Iv, Thomas F	Bozeman
Mckee, Neil	Stevensville
Moyer, Russ	Havre
Nedved, Dan	Kalispell
Olson, Joe	Geyser
Parsons, Pete	Helena
Patrick, Willard C	Helena
Peele, Bryan	Thompson Falls
Peterson, Eldon G	Whitefish
Pursley, Aaron	Big Sandy
Rodewald, Gary	Hamilton
Ruana Knife Works,	Bonner
Smith, Josh	Frenchtown
Sweeney, Coltin D	Missoula
Taylor, Shane	Miles City
Thill, Jim	Missoula
Weinand, Gerome M	Missoula
Yashinski, John L	Red Lodge

NC

Baker, Herb	Eden
Barefoot, Joe W.	Wilmington
Best, Ron	Stokes
Bisher, William (Bill)	Denton
Brackett, Jamin	Fallston
Britton, Tim	Bethania
Busfield, John	Roanoke Rapids
Crist, Zoe	Flat Rock
Drew, Gerald	Mill Spring
Edwards, Fain E	Topton
Fox, Paul	Claremont
Gaddy, Gary Lee	Washington
Goode, Brian	Shelby
Greene, Chris	Shelby
Gross, W W	Archdale
Gurganus, Carol	Colerain
Gurganus, Melvin H	Colerain
Johnson, Tommy	Troy
Laramie, Mark	Raeford
Livingston, Robert C	Murphy
Maynard, William N.	Fayetteville
Mclurkin, Andrew	Raleigh
Mcnabb, Tommy	Bethania
Mcrae, J Michael	Mint Hill
Parrish, Robert	Weaverville
Patrick, Chuck	Brasstown
Patrick, Peggy	Brasstown
Rapp, Steven J	Marshall
Santini, Tom	Pikeville
Scholl, Tim	Angier
Simmons, H R	Aurora
Sterling, Murray	Mount Airy
Summers, Arthur L	Concord
Sutton, S Russell	New Bern
Vail, Dave	Hampstead
Wacholz, Doc	Marble
Wagaman, John K	Selma
Walker, Don	Burnsville
Warren, Daniel	Canton
Whitley, L Wayne	Chocowinity
Wiggins, Bill	Canton
Williamson, Tony	Siler City

Wilson, Mike	Hayesville
Winkler, Daniel	Blowing Rock

ND

Kommer, Russ	Fargo
Pitman, David	Williston

NE

Archer, Ray And Terri	Omaha
Hielscher, Guy	Alliance
Jokerst, Charles	Omaha
Marlowe, Charles	Omaha
Moore, Jon P	Aurora
Mosier, Joshua J	Deshler
Schepers, George B	Shelton
Sloan, David	Diller
Suedmeier, Harlan	Nebraska City
Syslo, Chuck	Omaha
Tiensvold, Alan L	Rushville
Tiensvold, Jason	Rushville
Till, Calvin E And Ruth	Chadron

NH

Hill, Steve E	Goshen
Hitchmough, Howard	Peterborough
Hudson, C Robbin	Rummney
Macdonald, John	Raymond
Philippe, D A	Cornish
Saindon, R Bill	Goshen

NJ

Eden, Thomas	Cranbury
Fisher, Lance	Pompton Lakes
Grussenmeyer, Paul G	Cherry Hill
Knowles, Shawn	Great Meadows
Lesswing, Kevin	Bayonne
Licata, Steven	Boonton
Mccallen Jr., Howard H	So Seaside Park
Pressburger, Ramon	Howell
Sheets, Steven William	Mendham
Slee, Fred	Morganville
Viele, H J	Westwood
Yeskoo, Richard C	Summit

NM

Black, Tom	Albuquerque
Burnley, Lucas	Albuquerque
Cherry, Frank J	Albuquerque
Cordova, Joseph G	Bosque Farms
Cumming, Bob	Cedar Crest
Digangi, Joseph M	Santa Cruz
Duran, Jerry T	Albuquerque
Dyess, Eddie	Roswell
Fisher, Jay	Clovis
Garner, George	Albuquerque
Goode, Bear	Navajo Dam
Gunter, Brad	Tijeras
Hartman, Tim	Albuquerque
Hethcoat, Don	Clovis
Hume, Don	Albuquerque
Kimberley, Richard L.	Santa Fe
Leu, Pohan	Rio Rancho
Lewis, Tom R	Carlsbad
Lynn, Arthur	Galisteo
Macdonald, David	Los Lunas
Mallett, J.P.	Santa Fe
Mcdonald, Robin J	Albuquerque
Meshejian, Mardi	Santa Fe
Pollock, Wallace J	Reserve
Reid, Jim	Albuquerque
Rogers, Richard	Magdalena
Schaller, Anthony Brett	Albuquerque

Stalcup, Eddie — Gallup
Stetter, J. C. — Roswell
Terzuola, Robert — Albuquerque
Trujillo, Albert M B — Bosque Farms
Walker, Michael L — Pueblo Sur Taos
Wescott, Cody — Las Cruces

NV

Barnett, Van — Reno
Beasley, Geneo — Wadsworth
Bingenheimer, Bruce — Spring Creek
Cameron, Ron G — Logandale
Dellana, — Reno
George, Tom — Henderson
Hrisoulas, Jim — Henderson
Kreibich, Donald L. — Reno
Nishiuchi, Melvin S — Las Vegas
Thomas, Devin — Panaca
Tracy, Bud — Reno
Washburn, Arthur D — Pioche

NY

Baker, Wild Bill — Boiceville
Castellucio, Rich — Amsterdam
Davis, Barry L — Castleton
Farr, Dan — Rochester
Faust, Dick — Rochester
Hobart, Gene — Windsor
Johnson, Mike — Orient
Johnston, Dr. Robt — Rochester
Levin, Jack — Brooklyn
Loos, Henry C — New Hyde Park
Ludwig, Richard O — Maspeth
Lupole, Jamie G — Kirkwood
Manaro, Sal — Holbrook
Maragni, Dan — Georgetown
Mccornock, Craig — Willow
Meerdink, Kurt — Barryville
Page, Reginald — Groveland
Phillips, Scott C — Gouverneur
Rachlin, Leslie S — Elmira
Rappazzo, Richard — Cohoes
Rotella, Richard A — Niagara Falls
Scheid, Maggie — Rochester
Schippnick, Jim — Sanborn
Serafen, Steven E — New Berlin
Skiff, Steven — Broadalbin
Smith, Lenard C — Valley Cottage
Smith, Raymond L — Erin
Summers, Dan — Whitney Pt.
Szilaski, Joseph — Pine Plains
Turner, Kevin — Montrose
Welling, William — West Valley

OH

Bendik, John — Olmsted Falls
Busse, Jerry — Wauseon
Coffee, Jim — Norton
Collins, Lynn M — Elyria
Coppins, Daniel — Cambridge
Cottrill, James I — Columbus
Downing, Tom — Cuyahoga Falls
Downs, James F — Powell
Etzler, John — Grafton
Francis, John D — Ft. Loramie
Franklin, Mike — Aberdeen
Geisler, Gary R — Clarksville
Gittinger, Raymond — Tiffin
Glover, Ron — Mason
Greiner, Richard — Green Springs
Hinderer, Rick — Shreve
Hudson, Anthony B — Amanda
Humphrey, Lon — Newark

Imboden Ii, Howard L. — Dayton
Johnson, Wm. C. "Bill" — Enon
Jones, Roger Mudbone — Waverly
Kiefer, Tony — Pataskala
Longworth, Dave — Neville
Loro, Gene — Crooksville
Maienknecht, Stanley — Sardis
Mcdonald, Rich — Hillboro
Mcgroder, Patrick J — Madison
Mercer, Mike — Lebanon
Messer, David T — Dayton
Morgan, Tom — Beloit
Munjas, Bob — Waterford
O'Machearley, Michael — Wilmington
Panak, Paul S — Andover
Potter, Billy — Dublin
Ralph, Darrel — Galena
Rose, Derek W — Gallipolis
Rowe, Fred — Amesville
Salley, John D — Tipp City
Schuchmann, Rick — Cincinnati
Sheely, "Butch" Forest — Grand Rapids
Shinosky, Andy — Canfield
Shoemaker, Carroll — Northup
Shoemaker, Scott — Miamisburg
Spinale, Richard — Lorain
Stoddart, Jeff — Cincinnati
Strong, Scott — Beavercreek
Summers, Dennis K — Springfield
Thomas, Kim — Seville
Thourot, Michael W — Napoleon
Tindera, George — Brunswick
Trout, George H. — Wilmington
Votaw, David P — Pioneer
Ward, J J — Waverly
Worley, Joel A. — Maplewood
Wright, L T — Steubenville
Yurco, Mikey — Canfield
Stidham, Daniel — Gallipolis

OK

Baker, Ray — Sapulpa
Carrillo, Dwaine — Moore
Coye, Bill — Tulsa
Crenshaw, Al — Eufaula
Crowder, Gary L — Sallisaw
Damasteel Stainless Damascus, — Norman
Darby, David T — Cookson
Dill, Dave — Bethany
Duff, Bill — Poteau
Gepner, Don — Norman
Giraffebone Inc., — Norman
Heimdale, J E — Tulsa
Johns, Rob — Enid
Kennedy Jr., Bill — Yukon
Kirk, Ray — Tahlequah
Lairson Sr., Jerry — Ringold
Martin
Martin, John Alexander — Okmulgee
Mcclure, Jerry — Norman
Menefee, Ricky Bob — Blawchard
Miller, Michael E — Chandler
Parsons, Larry — Mustang
Shropshire, Shawn — Piedmont
Spivey, Jefferson — Yukon
Stanford, Perry — Broken Arrow
Tomberlin, Brion R — Norman
Williams, Michael — Broken Bow
Wingo, Gary — Ramona

OR

Bell, Gabriel — Coquille
Bell, Michael — Coquille
Bochman, Bruce — Grants Pass
Brandt, Martin W — Springfield

Buchanan, Thad — Prineville
Buchner, Bill — Idleyld Park
Busch, Steve — Oakland
Carter, Murray M — Hillsboro
Clark, Nate — Yoncalla
Coon, Raymond C — Damascus
Crowner, Jeff — Cottage Grove
Davis, Terry — Sumpter
Dowell, T M — Bend
Eirich, William — Bend
Frank, Heinrich H — Dallas
Gamble, Frank — Salem
Goddard, Wayne — Eugene
Harsey, William H — Creswell
Hilker, Thomas N — Williams
Horn, Jess — Eugene
House, Cameron — Salem
Kelley, Gary — Aloha
Lake, Ron — Eugene
Little, Gary M — Broadbent
Magruder, Jason — Talent
Martin, Gene — Williams
Martin, Walter E — Williams
Ochs, Eric — Sherwood
Olson, Darrold E — McMinnville
Pruyn, Peter — Grants Pass
Richard, Raymond — Gresham
Richards, Chuck — Salem
Rider, David M — Eugene
Sarganis, Paul — Jacksonville
Scarrow, Wil — Gold Hill
Schoeningh, Mike — North Powder
Schrader, Robert — Bend
Sevey Custom Knife, — Gold Beach
Sheehy, Thomas J — Portland
Shoger, Mark O — Beaverton
Sibert, Shane — Gladstone
Smith, Rick — Rogue River
Tendick, Ben — Eugene
Thompson, Leon — Gaston
Thompson, Tommy — Portland
Turner, Mike — Williams
Vallotton, Butch And Arey — Oakland
Vallotton, Rainy D — Umpqua
Vallotton, Shawn — Oakland
Vallotton, Thomas — Oakland
Ward, Ken — Grants Pass

PA

Anderson, Gary D — Spring Grove
Anderson, Tom — Manchester
Appleby, Robert — Shickshinny
Besedick, Frank E — Monongahela
Blystone, Ronald L. — Creekside
Candrella, Joe — Warminster
Clark, D E (Lucky) — Johnstown
Corkum, Steve — Littlestown
Darby, Rick — Levittown
Derespina, Richard — Willow Grove
Derespina, Richard — Willow Grove
Evans, Ronald B — Middleton
Frey Jr., W Frederick — Milton
Godlesky, Bruce F. — Apollo
Goldberg, David — Ft Washington
Gottschalk, Gregory J — Carnegie
Harner, Lloyd R. "Butch" — Hanover
Heinz, John — Upper Black Eddy
Hudson, Rob — Northumberland
Johnson, John R — New Buffalo
Jones, Curtis J — Washington
Malloy, Joe — Freeland
Marlowe, Donald — Dover
Mensch, Larry C — Milton
Miller, Rick — Rockwood
Moore, Ted — Elizabethtown

Morett, Donald	Lancaster
Nealy, Bud	Stroudsburg
Neilson, J	Wyalusing
Ogden, Bill	Avis
AVIS	
Ortega, Ben M	Wyoming
Parker, J E	Clarion
Root, Gary	Erie
Rose, Bob	Wagontown
Rupert, Bob	Clinton
Sass, Gary N	Sharpsville
Scimio, Bill	Spruce Creek
Sinclair, J E	Pittsburgh
Smith, Richard J.	Milford
Steigerwalt, Ken	Orangeville
Stroyan, Eric	Dalton
Takach, Andrew	Elizabeth
Valois, A. Daniel	Lehighton
Vaughan, Ian	Manheim
Whittaker, Robert E	Mill Creek

RI

Dickison, Scott S	Portsmouth
Jacques, Alex	East Greenwich
Mchenry, William James	Wyoming
Olszewski, Stephen	Coventry
Williams, Jason L	Wyoming
Wright, Richard S	Carolina

SC

Beatty, Gordon H.	Seneca
Branton, Robert	Awendaw
Brend, Walter	Ridge Springs
Cannady, Daniel L	Allendale
Cox, Sam	Gaffney
Denning, Geno	Gaston
Fecas, Stephen J	Anderson
Frazier, Jim	Wagener
Gainey, Hal	Greenwood
George, Harry	Aiken
Gregory, Michael	Belton
Hendrix, Jerry	Clinton
Hendrix, Wayne	Allendale
Hucks, Jerry	Moncks Corner
Kay, J Wallace	Liberty
Knight, Jason	Harleyville
Kreger, Thomas	Lugoff
Langley, Gene H	Florence
Lutz, Greg	Greenwood
Manley, David W	Central
Miles Jr., C R "Iron Doctor"	Lugoff
Odom Jr., Victor L.	North
Page, Larry	Aiken
Parler, Thomas O	Charleston
Peagler, Russ	Moncks Corner
Perry, Johnny	Inman
Sears, Mick	Kershaw
Smith, Ralph L	Taylors
Thomas, Rocky	Moncks Corner
Tyser, Ross	Spartanburg

SD

Boley, Jamie	Parker
Boysen, Raymond A	Rapid Ciy
Ferrier, Gregory K	Rapid City
Miller, Skip	Keystone
Thomsen, Loyd W	Oelrichs

TN

Accawi, Fuad	Clinton
Adams, Jim	Cordova
Bailey, Joseph D.	Nashville
Blanchard, G R (Gary)	Dandridge
Breed, Kim	Clarksville

Byrd, Wesley L	Evensville
Canter, Ronald E	Jackson
Casteel, Dianna	Monteagle
Casteel, Douglas	Monteagle
Claiborne, Ron	Knox
Clay, Wayne	Pelham
Conley, Bob	Jonesboro
Coogan, Robert	Smithville
Corby, Harold	Johnson City
Ewing, John H	Clinton
Harley, Larry W	Bristol
Harley, Richard	Bristol
Heflin, Christopher M	Nashville
Hughes, Dan	Spencer
Hurst, Jeff	Rutledge
Hutcheson, John	Chattanooga
Johnson, David A	Pleasant Shade
Johnson, Ryan M	Signal Mountain
Kemp, Lawrence	Ooltewah
Largin, Ken	Sevierville
Levine, Bob	Tullahoma
Marshall, Stephen R	Mt. Juliet
Mccarty, Harry	Blaine
Mcdonald, W J "Jerry"	Germantown
Moulton, Dusty	Loudon
Raley, R. Wayne	Collierville
Sampson, Lynn	Jonesborough
Smith, Newman L.	Gatlinburg
Taylor, C Gray	Fall Branch
Taylor, David	Rogersville
Vanderford, Carl G	Columbia
Ward, W C	Clinton
Wheeler, Gary	Clarksville
Williams Jr., Richard	Morristown

TX

Adams, William D	Burton
Alexander, Eugene	Ganado
Allen, Mike "Whiskers"	Malakoff
Appleton, Ron	Bluff Dale
Ashby, Douglas	Dallas
Baker, Tony	Allen
Barnes, Jim	Christoval
Barnes, Marlen R.	Atlanta
Barr, Judson C.	Irving
Batts, Keith	Hooks
Blackwell, Zane	Eden
Blum, Kenneth	Brenham
Bratcher, Brett	Plantersville
Brewer, Craig	Killeen
Broadwell, David	Wichita Falls
Brooks, Michael	Lubbock
Brown, Douglas	Fort Worth
Budell, Michael	Brenham
Bullard, Randall	Canyon
Burden, James	Burkburnett
Callahan, F Terry	Boerne
Carey, Peter	Lago Vista
Carpenter, Ronald W	Jasper
Carter, Fred	Wichita Falls
Champion, Robert	Amarillo
Chase, John E	Aledo
Chew, Larry	Weatherford
Childers, David	W. Spring
Churchman, T W (Tim)	Bandera
Cole, James M	Bartonville
Connor, John W	Odessa
Connor, Michael	Winters
Costa, Scott	Spicewood
Crain, Jack W	Granbury
Darcey, Chester L	College Station
Davidson, Larry	New Braunfels
Davis, Vernon M	Waco
De Mesa, John	Lewisville
Dean, Harvey J	Rockdale
Debaud, Jake	Dallas
Delong, Dick	Centerville
Dietz, Howard	New Braunfels

Dominy, Chuck	Colleyville
Dyer, David	Granbury
Eldridge, Allan	Ft. Worth
Elishewitz, Allen	New Braunfels
Epting, Richard	College Station
Eriksen, James Thorlief	Garland
Evans, Carlton	Gainesville
Fant Jr., George	Atlanta
Ferguson, Jim	San Angelo
Fortune Products, Inc.,	Marble Falls
Foster, Al	Magnolia
Foster, Norvell C	Marion
Fowler, Jerry	Hutto
Fritz, Jesse	Slaton
Fry, Jason	Abilene
Fuller, Bruce A	Baytown
Gann, Tommy	Canton
Garner, Larry W	Tyler
George, Les	Corpus Christi
Graham, Gordon	New Boston
Green, Bill	Sachse
Griffin, Rendon And Mark	Houston
Grimes, Mark	Bedford
Guinn, Terry	Eastland
Halfrich, Jerry	San Marcos
Halligan, Ed	San Antonio
Hamlet Jr., Johnny	Clute
Hand, Bill	Spearman
Hawkins, Buddy	Texarkana
Hayes, Scotty	Tesarkana
Haynes, Jerry	Gunter
Hays, Mark	Austin
Hemperley, Glen	Willis
Hicks, Gary	Tuscola
Horrigan, John	Burnet
Howell, Jason G	Lake Jackson
Hudson, Robert	Humble
Hughes, Lawrence	Plainview
Jackson, Charlton R	San Antonio
Jaksik Jr., Michael	Fredericksburg
Johnson, Ruffin	Houston
Keller, Bill	San Antonio
Kern, R W	San Antonio
Kious, Joe	Kerrville
Knipstein, R C (Joe)	Arlington
Ladd, Jim S	Deer Park
Ladd, Jimmie Lee	Deer Park
Lambert, Jarrell D	Granado
Laplante, Brett	McKinney
Lay, L J	Burkburnett
Lemcke, Jim L	Houston
Lennon, Dale	Alba
Lister Jr., Weldon E	Boerne
Lively, Tim And Marian	Marble Falls
Love, Ed	San Antonio
Lovett, Michael	Mound
Luchak, Bob	Channelview
Luckett, Bill	Weatherford
Majors, Charlie	Montgomery
Martin, Michael W	Beckville
Mcconnell Jr., Loyd A	Marble Falls
Merz Iii, Robert L	Katy
Miller, R D	Dallas
Minchew, Ryan	Pampa
Mitchell, Wm Dean	Warren
Moen, Jerry	Dallas
Moore, James B	Ft. Stockton
Neely, Greg	Bellaire
Nolen, Steve	Keller
Oates, Lee	La Porte
O'Brien, Mike J.	San Antonio
Odgen, Randy W	Houston
Ogletree Jr., Ben R	Livingston
Osborne, Warren	Waxahachie
Ott, Ted	Elgin
Overeynder, T R	Arlington
Ownby, John C	Murphy
Pardue, Joe	Spurger

Patterson, Pat	Barksdale
Pierce, Randall	Arlington
Polzien, Don	Lubbock
Powell, James	Texarkana
Powers, Walter R.	Lolita
Pugh, Jim	Azle
Ray, Alan W	Lovelady
Richardson Jr., Percy	Navasota
Roberts, Jack	Houston
Robinson, Charles (Dickie)	Vega
Rucker, Thomas	Nacogdoches
Ruple, William H	Pleasanton
Ruth, Michael G	Texarkana
Ruth, Jr., Michael	Texarkana
Scott, Al	Harper
Self, Ernie	Dripping Springs
Shipley, Steven A	Richardson
Sims, Bob	Meridian
Sloan, Shane	Newcastle
Smart, Steve	McKinney
Snody, Mike	Fredericksburg
Stokes, Ed	Hockley
Stone, Jerry	Lytle
Stout, Johnny	New Braunfels
Theis, Terry	Harper
Thuesen, Ed	Damon
Truncali, Pete	Garland
Turcotte, Larry	Pampa
Van Reenen, Ian	Amarillo
Vickers, David	Montgomery
Ware, Tommy	Onalaska
Watson, Daniel	Driftwood
Watts, Johnathan	Gatesville
Watts, Wally	Gatesville
Weever, John	Cleburne
White, Dale	Sweetwater
Whitley, Weldon G	Odessa
Wilcher, Wendell L	Palestine
Wilkins, Mitchell	Montgomery
Wilson, Curtis M	Burleson
Winn, Marvin	Frisco
Wolf Jr., William Lynn	Lagrange
Yeates, Joe A	Spring
Zboril, Terry	Caldwell
Zermeno, William D.	Houston

UT

Allred, Bruce F	Layton
Black, Earl	Salt Lake City
Ence, Jim	Richfield
Ennis, Ray	Ogden
Erickson, L.M.	Ogden
Hunter, Hyrum	Aurora
Johnson, Steven R	Manti
Jorgensen, Carson	Mt Pleasant
Lang, David	Kearns
Maxfield, Lynn	Layton
Nielson, Jeff V	Monroe
Nunn, Gregory	Castle Valley
Palmer, Taylor	Blanding
Peterson, Chris	Salina
Ricks, Kurt J.	Trenton
Strickland, Dale	Monroe
Velarde, Ricardo	Park City
Washburn Jr., Robert Lee	St George
Weeks, Ryan	Bountiful
Winn, Travis A.	Salt Lake City
Jenkins, Mitch	Manti
Johnson, Jerry	Spring City

VA

Apelt, Stacy E	Norfolk
Arbuckle, James M	Yorktown
Ball, Butch	Floyd
Ballew, Dale	Bowling Green
Batley, Mark S.	Wake
Batson, Richard G.	Rixeyville

Beverly Ii, Larry H	Spotsylvania
Catoe, David R	Norfolk
Chamberlain, Charles R	Barren Springs
Davidson, Edmund	Goshen
Douglas, John J	Lynch Station
Eaton, Frank L Jr	Stafford
Foster, Burt	Bristol
Goodpasture, Tom	Ashland
Harris, Cass	Bluemont
Hedrick, Don	Newport News
Hendricks, Samuel J	Maurertown
Herb, Martin	Richmond
Holloway, Paul	Norfolk
Jones, Barry M And Phillip G	Danville
Jones, Enoch	Warrenton
Kearney, Jarod	Swoope
Martin, Herb	Richmond
Mccoun, Mark	DeWitt
Metheny, H A "Whitey"	Spotsylvania
Mills, Michael	Colonial Beach
Murski, Ray	Reston
Norfleet, Ross W	Providence Forge
Parks, Blane C	Woodbridge
Pawlowski, John R	Newport News
Quattlebaum, Craig	Suffolk
Schlueter, David	Madison Heights
Tomes, P J	Shipman
Vanhoy, Ed And Tanya	Abingdon
Vestal, Charles	Abingdon
Ward, Ron	Rose Hill

VT

Bensinger, J. W.	Marshfield
Haggerty, George S	Jacksonville
Kelso, Jim	Worcester
Wulf, Derrick	Essex

WA

Amoureux, A W	Northport
Begg, Todd M.	Spanaway
Ber, Dave	San Juan Island
Berglin, Bruce	Mount Vernon
Boguszewski, Phil	Lakewood
Bromley, Peter	Spokane
Brothers, Robert L	Colville
Brown, Dennis G	Shoreline
Brunckhorst, Lyle	Bothell
Bump, Bruce D.	Walla Walla
Butler, John R	Shoreline
Campbell, Dick	Colville
Chamberlain, Jon A	E. Wenatchee
Conti, Jeffrey D	Bonney Lake
Conway, John	Kirkland
Crowthers, Mark F	Rolling Bay
D'Angelo, Laurence	Vancouver
Davis, John	Selah
Diaz, Jose	Ellensburg
Diskin, Matt	Freeland
Ferry, Tom	Auburn
Gray, Bob	Spokane
Greenfield, G O	Everett
Hansen, Lonnie	Spanaway
House, Gary	Ephrata
Hurst, Cole	E. Wenatchee
Keyes, Geoff P.	Duvall
Lisch, David K	Seattle
Norton, Don	Port Townsend
O'Malley, Daniel	Seattle
Padilla, Gary	Bellingham
Podmajersky, Dietrich	Seatlle
Rader, Michael	Wilkeson
Roeder, David	Kennewick
Rogers, Ray	Wauconda
Sanford, Dick	Montesano
Schempp, Ed	Ephrata

Schempp, Martin	Ephrata
Stegner, Wilbur G	Rochester
Sterling, Thomas J	Coupeville
Straub, Salem F.	Tonasket
Swyhart, Art	Klickitat
Wright, Kevin	Quilcene

WI

Atkins, Jim	Frederic
Boyes, Tom	West Bend
Brandsey, Edward P	Janesville
Bruner Jr., Fred Bruner Blades	Fall Creek
Carr, Joseph E.	Menomonee Falls
Coats, Ken	Stevens Point
Delarosa, Jim	Janesville
Haines, Jeff Haines Custom Knives Wauzeka	
Johnson, Richard	Germantown
Kanter, Michael	New Berlin
Kohls, Jerry	Princeton
Kolitz, Robert	Beaver Dam
Lary, Ed	Mosinee
Lerch, Matthew	Sussex
Maestri, Peter A	Spring Green
Martin, Peter	Waterford
Mikolajczyk, Glen	Caledonia
Millard, Fred G	Richland Center
Nelson, Ken	Pittsville
Niemuth, Troy	Sheboygan
Ponzio, Doug	Beloit
Rabuck, Jason	Springbrook
Revishvili, Zaza	Madison
Ricke, Dave	West Bend
Rochford, Michael R	Dresser
Roush, Scott	Washburn
Schrap, Robert G	Wauwatosa
Steinbrecher, Mark W	Pleasant Prairie
Wattelet, Michael A	Minocqua

WV

Derr, Herbert	St. Albans
Drost, Jason D	French Creek
Drost, Michael B	French Creek
Elliott, Jerry	Charleston
Jeffries, Robert W	Red House
Liegey, Kenneth R	Millwood
Maynard, Larry Joe	Crab Orchard
Morris, Eric	Beckley
Pickens, Selbert	Dunbar
Reynolds, Dave	Harrisville
Small, Ed	Keyser
Steingass, T.K.	Hedgesville
Tokar, Daniel	Shepherdstown
Wilson, Rw	Weirton
Wyatt, William R	Rainelle

WY

Alexander, Darrel	Ten Sleep
Ankrom, W.E.	Cody
Banks, David L.	Riverton
Barry, Scott	Laramie
Bartlow, John	Sheridan
Bennett, Brett C	Cheyenne
Draper, Audra	Riverton
Draper, Mike	Riverton
Fowler, Ed A.	Riverton
Friedly, Dennis E	Cody
Kilby, Keith	Cody
Rexroat, Kirk	Wright
Reynolds, John C	Gillette
Rodebaugh, James L	Carpenter
Ross, Stephen	Evanston
Spragg, Wayne E	Lovell
Whipple, Wesley A	Thermopolis

ARGENTINA

Ayarragaray, Cristian L.   Parana, Entre Rios
Bertolami, Juan Carlos   Neuquen
Gibert, Pedro   San Martin de los Andes, Neuquen
Kehiayan, Alfredo   Maschwitz, Buenos Aires
Rho, Nestor Lorenzo   Junin, Buenos Aires
Santiago, Abud   Buenos Aires

AUSTRALIA

Barnett, Bruce   Mundaring, WA
Bennett, Peter   Engadine, NSW
Brodziak, David   Albany, WA
Crawley, Bruce R   Croydon, VIC
Cross, Robert   Tamworth, NSW
Del Raso, Peter   Mt. Waverly, VIC
Gerner, Thomas   Walpole, WA
Giljevic, Branko   New South Wales
Green, William (Bill)   View Bank, VIC
Harvey, Max   Pert , WA
Hedges, Dee   Bedfordale, WA
Husiak, Myron   Altona, VIC
K B S, Knives   North Castlemaine, VIC
Maisey, Alan   Vincentia, NSW
Mcintyre, Shawn   Hawthornm, E VIC
Phillips, Alistair   Amaroo, ACT
Tasman, Kerley   Pt Kennedy, WA
Waters, Glenn   Hyland Park, NSW
Zemitis, Joe   Cardiff Heights, NSW

BELGIUM

Dox, Jan   Schoten
Monteiro, Victor   Maleves Ste Marie

BRAZIL

Bodolay, Antal   Belo Horizonte, MG
Bossaerts, Carl   Ribeirao Preto, SP
Campos, Ivan   Tatui, SP
Dorneles, Luciano Oliverira   Nova Petropolis, RS
Gaeta, Angelo   Centro Jau, SP
Gaeta, Roberto   Sao Paulo
Garcia, Mario Eiras   Caxingui, SP
Ikoma, Flavio   Presidente Prudente, SP
Lala, Paulo Ricardo P And Lala, Roberto P.   Presidente Prudente, SP
Neto Jr.,, Nelson And De Carvalho, Henrique M.   Braganca Paulista, SP
Paulo, Fernandes R   Lencois Paulista, SP
Petean, Francisco And Mauricio   Birigui, SP
Ricardo Romano, Bernardes   Itajuba MG
Sfreddo, Rodrigo Menezes   Nova Petropolis, RS
Vilar, Ricardo Augusto Ferreira   Mairipora, SP
Villa, Luiz   Itaim Bibi, SP
Villar, Ricardo   Mairipora, SP
Zakharov, Gladiston   Jacaret, SP

CANADA

Arnold, Joe   London, ON
Beauchamp, Gaetan   Stoneham, QC
Beets, Marty   Williams Lake, BC
Bell, Donald   Bedford, NS
Berg, Lothar   Kitchener ON
Beshara, Brent (Besh)   NL
Boos, Ralph   Edmonton, AB
Bourbeau, Jean Yves   Ile Perrot, QC
Bradford, Garrick   Kitchener, ON
Burke, Dan   Springdale, NL
Dallyn, Kelly   Calgary, AB
Debraga, Jose C.   Trois Rivieres, QC
Debraga, Jovan   Quebec
Deringer, Christoph   Cookshire, QC
Desaulniers, Alain   Cookshire, QC
Diotte, Jeff   LaSalle, ON
Doiron, Donald   Messines, QC
Doucette, R   Brantford, ON
Doussot, Laurent   St. Bruno, QC
Downie, James T   Ontario
Frigault, Rick   Golden Lake, ON
Ganshorn, Cal   Regina, SK
Garvock, Mark W   Balderson, ON
Gilbert, Chantal   Quebec City, QC
Haslinger, Thomas   Calgary, AB
Hayes, Wally   Essex, ON
Hindmarch, Garth   Carlyle, SK
Hofer, Louis   Rose Prairie, BC
Jobin, Jacques   Levis, QC
Kaczor, Tom   Upper London, ON
Lambert, Kirby   Regina, SK
Langley, Mick   Qualicum Beach, BC
Lay, R J (Bob)   Logan Lake, BC
Leber, Heinz   Hudson's Hope, BC
Lightfoot, Greg   Kitscoty, AB
Linklater, Steve   Aurora, ON
Loerchner, Wolfgang   Bayfield, ON
Lyttle, Brian   High River, AB
Maneker, Kenneth   Galiano Island, BC
Marchand, Rick   Wheatley, ON
Marzitelli, Peter   Langley, BC
Massey, Al   Mount Uniacke, NS
Mckenzie, David Brian   Campbell River, BC
Miville-Deschenes, Alain   Quebec
Nease, William   LaSalle, ON
Niro, Frank   Kamloops, B.C.
O'Hare, Sean   Grand Manan, NB
Olson, Rod   High River, AB
Painter, Tony   Whitehorse, YT
Patrick, Bob   S. Surrey, BC
Pepiot, Stephan   Winnipeg, MB
Piesner, Dean   Conestogo, ON
Ridley, Rob   Sundre, AB
Roberts, George A   Whitehorse, YT
Ross, Tim   Thunder Bay, ON
Schoenfeld, Matthew A   Galiano Island, BC
Stancer, Chuck   Calgary, AB
Storch, Ed   Mannville, AB
Stuart, Steve   Gores Landing, ON
Sylvester, David   Compton, QC
Tedford, Steven   Bewdley, ON
Tighe, Brian   St. Catharines, ON
Toner, Roger   Pickering, ON
Treml, Glenn   Thunder Bay, ON
Vanderkolff, Stephen   Mildmay, ON
Whitenect, Jody   Elderbank, NS
Young, Bud   Port Hardy, BC

DENMARK

Andersen, Henrik Lefolii   Fredensborg
Anso, Jens   Sporup
Henriksen, Hans J   Helsinge
Rafn, Dan C.   Hadsten
Strande, Poul   Dastrup
Vensild, Henrik   Auning
Willumsen, Mikkel   S Copenhagen

ENGLAND

Bailey, I.R.   Colkirk
Barker, Stuart   Oadby, Leicester
Boden, Harry   Derbyshire
Farid, Mehr R   Kent
Harrington, Roger   East Sussex
Jackson, Jim   High St. Bray
Morris, Darrell Price   Devon
Nowacki, Stephen R.   Southampton, Hampshire
Orford, Ben   Worcestershire
Penfold, Mick   Tremar, Cornwall
Stainthorp, Guy   Stroke-on-Trent
Wardell, Mick   N Devon
Wise, Donald   East Sussex
Wood, Alan   Brampton

FINLAND

Palikko, J-T   Helsinki
Ruusuvuori, Annssi   Piikkio
Tuominen, Pekka   Tossavanlahti
Vilppola, Markku   Turku

FRANCE

Bennica, Charles   Moules et Baucels
Chauzy, Alain   Seur-en-Auxios
Chomilier, Alain And Joris   Clermont-Ferrand
Doursin, Gerard   Pernes les Fontaines
Graveline, Pascal And Isabelle   Moelan-sur-Mer
Headrick, Gary   Juan Les Pins
Madrulli, Mme Joelle   Salon De Provence
Reverdy, Nicole And Pierre   Romans
Thevenot, Jean-Paul   Dijon
Viallon, Henri   Thiers

GERMANY

Balbach, Markus   WeilmŸnster
Becker, Franz   Marktl
Boehlke, Guenter
Borger, Wolf   Graben-Neudorf
Dell, Wolfgang   Owen-Teck
Drumm, Armin   Dornstadt
Faust, Joachim   Goldkronach
Fruhmann, Ludwig   Burghausen
Greiss, Jockl   Schenkenzell
Hehn, Richard Karl   Dorrebach
Herbst, Peter   Lauf a.d. Pegn.
Joehnk, Bernd   Kiel
Kressler, D F   Achim
Neuhaeusler, Erwin   Augsburg
Rankl, Christian   Munchen
Rinkes, Siegfried   Markterlbach
Selzam, Frank   Bad Koenigshofen
Steinau, Jurgen   Berlin
Tritz, Jean Jose   Hamburg
Wirtz, Achim   Wuerselen
Zirbes, Richard   Niederkail

GREECE

Filippou, Ioannis-Minas   Athens

IRELAND

Moore, Davy   Quin, Co Clare

ISRAEL

Shadmot, Boaz   Arava

ITALY

Albericci, Emilio   Bergamo
Ameri, Mauro   Genova
Ballestra, Santino   Ventimiglia
Bertuzzi, Ettore   Bergamo
Bonassi, Franco   Pordenone
Esposito, Emmanuel   Buttigliera Alta TO
Fogarizzu, Boiteddu   Pattada

Frizzi, Leonardo — Firenze
Garau, Marcello — Oristano
Giagu, Salvatore And Deroma Maria
Rosaria — Pattada (SS)
Ramondetti, Sergio — CHIUSA DI PESIO
(CN)
Riboni, Claudio — Truccazzano (MI)
Scordia, Paolo — Roma
Simonella, Gianluigi — Maniago
Toich, Nevio — Vincenza
Tschager, Reinhard — Bolzano

JAPAN

Aida, Yoshihito — Tokyo
Ebisu, Hidesaku — Hiroshima
Fujikawa, Shun — Osaka
Fukuta, Tak — Gifu
Hara, Kouji — Gifu
Hirayama, Harumi — Saitama
Hiroto, Fujihara — Hiroshima
Isao, Ohbuchi — Fukuoka
Ishihara, Hank — Chiba
Kagawa, Koichi — Kanagawa
Kanki, Iwao — Hyogo
Kansei, Matsuno — Gifu
Kato, Shinichi — Aichi
Katsumaro, Shishido — Hiroshima
Kawasaki, Akihisa — Hyogo
Keisuke, Gotoh — Oita
Koyama, Captain Bunshichi — Aichi
Mae, Takao — Osaka
Makoto, Kunitomo — Hiroshima
Matsuno, Kansei — Gifu-City
Matsusaki, Takeshi — Nagasaki
Michinaka, Toshiaki — Tottori
Narasada, Mamoru — NAGANO
Ryuichi, Kuki — Saitama
Sakakibara, Masaki — Tokyo
Sugihara, Keidoh — Osaka
Sugiyama, Eddy K — Oita
Takahashi, Masao — Gunma
Toshifumi, Kuramoto — Fukuoka
Uchida, Chimata — Kumamoto
Wada, Yasutaka — Nara
Yoshihara, Yoshindo — Tokyo
Yoshikazu, Kamada — Tokushima
Yoshio, Maeda — Okayama

MEXICO

Scheurer, Alfredo E Faes — Distrito Federal
Sunderland, Richard — Puerto Escondido, OA
Young, Cliff — San Miguel De Allende, GJ

NETHERLANDS

Sprokholt, Rob — Gatherwood
Van De Manakker, Thijs — Holland
Van Den Elsen, Gert — Tilburg
Van Eldik, Frans — Loenen
Van Ryswyk, Aad — Vlaardingen

NEW ZEALAND

Bassett, David J. — Auckland
Gunther, Eddie — Auckland
Knapton, Chris C. — Henderson, Aukland
Pennington, C A — Kainga Christchurch
Reddiex, Bill — Palmerston North
Ross, D L — Dunedin
Sandow, Brent Edward — Auckland
Sandow, Norman E — Howick, Auckland
Sands, Scott — Christchurch 9
Van Dijk, Richard — Harwood Dunedin

NORWAY

Bache-Wiig, Tom — Eivindvik
Sellevold, Harald — Bergen
Vistnes, Tor — Svelgen

RUSSIA

Kharlamov, Yuri — Tula

SLOVAKIA

Albert, Stefan — Filakovo 98604
Bojtos, Arpad — 98403 Lucenec
Kovacik, Robert — 98401 Lucenec
Laoislav, Santa-Lasky — 97637 Hrochot
Mojzis, Julius — 98511 Halic
Pulis, Vladimir — 96701 Kremnica

SOUTH AFRICA

Arm-Ko Knives, — Marble Ray , KZN
Baartman, George — Bela-Bela, LP
Bauchop, Robert — Munster, KN
Beukes, Tinus — Vereeniging, GT
Bezuidenhout, Buzz — Malvern, KZN
Boardman, Guy — New Germany, KZN
Brown, Rob E — Port Elizabeth, EC
Burger, Fred — Munster, KZN
Burger, Tiaan — Pretoria, GT
Dickerson, Gavin — Petit, GT
Fellows, Mike — Mossel Bay, SC
Grey, Piet — Naboomspruit, LP
Harvey, Heather — Belfast, MP
Harvey, Kevin — Belfast, LP
Herbst, Gawie — Akasia, GT
Herbst, Thinus — Akasia, GT
Horn, Des — Onrusrivier, WC
Klaasee, Tinus — George, WC
Kojetin, W — Germiston, GT
Lancaster, C G — Free State
Liebenberg, Andre — Randburg, GT
Mackrill, Stephen — Johannesburg, GT
Mahomedy, A R — Marble Ray, KZN
Mahomedy, Humayd A.R. — Marble Ray, KZN
Naude, Louis — Malmesbury, WC
Nelson, Tom — Wilropark, GT
Pienaar, Conrad — Free State
Prinsloo, Theuns — Free State
Rietveld, Bertie — Magaliesburg, GT
Russell, Mick — Port Elizabeth, EC
Schoeman, Corrie — Free State
Steyn, Peter — Freestate
Thorburn, Andre E. — Warmbaths, LP
Van Der Westhuizen, Peter — Mossel Bay, SC
Van Heerden, Andre — Pretoria, GT
Watson, Peter — La Hoff, NW

SOUTH AUSTRALIA

Edmonds, Warrick — Adelaide Hills

SPAIN

Cecchini, Gustavo T. — Sao Jose Rio Preto

SWEDEN

Bergh, Roger — Bygdea
Billgren, Per — Soderfors
Eklund, Maihkel — Farila
Embretsen, Kaj — Edsbyn
Hedlund, Anders — Brastad
Henningsson, Michael — Vastra Frolunda
(Gothenburg)
Hogstrom, Anders T — Johanneshov

Johansson, Anders — Grangesberg
Lundstrom, Jan-Ake — Dals-Langed
Lundstrom, Torbjorn (Tobbe) — Are
Nilsson, Jonny Walker — Arvidsjaur
Nordell, Ingemar — FSrila
Persson, Conny — Loos
Ryberg, Gote — Norrahammar
Styrefors, Mattias — Boden
Vogt, Patrik — Halmstad

SWITZERLAND

Roulin, Charles — Geneva
Soppera, Arthur — Ulisbach

UNITED ARAB EMIRATES

Kukulka, Wolfgang — Dubai

UNITED KINGDOM

Hague, Geoff — Quarley, Hampshire
Heasman, H G — Llandudno, N. Wales
Horne, Grace — Sheffield
Maxen, Mick — Hatfield, Herts

URUGUAY

Gonzalez, Leonardo Williams — Maldonado
Symonds, Alberto E — Montevideo

ZIMBABWE

Burger, Pon — Bulawayo

Not all knifemakers are organization-types, but those listed here are in good standing with these organizations.

the knifemakers' guild

2012 membership

a Les Adams, Douglas A. Alcorn, Mike "Whiskers" Allen, W. E. Ankrom

b Robert K. Bagley, Santino e Arlete Ballestra, Norman P. Bardsley, A. T. Barr, James J. Barry, III, John Bartlow, Barbara Baskett, Gene Baskett, Ron Best, Gary Blanchard ,Michael S. Blue, Arpad Bojtos, Philip W. Booth, Tony Bose, Dennis Bradley, Gayle Bradley, Edward Brandsey, W. Lowell Bray, Jr., George Clint Breshears, Richard E. Browne, Fred Bruner, Jr., John Busfield

c Harold J. "Kit" Carson, Michael Carter, Kevin Casey, Dianna Casteel, Douglas Casteel, William Chapo, Danial Chinnock, Howard F. Clark, Wayne Clay, Kenneth R. Coats, Blackie Collins, Bob F. Conley, Gerald Corbit, George Cousino, Colin J. Cox, Pat Crawford

d Alex K. Daniels, Jack Davenport, Edmund Davidson, John H Davis, William C. Davis, Dan Dennehy, Herbert K. Derr, William J. Dietzel, Mike Dilluvio, David Dodds, T. M. Dowell, Larry Downing, Tom Downing, James F. Downs, William Duff, Fred Durio, Will Dutton

e Jacob Elenbaas, Jim Elliott, William B. Ellis, James T. Eriksen, Carlton R. Evans

f Stephen J. Fecas, Cliff Fendley, Lee Ferguson, Linda Ferguson, Robert G. Flynt, Michael H. Franklin, John R Fraps, Dennis E. Friedly, Stanley Fujisaka, Bruce A. Fuller,

g Steve Gatlin, Warren Glover, Stefan Gobec, Richard R. Golden, Gregory J. Gottschalk ,Ernie Grospitch, Kenneth W. Guth

h Philip (Doc) L. Hagen, Gerald Halfrich, Marshall Chad Hall, Jim Hammond, Don L Hanson III, Koji Hara, Ralph Dewey Harris, Rade Hawkins, Earl Jay Hendrickson, Wayne Hendrix, Wayne G. Hensley, Gil Hibben, Wesley G. Hibben, R. Hinson, Steven W. Hoel, Kevin Hoffman, Desmond R. Horn, Jerry Hossom, Larry Hoststler, Durvyn Howard, Rob Hudson, Roy Humenick, Joseph Hytovick,

i Billy Mace Imel, Michael Irie

j James T. Jacks, Brad Johnson, Jerry L. Johnson, Keith R. Johnson, Ronald B. Johnson, Steven R. Johnson, William "Bill" C. Johnson, Enoch D. Jones, Jack Jones, Lonnie L Jones

k William L. Keeton, Bill Kennedy, Jr., Bill King, Harvey King, J. Kenneth King, Terry Knipschield

l Kermit Laurent, Paul M LeBetard, Gary E. LeBlanc, Tommy B. Lee, Kevin T. Lesswing, William S. Letcher, William L. Levengood, Jack Levin, Bob Levine, Steve Linklater, Ken Linton, Wolfgang Loerchner, R. W. Loveless, Schuyler Lovestrand, Don Lozier, Bill Luckett, Gail Lunn, Larry Lunn,

Ernest Lyle

m Stephen Mackrill, Riccardo Mainolfi, Joe Malloy, Tom Maringer, Herbert A. Martin, Charlie B. Mathews, Harry S. Mathews, Jerry McClure, Sandra McClure, Lloyd McConnell, W. J. McDonald, Mike Mercer, Ted Merchant, Robert L. Merz, III, Toshiaki Michinaka, James P. Miller, Stephen C. Miller, Dan Mink, Jim Minnick, Jerry Moen Jeff Morgan

n Bud Nealy, Corbin Newcomb, Larry Newton, Rick Noland, Ross W Norfleet

o Clifford W. O'Dell, Charles F. Ochs, III, Ben R. Ogletree, Jr., Warren Osborne, T. R. Overeynder, John E. Owens, Clifford W. O'Dell, Sean O'Hare

p Larry Page, Cliff Parker, Jerry Partridge, John R. Pawlowski, W. D. Pease, Alfred Pendray, John W. PerMar, Daniel Piergallini, Otakar Pok, Larry Pridgen, Jr. Joseph R. Prince, Theunis C. Prinsloo, Jim Pugh, Morris C. Pulliam,

r Jason Rabuck, James D. Ragsdale, Steven Rapp, Vernie Reed, John Reynolds, Ron F. Richard, Dave Ricke, Joseph Calvin Robinson, Michael Rochford, A. G. Russell

s Michael A. Sakmar, Hiroyuki Sakurai, Scott W. Sawby, Juergen Schanz, Mike Schirmer, Mark C. Sentz, Yoshinori Seto, Eugene W. Shadley, John I Shore, R. J. Sims, Jim Siska, Steven C. Skiff, Scott Slobodian, Ralph Smith, Marvin Solomon, Arthur Soppera, Jim Sornberger, David Steier, Murray Sterling, Russ Sutton, Charles C. Syslo

t Robert Terzuola, Leon Thompson, Michael A. Tison, Dan Tompkins, Bobby L. Toole, Reinhard Tschager, Ralph Turnbull

v Aas van Rijswijk, Donald Vogt

w George A. Walker, Edward Wallace, Charles B. Ward, Tom Watson, Charles G. Weeber, John S. Weever, Zachary Whitson, Wayne Whittaker, Donnie R. Wicker, RW Wilson, Stan Wilson, Daniel Winkler

y George L. Young, Mike Yurco

z Brad Zinker, Michael Zscherny

abs mastersmith listing

a David Anders, Jerome Anders, Gary D. Anderson, E. R. Russ Andrews II

b Gary Barnes, Aubrey G. Barnes Sr., James L. Batson, Jimmie H. Buckner, Bruce D. Bump, Bill Burke, Bill Buxton

c Ed Caffrey, Murray M. Carter, Kevin R. Cashen, Hsiang Lin (Jimmy) Chin, Jon Christensen, Howard F. Clark, Wade Colter, Michael Connor, James R. Cook, Joseph G. Cordova, Jim Crowell, Steve Culver

d Sava Damlovac, Harvey J. Dean, Christoph Deringer, Adam DesRosiers, Bill Dietzel, Audra L. Draper, Rick Dunkerley, Steve Dunn, Kenneth Durham

e Dave Ellis

f Robert Thomas Ferry III, Jerry Fisk, John S. Fitch, Joe Flournoy, Don Fogg, Burt Foster, Ronnie E. Foster, Timothy L Foster, Ed Fowler, Larry D. Fuegen, Bruce A. Fuller, Jack A. Fuller

g Tommy Gan, Bert Gaston, Thomas Gerner, Greg Gottschalk,

h Tim Hancock, Don .L Hanson III, Heather Harvey, Kevin Harvey, Wally Hayes, E. Jay Hendrickson, Don Hethcoat, John Horrigan, Rob Hudson

j Jim L. Jackson

k Joseph F. Keeslar, Keith Kilby, Ray Kirk, Hank Knickmeyer,

Jason Knight, Bob Kramer

l Jerry Lairson Sr., Mick Langley

m J. Chris Marks, John Alexander Martin, Roger D. Massey, Victor J. McCrackin, Shawn McIntyre, Hanford J. Miller, Wm Dean Mitchell

n Greg Neely, J. Neilson, Ron Newton, Douglas E. Noren

o Charles F. Ochs III

p Alfred Pendray, John L. Perry, Dan Petersen Ph.D., Timothy Potier

r Michael Rader, J. W. Randall, Kirk Rexroat, Linden W. Rhea, Dickie Robinson, James L. Rodebaugh, Kyle Royer, Raymond B. Rybar Jr.

s James P. Saviano, Stephen C. Schwarzer, Mark C. Sentz, Rodrigo Menezes Sfreddo, JD Smith, Josh Smith, Raymond L. Smith, Bill Sowell, H. Red St. Cyr, Charles Stout, Joseph Szilaski

t Shane Taylor, Jean-paul Thevenot, Jason Tiensvold, Brion Tomberlin, P. J. Tomes, Henry Torres

v Michael V. Vagnino Jr., Terry L. Vandeventer

w James L. Walker, John White, Michael L. Williams, Daniel Winkler

miniature knifemaker's society

Paul Abernathy, Gerald Bodner, Fred Cadwell, Barry Carithers, Kenneth Corey, Don Cowles, David J. Davis, Allen Eldridge, Linda Ferguson, Buddy Gaines, Larry Greenburg, Tom & Gwenn Guinn, Karl Hallberg, Bob Hergert, Laura Holmes, Brian Jacobson, Gary Kelley, R. F. Koebeman, Sterling Kopke, Gary E. Lack, Les Levinson, Henry C. Loos, Howard Maxwell, Mal Mele, Ray Mende, Toshiaki Michinaka, Paul Myer, Noriaki Narushima, Carol A. Olmsted, Allen R. Olsen, Charles Ostendorf, David Perkins, John Rakusan, Mark Rogers, Mary Ann Schultz, Jack Taylor, Valentin V. Timofeyev, Mike Viehman, Michael A. Wattelet, Kenneth P. Whitchard Jr., James D. Whitehead, Steve Williams, Carol A. Winold, Earl and

professional knifemaker's association

Sue Witsaman, John Yashinski
Mike Allen, Clay Allison, Pat Ankrom, Shane Atwood, Eddie Baca, John Bartlow, Scott Barry, Donald Bell,
Brett Bennett, Tom Black, Justin Bridges, Kenneth Brock, Lucas Burnley,Tim Cameron, Del Corsi, Joe Culpepper, Ray Ennis, Lee & Linda Ferguson, Chuck Fraley, Graham Fredeen, Bob Glassman, Guy Hielsher, Jay Higgins, Mike Irie, Mitch Jenkins, Harvey King, Todd Kopp, Jim Krause,Tom Krein, Tim Lambkin, Jim Largent, Ken Linton, Arthur Lynn, Jim Magee, Jerry & Sandy McClure, Clayton Miller, Michael Miller, Skip Miller, Ty Montell, Mike Mooney, Steve Myers, Fred Ott, William Pleins, James Poplin, Bill Post, Calvin Powell, Steve Powers, Peter Pruyn, Bill Redd, Steve Rollert, David Ruana, Dennis Ruana, Don Ruana, Terry Schreiner, Pepper Seaman, Walter Sherar, Eddie Stalcup, Craig Steketee, Douglas Stice, Mark Strauss, Kurt Swearingen, James Thrash, Ed Thuesen, Albert Trijillo, Pete Truncali, Charles Turnage, Dick Waites, Al Warren, Rod Watts, Hans Weinmueller, Harold Wheeler, R W Wilson, Michael Young, Monte Zavatta, Russ Zima, Don Zvonek.

state/regional associations

alaska interior knifemakers association
Frank Ownby, Fred DeCicco, Bob Hook, Jenny Day, Kent Setzer, Kevin Busk, Loren Wellnite, Mark Knapp, Matthew Hanson, Mel Harvey, Nate Miller, Richard Kacsur, Ron Miller, Terry Miller, Bob LaFrance, Randy Olsen

alaska knifemakers association
A.W. Amoureux, John Arnold, Bud Aufdermauer, Robert Ball, J.D. Biggs, Lonnie Breuer, Tom Broome, Mark Bucholz, Irvin Campbell, Virgil Campbell, Raymond Cannon, Christopher Cawthorne, John Chamberlin, Bill Chatwood, George Cubic, Bob Cunningham, Gordon S. Dempsey, J.L. Devoll, James Dick, Art Dufour, Alan Eaker, Norm Grant, Gordon Grebe, Dave Highers, Alex Hunt, Dwight Jenkins, Hank Kubaiko, Bill Lance, Bob Levine, Michael Miller, John Palowski, Gordon Parrish, Mark W. Phillips, Frank Pratt, Guy Recknagle, Ron Robertson, Steve Robertson, Red Rowell, Dave Smith, Roger E. Smith, Gary R. Stafford, Keith Stegall, Wilbur Stegner, Norm Story, Robert D. Shaw, Thomas Trujillo, Ulys Whalen, Jim Whitman, Bob Willis

arizona knifemakers association
D. "Butch" Beaver, Bill Cheatham, Dan Dagget, Tom Edwards, Anthony Goddard, Steve Hoel, Ken McFall, Milford Oliver, Jerry Poletis, Merle Poteet, Mike Quinn, Elmer Sams, Jim Sornberger, Glen Stockton, Bruce Thompson, Sandy Tudor, Charles Weiss

arkansas knifemakers association

Mike Allen, David Anders, Robert Ball, Reggie Barker, James Batson, Twin Blades, Craig Braschler, Kim and Gary Breed, Wheeler, Tim Britton, Benoni Bullard, Bill Buxton, J.R. Cook, Gary Crowder, James Crowell, Steve Culver, Jesse Davis, Jim Downie, Bill Duff, Fred Durio, Rodger Echols, Shawn Ellis, Lee Ferguson, Linda Ferguson, Jerry Fisk, Joe Flournoy, Ronnie Foster, James Glisson, Gordon Graham, Bob Ham, Douglas and Gail Hardy, Gary Hicks, Alan Hutchinson, Jack Jones, Lacy Key, Harvey King, Ray Kirk, Bill Kirkes, Jim Krause, Jerry Lairson, Ken Linton, Bill Luckett, Tad Lynch, Jim Magee, Roger Massey, Jerry McClure, Rusty McDonald, W.J. McDonald, Don McIntosh, Tony Metsala, Bill Miller, Skip Miller, Ronnie Mobbs, Sidney Moon, Gary Mulkey, Keith Murr, Steve Myers, Mark Nevling, Allen Newberry, Corbin Newcomb, Ron Newton, Chad Nichols, John Perry, Paul Piccola, Rusty Polk, Bill Post, J.W. Randall, Vernon Red, Lin Rhea, Ralph Richards, Ron Richerson, Bobby Rico, Dennis Riley, T.C. Roberts, Kenny Rowe, Kyle Royer, Mike Ruth, James Scroggs, Richard Self, Tex Skow, Mike Snider, Marvin Snider, Marvin Snider, Marvin Solomon, Craig Steketee, Ed Sticker, Charles Stout, Jeff Stover, Tim Tabor, Brian Thie, Brion Tomberlin, Russell Townsley, Leon Treiber, Pete Truncali, Terry Vandeventer, Charles Vestal, Jim Walker, John White, Mike Williams

australian knifemakers guild inc.

Peter Bald, Col Barn, Bruce Barnett, Denis Barrett, Alistair Bastian, David Brodziak, Stuart Burdett, Jim Deering, Peter Del Raso, Michael Fechner, Keith Fludder, John Foxwell, Thomas Gerner, Branko Giljevic, Stephen Gregory-Jones, Peter Gordon, Barry Gunston, Mal Hannan, Rod Harris, Glenn Henke, Matt James, Peter Kenney, Joe Kiss, Robert Klitscher, Maurie McCarthy, Shawn McIntyre, John McLarty, Ray Mende, Richard Moase, Adam Parker, Jeff Peck, Mike Petersen, Alistair Phillps, Mick Ramage, Wayne Saunders, Murray Shanaughan, Andre Smith, Jim Steele, Rod Stines, Doug Timbs, Stewart Townsend, Hardy Wangermann, Brendan Ware, Ross Yeats

california knifemakers association

Stewart Anderson, Elmer Art, Anton Bosch, Roger Bost, Clint Breshears, Christian Bryant, Mike Butcher, Joe Caswell, Marcus Clinco, Clow Richard, Mike Desensi, Parker Dunbar, Frank Dunkin, Vern Edler III, Stephanie Engnath, Robert Ewing, Chad Fehmie, Alex Felix, Jim Ferguson, Bob Fitlin, Brian Forrest, Dave Gibson, Joe Girtner, Jerry Goettig, Jeanette Gonzales, Russ Green, Tim Harbert, John Harris, Wm. R. 'Bill' Herndon, Neal A. Hodges, Jerid Johnson, Lawrence Johnson, David Kahn, David Kazsuk, Paul Kelso, Steve Koster, Robert Liguori, Harold Locke, R.W. Loveless, Gerald Lundgren, Gordon Melin, Jim Merritt, Russ Moody, Gerald Morgan, Mike Murphy, Tim Musselman, Jeff Mutz, Aram Nigoghossian, Bruce Oakley, Rich Orton, Barry E. Posner, Pat Randall, E. J. Robison, Valente Rosas, Clark Rozas, H. J. Schneider, Red St. Cyr, Chris Stanko, Bill Stroman, Tyrone Swader, Reinhardt Swanson, Tony Swatton, Billy Traylor, Tru-grit, Larry White, Stephen A. Williams

canadian knifemakers guild

Joe Arnold, John Benoit, Andre Benoit, Paul Bold, Guillaume Cote, Christoph Deringer, Alain Desaulniers, Sylvain Dion, Jim Downie, Eric Elson, Paul-Aime Fortier, Rick Frigault, Thomas Haslinger, Paul H. Johnston, Kirby Lambert, Greg Lightfoot, Steve Linklater, Wolfgang Loerchner, Brian Lyttle, David MacDonald, Antoine Marcal, James McGowan, Edward McRae, Mike Mossington, William Nease, Simone Raimondi, George Roberts, Paul Savage, Murray St. Amour, Stephen Stuart, David Sylvester, Brian Tighe, Stephen Vanderkolff, Craig Wheatley, Peter Wile, Elizabeth Loerchner, Fred Thynne, Rick Todd

florida knifemaker's association

Dick Atkinson, George Bachley, Mitch Baldwin, James Barry III, Dwayne Batten, Terry Betts, James H. Beusse Jr., Howard Bishop, Dennis Blaine, Dennis Blankenhem, Stephen A. Bloom, Dean Bosworth, John Boyce, W. Lowell Bray, Jr., Patrick R. Burris, Steve Butler, Norman Caesar, Tim Caldwell, Jason Clark, Lowell Cobb, William Cody, David Cole, Steve Corn, Jack Davenport, John Davis, Kenny Davis, Cary Desmon, Tim Caldwell, Jacob Elenbaas, Jim Elliot, William Ellis, Lynn Emrich, Tom Enos, Gary Esker, Frank Fischer, Todd Fischer, Mike Fisher, Travis Fletcher, Roger Gamble, Tony Garcia, James"Hoot" Gibson, Pedro Dick Gonzalez, Paul J. Granger, Ernie Grospitch, David Gruber, Chuck Harnage, Fred Harrington, R. Dewey Harris, Henry Heitler, Kevin Hoffman, Edward O. Holloway, Larry Hostetler, Stewart R. Hudson, Julie Hyman, Joe

"Hy" Hytovick, Tom Johanning, Richard Johnson, Roy Kelleher, Paul Kent, Bill King, Bryan Komula, George H. Lambert, William S. Letcher, Bill Levengood, Glenn A. Long, Ernie Lyle, Bob Mancuso, Stephen Mathewson, Michael Matthews, James McNiel, Faustina Mead, Steve Miller, Dan Mink, Martin L. Murphy, Gary Nelson, Larry Newton, J. Cliff Parker, Jerry D. Partridge, John W. PerMar Jr., Larry Patterson, Dan Piergallini, Terry Lee Renner, Calvin J. Robinson, Vince Ruano, Roberto Sanchez, Russell Sauls, Dave Semones, Ann Sheffield, Brad Shepherd, Bill Simons, Jimmie H. Smith, Fred Stern, Kent Swicegood, Timothy Tabor, , Dale Thomas, Wayne Timmerman, Michael Tison, Ralph Turnbull, Louis Vallet, Donald Vogt, Bruce Wassberg, Stan Wilson, Denny Young, Brad Zinker

georgia custom knifemakers' guild

Don R. Adams, Doug Adams, Dennis Bradley, Aaron Brewer, Mike Brown, Robert Busbee, Henry Cambron, Jim Collins, John Costa, Jerry Costin, Scott Davidson, Charles K. Dunn, Will Dutton, Emory Fennell, Stephan Fowler, Dean Gates, Warren Glover, George Hancox, Rade Hawkins, Wayne Hensley, Ronald Hewitt, Kevin Hoffman, Frank Jones, Davin Kates, Dan Masson, Charlie Mathews, Harry Mathews, Leroy Mathews, David McNeal, Dan Mink, James Mitchell, Ralph Mitchell, Sandy Morrisey, Jerry Partridge, Wes Peterson, James Poplin, Joan Poythress, Carey Quinn, Jim Ragsdale, Carl Rechsteiner, David Roberts, Andrew Roy, Joe Sangster, Jamey Saunders, Craig Schneeberger, Randy Scott, Ken Simmons, Nelson Simmons, Jim Small, Bill Snow, Don Tommey, Alex Whetsel, Mike Wilson, Patrick & Hillary Wilson, Robert A. Wright

knife group association of oklahoma

Mike "Whiskers" Allen, Ed Allgood, David Anders, Rocky Anderson, Tony and Ramona Baker, Jerry Barlow, Troy Brown, Dan Burke, Tom Buchanan, F. L. Clowdus Bill Coye, Gary Crowder, Steve Culver, Marc Cullip, David Darby, Voyne Davis, Dan Dick, Dave Dill, Lynn Drury, Bill Duff, Beau Erwin, David Etchieson, Harry Fentress, Lee Ferguson, Linda Ferguson, Daniel Fulk, Gary Gloden, Steve Hansen, Paul Happy, Calvin Harkins, Ron Hebb, Billy Helton, Ed Hites, Tim Johnston, Les Jones, Jim Keen,Bill Kennedy, Stew Killiam, Barbara Kirk, Ray Kirk, Nicholas Knack, Jerry Lairson, Sr., Al Lawrence, Ken Linton, Ron Lucus, Aidan Martin, Barbara Martin, Duncan Martin, John Martin, Jerry McClure, Sandy McClure, Rick Menefee, Ben Midgley, Michael E. Miller, Roy Miller, Ray Milligan, Duane Morganflash, Gary Mulkey, Jerald Nickels, Jerry Parkhurst, Chris Parson, Larry Parsons, Jerry Paul, Larry Paulen, Paul Piccola, Cliff Polk, Roland Quimby, Ron Reeves, Lin Rhea, Mike Ruth, Dan Schneringer, Terry Schreiner, Allen Shafer, Shawn Shropshire, Randell Sinnett, Clifford Smith, Jeremy Steely, Doug Sonntag, Perry Stanford, Mike Stegall, Gary Steinmetz, Mike Stott, Dud Hart Thomas, Brian Tomberlin, Tom Upton, Chuck Ward, Brett Wheat-Simms, Jesse Webb, Rob Weber, Joe Wheeler, Bill Wiggins, Joe Wilkie, Gary Wingo, Daniel Zvonek

knifemakers' guild of southern africa

Jeff Angelo, John Arnold, George Baartman, Francois Basson, Rob Bauchop, George Beechey, Arno Bernard, Buzz Bezuidenhout, Harucus Blomerus, Chris Booysen, Thinus Botha, Ian Bottomley, Peet Bronkhorst, Rob Brown, Fred Burger, Sharon Burger, Trevor Burger, William Burger, Brian Coetzee, Larry Connelly, Andre de Beer, André de Villiers, Melodie de Witt, Gavin Dickerson, Roy Dunseith, Mike Fellows, Leigh Fogarty, Werner Fourie, Andrew Frankland, Brian Geyer, Ettoré Gianferrari, Dale Goldschmidt, Stan Gordon, Nick Grabe, John Grey, Piet Gray, Heather Harvey, Kevin Harvey, Dries Hattingh, Gawie Herbst, Thinus Herbst, Greg Hesslewood, Des Horn, Nkosi Jubane, Billy Kojetin, Mark Kretschmer, Steven Lewis, Garry Lombard, Steve Lombard, Ken Madden, Abdur-Rasheed Mahomedy, Peter Mason, Edward Mitchell, George Muller, Günther Muller, Tom Nelson, Andries Olivier, Jan Olivier, Christo Oosthuizen, Cedric Pannell, Willie Paulsen, Nico Pelzer, Conrad Pienaar, David Pienaar, Jan Potgieter, Lourens Prinsloo, Theuns Prinsloo, Hilton Purvis, Derek Rausch, Chris Reeve, Bertie Rietveld, Melinda Rietveld, Dean Riley, John Robertson, Corrie Schoeman, Eddie Scott, Harvey Silk, Mike Skellern, Toi Skellern, Carel Smith, Ken Smythe, Graham Sparks, Peter Steyn, André Thorburn, Hennie Van Brakel, Fanie Van Der Linde, Johan van der Merwe, Van van der Merwe, Marius Van der Vyver, Louis Van der Walt, Cor Van Ellinckhuijzen, Andre van Heerden, Danie Van Wyk, Ben Venter, Willie Venter, Gert Vermaak, René Vermeulen, Erich Vosloo, Desmond, Waldeck, Albie Wantenaar, Henning Wilkinson, John Wilmot, Wollie Wolfaardt, Owen Wood

midwest knifemakers association

E.R. Andrews III, Frank Berlin, Charles Bolton, Tony Cates, Mike Chesterman, Ron Duncan, Larry Duvall, Bobby Eades, Jackie Emanuel, James Haynes, John Jones, Mickey Koval, Ron Lichlyter, George Martoncik, Gene Millard, William Miller, Corbin Newcomb, Chris Owen, A.D. Rardon, Archie Rardon, Max Smith, Ed Stewart, Charles Syslo, Melvin Williams

montana knifemaker's association

Peter C. Albert, Chet Allinson, Marvin Allinson, Tim & Sharyl Alverson, Bill Amoureux, Jan Anderson, Wendell Barnes, Jim & Kay Barth, Bob & Marian Beaty, Don Bell, Brett Bennett, Robert Bizzell, BladeGallery, Paul Bos, Daryl & Anna May Boyd, Chuck Bragg, Frederick Branch, Peter Bromley, Bruce Brown, Emil Bucharksky, Bruce & Kay Bump, Bill Burke, Alpha Knife Supply Bybee, Ed Caffrey, Jim & Kate Carroll, Murray Carter, Jon & Brenda Christensen, Norm Cotterman, Seith Coughlin, Bob Crowder, Mike Dalimata, John Davis, Maria DesJardins, Rich & Jacque Duxbury, Dan Erickson, Mel & Darlene Fassio, E.V. Ford, Eric Fritz, Dana & Sandy Hackney, Doc & Lil Hagen, Gary & Betsy Hannon, Eli Hansen, J.A. Harkins, Tedd Harris, Sam & Joy Hensen, Loren Higgins, Mickey Hines, Gerald & Pamela Hintz, Gary House, Tori Howe, Kevin Hutchins, Al Inman, Frank & Shelley Jacobs, Karl Jermunson, Keith Johnson, Don Kaschmitter, Steven Kelly, Dan & Penny Kendrick, Monte Koppes, Donald Kreuger, David Lisch, James Luman, Robert Martin, Max McCarter, Neil McKee, Larry McLaughlin, Mac & Nancy McLaughlin, Phillip Moen, Gerald Morgan, Randy Morgan, Dan & Andrea Nedved, Daniel O'Malley, Joe Olson, Collin Paterson, Willard & Mark Patrick, Jeffrey & Tyler Pearson, Brian Pender, James Poling, Chance & Kerri Priest, Richard Prusz, Greg Rabatin, Jim Raymond, Jim Rayner, Darren Reeves, John Reynolds, Ryan Robison, Gary Rodewald, Buster Ross, Ruana Knifeworks, Charles Sauer, Dean Schroeder, Michael Sheperes, Mike Smith, Gordon St. Clair, Terry Steigers, George Stemple, Dan & Judy Stucky, Art & Linda Swyhart, Jim Thill, Cary Thomas, James & Tammy Venne, Bill & Lori Waldrup, Jonathan & Doris Walther, Kenneth Ward, Michael Wattelet, Darlene Weinand, Gerome & Darlene Weinand, Daniel & Donna Westlind, Matt & Michelle Whitmus, Dave Wilkes, Mike & Sean Young

national independent cutlery association

Ron & Patsy Beck, Bob Bennett, Dave Bishop, Steve Corn, Dave Harvey, C.J. McKay, Mike Murray, Gary Parker, Rachel Schindler, Joe Tarbell

new england bladesmiths guild

Phillip Baldwin, Gary Barnes, Paul Champagne, Jimmy Fikes, Don Fogg, Larry Fuegen, Rob Hudson, Midk Langley, Louis Mills, Dan Maragni, Jim Schmidt, Wayne Valachovic and Tim Zowada

north carolina custom knifemakers' guild

Dr. James Batson, Wayne Bernauer, Tom Beverly, William "Bill" Bisher, Jamin Bracket, Mark Cary, Thomas Clegg, Ray Clontz, Travis Daniel, David Driggs, Russell Gardner, Talmage M. Hall, Koji Hara, John Hege, Curtis Iovito, Tommy Johnson, Barry and Phillip Jones, Frank Joyce, Carol Kelly, Tony Kelly, Robert Knight, Leon Lassiter, Gregory Manley, Mathew Manley, Aubrey McDonald, Tommy McNabb, Arthur McNeil, Christopher McNeil, William Morris, Van Royce Morton, Charles Ostendorf, James Poplin, Murphy Ragsdale, Kenneth Steve Randall, Bruce Ryan, Joel Sandifer, Tim Scholl, Andy Sharpe, Gene Smith, Octavio F. Soares, Arthur Summers, Russ Sutton, Bruce Turner.

ohio knifemakers association

Raymond Babcock, Van Barnett, Harold A. Collins, Larry Detty, Tom Downing, Jim Downs, Patty Ferrier, Jeff Flannery, James Fray, Bob Foster, Raymond Guess, Scott Hamrie, Rick Hinderer, Curtis Hurley, Ed Kalfayan, Michael Koval, Judy Koval, Larry Lunn, Stanley Maienknecht, Dave Marlott, Mike Mercer, David Morton, Patrick McGroder, Charles Pratt, Darrel Ralph, Roy Roddy, Carroll Shoemaker, John Smith, Clifton Smith, Art Summers, Jan Summers, Donald Tess, Dale Warther, John Wallingford, Earl Witsaman, Joanne Yurco, Mike Yurco

saskatchewan knifemakers guild

Dennis Allenback, Alton Vern, Broeksma Clarence, Brunas Irv, Bucharsky Emil, Clow Jim, Cook Murray, Crowder Bob, Dahlin Jim, Donald Kevin, Drayton Brian, Fehler Ray, Ganshorn Cal, Garling Dale, Greer Gary, Hamilton Wayne, Hartley John, Hazell Robert, Hebb Bryan, Hindmarch Garth, Holm Robert, Johnson Doug, Kreuger Donald, Laronge Paul, Macnamara Pat, Meeres Len, Morgan Brad, Nelson Ron, Nesdole Morris, Olafson Bryan, Parry Ben, Parry Blaine, Penner Greg, Popick Barry, Quickfall Jim, Robert Robson, Sainsbury Robert, Sali Carl, Senft Kim, Spasoff Don, Stinnon Dan,Vanderwekken Tim, Whitfield Trevor, Wilkes David, Williams Merle.

south carolina association of knifemakers

Douglas Bailey, Ken Black, Bobby Branton, Richard Bridwell,Gordo Brooks, Dan Cannady, Rodger Cassey, John Conn, Allen Corbet, Bill Dauksch, Geno Denning, Charlie Douan, Gene Ellison, Eddy Elsmore, Robbie Estabrook Jr., Lewis Fowler, Jim Frazier, Tally Grant, Jerry Hendrix, Wayne Hendrix, Johnny Johnson, Lonnie Jones, John Keaton, Jason Knight, Col. Thomas Kreger, Gene Langley, Tommy Lee, David Manley, Bill Massey, C.R. Miles, Gene Miller, Claude Montjoy, Patrick Morgan, Barry Meyers, Paul Nystrom Jr., Lee O'Quinn, Victor Odom Jr., Larry Page, James Rabb, Ricky Rankin, Rick Rockwood, John Sarratt, Gene Scaffe, Mick Sears, Ralph Smith, David Stroud, Rocky Thomas, Allen Timmons, Justin Walker, Mickey Walker, Woody Walker, Syd Willis Jr.

tennessee knifemakers association

John Bartlow, Doug Casteel, Harold Crisp, Larry Harley, John W. Walker, Harold Woodward, Harold Wright

texas knifemakers & collectors association

Doug Arnew, Doug Ashby, Ed Barker, George Blackburn, Zane Blackwell, Garrett Blackwell, David Blair, Gayle Bradley, Craig Brewer, Nathan Burgess, Stanley Buzek, Dennis Clark, Dwain Coats, Emil Colmenares, Stewart Crawford, Chester Darcey, Wesley Davis, Rorick Davis, Brian Davis, Harvey Dean, James Drouillard II, Stan Edge, Carlton Evans, Jesse Everett Jr., Sammy Fischer, Christopher Flo, Norvell Foster, Theodore Friesenhahn, Jason Fry, Les George, Mark Grimes, Don Halter, Johnny Hamlet, Glenn Hemperley, Roy Hinds, Darrel Holmquist, Mark Hornung, Karl Jakubik, Mickey Kaehr, Bill Keller, David Kinn, Greg Ledet, Jim Lemcke, Ken Linton, Michael LoGiudice, Paul Long, Eliot Maldonado, Glenn Marshall, Newton Martin, Riley Martin, Bob Merz, Jerry Moen, Don Morrow, Ted Munson, Clifford O'Dell, Tom Overeynder, John Ownby, Ronnie Packard, Glenn Parks, Pat Patterson, Garrett Patterson, Troy Patterson, Steven Patterson, William Petersen III, Jeff Petzke, Paul Piccola, Bill and Pat Post, Gary Powell, Rusty Preston, Martin Rizo, Thomas Rucker, Bill Ruple, Merle Rush, James Schiller, Dwight Schoneweis, Richard Self, Kirby Simmons, Adam Starr, Linda Stone, Wayne Stone, Johnny Stout, Katie Stout, Luke Swenson, Leon Treiber, Larry Turcotte, Charles Turnage, Jimmy Vasquez, David Vickers, Austin Walter, John Walts, Chuck Ward, Bruce Weber, John Weever, Harold Wheeler, Marvin Winn, John Wootters

The firms listed here are special in the sense that they make or market special kinds of knives made in facilities they own or control either in the U.S. or overseas. Or they are special because they make knives of unique design or function. The second phone number listed is the fax number.

sporting cutlers

A.G. RUSSELL KNIVES INC
2900 S. 26th St
Rogers, AR 72758-8571
800-255-9034 or 479-631-0130;
fax 479-631-8493
ag@agrussell.com; www.agrussell.com
The oldest knife mail-order company, highest quality. Free catalog available. In these catalogs you will find the newest and the best. If you like knives, this catalog is a must

AL MAR KNIVES
PO Box 2295
Tualatin, OR 97062-2295
503-670-9080; 503-639-4789
www.almarknives.com;
info@almarknives.com
Featuring our Ultralight™ series of knives. Sere 2000™ Shrike, Sere™, Operator™, Nomad™ and Ultraligh series™

ANZA KNIVES
C Davis
Dept BL 12 PO Box 710806
Santee, CA 92072-0806
619-561-9445; 619-390-6283
sales@anzaknives.com;
www.anzaknives.com

B&D TRADING CO.
3935 Fair Hill Rd
Fair Oaks, CA 95628

BARTEAUX MACHETES, INC.
1916 SE 50th St
Portland, OR 97215
503-233-5880
barteaux@machete.com; www.machete.com
Manufacture of machetes, saws, garden tools

**BEAR & SON CUTLERY
(FORMERLY BEAR MGC CUTLERY)**
1111 Bear Blvd., SW
Jacksonville, AL 36265 USA
256-435-2227; 800-3034
fax 256-435-9348
www.bearandsoncutlery.com
Folding pocket knives, fixed blades, specialty products

BECK'S CUTLERY & SPECIALTIES
7395-M Elevation Road
Benson, NC 27504
919-460-0203; 919-460-7772
beckscutlery@embarqmail.com;
www.BecksCutleryOnline.com

BENCHMADE KNIFE CO. INC.
300 Beavercreek Rd
Oregon City, OR 97045
503-655-6004; 800-800-7427
info@benchmade.com;
www.benchmade.com
Sports, utility, law enforcement, military, gift and semi custom

BERETTA U.S.A. CORP.
17601 Beretta Dr
Accokeek, MD 20607
800-636-3420 Customer Service
www.berettausa.com
Full range of hunting & specialty knives

BEST KNIVES / GT KNIVES
PO Box 151048
Fort Myers, FL 33914
800-956-5696; fax 941-240-1756
info@bestknives.com;
www.bestknives.com/gtknives.com
Law enforcement & military automatic knives

BLACKJACK KNIVES
PO Box 3
Greenville, WV 24945
304-832-6878; Fax 304-832-6550
knifeware@verizon.net;
www.knifeware.com

BLUE GRASS CUTLERY CORP.
20 E Seventh St PO Box 156
Manchester, OH 45144
937-549-2602; 937-549-2709 or 2603
sales @bluegrasscutlery.com;
www.bluegrasscutlery.com
Manufacturer of Winchester Knives, John Primble Knives and many contract lines

BOB'S TRADING POST
308 N Main St
Hutchinson, KS 67501
620-669-9441
www.gunshopfinder.com
Tad custom knives with Reichert custom sheaths one at a time, one-of-a-kind

BOKER USA INC
1550 Balsam St
Lakewood, CO 80214-5917
303-462-0662; 303-462-0668
sales@bokerusa.com; www.bokerusa.com
Wide range of fixed blade and folding knives for hunting, military, tactical and general use

BROWNING
One Browning Place
Morgan, UT 84050
800-333-3504; Customer Service:
801-876-2711 or 800-333-3288
www.browning.com
Outdoor hunting & shooting products

BUCK KNIVES INC.
660 S Lochsa St
Post Falls, ID 83854-5200
800-326-2825; Fax: 208-262-0555
www.buckknives.com
Sports cutlery

BULLDOG BRAND KNIVES
PO Box 23852
Chattanooga, TN 37421
423-894-5102; 423-892-9165
Fixed blade and folding knives for hunting and general use

BUSSE COMBAT KNIFE CO.
11651 Co Rd 12
Wauseon, OH 43567
419-923-6471; 419-923-2337
www.bussecombat.com;
info@bussecombat.com
Simple & very strong straight knife designs for tactical & expedition use

CAMILLUS C/O ACME UNITED CORP.
60 Round Hill Rd.
Fairfield, CT 06824
800-835-2263
www.camillusknives.com
info@camillusknives.com

CAS IBERIA INC.
650 Industrial Blvd
Sale Creek, TN 37373
423-332-4700
www.cashanwei.com
Extensive variety of fixed-blade and folding knives for hunting, diving, camping, military and general use. Japan ese swords and European knives.

CASE CUTLERY
W R & Sons
PO Box 4000
Owens Way
Bradford, PA 16701
800-523-6350; Fax: 814-368-1736
consumer-relations@wrcase.com
www.wrcase.com
Folding pocket knives

CHICAGO CUTLERY CO.
5500 Pearl St.
Rosemont, IL 60018
847-678-8600
www.chicagocutlery.com
Sport & utility knives.

CHRIS REEVE KNIVES
2949 S. Victory View Way
Boise, ID 83709-2946
208-375-0367; Fax: 208-375-0368
crknifo@chrisreeve.com;
www.chrisreeve.com
Makers of the award winning Yarborough/ Green Beret Knife; the One Piece Range; and the Sebenza and Mnandi folding knives

COAST CUTLERY CO
PO Box 5821
Portland, OR 97288
800-426-5858
www.coastcutlery.com;
staff@coastcutlery.com
Variety of fixed-blade and folding knives and multi-tools for hunting, camping and general use

COLD STEEL INC
3036-A Seaborg Ave.
Ventura, CA 93003
800-255-4716 or 805-650-8481
customerservice@coldsteel.com;
www.coldsteel.com
Wide variety of folding lockbacks and fixed-blade hunting, fishing and neck knives, as well as bowies, kukris, tantos, throwing knives, kitchen knives and swords

**COLONIAL KNIFE COMPANY
DIVISION OF COLONIAL CUTLERY
INTERNATIONAL**
PO Box 960
North Scituate, RI 02857
401-421-6500; Fax: 401-737-0054
colonialcutlery@aol.com;
www.colonialcutlery@aol.com or
www.colonialknifecompany.com
Collectors edition specialty knives. Special promotions. Old cutler, barion, trappers, military knives. Industrial knives-electrician.

COLUMBIA RIVER KNIFE & TOOL
18348 SW 126th Place
Tualatin, OR 97026
800-891-3100; 503-685-5015
info@crkt.com; www.crkt.com
Complete line of sport, work and tactical knives

CONDOR™ TOOL & KNIFE
Rick Jones, Natl. Sales Manager
7557 W Sand Lake Rd. #106
Orlando, FL 32819
407-354-3488; Fax: 407-354-3489
www.condortk.com
rtj@att.net

CRAWFORD KNIVES, LLC
205 N Center Drive
West Memphis, AR 72301
870-732-2452
www.crawfordknives.com
Folding knives for tactical and general use

CUTCO INTERNATIONAL
PO Box 810
Olean, NY 14760
716-372-3111
www.cutco.com
Household cutlery / sport knives

DAVID BOYE KNIVES
PO Box 1238
Dolan Springs, AZ 86441-1238
800-853-1617 or 928-767-4273
boye@ctaz.com; www.boyeknives.com
Boye Dendritic Cobalt boat knives

DUNN KNIVES
Steve Greene
PO Box 307, 1449 Nocatee St.
Intercession City, FL 33848
800-245-6483
s.greene@earthlink.net;
www.dunnknives.com
Custom knives

EMERSON KNIVES, INC.
1234 W. 254th St
Harbor City, CA 90710
310-539-5633; Fax: 310-212-7289
www.emersonknives.com
Hard use tactical knives; folding & fixed blades

EXTREMA RATIO SAS
Mauro Chiostri/Maurizio Castrati
Via Tourcoing 40/p
59100 Prato ITALY
0039 0574 584639; Fax: 0039 0574 581312
info@extremaratio.com;
www.extremaratio.com
Tactical/military knives and sheaths, blades and sheaths to customers specs

FALLKNIVEN AB
Granatvagen 8
S-961 43 Boden
SWEDEN
46-921 544 22; Fax: 46-921 544 33
info@fallkniven.se; www.fallkniven.com
High quality stainless knives

FAMARS
2091 Nooseneck Hill Road
Suite 200
Coventry, RI 02816
855-FAMARS1, Fax – 401-397-9191
famarsusa.com
info@famarsusa.com
FAMARS has been building guns for over 50 years. Known for their innovative design, quality, and craftsmanship. They have introduced their new line of gentleman's knives. Applying all the same principals they apply to their guns into their knives. Providing the best built products for many years to come.

FROST CUTLERY CO
PO Box 22636
Chattanooga, Tn 37422
800-251-7768; Fax: 423-894-9576
www.frostcutleryco.com
Wide range of fixed-blade and folding knives with a multitude of handle materials

GATCO SHARPENERS
PO Box 600
Getzville, NY 14068
716-646-5700; Fax: 716-646-5775
gatco@gatcosharpeners.com;
www.gatcosharpeners.com
Precision sharpening systems, diamond sharpening systems, ceramic sharpening systems, carbide sharpening systems, natural Arkansas stones

GERBER LEGENDARY BLADES
14200 SW 72nd Ave
Portland, OR 97224
503-639-6161; Fax: 503-684-7008
www.gerberblades.com
Knives, multi-tools, axes, saws, outdoor products

GROHMANN KNIVES LTD.
PO Box 40
116 Water St
Pictou, Nova Scotia B0K 1H0
CANADA
888-756-4837; Fax: 902-485-5872
www.grohmannknives.com
Fixed-blade belt knives for hunting and fishing, folding pocketknives for hunting and general use. Household cutlery.

H&B FORGE CO.
235 Geisinger Rd
Shiloh, OH 44878
419-895-1856
hbforge@direcway.com; www.hbforge.com
Special order hawks, camp stoves, fireplace accessories, muzzleloading accroutements

HISTORIC EDGED WEAPONRY
1021 Saddlebrook Dr
Hendersonville, NC 28739
828-692-0323; 828-692-0600
histwpn@bellsouth.net
Antique knives from around the world; importer of puukko and other knives from

Norway, Sweden, Finland and Lapland; also edged weaponry book "Travels for Daggers" by Eiler R. Cook

JOY ENTERPRISES-FURY CUTLERY
Port Commerce Center III
1862 M.L. King Jr. Blvd
Riviera Beach, FL 33404
800-500-3879; Fax: 561-863-3277
mail@joyenterprises.com;
www.joyenterprises.com;
www.furycutlery.com
Fury™ Mustang™ extensive variety of fixed-blade and folding knives for hunting, fishing, diving, camping, military and general use; novelty key-ring knives. Muela Sporting Knives. KA-BAR KNIVES INC. Fury Tactical, Muela of Spain, Mustang Outdoor Adventure

KA-BAR KNIVES INC
200 Homer St
Olean, NY 14760
800-282-0130; Fax: 716-790-7188
info@ka-bar.com; www.ka-bar.com

KATZ KNIVES
10924 Mukilteo Speedway #287
Mukilteo, WA 98275
480-786-9334; 480-786-9338
katzkn@aol.com; www.katzknives.com

KELLAM KNIVES WORLDWIDE
PO Box 3438
Lantana, FL 33462
800-390-6918; Fax: 561-588-3186
info@kellamknives.com;
www.kellamknives.com
Largest selection of Finnish knives; handmade & production
KAI USA Ltd.
18600 SW Teton Avenue
Tualatin, Oregon 97062
503 682-1966; Fax: 503 682-7168
www.kershawknives.com

KLOTZLI (MESSER KLOTZLI)
Hohengasse 3 CH 3400
Burgdorf
SWITZERLAND
(34) 422-23 78; Fax: (34) 422-76 93
info@klotzli.com; www.klotzli.com
High-tech folding knives for tactical and general use

KNIFEWARE INC
PO Box 3
Greenville, WV 24945
304-832-6878; Fax: 304-832-6550
knifeware@verizon.net; www.knifeware.com
Blackjack and Big Country Cross reference Big Country Knives see Knifeware Inc.

KNIGHTS EDGE LTD.
5696 N Northwest Highway
Chicago, IL 60646-6136
773-775-3888; Fax: 773-775-3339
sales@knightsedge.com;
www.knightsedge.com
Medieval weaponry, swords, suits of armor, katanas, daggers

KNIVES OF ALASKA, INC.
Charles or Jody Allen
3100 Airport Dr
Denison, TX 75020
800-572-0980; 903-786-7371
info@knivesofalaska.com;
www.knivesofalaska.com
High quality hunting & outdoorsmen's knives

KNIVES PLUS
2467 40 West
Amarillo, TX 79109
800-687-6202
www.knivesplus.com
Retail cutlery and cutlery accessories since 1987; free catalog available

LEATHERMAN TOOL GROUP, INC.
12106 N.E. Ainsworth Circle
Portland, OR 97220
800-847-8665; Fax: 503-253-7830
www.leatherman.com;
dsales@leatherman.com

LONE WOLF KNIVES
300 Beavercreek Rd
Oregon City, OR 97045
503-431-6777
customerservice@lonewolfknives.com;
www.lonewolfknives.com

LONE STAR WHOLESALE
2401 Interstate 40 W
Amarillo, TX 79105
806-356-9540; Fax 806-359-1603
knivesplus@knivesplus.com
Great prices, dealers only, most major brands

MARBLE'S OUTDOORS
420 Industrial Park
Gladstone, MI 49837
906-428-3710; Fax: 906-428-3711
info@marblescutlery.com;
www.marblesoutdoors.com

MASTER CUTLERY INC
701 Penhorn Ave
Secaucus, NJ 07094
888-227-7229; Fax: 201-271-7228
www.mastercutlery.com
Largest variety in the knife industry

MASTERS OF DEFENSE KNIFE CO.
BlackHawk Products Group
4850 Brookside Ct
Norfolk, VA 23502
800-694-5263; 888-830-2013
www.blackhawk.com/catalog/Knives,19.htm
Fixed-blade and folding knives for tactical and general use

MCCANN INDUSTRIES
132 S 162nd PO Box 641
Spanaway, WA 98387
253-537-6919; Fax: 253-537-6993
mccann.machine@worldnet.att.net;
www.mccannindustries.com

MEYERCO USA
4481 Exchange Service Dr
Dallas, TX 75236
214-467-8949; 214-467-9241
www.meyercousa.com
Folding tactical, rescue and speed-assisted pocketknives; fixed-blade hunting and fishing designs; multi-function camping tools and machetes

MICROTECH KNIVES
300 Chestnut Street Ext.
Bradford, PA 16701
814-363-9260; Fax: 814-363-9284
mssweeney@microtechknives.com;
www.microtechknives.com
Manufacturers of the highest quality production knives

MORTY THE KNIFE MAN, INC.
P.O. Box 152787
Cape Coral, FL 33915
1-800-247-2511
info@mtkm.com;
www.mortytheknifeman.com

MUSEUM REPLICAS LTD.
P.O. Box 840
2147 Gees Mill Rd
Conyers, GA 30012
800-883-8838; Fax: 770-388-0246
www.museumreplicas.com
Historically accurate & battle-ready swords & daggers

MYERCHIN, INC.
14765 Nova Scotia Dr
Fontana, CA 92336
909-463-6741; 909-463-6751
myerchin@myerchin.com;
www.myerchin.com
Rigging/ Police knives

NATIONAL KNIFE DISTRIBUTORS
756 S Church St
Forest City, NC 28043
800-447-4342; 828-245-5121
nkdi@nkdi.com; www.nkdi.com
Benchmark pocketknives from Solingen, Germany

NORMARK CORP.
10395 Yellow Circle Dr
Minnetonka, MN 55343-9101
800-874-4451; 612-933-0046
www.rapala.com
Hunting knives, game shears and skinning ax

ONTARIO KNIFE CO. & QUEEN CUTLERY CO.
26 Empire St.
Franklinville, NY 14737
800-222-5233; 800-299-2618
sales@ontarioknife.com;
www.ontarioknife.com
Fixed blades, tactical folders, military & hunting knives, machetes

OUTDOOR EDGE CUTLERY CORP.
9500 W 49th Ave., #A-100
Wheat Ridge, CO 80033
800-447-3343; 303-530-7020
info@outdooredge.com;
www.outdooredge.com

PACIFIC SOLUTION MARKETING, INC.
1220 E. Belmont St.
Ontario, CA 91761
Tel: 877-810-4643
Fax: 909-930-5843
sales@pacificsolution.com
www.pacificsolution.com
Wide range of folding pocket knives, hunting knives, tactical knives, novelty knives, medieval armors and weapons as well as hand forged samurai sword and tantos.

PILTDOWN PRODUCTIONS
Errett Callahan
2 Fredonia Ave
Lynchburg, VA 24503
434-528-3444
www.errettcallahan.com

QUEEN CUTLERY COMPANY
PO Box 500
Franklinville, NY 14737
800-222-5233; 800-299-2618
sales@ontarioknife.com;
www.queencutlery.com
Pocket knives, collectibles, Schatt & Morgan, Robeson, club knives

QUIKUT
118 East Douglas Road PO Box 29
Walnut Ridge, AR 72476
800-338-7012; Fax: 870-886-9162
www.quikut.com

RANDALL MADE KNIVES
PO Box 1988
Orlando, FL 32802
407-855-8075; Fax: 407-855-9054
grandall@randallknives.com;
www.randallknives.com
Handmade fixed-blade knives for hunting, fishing, diving, military and general use

REMINGTON ARMS CO., INC.
PO Box 700
870 Remington Drive
Madison, NC 27025-0700
800-243-9700; Fax: 336-548-7801
www.remington.com

SANTA FE STONEWORKS
3790 Cerrillos Rd.
Santa Fe, NM 87507
800-257-7625; Fax: 505-471-0036
knives@rt66.com;
www.santafestoneworks.com
Gem stone handles

SARCO CUTLERY LLC
449 Lane Dr
Florence AL 35630
256-766-8099
www.sarcoknives.com
Etching and engraving services, club knives, etc. New knives, antique-collectible knives

SOG SPECIALTY KNIVES & TOOLS, INC.
6521 212th St SW
Lynnwood, WA 98036
425-771-6230; Fax: 425-771-7689
info@sogknives.com; www.sogknives.com
SOG assisted technology, Arc-Lock, folding knives, specialized fixed blades, multi-tools

SPYDERCO, INC.
820 Spyderco Way
Golden, CO 80403
800-525-7770; 303-278-2229
sales@spyderco.com;
www.spyderco.com
Knives and sharpeners

SWISS ARMY BRANDS INC.
15 Corporate Dr.
Orangeburg, NY 10962
800-431-2994; 914-425-4700
www.swissarmy.com
Folding multi-blade designs and multi-tools for hunting, fishing, camping, hiking, golfing and general use. One of the original brands (Victorinox) of Swiss Army Knives

TAYLOR BRANDS LLC
PO Box 1638
Kingsport, TN 37663
800-251-0254; Fax: 423-247-5371
info@taylorbrandsllc.com;
www.taylorbrands.com
Fixed-blade and folding knives for tactical, rescue, hunting and general use. Also provides etching, engraving, scrimshaw services.

TIGERSHARP TECHNOLOGIES
1002 N Central Expwy Suite 499
Richardson TX 75080
888-711-8437; Fax: 972-907-0716
www.tigersharp.com

TIMBERLINE KNIVES
7223 Boston State Rd.
Boston, NY 14075
800-548-7427; Fax: 716-646-5775
www.timberlineknives.com
*High technology production knives for
professionals, sporting, tradesmen & kitchen*

TINIVES
1725 Smith Rd
Fortson, GA 31808
888-537-9991; 706-322-9892
*High-tech folding knives for tactical, law
enforcement and general use*

TRU-BALANCE KNIFE CO.
PO Box 140555
Grand Rapids, MI 49514
(616) 647-1215

TURNER, P.J., KNIFE MFG., INC.
P.O. Box 1549
164 Allred Rd
Afton, WY 83110
307-885-0611
pjtkm@silverstar.com;
www2.silverstar.com/turnermfg

UTICA CUTLERY CO
820 Noyes St
PO Box 10527
Utica, NY 13503-1527
800-879-2526; Fax: 315-733-6602
info@uticacutlery.com; www.uticacutlery.com
*Wide range of folding and fixed-blade designs,
multi-tools and steak knives*

WARNER, KEN
PO Box 3
Greenville, WV 24945
304-832-6878; 304-832-6550
www.kenwarnerknives.com

WENGER NORTH AMERICA
15 Corporate Dr
Orangeburg, NY 10962
800-267-3577 or 800-447-7422
www.wengerna.com
*One of the official makers of folding multi-
blade Swiss Army knives*

WILD BOAR BLADES
PO Box 328
Toutle, WA 98649
360-601-1927
info@wildboarblades.com;
www.wildboarblades.com
*Wild Boar Blades is pleased to carry a full line
of Kopromed knives and kitchenware imported
from Poland*

WORLD CLASS EXHIBITION KNIVES
Cary Desmon
941-504-2279
www.withoutequal.com
Carries an extensive line of Pius Lang knives

WILLIAM HENRY STUDIO
3200 NE Rivergate St
McMinnville, OR 97128
503-434-9700; Fax: 503-434-9704
www.williamhenrystudio.com
*Semi-custom folding knives for hunting and
general use; some limited editions*

WUU JAU CO. INC
2600 S Kelly Ave
Edmond, OK 73013
800-722-5760; Fax: 877-256-4337
mail@wuujau.com; www.wuujau.com
*Wide variety of imported fixed-blade and
folding knives for hunting, fishing, camping,
and general use. Wholesale to knife dealers
only*

WYOMING KNIFE CORP.
101 Commerce Dr
Ft. Collins, CO 80524
970-224-3454; Fax: 970-226-0778
wyoknife@hotmail.com;
www.wyomingknife.com

XIKAR INC
PO Box 025757
Kansas City MO 64102
888-266-1193; fax: 405-340-5965
info@xikar.com; www.xikar.com
Gentlemen's cutlery and accessories

importers

A.G. RUSSELL KNIVES INC
2900 S. 26th St.
Rogers, AR 72758-8571
800-255-9034 or 479-631-0130;
fax 479-631-8493
ag@agrussell.com; www.agrussell.com
*The oldest knife mail-order company, highest
quality. Free catalog available. In these
catalogs you will find the newest and the
best. If you like knives, this catalog is a must.
Celebrating over 40 years in the industry*

ADAMS INTERNATIONAL KNIFEWORKS
8710 Rosewood Hills
Edwardsville, IL 62025
Importers & foreign cutlers

AITOR-BERRIZARGO S.L.
P.I. Eitua PO Box 26
48240 Berriz Vizcaya
SPAIN
946826599; 94602250226
info@aitor.com; www.aitor.com
Sporting knives

ATLANTA CUTLERY CORP.
2147 Gees Mill Road
Conyers, Ga 30012
800-883-0300; Fax: 770-388-0246
custserve@atlantacutlery.com;
www.atlantacutlery.com
Exotic knives from around the world

BAILEY'S
PO Box 550
Laytonville, CA 95454
800-322-4539; 707-984-8115
baileys@baileys-online.com;
www.baileys-online.com

BELTRAME, FRANCESCO
Fratelli Beltrame F&C snc Via dei Fabbri
15/B-33085 MANIAGO (PN)
ITALY
39 0427 701859
www.italianstiletto.com

BOKER USA, INC.
1550 Balsam St
Lakewood, CO 80214-5917
303-462-0662; 303-462-0668
sales@bokerusa.com; www.bokerusa.com
Ceramic blades

CAMPOS, IVAN DE ALMEIDA
R. Stelio M. Loureiro, 205
Centro, Tatui
BRAZIL
00-55-15-33056867
www.ivancampos.com

C.A.S. HANWEI, INC.
650 Industrial Blvd
Sale Creek, TN 37373
423-332-4700; 423-332-7248
info@casiberia.com; www.casiberia.com

CLASSIC INDUSTRIES
1325 Howard Ave, Suite 408
Burlingame, CA 94010

COAST CUTLERY CO.
8033 NE Holman St.
Portland, OR 97218
800-426-5858
staff@coastcutlery.com;
www.coastcutlery.com

COLLECTION INFORMATION CO.,LTD.
Akanabe Hongo 1-49 Ginancho
Gifu city, Gifu, JAPAN
81 58 274 1960; 81 58 273 7369
www.samurai-nippon.net

COLUMBIA PRODUCTS CO.
1622 Browning
Irvine, CA 92606-4809
949.474.0777; fax: 949.474.1191
www.columbiasinks.com

COLUMBIA PRODUCTS INT'L
PO Box 8243
New York, NY 10116-8243
201-854-3054; Fax: 201-854-7058
nycolumbia@aol.com;
http://www.columbiaproducts.homestead.
com/cat.html
Pocket, hunting knives and swords of all kinds

COMPASS INDUSTRIES, INC.
104 West 29th Street
New York, NY 10001
800-221-9904; Fax: 212-353-0826
jeff@compassindustries.com;
www.compassindustries.com
Imported pocket knives

CONAZ COLTELLERIE
Dei F.Lli Consigli-Scarperia
Via G. Giordani, 20
50038 Scarperia (Firenze)
ITALY
36 55 846187; 39 55 846603
conaz@dada.it; www.consigliscarperia.
com
*Handicraft workmanship of knives of the
ancient Italian tradition. Historical and
collection knives*

CONSOLIDATED CUTLERY CO., INC.
696 NW Sharpe St
Port St. Lucie, FL 34983
772-878-6139

CRAZY CROW TRADING POST
PO Box 847
Pottsboro, TX 75076
800-786-6210; Fax: 903-786-9059
info@crazycrow.com; www.crazycrow.com
Solingen blades, knife making parts & supplies

DER FLEISSIGEN BEAVER
(The Busy Beaver)
Harvey Silk
PO Box 1166
64343 Griesheim
GERMANY
49 61552231; 49 6155 2433
Der.Biber@t-online.de
*Retail custom knives. Knife shows in Germany
& UK*

EXTREMA RATIO SAS
Mauro Chiostri; Mavrizio Castrati
Via Tourcoing 40/p
59100 Prato (PO)
ITALY
0039 0574 58 4639; 0039 0574 581312
info@extremarazio.com;
www.extremaratio.com
Tactical & military knives manufacturing

FALLKNIVEN AB
Granatvagen 8
S-961 Boden
SWEDEN
46 92154422; 46 92154433
info@fallkniven.se
www.fallkniven.com
High quality knives

FREDIANI COLTELLI FINLANDESI
Via Lago Maggiore 41I-21038
LeggiunoITALY

**GIESSER MESSERFABRIK GMBH,
JOHANNES**
Raiffeisenstr 15
D-71349 Winnenden
GERMANY
49-7195-1808-29
info@giesser.de; www.giesser.de
Professional butchers and chef's knives

HILTARY INDUSTRIES
Elliott Glasser
6060 E Thomas Rd
Scottsdale, AZ 85257
480-425-0700
usgrc@usgrc.biz

HIMALAYAN IMPORTS
3495 Lakeside Dr
Reno, NV 89509
775-825-2279
unclebill@himalayan-imports.com; www.
himilayan-imports.com

**IVAN DE ALMEIDA CAMPOS-KNIFE
DEALER**
R. Xi De Agosto
107, Centro, Tatui, Sp 18270
BRAZIL
55-15-251-8092; 55-15-251-4896
campos@bitweb.com.br

JOY ENTERPRISES
1862 M.L. King Blvd
Riviera Beach, FL 33404
800-500-3879; 561-863-3277
mail@joyenterprises.com;
www.joyenterprises.com
Fury™, Mustang™, Hawg Knives, Muela

KELLAM KNIVES WORLDWIDE
PO Box 3438
Lantana, FL 33462
800-390-6918; 561-588-3186
info@kellamknives.com;
www.kellamknives.com
Knives from Finland; own line of knives

KNIFE IMPORTERS, INC.
11307 Conroy Ln
Manchaca, TX 78652
512-282-6860, Fax: 512-282-7504
Wholesale only

KNIGHTS EDGE
5696 N Northwest Hwy
Chicago, IL 60646
773-775-3888; 773-775-3339
www.knightsedge.com
*Exclusive designers of our Rittersteel,
Stagesteel and Valiant Arms and knightedge
lines of weapon*

LINDER, CARL NACHF.
Erholungstr. 10
D-42699 Solingen
GERMANY
212 33 0 856; Fax: 212 33 71 04
info@linder.de; www.linder.de

MARTTIINI KNIVES
PO Box 44 (Marttiinintie 3)
96101 Rovaniemi
FINLAND

MATTHEWS CUTLERY
PO Box 185
Moultrie, GA 31776
877-428-3599
www.matthewscutlery.com

MESSER KLÖTZLI
PO Box 104
Hohengasse 3, Ch-3402 Burgdorf
SWITZERLAND
034 422 2378; 034 422 7693
info@klotzli.com; www.klotzli.com

MUSEUM REPLICAS LIMITED
2147 Gees Mill Rd
Conyers, GA 30012
800-883-8838
www.museumreplicas.com

NICHOLS CO.
Pomfret Rd
South Pomfret, VT 05067
*Import & distribute knives from EKA (Sweden),
Helle (Norway), Brusletto (Norway), Roselli
(Finland). Also market Zippo products, Snow,
Nealley axes and hatchets and snow & Nealley
axes*

NORMARK CORP.
Craig Weber
10395 Yellow Circle Dr
Minnetonka, MN 55343

PRODUCTORS AITOR, S.A.
Izelaieta 17
48260 Ermua
SPAIN
943-170850; 943-170001
info@aitor.com
Sporting knives

PROFESSIONAL CUTLERY SERVICES
9712 Washburn Rd
Downey, CA 90241
562-803-8778; 562-803-4261
*Wholesale only. Full service distributor of
domestic & imported brand name cutlery.
Exclusive U.S. importer for both Marto Swords
and Battle Ready Valiant Armory edged weapons*

SCANDIA INTERNATIONAL INC.
5475 W Inscription Canyon Dr
Prescott, AZ 86305
928-442-0140; Fax: 928-442-0342
mora@cableone.net; www.frosts-scandia.
com
Frosts knives of Sweden

STAR SALES CO., INC.
1803 N. Central St
Knoxville, TN 37917
800-745-6433; Fax: 865-524-4889
www.starknives.com

SVORD KNIVES
Smith Rd., RD 2
Waiuku, South Auckland
NEW ZEALAND
64 9 2358846; Fax: 64 9 2356483
www.svord.com

SWISS ARMY BRANDS LTD.
The Forschner Group, Inc.
One Research Drive
Shelton, CT 06484
203-929-6391; 203-929-3786
www.swissarmy.com

TAYLOR BRANDS, LLC
1043 Fordtown Road
Kingsport, TN 37663
800-251-0254; Fax: 423-247-5371
info@taylorbrandsllc.com;
www.taylorbrands.com
*Fixed-blade and folding knives for tactical,
rescue, hunting and general use. Also provides
etching, engraving, scrimshaw services.*

UNITED CUTLERY CORP.
475 US Hwy 319 S
Moultrie, GA 31768
800-548-0835; 229-890-6669

fax: 229-551-0182
order@unitedcutlery.com;
Harley-Davidson ® Colt ® , Stanley ®, U21 ®,
Rigid Knives ®, Outdoor Life ®, Ford ®, hunting,
camping, fishing

UNIVERSAL AGENCIES INC
4690 S Old Peachtree Rd, Suite C
Norcross, GA 30071-1517
678-969-9147; Fax: 678-969-9169
info@knifecupplies.com;
www.knifesupplies.com;
www.thunderforged.com; www.uai.org
Serving the cutlery industry with the finest
selection of India Stag, Buffalo Horn,
Thurnderforged ™ Damascus. Mother of Pearl,
Knife Kits and more

VALOR CORP.
1001 Sawgrass Corp Pkwy
Sunrise, FL 33323
800-899-8256; Fax: 954-377-4941
www.valorcorp.com
Wide variety of imported & domestic knives

WENGER N. A.
15 Corporate Dr
Orangeburg, NY 10962
800-431-2996
www.wengerna.com

WILD BOAR BLADES
PO Box 328
Toutle, WA 98649
360-601-1927
www.wildboarblades.com

Carries a full line of Kopromed knives and
kitchenware imported from Poland

WORLD CLASS EXHIBITION KNIVES
Cary Desmon
941-504-2279
www.withoutequal.com

ZWILLING J.A. HENCKELS USA
171 Saw Mill River Rd
Hawthorne, NY 10532
800-777-4308; Fax: 914-747-1850
info@jahenckels.com;
www.jahenckels.com
Kitchen cutlery, scissors, gadgets, flatware and
cookware

knife making supplies

AFRICAN IMPORT CO.
Alan Zanotti
22 Goodwin Rd
Plymouth, MA 02360
508-746-8552; 508-746-0404
africanimport@aol.com
Ivory

ALABAMA DAMASCUS STEEL
PO Box 54
WELLINGTON, AL 36279
256-892-2950
sales@alabamadamascussteel.com
www.alabamadamascussteel.com
We are a manufacturer of damascus steel
billets & blades. We also offer knife supplies.
We can custom make any blade design that
the customer wants. We can also make custom
damascus billets per customer specs.

AMERICAN SIEPMANN CORP.
65 Pixley Industrial Parkway
Rochester, NY 14624
800-724-0919; Fax: 585-247-1883
www.siepmann.com
CNC blade grinding equipment, grinding
wheels, production blade grinding services.
Sharpening stones and sharpening equipment

ANKROM EXOTICS
Pat Ankrom
306 1/2 N. 12th
Centerville, Iowa 52544
641-436-0235
ankromexotics@hotmail.com
www.ankromexotics.com
Stabilized handle material; Exotic burls
and hardwoods from around the world;
Stabilizing services available

ATLANTA CUTLERY CORP.
2147 Gees Mill Rd. Box 389
Conyers, Ga 30012
770-922-7500; Fax: 770-918-2026
custserve@atlantacutlery.com;
www.atlantacutlery.com

BLADEMAKER, THE
Gary Kelley
17485 SW Phesant Ln
Beaverton, OR 97006
503-649-7867
garykelly@theblademaker.com;
www.theblademaker.com
Period knife and hawk blades for hobbyists
& re-enactors and in dendritic D2 steel.
"Ferroulithic" steel-stone spear point, blades
and arrowheads

BOONE TRADING CO., INC.
PO Box 669
562 Coyote Rd
Brinnon, WA 98320
800-423-1945; Fax: 360-796-4511
www.boonetrading.com
Ivory of all types, bone, horns

BORGER, WOLF
Benzstrasse 8
76676 Graben-Neudorf
GERMANY
wolf@messerschmied.de;
www.messerschmied.de

BOYE KNIVES
PO Box 1238
Dolan Springs, AZ 86441-1238
800-853-1617; 928-767-4273
info@boyeknives.com;
www.boyeknives.com
Dendritic steel and Dendritic cobalt

BRONK'S KNIFEWORKS
Lyle Brunckhorst
Country Village
23706 7th Ave SE, Suite B
Bothell, WA 98021
425-402-3484
bronks@bronksknifeworks.com;
www.bronksknifeworks.com
Damascus steel

CRAZY CROW TRADING POST
PO Box 847
Pottsboro, TX 75076
800-786-6210; Fax: 903-786-9059
info@crazycrow.com; www.crazycrow.com
Solingen blades, knife making parts & supplies

CULPEPPER & CO.
Joe Culpepper
P.O. Box 690
8285 Georgia Rd.
Otto, NC 28763
828-524-6842; Fax: 828-369-7809
culpepperandco@verizon.net
www.knifehandles.com http://www.
knifehandles.com
www.stingrayproducts.com <http://www.
stingrayproducts.com>
Mother of pearl, bone, abalone, stingray,
dyed stag, blacklip, ram's horn, mammoth
ivory, coral, scrimshaw

CUSTOM FURNACES
PO Box 353
Randvaal, 1873
SOUTH AFRICA
27 16 365-5723; 27 16 365-5738
johnlee@custom.co.za
Furnaces for hardening & tempering of knives

DAMASCUS-USA CHARLTON LTD.
149 Deans Farm Rd
Tyner, NC 27980-9607
252-221-2010
rcharlton@damascususa.com;
www.damascususa.com

DAN'S WHETSTONE CO., INC.
418 Hilltop Rd
Pearcy, AR 71964
501-767-1616; 501-767-9598
questions@danswhetstone.com;
www.danswhetstone.com
Natural abrasive Arkansas stone products

**DIAMOND MACHINING TECHNOLOGY,
   INC. DMT**
85 Hayes Memorial Dr
Marlborough, MA 01752
800-666-4DMT
dmtsharp@dmtsharp.com;
www.dmtsharp.com
Knife and tool sharpeners-diamond, ceramic
and easy edge guided sharpening kits

DIGEM DIAMOND SUPPLIERS
7303 East Earll Drive
Scottsdale, Arizona 85251
602-620-3999
eglasser@cox.net
#1 international diamond tool provider. Every
diamond tool you will ever need 1/16th of an
inch to 11'x9'. BURRS, CORE DRILLS, SAW
BLADES, MILLING SHAPES, AND WHEELS

DIXIE GUN WORKS, INC.
PO Box 130
Union City, TN 38281
800-238-6785; Fax: 731-885-0440
www.dixiegunworks.com
Knife and knifemaking supplies

EZE-LAP DIAMOND PRODUCTS
3572 Arrowhead Dr
Carson City, NV 89706
800-843-4815; Fax: 775-888-9555
sales@eze-lap.com; www.eze-lap.com
Diamond coated sharpening tools

FLITZ INTERNATIONAL, LTD.
821 Mohr Ave
Waterford, WI 53185
800-558-8611; Fax: 262-534-2991
info@flitz.com; www.flitz.com
Metal polish, buffing pads, wax

FORTUNE PRODUCTS, INC.
2010A Windy Terrace
Cedar Park, Texas 78613
1-800-742-7797; Fax: 1-800-600-5373
www.accusharp.com
AccuSharp knife sharpeners

GALLERY HARDWOODS
Larry Davis
Eugene, Oregon 97403
www.galleryhardwoods.com
Stabilized exotic burls and woods

GILMER WOOD CO.
2211 NW St Helens Rd
Portland, OR 97210
503-274-1271; Fax: 503-274-9839
www.gilmerwood.com

GREEN RIVER LEATHER, INC.
1100 Legion Park Rd.
Greensburg, KY 42743
270-932-2212; Fax: 270-299-2471
sherrylott@alltel.net;
www.greenriverleather.com
Complete line of veg tan and exotic leathers, shethmaking hardware, thread, dyes, finishes, etc.

GRS CORP.
D.J. Glaser
PO Box 1153
Emporia, KS 66801
800-835-3519; Fax: 620-343-9640
glendo@glendo.com; www.glendo.com
Engraving, equipment, tool sharpener, books/ videos

HALPERN TITANIUM INC.
Les and Marianne Halpern
PO Box 214
4 Springfield St
Three Rivers, MA 01080
888-283-8627; Fax: 413-289-2372
info@halperntitanium.com;
www.halperntitanium.com
Titanium, carbon fiber, G-10, fasteners; CNC milling

HAWKINS KNIVE MAKING SUPPLIES
110 Buckeye Rd
Fayetteville, GA 30214
770-964-1177; Fax: 770-306-2877
Sales@hawkinsknifemakingsupplies.com
www.HawkinsKnifeMakingSupllies.com
All styles

HILTARY-USGRC
6060 East Thomas Road
Scottsdale, AZ 85251
Office: 480-945-0700
Fax: 480-945-3333
usgrc@cox.net
Gibeon Meteorite, Recon Gems, Diamond cutting tools, Exotic natural minerals, garaffe bone. Atomic absorbtion/ spectographic analyst, precisious metal

HOUSE OF TOOLS LTD.
#54-5329 72 Ave. S.E.
Calgary, Alberta
CANADA T2C 4X
403-640-4594; Fax: 403-451-7006

INDIAN JEWELERS SUPPLY CO.
Mail Order: 601 E Coal Ave
Gallup, NM 87301-6005
2105 San Mateo Blvd NE
Albuquerque, NM 87110-5148
505-722-4451; 505-265-3701
orders@ijsinc.com; www.ijsinc.com
Handle materials, tools, metals

INTERAMCO INC.
5210 Exchange Dr
Flint, MI 48507
810-732-8181; 810-732-6116
solutions@interamco.com
Knife grinding and polishing

JANTZ SUPPLY / KOVAL KNIVES
PO Box 584
309 West Main
Davis, OK 73030
800-351-8900; 580-369-2316
jantz@brightok.net; www.knifemaking.com
Pre shaped blades, kit knives, complete knifemaking supply line

JOHNSON, R.B.
I.B.S. Int'l. Folder Supplies
Box 11
Clearwater, MN 55320
320-558-6128; 320-558-6128
www.rbjohnsonknives.com
Threaded pivot pins, screws, taps, etc.

JOHNSON WOOD PRODUCTS
34897 Crystal Rd
Strawberry Point, IA 52076
563-933-6504

K&G FINISHING SUPPLIES
1972 Forest Ave
Lakeside, AZ 85929
800-972-1192; 928-537-8877
www.johnsonwoodproducts.com
Full service supplies

KOWAK IVORY
Roland and Kathy Quimby
(April-Sept): PO Box 350
Ester, AK 99725
907-479-9335
(Oct-March)
PO Box 693
Bristow, OK 74010
918-367-2684
sales@kowakivory.com;
www.kowakivory.com
Fossil ivories

LITTLE GIANT POWER HAMMER
Harlan "Sid" Suedmeier
420 4th Corso
Nebraska City, NE 68410
402-873-6603
www.littlegianthammer.com
Rebuilds hammers and supplies parts

LIVESAY, NEWT
3306 S Dogwood St
Siloam Springs, AR 72761
479-549-3356; 479-549-3357
http://newtlivesayknives.com/
Combat utility knives, titanium knives, sportsmen knives, custom made orders taken on knives and after market Kydex© sheaths for commercial or custom cutlery

LOHMAN CO., FRED
3405 NE Broadway
Portland, OR 97232
503-282-4567; Fax: 503-287-2678
lohman@katana4u.com;
www.japanese-swords.com

M MILLER ORIGINALS
Michael Miller
2960 E Carver Ave
Kingman AZ 86401
928-757-1359
mike@milleroriginals.com;
www.mmilleroriginals.com
Supplies stabilized juniper burl blocks and scales

MARKING METHODS, INC.
Sales
301 S. Raymond Ave
Alhambra, CA 91803-1531
626-282-8823; Fax: 626-576-7564
experts@markingmethods.com;
www.markingmethods.com
Knife etching equipment & service

MASECRAFT SUPPLY CO.
254 Amity St
Meriden, CT 06450
800-682-5489; Fax: 203-238-2373
info@masecraftsupply.com;
www.masecraftsupply.com
Natural & specialty synthetic handle materials & more

MEIER STEEL
Daryl Meier
75 Forge Rd
Carbondale, IL 62903
618-549-3234; Fax: 618-549-6239
www.meiersteel.com

NICO, BERNARD
PO Box 5151
Nelspruit 1200
SOUTH AFRICA
011-2713-7440099; 011-2713-7440099
bernardn@iafrica.com

NORRIS, MIKE
Rt 2 Box 242A
Tollesboro, KY 41189
606-798-1217
Damascus steel

NORTHCOAST KNIVES
17407 Puritas Ave
Cleveland, Ohio 44135
216-265-8678
www.NorthCoastKnives.com
Tutorials and step-by-step projects. Entry level knifemaking supplies.

OSO FAMOSO
PO Box 654
Ben Lomond, CA 95005
831-336-2343
oso@osofamoso.com;
www.osofamoso.com
Mammoth ivory bark

OZARK KNIFE & GUN
3165 S Campbell Ave
Springfield, MO 65807
417-886-CUTT; 417-887-2635
danhoneycutt@sbcglobal.net
28 years in the cutlery business, Missouri's oldest cutlery firm

PARAGON INDUSTRIES, INC. L. P.
2011 South Town East Blvd
Mesquite, TX 75149-1122
800-876-4328; Fax: 972-222-0646
info@paragonweb.com;
www.paragonweb.com
Heat treating furnaces for knifemakers

POPLIN, JAMES / POP'S KNIVES & SUPPLIES
103 Oak St
Washington, GA 30673
706-678-5408; Fax: 706-678-5409
www.popsknifesupplies.com

PUGH, JIM
PO Box 711
917 Carpenter
Azle, TX 76020
817-444-2679; Fax: 817-444-5455
Rosewood and ebony Micarta blocks, rivets for Kydex sheaths, 0-80 screws for folders

RADOS, JERRY
134 Willie Nell Rd
Colombia, KY 42728
815-405-5061
jerry@radosknives.com;
www.radosknives.com
Damascus steel

REACTIVE METALS STUDIO, INC.
PO Box 890
Clarksdale, AZ 86324
800-876-3434; 928-634-3434; Fax: 928-634-6734
info@reactivemetals.com; www.reactivemetals.com

R. FIELDS ANCIENT IVORY
Donald Fields
P.O. BOX 295
ARCADIA, FL. 34265
863-993-1138
http://fieldsancientivory.com
Selling ancient ivories; Mammoth, fossil & walrus

RICK FRIGAULT CUSTOM KNIVES
3584 Rapidsview Dr
Niagara Falls, Ontario
CANADA L2G 6C4
905-295-6695
Selling padded zippered knife pouches with an option to personalize the outside with the marker, purveyor, stores-address, phone number, email web-site or any other information needed. Available in black cordura, mossy oak camo in sizes 4"x2" to 20"x4.5"

RIVERSIDE MACHINE
201 W Stillwell
DeQueen, AR 71832
870-642-7643; Fax: 870-642-4023
uncleal@riversidemachine.net
www.riversidemachine.net

SAKMAR ENTERPRISES, LLC
903 S Latson Rd # 257
Howell, MI 48843
sakmarent@yahoo.com
Mokume bar stock. Retail & wholesale

SANDPAPER, INC. OF ILLINOIS
P.O. Box 2579
Glen Ellyn, IL 60138
630-629-3320; Fax: 630-629-3324
sandinc@aol.com; www.sandpaperinc.com
Abrasive belts, rolls, sheets & discs

SCHEP'S FORGE
PO Box 395
Shelton, NE 68876-0395

SENTRY SOLUTIONS LTD.
PO Box 214
Wilton, NH 03086
800-546-8049; Fax: 603-654-3003
info@sentrysolutions.com;
www.sentrysolutions.com
Knife care products

SHEFFIELD KNIFEMAKERS SUPPLY, INC.
PO Box 741107
Orange City, FL 32774
386-775-6453
email@sheffieldsupply.com;
www.sheffieldsupply.com

SHINING WAVE METALS
PO Box 563
Snohomish, WA 98291
425-334-5569
info@shiningwave.com;
www.shiningwave.com
A full line of mokume-gane in precious and non-precious metals for knifemakers, jewelers and other artists

SMITH'S
747 Mid-America Boulevard
Hot Springs, AR 71913-8414
1-800-221-4156; Fax: 501-321-9232
www.smithsproducts.com

SMOLEN FORGE, INC.
Nick Smolen
S1735 Vang Rd
Westby, WI 54667
608-634-3569; Fax: 608-634-3869
smoforge@mwt.net;
www.smolenforge.com
Damascus billets & blanks, Mokume gane billets

SOSTER SVENSTRUP BYVEJ 16
Søster Svenstrup Byvej 16
4130 Viby Sjælland
Denmark
45 46 19 43 05; Fax: 45 46 19 53 19
www.poulstrande.com

STAMASCUS KNIFEWORKS INC.
Ed VanHoy
24255 N Fork River Rd
Abingdon, VA 24210
276-944-4885; Fax: 276-944-3187
stamascus@centurylink.net;
www.stamascusknifeworks.com
Blade steels

STOVER, JEFF
PO Box 43
Torrance, CA 90507
310-532-2166
edgedealer1@yahoo.com;
www.edgedealer.com
Fine custom knives, top makers

TEXAS KNIFEMAKERS SUPPLY
10649 Haddington Suite 180
Houston TX 77043
713-461-8632; Fax: 713-461-8221
sales@texasknife.com;
www.texasknife.com
Working straight knives. Hunters including upswept skinners and custom walking sticks

TRU-GRIT, INC.
760 E Francis Unit N
Ontario, CA 91761
909-923-4116; Fax: 909-923-9932
www.trugrit.com
The latest in Norton and 3/M ceramic grinding belts. Also Super Flex, Trizact, Norax and Micron belts to 3000 grit. All of the popular belt grinders. Buffers and variable speed motors. ATS-34, 440C, BG-42, CPM S-30V, 416 and Damascus steel

FINE TURNAGE PRODUCTIONS
Charles Turnage
1210 Midnight Drive
San Antonio, TX 78260
210-352-5660
cat41259@aol.com
www.fineturnage.com
Specializing in stabilized mammoth tooth and bone, mammoth ivory, fossil brain coral, meteorite, etc.

UNIVERSAL AGENCIES INC
4690 S Old Peachtree Rd, Suite C
Norcross, GA 30071-1517
678-969-9147; Fax: 678-969-9169
info@knifecupplies.com;
www.knifesupplies.com;
www.thunderforged.com; www.uai.org
Serving the cutlery industry with the finest selection of India Stag, Buffalo Horn, Thurnderforged ™ Damascus. Mother of Pearl, Knife Kits and more

WASHITA MOUNTAIN WHETSTONE CO.
PO Box 20378
Hot Springs, AR 71903-0378
501-525-3914; Fax: 501-525-0816
wmw@hsnp

WEILAND, J. REESE
PO Box 2337
Riverview, FL 33568
813-671-0661; 727-595-0378
www.reeseweilandknives.com
rwphil413@earthlink.net
Folders, straight knives, etc.

WILD WOODS
Jim Fray
9608 Monclova Rd
Monclova, OH 43542
419-866-0435

WILSON, R.W.
PO Box 2012
113 Kent Way
Weirton, WV 26062
304-723-2771

WOOD CARVERS SUPPLY, INC.
PO Box 7500-K
Englewood, FL 34223
800-284-6229; 941-460-0123
info@woodcarverssupply.com;
www.woodcarverssupply.com
Over 2,000 unique wood carving tools

WOOD LAB
Michael Balaskovitz
P.O. Box 222
Hudsonville, MI 49426
616-322-5846
michael@woodlab.biz;
www.woodlab.biz
Acrylic stabilizing services and materials

WOOD STABILIZING SPECIALISTS INT'L, LLC
2940 Fayette Ave
Ionia, IA 50645
800-301-9774; 641-435-4746
mike@stabilizedwood.com;
www.stabilizedwood.com
Processor of acrylic impregnated materials

ZOWADA CUSTOM KNIVES
Tim Zowada
4509 E. Bear River Rd
Boyne Falls, MI 49713
231-348-5416
tim@tzknives.com; www.tzknives.com
Damascus, pocket knives, swords, Lower case gothic tz logo

mail order sales

A.G. RUSSELL KNIVES INC
2900 S. 26th St
Rogers, AR 72758-8571
800-255-9034 or 479-631-0130;
fax 479-631-8493
ag@agrussell.com; www.agrussell.com
The oldest knife mail-order company, highest quality. Free catalog available. In these catalogs you will find the newest and the best. If you like knives, this catalog is a must

ARIZONA CUSTOM KNIVES
Julie Hyman
2225 A1A South, Ste. B9
St. Augustine, FL 32080
904-460-0009
sharptalk@arizonacustomknifes.com;
www.arizonacustomknives.com
Color catalog $5 U.S. / $7 Foreign

ARTISAN KNIVES
Ty Young
206-407-3855
ty@artisanknives.com;
www.artisanknives.com
Feature master artisan knives and makers in a unique "coffee table book" style format

ATLANTA CUTLERY CORP.
P.O.Box 839
Conyers, Ga 30012
800-883-0300; Fax: 770-388-0246
custserve@atlantacutlery.com;
www.atlantacutlery.com

ATLANTIC BLADESMITHS/PETER STEBBINS
50 Mill Rd #221
Littleton, MA 01460
978-952-6448
Sell, trade, buy; carefully selected handcrafted, benchmade and factory knives

BALLARD CUTLERY
1495 Brummel Ave.
Elk Grove Village, IL 60007
847-228-0070

BECK'S CUTLERY SPECIALTIES
7395-M Elevation Road
Benson, North Carolina 27504
919-902-9416
beckscutlery@mindspring.com;
www.beckscutlery.com
Knives

BLADEGALLERY, INC. / EPICUREAN EDGE, THE
107 Central Way
Kirkland, WA 98033
425-889-5980; Fax: 425-889-5981
info@bladegallery.com;
www.bladegallery.com
Bladegallery.com specializes in hand-made one-of-a-kind knives from around the world. We have an emphasis on forged knives and high-end gentlemen's folders

BLUE RIDGE KNIVES
166 Adwolfe Rd
Marion, VA 24354
276-783-6143; 276-783-9298
onestop@blueridgeknives.com;
www.blueridgeknives.com
Wholesale distributor of knives

BOB NEAL CUSTOM KNIVES

LES ROBERTSON
P.O. Box 1367
Evans, Ga 30809
706-650-0252
customknives@comcast.net;
www.bobnealcustomknives.com
Exclusive limited edition custom knives-sets & single

BOB'S TRADING POST
308 N Main St
Hutchinson, KS 67501
620-669-9441
bobstradingpost@cox.net;
www.gunshopfinder.com
Tad custom knives with reichert custom sheaths one at a time, one of a kind

BOONE TRADING CO., INC.
PO Box 669
562 Coyote Rd
Brinnon, WA 98320
800-423-1945; Fax: 360-796-4511
www.boonetrading.com
Ivory of all types, bone, horns

CARMEL CUTLERY
Dolores & 6th
PO Box 1346
Carmel, CA 93921
831-624-6699; 831-624-6780
ccutlery@ix.netcom.com;
www.carmelcutlery.com
Quality custom and a variety of production pocket knives, swords; kitchen cutlery; personal grooming items

CUTLERY SHOPPE
3956 E Vantage Pointe Ln
Meridian, ID 83642-7268
800-231-1272; Fax: 208-884-4433
order@cutleryshoppe.com;
www.cutleryshoppe.com
Discount pricing on top quality brands

CUTTING EDGE, THE
2900 South 26th St
Rogers, AR 72758-8571
800-255-9034; Fax: 479-631-8493
ce_info@cuttingedge.com;
www.cuttingedge.com
After-market knives since 1968. They offer about 1,000 individual knives for sale each month. Subscription by first class mail, in U.S. $20 per year, Canada or Mexico by air mail, $25 per year. All overseas by air mail, $40 per year. The oldest and the most experienced in the business of buying and selling knives. They buy collections of any size, take knives on consignment. Every month there are 4-8 pages in color featuring the work of top makers

DENTON, JOHN W.
703 Hiawassee Estates
Hiawassee, GA 30546
706-781-8479
jwdenton@windstream.net
Loveless knives

DUNN KNIVES
Steve Greene
PO Box 307, 1449 Nocatee St.
Intercession City, FL 33848
800-245-6483
s.greene@earthlink.net;
www.dunnknives.com
Custom knives

FAMARS
2091 Nooseneck Hill Road
Suite 200
Coventry, RI 02816
855-FAMARS1, Fax – 401-397-9191
famarsusa.com
info@famarsusa.com
FAMARS has been building guns for over 50 years. Known for their innovative design, quality, and craftsmanship. They have introduced their new line of gentleman's knives. Applying all the same principals they apply to their guns into their knives. Providing the best built products for many years to come.

FAZALARE INTERNATIONAL ENTERPRISES
PO Box 7062
Thousand Oaks, CA 91359
805-496-2002
ourfaz@aol.com
Handmade multiblades; older case; Fight'n Rooster; Bulldog brand & Cripple Creek

FROST CUTLERY CO.
PO Box 22636
Chattanooga, TN 37422
800-251-7768; Fax: 423-894-9576
www.frostcutlery.com

GENUINE ISSUE INC.
949 Middle Country Rd
Selden, NY 11784
631-696-3802; 631-696-3803
gicutlery@aol.com
Antique knives, swords

GEORGE TICHBOURNE CUSTOM KNIVES
7035 Maxwell Rd #5
Mississauga, Ontario L5S 1R5
CANADA
905-670-0200
sales@tichbourneknives.com;
www.tichbourneknives.com
Canadian custom knifemaker has full retail knife store

GODWIN, INC. G. GEDNEY
PO Box 100
Valley Forge, PA 19481
610-783-0670; Fax: 610-783-6083
sales@gggodwin.com;
www.gggodwin.com
18th century reproductions

GUILD KNIVES
Donald Guild
320 Paani Place 1A
Paia, HI 96779
808-877-3109
don@guildknives.com;
www.guildknives.com
Purveyor of custom art knives

HOUSE OF TOOLS LTD.
#136, 8228 Macleod Tr. SE
Calgary, Alberta, Canada
T2H 2B8

**JENCO SALES, INC. / KNIFE
    IMPORTERS, INC.**
PO Box 1000
11307 Conroy Ln
Manchaca, TX 78652
800-531-5301; fax:800-266-2373
jencosales@sbcglobal.net

KELLAM KNIVES WORLDWIDE
PO Box 3438
Lantana, FL 33462
800-390-6918; 561-588-3185
info@kellamknives.com;
www.kellamknives.com
*Largest selection of Finnish knives; own line
of folders and fixed blades*

KNIFEART.COM
13301 Pompano Dr
Little Rock AR 72211
501-221-1319; Fax: 501-221-2695
www.knifeart.com
*Large internet seller of custom knives &
upscale production knives*

KNIFEPURVEYOR.COM LLC
646-872-0476
mdonato@knifepurveyor.com
www.knifepurveyor.com
*Owned and operated by Michael A. Donato
(full-time knife purveyor since 2002). We
buy, sell, trade, and consign fine custom
knives. We also specialize in buying and
selling valuable collections of fine custom
knives. Our goal is to make every transaction
a memorable one.*

KNIVES PLUS
2467 I 40 West
Amarillo, TX 79109
800-687-6202
salessupport@knivesplus.com; www.
knivesplus.com
*Retail cutlery and cutlery accessories since
1987*

KRIS CUTLERY
2314 Monte Verde Dr
Pinole, CA 94564
510-758-9912 Fax: 510-223-8968
kriscutlery@aol.com; www.kriscutlery.com
Japanese, medieval, Chinese & Philippine

LONE STAR WHOLESALE
2407 W Interstate 40
Amarillo, TX 79109
806-356-9540
*Wholesale only; major brands and
accessories*

MATTHEWS CUTLERY
PO Box 185
Moultrie, GA 31776
877-428-3599
www.matthewscutlery.com

MOORE CUTLERY
PO Box 633
Lockport, IL 60441
708-301-4201
www.knives.cx
*Owned & operated by Gary Moore since 1991
(a full-time dealer). Purveyor of high quality
custom & production knives*

MORTY THE KNIFE MAN, INC.
P.O. Box 152787
Cape Coral, FL 33915
1-800-247-2511
info@mtkm.com;
www.mortytheknifeman.com

MUSEUM REPLICAS LIMITED
2147 Gees Mill Rd
Conyers, GA 30012
800-883-8838
www.museumreplicas.com
*Historically accurate and battle ready swords
& daggers*

NORDIC KNIVES
1634-C Copenhagen Drive
Solvang, CA 93463
805-688-3612; Fax: 805-688-1635
info@nordicknives.com;
www.nordicknives.com
Custom and Randall knives

**PARKERS' KNIFE COLLECTOR
    SERVICE**
6715 Heritage Business Court
Chattanooga, TN 37422
615-892-0448; Fax: 615-892-9165

PLAZA CUTLERY, INC.
3333 S. Bristol St., Suite 2060
South Coast Plaza
Costa Mesa, CA 92626
866-827-5292; 714-549-3932
dan@plazacutlery.com;
www.plazacutlery.com
*Largest selection of knives on the west coast.
Custom makers from beginners to the best.
All customs, William Henry, Strider, Reeves,
Randalls & others available online by phone*

QUINTESSENTIAL CUTLERY
320 - 217 - 9002
gshaw@quintcut.com
www.quintcut.com
*Specializing in investment-grade custom
knives and early makers*

ROBERTSON'S CUSTOM CUTLERY
4960 Sussex Dr
Evans, GA 30809
706-650-0252; 706-860-1623
rccedge@csranet.com; www.
robertsoncustomcutlery.com
*World class custom knives, Vanguard knives-
Limited exclusive design*

**SMOKY MOUNTAIN KNIFE WORKS,
    INC.**
2320 Winfield Dunn Pkwy
PO Box 4430
Sevierville, TN 37864
800-251-9306; 865-453-5871
info@smkw.com; www.eknifeworks.com
*The world's largest knife showplace, catalog
and website*

VOYLES, BRUCE
PO Box 22007
Chattanooga, TN 37422
423-238-6753; Fax: 423-238-3960
bruce@jbrucevoyles.com;
www.jbrucevoyles.com
Knives, knife auctions

knife services

appraisers

Levine, Bernard, P.O. Box 2404, Eugene,
    OR, 97402, 541-484-0294, brlevine@
    ix.netcom.com
Russell, A.G., Knives Inc, 2900 S. 26th
    St., Rogers, AR 72758-8571, phone
    800-255-9034 or 479-631-0130, fax
    479-631-8493, ag@agrussell.com,
    www.agrussell.com
Vallini, Massimo, Via G. Bruno 7, 20154
    Milano, ITALY, 02-33614751, massimo_
    vallini@yahoo.it, Knife expert

custom grinders

McGowan Manufacturing Company,
    4854 N Shamrock Pl #100, Tucson,
    AZ, 85705, 800-342-4810, 520-219-
    0884, info@mcgowanmfg.com, www.
    mcgowanmfg.com, Knife sharpeners,
    hunting axes
Peele, Bryan, The Elk Rack, 215 Ferry St.
    P.O. Box 1363, Thompson Falls, MT,
    59873
Schlott, Harald, Zingster Str. 26, 13051
    Berlin, GERMANY, 049 030 9293346,
    harald.schlott@T-online.de, Custom
    grinder, custom handle artisan, display
    case/box maker, etcher, scrimshander
Wilson, R.W., P.O. Box 2012, Weirton, WV,
    26062

custom handles

Cooper, Jim, 1221 Cook St, Ramona, CA,
    92065-3214, 760-789-1097, (760) 788-
    7992, jamcooper@aol.com
Burrows, Chuck, dba Wild Rose Trading
    Co, 289 Laposta Canyon Rd, Durango,
    CO, 81303, 970-259-8396, chuck@
    wrtcleather.com
Fields, Donald, 790 Tamerlane St,
    Deltona, FL, 32725, 386-532-9070,
    donaldfields@aol.com, Selling ancient
    ivories; mammoth & fossil walrus
Grussenmeyer, Paul G., 310 Kresson Rd,
    Cherry Hill, NJ, 08034, 856-428-1088,
    856-428-8997, pgrussentne@comcast.
    net, www.pgcarvings.com

Holland, Dennis K., 4908-17th Pl., Lubbock, TX, 79416

Imboden II, Howard L., hi II Originals, 620 Deauville Dr., Dayton, OH, 45429

Kelso, Jim, 577 Collar Hill Rd, Worcester, VT, 05682, 802-229-4254, (802) 223-0595

Knack, Gary, 309 Wightman, Ashland, OR, 97520

Marlatt, David, 67622 Oldham Rd., Cambridge, OH, 43725, 740-432-7549

Mead, Dennis, 2250 E. Mercury St., Inverness, FL, 34453-0514

Myers, Ron, 6202 Marglenn Ave., Baltimore, MD, 21206, 410-866-6914

Saggio, Joe, 1450 Broadview Ave. #12, Columbus, OH, 43212, jvsag@webtv.net, www.j.v.saggio@worldnet.att.net, Handle Carver

Schlott, Harald, Zingster Str. 26, 13051 Berlin, GERMANY, 049 030 9293346, harald.schlott@T-online.de, Custom grinder, custom handle artisan, display case/box maker, etcher, scrimshander

Snell, Barry A., 4801 96th St. N., St. Petersburg, FL, 33708-3740

Vallotton, A., 621 Fawn Ridge Dr., Oakland, OR, 97462

Watson, Silvia, 350 Jennifer Lane, Driftwood, TX, 78619

Wilderness Forge, 315 North 100 East, Kanab, UT, 84741, 435-644-3674, bhatting@xpressweb.com

Williams, Gary, (GARBO), PO Box 210, Glendale, KY, 42740-2010

display cases and boxes

Bill's Custom Cases, P O Box 603, Montague, CA, 96064, 530-459-5968, billscustomcases@earthlink.net

Brooker, Dennis, Rt. 1, Box 12A, Derby, IA, 50068

Chas Clements' Custom Leathercraft, Chas, 1741 Dallas St., Aurora, CO, 80010-2018, 303-364-0403, GRYPHONS@ HOME.NET, Display case/box maker, Leatherworker, Knife appraiser

Freund, Steve, Tomway LLC, 1646 Tichenor Court, Atlanta, GA, 30338, 770-393-8349, steve@tomway.com, www.tomway.com

Gimbert, Nelson, P.O. Box 787, Clemmons, NC, 27012

McLean, Lawrence, 12344 Meritage Ct, Rancho Cucamonga, CA, 91739, 714-848-5779, lmclean@charter.net

Miller, Michael K., M&M Kustom Krafts, 28510 Santiam Highway, Sweet Home, OR, 97386

Miller, Robert, P.O. Box 2722, Ormond Beach, FL, 32176

Retichek, Joseph L., W9377 Co. TK. D, Beaver Dam, WI, 53916

Robbins, Wayne, 11520 Inverway, Belvidere, IL, 61008

S&D Enterprises, 20 East Seventh St, Manchester, OH, 45144, 937-549-2602, 937-549-2602, sales@s-denterprises. com, www.s-denterprises.com, Display case/ box maker. Manufacturer of aluminum display, chipboard type displays, wood displays. Silk screening or acid etching for logos on product

Schlott, Harald, Zingster Str. 26, 13051 Berlin, GERMANY, 049 030 9293346, harald.schlott@T-online.de, Custom grinder, custom handle artisan, display case/box maker, etcher, scrimshander

engravers

Adlam, Tim, 1705 Witzel Ave., Oshkosh, WI, 54902, 920-235-4589, www.adlamngraving.com

Alfano, Sam, 36180 Henry Gaines Rd., Pearl River, LA, 70452

Allard, Gary, 2395 Battlefield Rd., Fishers Hill, VA, 22626

Alpen, Ralph, 7 Bentley Rd., West Grove, PA, 19390, 610-869-7141

Baron, David, Baron Technology Inc., 62 Spring Hill Rd., Trumbull, CT, 06611, 203-452-0515, bti@baronengraving.com, www. baronengraving.com, Polishing, plating, inlays, artwork

Bates, Billy, 2302 Winthrop Dr. SW, Decatur, AL, 35603, bbrn@ aol.com, www.angelfire.com/al/billybates

Bettenhausen, Merle L., 17358 Ottawa, Tinley Park, IL, 60477

Blair, Jim, PO Box 64, 59 Mesa Verde, Glenrock, WY, 82637, 307-436-8115, jblairengrav@msn.com

Bonshire, Benita, 1121 Burlington, Muncie, IN, 47302

Boster, A.D., 3000 Clarks Bridge Rd Lot 42, Gainesville, GA, 30501, 770-532-0958

Brooker, Dennis B., Rt. 1 Box 12A, Derby, IA, 50068

Churchill, Winston G., RFD Box 29B, Proctorsville, VT, 05153

Collins, Michael, Rt. 3075, Batesville Rd., Woodstock, GA, 30188

Cupp, Alana, PO Box 207, Annabella, UT, 84711

Dashwood, Jim, 255 Barkham Rd., Wokingham, Berkshire RG11 4BY, ENGLAND

Dean, Bruce, 13 Tressider Ave., Haberfield, N.S.W. 2045, Sydney, AUSTRALIA, 02 97977608

DeLorge, Ed, 6734 W Main St, Houma, LA, 70360, 504-223-0206

Dickson, John W., PO Box 49914, Sarasota, FL, 34230

Dolbare, Elizabeth, PO Box 502, Dubois, WY, 82513-0502

Downing, Jim, PO Box 4224, Springfield, MO, 65808, 417-865-5953, www.thegunengraver.com, Scrimshander

Duarte, Carlos, 108 Church St., Rossville, CA, 95678

Dubben, Michael, 414 S. Fares Ave., Evansville, IN, 47714

Dubber, Michael W., 8205 Heather Pl, Evansville, IN, 47710-4919

Eklund, Maihkel, Föne 1111, S-82041 Färila, SWEDEN, www. art-knives.com

Eldridge, Allan, 1424 Kansas Lane, Gallatin, TN, 37066

Ellis, Willy B, Willy B's Customs by William B Ellis, 4941 Cardinal Trail, Palm Harbor, FL, 34683, 727-942-6420, www.willyb.com

Engel, Terry (Flowers), PO Box 96, Midland, OR, 97634

Flannery Engraving Co., Jeff, 11034 Riddles Run Rd., Union, KY, 41091, engraving@fuse.net, http://home.fuse.net/ engraving/

Foster, Norvell, Foster Enterprises, PO Box 200343, San Antonio, TX, 78220

Fountain Products, 492 Prospect Ave., West Springfield, MA, 01089

Gipe, Sandi, Rt. 2, Box 1090A, Kendrick, ID, 83537

Glimm, Jerome C., 19 S. Maryland, Conrad, MT, 59425

Gournet, Geoffroy, 820 Paxinosa Ave., Easton, PA, 18042, 610-559-0710, www.geoffroygournet.com

Halloran, Tim 316 Fence line Dr. Blue Grass, IA 52726 563-381-5202

Harrington, Fred A., Winter: 3725 Citrus, Summer: 2107 W Frances Rd Mt Morris MI 48458-8215, St. James City, FL, 33956, Winter: 239-283-0721 Summer: 810-686-3008

Henderson, Fred D., 569 Santa Barbara Dr., Forest Park, GA, 30297, 770-968-4866

Hendricks, Frank, 396 Bluff Trail, Dripping Springs, TX, 78620, 512-858-7828

Hochstrat, Brian, bhsaddles.com, brian@bhsaddles.com

Holder, Pat, 7148 W. Country Gables Dr., Peoria, AZ, 85381

Ingle, Ralph W., 151 Callan Dr., Rossville, GA, 30741, 706-858-0641, riengraver@aol.com, Photographer

Johns, Bill, 1716 8th St, Cody, WY, 82414, 307-587-5090

Kelly, Lance, 1723 Willow Oak Dr., Edgewater, FL, 32132

Kelso, Jim, 577 Coller Hill Rd, Worcester, VT, 05682

Koevenig, Eugene and Eve, Koevenig's Engraving Service, Rabbit Gulch, Box 55, Hill City, SD, 57745-0055

Kostelnik, Joe and Patty, RD #4, Box 323, Greensburg, PA, 15601

Kudlas, John M., 55280 Silverwolf Dr, Barnes, WI, 54873, 715-795-2031, jkudlas@cheqnet.net, Engraver, scrimshander

Lark, David, 6641 Schneider Rd., Kingsley, MI 49649, Phone: 231-342-1076 dblark58@yahoo.com

Limings Jr., Harry, 959 County Rd. 170, Marengo, OH, 43334-9625

Lindsay, Steve, 3714 West Cedar Hills Drive, Kearney, NE, 68847

Lyttle, Brian, Box 5697, High River AB CANADA, T1V 1M7

Lytton, Simon M., 19 Pinewood Gardens, Hemel Hempstead, Herts. HP1 1TN, ENGLAND

Mason, Joe, 146 Value Rd, Brandon, MS, 39042, 601-824-9867, www.joemasonengraving.com

McCombs, Leo, 1862 White Cemetery Rd., Patriot, OH, 45658

McDonald, Dennis, 8359 Brady St., Peosta, IA, 52068

McLean, Lawrence, 12344 Meritage Ct, Rancho Cucamonga, CA, 91739, 714-848-5779, lmclean@charter.net

Meyer, Chris, 39 Bergen Ave., Wantage, NJ, 07461, 973-875-6299

Minnick, Joyce, 144 N. 7th St., Middletown, IN, 47356

Morgan, Tandie, P.O. Box 693, 30700 Hwy. 97, Nucla, CO, 81424

Morton, David A., 1110 W. 21st St., Lorain, OH, 44052

Moulton, Dusty, 135 Hillview Ln, Loudon, TN, 37774, 865-408-9779

Muller, Jody & Pat, PO Box 35, Pittsburg, MO, 65724, 417-852-4306/417-752-3260, mullerforge@hotmail.com, www.mullerforge.com

Nelida, Toniutti, via G. Pasconi 29/c, Maniago 33085 (PN), ITALY

Nilsson, Jonny Walker, Tingsstigen 11, SE-933 33 Arvidsjaur, SWEDEN, +(46) 960-13048, 0960.13048@telia.com, www.jwnknives.com

Nott, Ron, Box 281, Summerdale, PA, 17093

Parsons, Michael R., McKee Knives, 7042 McFarland Rd, Indianapolis, IN, 46227, 317-784-7943

Patterson, W.H., P.O. Drawer DK, College Station, TX, 77841

Peri, Valerio, Via Meucci 12, Gardone V.T. 25063, ITALY

Pilkington Jr., Scott, P.O. Box 97, Monteagle, TN, 37356, 931-924-3400, scott@pilkguns.com, www.pilkguns.com

Poag, James, RR1, Box 212A, Grayville, IL, 62844

Potts, Wayne, 1580 Meade St Apt A, Denver, CO, 80204

Rabeno, Martin, Spook Hollow Trading Co, 530 Eagle Pass, Durango, CO, 81301

Raftis, Andrew, 2743 N. Sheffield, Chicago, IL, 60614

Riccardo Fine Hand Engraving, David Riccardo, Buckley MI, 231-269-3028, riccardoengraving.com

Roberts, J.J., 7808 Lake Dr., Manassas, VA, 20111, 703-330-0448, jjrengraver@aol.com, www.angelfire.com/va2/ engraver

Robidoux, Roland J., DMR Fine Engraving, 25 N. Federal Hwy. Studio 5, Dania, FL, 33004

Rosser, Bob, Hand Engraving, 2809 Crescent Ave Ste 20, Homewood, AL, 35209-2526, www.hand-engravers.com

Rudolph, Gil, 20922 Oak Pass Ave, Tehachapi, CA, 93561, 661-822-4949, www.gtraks@csurfers.net

Rundell, Joe, 6198 W. Frances Rd., Clio, MI, 48420

Schickl, L., Ottingweg 497, A-5580 Tamsweg, AUSTRIA, 0043 6474 8583, Scrimshander

Schlott, Harald, Zingster Str. 26, 13051 Berlin, GERMANY, 049 030 9293346, 049 030 9293346, harald.schlott@T-online.de, www.gravur-kunst-atelier.de.vu, Custom grinder, custom handle artisan, display case/box maker, etcher, scrimshander

Schönert, Elke, 18 Lansdowne Pl., Central, Port Elizabeth, SOUTH AFRICA

Shaw, Bruce, P.O. Box 545, Pacific Grove, CA, 93950, 831-646-1937, 831-644-0941

Simmons, Rick W., 3323 Creek Manor Dr., Kingwood, TX, 77339, 504-261-8450, exhibitiongrade@gmail.com www.exhibitionengraver.com

Slobodian, Barbara, 4101 River Ridge Dr., PO Box 1498, San Andreas, CA 95249, 209-286-1980, fax 209-286-1982, barbara@dancethetide.com. Specializes in Japanese-style engraving.

Smith, Ron, 5869 Straley, Ft. Worth, TX, 76114

Smitty's Engraving, 21320 Pioneer Circle, Hurrah, OK, 73045, 405-454-6968, smittys.engraving@prodigy.net, www.smittys-engraving.us

Spode, Peter, Tresaith Newland, Malvern, Worcestershire WR13 5AY, ENGLAND

Swartley, Robert D., 2800 Pine St., Napa, CA, 94558

Takeuchi, Shigetoshi, 21-14-1-Chome kamimuneoka Shiki shi, 353 Saitama, JAPAN

Theis, Terry, 21452 FM 2093, Harper, TX, 78631, 830-864-4438

Valade, Robert B., 931 3rd Ave., Seaside, OR, 97138, 503-738-7672, (503) 738-7672

Waldrop, Mark, 14562 SE 1st Ave. Rd., Summerfield, FL, 34491

Warenski, Julie, 590 East 500 N., Richfield, UT, 84701, 435-896-5319, julie@warenskiknives.com, www.warenskiknives.com

Warren, Kenneth W., P.O. Box 2842, Wenatchee, WA, 98807-2842, 509-663-6123, (509) 663-6123

Whitehead, James 2175 South Willow Ave. Space 22 Fresno, CA 93725 559-412-4374 jdwmks@yahoo.com

Whitmore, Jerry, 1740 Churchill Dr., Oakland, OR, 97462

Winn, Travis A., 558 E. 3065 S., Salt Lake City, UT, 84106

Wood, Mel, P.O. Box 1255, Sierra Vista, AZ, 85636

Zietz, Dennis, 5906 40th Ave., Kenosha, WI, 53144

Zima, Russ, 7291 Ruth Way, Denver, CO, 80221, 303-657-9378, www.rzengraving.com

etchers

Baron Technology Inc., David Baron, 62 Spring Hill Rd., Trumbull, CT, 06611

Famars, 2091 Nooseneck Hill Road, Suite 200, Coventry, RI 02816, 855-FAMARS1, Fax – 401-397-9191, famarsusa.com, info@famarsusa.com

Fountain Products, 492 Prospect Ave., West Springfield, MA, 01089

Hayes, Dolores, P.O. Box 41405, Los Angeles, CA, 90041

Holland, Dennis, 4908 17th Pl., Lubbock, TX, 79416

Kelso, Jim, 577 Collar Hill Rd, Worcester, VT, 05682

Larstein, Francine, FRANCINE ETCHINGS & ETCHED KNIVES, 368 White Rd, Watsonville, CA, 95076, 800-557-1525/831-426-6046, 831-684-1949, francine@francinetchings.com, www.boyeknivesgallery.com

Lefaucheux, Jean-Victor, Saint-Denis-Le-Ferment, 27140 Gisors, FRANCE

Mead, Faustina L., 2550 E. Mercury St., Inverness, FL, 34453-0514, 352-344-4751, scrimsha@infionline.net, www.scrimshaw-by-faustina.com

Myers, Ron, 6202 Marglenn Ave., Baltimore, MD, 21206, (acid) etcher

Nilsson, Jonny Walker, Tingsstigen 11, SE-933 33 Arvidsjaur, SWEDEN, +(46) 960-13048, 0960.13048@telia.com, www.jwnknives.com

Schlott, Harald, Zingster Str. 26, 13051 Berlin, GERMANY, 049 030 9293346, harald.schlott@T-online.de, Custom grinder, custom handle artisan, display case/box maker, etcher, scrimshander

Vallotton, A., Northwest Knife Supply, 621 Fawn Ridge Dr., Oakland, OR, 97462

Watson, Silvia, 350 Jennifer Lane, Driftwood, TX, 78619

heat treaters

Bay State Metal Treating Co., 6 Jefferson Ave., Woburn, MA, 01801

Bos Heat Treating, Paul, Shop: 1900 Weld Blvd., El Cajon, CA, 92020, 619-562-2370 / 619-445-4740 Home, PaulBos@BuckKnives.com

Holt, B.R., 1238 Birchwood Drive, Sunnyvale, CA, 94089

Kazou, Okayusu, 12-2 1 Chome Higashi, Ueno, Taito-Ku, Tokyo, JAPAN, 81-33834-2323, 81-33831-3012

Metal Treating Bodycote Inc., 710 Burns St., Cincinnati, OH, 45204

O&W Heat Treat Inc., One Bidwell Rd., South Windsor, CT, 06074, 860-528-9239, (860) 291-9939, owht1@aol.com

Paul Bos Heat Treating, 660 S. Lochsa St. Post Falls, ID 83854,208-262-0500

Progressive Heat Treating Co., 2802 Charles City Rd, Richmond, VA, 23231, 804-545-0010, 804-545-0012

Texas Heat Treating Inc., 303 Texas Ave., Round Rock, TX, 78664

Texas Knifemakers Supply, 10649 Haddington, Suite 180, Houston, TX, 77043

Tinker Shop, The, 1120 Helen, Deer Park, TX, 77536

Valley Metal Treating Inc., 355 S. East End Ave., Pomona, CA, 91766

Wilderness Forge, 315 North 100 East, Kanab, UT, 84741, 435-644-3674, bhatting@xpressweb.com

Wilson, R.W., P.O. Box 2012, Weirton, WV, 26062

leather workers

Abramson, David, 116 Baker Ave, Wharton, NJ, 07885, lifter4him1@aol.com, www.liftersleather.com

Bruner, Rick, 7756 Aster Lane, Jenison, MI, 49428, 616-457-0403

Burrows, Chuck, dba Wild Rose Trading Co, 289 Laposta Canyon Rd, Durango, CO, 81303, 970-259-8396, chuck@wrtcleather.com

Clements' Custom Leathercraft, Chas, 1741 Dallas St., Aurora, CO, 80010-2018

Cole, Dave, 620 Poinsetta Dr., Satellite Beach, FL 32937, 321-773-1687, www.dcknivesandleather.blademakers.com. Custom sheath services.

Cooper, Harold, 136 Winding Way, Frankfort, KY, 40601

Cooper, Jim, 1221 Cook St, Ramona, CA, 92065-3214, 760-789-1097, 760-788-7992, jamcooper@aol.com

Cow Catcher Leatherworks, 3006 Industrial Dr, Raleigh, NC, 27609

Cubic, George, GC Custom Leather Co., 10561 E. Deerfield Pl., Tucson, AZ, 85749, 520-760-0695, gcubic@aol.com

Dawkins, Dudley, 221 N. Broadmoor Ave, Topeka, KS, 66606-1254, 785-235-3871, dawkind@sbcglobal.net, ABS member/knifemaker forges straight knives

Evans, Scott V, Edge Works Mfg, 1171 Halltown Rd, Jacksonville, NC, 28546, 910-455-9834, (910) 346-5660, edgeworks@coastalnet.com, www.tacticalholsters.com

Genske, Jay, 283 Doty St, Fond du Lac, WI, 54935, 920-921-8019/Cell Phone 920-579-0144, jaygenske@hotmail.com, Custom Grinder, Custom Handle Artisan

Green River Leather, 1100 Legion Park Road, PO BOX 190, Greensburg, KY, 42743, Phone: 270-932-2212 fax: 270-299-2471 email: info@greenriverleather.com

Hawk, Ken, Rt. 1, Box 770, Ceres, VA, 24318-9630

Homyk, David N., 8047 Carriage Ln., Wichita Falls, TX, 76306

John's Custom Leather, John R. Stumpf, 523 S. Liberty St, Blairsville, PA, 15717, 724-459-6802, 724-459-5996

Kelley, Jo Ann, 52 Mourning Dove Dr., Watertown, WI 53094, 920-206-0807, ladybug@ticon.net, www.hembrookcustomknives.com. Custom leather knife sheaths $40 to $100; making sheaths since 2002.

Kravitt, Chris, HC 31 Box 6484, Rt 200, Ellsworth, ME, 04605-9805, 207-584-3000, 207-584-3000, sheathmkr@aol.com, www.treestumpleather.com, Reference: Tree Stump Leather

Larson, Richard, 549 E. Hawkeye, Turlock, CA, 95380

Layton, Jim, 2710 Gilbert Avenue, Portsmouth, OH, 45662

Lee, Randy, P.O. Box 1873, 270 N 9th West, St. Johns, AZ, 85936, 928-337-2594, 928-337-5002, randylee@randyleeknives.com, info@randyleeknives.com, Custom knifemaker; www.randyleeknives.com

Long, Paul, 108 Briarwood Ln W, Kerrville, TX, 78028, 830-367-5536, PFL@cebridge.net

Lott, Sherry, 1100 Legion Park Rd., Greenburg, KY 42743, phone 270-932-2212, fax 270-299-2471, sherrylott@alltel.net

Mason, Arne, 258 Wimer St., Ashland, OR, 97520, 541-482-2260, (541) 482-7785, www.arnemason.com

McGowan, Liz, 12629 Howard Lodge Dr., Winter Add-2023 Robin Ct Sebring FL 33870, Sykesville, MD, 21784, 410-489-4323

Metheny, H.A. "Whitey", 7750 Waterford Dr., Spotsylvania, VA, 22553, 540-582-3228 Cell 540-542-1440, 540-582-3095, nametheny@aol.com, www.methenyknives.com

Miller, Michael K., 28510 Santiam Highway, Sweet Home, OR, 97386

Mobley, Martha, 240 Alapaha River Road, Chula, GA, 31733

Morrissey, Martin, 4578 Stephens Rd., Blairsville, GA, 30512

Niedenthal, John Andre, Beadwork & Buckskin, Studio 3955 NW 103 Dr., Coral Springs, FL, 33065-1551, 954-345-0447, a_niedenthal@hotmail.com

Neilson, Tess, RR2 Box 16, Wyalusing, PA, 18853, 570-746-4944, www.mountainhollow.net, Doing business as Neilson's Mountain Hollow

Parsons, Larry, 1038 W. Kyle, Mustang, OK 73064 405-376-9408 s.m.parsons@sbcglobal.net

Parsons, Michael R., McKee Knives, 7042 McFarland Rd, Indianapolis, IN, 46227, 317-784-7943

Poag, James H., RR #1 Box 212A, Grayville, IL, 62844

Red's Custom Leather, Ed Todd, 9 Woodlawn Rd., Putnam Valley, NY, 10579, 845-528-3783

Rowe, Kenny, 3219 Hwy 29 South, Hope, AR, 71801, 870-777-8216, 870-777-0935, rowesleather@yahoo.com, www.knifeart.com or www.theedgeequipment.com

Schrap, Robert G., 7024 W. Wells St., Wauwatosa, WI, 53213-3717, 414-771-6472, (414) 479-9765, knifesheaths@aol.com, www.customsheaths.com

Strahin, Robert, 401 Center St., Elkins, WV, 26241, *Custom Knife Sheaths

Tierney, Mike, 447 Rivercrest Dr., Woodstock ON CANADA, N4S 5W5

Turner, Kevin, 17 Hunt Ave., Montrose, NY, 10548

Velasquez, Gil, 7120 Madera Dr., Goleta, CA, 93117

Walker, John, 17 Laber Circle, Little Rock, AR, 72210, 501-455-0239, john.walker@afbic.com

Watson, Bill, #1 Presidio, Wimberly, TX, 78676

Whinnery, Walt, 1947 Meadow Creek Dr., Louisville, KY, 40218

Williams, Sherman A., 1709 Wallace St., Simi Valley, CA, 93065

miscellaneous

Hendryx Design, Scott, 5997 Smokey Way, Boise, ID, 83714, 208-377-8044, www.shdsheaths@msn.com Kydex Sheath Maker

Robertson, Kathy, Impress by Design, PO Box 1367, Evans, GA, 30809-1367, 706-650-0982, (706) 860-1623, impressbydesign@comcast.net, Advertising/graphic designer

Strahin, Robert, 401 Center St., Elkins, WV, 26241, 304-636-0128, rstrahin@copper.net, *Custom Knife Sheaths

photographers

Alfano, Sam, 36180 Henery Gaines Rd., Pearl River, LA, 70452

Allen, John, Studio One, 3823 Pleasant Valley Blvd., Rockford, IL, 61114

Balance Digital, Rob Szajkowski, 261 Riverview Way, Oceanside, CA 92057, 760-815-6131, rob@balancedigital.com, www.balancedigital.com

Bilal, Mustafa, Turk's Head Productions, 908 NW 50th St., Seattle, WA, 98107-3634, 206-782-4164, (206) 783-5677, mustafa@turkshead.com, www.turkshead.com, Graphic design, marketing & advertising

Bogaerts, Jan, Regenweg 14, 5757 Pl., Liessel, HOLLAND

Box Photography, Doug, 1804 W Main St, Brenham, TX, 77833-3420

Brown, Tom, 6048 Grants Ferry Rd., Brandon, MS, 39042-8136

Butman, Steve, P.O. Box 5106, Abilene, TX, 79608

Calidonna, Greg, 205 Helmwood Dr., Elizabethtown, KY, 42701

Campbell, Jim, 7935 Ranch Rd., Port Richey, FL, 34668

Cooper, Jim, Sharpbycoop.com photography, 9 Mathew Court, Norwalk, CT, 06851, jcooper@sharpbycoop.com, www.sharpbycoop.com

Courtice, Bill, P.O. Box 1776, Duarte, CA, 91010-4776

Crosby, Doug, RFD 1, Box 1111, Stockton Springs, ME, 04981

Danko, Michael, 3030 Jane Street, Pittsburgh, PA, 15203

Davis, Marshall B., P.O. Box 3048, Austin, TX, 78764

Earley, Don, 1241 Ft. Bragg Rd., Fayetteville, NC, 28305

Ehrlich, Linn M., 1850 N Clark St #1008, Chicago, IL, 60614, 312-209-2107

Etzler, John, 11200 N. Island Rd., Grafton, OH, 44044

Fahrner, Dave, 1623 Arnold St., Pittsburgh, PA, 15205

Faul, Jan W., 903 Girard St. NE, Rr. Washington, DC, 20017

Fedorak, Allan, 28 W. Nicola St., Amloops BC CANADA, V2C 1J6

Fox, Daniel, Lumina Studios, 6773 Industrial Parkway, Cleveland, OH, 44070, 440-734-2118, (440) 734-3542, lumina@en.com

Francesco Pachi, Loc. Pometta 1, 17046 Sassello (SV) ITALY, 0039 19 720086, www.pachi-photo.com, info@pachi-photo.com

Freiberg, Charley, PO Box 42, Elkins, NH, 03233, 603-526-2767, charleyfreiberg@tos.net

Gardner, Chuck, 116 Quincy Ave., Oak Ridge, TN, 37830

Gawryla, Don, 1105 Greenlawn Dr., Pittsburgh, PA, 15220

Goffe Photographic Associates, 3108 Monte Vista Blvd., NE, Albuquerque, NM, 87106

Graham, James, 7434 E Northwest Hwy, Dallas, TX, 75231, 214-341-5138, jamie@jamiephoto.com, www.jamiephoto.com, Product photographer

Graley, Gary W., RR2 Box 556, Gillett, PA, 16925

Griggs, Dennis, 118 Pleasant Pt Rd, Topsham, ME, 04086, 207-725-5689

Hanusin, John, Reames-Hanusin Studio, PO Box 931, Northbrook, IL, 60065 0931

Hardy, Scott, 639 Myrtle Ave., Placerville, CA, 95667

Hodge, Tom, 7175 S US Hwy 1 Lot 36, Titusville, FL, 32780-8172, 321-267-7989, egdoht@hotmail.com

Holter, Wayne V., 125 Lakin Ave., Boonsboro, MD, 21713, 301-416-2855, mackwayne@hotmail.com

Hopkins, David W, Hopkins Photography inc, 201 S Jefferson, Iola, KS, 66749, 620-365-7443, nhoppy@netks.net

Kerns, Bob, 18723 Birdseye Dr., Germantown, MD, 20874

LaFleur, Gordon, 111 Hirst, Box 1209, Parksville BC CANADA, V0R 270

Lear, Dale, 6544 Cora Mill Rd, Gallipolis, OH, 45631, 740-245-5482, dalelear@yahoo.com, Ebay Sales

LeBlanc, Paul, No. 3 Meadowbrook Cir., Melissa, TX, 75454

Lester, Dean, 2801 Junipero Ave Suite 212, Long Beach, CA, 90806-2140

Leviton, David A., A Studio on the Move, P.O. Box 2871, Silverdale, WA, 98383, 360-697-3452

Long, Gary W., 3556 Miller's Crossroad Rd., Hillsboro, TN, 37342

Long, Jerry, 402 E. Gladden Dr., Farmington, NM, 87401

Lum, Billy, 16307 Evening Star Ct., Crosby, TX, 77532

McCollum, Tom, P.O. Box 933, Lilburn, GA, 30226

Mitch Lum Website and Photography, 22115 NW Imbrie Dr. #298, Hillsboro, OR 97124, mitch@mitchlum.com, www.mitchlum.com, 206-356-6813

Moake, Jim, 18 Council Ave., Aurora, IL, 60504

Moya Inc., 4212 S. Dixie Hwy., West Palm Beach, FL, 33405

Norman's Studio, 322 S. 2nd St., Vivian, LA, 71082

Owens, William T., Box 99, Williamsburg, WV, 24991

Pachi, Francesco, Loc. Pometta 1, 17046 Sassello (SV) ITALY Tel-fax: 0039 019 720086, www.pachi-photo.com

Palmer Studio, 2008 Airport Blvd., Mobile, AL, 36606

Payne, Robert G., P.O. Box 141471, Austin, TX, 78714

Photography by Kayla Minchew, 2510 Mary Ellen, Pampa, TX, 79065, 806-669-3933, www.knifephotosbykayla.com

Pigott, John, 9095 Woodprint LN, Mason, OH, 45040

Point Seven, 6450 Weatherfield Ct., Unit 2A, Maumee, OH, 43537, 419-243-8880, 877-787-3836, www.pointsevenstudios.com

Professional Medica Concepts, Patricia Mitchell, P.O. Box 0002, Warren, TX, 77664, 409-547-2213, pm0909@wt.net

Rasmussen, Eric L., 1121 Eliason, Brigham City, UT, 84302

Rhoades, Cynthia J., Box 195, Clearmont, WY, 82835

Rice, Tim, PO Box 663, Whitefish, MT, 59937

Richardson, Kerry, 2520 Mimosa St., Santa Rosa, CA, 95405, 707-575-1875, kerry@sonic.net, www.sonic.net/~kerry

Ross, Bill, 28364 S. Western Ave. Suite 464, Rancho Palos Verdes, CA, 90275

Rubicam, Stephen, 14 Atlantic Ave., Boothbay Harbor, ME, 04538-1202

Rush, John D., 2313 Maysel, Bloomington, IL, 61701

Schreiber, Roger, 429 Boren Ave. N., Seattle, WA, 98109

Semmer, Charles, 7885 Cyd Dr., Denver, CO, 80221

Silver Images Photography, 2412 N Keystone, Flagstaff, AZ, 86004

Slobodian, Scott, 4101 River Ridge Dr., P.O. Box 1498, San Andreas, CA, 95249, 209-286-1980, (209) 286-1982, www.slobodianswords.com

Smith, Earl W., 5121 Southminster Rd., Columbus, OH, 43221

Smith, Randall, 1720 Oneco Ave., Winter Park, FL, 32789

Storm Photo, 334 Wall St., Kingston, NY, 12401

Surles, Mark, P.O. Box 147, Falcon, NC, 28342

Third Eye Photos, 140 E. Sixth Ave., Helena, MT, 59601

Thurber, David, P.O. Box 1006, Visalia, CA, 93279

Tighe, Brian, RR 1, Ridgeville ON CANADA, L0S 1M0, 905-892-2734, www.tigheknives.com

Towell, Steven L., 3720 N.W. 32nd Ave., Camas, WA, 98607, 360-834-9049, sltowell@netscape.net

Valley Photo, 2100 Arizona Ave., Yuma, AZ, 85364

Verno Studio, Jay, 3030 Jane Street, Pittsburgh, PA, 15203

Ward, Chuck, 1010 E North St, PO Box 2272, Benton, AR, 72018, 501-778-4329, chuckbop@aol.com

Weyer International, 6466 Teal Rd., Petersburgh, MI, 49270, 419-534-2020, law-weyerinternational@msn.com, Books

Wise, Harriet, 242 Dill Ave., Frederick, MD, 21701

Worley, Holly, Worley Photography, 6360 W David Dr, Littleton, CO, 80128-5708, 303-257-8091, 720-981-2800, hsworley@aol.com, Products, Digital & Film

scrimshanders

Adlam, Tim, 1705 Witzel Ave., Oshkosh, WI, 54902, 920-235-4589, www.adlamngraving.com

Alpen, Ralph, 7 Bentley Rd., West Grove, PA, 19390, 610-869-7141

Anderson, Terry Jack, 10076 Birnamwoods Way, Riverton, UT, 84065-9073

Bailey, Mary W., 3213 Jonesboro Dr., Nashville, TN, 37214, mbscrim@aol.com, www.members.aol.com/mbscrim/ scrim.html

Baker, Duane, 2145 Alum Creek Dr., Cambridge Park Apt. #10, Columbus, OH, 43207

Barrows, Miles, 524 Parsons Ave., Chillicothe, OH, 45601

Brady, Sandra, P.O. Box 104, Monclova, OH, 43542, 419-866-0435, (419) 867-0656, sandyscrim@hotmail.com, www.knifeshows.com

Beauchamp, Gaetan, 125 de la Riviere, Stoneham, PQ, G0A 4P0, CANADA, 418-848-1914, (418) 848-6859, knives@gbeauchamp.ca, www.beauchamp.cjb.net

Bellet, Connie, PO Box 151, Palermo, ME, 04354 0151, 207-993-2327, phwhitehawk@gwi.net

Benade, Lynn, 2610 Buckhurst Dr, Beachwood, OH, 44122, 216-464-0777, llbnc17@aol.com

Bonshire, Benita, 1121 Burlington Dr., Muncie, IN, 47302

Boone Trading Co. Inc., P.O. Box 669, Brinnon, WA, 98320, 800-423-1945, ww.boonetrading.com

Bryan, Bob, 1120 Oak Hill Rd., Carthage, MO, 64836

Burger, Sharon, Cluster Box 1625, Forest Hills/KLOOF 3624, KZN, South Africa, cell: +27 83 7891675, tel/fax: +27 31 7621349, scribble@iafrica.com, www.kgsa.co.za/members/sharonburger

Byrne, Mary Gregg, 1018 15th St., Bellingham, WA, 98225-6604

Cable, Jerry, 332 Main St., Mt. Pleasant, PA, 15666

Caudill, Lyle, 7626 Lyons Rd., Georgetown, OH, 45121

Cole, Gary, PO Box 668, Naalehu, HI, 96772, 808-929-9775, 808-929-7371, www.community.webshots.com/album/11836830uqyeejirsz

Collins, Michael, Rt. 3075, Batesville Rd., Woodstock, GA, 30188

Conover, Juanita Rae, P.O. Box 70442, Eugene, OR, 97401, 541-747-1726 or 543-4851, juanitaraeconover@yahoo.com

Courtnage, Elaine, Box 473, Big Sandy, MT, 59520

Cover Jr., Raymond A., Rt. 1, Box 194, Mineral Point, MO, 63660

Cox, J. Andy, 116 Robin Hood Lane, Gaffney, SC, 29340

Dietrich, Roni, Wild Horse Studio, 1257 Cottage Dr, Harrisburg, PA, 17112, 717-469-0587, ronimd@aol

DiMarzo, Richard, 2357 Center Place, Birmingham, AL, 35205

Dolbare, Elizabeth, PO Box 502, Dubois, WY, 82513-0502

Eklund, Maihkel, Föne 1111, S-82041 Färila, SWEDEN, +46 6512 4192, maihkel.eklund@swipnet.se, www.art-knives.com

Eldridge, Allan, 1424 Kansas Lane, Gallatin, TN, 37066

Ellis, Willy b, Willy B's Customs by William B Ellis, 4941 Cardinal Trail, Palm Harbor, FL, 34683, 727-942-6420, www.willyb.com

Fisk, Dale, Box 252, Council, ID, 83612, dafisk@ctcweb.net

Foster Enterprises, Norvell Foster, P.O. Box 200343, San Antonio, TX, 78220

Fountain Products, 492 Prospect Ave., West Springfield, MA, 01089

Gill, Scott, 925 N. Armstrong St., Kokomo, IN, 46901

Halligan, Ed, 14 Meadow Way, Sharpsburg, GA, 30277, ehkiss@bellsouth.net

Hands, Barry Lee, 26192 East Shore Route, Bigfork, MT, 59911

Hargraves Sr., Charles, RR 3 Bancroft, Ontario CANADA, K0L 1C0

Harless, Star, c/o Arrow Forge, P.O. Box 845, Stoneville, NC, 27048-0845

Harrington, Fred A., Summer: 2107 W Frances Rd, Mt Morris MI 48458 8215, Winter: 3725 Citrus, St. James City, FL, 33956, Winter 239-283-0721, Summer 810-686-3008

Hergert, Bob, 12 Geer Circle, Port Orford, OR, 97465, 541-332-3010, hergert@harborside.com, www.scrimshander.com

Hielscher, Vickie, 6550 Otoe Rd, P.O. Box 992, Alliance, NE, 69301, 308-762-4318, g-hielsc@bbcwb.net

High, Tom, 5474 S. 112.8 Rd., Alamosa, CO, 81101, 719-589-2108, scrimshaw@vanion.com, www.rockymountainscrimshaw.com, Wildlife Artist

Himmelheber, David R., 11289 40th St. N., Royal Palm Beach, FL, 33411

Holland, Dennis K., 4908-17th Place, Lubbock, TX, 79416

Hutchings, Rick "Hutch", 3007 Coffe Tree Ct, Crestwood, KY, 40014, 502-241-2871, baron1@bellsouth.net

Imboden II, Howard L., 620 Deauville Dr., Dayton, OH, 45429, 937-439-1536, Guards with the "Last Wax Technic"

Johnson, Corinne, W3565 Lockington, Mindora, WI, 54644

Johnston, Kathy, W. 1134 Providence, Spokane, WA, 99205

Karst Stone, Linda, 903 Tanglewood Ln, Kerrville, TX, 78028-2945, 830-896-4678, 830-257-6117, karstone@ktc.com

Kelso, Jim, 577 Coller Hill Rd, Worcester, VT, 05682

Kirk, Susan B., 1340 Freeland Rd., Merrill, MI, 48637

Koevenig, Eugene and Eve, Koevenig's Engraving Service, Rabbit Gulch, Box 55, Hill City, SD, 57745-0055

Kostelnik, Joe and Patty, RD #4, Box 323, Greensburg, PA, 15601

Lemen, Pam, 3434 N. Iroquois Ave., Tucson, AZ, 85705

Martin, Diane, 28220 N. Lake Dr., Waterford, WI, 53185

McDonald, René Cosimini-, 14730 61 Court N., Loxahatchee, FL, 33470

McFadden, Berni, 2547 E Dalton Ave, Dalton Gardens, ID, 83815-9631

McGowan, Frank, 12629 Howard Lodge Dr., Winter Add-2023 Robin Ct Sebring FL 33870, Sykesville, MD, 21784, 863-385-1296

McGrath, Gayle, PMB 232 15201 N Cleveland Ave, N Ft Myers, FL, 33903

McLaran, Lou, 603 Powers St., Waco, TX, 76705

McWilliams, Carole, P.O. Box 693, Bayfield, CO, 81122

Mead, Faustina L., 2550 E. Mercury St., Inverness, FL, 34453-0514, 352-344-4751, scrimsha@infionline.net, www.scrimshaw-by-faustina.com

Mitchell, James, 1026 7th Ave., Columbus, GA, 31901

Moore, James B., 1707 N. Gillis, Stockton, TX, 79735

Ochonicky, Michelle "Mike", Stone Hollow Studio, 31 High Trail, Eureka, MO, 63025, 636-938-9570, www.bestofmissourihands.com

Ochs, Belle, 124 Emerald Lane, Largo, FL, 33771, 727-530-3826, chuckandbelle@juno.com, www.oxforge.com

Pachi, Mirella, Via Pometta 1, 17046 Sassello (SV), ITALY, 019 720086, WWW.PACHI-KNIVES.COM

Parish, Vaughn, 103 Cross St., Monaca, PA, 15061

Peterson, Lou, 514 S. Jackson St., Gardner, IL, 60424

Pienaar, Conrad, 19A Milner Rd., Bloemfontein 9300, SOUTH AFRICA, Phone: 027 514364180 fax: 027 514364180

Poag, James H., RR #1 Box 212A, Grayville, IL, 62844

Polk, Trena, 4625 Webber Creek Rd., Van Buren, AR, 72956

Purvis, Hilton, P.O. Box 371, Noordhoek, 7979, SOUTH AFRICA, 27 21 789 1114, hiltonp@telkomsa.net, www.kgsa.co.za/member/hiltonpurvis

Ramsey, Richard, 8525 Trout Farm Rd, Neosho, MO, 64850

Ristinen, Lori, 14256 County Hwy 45, Menahga, MN, 56464, 218-538-6608, lori@loriristinen.com, www.loriristinen.com

Roberts, J.J., 7808 Lake Dr., Manassas, VA, 22111, 703-330-0448, jjrengraver@aol.com, www.angelfire.com/va2/ engraver

Rudolph, Gil, 20922 Oak Pass Ave, Tehachapi, CA, 93561, 661-822-4949, www.gtraks@csurfers.net

Rundell, Joe, 6198 W. Frances Rd., Clio, MI, 48420

Saggio, Joe, 1450 Broadview Ave. #12, Columbus, OH, 43212, 614-481-1967, jvsaggio@earthlink.net, www.j.v.saggio@worldnet.att.net

Sahlin, Viveca, Konstvaktarevagem 9, S-772 40 Grangesberg, SWEDEN, 46 240 23204, www.scrimart.use

Satre, Robert, 518 3rd Ave. NW, Weyburn SK CANADA, S4H 1R1

Schlott, Harald, Zingster Str. 26, 13051 Berlin, 929 33 46, GERMANY, 049 030 9293346, 049 030 9293346, harald.schlott@t-online.de, www.gravur-kunst-atelier.de.vu

Schulenburg, E.W., 25 North Hill St., Carrollton, GA, 30117

Schwallie, Patricia, 4614 Old Spartanburg Rd. Apt. 47, Taylors, SC, 29687

Selent, Chuck, P.O. Box 1207, Bonners Ferry, ID, 83805

Semich, Alice, 10037 Roanoke Dr., Murfreesboro, TN, 37129

Shostle, Ben, 1121 Burlington, Muncie, IN, 47302

Smith, Peggy, 676 Glades Rd., #3, Gatlinburg, TN, 37738

Smith, Ron, 5869 Straley, Ft. Worth, TX, 76114

Stahl, John, Images In Ivory, 2049 Windsor Rd., Baldwin, NY, 11510, 516-223-5007, imivory@msn.com, www.imagesinivory.org

Steigerwalt, Jim, RD#3, Sunbury, PA, 17801

Stuart, Stephen, 15815 Acorn Circle, Tavares, FL, 32778, 352-343-8423, (352) 343-8916, inkscratch@aol.com

Talley, Mary Austin, 2499 Countrywood Parkway, Memphis, TN, 38016, matalley@midsouth.rr.com

Thompson, Larry D., 23040 Ave. 197, Strathmore, CA, 93267

Toniutti, Nelida, Via G. Pascoli, 33085 Maniago-PN, ITALY

Trout, Lauria Lovestrand, 1555 Delaney Dr, No. 1723, Talahassee, FL, 32309, 850-893-8836, mayalaurie@aol.com

Tucker, Steve, 3518 W. Linwood, Turlock, CA, 95380

Tyser, Ross, 1015 Hardee Court, Spartanburg, SC, 29303

Velasquez, Gil, Art of Scrimshaw, 7120 Madera Dr., Goleta, CA, 93117

Wilderness Forge, 475 NE Smith Rock Way, Terrebonne, OR, 97760, bhatting@xpressweb.com

Williams, Gary, PO Box 210, Glendale, KY, 42740, 270-369-6752, garywilliam@alltel.net

Winn, Travis A., 558 E. 3065 S., Salt Lake City, UT, 84106

Young, Mary, 4826 Storeyland Dr., Alton, IL, 62002

organizations

AMERICAN BLADESMITH SOCIETY
c/o Office Manager, Cindy Sheely; P. O. Box 160, Grand Rapids, Ohio 45522; cindy@americanbladesmith.com; (419) 832-0400; Web: www.americanbladesmith.com

AMERICAN KNIFE & TOOL INSTITUTE***
David Kowalski, Comm. Coordinator, AKTI; DEPT BL2, 22 Vista View Ln, Cody, WY 82414-9606,(307) 587-8296 Fax: (307) 587-8296 Web: communications@akti.org; www.akti.org

AMERICAN KNIFE THROWERS ALLIANCE
c/o Bobby Branton; PO Box 807; Awendaw, SC 29429; www.AKTA-USA.com

BAY AREA KNIFE COLLECTOR'S ASSOCIATION
Dana Hermes BAKCA Inc. P.O. Box 3274
San Ramon, CA. 94583; Web: www.bakcainc.org

ARKANSAS KNIFEMAKERS ASSOCIATION
David Etchieson, 60 Wendy Cove, Conway, AR 72032; Web: www.arkansasknifemakers.com

CALIFORNIA KNIFEMAKERS ASSOCIATION
c/o admin@calknives.org; http://www.calknives.org/
Dedicated to teaching and improving knifemaking

CANADIAN KNIFEMAKERS GUILD
c/o Peter Wile; RR # 3; Bridgewater N.S. CANADA B4V 2W2; 902-543-1373; www.ckg.org

CUSTOM KNIFE COLLECTORS ASSOCIATION
c/o Jim Treacy, PO Box 5893, Glen Allen, VA 23058-5893; E-mail: customknifecollectorsassociation@yahoo.com; Web: www.customknifecollectorsassociation.com
The purpose of the CKCA is to recognize and promote the artistic significance of handmade knives, to advnace their collection and conservation, and to support the creative expression of those who make them. Open to collectors, makers purveyors, and other collectors. Has members from eight countries. Produced a calednar which features custom knives either owned or made by CKCA members.

CUTTING EDGE, THE
A. G. Russell Knives, Inc.,2900 South 26th St.
Rogers, AR 72758-8571; ce-info@cuttingedge.com
After-market knives since 1968. We offer about 1,000 individual knives each month. The oldest and the most experienced in the business of buying and selling knives. We buy collections of any size, take knives on consignment or we will trade. Web: www.cuttingedge.com

FLORIDA KNIFEMAKERS ASSOCIATION
c/o President, Dan Mink, PO Box 861, Crystal beach, Florida, 34681 (727) 786 5408; Web: www.floridaknifemakers.org

JAPANESE SWORD SOCIETY OF THE U.S.
c/o Barry Hennick; barry@hennick.ca; PO Box 712; Breckenridge, TX 76424; http://www.jssus.org/

KNIFE COLLECTORS CLUB INC, THE
2900 S. 26th St., US 540 Exit 81, Rogers, AR 72758-8571 479-631-0130; 479-631-8493; ag@agrussell.com; Web:www.club@k-c-c.com
The oldest and largest association of knife collectors. Issues limited edition knives, both handmade and highest quality production, in very limited numbers. The very earliest was the CM-1, Kentucky Rifle

KNIFE WORLD
PO Box 3395; Knoxville, TN 37927; 800-828-7751; 865-397-1955; 865-397-1969; knifepub@knifeworld.com
Publisher of monthly magazine for knife enthusiasts and world's largest knife/cutlery bookseller. Web: www.knifeworld.com

KNIFEMAKERS GUILD
Knifemakers Guild, Box 922, New Castle, IN 47362; (765) 529-1651; Web: www.knifemakersguild.com

KNIFEMAKERS GUILD OF SOUTHERN AFRICA, THE
c/o Carel Smith; PO Box 1744; Delmars 2210; SOUTH AFRICA; carelsmith@therugby.co.za; Web:www.kgsa.co.za

KNIVES ILLUSTRATED
c/o David Beckler,4635 McEwen Road, Dallas, TX 75244; 972-448-9173 knivesillustrated@yahoo.com; Web:www.knivesillustrated.com
All encompassing publication focusing on factory knives, new handmades, shows and industry news, plus knifemaker features, new products, and travel pieces

MONTANA KNIFEMAKERS' ASSOCIATION, THE
14440 Harpers Bridge Rd; Missoula, MT 59808; 406-543-0845; http://www.montanaknifemakers.com
Annual book of custom knife makers' works and directory of knife making supplies; $19.99

NATIONAL KNIFE COLLECTORS ASSOCIATION
PO Box 21070; Chattanooga, TN 37424; 423-892-5007; 423-899-9456; info@nationalknife.org; Web: www.nationalknife.org

NEO-TRIBAL METALSMITHS
Tai Goo Knives,Attn: Tai Goo,P.O. Box 1854,Cortaro, AZ 85652-1854 USA; Web: www.neo-tribalmetalsmiths.com

NEW ENGLAND CUSTOM KNIFE ASSOCIATION
George R. Rebello, President; 686 Main Rd; Brownville, ME 04414; Web: http://www.necka.net/

NORTH CAROLINA CUSTOM KNIFEMAKERS GUILD
c/o 2112 Windy Woods Drive, Raleigh, NC 27607 (919) 834-4693; Web: http://ncknifeguild.org/

NORTH STAR BLADE COLLECTORS
PO Box 20523, Bloomington, MN 55420; http://www.nsbc.us

OHIO KNIFEMAKERS ASSOCIATION
c/o Jerry Smith, Anvils and Ink Studios, P.O. Box 151 Barnesville, Ohio 43713; Web: http://www.oocities.org/ohioknives/

OREGON KNIFE COLLECTORS ASSOCIATION
Web: www.oregonknifeclub.org

ROCKY MOUNTAIN BLADE COLLECTORS ASSOCIATION
Mike Moss. Pres., P.O. Box 324, Westminster, CO 80036

RESOURCE GUIDE AND NEWSLETTER / AUTOMATIC KNIVES
LATAMA P.O. Box 721. Montauk, NY 11954; 631-668-5995; Web: www.thenewsletter.com

SOUTH CAROLINA ASSOCIATION OF KNIFEMAKERS
c/o Victor Odom, Jr., Post Office Box 572, North, SC 29112
(803) 247-5614; Web: www.scak.org

SOUTHERN CALIFORNIA BLADES
SC Blades, PO Box 1140, Lomita, CA 90717; Web: www.
scblades.com

TEXAS KNIFEMAKERS & COLLECTORS ASSOCIATION
TKCA PO Box 234,Eden, TX 76837; 325-869-8821;
Web:www.tkca.org

TACTICAL KNIVES
Harris Publications; 1115 Broadway; New York, NY 10010;
Web: http://www.tactical-life.com

publications

BLADE
700 E. State St., Iola, WI 54990-0001; 715-445-2214; Web:
www.blademag.com
The world's No. 1 knife magazine

KNIFE WORLD
PO Box 3395, Knoxville, TN 37927; www.knifeworld.com

KNIVES ILLUSTRATED
265 S. Anita Dr., Ste. 120, Orange, CA 92868; 714-939-9991;
knivesillustrated@yahoo.com; Web: www.knivesillustrated.
com
*All encompassing publication focusing on factory knives, new
handmades, shows and industry news*

**RESOURCE GUIDE AND NEWSLETTER / AUTOMATIC
KNIVES**
2269 Chestnut St., Suite 212, San Francisco, CA 94123;
415-731-0210; Web: www.thenewsletter.com

TACTICAL KNIVES
Harris Publications, 1115 Broadway, New York, NY 10010;
Web: www.tacticalknives.com

WEYER INTERNATIONAL BOOK DIVISION
2740 Nebraska Ave., Toledo, OH 43607-3245